2340491
9-1207

CO-ATX-289

VISUALIZING THE TRAGIC

Visualizing the Tragic

Drama, Myth, and Ritual in Greek Art and Literature

Essays in Honour of Froma Zeitlin

Edited by
Chris Kraus, Simon Goldhill,
Helene P. Foley, Jaś Elsner

OXFORD
UNIVERSITY PRESS

OXFORD
UNIVERSITY PRESS

Great Clarendon Street, Oxford OX2 6DP

Oxford University Press is a department of the University of Oxford.
It furthers the University's objective of excellence in research, scholarship,
and education by publishing worldwide in

Oxford New York

Auckland Cape Town Dar es Salaam Hong Kong Karachi
Kuala Lumpur Madrid Melbourne Mexico City Nairobi
New Delhi Shanghai Taipei Toronto

With offices in

Argentina Austria Brazil Chile Czech Republic France Greece
Guatemala Hungary Italy Japan Poland Portugal Singapore
South Korea Switzerland Thailand Turkey Ukraine Vietnam

Oxford is a registered trade mark of Oxford University Press
in the UK and in certain other countries

Published in the United States
by Oxford University Press Inc., New York

© Oxford University Press 2007

The moral rights of the author have been asserted
Database right Oxford University Press (maker)

First published 2007

All rights reserved. No part of this publication may be reproduced,
stored in a retrieval system, or transmitted, in any form or by any means,
without the prior permission in writing of Oxford University Press,
or as expressly permitted by law, or under terms agreed with the appropriate
reprographics rights organization. Enquiries concerning reproduction
outside the scope of the above should be sent to the Rights Department,
Oxford University Press, at the address above

You must not circulate this book in any other binding or cover
and you must impose the same condition on any acquirer

British Library Cataloguing in Publication Data
Data available

Library of Congress Cataloging in Publication Data
Data available

Typeset by SPI Publisher Services, Pondicherry, India
Printed in Great Britain
on acid-free paper by
Biddles Ltd., King's Lynn, Norfolk

ISBN 978–0–19–927602–8

1 3 5 7 9 10 8 6 4 2

PA
3014
.T66
V57
2007

For Froma,
with all our love

The Red-Gold Border

Ruth Padel

If an eye wants to know itself, he said,
it looks into the thing most like it in the world:
another eye. Closed-bracket algebra of lovers,
watching their twin flames flicker
in the burnished pick-up mirror of each other.

Though Plato doesn't add it, let's pretend
Socrates sighed then; leaned against the glow
of Alcibiades in shadow, loose
red-gold-bordered tunic opening to show
bronze thighs (and look, one knee up) splayed

on the cushioned bench, little duck-tail rivulets
of sweat-curled dark hair feathering
those famous soldier's muscles. Close, too close, beside
the snub-nosed simian recusenik
chopping logic in the sweet-oil light

as Samian wine went round the board
and flute-girls danced in panther-spotted *chitons*.
Yes; his golden boy, out always to seduce,
who'd grow up to destroy
the white imperial city he adored.

'The Red-Gold Border' from *The Soho Leopard* by Ruth Padel, published by Chatto & Windus (London, 2004). Reprinted by permission of the Random House Group Ltd.

Preface

This book has a double purpose: to honour our friend Froma Zeitlin, and to explore the avenues that her own distinctive scholarly voice has so fruitfully opened up in the areas of Greek tragedy and its antecedents, influences, and representations. The papers that follow speak eloquently of her importance in the field; we hope that she will enjoy this volume as a token of our immense regard for her.

Such is Froma's standing, and significance, in the study of Greek literature that this volume could easily have been filled many times over with papers by other distinguished scholars, including former students and other younger members of the field. We would like to thank Froma's colleagues at Princeton for helpful advice during the process of putting the volume together. We gratefully acknowledge permission from the Metropolitan Museum of Art (New York) to reprint the cover illustration, Gustave Moreau's *Oedipus and the Sphinx*, 1864. The Department of Classics at Yale generously covered the expenses incurred in photographic permissions and preparing the manuscript for the press; CSK would especially like to thank Ornella Rossi for her hard work and sharp eyes and Marta Steele for her quick, thorough indexing. The editorial team at OUP has been characteristically helpful: in particular we would like to thank Hilary O'Shea for taking the project on—and Jenny Wagstaffe for coping with the process—despite the daunting prospect of dealing with four editors; Leofranc Holford-Strevens for translating the original French (the papers of Frontisi-Ducroux, Lissarrague, Vernant, and Vidal-Naquet); and Ian McAuslan for his expert editing. We have tried to be consistent within chapters in transliterating Greek, but inconsistencies will inevitably remain.

New Haven, Cambridge, New York, Oxford
March 2007

Contents

Notes on Contributors   xiii
Illustrations   xviii

Editors' Introduction   1

I. VISUALIZING TRAGEDY FROM ELSEWHERE

1. Notes on Tragic Visualizing in the *Iliad*   19
   Laura M. Slatkin

2. Outer Limits, Choral Space   35
   Richard P. Martin

3. Visualizing the Choral: Epichoric Poetry, Ritual,
   and Elite Negotiation in Fifth-Century Thebes   63
   Leslie Kurke

II. DRAMA ON DRAMA

4. Euripides and Aristophanes: What does Tragedy Teach?   105
   Pietro Pucci

5. What's in a Wall?   127
   Simon Goldhill

III. DRAMA AND VISUALIZATION:
THE IMAGES OF TRAGEDY AND MYTH

6. Looking at Shield Devices: Tragedy and Vase Painting   151
   François Lissarrague

7. The Invention of the Erinyes   165
   Françoise Frontisi-Ducroux

8. A New Pair of Pairs: Tragic Witnesses in Western
   Greek Vase Painting?   177
   Oliver Taplin

9. Medea in Eleusis, in Princeton   197
    Luca Giuliani and Glenn W. Most

        IV. VISUALIZING DRAMA: THE DIVINITIES
               OF TRAGEDY AND COMEDY

10. Tragedy Personified   221
    Edith Hall

11. *Nikê's* Cosmetics: Dramatic Victory, the End of Comedy,
    and Beyond   257
    Peter Wilson

12. Everything to do with Dionysus? (Medelhavsmuseet,
    Stockholm, inv. MM 1962:7 / *ABV* 374 no. 197)   288
    John Henderson

         V. THE HISTORY OF TRAGIC VISION

13. Philostratus Visualizes the Tragic: Some Ecphrastic and
    Pictorial Receptions of Greek Tragedy in the Roman Era   309
    Jaś Elsner

14. Pulling the Other? Longus on Tragedy   338
    Ewen Bowie

15. Envisioning the Tragic Chorus on the Modern Stage   353
    Helene P. Foley

                    VI. CODA

16. Rencontre avec Froma   381
    †*Jean-Pierre Vernant*

17. Présence de Froma Zeitlin   388
    †*Pierre Vidal-Naquet*

References   398
Index Locorum   427
General Index   443

Notes on Contributors

Ewen Bowie has been E. P. Warren Praelector in Classics at Corpus Christi College, Oxford, since 1965. He has published numerous articles and contributions to collective volumes on the Greek literature and culture of the first three centuries CE, and has also worked on early Greek elegiac and iambic poetry, on Attic Old Comedy, and on Hellenistic poetry. He is currently completing a commentary on Longus, *Daphnis and Chloe.*

Jaś Elsner is Humfry Payne Senior Research Fellow in Classical Art and Archaeology at Corpus Christi College, Oxford, and Visiting Professor in Art History and Classics at the University of Chicago. His next book is *Roman Eyes: Visuality and Subjectivity in Roman Art.*

Helene P. Foley is Professor of Classics, Barnard College, Columbia University. She received her BA from Swarthmore College, an MAT and MA from Yale University, and a Ph.D. from Harvard University. She is the author of books and articles on Greek epic and drama, on women and gender in antiquity, and on modern performance and adaptation of Greek drama. Her books include *Ritual Irony: Poetry and Sacrifice in Euripides* (Ithaca, 1985), *The Homeric Hymn to Demeter* (Princeton, 1994), and *Female Acts in Greek Tragedy* (Princeton and Oxford, 2001). She is co-author of *Women in the Classical World: Image and Text* (New York and Oxford, 1994) and editor of *Reflections of Women in Antiquity* (New York and London, 1981). She is currently working on performance and adaptation of Greek tragedy in the U.S.

Françoise Frontisi-Ducroux is honorary Sous-directrice of the Collège de France and a member of the Centre Louis Gernet, Paris. Her research centres on religion (particularly on the figure of Dionysus), myth, and ancient Greek concepts of the gaze and of images. Her books include *Dédale. Mythologie de l'artisan en Grèce ancienne* (Paris, 1975; new edition, La Découverte, 2000).

Luca Giuliani has been Curator for Greek vases at the Antikenmuseum in Berlin (1982–92), Professor of Classical Archaeology at the University of Freiburg (1992–8), and since 1998 has been the Professor of Classical Archaeology at the Ludwig-Maximilians-Universität in Munich. His most recent book is *Bild und Mythos: Geschichte der Bilderzählung in der griechischen Kunst* (Munich, 2003).

Simon Goldhill is Professor of Greek at Cambridge University. He has published very widely on all aspects of Greek literature and culture, and is in demand as a lecturer all over the world. He appears regularly on radio and TV on the ancient and modern world.

Edith Hall, after holding posts at the Universities of Cambridge, Reading, Oxford, and Durham, in 2006 was appointed to a Research Chair in the departments of Classics and of Drama & Theatre at Royal Holloway, University of London. She is also co-founder and co-director of the Archive of Performances of Greek and Roman Drama. Her books include *Inventing the Barbarian* (Oxford, 1989), an edition of Aeschylus' *Persians* (Warminster, 1996), *Greek Tragedy and the British Theatre 1660–1914* (Oxford, 2005, co-authored with Fiona Macintosh), and *The Theatrical Cast of Athens: Interactions between Ancient Greek Drama and Society* (Oxford, 2006). She is also co-editor of several collections of essays, including *Greek and Roman Actors* (Cambridge, 2002, co-edited with Pat Easterling), and *Dionysus since 69: Greek Tragedy at the Dawn of the Third Millennium* (Oxford, 2004). She is currently writing a book on the reception of the *Odyssey* and editing collections of essays on the performance history of Aristophanes and on ancient pantomime.

John Henderson is Professor of Classics at the University of Cambridge and Fellow of King's College. Among his recent books are: *The Triumph of Art at Thorvaldsens Museum: 'Løve' in Copenhagen* (Copenhagen, 2005), *Morals and Villas in Seneca's Letters: Places to Dwell* (Cambridge, 2004), and *Pliny's Statue: the Letters, Self-Portraiture and Classical Art* (Exeter, 2002).

Chris Kraus has taught at New York University, University College London, and Oriel College, Oxford; she is at present Professor and Chair of Classics at Yale. Her research interests lie primarily in Latin prose style, narrative, and historiography, but she treasures her time as an undergraduate studying Greek tragedy with Froma at Princeton and occasionally ventures to publish in that field. She is currently working (with A. J. Woodman) on a commentary on Tacitus, *Agricola.*

Leslie Kurke is Professor of Classics and Comparative Literature at the University of California, Berkeley. She is the author of *The Traffic in Praise: Pindar and the Poetics of Social Economy* (Ithaca and London, 1991) and *Coins, Bodies, Games, and Gold: The Politics of Meaning in Archaic Greece* (Princeton, 1999). With Carol Dougherty, she is co-editor of *Cultural Poetics in Archaic Greece: Cult, Performance, Politics* (Cambridge, 1993) and *The Cultures within Ancient Greek Culture: Contact, Conflict, Collaboration* (Cambridge, 2003). She is currently working on the figure of Aesop as a form of mediation between high and popular cultures in ancient Greece.

François Lissarrague is Directeur d'Études, École des Hautes Études en Sciences Sociales (Anthropology and Images; the Greek experience). He is the author of several books on ancient Greek imagery, among them *The Aesthetics of the Greek Banquet* (Princeton, 1990) and *Greek Vases: The Athenians and their Images* (Riverside, 2001).

Richard P. Martin is the Antony and Isabelle Raubitschek Professor of Classics at Stanford University. He is currently working on two Homeric projects, *Rhapsodizing Homer* (about the meaning of ancient competitive performance for our understanding of the poems of Homer, Hesiod, and the Hymns) and *The Last Hero Song: Telemachus and the Generation of the Odyssey* (about the self-consciousness of the *Odyssey* in terms of the end of a tradition); he is also interested in Greek myth, religion, and Greek lyric in relation to art and music. His books include *The Language of Heroes: Speech and Performance in the Iliad* (Ithaca, 1989) and *Myths of the Ancient Greeks* (New York, 2003).

Glenn W. Most is Professor of Greek Philology at the Scuola Normale Superiore di Pisa and Professor of Social Thought, Classics, and Comparative Literature at the University of Chicago. He has written widely on ancient and modern literature and philosophy, on art history, and the classical tradition. His most recent books are *Doubting Thomas* (Cambridge, MA, 2005) and a translation of Sebastiano Timpanaro's *Genesis of Lachmann's Method* (Chicago, 2005).

Ruth Padel, an award-winning poet, Chair of the UK Poetry Society, and Fellow of the Royal Society of Literature, has published six collections of poetry. Froma encouraged her to publish two books from her D.Phil. (begun under E. R. Dodds) with Princeton University Press. Non-fiction since includes *I'm A Man* (on rock music, modern masculinity, and Greek myth), *52 Ways of Looking at a Poem* (readings in contemporary British poetry), and *Tigers in Red Weather*, a travel-memoir (with poems in the back) on where and how wild tigers live now.

Pietro Pucci teaches Greek literature at Cornell University. His recent books are *Xenophon, Socrates' Defense*: Introduction and Commentary (Amsterdam, 2002) and *Sofocle, Filottete: Introduzione e Commento* (Rome, 2003).

Laura M. Slatkin teaches at NYU and at the University of Chicago. She has published *The Power of Thetis: Allusion and Interpretation in the Iliad* (Berkeley and Oxford, 1991) and articles on Greek epic and drama. She co-edited (with Nicole Loraux and Gregory Nagy) *Histories of Post-War French Thought* vol. 2, *Antiquities: Rewriting the Past, Rethinking the Present* (New York, 2001).

Oliver Taplin is a Professor of Classics at Oxford University and a Tutorial Fellow of Magdalen College. His first book was *The Stagecraft of Aeschylus* (Oxford, 1977); his latest, *Pots and Plays. Interactions between Tragedy and Greek Vase-Painting of the Fourth Century BCE*, is to be published by Getty Museum Publications.

†**Jean-Pierre Vernant** was co-founder and first director of the Centre Louis Gernet at the École des Hautes Études en Sciences Sociales, and Professor of the Comparative Study of Ancient Religions at the Collège de France. A major player in the French resistance during the Second World War, he was perhaps the dominant figure in French Classics in the post-War period, having been founding father generally of the whole 'structuralist' approach to Classics, which revolutionized interpretations of Greek myth, text, and image. He was author of a series of classic books and articles on Greek mythology including *Les origines de la pensée grecque* (Paris, 1962), *Mythe et pensée chez les Grecs* (Paris, 1965), *Mythe et société en Grèce ancienne* (Paris, 1974) and *Mortals and Immortals* (Princeton, 1991, translated by Froma Zeitlin).

†**Pierre Vidal-Naquet** was Directeur d'Études at the École des Hautes Études en Sciences Sociales. He was probably the most influential, because the most historically aware, of the members of the 'structuralist' movement in French Classics, and was author of a number of fundamental works, many collected in *Le chasseur noire* (Paris, 1981), as well as a group of important books co-written with Jean-Pierre Vernant including *Mythe et tragédie en Grèce ancienne* (Paris, 1973 and 1986) and *Oedipe et ses mythes* (Brussels, 1988). As a politically involved intellectual, he was notable for his denunciation of torture by the French State during the Algerian war in *La torture dans la République: Essai d'histoire et de politique contemporaines* (Paris, 1983), and for his fight against Holocaust revisionism in *Les assassins de la mémoire* (Paris, 1987). His last book was *L'Atlantide: Petite histoire d'un mythe platonicien* (Paris, 2005).

Peter Wilson is Professor of Classics in the Department of Classics and Ancient History at the University of Sydney. He previously held posts at the University of Warwick and the University of Oxford. His research centres on the history of the Greek theatre, and publications include *The Athenian Institution of the* Khoregia: *the Chorus, the City, and the Stage* (Cambridge, 2000) and, with Penelope Murray, *Music and the Muses: the culture of* mousikē *in the Classical Athenian City* (Oxford, 2004). He is currently engaged on a large project (in collaboration with Eric Csapo), funded by the Australian Research Council, to write a new social and economic history of the classical theatre.

Illustrations

2.1 Drawing of a verse inscription on a marble tripod base from the Acropolis at Athens (*IG* I³ 833). *c.*500–480 BCE. (After Peppa-Delmousou, 1971). 39

6.1a and b Drawings after a red-figure psykter attributed to Oltos, showing hoplites with shields. Attic, *c.*510 BCE. 153

6.2 Drawing from the exterior of a damaged red-figure cup attributed to Macron, showing hoplites carrying shields that together depict a black-figure centauromachy with Heracles. Attic, *c.*490 BCE. 154

6.3 Drawing from the exterior of a damaged red-figure cup attributed to the Cleophrades Painter, showing Heracles fighting the Amazons. Attic, *c.*500 BCE. 157

6.4 Drawing from the exterior of a red-figure cup attributed to Macron, showing Achilles killing Troilus. Attic, *c.*490 BCE. 158

6.5 Red-figure pelike attributed to the Harrow Painter, showing a warrior with a shield whose device is a centaur playing a barbiton. Attic, *c.*470 BCE. 159

6.6 Drawing from a red-figure column crater attributed to the Cleveland Painter, showing Caeneus fighting the centaurs. Attic, *c.*470 BCE. 160

6.7 Red-figure column crater attributed to the Pan Painter, showing Caeneus fighting the centaurs. Attic, *c.*470 BCE. 161

8.1 Detail from a red-figure amphora attributed to the Darius Painter. Obverse, showing the death of Atreus. South Italian, *c.*340–330 BCE. Museum of Fine Arts, Boston. Collection of Shelby White and

Leon Levy and Gift of the Jerome Levy Foundation.
Photo: Museum of Fine Arts, Boston.   181

8.2   Red-figure amphora attributed to the Darius
       Painter. Obverse, detail showing a winged figure
       labelled *ΠΟΙΝΗ* (Revenge) and two females
       labelled *ΔΜΩΙΑΙ* (Maids). South Italian,
       *c.*340–330 BCE. Museum of Fine Arts, Boston.
       Collection of Shelby White and Leon Levy and
       Gift of the Jerome Levy Foundation.
       Photo: Museum of Fine Arts, Boston.   182

8.3   Detail from red-figure amphora attributed to the
       Darius Painter. Obverse, showing Heracles being
       supplicated by Laomedon, King of Troy, and
       his son Priam. South Italian, *c.*340–330 BCE.
       Musée d'art et d'histoire, Geneva. Photo:
       Museum (Maurice Aeschimann).   184

8.4   Red-figure amphora attributed to the Darius
       Painter. Obverse, detail showing two Trojan
       spearmen labelled *ΦΡΥΓΕΣ* (Phrygians) observing
       the main action. South Italian, *c.*340–330 BCE.
       Musée d'art et d'histoire, Geneva.
       Photo: Museum (Maurice Aeschimann).   186

9.1   Red-figure volute crater attributed to the
       Darius Painter, showing Medea at Eleusis.
       South Italian, *c.*340–330 BCE. Princeton
       University Art Museum, Carl Otto von
       Kienbusch Jr. Memorial Collection Fund.
       Photo: Trustees of Princeton University.   198

9.2   Red-figure amphora, ascribed to the Darius
       Painter, showing Medea fleeing from Corinth
       in a chariot pulled by serpents with a dead child
       behind her and Jason in pursuit. South Italian,
       *c.*340–330 BCE. Museo Nazionale, Naples.
       Photo: Soprintendenza archeologica
       delle Province di Napoli e Caserta.   200

9.3   Red-figure amphora, ascribed to the Darius
       Painter. Detail of Fig. 9.2, showing Medea
       fleeing from Corinth in a chariot pulled by
       serpents with a dead child behind her and

Jason in pursuit. South Italian, *c.*340–330 BCE. Museo Nazionale, Naples. Photo: Soprintendenza archeologica delle Province di Napoli e Caserta.   204

9.4   Red-figure volute crater attributed to the Darius Painter, showing Phrixus and Athamas before an altar. South Italian, *c.*340–330 BCE. Antikensammlung, Staatliche Museen zu Berlin. Photo: Johannes Laurentius.   208

10.1   Red-figure crater painted by a member of the Polygnotus Group. Athenian *c.*440–430 BCE. Musée Antoine Vivenel, Compiègne. Photo: Museum.   225

10.2   Red-figure crater painted by a member of the Polygnotus Group. Detail of Fig. 10.1, showing a personification of Tragedy, with a thyrsus and crouching leveret. Athenian, *c.*440 BCE. Musée Antoine Vivenel, Compiègne. Photo: Museum.   226

10.3   Detail from the neck of a red-figure volute crater attributed to the Leucippid Painter, showing two satyrs approaching maenads named *Kômôidia* and *Tragôidia* (with thyrsos). Athenian, *c.*430 BCE. Metropolitan Museum of Art, New York. Photo: Museum.   230

10.4   Red-figure oinochoe, showing a satyr approaching the sleeping figure of Tragedy. Athenian, *c.*430 BCE. Ashmolean Museum, Oxford. Photo: Museum.   232

10.5a   Drawing of a red-figure pelike now in Barcelona, with Apollo, Dionysus, and personifications of Tragedy (?) and Comedy. Athenian, late fifth century. Archaeological Museum of Catalonia, Barcelona. Drawing by Christina Unwin.   234

10.5b   Detail of Fig. 10.5a, showing the fragment with a satyr holding a jug and the now largely lost figure probably to be identified as Tragedy. Archaeological Museum of Catalonia, Barcelona. Photo: Museum.   235

10.6 Detail from a red-figure volute crater, known as the Pronomos vase, showing Dionysus, Ariadne, Himeros, and a figure here identified as Tragedy. Found in Ruvo, Apulia. *c.*400 BCE. Museo Nazionale, Naples. Photo: François Lissarrague. 236

10.7 Figure of Comedy from a statue group dedicated in the Dionysion in Thasos. Marble. Mid to late fourth century BCE. Photo: Archaeological Museum, Thasos. 245

10.8 Head of Tragedy as the mask of a blind old man, from the Dionysion in Thasos. Marble. Mid to late fourth century BCE. Photo: Archaeological Museum, Thasos. 246

12.1 Black-figure neck amphora signed by Amasis as potter, showing Athene and Poseidon. Athenian, late sixth century BCE. Obverse *ABV* 64.28. Cabinet des Médailles (1863, Luynes Collection), Bibliothèque Nationale de France 222, Paris. 291

12.2 Black-figure neck amphora signed by Amasis as potter, showing Dionysus with two maenads. Athenian, late sixth century BCE. Reverse *ABV* 64.28. Cabinet des Médailles (1863, Luynes Collection), Bibliothèque Nationale de France 222, Paris. 291

12.3 Black-figure neck amphora of the Leagros Group. Late sixth century BCE. Obverse, showing a male mounting a chariot. Medelhavsmuseet, Stockholm, inv. MM1962:7 / *ABV* 374 no. 197. 294

12.4 Black-figure neck amphora of the Leagros Group. Late sixth century BCE. Reverse, showing Dionysos with a consort and satyrs. Medelhavsmuseet, Stockholm, inv. MM1962:7 / *ABV* 374 no.197. 296

12.5 Detail of Fig. 12.4. 299

12.6 Marble hero relief from Chrysapha (Laconia). Mid sixth century BCE. Staatliche Museen, Berlin 731. 301

12.7 Transcription of image from black-figure hydria from Vulci, at Berlin: Cook (1940) 1049, fig. 842. 303

13.1   The death of Pentheus, wall painting from the
        House of the Vettii, Pompeii (vi.15.1, triclinium n).
        About 70 CE. Photograph: DAI Rome, Inst.
        Neg. 34.1678.   317

13.2   The death of Pentheus, carved relief front of the
        marble funerary urn of Cassius, now in the
        Museum of Fine Arts, Boston (Benjamin and
        Lucy Rowland Fund). About 200 CE. Photo:
        Museum of Fine Arts, Boston.   318

13.3   Agave with the head of Pentheus, bas relief
        from a marble candelabrum base now in the
        Museo Archeologico, Venice. Perhaps first
        quarter of the second century CE. Photo:
        DAI Rome, Inst. Neg. 82.519.   319

13.4   The death of Hippolytus, carved relief from the
        left end of a marble sarcophagus, now in San
        Nicola, Agrigento. Perhaps second quarter of
        the third century CE. Photo: DAI Rome,
        Inst. Neg. 71.854.   324

Editors' Introduction[1]

Athenian tragedy of the fifth century BCE became an international and a canonical genre with remarkable rapidity. There are plenty of reasons for expecting that tragedy might not have had such an impact with such speed. The performance of tragedy is closely linked to the city of Athens both through the festival of the Great Dionysia and through the scripts of the plays themselves, which set its stories of calamitous civic breakdown in the other cities of Greece, and praise Athens when the opportunity arises. The cost of mounting a tragedy was large, not least since it takes a good while to train and equip a chorus, actors, and musicians. A theatre may often have been a temporary site, but even so to seat a large audience and stage a trilogy required considerable effort and material resources. Yet Aeschylus was invited to stage plays in Sicily before the middle of the fifth century, Euripides moved to Macedon at the end of his career; theatres in Delphi and Delos had already been built in the fourth century; travelling companies visited cities of varying sizes; and, perhaps most poignantly, the few Athenians to survive the mines of Syracuse, after the disastrous Athenian military expedition against Sicily, owed their lives to the fact that they had learnt some Euripidean verses off by heart and could perform them for their impressed captors. Tragedy became not merely international but of canonical status. Official versions of the plays of Aeschylus, Sophocles, and Euripides were produced and guarded by the State. By the fourth century these were already the classics: Aeschylus was guaranteed

---

[1] Though this Introduction was written collaboratively, the lion's share was done by SDG, whose original we worked from. The other editors would like to thank him for blazing the trail!

reperformance, and Aristotle, a non-Athenian from Stagira, was not alone in thinking that the plays of Sophocles and Euripides constituted the golden age of drama.

Modern critics have cogently outlined reasons for the rise of tragedy. The plays themselves, as with Panhellenic epic, have a strong tendency towards universalism rather than the parochialism of, say, comedy: Sophocles' play is explicit that Oedipus is an example for all mankind (*OT* 1186–97). The genre of drama appealed strongly to the Greek sense of competition and to performance—the *agon* was a central institution for Greek culture as much as it is for Athenian drama.² The emotional power of tragedy, or rather the enactment of such emotional power and its effect on the spectators, offered a new and hugely stirring form, that took the allure of epic themes to a new level of audience engagement. Tragedy's ability to explore issues of burning concern in the post-Persian war society of Greece spoke across local affiliations and domestic politics.³ The sheer beauty and force of the poetry offered a compelling rewriting of the grandeur of Homer for the contemporary polis. These factors can all be claimed to have made tragedy a genre that travelled far beyond its first performances both chronologically and spatially.

In this volume, however, we are interested not so much in explaining the causes of the spread of tragedy. Rather, we set out to trace the process of its growth and dissemination. 'Reception' has become a buzzword of contemporary classical studies. In the study of the classical tradition, there is within the modern academy considerable interest in moving away from the project of simply tracing who read what texts at what point in history (important though such empirical histories are) towards exploring a more dynamic sense of how a genre in the ancient world comes into being and how the ancient world becomes part of later societies. How does a new genre like tragedy relate to literary and cultural traditions? How, in turn, does tragedy become part of a classical tradition? What affiliations are being created by appeals to classical antiquity, and how? What ideological, intellectual, cultural work do such images of the past perform? What role does forgetting or selective memory play in these constructed ties? These and other, interrelated questions have changed the ways in

---

² See Osborne (1993).   ³ See Taplin (1999).

which the privileged place of the classical past in the modern West is comprehended, as well as changing our understanding of tragedy as a cultural event of the classical city.

Tragedy is a remarkably important test case through which to make such explorations of how a genre becomes privileged and of what the cultural effects of its continuing appropriation are. This process begins in the fifth century itself, where we can see Athenian tragedy at one level through the lens of how it adopts and adapts the strategies of earlier privileged textual and performance histories (such as Homer in particular), finding its place within cultural and literary traditions. At another level, we can view tragedy through the lens of contemporary fifth-century responses in literature and in other media. Comedy, as evidenced by the so-called Old Comedy of Aristophanes, loves to parody and play with the resources of its cousin, tragedy. Not only is the grand language of tragedy mocked (and imitated) on the comic stage, but also the tragic playwrights, Aeschylus and Euripides appear as figures on stage, and their tragic plots are raided and manipulated for comic extravaganzas. Comedy has proved a remarkably long-lived influence on the critical reception of tragedy, especially through a play like the *Frogs* of Aristophanes. But tragedy itself is not a static genre. Euripides in particular is celebrated for his self-conscious intertextual play with earlier tragedy, most famously in the games he plays with the recognition scene of Aeschylus' *Libation Bearers* in his *Electra*—an episode whose explicit literary self-awareness so outraged the great Eduard Fraenkel that he proposed deleting the whole scene.[4] To see how tragedy develops an awareness of itself as a genre, one starting point must be the plays themselves.

Tragedy's dominance of the cultural imagination, however, is vividly reflected in other genres and other media too. Polytheistic myth loves to let a thousand stories bloom: like an expanding and intertwining network of ivy, there are multiple, interrelated versions of the most familiar mythic narratives, each told for specific purpose and with specific purchase. Yet some of tragedy's figures were so celebrated that they came to represent *the* paradigmatic account: Euripides' *Hippolytus* or *Medea* changes the way that the figures of Hippolytus

---

[4] Fraenkel (1950: iii.815–26).

or Medea are represented and understood ever after. Now an orator can rant: 'What should I call him? Oedipus? Aegisthus?' (Andocides 1.129) and expect his audience to recall through his insult the grim narrative of tragic transgression.

The city of Athens was not just a city of words, but also a city of images. The picturing of mythic narratives which survives on ceramics in particular, both influenced the potential of tragedy's staging and was influenced by tragedy's performances. It is hard to find many pots which directly illustrate particular performances of specific tragedies.[5] Yet the repertoire of Athenian imagery—and from the fourth century onwards imagery from the rest of the Greek-speaking world too—shows a fascinating dynamic relation with the stage. At one level, we see apparently direct echoes of tragic narrative in the portrayal of mythic figures. Medea now appears in the dragon-drawn chariot of the Sun God, echoing the novel ending of Euripides' play. But we also see more diffuse reflections of tragedy's obsession with revenge, and, at the most sophisticated level, a fascination with the connection between representation and the world of the theatre. The Pronomos vase, for example, one of the most famous examples of ancient painted pottery, shows actors in the various stages of dressing up as satyrs for a satyr play, juxtaposed against 'real' satyrs, dancing for Dionysus. The combination of men dressing up until they become indistinguishable from mythic characters in religious worship, all represented by the painter's skill on the surface of the vase, seems to reflect on the power and playfulness of mimesis in a highly suggestive and pointed manner. The fifth-century enlightenment, with its complex intellectual debates about vision, perception, and representation, is fuelled by the event of theatre, much as the plays of the period engage with such concerns. We should not be surprised that the work of the painters of pots should also participate in such a cultural moment.

This intricate reception—appropriation, privileging, reading, re-presenting—of tragedy continued over the centuries, even and especially when Greece became part of the Roman Empire.[6] Tragedy was taught in schools and was an integral part of the education of a Greek gentleman: *paideia*—education, culture—made the

---

[5] See Green (1994); Trendall and Webster (1970).   [6] See Easterling (1997*b*).

pepaideumenos, the cultivated, sophisticated man, and knowing tragedy was part of the expectation of a civilized citizen of the Roman Empire. Philostratus, the third-century intellectual associated closely with the court of Julia Domna, wrote a biography of Apollonius of Tyana, the wandering miracle worker and sage. Apollonius travels to India to learn the wisdom of the East and, in a scene as familiar from modern cartoons as from ancient stereotypes, struggles to reach the guru who will tell him the secrets of the universe. This guru quotes Euripides. It is a wonderful and very funny moment that bears elegant testimony to the place of tragedy at the pinnacle of man's knowledge of the world. The texts of the so-called Second Sophistic repeatedly reflect on the inheritance of tragedy—from the literary-critical comparison of three versions of *Philoctetes* offered by Dio of Prusa, to the rhetorical outbursts of a lover whose boyfriend has been dragged to death by his horse like a new Hippolytus, as portrayed in *Leucippe and Clitophon*, the novel of Achilles Tatius. So too the visual arts from the Hellenistic period onwards revelled in the psychological and physical torments of tragic narratives, as did the poetry and prose reflecting on that art. Tragedy became part of the furniture of the Greek mind.

In the modern West too, of course, Athenian tragedy, often mediated through the Roman plays of Seneca, has continued to have a major impact not just in the history of theatre, but also in the history of thought. Hegel's Antigone is essential to his philosophy, and also dominates modern critical readings of *Antigone*;[7] Wagner thought the *Ring* and the Bayreuth Festival would rediscover the true and pure art of Greek tragedy for the modern age: 'it would be better to be half a day a Greek in the presence of the Art-work of tragedy, than to be all eternity an—unGreek *God*!'[8] Sartre, T. S. Eliot, Eugene O'Neill nourished their theatre on Greek tragedy. Indeed, the last thirty-five years have witnessed the most extraordinary flourishing of ancient tragedy on the modern stage. There has been scarcely a year without a major production of Greek tragedy in London, New York, Paris, and Berlin. The engagement of modern culture with ancient tragedy shows no sign of abating.

---

[7] See Steiner (1984); Leonard (2005).   [8] Wagner (1892–9: i.35).

The appropriation, influence, and cultural power of tragedy—its becoming a genre—constitutes one connecting theme of the essays in this book. We hope that our discussion of the variety of dynamic forms of this long-running multidisciplinary engagement with tragedy will make a significant contribution to the current debate about how the literature and art of the classical world become the classical tradition. And we hope that this very broad, multidirectional sense of 'reception' will prove productive for others, as it has for us. But it should be clear that to attempt to deal with all of the potential angles of such an intricate and far-reaching thematic would not be possible in any one volume. Our second focus narrows down such a frame to one central concern: visualization.

Theatre is different from epic and other forms of ancient poetry because of its commitment to embodied enactment before spectators. The modality of the visual is an ineluctable constituent of theatre. *To theatron*, 'the theatre', in Greek means 'the place for looking'; a seat in the theatre is called a *thea*, a 'sight', 'viewing'; the audience is made up of *theatai*, 'spectators', 'lookers'; and the fund which supported the attendance of citizens in the theatre was called the *theorikon*. *Theoria* (from which comes our modern word, 'theory') names the process of attending a festival as a participant observer—which turns the act of watching in the theatre away from a merely aesthetic experience towards the active role of a citizen of democracy, participating in a festival and an institution of the city.[9] The visual is an integral element of theatre. Plato may have mistrusted perception as a route to knowledge, and Aristotle, inheriting and systematizing his master's distaste, may have declared that visual spectacle (*opsis*) was the least significant element of drama (*Po.* 6.19; 1450[b]). But its very vocabulary marks theatre as a key institution of the city's visual culture.

The dramas of this institution repeatedly reflect on this condition. The language of sight runs through the discourse of Sophocles' *Oedipus Tyrannus*, as Oedipus approaches his self-blinding, a gesture which embodies his despair at his own ignorance.[10] Euripides' *Bacchae* takes

---

[9] See Goldhill (2000*b*), and Nightingale (2004); see Goldhill (2000*a*) and Rhodes (2003).
[10] See Segal (1981: 207–48).

as its dramatic premise the need to perceive and recognize the god Dionysus, whose power is the power of transformation, disguise, and deception. 'Now you see what you should see', says Dionysus, as the possessed Pentheus observes, 'I seem to see two suns, two cities' (*Ba.* 918–24). Aeschylus composes a satyr play, in which the satyrs come face to face with sculptures of satyrs, and comment on the mimesis in the language of art theory.[11] The close linguistic and conceptual connection between seeing and knowing in Greek (*idein/ eidenai*) always encourages the discourse of sight in theatre to cue the broadest tragic concerns with man's understanding of the world. Athenian theatre repeatedly exposes for its spectators the anxieties and false hopes of human knowledge, and the discourse of sight is essential to this fundamental issue.

Theatrical performance's work of visualization is of signal importance, then, for the functioning of theatre as theatre and for the thematic texture of the dramas themselves. For the painter, visualizing myth is no less a necessary process. The cultural imagination which produced the images on Athenian ceramics is deeply influenced by tragedy's representation of myth on stage (though it is harder to show the likely influence of the idealist art of the fifth century on the representations of the heroes in the theatre). Yet the influence rarely takes the form of simple illustration. It needs considerable care to articulate how tragedy is visualized, or re-visualized, in the city of images—and this makes such imagery a fascinating sphere in which to explore the process of cultural engagement with theatre. From this other medium, how does tragedy look?

The rhetoricians who trained the educated elite of the Hellenistic cities and the Greeks of the Roman Empire developed a full theory of visualization, under the heading of *enargeia*, which is often translated as 'vividness', but which is defined as 'the power to bring an event before the eyes of an audience as if they were there themselves'. *Enargeia* is one of 'the *aretai* [virtues] of ecphrasis', the power of good description.[12] So writers of Hellenistic epigrams, like the masters of second- and third-century CE Greek prose, station themselves before pictures of tragic heroes and heroines and explore

---

[11] See Zeitlin (1994: 138–47).
[12] Theon, *Prog.* 11; Hermog., *Prog.* 10; see Zanker (1981); Webb (1997; 1999).

through words what it is like to look at these portrayals; and they strive to bring the images alive for us, the readers.[13] This is an archetypal process of re-visualizing tragedy: responding with as much vividness as possible to an artistic portrait of a tragic figure, itself a response to the texts, which we are all presumed to have read and absorbed. It captures precisely the intricate cultural work that is concealed in the phrase 'the reception of tragedy'. Just as every performance has to create its own visualization of ancient tragedy, so too art and the verbal interpretations of these artworks, are actively forming and formulating the classical tradition.

The fecundity of this idea of visualization is clear from the range of approaches and material which this book includes. The first section of the book, 'Visualizing Tragedy from Elsewhere', looks at tragedy very much from the outside, providing a set of contrasts and forebears for the central sections of the volume. It should be clear that to appreciate Athenian tragedy as an institution, the viewpoint of other cities, other genres, and other times will help specify and define its particular development. We begin with Laura Slatkin's study of Homer's intimations of tragic visualization. Tragedy is veined with the language of Homer, and in the most profound way *written through* epic. It would not be possible to discuss tragedy and visualization without a treatment of Homer's master-text. Tragedy takes place, finds its place, through its reworking of Homer for the contemporary city. Slatkin shows how the *Iliad*'s sense of the visual prefigures the obsessions of the tragic imagination. Richard Martin turns to a genre of sung poetry, the dithyramb, performed, like tragedy, at the festivals of Dionysus at Athens. The dithyramb involved more performers than tragedy, was closely related to the worship of the god, and was a genre where literary and musical innovation was crucial; yet its representation in the city and beyond is quite different from that of tragedy. Martin looks at how the dithyramb enters the long-term discourse of the city—its memorialization through monuments—and thus links the two themes of reception and visualization, and through the different viewpoint of the genre of dithyramb lets us see the genre of tragedy in a far richer context. Thebes is the tragic city *par excellence*, the city of

---

[13] See Goldhill (1994*a*) and (forthcoming *b*).

Oedipus and Pentheus, an inverted version of Athens. Leslie Kurke takes a Pindaric poem centred on a particular rite in Thebes and shows how it is read and reread over history. We have here a rite more to do with aristocratic competition than democratic politics, choral poetry without the play of actors and, above all, a poem with a strong localized politics. As on the tragic stage, so in such literary history Thebes provides a pointed contrast for Athens. This first section thus provides a cultural and literary tradition against and within which tragedy develops as a genre. It shows how the new and provocative discourse of tragedy is formed within a process of 'reception'.

The second section, 'Drama on Drama', looks at how the genre of tragedy is formulated through the theatre itself. First Pietro Pucci takes on comedy and its appropriation of tragedy. He explores not just how comedy mocks tragedy's claims to teach, nor just how comedy redrafts tragedy's politics, but also how comedy plays with the props of tragedy, using the *visual* resources of theatre to construct its humour and its own aesthetic. Simon Goldhill takes a specific act of tragic visualization, the representation of the walls of Thebes in Euripides' *Phoenissae*, and investigates how such visualization is developed through a set of literary and political expectations first from Homer and the fifth-century city, and second, from tragedy itself, and from Aeschylus' *Seven Against Thebes* in particular. Together, these two chapters show how the idea of a genre of tragedy is constructed within drama itself—an internal dynamic of reception—and how the visualization integral to theatrical performance plays a formative role in such a process.

The third section, 'Drama and Visualization: The Images of Tragedy and Myth', focuses on visual images. François Lissarrague, like Goldhill, starts from Aeschylus' *Seven Against Thebes*. He notes how the shield blazons in the tragedy are described in such a way as to construct a system of significant images. He compares this with images of shield blazons painted on cups, and specifically images of centaurs and Heracles, to show how it is possible to see such structured systems already present in Athenian representational norms. This, he suggests, may indicate the influence of painted pots on tragedy's language. How tragedy visualizes in words may be formed in part through how artists visualize myth on pots. A similar interplay between tragedy's language and images from art is analysed by Françoise Frontisi-Ducroux with regard to the Erinyes. The Furies make an appearance on stage in the *Eumenides* of Aeschylus; in the *Libation Bearers* they are invisible and seeing them is a sign of Orestes' madness. Visualizing the Erinyes—their gradual embodiment— is central thus to the dramatic narrative of the *Oresteia*. Frontisi-Ducroux tries to explain why the appearance of the Furies was said to be so frightening, and how the artistic record helps us comprehend Aeschylus' novelty. Oliver Taplin directs our gaze to marginal and anonymous pairs of figures on certain vases (which depict some well-known mythic narratives much beloved of tragedians). He suggests that the fact that these figures are given labels but not names (*dmôiai*, for example, 'maidservants') indicates a desire to construct a choral presence in these visual representations: that is, an anonymous group who bear witness to tragic events, who mediate and direct our gaze at events, and who are survivors. From this we can appreciate how tragic theatre affects representational strategies of myth in an indirect and diffuse manner, and not by a desire for evident theatrical illustration. Finally in this section, Luca Giuliani and Glenn Most look at some surprising images of Medea, and try to read how mythic narratives, whether influenced or untouched by tragedy, may be read from the fragmented cues of the visual field. In this section, we see how the visual medium of tragedy is intertwined—another dynamic relation of reception—with the visual medium of painting.

The fourth section, 'Visualizing Drama: The Divinities of Tragedy and Comedy', takes three divinities closely associated with theatre and explores what their visualization in the artistic record can reveal. Edith Hall looks at the figure of *Tragoedia* (Tragedy) herself, pictured as a divine female, who appears on pots from the 440s BCE. The image of Tragedy is instrumental in the construction of the idea of the genre of tragedy, she argues, and the shifting nature of the imagery of Tragedy as a figure reflects shifting conceptualizations of the genre. Visualizing Tragedy—here in a most literal form— becomes thereby a significant factor in the literary history of the genre. Peter Wilson focuses on the more familiar figure of Victory, whose winged arrival is depicted throughout the city of Athens, from Pheidias' statue of Athena Parthenos to a host of lowly cups. Victory is the culmination of the dramatic festival as a contest (and no doubt much sought after by playwrights and liturgists alike), but Wilson shows how both tragedy and comedy take a more questioning view of the value of winning. In particular, comedy unpicks the ideology of self-confidence in such imagery by depicting the ugliness, selfishness, and violence involved in triumph. Like Hall, Wilson explores the space between the verbal texts and the visual imagery of the city—the space where visualization is at stake. John Henderson turns to Dionysus, the god of theatre himself, and anatomizes the imagery of Dionysiac religion on two particular cups. How is the god (to be) visualized? Henderson investigates how Dionysiac distortion of perception—along with his standard accompaniments of the whirling dance of the chorus, the delights of wine and dressing up—affects the space and question of visualization. In the arena of Dionysiac vision, a certain self-reflexivity is required. (How do pots see you?) What is imaged in these intricate pictures, argues Henderson, is a question about seeing itself. Henderson brings the Dionysiac images on two drinking cups into the intellectual world of the sophists and Plato, where perception, intellectual comprehension of divinity, and changing models of the self are major topics of intellectual concern. Visualization here is not merely an artistic or verbal process but a question about the self's engagement with the world.

The fifth and final section, 'The History of Tragic Vision', looks at paradigmatic moments of the later reception of tragedy. Jaś Elsner opens Philostratus' *Imagines* on the pages where he describes paintings of Hippolytus and other tragic heroes. Elsner brings out carefully Philostratus' witty awareness of the intellectual playfulness inherent in his game of representing in words an artist's rendition of a tragic text from long ago. Philostratus revels in the rhetorician's love of visualization as one of the key weapons in his armoury. Ewen Bowie treads a completely opposite path. He shows how Longus' novel, *Daphnis and Chloe*, which loves to parade its *paideia* through literary echo and witty reference, only rarely seems to make any verbal or conceptual nods towards tragedy. Bowie reads this as a sign of a specific ideological strategy. In tragedy, *eros* is never simply happy or successful, never between equals, never allowed as a positive emotion in a woman. The novel, as Foucault and others have argued, is a sign and symptom of a shift in attitudes towards sexuality and specifically towards the possibilities of long-lasting heterosexual affection within marriage. Longus does significantly and carefully echo tragedy's description of the symptoms of passion, only to fit them into a quite different narrative. The rejection of the language of tragedy becomes a silencing of an unwanted set of associations in the new world of the erotic novel. Finally, Helene Foley offers as a paradigmatic case of the reperformance of tragedy the attempts of modern theatrical practitioners to deal with the chorus of Athenian tragedy on the contemporary stage. She looks at how hard it has proved to envisage a collective body which can comment in an authoritative way on the action, what the costs are of the solutions directors have hazarded, and how such attempts have drawn on multicultural theatrical traditions. As the first section looked at different choruses in dithyramb and Theban ritual, so we end with the different world of modernity trying to come to terms with the chorus of tragedy. This final section is both a demonstration of how tragedy is part of a process of reception over the centuries, and how visualization plays a crucial role in this process.

The five sections of the volume, then, take a multidisciplinary and variegated perspective on the central issue of how we might understand the diffuse formation of the genre of tragedy through the central category of visualization.

But there is another motivating force for this volume. It is written in honour of Froma Zeitlin, and dedicated to her with love and deepest respect from what is only a selection of her friends in the field of classics. The topics on which we have written, the texts and images we have chosen for exposition, the whole subject of the book, is prompted by the intellectual interests of someone who has inspired, educated, and thrilled all the authors in this volume over many years. The late Jean-Pierre Vernant and Pierre Vidal-Naquet, whose work has been so influential on modern perspectives on tragedy, end this volume with two, very personal recollections of how they shared an intellectual life with Froma Zeitlin.

'Visualizing the Tragic' could have been the title of a large collection of Zeitlin's essays. Her earliest published work was on Aeschylus, and her essays on sacrificial imagery and on the dynamics of misogyny in the *Oresteia* show from the start her extraordinary range of talents. It is a matter of great pride to her that none of her work, however provocative or groundbreaking, shows anything less than the highest standards of traditional, technical classical scholarship. At the same time, her work demonstrates an equally scholarly understanding of anthropological studies of myth and ritual. Sacrifice is a central religious rite of Greek culture and needs to be understood as such, and not just as a literary motif. Similarly, understanding the language of misogyny in the *Oresteia* requires an appreciation of how the trilogy works with mythic narratives of the place of women, as well as a comprehension of the role of women in the family and state in the fifth century. These studies of Aeschylus were extraordinarily timely. 'The Dynamics of Misogyny' was a foundational text not only for the new approaches to Greek tragedy which have dominated the academy since the 1970s, but also for generations of feminist scholarship. Zeitlin does not just work on tragedy: she has changed the way we all work on tragedy.

Theatre has remained a mainstay of Zeitlin's career. In 1982 she published *Under the Sign of the Shield*, on Aeschylus' *Seven Against Thebes*, which demonstrates her flair for close reading as well as her understanding of the deep structures of social thought in tragic narrative. It is a play that brings the topic of visualization to the fore, with its famous central scene of Eteocles hearing and responding to the description of the shield blazons of the seven champions ranged against the seven gates of Thebes. A series of seminal articles over the same decades have made a huge impact, especially 'The Closet of Masks' and 'Playing the Other' (which later became the title of a volume of her collected essays). 'The Closet of Masks' was a trendsetting essay on Euripidean self-consciousness, which took the debate about his sophistication and literariness to a new level of literary sophistication. 'Playing the Other' was nothing less than a general view of tragedy's strategies of representation, which focused with brilliant economy on how tragedy represents other cities at other times and involves people other than the male, citizen audience. Her celebrated essay on the *Thesmophoriazusae* of Aristophanes, 'Travesties of Gender and Genre', is still the best account of how comedy hijacks tragedy, and how the representation of women is intimately connected with the transgressive world of comedy and its literary aesthetics. The fascination with gender and drama also motivates Zeitlin's fine essays on Euripides' *Hippolytus* and *Ion*. In recent years, the modern reception of tragedy has been the subject of her remarkable essay on 'Dionysus in 69', Schechner's adaptation of Euripides' *Bacchae* in New York in 1968.

This sequence of long essays—a form of publication she has made her own—represents an extremely important and influential body of work. Tragedy and the theatre are never far from Zeitlin's work—but she travels throughout the ancient world herself. Her work on the novel is broad: she delivered the Sather lectures precisely on visualization and the prose of the Second Sophistic, an early foretaste of which can be enjoyed in a celebrated essay on mimesis and *Daphnis and Chloe*. She has published on Homer; on Petronius; on Hesiod. She has also co-edited two of the most influential collections of essays on what became burning issues in the field. *Before Sexuality* responds to the new histories of sexuality associated with Foucault and others; and *Nothing to Do with Dionysos?* opens up the issue of the social context of Greek drama.

It is typical that Froma Zeitlin should have been in at the beginning of what became such important topics of debate, and also typical that she should have been instrumental in producing volumes that were so influential in these debates. There are two reasons for this. First, her work has always insisted on taking on the biggest questions. In a field which so often delights in the trees at the expense of the forest, this refreshing willingness to broach major intellectual projects has made Zeitlin a classicist whose work has a special purchase in other fields. She is passionate about thinking hard: but she is beholden to no single methodological school. She has always had a distaste for the 'Girardian' reading of this or the 'Lacanian' reading of that. For her, it is the ancient material, not a predigested modern theory, which must dictate the critical framework. Second, she is fantastic at bringing people together, and at seeing the potential of others. Froma Zeitlin was influential in mediating the exciting new work associated with the Centre Louis Gernet in Paris for an English-speaking audience (and several of the Centre's luminaries write in this volume). And she loves to say 'Have you met . . . ?', 'I must get you to see . . .'. The authors of this volume include only one person who has actually studied as a graduate student with Froma Zeitlin, namely Leslie Kurke (who at Princeton worked mainly with Richard Martin). Glenn Most and Richard Martin were formerly her colleagues at Princeton. Otherwise, we are all those who have come into her orbit—and stayed there for decades, in her network of friends and intellectual allies. And the volume could have had three times as many contributors without difficulty.

This brief intellectual biography has left out much: it does not mention her recent and characteristically all-embracing interest in Holocaust literature, her teaching, or her lecturing. But it does help explain the choices of the subjects of each chapter above: each scholar has chosen a particular aspect of Zeitlin's work that stimulates reflection, critical commentary, new argument. But what such an intellectual biography cannot explain is why we wanted to write this volume. For all of us, it is a deep affection based first on her intellectual generosity and fecundity. Froma bubbles over with ideas, freely given, generously critical, explosively insightful, passionately engaged. It is also based on her capacity for friendship and support: long conversations, late nights, loud laughter, intense absorption in the moment of companionship. It is in such a spirit that this book is dedicated to her.

I

Visualizing Tragedy from Elsewhere

1

Notes on Tragic Visualizing in the *Iliad*

Laura M. Slatkin

The *Iliad* is a poem of shocking visions. Drawing attention throughout to what its characters perceive, to their experience of viewing, the poem dwells on the impact of the sights that confront them and on the act of seeing itself. Whether from distant vantage points (the fiery head of Achilles appearing to the Trojans) or those close by (the view of Hector's neck as Achilles takes fatal aim), confrontations with things seen place the unfolding of the poem before the audience's eyes, even as the events are realized in the experience of its characters.[1] At such moments, what they are seeing we are seeing; the audience shares their line of vision. In the discussion that follows, I hope to suggest how the characters' lines of vision, in the various directions they take, may offer additional perspective on the *Iliad*'s stringent and subtle intimations of tragedy.

Central to the scenes of battle, one after another, is the act of catching sight—of a wounded or fallen comrade or brother. Those glimpses through which warriors become aware of their comrades in ultimate peril on the battlefield are what impel them most often to enter the fray.[2] The urgent, galvanizing verb in the dynamics of battle is none other than ἐνόησε (*enoêse*) 'he noticed':[3] at the sight of a fallen fellow warrior, the fighters—pitying, grieving, vengeful—risk

---

[1] See Bakker (1999).

[2] As Bernard Fenik's analysis of battle scenes has demonstrated; see Fenik (1968).

[3] The semantic range of νοέω in the *Iliad* includes not only 'taking note of', 'observing', but 'having in mind', 'bearing in awareness'.

everything.[4] An elaborated instance of this, decisive for the poem's plot, is Achilles' sighting—*enoêse*[5]—of the wounded Machaon, which prompts him to send Patroclus to the ships of the Achaeans.[6] Thus we understand that Ajax's plea to Zeus: 'don't kill us in the darkness, kill us in the light' (17.645–7), is, in part, an appeal to be able to lay eyes on one's comrades, to see and be seen, an appeal on behalf of the opportunity to enact solidarity among the fighting men.

The scenes of carnage on which that light shines are viewed face to face in the poem's full-frontal depiction of the war's brutality. Witnessing, we are made aware, is a crucial dimension of the fighters' courage; the capacity to see is inseparable from the heroic endeavours that earn them glory. No warrior ever averts his eyes from those images of lacerated flesh, of bodies subjected to death blows, of disfigured and dismembered remnants of the human corpses.[7] By creating for its audience alternative images, in the similes that translate the horror of slaughter and mutilation into figures of peace and productivity,[8] the narrative only reinforces the relentless cruelty

---

[4] Among many examples:

> τὸν δ' ὡς οὖν ἐνόησε Κόων ἀριδείκετος ἀνδρῶν
> πρεσβυγενὴς Ἀντηνορίδης, κρατερόν ῥά ἑ πένθος
> ὀφθαλμοὺς ἐκάλυψε κασιγνήτοιο πεσόντος.
> στῆ δ' εὐράξ σὺν δουρὶ λαθὼν Ἀγαμέμνονα δῖον,
> νύξε δέ μιν κατὰ χεῖρα μέσην ἀγκῶνος ἔνερθε,
> ἀντικρὺ δὲ διέσχε φαεινοῦ δουρὸς ἀκωκή.   (11.248–53)

When Koön, conspicuous among the fighters, caught sight of him,
he who was Antenor's eldest born, the strong sorrow
misted about his eyes for the sake of his fallen brother.
He came from the side and unobserved at great Agamemnon
and stabbed with his spear at the middle arm, underneath the elbow,
and the head of the glittering spear cut its way clean through.

(All translations are from Lattimore [1961], with some alterations.)

[5] τὸν δὲ ἰδὼν ἐνόησε ποδάρκης δῖος Ἀχιλλεύς (11.599: ('And swift-footed, brilliant Achilleus, watching, observed him').

[6] On pity as motivating warriors to action, see Kim (2000: ch. 2).

[7] See Scarry (1987) for a trenchant discussion of the contemporary (as well as ancient) figurative language and discourses of physical suffering.

[8]
> πάντῃ δὴ πύργοι καὶ ἐπάλξιες αἵματι φωτῶν
> ἐρράδατ' ἀμφοτέρωθεν ἀπὸ Τρώων καὶ Ἀχαιῶν.
> ἀλλ' οὐδ' ὣς ἐδύναντο φόβον ποιῆσαι Ἀχαιῶν,
> ἀλλ' ἔχον ὥς τε τάλαντα γυνὴ χερνῆτις ἀληθής,
> ἥ τε σταθμὸν ἔχουσα καὶ εἴριον ἀμφὶς ἀνέλκει
> ἰσάζουσ', ἵνα παισὶν ἀεικέα μισθὸν ἄρηται·   (12.430–5)

of what the fighting men stare down. Such similes also point to the broader conceptual paradigms the poem everywhere encodes: those norms governing peaceful, as well as martial, activity—indeed the mutual implication of those norms, that broader cultural system underlying early epic, in which men must work, strive, labour, and die, and forever live apart from the gods.

The all-too-mortal condition of human experience underlies the powerful epic figuration of human seeing, from sight as stimulus-to-battle to other, less furious modes of seeing. At the other extreme from the constantly presented views of wounded comrades, the poem highlights an extraordinary mode of seeing—one that estranges the activity of cognition and the faculty of vision. To behold the gods, as it were, in their own persons—this is given to few mortals, and the poem describes such beholding as phenomenologically unlike any other experience of seeing. The scene in which Athene enables Diomedes' *aristeia*, in book 5, begins with her making such vision possible for him—a process at once physical and metaphysical that requires her explanation:

> ἀχλὺν δ' αὖ τοι ἀπ' ὀφθαλμῶν ἕλον ἣ πρὶν ἐπῆεν,
> ὄφρ' εὖ γιγνώσκῃς ἠμὲν θεὸν ἠδὲ καὶ ἄνδρα   (5.127–8)

> The mist that was formerly on your eyes I have taken away,
> so that you may well recognize the god and the man.

Such seeing marks the viewer, sets him apart from those who share his line of sight but not his condition of perception—the mist is still upon their eyes. Human vision, however acute, is understood then to be always shuttered, always dimmed by mortality.[9] That shadow that keeps the god beyond human sight is an extension of the final *achlus* that covers the eyes of the warrior once and for all.

> Everywhere the battlements and the bastions were awash
> with men's blood shed from both sides, Achaian and Trojan.
> But even so they could not drive panic among the Achaians,
> But held evenly as the scales which a careful widow
> holds, taking it by balance beam, and weighs her wool evenly,
> at either end, working to win a pitiful wage for her children.

---

[9] See Vernant (1989) for a discussion of the comparison between human and divine faculties.

Μηριόνης δ' Ἀκάμαντα κιχεὶς ποσὶ καρπαλίμοισι
νύξ' ἵππων ἐπιβησόμενον κατὰ δεξιὸν ὦμον·
ἤριπε δ' ἐξ ὀχέων, κατὰ δ' ὀφθαλμῶν κέχυτ' **ἀχλύς**.   (16.342–4)

Meriones on his agile feet overtaking Akamas
stabbed him in the right shoulder as he climbed up behind his horses;
he hurtled from the chariot and the mist drifted over his eyes.

When an especially fierce and evidently fearless combatant bears
down on his opponents, those facing him will ask whether it is a man
they see before them, or a god.[10] Visual undecidability presents a
cognitive impasse: and of course, whether one beholds a god or a
man may make all the mortal difference. At the end, what Hector
understands is the *meaning* of his inability to see Athene for who she
is—that it is a *sign* of his impending death, not simply its cause.

Ἕκτωρ δ' ἔγνω ᾗσιν ἐνὶ φρεσὶ φώνησέν τε·
"ὢ πόποι, ἦ μάλα δή με θεοὶ θάνατονδὲ κάλεσσαν·
Δηΐφοβον γὰρ ἔγωγ' ἐφάμην ἥρωα παρεῖναι·
ἀλλ' ὁ μὲν ἐν τείχει, ἐμὲ δ' ἐξαπάτησεν Ἀθήνη.
νῦν δὲ δὴ ἐγγύθι μοι θάνατος κακός, οὐδ' ἔτ' ἄνευθεν...   (22.296–300)

And Hektor knew the truth inside his heart, and spoke aloud:
'No use. Here at last the gods have summoned me deathward.
I thought Deïphobos the hero was here next to me,
but he is on the wall, and Athene deceived me.
And now evil death is beside me, and no longer far away...'

From the outset, the poem represents the distinctiveness of
Achilles—his special case of rapprochement with the gods—as a
matter of his ability to behold them vis-à-vis.[11] When he turns to
see Athene, at the opening of the poem, he needs no mist-lifting
intervention to know her at once; in fact, in book 20, Poseidon can
save Aeneas from death at Achilles' hands only by shedding a mist
upon Achilles, to make him see (or not see) as others do.[12]

---

[10] See, for example, the conversation between Aeneas and Lycaon, at 5.179–87;
Diomedes' speech to Glaucus at 6.123–43.

[11] On the special visual perceptiveness of Achilles, see Robinson (1999: especially
3 n. 4).

[12]   ἷξε δ' ὅθ' Αἰνείας ἠδ' ὁ κλυτὸς ἦεν Ἀχιλλεύς.
        αὐτίκα τῷ μὲν ἔπειτα κατ' ὀφθαλμῶν χέεν ἀχλὺν
        Πηλεΐδῃ Ἀχιλῆϊ· ὁ δὲ μελίην εὔχαλκον
        ἀσπίδος ἐξέρυσεν μεγαλήτορος Αἰνείαο·
        καὶ τὴν μὲν προπάροιθε ποδῶν Ἀχιλῆος ἔθηκεν.   (20.320–4)

The metaphysics of vision alternately close and expose—as well as embody—the gap between the godlike and the god, and more generally, between the figurative and the literal. When the narrative says, for example, that Hector 'recognized' the scales of Zeus (γνῶ γὰρ Διὸς ἱρὰ τάλαντα 16.658), has he actually seen something, or is the poem making a metaphor? The poem, in its attention to the act of seeing, creates an ambiguous space in which such questions arise, and unsettles our sense of how the world is and is not comprehensible, of what its characters can and cannot know: at any moment the mist may descend on us and return us to shrouded, provisional 'seeing'.

The trauma of seeing afflicts the gods as well, unimpeded though their vision is; and correspondingly, it both joins them to and separates them from the human realm. The scene in which Zeus witnesses Sarpedon's final confrontation with Patroclus and, overcome with pity, is moved to intervene, recalls those many instances in which heroes, catching sight of a kinsman or ally in desperate straits on the battlefield, throw caution aside to rush to the rescue—or to avenge. Powerless to save Sarpedon, Zeus resembles Sarpedon's warrior-companion Glaucus, filled with sorrow at being unable to protect his friend.

> τοὺς δὲ ἰδὼν ἐλέησε Κρόνου πάϊς ἀγκυλομήτεω,
> Ἥρην δὲ προσέειπε κασιγνήτην ἄλοχόν τε·
> "ὤ μοι ἐγών, ὅ τέ μοι Σαρπηδόνα φίλτατον ἀνδρῶν
> μοῖρ᾽ ὑπὸ Πατρόκλοιο Μενοιτιάδαο δαμῆναι." (16.431–4)

And watching them the son of crooked-minded Kronos
felt pity, and spoke to Hera, his sister and his wife:
'Ah me, that it is destined for the dearest of men to me, Sarpedon,
to go down under the hands of Menoitios' son Patroklos.'

Such a scene broaches another dimension of the Iliadic uses of seeing. Beyond the many occasions when seeing spurs the action of the poem, we find another narratological function, in which the act of seeing arrests, suspends, or dilates poetic action, authorizing the inner life of its characters by elaborating their responses, their

[Poseidon] came to where Aeneas was, and renowned Achilleus.
There quickly he drifted a mist across the eyes of one fighter,
Achilleus, Peleus' son, and from the shield of Aeneas
of the great heart pulled loose the strong bronze-headed ash spear
and laid it down again before the feet of Achilleus.

understandings (or struggle toward), and the mental structures and cultural paradigms governing such comprehension. Through such stunned or wondrous seeing, characters begin to perceive and articulate, within the poem, a way to understand the stakes of the poem and its action, and to model for us, in their complex responses, our own responses.

Here we may think of those instances in which seeing stops people in their tracks, and characters even pause to remark in amazement on what their eyes present them with: ὦ πόποι, ἦ μέγα θαῦμα τόδ' ὀφθαλμοῖσιν ὁρῶμαι ('Can this be? Here is a strange thing I see with my own eyes')—as when Thoas observes the wounded Hector[13] return to battle, or when Achilles happens upon Lycaon, the Trojan boy whom he had lately captured and sold.[14] The scathing mockery of Achilles' address to his victim modulates into his self-description, his invitation to the suppliant to ponder the body whose knees he is

---

[13]   ὅ σφιν ἐϋφρονέων ἀγορήσατο καὶ μετέειπεν·
       "ὦ πόποι, ἦ μέγα θαῦμα τόδ' ὀφθαλμοῖσιν ὁρῶμαι,
       οἷον δ' αὖτ' ἐξαῦτις ἀνέστη κῆρας ἀλύξας
       Ἕκτωρ· ἦ θήν μιν μάλα ἔλπετο θυμὸς ἑκάστου
       χερσὶν ὑπ' Αἴαντος θανέειν Τελαμωνιάδαο.
       ἀλλά τις αὖτε θεῶν ἐρρύσατο καὶ ἐσάωσεν
       Ἕκτορ', ὃ δὴ πολλῶν Δαναῶν ὑπὸ γούνατ' ἔλυσεν."   (15.285–91)

       [Thoas] in kind intention now spoke forth and addressed them:
       'Can this be? Here is a strange thing I see with my own eyes,
       how this Hektor has got to his feet once more, and eluded
       the death spirits. I think in each of us the heart had high hope
       he was killed under the hands of Telamonian Ajax.
       Now someone of the gods has come to his help and rescued
       Hektor, who has unstrung the knees of so many Danaans.'

Other examples at 13.99, 20.344, 21.54. Especially poignant is Zeus' exclamation (22.168–70), which varies the formula to express not irony, or vexation, but sorrow, at the sight of Hector pursued by Achilles:

       ὦ πόποι ἦ φίλον ἄνδρα διωκόμενον περὶ τεῖχος
       ὀφθαλμοῖσιν ὁρῶμαι· ἐμὸν δ' ὀλοφύρεται ἦτορ
       Ἕκτορος.

       'Ah me, this is a man beloved whom now my eyes watch
       being chased around the wall; my heart is mourning for Hektor.'

[14]   ὦ πόποι, ἦ μέγα θαῦμα τόδ' ὀφθαλμοῖσιν ὁρῶμαι·
       ἦ μάλα δὴ Τρῶες μεγαλήτορες οὕς περ ἔπεφνον
       αὖτις ἀναστήσονται ὑπὸ ζόφου ἠερόεντος,
       οἷον δὴ καὶ ὅδ' ἦλθε φυγὼν ὕπο νηλεὲς ἦμαρ

grasping, so that Lycaon may measure the disparity between the
stature and the vulnerability of the man about to kill him:

"οὐχ ὁράᾳς οἷος καὶ ἐγὼ καλός τε μέγας τε;
πατρὸς δ' εἴμ' ἀγαθοῖο, θεὰ δέ με γείνατο μήτηρ·
ἀλλ' ἔπι τοι καὶ ἐμοὶ θάνατος καὶ μοῖρα κραταιή·
ἔσσεται ἢ ἠὼς ἢ δείλη ἢ μέσον ἦμαρ,
ὁππότε τις καὶ ἐμεῖο Ἄρῃ ἐκ θυμὸν ἔληται
ἢ ὅ γε δουρὶ βαλὼν ἢ ἀπὸ νευρῆφιν ὀϊστῷ."   (21.108–113)

'Do you not see what I am like, how huge, how splendid
and born of a noble father, and the mother who bore me a goddess?
Yet even death and powerful destiny stand over me also,
and there shall be a dawn or an afternoon or a noontime
when some man in the fighting will take the life from me also
either with a spearcast or an arrow flown from the bowstring.'

Here Achilles relinquishes irony to propose a pause, a reflection,
which is also a condensed commentary on the fatality of the undertakings of the warrior-hero.

Astonished seeing may beget fear, as in the case of the Trojan
charioteers, stunned at the sight of Achilles (18.225–7); elsewhere it
begets desire, as in the case of Helen. While the truce in preparation
for the duel over her interrupts the momentum of the plot, it is
Helen's first appearance in the poem that seems not only to arrest
the poem's action, but, as it were, to stop time altogether, in the
response that brings mortal and immortal temporalities, as well as

"Λῆμνον ἐς ἠγαθέην πεπερημένος· οὐδέ μιν ἔσχε
πόντος ἁλὸς πολιῆς, ὃ πολέας ἀέκοντας ἐρύκει.
ἀλλ' ἄγε δὴ καὶ δουρὸς ἀκωκῆς ἡμετέροιο
γεύσεται, ὄφρα ἴδωμαι ἐνὶ φρεσὶν ἠδὲ δαείω
ἢ ἄρ' ὁμῶς καὶ κεῖθεν ἐλεύσεται, ἤ μιν ἐρύξει
γῆ φυσίζοος, ἥ τε κατὰ κρατερόν περ ἐρύκει."   (21.54–63)

'Can this be? Here is a strange thing that my eyes look on.
Now the great-hearted Trojans, even those I have killed already,
will stand and rise up again out of the gloom and the darkness
as this man has come back and escaped the day without pity
though he was sold into sacred Lemnos; but the main of the grey sea
could not hold him, though it holds back many who are unwilling.
But come now, he must be given a taste of our spearhead
so that I may know inside my heart and make certain
whether he will come back even from there, or the prospering
earth will hold him, she who holds back even the strong man.'

appearances (however transiently) into alignment. At the sight of Helen, the old men on the wall of Troy become young again: too elderly to fight they may be, but they feel the unarguable power of a visage that is 'like the immortals'. At this hiatus—within a controlled rearrangement of the narrative's temporal logic, in which the beginning of the conflict between Greeks and Trojans is superimposed on its closing[15]—the sight of Helen trumps any impulse to reproach; and this sight prompts a reflection that justifies the war's beginning and its continuing, much as it keeps alive hopes for an unlikely ending:

> οἱ δ' ὡς οὖν εἴδονθ' Ἑλένην ἐπὶ πύργον ἰοῦσαν,
> ἦκα πρὸς ἀλλήλους ἔπεα πτερόεντ' ἀγόρευον·
> "οὐ νέμεσις Τρῶας καὶ ἐϋκνήμιδας Ἀχαιοὺς
> τοιῇδ' ἀμφὶ γυναικὶ πολὺν χρόνον ἄλγεα πάσχειν·
> αἰνῶς ἀθανάτῃσι θεῆς εἰς ὦπα ἔοικεν·
> ἀλλὰ καὶ ὣς τοίη περ ἐοῦσ' ἐν νηυσὶ νεέσθω,
> μηδ' ἡμῖν τεκέεσσί τ' ὀπίσσω πῆμα λίποιτο." (3.154–60)

And these, as they saw Helen along the tower approaching,
murmuring softly to each other uttered their winged words:
'Surely there is no blame on Trojans and strong-greaved Achaians
if for long time they suffer hardship for a woman like this one.
She is terribly like the immortal goddesses in her face.
Still, though she be such, let her go away in the ships, lest
she be left behind, a grief to us and our children.'

In the *Teichoskopiê*, the sudden vision of Helen puts the poem's internal clock, as well as nature's temporal ordinance, temporarily on hold. So too, at a later moment, the sight of Hera, radiant and desirable as never before, momentarily suspends the narrative and returns Zeus (unageing as he is) to early days as he gazes at her.

> ἴδε δὲ νεφεληγερέτα Ζεύς.
> ὡς δ' ἴδεν, ὥς μιν ἔρως πυκινὰς φρένας ἀμφεκάλυψεν,
> οἷον ὅτε πρῶτόν περ ἐμισγέσθην φιλότητι
> εἰς εὐνὴν φοιτῶντε, φίλους λήθοντε τοκῆας. (14.293–6)

And Zeus who gathers the clouds saw her,
and when he saw her desire enfolded his close heart
as much as at that time they first went to bed together
and lay in love, and their dear parents knew nothing of it.

---

[15] See Bergren (1979).

The poem emphasizes, by reiterating, the instantaneous, overpowering effect of his seeing:[16] but here while Zeus, amazed by Hera, shifts his focus away from the battlefield, the war continues unabated. With Zeus looking elsewhere, the poem does not so much freeze the action as show the breach between parallel universes. Zeus' shift of attention means that the progress of the battle goes awry but not that the battle itself stops: even if the erotically dazzled Zeus has turned his gaze elsewhere, threatened the battle plan, and jeopardized the promised outcome, what is never threatened is the general human condition of mortality over and against the gods' radically separate purview, immortality. Gods may be deceived by or through their eyes, but this can never register, as it does for the human characters, the metaphysical and ontological limits of their seeing.

It is finally θαῦμα ('wonder'), self-evidently and preeminently a condition of seeing in Homeric poetry,[17] that makes possible the poem's ultimate meditation on the conditions of human well-being and travail, attachment and loss, devotion and bereavement. The admiration and awe that Achilles proposes to summon from Lycaon are realized in a scene that—by the prior logic of the narrative—should lead as that earlier episode does, to the slaying of the suppliant; instead, the mutuality of astonished beholding allows for a transformed outcome.

ὡς δ' ὅτ' ἂν ἄνδρ' ἄτη πυκινὴ λάβῃ, ὅς τ' ἐνὶ πάτρῃ
φῶτα κατακτείνας ἄλλων ἐξίκετο δῆμον,
ἀνδρὸς ἐς ἀφνειοῦ, θάμβος δ' ἔχει εἰσορόωντας,
ὡς Ἀχιλεὺς θάμβησεν ἰδὼν Πρίαμον θεοειδέα·
θάμβησαν δὲ καὶ ἄλλοι, ἐς ἀλλήλους δὲ ἴδοντο.   (24.480–4)

. . .

---

[16] ἀμφικαλύπτω, the verb used here of the *erôs* that envelops the dazed Zeus and blinkers him, is the verb that regularly describes the obscuring mist by which the sight of mortals is shrouded, the darkness that covers their eyes in death (see e.g. 20.417); that misty *erôs* materializes into the cloud that hides the couple's lovemaking, preventing Zeus from seeing as well as being seen. Yet his vulnerability to the *erôs* that enfolds him and blinds him to the action below represents merely his temporary loss of control over the poem's movement before he reasserts it by announcing its plot. My thanks to Chris Kraus for helping me to think about this comparison.

[17] See Prier (1989: ch. 1), for the observation that θάμβος occurs exclusively in the context of the verbs (εἰς)οράω and δέρκομαι in both *Iliad* and *Odyssey*.

ἤτοι Δαρδανίδης Πρίαμος θαύμαζ᾿ Ἀχιλῆα
ὅσσος ἔην οἷός τε· θεοῖσι γὰρ ἄντα ἐῴκει·
αὐτὰρ ὁ Δαρδανίδην Πρίαμον θαύμαζεν Ἀχιλλεὺς
εἰσορόων ὄψίν τ᾿ ἀγαθὴν καὶ μῦθον ἀκούων.   (24.629–32)

As when dense disaster closes on one who has murdered
a man in his own land, and he comes to the country of others,
to a man of substance, and wonder seizes on those who behold him,
so Achilleus wondered as he looked on Priam, a godlike
man, and the rest of them wondered also, and looked at each other.

···

Priam, son of Dardanos, gazed upon Achilleus, wondering
at his size and beauty, for he seemed like an outright vision
of gods. Achilleus in turn gazed on Dardanian Priam
and wondered, as he saw his brave looks and listened to him talking.

Introduced by a simile that makes amazed seeing its subject (as other
similes figure running, etc.), the encounter of Priam and Achilles both
arrests the action of the poem and, as their agreement makes plain,
guarantees its continuity. Their exchange distils an understanding,
an acceptance, of the war and its casualties as inevitable, divinely
ordained as the overarching structure within which the human portion of elation and suffering, achievement and defeat, are mingled.

The operations of seeing, then, as foregrounded in the contexts
noted above, establish and reiterate the poem's dominant consciousness, linking present experience to traditional norms—the perspective through which the war's dire toll takes concrete shape and is
reintegrated into its triumph, its power to make memorable and to
endow with glory the lives it encompasses. Seeing comes to mean
many things: to see is to take aim, know, wonder, desire, fear, be
summoned to action, record in memory; it comes to mean, one
might say, what stands forth as the substance of the poem. What is
seen is what will be honoured and mourned, and is thus what will
be recalled, celebrated, preserved. 'Seeing' encodes what has been
able to be seen: to have been cited, selected, arranged, sung, resung,
as worthy of notice.

Epic sings, that is, what is *a priori* of epic value, what can be
integrated into epic song. Yet beyond these always already valorized
sights—tested, scrutinized, interrogated as they are in this most
reflexive epic—the *Iliad* extends itself to an even more surprising

perspective, a harrowing form of visualization that reaches beyond what epic praise and commemoration can reintegrate.

It may seem tautological to observe that epic valorizes what epic cites, says, sees, puts before our eyes and ears; yet the whole operation of *the song itself as sign and saying of value*, as remembrance of glory, is the marker of epic ideology *per se*. Epic song constantly announces itself as recuperative: however terrible the deaths, however grievous the hurts, they are sung and, in being sung, reintegrated as matters of glorious note; and those who shame themselves within epic receive as well their notice of blame.

Yet the *Iliad* shows itself capable of imagining a futurity in which remembrance does not recuperate, in which to see and to note is to destroy rather than to confirm epic value, in which irreconcilable outcomes and values are not part of a glorious strife, praise or blame, but rather an index of irretrievable loss. It is no surprise that these moments involve women and the aged and children, those who need refuge, those excluded from *kleos*—from the workings of Iliadic value—those who will bear on their bodies the horrors of war but whose fates will not be sung by the epic of war.[18] It is this very residue of epic that the Athenian dramatists discover; tragedy will address what cannot be re-incorporated, and will envision what the *Iliad* keeps from view—female heroes, widowed mothers, sacrificed daughters, the chorus of the exiled.[19] That this shift in genre reflects as well a historic shift in socio-political organization suggests that visualization, in epic, tragedy, or any genre, lends itself to our diagnosing and historicizing the political economy of 'sight'.

It is given to Hector to see not only beyond his own death but beyond epic. In *Iliad* 6, as Hector anticipates his approaching death on the field of battle, the defeat of the Trojans, and the fall of their city, he voices his anguish—his greatest—at Andromache's inevitable duress by depicting an imagined scene of her servitude: he envisions her led off into servitude by an armoured warrior—a picture that

---

[18] One might say that the *Iliad* is built on the stories of those victims of war—wives, children, aged parents—who can take no part in the conflict yet serve to attest the miseries of its outcome; but their testimonies remain always reactive, muted, secondary to the valorized stories of the agents of war.

[19] See Zeitlin (1996*b*).

modulates into images of her weaving at a stranger's loom and drawing water from an Argive well.

> "ἀλλ᾽ οὔ μοι Τρώων τόσσον μέλει ἄλγος ὀπίσσω,
> οὔτ᾽ αὐτῆς Ἑκάβης οὔτε Πριάμοιο ἄνακτος
> οὔτε κασιγνήτων, οἵ κεν πολέες τε καὶ ἐσθλοὶ
> ἐν κονίῃσι πέσοιεν ὑπ᾽ ἀνδράσι δυσμενέεσσιν,
> ὅσσον σεῦ, ὅτε κέν τις Ἀχαιῶν χαλκοχιτώνων
> δακρυόεσσαν ἄγηται ἐλεύθερον ἦμαρ ἀπούρας·
> καί κεν ἐν Ἄργει ἐοῦσα πρὸς ἄλλης ἱστὸν ὑφαίνοις,
> καί κεν ὕδωρ φορέοις Μεσσηΐδος ἢ Ὑπερείης
> πόλλ᾽ ἀεκαζομένη, κρατερὴ δ᾽ ἐπικείσετ᾽ ἀνάγκη·
> καί ποτέ τις εἴπῃσιν ἰδὼν κατὰ δάκρυ χέουσαν·
> Ἕκτορος ἥδε γυνὴ ὃς ἀριστεύεσκε μάχεσθαι
> Τρώων ἱπποδάμων ὅτε Ἴλιον ἀμφεμάχοντο.
> ὥς ποτέ τις ἐρέει· σοὶ δ᾽ αὖ νέον ἔσσεται ἄλγος
> χήτεϊ τοιοῦδ᾽ ἀνδρὸς ἀμύνειν δούλιον ἦμαρ.
> ἀλλά με τεθνηῶτα χυτὴ κατὰ γαῖα καλύπτοι
> πρίν γέ τι σῆς τε βοῆς σοῦ θ᾽ ἑλκηθμοῖο πυθέσθαι."   (6.450–65)

'But it is not so much the pain to come of the Trojans
that troubles me, not even of Priam the king nor Hekabe,
not the thought of my brothers who in their numbers and valour
shall drop in the dust under the hands of men who hate them,
as troubles me the thought of you, when some bronze-armoured
Achaian leads you off, taking away your day of liberty,
in tears; and in Argos you must work at the loom of another,
and carry water from the spring Messeis or Hypereia,
all unwilling, but strong will be the necessity upon you;
and some day seeing you shedding tears a man will say of you:
'This is the wife of Hektor, who was ever the bravest fighter
of the Trojans, breakers of horses, in the days when they
    fought about Ilion.'
So will one speak of you; and for you it will be yet a fresh grief,
to be widowed of such a man who could fight off the day
    of your slavery.
But may I be dead and the piled earth hide me under before I
hear you crying and know by this that they drag you captive.'

In expressing his despair at the dreaded conclusion of the war, Hector reinforces the pathos of what awaits her by representing Andromache's impending condition as a spectacle—a representation underscored by the inclusion, in the scene he pictures, of an anonymous observer, a spectator whose reaction, as Hector ventriloquizes it, is (in effect) 'Look at this! What a sight!'

Hector's visualization of a future scene of beholding, of retrospection, refracts all that the epic provides as aspiration and consolation, recasting its compensations by representing a post-Iliadic world and post-epic framework. Andromache's 'what if?' plea—what if Hector were not to return to battle?—elicits a response from Hector that begins by affirming his obligation as a warrior to the larger social entity; yet it is the image he then visualizes that brings to the fore concerns that praise and blame do not answer—any more than does divine purpose—and implicitly critiques them. The reward of earned renown, of the glorious name that will be on the lips of subsequent generations, is, in this image, utterly unequal to the bitter desolation that Hector, foreseeing, dramatizes.

The scene of Andromache enslaved and grieving is necessarily one from which he will be absent: thus Hector puts himself outside the picture he creates, offstage, so to speak, and prospectively imagines an onlooker who observes what he himself—a presence only in memory—cannot see, but whose reaction he can know. Far from redeeming Andromache's loss, the spectator's retrospective tribute to her peerless husband will intensify her grief; his anonymous exclamation—is he Greek or Trojan?—of homage to Hector, framed by pity for Andromache, is a source of unbearable pain for Hector. The hero produces in his mind's eye the one sight that he must turn away from, for all the battlefield horrors he has looked upon.

Through the visualizing of a sight that cannot be countenanced,[20] the epic marks the limits of its own terrain of exploration, prefiguring a new horizon of pity and fear, in which, as Froma Zeitlin has so illuminatingly shown, the subjectivity of the other is brought into view and plays a defining role.[21] Much as the enactment of Hector's visual imagination expresses his most profound and intimate anxiety,

---

[20] From this sight the final ἀχλύς will be Hector's welcome protection.

[21] Zeitlin (1996a). Froma Zeitlin's work, more broadly, has modelled for us a dialectical criticism wholly alive to the richnesses and contradictions—particularly those involving gender—in Greek epic and drama; her scholarship has animated my thinking (like that of so many others) in this essay and elsewhere.

the despair of Priam and Andromache are conveyed through scenes in the mind's eye, in two episodes that, similarly, foreshadow a post-heroic world.

In book 22, Priam pleads with Hector not to face Achilles in battle, entreating his son to have pity on a wretched father. Priam delineates the family's imminent destruction, and his own death in particular, when the city has fallen. Conjuring up a scene of terror, in which his own dogs go in for the kill, he meditates on the abhorrence of such a gruesome vision as it would look to a spectator: it will appear not as heroic deaths do, but as the 'most pitiful' mortal sight.

> "αὐτὸν δ' ἂν πύματόν με κύνες πρώτῃσι θύρῃσιν
> ὠμησταὶ ἐρύουσιν, ἐπεί κέ τις ὀξέϊ χαλκῷ
> τύψας ἠὲ βαλὼν ῥεθέων ἐκ θυμὸν ἕληται,
> οὓς τρέφον ἐν μεγάροισι τραπεζῆας θυραωρούς,
> οἵ κ' ἐμὸν αἷμα πιόντες ἀλύσσοντες περὶ θυμῷ
> κείσοντ' ἐν προθύροισι. νέῳ δέ τε πάντ' ἐπέοικεν
> ἀρηϊκταμένῳ δεδαϊγμένῳ ὀξέϊ χαλκῷ
> κεῖσθαι· πάντα δὲ καλὰ θανόντι περ ὅττι φανήῃ·
> ἀλλ' ὅτε δὴ πολιόν τε κάρη πολιόν τε γένειον
> αἰδῶ τ' αἰσχύνωσι κύνες κταμένοιο γέροντος,
> τοῦτο δὴ οἴκτιστον πέλεται δειλοῖσι βροτοῖσιν."　　(22.66–76)

'And myself last of all, my dogs in front of my doorway
will rip me raw, after some man with stroke of the sharp bronze,
or with spearcast, has torn the life out of my body;
those dogs I raised in my halls to be at my table, to guard my
gates, who will lap my blood in the savagery of their anger
and then lie down in my courts. For a young man all is decorous
when he is cut down in battle and torn with the sharp bronze,
　　and lies there
dead, and though dead still all that shows about him is beautiful;
but when an old man is dead and down, and the dogs mutilate
the grey head and the grey beard and the parts that are secret,
this, for all sad mortality, is the sight most pitiful.'

In an even more hopeless moment, Andromache expresses her dread at the news of Hector's death by elaborating an image of Astyanax as an outcast in his own community, once Hector is no longer alive. She pictures in detail a scene, complete with dialogue, in which the boy appeals to his father's former companions for sustenance, imploring them and even tugging at their garments. At best, some will pity him, and keep him alive for future sorrow.

> "οὔτε σὺ τούτῳ
> ἔσσεαι Ἕκτορ ὄνειαρ, ἐπεὶ θάνες, οὔτε σοὶ οὗτος.
> ἤν περ γὰρ πόλεμόν γε φύγῃ πολύδακρυν Ἀχαιῶν,
> αἰεί τοι τούτῳ γε πόνος καὶ κήδε᾽ ὀπίσσω
> ἔσσοντ᾽· ἄλλοι γάρ οἱ ἀπουρίσσουσιν ἀρούρας.
> ἦμαρ δ᾽ ὀρφανικὸν παναφήλικα παῖδα τίθησι·
> πάντα δ᾽ ὑπεμνήμυκε, δεδάκρυνται δὲ παρειαί,
> δευόμενος δέ τ᾽ ἄνεισι πάϊς ἐς πατρὸς ἑταίρους,
> ἄλλον μὲν χλαίνης ἐρύων, ἄλλον δὲ χιτῶνος·
> τῶν δ᾽ ἐλεησάντων κοτύλην τις τυτθὸν ἐπέσχε·
> χείλεα μέν τ᾽ ἐδίην᾽, ὑπερῴην δ᾽ οὐκ ἐδίηνε.
> τὸν δὲ καὶ ἀμφιθαλὴς ἐκ δαιτύος ἐστυφέλιξε,
> χερσὶν πεπληγὼς καὶ ὀνειδείοισιν ἐνίσσων·
> 'ἔρρ᾽ οὕτως· οὐ σός γε πατὴρ μεταδαίνυται ἡμῖν.'
> δακρυόεις δέ τ᾽ ἄνεισι πάϊς ἐς μητέρα χήρην
> Ἀστυάναξ, ὃς πρὶν μὲν ἑοῦ ἐπὶ γούνασι πατρὸς
> μυελὸν οἶον ἔδεσκε καὶ οἰῶν πίονα δημόν."   (22.485–501)

'You cannot help him,
Hektor, any more, since you are dead. Nor can he help you.
Though he escape the attack of the Achaians with all its sorrows,
yet all his days for your sake there will be hard work for him
and sorrows, for others will take his lands away from him. The day
of bereavement leaves a child with no agemates to befriend him.
He bows his head before every man, his cheeks are bewept, he
goes, needy, a boy among his father's companions,
and tugs at this man by the mantle, that man by the tunic,
and they pity him, and one gives him a tiny drink from a goblet,
enough to moisten his lips, not enough to moisten his palate.
But one whose parents are living beats him out of the banquet
hitting him with his fists and in words also abuses him:
"Get out, you! Your father is not dining among us."
And the boy goes away in tears to his widowed mother,
Astyanax, who in days before on the knees of his father
would eat only the marrow or the flesh of sheep that was fattest.'

The looming, irremediable dissolution of their world—a world no longer to be sustained by *aidôs* and beyond the reach of glory—is represented by the *Iliad* through the recognitions Hector, Priam, and

Andromache experience, each envisaging a scene in which the consolations of epic have no place. As the characters visualize the inevitable—τὸ ἀναγκαῖον, in Aristotle's term (*Po.* 1451ᵃ)—pity for that necessary unfolding is transferred to the onlooker: to ourselves. Within epic, even against it, we can begin to discern the lineaments of a new imaginative structure. Here Homeric epic shows its strength and its limit—its strength precisely by tracking the underside of its limit: and here, at that threshold, it points toward what tragedy will put on the stage.[22]

[22] I am grateful to the editors of this volume for their solidarity and their exceptionally generous and incisive engagement with this essay; my thanks as well to Sharon James, Maureen McLane, and Gloria Ferrari Pinney for stimulating conversation—and, as always, to Froma.

2

Outer Limits, Choral Space

Richard P. Martin

The Theatre of Dionysus as an arena for citizenship was every bit as politicized as the assembly area on the Pnyx, a few hundred yards from spectators' seats on the slope of the Acropolis, or as the agora, on the other side of the hill. The similarities among these public performance venues, and the implications of their overlaps, have over the past three decades occupied critics of Athenian tragedy and comedy, as part of a much-needed larger effort to reimagine the cultural negotiations and contextualized meanings that one-time, live performance enabled. Froma Zeitlin's work has been central in revitalizing the study of Greek drama along these lines. It is a pleasure to be able to offer this brief paradramatic paper as a token of the gratitude I owe for her deep personal generosity and unmatched scholarly inspiration during our years together at Princeton (1981–99).

Apart from their involvement in such ongoing cultural negotiations, the consumers of Athenian drama, citizens and others, also encountered, in their everyday lives outside the theatre, reverberations of performance after the music and dancing stopped. This ambient 'noise' of drama also demands imaginative reconstruction; the interacting echoes have to be heard. Some were in the air, such as the choral songs of Phrynichus and Euripides that spectators preserved in memory and performed for pleasure.[1] Others were literally

---

[1] On Phrynichus' sweet songs, see Ar. *Wasps* 220, *Birds* 748; on those of Euripides, see the famous anecdote about the Athenians in Sicily whose lives were saved because they could recite his verses: Plu. *Nic.* 29.2–3.

in the ground, especially in the form of monuments commemorating performance set up by the victorious producers. On the way to the Theatre of Dionysus, on the Street of Tripods, one would have passed dozens of such choregic assertions. On the Acropolis summit behind the theatre, further monuments of performance could be seen and admired, within the wider context of dedications to the gods.[2] Svenbro, Calame, and Day, among others, have taught us to read dedications as being inherently dramatic, even 'performative' in the stricter speech-act sense.[3] From this viewpoint, the inscriptional echo of a dramatic performance can itself become a theatricalization, a monologue turning into dialogue as its script gets voiced by passers-by.

This hum of voices—songs in memory, speaking stones—amplified the 'buzz' about performance that must have permeated ancient Athens as it does large swathes of modern Los Angeles. An inventory of just the verbal offshoots of dramatic competitions in the fifth through fourth centuries BCE would have to include (apart from the actual dramatic texts), casual compliments, abuse, or anecdotes about poets and actors; oratory and history in which they are mentioned; reminiscences of performances; official didascalic records of the winners; choregic inscriptions; sepulchral inscriptions of those who had once been involved in performance; talk at symposia; and songs, poems, and prose works (such as Plato's *Symposium* and the *Epidêmiai* of Ion of Chios) that are based wholly or in part on performers and their art. And of course the visual inventory, from vases to portrait busts, extended the impact of the stage even further in space and time.[4]

---

[2] Wilson (2000: 198–262) provides an indispensable guide to all issues relating to choregic monuments. See also Paus. 1.20.1; Hurwit (1999: 257–9). Examples with metrical inscriptions from the Acropolis include Hansen (1983: no. 253, possibly no. 230).

[3] Svenbro (1993); Calame (1995: 116–36); Day (1994; 2000); also important for this question is Depew (1997). On speech-act theory in the interpretation of archaic Greek texts, see Martin (1989).

[4] Basic collections of, and essays about, these materials: Ruck (1967); Mette (1977); Winkler and Zeitlin (1990); Kurke and Dougherty (1993; 2003); Csapo and Slater (1995); Goldhill and Osborne (1999); Easterling and Hall (2002). Ford (2002: 190–4) discusses Ion of Chios, and the role of poetry-quoting in fifth-century displays of stylish aristocratic sophistication (*dexiotês*).

Nor should we limit our inventory-making to stage drama strictly defined. As recent scholarship has increasingly emphasized, the dithyrambic contests at several festivals in Athens ranked in civic importance as high if not higher than tragedy, comedy, and satyr-play. Diachronically, some form of dithyramb influenced the evolution of tragedy—or so we are assured by Aristotle (*Po.* 1449ª9–24). What the exact contribution might have been, and what the form and content of these cult songs were, will most likely remain opaque as long as we possess only the scrappy mentions of dithyramb, and a few disputed texts, before the complete renovation of the genre late in the fifth century BCE, apparently in conjunction with the rise of New Music.[5] Synchronically, we should try to imagine an audience for stage drama at the Dionysia whose memories and attention had been focused just days before on the choral competitions among the ten tribes, each vying for the prize with one chorus apiece of fifty men and another of fifty boys. Given the state funds involved, the prestige accorded producers and composer-choreographers (*khorodidaskaloi*), opportunity for inventive agonistic display, length of training in song and dance, and likelihood that their friends and family members were actually competing, the dithyramb experience cannot have failed to colour an Athenian audience's reaction to the stage genres. To a great extent, dithyramb must have shared much more than performance space with its ultimately longer-lived congeners. In what follows, I shall argue on the basis of an 'echo' text, an early monument to dithyrambic victory, that one shared element was a particular way of conceptualizing choral space, evident still in metapoetic form on stone and in script.

Before turning to the inscription in question, it will be worthwhile to recall the format of another 'echo' already mentioned, the typical choregic inscription. Numerous texts record the bare facts of victory in dithyrambic and tragic contests and give prominent mention to the sponsoring citizen (*khorêgos*).[6] The standard form can be seen,

---

[5] On the Aristotle passage see Leonhardt (1991); on the New Music, Martin (2003) and Csapo (2004); for the remains of dithyramb and testimonia to it, see Ieranò (1997). I look forward to publication of the excellent Oxford conference on dithyramb organized by Barbara Kowalzig and Peter Wilson in July 2004.

[6] For the fifth century, see *IG*³ 957–62 (Dionysia) and 963–6 (Thargelia); also, Ieranò (1997: 331–4).

for example, in *IG*³ 961 commemorating a dithyrambic victory of the late fifth century BCE:

Οἰνεὶς ἐνίκα παίδον/ Εὐρυμένε[s] Μελετέονος ἐχορέγε/ Νικόστρατος ἐδίδασκε

The tribe which won (Oineis) with a chorus of boys, the funding *khorêgos* (Eurumenes) and the instructor of the chorus (the poet who wrote the piece and rehearsed the production) are mentioned. A similar format is used in commemoration of a *khorêgos* for the Thargelia (*IG*³ 966), at which two tribes usually joined in entering a chorus in competition and both won mention in the inscription:

[Ἐ]ρυξίας Ἐρυξιμάχο
Κυδαθηναιεὺς ἐχορήγε
Πανδιονίδι Ἐρεχθηίδι παίδων.

Eryxias son of Eryximachus acted as *khorêgos* for
(the tribes) Pandionis and Erechtheis with a chorus of boys.

Such inscriptions are priceless for increasing our knowledge of Athenian musical and theatrical history, but they provide no perspective on the performance itself. A related, smaller, but richer category comprises dedications of tripods made by the winning musicians or sponsors of choral events at the Dionysia, Thargelia, and Panathenaic festivals. This tradition of making dedications was practised on the Athenian Acropolis from the sixth century until about 480 BCE.[7] It is with one such text—perhaps the earliest epigraphic attestation of choral poetry in Athens—that I would like to begin my exploration. From an internal analysis of the lacunose inscribed poem, we can move to an external comparison with one aspect of the poetics of Athenian tragic choruses.

The epigram appears on a rectangular tripod base of Pentelic marble, part of which was found in March 1836 on the Acropolis east of the Parthenon (Figure 1).[8] Dated to about 500–480 BCE, the

---

[7] Dedications after victory form part of the larger set of Acropolis dedications, for which see Raubitschek (1949); those bearing verse inscriptions have been collected and edited by Hansen (1983: 99–158). See further on the forms of tripod dedication Amandry (1976).

[8] A second fragment was found between the Theatre of Dionysus and the Herodeion; a third piece, without provenance, was kept in the Acropolis Museum until

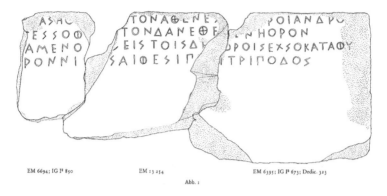

EM 6694; IG I³ 850   EM 13 154   EM 6395; IG I³ 673; Dedic. 323

Abb. 1

Fig. 2.1 Drawing of a verse inscription on a marble tripod base from the Acropolis at Athens (*IG* I³ 833). *c*.500–480 BCE.

inscribed stone is now in the Epigraphical Museum in Athens, where I have examined it on two occasions. The following text is that printed as *IG* I³ 833 *bis* following a new join made by Dina Peppa-Delmousou (and including her restoration of the first line, not adopted by Lewis and Jeffery):

[νικε]σας ho[δε ᾧ πρῶ]τον Ἀθένεσ[ιν χο]ροι ἀνδρο[ν]/
[_]τες σοφ[ίες] τόνδ' ἀνέθε[κ]εν hόρον/
[εὐχσ]άμενο[ς· π]λείστοις δὲ [χ]οροῖς ἔχσο κατὰ φῦ[λα]/
[ἀνδ]ρον νι[κε]σαί φεσὶ π[ερ]ὶ τρίποδος.

...dedicated this boundary marker of (lovely? practised?) poetic wisdom after (winning?) for the first time at Athens with a men's chorus. But outside, among the races of men, he says [or perhaps, the *marker* declares] he was victorious, for a tripod, with the most choruses.[9]

1956, when it was transferred to the Epigraphical Museum. On the form of the base see Amandry (1976: 16).

[9] Peppa-Delmousou (1971). For full apparatus and further bibliography see Lewis and Jeffery (1994: 616–17) and Hansen (1983: 144–5); the latter (p. 261) prefers Gallavotti's supplement *aske]tês* instead of Peppa-Delmousou's suggestion *himer]tês*. Wilson (2000: 217) speculates that the cryptic phrase *peri tripodos* ('about the tripod') could refer to the prize standing on this very base (thus, the inscription is literally 'around' the tripod) or that the poet won 'with respect to a tripod', which might imply a further tension between potential displayers of the prize, the *khorêgos* and the poet.

Several unusual features of this poem invite attention, especially since the poetics—as opposed to the textual restoration—of this piece have not been much discussed. The identity of the dedicator, for one thing, remains a problem. Gallavotti thought it was Simonides, commemorating his dithyrambic victory of 477/6.[10] He was encouraged to conclude this by two (possibly later) epigrams, one mentioning a *pinax* dedication by Simonides following 56 dithyrambic victories, the other a victory by the poet at age eighty.[11] But Podlecki points out that this forces us to the unlikely conclusion that a poet who had won, by his own testimony, so often afield by that date had never won in Athens until the event commemorated.[12] The inscription seems to be complete in two couplets, but there is no obvious place for the name Simonides, or convincing restoration of another name.[13] We should contrast the format with that of the typical choregic monument which, as we have seen, explicitly states the name of the producer and makes room for mentioning the winning tribe but not always the *khorodidaskalos*. It seems that the poem in question is thus a hybrid of choregic inscription and personal dedication; of the latter genre, it blends two subtypes, agonistic victory dedication with what we might call 'testament of art'.[14] The

---

[10] Gallavotti (1975: 166–71).

[11] The poems are Page (1975) Simonides XXVII (= *AP* 6.213) and XXVIII (= Syrian. *In Hermog.* i p. 86R). For commentary, see Page (1981: 241–3). It is worth noting that the final phrase of line 3 in the former (χορὸν ἀνδρῶν: Page edition line 183) is almost identical to the end of the tripod inscription's first line. The latter poem (Page edition lines 185–90) is a neatly stylized version of choregic inscriptions of the type mentioned above, giving, in typical order, tribe (Antiochis), *khorêgos* (Aristeides), chorus type (men's) and *didaskalos* (Simonides). The archon mentioned (Adeimantos, line 185) dates the victory to 477/6 BCE. See further Pickard-Cambridge (1962: 15–16) and Podlecki (1981: 97).

[12] Podlecki (1981: 100). His further argument that the poem is not up to the level of Simonidean style should be disregarded; as I hope to show the poem is quite complex in form and diction.

[13] See the commentary in Lewis and Jeffery (1994: 617) for earlier suggestions. Probably the dedicator's name was on a separate adjacent stone: for parallels see Hansen (1983: 144). Hansen (1989: 302) records Day's rejection, based on autopsy, of - σ - as the first letter of the first line and therefore prefers Lewis' suggestion Διαγο]ρας. Podlecki (1981: 100) had rejected Lewis's restoration on chronological grounds (as Diagoras was a mid-fifth-century poet) and offered instead Βακχια]δας (an earlier Sicyonian poet); but Hansen (1989: 302) finds this name 'spatio non aptum'.

[14] For the former see Ebert (1972). An interesting early example of the latter is *IG*I³ 766 (= Raubitschek [1949] no. 224 = Hansen [1983] no. 230), which Friedländer (1948) translates (on the basis of Hiller's restoration): 'It is well for the skilled

fifth-century monuments recorded the names of victorious *khorêgos* and *tribê*; that of the poet could be on private memorials but was not inscribed on official records. It is apparent that we are dealing with a sort of hybrid commemorative text.[15]

Another interesting feature about the poem is the contrast made between the Athenian victory, which it commemorates, and the string of other poetic successes. At first sight, it appears that the dedicator speaks somewhat defensively, as if to cover his failure to appear or win previously in Athens by reference to his out-of-state victories, *ekso kata phula andrôn*. But the statement can also be read as a variation on a well-known trope that we see in the *Hymn to Apollo* and in the *Theognidea*. When the narrator of the *Hymn* instructs the chorus of Delian maidens to inform future enquirers of his own excellence at song, he promises to compensate them for the favour by spreading their fame (174–5):

> ἡμεῖς δ' ὑμέτερον κλέος οἴσομεν ὅσσον ἐπ' αἶαν
> ἀνθρώπων στρεφόμεσθα πόλεις εὖ ναιεταώσας·

> And we will bear your fame as far on earth
> as we go in wandering to men's well-inhabited cities.

The same elements—fame being spread, wandering, recompense—occur in a variation of this motif, as Theognis contrasts his bestowal of fame on Cyrnus with the young man's refusal to respect him (237–47):

I have given you wings with which you will fly, soaring easily, over the boundless sea and all the land (κατὰ γῆν πᾶσαν). You will be present at every dinner and feast, lying on the lips of many, and lovely youths accompanied by the clear sounds of pipes will sing of you in orderly fashion with beautiful, clear voices. And whenever you go to Hades' house of wailing, down in the dark earth's depths, never even in death will you lose your fame (κλέος) but you will be in men's thoughts, your name ever immortal

---

craftsmen to show their cunning (σοφοῖσι σο[φ]ίζεσθ[αι]) according to their craft, for whoso possesses a craft possesses a better life'. Cf. the tripod epigram's emphasis on *sophia*. Other dedications apparently by craftspeople or performers are Hansen (1983) nos. 235, 252, 253, 271, 306.

[15] On the usual inscriptional format see Pickard-Cambridge (1962: 36), Page (1981: 242).

(ἄφθιτον), Cyrnus, as you roam throughout the land of Greece (καθ᾽ Ἑλλάδα γῆν στρωφώμενος) and among the islands.[16]

As in such poetic self-representations, the point of the tripod verses can be that the dedicator advertises both the power of the medium, in this case choral art, and himself as *khorodidaskalos*, or as poet. This is a man with travel experience; by the same token, the fame of Athens will be increased when he performs in other places, if, like the blind man of Chios in the *Hymn to Apollo*, he calls to mind his previous experiences with choruses. His fulfilment of a vow at this point (reading εὐξάμενος in line 3) is thus also an implicit promise or guarantee of his future behaviour. Not only does he travel but he makes good his word.[17]

Keeping in mind these considerations about the spatial and temporal claims made by this poem, we may turn now to the most unusual feature of this composition: the use of the word *horos*, 'boundary marker', to describe (at least as it appears) the tripod that is being dedicated. Thus far I have found no parallel for this usage in dedicatory inscriptions.[18] The closest parallel to the tripod dedication comes in an epigram attributed in the *Palatine Anthology* to 'Bacchylides or Simonides'. This poem, seemingly a dedication by the tribal chorus itself, gives in a stylized form the basic information of a choregic inscription (*A.P.* 13.28):

> Πολλάκι δὴ φυλῆς Ἀκαμαντίδος ἐν χοροῖσιν ὧραι
> ἀνωλόλυξαν κισσοφόροις ἐπὶ διθυράμβοις
> αἱ Διονυσιάδες, μίτραισι δὲ καὶ ῥόδων ἀώτοις

---

[16] Translation by Gerber (1999: 209). As the poet goes on to say 'not on horseback but the Muses' gifts will send you' (lines 249–50), Cyrnus' wandering might be metaphorical.

[17] For the formulaic *euxamenos* in dedications cf. e.g. Hansen (1983) nos. 202–3, 237, 241, etc.

[18] A less likely possibility is that *horos* describes only the stone base of the tripod. Podlecki (1981: 101) sidesteps the problem of the meaning of *horos* in the poem by remarking that the base may *not* have held a tripod, so that the *horos* would be the stone itself. But he does not pursue the idea. Kaibel (1878) no. 923 imagined that the victor actually set up the tripod with base as a boundary marker somewhere in Athens, but his reading relied on the right-hand segment of the base alone, the only portion available at the time. Raubitschek (1949: 346) noted that the find-spot on the Acropolis meant that 'there is no reason to doubt that the dedication was set up there'. The index to *IG* I³ lists no other example of the word except as used on actual boundary stones (on which see below).

σοφῶν ἀοιδῶν ἐσκίασαν λιπαρὰν ἔθειραν,
οἳ τόνδε τρίποδά σφισι μάρτυρα Βακχίων ἀέθλων 5
ἔθηκαν· κείνους δ Ἀντιγένης ἐδίδασκεν ἄνδρας,
εὖ δ᾽ ἐπιθηνεῖτο γλυκερὰν ὄπα Δωρίοις Ἀρίστων
Ἀργεῖος ἡδὺ πνεῦμα χέων καθαροῖς ἐν αὐλοῖς,
τῶν ἐχορήγησεν κύκλον μελίγηρυν Ἱππόνικος,
Στρούθωνος υἱός, ἅρμασιν ἐν Χαρίτων φορηθείς 10
αἵ οἱ ἐπ᾽ ἀνθρώπους ὄνομα κλυτὸν ἀγλαάν τε νίκαν
θῆκαν ἰοστεφάνων θεᾶν ἕκατι Μοισᾶν.

Often indeed the Seasons of the Dionysia have shouted for joy among *khoroi* of the Acamantid *phyle* at the ivy-bearing dithyrambs, and with headbands of finest roses have shadowed the shiny hair of skilled singers, who have set up this tripod for themselves as witness to their Bacchic struggles. Antigenes trained these men; and Argive Ariston fostered their sweet voice well, blowing a sweet strain on his pure, Dorian aulos. Hipponicos son of Strouthon was *khoregos* of their honey-voiced cyclical *khoros*, borne in the chariot of the Charites, who set a glorious name and bright victory on men by the grace of the violet-garlanded goddesses, the Muses.[19]

Amidst a swarm of metaphors, the tripod is described in line 5 as a witness (*martura*) of the contests. We will return to this legal metaphor shortly. For now, let us explore the functionally similar but semantically different word *horos*. Although it is apparently unique in dedicatory inscriptions, this word is common on another type of archaeological monument in the sixth and fifth centuries, actual boundary stones, a coincidence that once again underscores the hybrid nature of the tripod poem.[20] The body of literature on the phenomenon of Athenian *horos* inscriptions shows that this one word must have had powerful resonance for an Athenian audience precisely at the period of the tripod epigram. For if this dedication was made on the Acropolis at the period suggested—500 to 470 BCE—the original viewers and reperformers of the epigram would

[19] Page (1975) prints the poem as Bacchylides III (lines 438–49) = Simonides 148 в. Translation by Wilson (2000: 121), who astutely interprets the dedication's ideology and style. See further Wilamowitz (1913: 218–22).

[20] The boundaries of tombs (*IGI³*), public spaces, or cult sites have yielded a number of *horos* stones. The uses of *horos* markers in post-fifth-century Athenian land and credit dealings are analysed by Finley (1985): none of his three categories is relevant to my interpretation of the tripod epigram.

be seeing and speaking a word employed for a quite specific purpose just down the slope in the Athenian agora. Boundary markers dating to around 500 BCE have been found bearing the inscription *horos eimi tês agorâs*, 'I am the boundary of the marketplace'.[21]

In this connection, it is worth recalling a penetrating study of these and similar *horoi* by my erstwhile Princeton colleague Josh Ober.[22] First, he notes that the *horos* functions as a speech act, informing its reader that a border has been established and commanding the reader to act accordingly. To function in this way, Ober observes, certain basic premises about the *horos* must be granted: 'Both the veracity and felicity of any given *horos*' claim to mark a boundary is a direct function of its specific location'. He goes on to say, 'If someone were to pull up the agora *horos* and carry it somewhere else, the statement it proclaims would no longer be accurate, since it would no longer mark a boundary of the agora'.[23] Both a constative speech act (declaring something) and a performative speech act (making something happen), the *horos* inscription acts like a permanent assertion of authority in the landscape—but is activated only when placed properly in that landscape.

When we return to the tripod epigram with this view of the social meaning of *horos*, the daring artistry of the little poem on the monument base begins to emerge. By designating the tripod a 'boundary', the poet poses several paradoxes. First of all, how does something like a tripod, which can circulate in prestige contexts involving agonistic achievement, achieve immobility and become a permanent mark on the landscape?[24] The answer must reside in a provocative prolepsis: this tripod by the *very act* of dedication, placement on its stand, and poetic declaration by the epigram is *not* going to move any more.[25] Put another way, the dedicator's

[21] Wycherley (1957: 218) lists several late-sixth-century examples.

[22] Ober (1995). He further develops these notions in an analysis of the political implications of the early Athenian *horoi* (in Blok and Lardinois [2006]).

[23] Ober (1995: 91–2).

[24] For the image of a circulating tripod in contestation, see the stories of the Seven Sages with my analysis (Martin 1993). The story of Hesiod's dedication of a tripod won at the games for Amphidamas (*Op.* 654–9) is also relevant. Podlecki (1981) adds the dedication by Echembrotus after a Pythian victory, recorded in Pausanias.

[25] We might compare rhetorical assertions surrounding any sports trophy (whether the Stanley Cup in hockey, the America's Cup in yachting, or the axe

gesture thus becomes a metaphor for the choral victory. Just as the victory event establishes a new mark in the field of music, so the tripod thereby won creates a new bounded space in the civic land-scape and, like a *horos* stone, declares its precise and proper location.

This introduces a second paradox: the dedication after all com-memorates a victory with the men's chorus. Such a dithyrambic chorus would have danced in a circular motion; recall that 'cyclic' is another word for dithyrambic in the testimonia for such perform-ances.[26] Thus, the dedication imposes a limit on the precise sort of poetic *sophiê* that, in performance, produces a *limitless*, unbroken ring. The unbounded and ideally unending force of the dithyramb as ritual act (its praise of Dionysus or Apollo) is contained and summed up in four squared-off lines. We can go further in this vein: if the permanence asserted by the inscription proclaims a fact in the realm of performance—'this is the new boundary'—there is yet another paradox in making this assertion about a *horos* within an agonistic context. For in the realm of athletic events, with which dithyrambic contests ran in parallel, a boundary mark can also represent a challenge. Rather than saying 'don't go beyond this point', the *horos* in such a context says in effect the opposite, 'Try to surpass this'. As we shall see shortly, this double function of the boundary is made explicit in Homeric poetry.[27]

Here we can contrast the epigram attributed to Bacchylides in which the tripod is called a *martus*. This 'witness', in attesting to the truth of the victory by the Acamantis tribe, can always respond to a challenge, but does not itself offer a challenge. Also, witnesses generally, unlike boundary marks, move around. In this regard, they are more like prestige tripods. In a trimeter poem attributed

---

awarded to the winner of the annual Stanford–Berkeley football game). Fans after victory will always claim that the prize in question is immovable, 'home to stay', and so forth.

[26] See testimonia in Ieranò (1997: 32–6).

[27] A later expression of this trope, applied to art, comes in the interesting epigram that the painter Parrhasius is said to have written in his own praise (*apud* Ath. 12.543e): 'I say the following, though to hearers who do not believe: I assert that the clear goals (*termata … saphê*) of this art have been reached by my hand. A boundary (*ouros*) has been set that will not be surmounted (*anuperblêtos*). But nothing for mortals is without blame.'

to Solon, the lawmaker's role as liberator is actually highlighted by an inversion of the regular complementary relationship of moving witness and unmoved marker (36W², lines 3–7):

συμμαρτυροίη ταῦτ' ἂν ἐν δίκηι Χρόνου
μήτηρ μεγίστη δαιμόνων Ὀλυμπίων
ἄριστα, Γῆ μέλαινα, τῆς ἐγώ ποτε
ὅρους ἀνεῖλον πολλαχῆι πεπηγότας,
πρόσθεν δὲ δουλεύουσα, νῦν ἐλευθέρη.

I call as witness in the court of Time
the mighty mother of the Olympian gods,
dark earth, from whom I lifted boundary stones
that did beset her—slave before, now free.[28]

Here the earth, an unmoving thing, is said to be a potential witness to the action of Solon, who radically shifted social relations in Athens by making the previously immovable (*pepêgotas*) *horoi* stones move. Both Solon's behaviour, and the poem commemorating it, are exceptional.[29]

Thus far the examination of the highly charged semantic field of the word *horos* has led to a contrast with the functionally similar *martus*. It is time now to move to a somewhat larger issue, namely the relationship between these epigrams *about* performances to the texts that purport to represent actual performances.[30] To do so, we must focus once more on *martus* and *horos*. Although they may be contrasted, in one key way that is important for questions of performance, they are quite similar. For the metaphor of the 'witness' and that of the 'boundary marker' can be applied *by the poetic performer* to his own role. In the case of *martus*, that is to say, the epigram attributed to Bacchylides uses a metaphor for the tripod, which a genre practised by Bacchylides (the *epinikion*) uses for the poetic 'I'—whether we want to call this the composer, *khorêgos*, or chorus. We find the

---

[28] West (1993: 82).

[29] On the *horos* in Solon's poetry, see my article in Blok and Lardinois (2006).

[30] It is worth noting that Wilson (2000) following Wilamowitz (1913: 222–3) sees 'Bacchylides III' (above) as exhibiting the style and diction of the very genre it commemorates, the dithyramb. I propose a similar mirror effect for the tripod inscription under consideration.

metaphor most clearly in the surviving choral poems of Pindar. *Olympian* 4 begins with a striking use of this trope (lines 1–3):

> Ἐλατὴρ ὑπέρτατε βροντᾶς ἀκαμαντόποδος
> Ζεῦ· τεαὶ γὰρ ὧραι
> ὑπὸ ποικιλοφόρμιγγος ἀοιδᾶς ἑλισσόμεναί μ'
> ἔπεμψαν
> ὑψηλοτάτων μάρτυρ' ἀέθλων·

Driver most high of thunder with untiring feet, Zeus; on you I call because your Horai in their circling round have sent me, accompanied by song with the lyre's varied tones, as a witness of the loftiest games.[31]

That the metaphor had a wider choral application is evident from Pindar's second *partheneion*. In this poem, the voice of the narrator is that of a young woman in a laurel-bearing procession (fr. 94b S—M lines 38–45):

> πιστὰ δ' Ἀγασικλέει
> μάρτυς ἤλυθον ἐς χορόν
> ἐσλοῖς τε γονεῦσιν
> ἀμφὶ προξενίαισι· τί-
> μαθεν γὰρ τὰ πάλαι τὰ νῦν
> τ' ἀμφικτιόνεσσιν
> ἵππων τ' ὠκυπόδων πο[λυ-
> γνώτοις ἐπὶ νίκαις ...

As a faithful witness for Agasicles I have come to the dance and for his noble parents because of their hospitality, for both of old and still today they have been honoured by their neighbours for their celebrated victories with swift-footed horses... [32]

The first person declares that she has come as a witness to the boy *daphnêphoros* Agasicles. It is significant in this passage that the praise by the girl shifts into the epinician style with praise of the boy's family's good luck at horse racing. It is hard to tell whether we have a case of one genre of discourse embedded in another. If so, perhaps the *partheneion* context has the older claim to the metaphor. An earlier example of the trope does appear in Alcman's *partheneion* (1P lines 39–43):

---

[31] Translation by Race (1997a: 89).
[32] Translation by Race (1997b: 327). For a discussion of P. fr. 94b see Kurke in this volume.

ἐγὼν δ' ἀείδω
Ἀγιδῶς τὸ φῶς·ὁρῶ
F' ὦτ' ἄλιον, ὅνπερ ἄμιν
Ἀγιδὼ μαρτύρεται
φαίνην·

And so I sing of the brightness of Agido: I see her like the sun, which Agido summons to shine on us as our witness. (tr. Campbell)

Here it is already highly complex: the choral first-person sings of Agido. That woman, in turn, is said to call on the sun to shine as witness for the chorus. But at the same time, Agido is emphatically *like* the sun (ὦτ' ἄλιον). Thus the chorus places the guarantor of its performance within the group itself.[33]

On the basis of these examples, we can say that an old motif of 'giving witness' to and through the means of the choral performance itself extends beyond the outer limits of performance, into the retrospective poetry used to commemorate choral victories. In other words, the *echo* text (commemorative stone) takes up a primary metaphor that can occur in the *performance* text. For the sake of symmetry we should ask: does the same thing apply to the metaphor of the boundary marker? At first sight, it does not seem to be the case. The word *horos* does not appear in Pindar; it is used only once in Bacchylides, in a phrase about the 'boundary of life' (B. 5.144)—and not in reference to the chorus. Yet there are two points that lead one to believe the marker metaphor can be implicit in choral self-description.

First, another trimeter poem of Solon shows that this metaphor, too, can be applied to a poetic performer—apparently a solo composer/ performer of iambics (37W² lines 7–10):

οὐκ ἂν κατέσχε δῆμον, οὐδ' ἐπαύσατο
πρὶν ἀνταράξας πῖαρ ἐξεῖλεν γάλα·
ἐγὼ δὲ τούτων ὥσπερ ἐν μεταιχμίωι
ὅρος κατέστην.

He would not have restrained the masses nor would he have stopped until he had stirred up the milk and got rid of the cream. But I stood in no-man's-land between them like a boundary marker. (tr. Gerber)

---

[33] On the complicated deictic imagination underlying this composition see now Peponi (2004).

These lines quoted by Aristotle (*Ath.* 12.5) feature Solon describing his self-positioning and fixity between two warring camps—in the *metaikhmion*—the land between spears. Here he has set himself up as a *horos*.[34] The association of landscape with *horos* is of course natural; these stones are pegged to the soil. But land with *horoi* in it becomes something else: it is land that has been made subject to a declarative speech act, a demarcated social and often civic space. Now as Pausanias tells us (3.11.9), exactly such a civic space in the centre of Sparta was known as the *khoros*. The equivalent space at Athens would be the agora, which, as we have seen, was bounded by *horoi*.

The picture that I am now sketching—the *khoros* as a space that is assumed to be defined by the *horos*—has already been staked out by the anonymous composer and/or inscriber of the tripod epigram with which I began. An unnoticed aspect of the poetic technique in this epigram is its wordplay. We have χο]ροι ἀνδρο[ν] ending line 1. Line 2 ends with ἀνέθε[κ]εν hόρον. Line 3 places [χ]οροῖς at the hephthemimeral caesura. And line 4 starts (probably) with [ἀνδ]ρον. In fact the syntax at this juncture is ambiguous. Does the genitive *andrôn* go with *khorois* or *phula*—'dances', or 'races', of men? It could be that the poet's desire for chiasmus and symmetry is what prompted this placement of the genitive, which in turn produces the slight hesitation about the word's affiliation.[35]

In short, the word *horos*, already so unusual for this context, is framed in the poem by the word *khoros*. This constitutes a visual and verbal pun, since the *horoi* are supposed to be the bounding artefacts, the outside, not the middle. I want to stress the visual aspect of this arrangement, as we know this poem was meant for seeing as well as enunciation. A look at the drawing of the stone (Fig. 2.1) reveals more clearly the perfect chiastic figure that is made by the *r/o*

[34] For the role of metaphor in political representation, see Martin 2006; and on the *metaikhmion* see further Goldhill (ch. 5 of this volume).

[35] For the supplement, see Peek (1974). Podlecki (1981: 101) remarks that the genitive placement is 'either infelicitous or something approaching conscious wordplay'. His further disparagement ('Whoever the poet was, he was more accomplished at dithyramb than at epigram...') hints at the former; in this paper I have sought to demonstrate that the latter is much more likely.

characters of *khoroi* and the *o/r* of *horon*. Visually, in the pre-Ionic local Athenian alphabet, the punning effect is even more striking as both long and short /o/ are written with one and the same letter form. A more ambitious pun relies on the same lack of a distinction between the sign for long and short /e/ sounds.[36] On the top line of our middle fragment one can read the word *Athenesi* 'at Athens'. Directly below, in line 2, is the key declarative word of this inscription, *anetheken*. This time, the chiastic *figura* comprises a reversal of syllables rather than letters: *the-ne/ne-the*. In short, we have here a carefully choreographed visual and verbal poetic performance on stone, a dance of the letters several generations before the infamous Letter Show (*Grammatikê Theôria*) of the Athenian comic poet Callias with its singing and moving alphabet chorus.[37] This elaborate poetic foregrounding of *khoros* as it is linked with *horos* now opens a further question: is there at play in choral poetry itself an implicit association of the performance group and boundaries?

My overall assumption is grounded in what we can call 'social poetics', an approach that demands that we take metaphors seriously as part of the way social behaviour is organized and talked about. This is to say that the inscribed poem can relate to choral performances in two ways, both as a direct mirroring of the poetic tropes expressed in dramatic choruses, and at a higher level, as a cognate expression of an underlying metaphor-set in Athenian, or even Greek, culture as a whole. These two routes are complementary: put another way, poetry—on stage or on stone—elicits the otherwise unexpressed but central social-poetic systems at work. Conscious artistry collaborates with unconscious cognitive structures to produce a consistent signal about associations that matter.

It is in the dramatic poetry of Euripides and Aeschylus that one can see this underlying association of 'chorus' and 'boundaries'

---

[36] A curious sidenote: Simonides was credited with introducing the sign for *êta* at Athens (*Suda*). If the rather odd tradition is authentic, it could be another strike against his being author of this poem, presuming he had anything to do with the inscribing process. It may be objected that the verbal patterns I here describe could have arisen only from the *inciser*'s, not the poet's, design, but this assumes there could be no cases of collaboration in creating poetic inscriptions. In fact, it is more economical to assume that poets oversaw the process and acted as prompters.

[37] The most recent full study of this drama is Rosen (1999).

played out. It might seem to be a baiting-and-switching of my audience at this stage, to introduce the theme of outer limits via a dedication for dithyrambic performance and get my results out of tragedy. But that in a way is exactly the point: that a fruitful interplay and crossover among dramatic and non-dramatic forms, scripts and echo texts, existed in classical Athens. In practical terms, there are good bridging mechanisms to ease the crossover. Dramatists were not confined to stage pieces after all: we hear of Sophocles composing a paean and Euripides an epinician, while Aeschylus composed an epitaph (his own)—although it is unclear if that was in verse. It is inevitable that the representational strategies of non-dramatic choral poetry surface inside dramatic choruses, when the mood calls for it. A prime example is that of the *thrênos* as it is stylized and embedded in tragedy. Similarly, there are 'epinician' choral moments in both tragedy and comedy.[38] The interpretative problem in the case of the boundary motif is that the traces of it appear only at the margins—in Solon and a stone, not in surviving non-dramatic choral texts.

In two important passages of tragic poetry, if we assume the implicit association of a *khoros* with boundaries we gain broader textual coherence and increased dramatic force. Let us begin with the chronologically later example, from the second stasimon of Euripides' *Heracles*. After cursing old age in the first strophe, the old men of the chorus express their wish that there could be a reward for virtue—namely a double youth (lines 655–72):

> εἰ δὲ θεοῖς ἦν ξύνεσις
> καὶ σοφία κατ᾽ ἄνδρας,
> δίδυμον ἂν ἥβαν ἔφερον,
> φανερὸν χαρακτῆρ᾽ ἀρετᾶς
> ὅσοισιν μέτα, καὶ θανόντες   660
> εἰς αὐγὰς πάλιν ἁλίου
> δισσοὺς ἂν ἔβαν διαύλους,
> ἁ δυσγένεια δ᾽ ἁπλοῦν ἂν
> εἶχε ζόας βίοτον,
> καὶ τῶιδ᾽ ἂν τούς τε κακοὺς ἦν   665
> γνῶναι καὶ τοὺς ἀγαθούς,
> ἴσον ἅτ᾽ ἐν νεφέλαισιν ἄ-

---

[38] e.g. S. *Tr.* 498–530, Ar. *Ach.* 1227–34.

στρων ναύταις ἀριθμὸς πέλει.
νῦν δ' οὐδεὶς ὅρος ἐκ θεῶν
χρηστοῖς οὐδὲ κακοῖς σαφής,   670
ἀλλ' εἱλισσόμενός τις αἰ-
ὼν πλοῦτον μόνον αὔξει.

If the gods had intelligence
and wisdom regarding men's affairs,
those who excel would win a double youth,
a clear sign (*kharaktêra*) of their excellence.
And after their death they would run a double course and
come back to the rays of the sun
but the ignoble would have
a single life to live
and by this it would be possible to recognize
both the good and the bad
just as among the clouds
sailors can count the stars
but as things are now there is no marker from the gods
that is clear for the noble and the base
but a lifetime as it rolls along
only increases wealth.[39]

The passage centres on an inscriptional image: in an ideal world, the excellent people would have the stamp of divine approval, an indelible *kharaktêr* (659).[40] 'A second life is odd as a distinguishing mark', as Bond notes.[41] Perhaps stranger is the rapid shift from the immobile, symbolic mark, in the sphere of *nomos*, to this ultimate image of *phusis* (a new life) and thence to the language of athletics, in the image of the double course (δισσοὺς ἂν ἔβαν διαύλους). Yet, this shift constitutes a repetition of sorts because the two-length run in a stadium (*diaulos*) places us back in the land of clear markers, where a *terma* or *sêma* provides for runners the all-important turning point.[42] This sequence of images remains counterfactual in the old men's fantasy of distinct markers: as things are, they say, there exists no clear boundary stone (οὐδεὶς ὅρος ... σαφής) from the gods, for

[39] All translations of the *Heracles* are from Halleran (1988).

[40] On the complex associations of this term in the symbolic realm of coinage, see Kurke (1999: 320–5 and esp. 324 n. 54 on the use of the word in Euripides).

[41] Bond (1988: 233).

[42] See on the vocabulary surrounding this image Nagy (1983).

either the noble or the base. Instead, a lifetime as it rolls or whirls around (εἰλισσόμενος) increases only wealth (rather than the length of one's life). As well as being appropriate to the decrepit state of the chorus members, theirs is an aristocratic attitude which decries the lack of social and ethical markers. A close parallel, that I have not seen cited, comes in the *Theognidea* (226–9):

> Πλούτου δ' οὐδὲν τέρμα πεφασμένον ἀνθρώποισιν·
> οἳ γὰρ νῦν ἡμῶν πλεῖστον ἔχουσι βίον,
> διπλάσιον σπεύδουσι. τίς ἂν κορέσειεν ἅπαντας;
> χρήματά τοι θνητοῖς γίνεται ἀφροσύνη.

Of wealth no limit is revealed to men, since those of us who now have the greatest livelihood are eager to double it. What could satisfy everyone? In truth possessions result in folly for mortals. (tr. Gerber)

As in *Her.* 669–72, the problem here with wealth is its lack of any boundary (*terma*): to the sage adviser, money is madness, causing those who already have the most to double their efforts at getting more. Theognidean poetry offers this as a simple maxim about limitations, in a fashion less condensed and less bold than the choral passage. By contrast, the thought in Euripides has a theological dimension: because the gods have not established a *horos*, not only is there no means of distinguishing virtue (*aretê*); people are concomitantly given free rein to range all over in pursuit of wealth. The logic seems to be that a marker (*kharaktêr*) of virtue would also provide a boundary (*horos*) for acquisition; the unspoken corollary must be that only the truly good should get rich. One feature joins together the moralizing of Theognis and Euripides: the present state of affairs is due in large part to lack of *sophia* among men (cf. *HF* 656).[43]

What does this talk of boundaries have to do with a chorus? As we read further in the second stasimon of the *Heracles*, the old men's musings turn metapoetic, to talk about song-making itself. In an implicit rejection of the money-grubbing whirl of life unbounded (671–2), the singers promise themselves a different kind of perpetuity, endless song (673–7):

---

[43] The related desire for a way to distinguish base from noble is expressed in the Theognidean corpus through the image of the touchstone: Kurke (1999: 42–4 and 53–5).

> I will not cease mixing together
> the Graces and the Muses,
> the sweetest yoking.
> May I never live without music
> but may I always be crowned.

As celebrators of Heracles' victory, of course, they are already crowned, so the visual cue reinforces the sense that their promise of devotion will hold true. There may also be a metadramatic prolepsis, alluding to anticipated victory (and thus crowning) at the Dionysia of the actual dramatic *choreutae*. The promise is embodied by changes of tense and mood, from the 'performative future' (673 *pausomai*) and optatives (676–7) to present indicatives (679 *keladô*, 681 *aeidô*). A ring composition takes the singers back to the future at line 685: 'In no way will we abandon (*katapausomen*) the Muses who set me dancing (*m'ekhoreusan*)'.[44] Such elaboration concerning their own choral medium sets the stage for the next lines (687–94):

> παιᾶνα μὲν Δηλιάδες
> ⟨ναῶν⟩ ὑμνοῦσ' ἀμφὶ πύλας
> τὸν Λατοῦς εὔπαιδα γόνον,
> εἰλίσσουσαι καλλίχοροι·   690
> παιᾶνας δ' ἐπὶ σοῖς μελάθροις
> κύκνος ὡς γέρων ἀοιδὸς
> πολιᾶν ἐκ γενύων
> κελαδήσω·

> The Delian maidens around the temples' doors
> whirling in their beautiful dances
> sing a paean in praise
> of Leto's noble child.
> I will sing paeans in celebration
> at your house,
> an old singer like a swan
> from a white throat.

As commentators have seen, the *men/de* construction of 687/691 contrasts the places of performance (Delos/Thebes) while at the same time making a parallel between the young women who praise Apollo and the old men who will sing like Apollo's sacred bird (albeit to

---

[44] For alternate readings that change the tenses, see Bond (1988: 241).

honour Heracles).[45] I would argue that part of the overarching symmetry uniting the two choruses has to do with their sense of limit and control: the verb which recurs at 690, describing the Delian maidens' dance (*heilissousai*), brings to mind the uncontrolled life of acquisition (671 *heilissomenos*). But the young women are, by contrast, graceful performers (*kallikhoroi*).[46] Their song and dance performance is ideally contained within a festival context, and its praise of Apollo enters into an economy of proper exchange, in which reciprocal favour (*kharis*) passes from mortals to gods and back. Their action is the opposite of, and the remedy against, the unrestrained one-way acquisition of the unbordered life.[47] Although both Deliades and the old men of the *Heracles* chorus are presented as enacting timeless, perpetual praise (cf. *ou katapausomen*), the audience is well aware that the requirements of actual performance check all choral activity, and moreover that this is the proper and expected end for ritual. Drama reinforces the stop-and-start nature of choral song through its rigid structure of episodes and stasima. I would go further: chorality in Greek culture is itself the most conspicuous marker of social- and self-control, of bodily comportment and the civil order that flows from it. One does not have to be Plato to appreciate that the very image of enthusiastic song and movement, enacted by a group, paced to rhythm and sculpted by dance, transmits powerful messages about harmony and *kosmos*.[48]

As so often happens in Greek myth, art, and literature, positive predications are reinforced by (sometimes spectacular) examples of a similar but negative type. The good social order embodied in bounded choral dance dissolves when dancers lose control. In several tragic scenes alluding to this phenomenon, the verb *helisso* appears.[49] Euripides' *Bacchae*, staging a disruption already latent in a number of Dionysiac myths concerning dangerous females, speaks of the god

[45] Bond (1988: 243–4).

[46] Reading Hermann's emendation as opposed to the Laurentian's *kallikhoron* (the adjective modifying Apollo): see Bond (1988: 245). On this passage as a whole see Henrichs (1996: 59–60).

[47] On the economy of *kharis* as expressed in Pindaric choruses, see Kurke (1991: esp. 66–70).

[48] On dance and social order see Wilson (2003).

[49] Henrichs (1995; 1996) in his valuable wide-ranging surveys does not note this connotation of the verb.

leading worshippers as they whirl (569–70 εἰλισσομένας μαινάδας
ἄξει). Another instance in Euripides shows the chorus of Phoenician
women imagining the whirl of dance as an escape from the disaster
that threatens Thebes (*Ph.* 234–8):

> εἰ-
> λίσσων ἀθανάτους θεοῦ
> χορὸς γενοίμαν ἄφοβος
> παρὰ μεσόμφαλα γύαλα Φοί-
> βου Δίρκαν προλιποῦσα.

> May I dance in honour of the deathless ones
> and dance in the god's honour free from fear,
> leaving Dirce for Phoebus' vale
> at the earth's navel. (tr. Kovacs)

And in the *Iphigeneia at Aulis* the chorus uses this highly marked verb
helisso as it recalls the celebration of the wedding of Peleus and Thetis,
at which the fifty Nereids performed circular dances (1054–7):

> παρὰ δὲ λευκοφαῆ ψάμαθον
> εἰλισσόμεναι κύκλια
> πεντήκοντα κόραι Νηρέως
> γάμους ἐχόρευσαν.

> Upon the white-gleaming sand
> Nereus' fifty daughters
> trod their whirling measures
> and danced the nuptials. (tr. Kovacs)

Here, cosmic order appears perfect, so long as we do not remember
the later narrative of Achilles' family and fate.

In a system of multiple interconnected metaphors, we have seen
horos standing for an enclosing boundary, but also a challenging
marker of limits not yet passed. The difference is akin to the grammatical distinction of imperative (one should not go) from indicative
(one has not gone). In this regard, the semantics of *horos* verge on
another noun, *terma* in its sense of 'endpoint'. In the imagery of the
Heracles chorus, as we saw, *horos* and *kharaktêr* are concatenated with
the footrace (*diaulos*), and thus with an implicit *terma*. Furthermore,
as we saw, boundary imagery gravitates to passages in which the
ethical problem of wealth is raised. With these associations in mind,

we can turn from Euripides' *Heracles* to another rich passage from a tragic chorus, Aeschylus' *Agamemnon* (773–81):

> Δίκα δὲ λάμπει μὲν ἐν
> δυσκάπνοις δώμασιν,
> τὸν δ' ἐναίσιμον τίει·   775
> τὰ χρυσόπαστα δ' ἔδεθλα σὺν
> πίνωι χερῶν παλιντρόποις
> ὄμμασι λιποῦσ' ὅσια προσέβα
> †τοῦ, δύναμιν οὐ σέβουσα πλού-
> του παράσημον αἴνωι·   780
> πᾶν δ' ἐπὶ τέρμα νωμᾶι.

But Righteousness shines in smoke-begrimed dwellings and esteems the virtuous man. From gilded mansions, where men's hands are foul, she departs with averted eyes and makes her way to pure homes; she does not worship the power of wealth stamped counterfeit by the praise of men, and she guides all things to their proper end.[50]

Boundary language has here led us to *the* central theme of early Greek literature, the nature of justice. In the imagery of the *Agamemnon* chorus, personified *Dikê* shuns the wrongly stamped (*parasêmon*) coin of gain and acts like a chariot-driver on a racecourse, heading without deviation to the *terma*. As in the *Heracles* passage above, inscribed signs and boundaries come together in the poetic imagination. The chain of thought is typically dense, laden with meanings dependent on the further connotations of religious imagery, interwoven with strands of democratic ideology. The verses weigh up wealth and flattery: just persons get money or give praise in the right proportions. Lines 779–80 imply that *Dikê* is beyond reputation, that it will head for the truth even if others are bribed to praise the rich. The chorus's observation might sound like a rejection of the entire system of aristocratic achievement in the polis. But it shares with a mainstay of that system, the poetry of Pindar, a key tenet: that only properly proportioned praise is legitimate. The next lines make this explicit (782–6):

> ἄγε δὴ βασιλεῦ, Τροίας πτολίπορθ',
> Ἀτρέως γένεθλον,

---

[50] Translations of Aeschylus are from Smyth (1926).

πῶς σε προσείπω; πῶς σε σεβίξω   785
μήθ' ὑπεράρας μήθ' ὑποκάμψας
καιρὸν χάριτος;

All hail, my King, sacker of Troy, off-spring of Atreus! How shall I greet you?
How shall I do you homage, not overshooting or running short of the due
measure of courtesy (*kharis*)?

Whether one praises athletes or kings, the central problem is: how far
do you go? Praise can get out of hand just as choral dance can go too
far. In addition, *dikê* cuts both ways: the hero, leader, or athlete must
not exceed in excelling. The poet's restraint thus functions as a model
for his addressee.

Put in this context, that a poet's monument (the stone we have in
front of us) should characterize itself as a *horos*, becomes all the more
appropriate. It is a 'boundary of poetry' now in three senses: the
horos marks ownership (it is the poet's own *sophia* that is commemorated); it is also a marker of self-control and of repose as contrasted
with movement (that is, the *khoros*); in this stability, it acts as a
terminus or limit, asserting that the poet does not go too far in
displaying either praise or wealth.[51]

But third—as we hinted earlier—the boundary *horos* is the ultimate limit. This tripod dedication, in other words, can function as a
trophy in the modern sense. The prize announces to any audience
that 'this is the record'. In agonistic contexts the trophy is a provo-
cation to go beyond. Both mark ultimate achievement but also set the
mark for further challenge. We can see how this works already in
Homeric verse (*Od.* 8.190–6) when Odysseus in disguise throws the
discus, which flies over all the other *sêmata* (markers for throws).
Athena puts the *termata* down (they seem to be the same as markers)
and makes the brief declaration: 'Even a blind man, stranger, could
distinguish this marker (*to sêma*)'. Another Homeric passage (*Il.*
23.309–10) brings together the turning point of a race (called *termata*) with the verb we already concentrated on in speaking of the
chorus, *helissemen*, in the context of a horse race at funeral games. So
an analogy begins to emerge: dance and athletics both need *termata*,
both as restraint and as competition. This should not be surprising,

---

[51] For the danger of overstepping in praise, see Pindar *N.* 7.70–3.

as long as we keep in mind that ancient Greek dance was not clearly distinguished from athletics (cf. the competitive dance in armour called the *pyrrhikê*). The Homeric diction in the same extended passage (*Il.* 23.329–33) gives us a glimpse into the importance of authority and speech for establishing markers: Achilles, the authorized master of games at this moment, linguistically marks the marker: *kai nun termat' ethêke*.[52]

Our explications, like choral dances, can traipse beyond boundaries; therefore I return now to the stone. Following the trail of semantic associations, we have seen that *horos* has a relationship to *terma*; which word, in turn, shows us in context the essential role of authorized persons in declaring the status of marker. And the association has an agonistic edge to it. If we look again at the assertion of 'so-and-so dedicated this boundary stone' and think of the poem this time in a totalizing agonistic realm (that of dithyramb, but also Athenian elite life), we see more point to the phrase *pleistois khorois ekso* in line 3.

Instead of reading it as an excuse (well, I have *not* won at Athens but I *did* win a lot elsewhere), we can turn it around. The dedicator has triumphed at Athens, after having won 'with the most' victories elsewhere. Thus, it is an assertion that the poet has really arrived, quite literally made it to the heights (a built-in metaphor for Acropolis dedications). The miniature rhetorical move is wonderfully tactful, because it treats Athens as the biggest event, at the same time as it declares our poet to be the big-time winner everywhere else, a Tiger Woods of professional dithyramb.

Let me end with one more possibility for the phrase with which we began: the *sophiês horos* 'endpoint, boundary of poetry'. Although I have thus far teased out meanings for this phrase by reference to parallels in diction and theme, I have not tugged too hard on the more basic grammatical point: what kind of genitive *is* this? We might most easily have assumed that it is limiting, in the way that *horos agoras* names the boundaries 'belonging to the agora'. But *sophiês* can also be taken as genitive of material or contents, in the way that *herkos odontôn* means not 'a barrier *belonging to* the teeth', but rather '*consisting of* the teeth' (Smyth 1956: §1323). The *horos*

---

[52] Similarly in *Il.* 23.358–9.

sophiês is then a boundary *made of* poetry—as, of course, in the solidity of these verses on stone, it is. But this introduces a further question: what exactly is the reference point here, the tripod and all it signifies, or the poetic inscription on its base? Why would one want in this way to bring attention to the poem itself as *horos*?

There is a tension produced by the very act of choral performance in competition. It has to end (otherwise all order is lost—the nightmare of Bacchic debacle), but it should not end in its function as an act of praise to gods by dancers performing for the community (and their tribes). After the music died, one could have resorted to a plain prose inscription detailing the results. But a poet's victory by being inscribed as another *poem* continues not only the medium (albeit with different metre) but the message of competition: try to beat not just this winning dithyramb but the latest poem commemorating it. Of course by being such a clever and complex assertion using an old word in an entirely new context (*horos*), the poem proves itself to be the boundary it embodies, the *ne plus ultra* of this kind of epigram. In the end of the archaic period, it seems, when literacy, thanks to the *polis*, had begun to spread even further, poets like Pindar and Bacchylides might have been thinking more consciously of what would happen to their work *after* the moment of performance. Would one's song continue to appear better than a rival's—or rivals' to come—*sub specie aeternitatis*? Homeric poetry had been self-assured about the poetic glory (*kleos*) it conferred: mortals suffered and died to be *aoidimos*, a topic for song.[53] But the world of the sixth and fifth centuries BCE brought the need for inscription on a grander scale.[54] From our perspective, it seems poets would want to produce written texts so as to control future reperformance of their songs. The Acropolis tripod dedication we have analysed shares the same concern and so mutates *khoros* into *horos* (of course, the better solution would be to inscribe an entire composition, as we hear happened with Pindar's *Olympian 7* in Rhodes—but that required public expense).

[53] *Il.* 6.357–8.
[54] The example of the tyrants, experts at inscribing, must have rubbed off on their poet clients: see the case studies in Steiner (1994).

It may be interesting that Pindar himself, a poet who thought deeply about this problematic, makes a visual paradigm of it. In a reverse move (from the tripod epigram), he transmutes, at the end of *Pythian 9*, a *horos* into a *khoros* (lines 111–14):

πατὴρ δὲ θυγατρὶ φυτεύων
κλεινότερον γάμον, ἄκουσεν Δαναόν ποτ᾽ ἐν Ἄργει
οἷον εὗρεν τεσσαράκοντα καὶ ὀκ-
τὼ παρθένοισι πρὶν μέσον ἆμαρ, ἑλεῖν
ὠκύτατον γάμον· ἔστασεν γὰρ ἅπαντα **χορόν**
ἐν **τέρμασιν** αὐτίκ᾽ ἀγῶνος·

But her father, planning a more glorious marriage for his daughter, had heard how in Argos Danaos in his day had devised a means to gain a most speedy marriage for his forty-eight unwed daughters before noon: at once he placed the whole **throng** at the **finish line** of the contest... [55]

The ode concludes with a recollection of the Libyan forefathers of the victor, Telesicrates of Cyrene, recalling how one of them, Antaeus, once managed a bride contest for his daughter. Pindar takes a step further back into the past. Antaeus, he says, wanting to make an impressive wedding, did something already mythic in his own time. His mythic model, Danaus, had once ordered suitors to run for their wives (his daughters): first to win, first wed. Antaeus, the later king, made the competition fiercer because he had only one daughter to give away as a racing prize. He adorned the trophy girl and set her up as the *telos akron* (118 'ultimate goal'). The one who managed first to reach her and touch her garment would win her (*P.* 9.117–20).

As with his own poetry of hymnic, choral dance and song, Pindar envisions the contest event in live performance terms, with a group of young girls inscribed within it. His poem (for a race in armour, 474 BCE) is all about racing, winning, getting a girl. Apollo, the victor, and his ancestors are all drawn into the action. It also embeds a significant moment of 'hearing', as Antaeus 'heard about' (112 *akousen*) the earlier episode. In other words, it revolves around a scenario of oral tradition. The mythic reward offered by Danaus was not just a 'throng' of girls but a *khoros* at the *termata*. In a perfect mirroring of Pindar's own poetic economy, the winner achieves a chorus. Live

[55] Translation by Race (1997*a*).

performance, like the processes of marriage and nature celebrated in this poem, keeps poet and victor's names alive, as other people will hear about both achievements, the event and its echo (just as Antaeus heard of Danaus' clever device). In one of the many ironies of Greek literary history, Pindar's poetry, which envisions and privileges the *non*-written primacy of live performance, became textualized and canonical. But the composer of so many winning dithyrambs, who proudly crafted his own perpetual *horos sophiês*, had his work disappear, except for a damaged stone base in the Epigraphical Museum.[56]

[56] I wish to thank members of the Coralie *thiasos* and of the American School of Classical Studies at Athens, in particular its director Prof. Stephen Tracy, for enabling shorter presentations of this paper and offering valuable critiques.

3

Visualizing the Choral: Epichoric Poetry, Ritual, and Elite Negotiation in Fifth-Century Thebes

Leslie Kurke

I. BACKGROUND: RECONSTRUCTING THEBAN CHORALITY

All Greek choral poetry of the archaic and classical periods was composed for a religious context—indeed, choral poetry provided the script for ritual performance and, as such, was intended to act on the world. In the domain of tragedy, no one has articulated this more clearly or played out its implications more fully than Froma Zeitlin. Zeitlin has changed the way we read tragedy by insisting that we attend to its broader social context—in particular, to its religious or ritual dimension as central to the meaning of tragedy and to its effects on the world.[1] I had the great good fortune to study with Froma Zeitlin as a graduate student, and her teaching and methods of reading had an enduring influence on my approach to Greek literature. Here I want to offer her, as a small token of gratitude for that profound impact, an essay that extends her characteristic cluster of issues beyond Athens and tragedy to contemporary choral poetry. For recent discussions of Greek *mimesis* as 'ritual re-enactment' have recognized many of the elements of drama already present in archaic choral poetry. Thus

---

[1] See e.g. Zeitlin (1965; 1966; 1970; 1982a; 1993) and many of the essays collected in Zeitlin (1996a). See also the important discussion of Foley (1985).

Gregory Nagy has offered a reconstruction of the repeated performance tradition of Alcman's first *partheneion* in which two girls re-enact
the roles of the two royal chorus leaders Hagesichora and Agido,
themselves ritually re-enacting the roles of the Leucippides from the
poem's myth. In the reconstruction of Nagy and other scholars, the
whole performance was staged with complex choreography, elaborate
costumes, and props (thus Nagy 1990: 42–5, 343–52, 373–8; cf.
Calame 1997, Peponi 2004, and, on the pervasive theatricalization
of Greek culture in general, Bassi 1998). This culturally thicker notion
of *mimesis* suggests that there was a significant choral 'baseline' even
before the emergence of full-scale drama. Thus we need to think about
choral performance in its complex social and religious embedding as
the substrate or background to tragedy, to be able to see what is the
same and what is distinctive or different about tragedy's appropriation
of choral forms. This paper represents an exercise in 'visualizing the
choral' as an essential precondition for 'visualizing the tragic'. Or, to
take up Richard Martin's metaphor drawn from a different realm of
sense perception, I would contend that all Greece, with its multiple,
diverse choral forms, serves as the echo chamber for tragedy—the
context in which we need to hear competing and conflicting cultural
conversations and contestations.

   For all of this, I find it irresistible to turn to Thebes, partly because
I am a Pindarist, but also as a kind of homage to Froma Zeitlin's own
brilliant work on Thebes as a topos or 'commonplace' on the Athenian tragic stage. In two now classic essays, Zeitlin analysed how
Thebes offered an 'other place' wherein Attic tragedy could confront
and explore issues of the unstable boundaries of self and society, the
collapse of distinctions, and the impossibility of escaping the pull of
a destructive mythic past (Zeitlin 1990*b*, 1993). I would like
here to shift the focus, to try to imagine the process of self- and
civic-constitution through choral performance at home in Thebes.
This is then a preliminary chapter toward a larger study of Theban
ritual and choral poetics; for the brief compass of this paper, I will
focus on Pindar's so-called second *partheneion* (fr. 94b SM) and its
attendant ritual of the Daphnephoria. But I must begin with a
disclaimer. Inevitably, we have a great deal more data (both literary
and epigraphic) for Athenian developments of the fifth and fourth
centuries; this difference in quantity and quality of source material

entails that our reconstruction of choral and cultic landscapes outside of Athens must perforce be more schematic and more speculative, painstakingly built up from sources that are haphazard, lacunose, and wildly divergent in date. Acutely aware of these limitations, I offer the following as an imaginative reconstruction of Theban choral and ritual forms.

Pindar fr. 94b was originally published from papyrus in 1904.[2] It appears to represent the only preserved remnant of archaic or classical maiden song of any length outside of the *Partheneia* of Alcman. As such, this text is a fascinating and tantalizing document: unfortunately very fragmentary, but still recognizably epichoric (in contrast to the more Panhellenic epinicia) and intimately embedded in the specificities of cult practice. It thus seems a promising starting point for reconstructing the choral and cultic landscape of Thebes; as I will suggest, read with and against other sources for the ritual, it will help us delineate a characteristically Theban chorality.

The poem itself makes clear that it was sung by a chorus of *parthenoi* on the occasion of the Theban Daphnephoria (the female speaker refers to 'holding a shining branch of laurel', 7–8). The bulk of what we know about the Theban Daphnephoria and its complex cast of characters comes to us from much later sources (Pausanias and Proclus *apud* Photius); I will be reviewing this material in detail below. When the fragment was first discovered on papyrus, scholars immediately read it against, and in the light of, these much later reports of the ritual. Beyond identifying and reconstructing the poem's ritual context, what little scholarly discussion there has been of Pindar's fragment has focused mainly on the textual corruption of lines 19–20 and the exact relations among the many named individuals in the poem: Aeoladas (9), his son Pagondas (10), Agasicles (39), Damaena (66), and Andaesistrota (71).[3] For the latter, Luigi Lehnus

---

[2] As *P. Oxy.* 659; see Grenfell and Hunt (1904: 50–60).

[3] For discussion of textual issues, see Farnell (1932: 427–8), Most (1986), Ferrari (1991: 390–6); for the *dramatis personae* and their relations to one another, see Wilamowitz (1922: 435, 553), Sbordone (1940: 33–4), Lehnus (1984: 83–5), Calame (1997: 60–2). Stehle (1997: 93–100) represents a notable exception to the general trend of scholarship on fr. 94b, since she offers a nuanced literary reading that focuses mainly on issues of gender and the complexities of self-presentation of Pindar's maiden chorus. My reading will build on and complement hers, devoting greater attention to the ritual, social, and political aspects of the poem in performance.

made a major contribution to the understanding of the genealogical connections among the ritual participants when he improved the text of line 66 based on a reinspection of the papyrus. Reading Δαμαίνας πά[τε]ρ in place of Grenfell-Hunt's Δαμαίνας πα[î], Lehnus was able to propose a consistent and economical interpretation of all the poem's relational references and assign each actor a plausible role within the ritual: Aeoladas the grandfather, Pagondas and Andaesistrota the adult parents of Agasicles, the παῖς ἀμφιθαλής, and of Damaena, the leader of the maiden chorus.[4] Lehnus also, following Grenfell-Hunt, identified the poem's Pagondas, son of Aeoladas, with the Boeotarch who, according to Thucydides, played a decisive role in the battle of Delium in 424 BCE (Th. 4.90–6); he therefore concluded that this must be a late composition of Pindar's.[5] I will return below to the question of the poem's date.

When scholars have considered the poem from a literary perspective, they have often remarked on its seeming generic mixture of *partheneion* and epinician elements. An extreme version of this is represented by Albert Schachter, in his somewhat disgruntled assessment of the poem:

The daphnephoric hymn, we are told by Proklos, is a hymn in honour of Apollo; but, in this poem the maiden undertakes to sing in honour of the house of Aiolidas and his son Pagondas, and proceeds to do so. Apollo appears only once in the text, and even then only by grace of a restoration...On balance I find it impossible to decide whether or not

---

[4] Lehnus (1984: 83–5). Lehnus's reconstruction is accepted by Herwig Maehler, who includes with the text of the poem a genealogical chart based on it in his latest edition of the Pindar fragments (Maehler 2001: 95). On this reconstruction, Pagondas, as Agasicles' nearest adult male relative, would thus be the *kôpô*-bearer (see § 2 below). Calame (1997: 61 n. 156) objects that 'nothing in Pindar's text shows that Agasicles and Damaena are such close relatives, nor that Andaesistrota is the wife of Pagondas'. But in fact I take Pindar's lines 36–7 (ἀνδρὸς δ' οὔτε γυναικός, ὧν θάλεσσιν ἔγκειμαι, χρή με λαθεῖν ἀοιδὰν πρόσφορον) to be a punning reference to the *pais amphithalês* Agasicles (whose name immediately follows). At the same time, Pindar's oddly specific phrase ἀνδρὸς δ' οὔτε γυναικός suggests that the poem celebrates not just the father of the *pais amphithalês*, but also his *mother* (Andaesistrota?), while (as Lehnus 1984: 85 points out) the plural θάλεσσιν, if it is not just a poetic plural, would appropriately designate both Agasicles and Damaena, if they are brother and sister and children of Pagondas.

[5] Grenfell and Hunt (1904: 51), Lehnus (1984: 77–8). Cf. Wilamowitz (1922: 436–7).

this hymn is daphnephoric. It is a Theban hymn, but seems to honour a noble family rather than the Ismenian god. In this respect it has more in common with the epinicia than with what one might expect of a daphnephoric hymn. (Schachter 1981: 85)

Clearly, as far as Schachter is concerned, the poem contravenes his expectations of what a proper *daphnêphorikon* should contain. But, of course, this just begs the question: given that we have almost no surviving fragments of *daphnêphorika*, what should we expect from a daphnephoric hymn? I will attempt here to explain this so-called problem of generic mixture by reinserting Pindar's fragmentary poem, as much as possible, in its historical and ritual contexts.

It should be said that Lehnus had already effectively answered Schachter's doubts, noting that the supplement [Λοξ]ίας in line 3 is almost certain and that (more importantly) the Theban Daphnephoria is a festival at once civic and familial. In so far as a single aristocratic house plays a leading role in the event, commemoration of its glories (including athletic victories) is entirely appropriate; and this lends a 'para-epinician' cast to parts of the maiden song.[6] Lehnus's response to Schachter is descriptively correct, but it does not tackle the question of why poem and rite alike would be constructed this way: why should the ritual award such a prominent role to a single aristocratic family, so that Pindar's poem appropriately interweaves generic elements of *partheneion* and epinician? A merely descriptive answer runs the risk of portraying Pindar as simply unable to help himself—as if the celebration of athletic victories is an automatic impulse for the poet, an epinician reflex entirely incidental to the civic and cultic project of the poem.

Thus, rather than taking for granted that the Theban Daphnephoria is a 'family affair', I would like to consider why this is from the perspective of ritual or, perhaps better, ritualization. Following the lead of much recent critical discussion of ritual, I start from the assumption that ritual does not merely passively reflect some

---

[6] Lehnus (1984: 77, 80–1), quoting Bowra (1961: 47): 'in Pindar's δαφνηφορικόν for Agasicles ... the whole festival is a family affair'. Contra Schachter, it is also worth noting Severyns' point (1938: 2.211, 229) that Proclus specifically categorizes the *partheneion* as a 'mixed genre' because it combines praise of gods and men in one poem; cf. D'Alessio (2000: 259–60).

pre-existent instituted order; instead, by a process of ritualization, certain marked or privileged acts constitute the very order they pretend to represent, while endowing it with an aura of cosmic legitimacy. It is this that Catherine Bell refers to as 'redemptive hegemony' as the goal and end product of ritualized activity, while Clifford Geertz makes a similar point when he asserts that ritual does not simply represent power that is elsewhere: it just *is* power.[7] Thus I would suggest that the ritual of the Theban Daphnephoria serves periodically to constitute and legitimate a certain hierarchical social and political order. And, viewed from the perspective of ritualization, choral poetry provides the script for this mystificatory process: thus 'generic mixture' can be understood only by being grounded in the needs of the broader historical context and of the particular ritual occasion. I will therefore consider each of these in turn: first, what we can reconstruct about the history of Thebes in the archaic and classical period; second (in the next section), the specifics of the Daphnephoria ritual as these are reported by other, late sources.

In the sixth and first half of the fifth century (at least according to Theban speakers in Thucydides), Thebes was a narrow oligarchy, dominated by a small number of elite families (Th. 3.62.3–4). The existence of this extremely narrow oligarchy is confirmed by the treatment of Thebes by the Greek allies after the Persian Wars. For although Thebes and most of Boeotia allied themselves and fought with the Persians in 480–479, the city as a whole got off surprisingly lightly: the allies besieged Thebes and ravaged its territory immediately after the battle of Plataea, but in the end punished only a small group of Theban leaders (Hdt. 9.86–8). After the battle of Oenophyta in 457 BCE, the victorious Athenians set up democracies or pro-Athenian oligarchies in many cities of Boeotia, including a democratic regime within Thebes itself. A glancing reference in Aristotle implies that this new Theban government was overthrown not long after it was instituted because of its disorganization and incompetence (Arist. *Pol.* 1302[b]27–30). These developments suggest a fairly stable oligarchic regime within the city: at least according to

---

[7] Bell (1992), Geertz (1980: 121–36). For a fuller exposition of Bell's model of ritualization, see Kurke (2005: 81–4).

Thucydides' representation of Thebes' tendentious self-defence in 427, there was a shift from the control of a very few elite families to a broader-based oligarchy after the Persian Wars.[8] The 450s, then, saw the brief imposition of a democratic regime and *stasis* or revolution that restored Thebes' traditional oligarchy.

In this same period, the history of Thebes is inseparable from the city's attempt to organize and control all of Boeotia. Traditionally, scholars have assumed an organized Boeotian 'League' already in the late sixth century, but Emily Mackil has recently challenged that reconstruction as an anachronistic retrojection of the later fifth- and fourth-century institution on to an earlier period.[9] Mackil instead urges caution; as she notes, in dedicatory inscriptions from the early fifth century, as in later references in fifth-century literary texts, there is often a slippage between 'Boiotoi' and 'Thebans', so that we should probably understand the former term in this period as *normative* rather than *descriptive*. As Mackil observes, 'prior to 457 the "Boiotoi" seem actually to have been Theban élites attempting to appropriate the name of the region in their bid for hegemony'.[10] Mackil herself suggests that the first half of the fifth century witnessed the

---

[8] On the tendentiousness of the Theban speaker's claims here, see Hornblower (1991: 456–7).

[9] Many details of Boeotian political and military history in the archaic and classical period are obscure or disputed, since we rely for this period almost entirely on brief references in Herodotus, Thucydides, and Aristotle (the anonymous *Hellenica Oxyrhynchia*, first published in 1908, provides an invaluable description of the constitution of the Boeotian *koinon*, but covers only the period 447–387 BCE). For the traditional view of the existence of the Boeotian *koinon* in the late sixth century, see e.g. Larsen (1968: 29–30); Buck (1972; 1979: 107–20); Ducat (1973). Demand (1982: 17–20) and Hansen (1995: 30–2) express scepticism about the existence of a formal *koinon* already in the late sixth century, while Mackil (2003) offers a thoroughgoing re-evaluation of the evidence. I shall in general follow Mackil and avoid using the terms 'league' or 'federal league' as translations of *koinon*, regarding them as anachronistic and misleading.

[10] For the broader argument, see Mackil (2003, chs. 3–5); quotation from p. 251. As Mackil points out, there are only two 'bits of tolerably good evidence for the existence of a Boiotian *koinon* prior to 447' (2003: 275 n. 222): (i) Herodotus' report of a 'Boiotian' attack on Plataia of 519 to force that city to 'take part in the Boiotians' (τελέειν ἐς Βοιωτούς, Hdt. 6.108.5; cf. Th. 3.68.5); (ii) Herodotus' mention of Boeotarchs in the aftermath of the battle of Plataea in 479 BCE (Hdt. 9.15.1). The former, the attack of Thebes on Plataea in 519, Mackil sees as the depradation of a single expansionist city, rather than as the first unified action of a 'federal league'. The latter, Herodotus' use of the term Boeotarchs in his account of the events of 479,

gradual coalescence of the region, while the organized *koinon* first crystallized only after the battle of Coronea, in which a coalition of Boeotian cities joined forces in 447 to drive Athens out of Boeotia after her ten-year occupation. This reconstruction has the advantage of respecting the historical specificity of the early-fifth-century data, while Mackil's proposed *terminus post quem* of 447 corresponds to the evidence of our only written source on the Boeotian *koinon*, the *Hellenica Oxyrhynchia*.

Finally, Mackil's comparative study of three ancient *koina* (the Boeotian, Achaean, and Aetolian) traces out the patterns of older, informal economic and cultic networks that seem in each case to underlie and enable the eventual development of the organized political institutions of the *koinon*. Mackil thereby restores to the picture dynamic patterns of mutual advantage and agency that informed the coalescence of a region and a multi-polis political organization (Mackil 2003, chs. 2–4).

The gains of this kind of historically respectful, holistic analysis of *koinon* formation for the reading of Pindar's Theban poems is enormous. For if Mackil is right in her reconstruction and her dating, Pindar's several Theban poems fall right in the period of the active efforts of the Theban elite to constitute a broader Boiotian unity and identity under their own leadership. And here, the historical argument converges with the modelling of ritual—or ritualization—as an active, shaping force within cultural formations: for Pindar's choral odes written for Theban occasions, as the scripts for such ritualization, could very well preserve traces of this process. That is to say, we may be able to find in these poems the micro-mechanics of the ideological work necessary to bring the Boiotian *koinon* into being. This applies to all Pindar's Theban poems, but would seem to be particularly important for fr. 94b, since this fragment may date to the very moment of the crystallization of the *koinon* (if we are right

---

Mackil connects with Thucydides' conflation of 'Boiotoi' and Thebans (as implied by the reference to the region 'previously called Kadmeis', Th. 1.12.3; as Mackil points out, Cadmus is only ever associated with the city of Thebes). That is, the Boeotarchs may have been leaders of some sub-group of all the Boeotians, constituted under Theban leadership in the late archaic period (Mackil 2003: 275–80, cf. 309–12). For similar caution about the probative value of these fifth-century references for the existence of an institutionalized *koinon* before 447/6, see Hansen (1995: 31–2).

to identify the poem's Pagondas with the Theban commander at Delium in 424 BCE).[11]

Whenever exactly we date the formation of the Boeotian *koinon*, once established, it was a remarkably stable form. As J. A. O. Larsen observes, 'The Boeotian constitution of 447 was on the whole unusually successful. It lasted with little change for two generations—longer, for instance, than the period from the development of extreme democracy in Athens under Pericles to the oligarchic revolutions of 411 and 404' (Larsen 1968: 36). How to account for this endurance and broad-based support? Since it was by and large not a matter of military domination within each city or by one city of the rest of the *koinon*, such stability strongly suggests successful consensus- and community-building at several different levels: within the different factions among the ruling elite; between the Theban elite and the civic population at large; and finally, between the Thebans struggling to establish their role as leading city and the other participants in the *koinon*. All three of these levels, I would suggest, are effectively addressed by the ritual of the Daphnephoria.

II. READING THE RITUAL: THEBAN AND BOEOTIAN COMMUNITY-BUILDING

But what of the ritual and the specific ritual context of Pindar's poem? As often in the domain of Greek religion, our knowledge of the Theban Daphnephoria ritual is haphazard and lacunose, dependent on partial reports in different sources that stretch over a millennium: besides Pindar's fragmentary poem, we have a brief mention of the *daphnaphoros* priesthood in Pausanias (second century CE) and a

---

[11] Cf. Kowalzig (2002: 229–70, esp. 231, 251) for a similar formulation about the constitutive work of 'choral song-dance' in the formation of the Boiotian *koinon*. As Barbara Kowalzig points out to me, the exact dating of the creation of the Boiotian *koinon* does not in fact materially affect the argument presented here, since, whether we accept the traditional late-sixth-century date or Mackil's mid-fifth-century date, contestation over what constituted a unified Boiotian identity certainly spanned the first half of the fifth century (the period when all of Pindar's Theban poems must have been composed).

detailed description of the Daphnephoria procession recorded by
Proclus (fifth century CE), then epitomized by the learned and indus-
trious ninth-century Byzantine Patriarch Photius (Proc. *Chrest. apud*
Photius *Bibl.* Cod. 239, pp. 321a–b Bekker). Pausanias, having
described the topography and sculptures of the Theban Ismenion,
pauses to observe:

This I know still occurs even in my time in Thebes. They make a boy of a
distinguished house, who is himself good-looking and strong (παῖδα οἴκου
τε δοκίμου καὶ αὐτὸν εὖ μὲν εἴδους, εὖ δὲ ἔχοντα καὶ ῥώμης) the yearly priest
for Apollo Ismenios. And they call him *daphnêphoros*,[12] for the boys wear
crowns of laurel branches. And I am not clear, if it was equally established for
all of them, when they had completed their service as *daphnaphoroi*
(δαφνηφορήσαντας) to dedicate a bronze tripod to the god. But I do not
think it was the custom for all of them [to do so], since I did not see many
[tripods] dedicated there. But the more well-to-do of the boys do dedicate
them. But the most conspicuous tripod, both for its antiquity and for the
glory of the dedicant, is the dedication of Amphitryon for Heracles' service
as *daphnêphoros*. (Paus. 9.10.4)

Proclus, in a fascinating section on maiden songs, informs us that the
Daphnephoria is a festival held once every eight years in Boeotia, in
which a chorus of girls sings a hymn to Apollo while processing in
turn to his shrines of the Ismenion and Chalazion or Galaxion (all
three probably in the neighbourhood of Thebes).[13] Proclus proceeds
to offer an aetiology and a detailed account of the ritual:

For in Boeotia the priests conveying laurel [branches] every eight years to the
[shrines] of Apollo used to celebrate him through a chorus of maidens. And
[this] is the cause: however many of the Aeolians used to inhabit Arne
and the territory around it, at the behest of an oracle rose up from there
and, settling down in front of Thebes, were trying to sack it, previously held

---

[12] In this instance alone, Pausanias uses the local dialect form of the title
(δαφναφόρος)—presumably picked up from a native source (perhaps a guide in
the temple or a local Theban antiquarian?; cf. Habicht 1985: 144–5; Jones 2001).

[13] The two different manuscript traditions of Photius actually provide two different cult titles for the chorus's second destination: A reads Χαλαζίου, M reads
γαλαξίου. R. Henry, editor of the Belles Lettres edition of Photius, prefers Chalazios;
Schachter (1981: 48–9) prefers Galaxios. Since we have no secure location for either
shrine (though both were probably close to Thebes), this makes little difference for
my argument.

by the Pelasgians. Since there was a festival of Apollo common to both groups, they made truces and, cutting laurel branches, the one group from Helicon, the other from [the territory] near the River Melas, they were conveying them for Apollo. And Polematas, the one leading the Boeotians, had a dream in which it seemed that a young man gave him a panoply and commanded that laurel bearers every nine years make prayers to Apollo. On the third day afterwards, he attacks and conquers the enemy, and himself was instituting the Daphnephoria. And from there the custom has been continuously maintained.

The Daphnephoria: They cover a log of olive wood with laurel branches and variegated flowers and at the top a bronze sphere is fitted, and from this they hang smaller spheres. And in the middle of the log putting around a smaller [sphere] than the one at the top they fasten to it purple wreaths; but the bottom of the log they cover in a saffron robe (τὰ δὲ τελευταῖα τοῦ ξύλου περιστέλλουσι κροκωτῷ). And of these, the uppermost sphere signifies the sun (with which they identify Apollo), but the sphere placed underneath [signifies] the moon, and the smaller spheres attached to them the stars and constellations, and the wreaths the cycle of the year—since they make these 365. And a boy with both parents living (παῖς ἀμφιθαλής) leads the Daphnephoria, and his nearest male relative carries the covered log which they call κωπώ.[14] And the *daphnêphoros* himself, following, holds on to the laurel branch, with his hair loose, wearing a golden crown and garbed in a shining robe that reaches to his feet, and wearing high boots(?) (ἐπικρατίδας or ἰφικρατίδας).[15] Him a chorus of maidens follows, holding forth branches for supplication [and] singing hymns. And they used to convey the daphnephoria in procession to [the shrines] of Apollo Ismenios and Chalazios [or Galaxios]. (Proclus *apud* Photius *Bibl.* Cod. 239, pp. 321a35–b32 Bekker)

At first sight, these two accounts, so disparate in time from Pindar's poem and from each other, seem to diverge wildly in details: where Proclus speaks of a procession held once every eight years, Pausanias describes a yearly priesthood and the dedication of a tripod. In contrast,

---

[14] Or κώπω. The word occurs only here and in the Scholia to Clem. Al. *Protr.* (clearly based on the same text of Proclus or his source[s]), and the manuscripts of Photius offer two different accentuations. Severyns (1938: 1.97–8) prefers the paroxytone accent as characteristically Boeotian/ West Aeolic (since he regards this as a Boeotian dialect word); Schönberger (1942), Chantraine (1968–80 s.v. κώπη), and Schachter (1981: 83 n. 3) opt for the oxytone accent as characteristic of compounds in −ω.

[15] Again, the two manuscript traditions of Photius offer two different terms here (A reads ἐπικρατίδας; M reads ἰφικρατίδας); see discussion n. 35 below.

Proclus' version and the fifth-century ritual as reconstructable from Pindar's poem appear much closer on points of detail than either one seems in relation to Pausanias' account. But even between Proclus' report and Pindar's poem there are discrepancies. Thus Proclus' cast of characters consists of a *pais amphithalês* leading the procession; his nearest adult male relative bearing the *kôpô*; following him, the *daphnêphoros* holding on to a laurel branch wrapped around the *kôpô*; and finally the maiden chorus (thus Severyns 1938: 2.220–1, Schachter 1981: 83–4). Pindar's poem, even in its fragmentary state, does not seem to allow space for the *daphnêphoros*, for at one point it mentions the first girl of the maiden chorus following immediately behind the *kôpô* (fr. 94b.67–70).

Most scholars who have discussed Pindar's poem or the rite of the Daphnephoria have simply ignored these differences of detail among the three accounts, seamlessly merging them together to produce a single, timeless narrative of the ritual.[16] On the other hand, a few scholars, disturbed by the discrepancies, have denied that these sources can be put together at all: thus A. Severyns, in his edition and commentary on Photius Cod. 239, denied that Pausanias' discussion had any relevance for the rite as described by Proclus, while Franco Ferrari challenged the utility of attempting to combine Pausanias' 'priesthood' with the details of the rite and with Pindar's fragment (Severyns 1938: 2.221, 225–8; Ferrari 1991: 396).

Rather than follow either of these routes, which depend either on the complete elision of difference or on the utter segregation of the few sources we have, I would like to shift the level of comparison from that of specific details to that of structural system. For that purpose, I will first offer a reading of the ritual as represented by the two later sources, attempting to account for as many details as possible (which, to my knowledge, has never been done),[17] and then to compare that reading in its main structural outlines to the

---

[16] Thus Wilamowitz (1922: 433–5); Sbordone (1940: 30, 33–4); Brelich (1969: 413 n. 238); Bernardini (1989); Calame (1997: 59–62, 103). Thus also Snell and Maehler (1975); Maehler (2001: ad loc.).

[17] Scholars have either focused only on specific details (the *kôpô*; the laurel bearing; the *pais amphithalês*; the maiden chorus), or, when they have analysed the ritual as a whole (e.g. Severyns 1938, Schachter 1981), the analysis has been vitiated by nineteenth-century assumptions about how ritual works: see discussion in text below.

fragmentary remains of Pindar's poem. What I hope to demonstrate by reading the rite and the poem separately in the first instance is that there are certain structural or family resemblances that justify reading them together, even if we cannot pinpoint very precisely in time the ritual as described by the later sources. Thus I will suggest that the later reports of the rite and the fragmentary remains of Pindar's poem mutually illuminate each other.

At the same time, the reading offered here is predicated on certain assumptions about the accounts of Pausanias and Proclus:

1. Pausanias is generally regarded as a reliable guide, especially for sites and objects for which he was an eyewitness.[18] In this case, his account of the yearly priesthood is attached to and inspired by objects he would have seen—tripods dedicated in the Theban Ismenion.

2. The accounts of Pausanias and Proclus are not irreconcilable; they differ because they are conditioned by their authors' different interests and focus. Thus (as noted) Pausanias' brief account of the yearly *daphnaphoros* priesthood occurs in the context of his description of the Theban Ismenion, inspired by the priests' dedicatory tripods commemorating their service. Proclus' account, by contrast, is part of a compendium of different kinds of choral song (here 'maiden song') performed in different ritual contexts in the Greek cities; thus Proclus' interest is focused entirely on the ritual procession, its participants, and accompanying song, and not at all on the duration or memorials of the priesthood.

3. I assume that the Theban Daphnephoria was not still being celebrated in the fifth century CE; that is, that Proclus is not offering an eyewitness account. If he is not, then we must assume that his complex narrative, full of circumstantial detail, comes from *somewhere*. Certain elements of Proclus' account are clearly late: thus the 365 fillets on the *kôpô* and the elaborate astronomical symbolism reflect a post-Julian calendrical system and post-Ptolemaic knowledge of astronomy.[19] But what of all the rest of the circumstantial detail in

---

[18] For Pausanias' reliability as an eyewitness, see Habicht (1985: 28–94, 144–51).

[19] On Proclus, his *Chrestomathy*, and his astronomical interests, see Wilson (1996: 37–41, 44); for Proclus' interpretation of the symbolism of the *kôpô* as a late superimposition, see Nilsson (1906: 165), Wilamowitz (1922: 433 with n. 1),

Proclus' account? The aetiology of the festival, linking it to the military victory of the Ur-Boeotians? The precise locations from which the original laurel branches were culled? The strange terms—the *kôpô* log and the *epikratides* or *iphikratides* for the footwear of the *daphnêphoros*? The fact is that we have different, earlier sources for each of these elements, grounding them in the context of Theban and Boeotian ritual and its symbolic logic—so that, even if the ensemble is a late antique fantasy, it is a fantasy based on something.[20]

On the basis of these assumptions, I think it is possible to make use of these two late accounts to reconstruct the ritual behind Pindar's poem. Indeed, the proof and justification for this procedure lies in the striking structural parallels detectable between elements of the rite and of the poem: for that purpose, I will focus here on just three specific elements that seem to me to speak to or reveal the different levels of community-building that the rite and priesthood achieve.

1. Levels of negotiation within Thebes. Pausanias' report of a yearly priesthood confirms what we would have expected anyway: some

Schachter (1981: 84 n. 2), Mackil (2003: 239 n. 105). Intriguingly, Wilson (1996: 39–40) expresses doubt that the Proclus whose *Chrestomathy* Photius epitomated was, in fact, the fifth-century Neoplatonic philosopher at all; he thinks, given the contents of the *Chrestomathy*, that 'it looks more like the work of a teacher of literature than a philosopher' (Wilson 1996: 39). This was already the conclusion of R. Beutler who, in the *RE* article on the Neoplatonic philosopher Proclus, categorizes the *Chrestomathy* among the 'Ps.-proklische Schriften' (Beutler 1957: coll. 207–8, with extensive citation of earlier bibliography). Alan Cameron and Richard Hunter have voiced these same doubts to me; Cameron thinks that the summary of the epic cycle is much more likely to derive from a second-century CE *grammatikos*; Hunter suggests that this might be Proclus of Naucratis, who was a teacher of Philostratus in Athens (see Philostr. *VS* 2.21).

[20] Some of these other sources will receive more detailed discussion in the text. Briefly: (i) Military invasion of Ur-Boeotians from Thessaly connected with the Thebans—Kowalzig (2002: 229–70) sees this as a prominent theme of early fifth-century mythmaking, based on sources going back to Pindar, Bacchylides, and Thucydides; (ii) Locations from which laurel culled—Mackil (2003: 240–3) has suggested a link to the shrine of Apollo Tegyraios near the River Melas (Plu. *Pel.* 16.3–6); (iii) The *kôpô*-log—the log (but not the name) attested for the Boeotian Daedala festival by Plutarch fr. 157; (iv) The different names for the *daphnêphoros'* footwear—D.S. 15.44, Ath. 11.471b (citing Clearchus), Pollux 7.89, Alciphr. 3.57, Dam. *Isid.* 89 all mention '*iphikratides*', while Photius' *Lexicon* calques '*iphikratides*' as '*epikratides*' (entry perhaps based on this passage in Proclus? See discussion in n. 35 below).

kind of instituted rotation among the different aristocratic houses whose sons occupy the yearly priesthood as *daphnêphoros*. (For the immense political prestige attached to such religious office, we might think of the parallel of elite Athenian girls serving as *kanêphoroi* in the Panathenaic procession.) For it seems that the *daphnêphoros* also played a prominent role in the procession of the Daphnephoria, if indeed it is legitimate to put together Pausanias' testimony and Proclus'.

But what Pausanias has to say about the tripods dedicated in the Theban Ismenion is also very suggestive. If the spottiness of tripod dedications observed by the Periegete is not simply the result of hundreds of years of depredations and urban decay in Thebes, Pausanias' hesitant remarks may instead suggest evidence of elite competition still preserved in the material record of his time.[21] That is to say, we might imagine the rotation of the yearly priesthood originally instituted to defuse or moderate competition among a narrow group of ruling elite families that might otherwise erupt in *stasis* and civil upheaval. But what Pausanias' *aporia* may imply is that the tripod dedication to commemorate the priesthood then itself became another locus for elite competitive display. In these terms, Pausanias' observation that only the wealthier boys (εὐδαιμονέστεροι τῶν παίδων) dedicated tripods is telling.

I would like to connect this dim echo of elite competition that we may catch in Pausanias with the critique of oligarchy Herodotus puts into the mouth of Darius in his fantasized Persian debate on the constitutions—for these views surely conform to broader Greek stereotypes about this form of political regime in a period more or less contemporary with Pindar's poem:[22]

---

[21] Schachter (1981: 83) suggests that the spottiness of tripod dedications observed by Pausanias may be explicable by the repeated sacks of Thebes, but this 'common-sensical' explanation in fact fails to account for the fact that *any* tripods were preserved to be seen by the Periegete. In reading evidence of elite competition in the material record, I take my inspiration from Peter Wilson's brilliant discussion of the choregic monuments in Athens (cf. Wilson 2000: 120–3, 198–262).

[22] The traditional nature of Herodotus' formulation here is confirmed by the close parallels of thought and diction with Theognis 39–52; on this correspondence, see Nagy (1990: 181–2, 369).

ἐν δὲ ὀλιγαρχίῃ πολλοῖσι ἀρετὴν ἐπασκέουσι ἐς τὸ κοινὸν ἔχθεα ἴδια ἰσχυρὰ
φιλέει ἐγγίνεσθαι· αὐτὸς γὰρ ἕκαστος βουλόμενος κορυφαῖος εἶναι γνώμῃσί τε
νικᾶν ἐς ἔχθεα μεγάλα ἀλλήλοισι ἀπικνέονται, ἐξ ὧν στάσιες ἐγγίνονται, ἐκ δὲ
τῶν στασίων φόνος, ἐκ δὲ τοῦ φόνου ἀπέβη ἐς μουναρχίην . . .   (Hdt. 3.82.3)

But in oligarchy, with many cultivating achievement in the public sphere,
strong private animosities tend to develop. Since each man wishes himself to
be the leading figure and to conquer with his counsels, they reach the point
of great feuds with each other, from which civil strife develops, and from
strife murder, and from murder it devolves to monarchy.

As we shall see, this passage contains some striking dictional parallels
with Pindar's *partheneion* fragment. For now, it is worth noting
that on this model it is the 'cultivation of achievement in the
public sphere' by individual members within the ruling elite that
tends to degenerate into animosities, civil war, and murder. And
I find it striking that in this context, Herodotus uses κορυφαῖος
(which I have translated 'leading figure') to characterize each
oligarchic leader's aspiration. This is a very general term, derived
from κορυφή—'top' or 'summit'—but it seems to function equally in
the political and choral spheres (by the time of Aristophanes,
κορυφαῖος without qualification can mean 'chorus leader').[23] Nor is
this complete interpenetration of political and choral domains surprising—this is exactly what we would expect for the archaic period.
Still, it seems significant that this word, with its fusion of political
and choral 'leadership', occurs in the debate on the constitutions *only*
for oligarchy. It is almost as if the Theban Daphnephoria attempts to
substitute the role of choral *koruphaios* for its political equivalent,
alloting to each of a small number of ruling houses in turn the
privilege of leading the chorus and the ritual, precisely in order
to forestall the downward spiral of animosities which Herodotus'
Darius catalogues.[24]

---

[23] Cf. Ar. *Pl.* 953, Arist. *Pol.* 1277ª 11. The term also occurs in D. 21.60, but is there
likely to be the intrusion of a marginal gloss into the text: see MacDowell (1990: 281);
for a different view on this passage, see Slater (1997), Wilson (2000: 358 n. 50). Nagy
(1990: 366 n. 145, 368–9) assumes that Herodotus is using a choral image here,
though he does not identify it specifically with oligarchy. See also Wilson (2000:
358 n. 50): 'The frequent analogy between choral and political forms of organisation
makes the use of the term in early choral contexts probable.'

[24] Cf. Wilson (2003) on the effects of dithyramb and dithyrambic competition to
allay civic *stasis*.

But it is not just intra-elite competition for which the festival provides a controlled outlet; the ritual spotlighting of a single noble family also speaks to the broader community of Thebes, affirming—indeed staging—the cosmic propriety of oligarchic leadership. In fact, Herodotus' Darius also implicitly acknowledges this level with the phrase ἐς τὸ κοινόν. It is not enough for individual oligarchic leaders to 'cultivate their virtue' or 'achievement' just among themselves; they need the whole city as admiring audience and witness. And if we may accept Pausanias' report of the dedication of tripods as actually connected to the same rite, such a practice would serve both these levels of ritualized negotiation. The individual wealthy *daphnêphoros* (or more likely, his father) would thus leave a permanent record of his moment in the cultic spotlight for his fellow aristocrats and for the city at large. Inscribed for all to see and dedicated in the Ismenion, the tripods would link each dedicating father and son in a continuous sequence of emulation stretching back to Amphitryon and Heracles.

2. The ritual, as Proclus narrates it to us, carefully links Thebes to the rest of Boeotia geographically; this is achieved particularly through the rite's historical *aition*. Proclus' aetiology makes the Daphnephoria into a commemoration and celebration of the beginnings of Boeotian identity and control of the territory. Nor is this a narrative that applies narrowly to Thebes, for the odd detail that the two groups of belligerents gathered their laurel branches from the areas of Helicon and the River Melas (near Orchomenos), respectively, situates this activity around Lake Copaïs far from the city of Thebes. Emily Mackil has suggested connecting the specific detail of the River Melas with the shrine of Apollo Tegyraios, which (according to Plutarch) was an oracular shrine to Apollo situated just below the marshes of the River Melas:

A little below the marshes [of the River Melas] there is a temple of Apollo Tegyraios and an oracle which has been abandoned for no long time, but which was at its height down to the time of the Persian Wars, when Echecrates was the prophet. And here they tell the story that the god was born; and the nearby mountain is called Delos and beside it the diffusions of the River Melas cease, and behind the temple two springs break forth from a source marvellous for its sweetness, abundance, and coldness. One of these we call 'Palm' and the other 'Olive', up to the present day. (Plu. *Pel.* 16.3–4)

Already in 1967, Albert Schachter had suggested that this shrine
belonged to a common 'Boiotian cult type' that also included the
Theban Ismenion (based on certain common distinctive features: a
shrine situated on a hill, with two springs behind, where a male
prophet officiated). And, while Schachter took this iteration of
a single cult as evidence for an original ethnic identity of the
Boeotians in the dim period of their migration into the territory,
Mackil argues instead that it represents a deliberate construction of
cult links—probably in the early fifth century.[25] The associations of
the ritual with the Lake Copaïs region are also visible in the name
given to the ornamented log borne in the procession—κωπώ, which
scholars have plausibly connected etymologically with Κωπαΐς
(Schönberger 1942: 89, Schachter 1981: 79).

3. The Daphnephoria ritual—again as narrated by Proclus—is a
bizarre hybrid. Why does it combine the carrying of an olive log with
laurel branches? The hybrid nature of the ritual has not escaped the
notice of scholars, but it has generally been 'explained' as a diachronic accretion—as the amalgamation of two different, originally
distinct rituals. Thus Severyns saw an 'original' agrarian ritual of the
Boeotian countryside, likely to have been annual, which involved
the bearing of the κωπώ, an adorned log akin to the maypole.
Superimposed on this older rite, Severyns suggested, perhaps under
Delphic influence, was the Apolline Daphnephoria, which made
the festival enneateric and attached it to Apollo's shrines in the
neighbourhood of Thebes (Severyns 1938: 2.218–19; cf. Nilsson
1906: 164–5). Likewise Albert Schachter:

there appear originally to have been two separate processions, one Apolline,
in which the laurel was borne to his sanctuaries, the other non- or
pre-Apolline, in which an adorned log (the κωπώ is a ξύλον, not a branch)
was borne. They were linked together by having the daphnephoros hold on
to the laurel attached to the log. The Daphnephoria proper suggests, by its

---

[25] Schachter (1967: 6–13); cf. Schachter (1981: 75). Mackil (2003: 240–3); cf. also
Kowalzig (2002: 251–70) for the late sixth/ early fifth century as the likely period for
the assimilation of Apollo Ismenios to the 'Daphnephoric' Apollo of the Lake Copaïs
region. Intriguingly, D'Alessio (2000) has identified Plutarch's Echecrates (prophet of
Apollo Tegyraios at the time of the Persian Wars) with the Echecrates named in
Pi. fr. dub. 333 SM—a fragment which, D'Alessio argues, may in fact be a remnant of
a Pindaric *partheneion*, sung by a maiden chorus from Orchomenos.

name and character, that it was introduced under Delphic influence. The log procession is one manifestation of a pan-Boiotian rite known to have been celebrated in southern Boiotia, but which may also have been celebrated in the Kopais region. (Schachter 1981: 85)

Neither of these scholars makes any attempt to explain why these two diverse rituals would have been sutured together; both, I suspect, still adhere to a nineteenth-century antiquarian model that sees religion as the random (almost instinctive) accretion and preservation of older elements. But I would suggest instead that we should understand the Daphnephoria ritual as a deliberate hybrid, a festival crafted to suture together the city of Thebes and the Boeotian countryside. Thus, we should pay particular attention to Schachter's point about the geographic distribution of 'log processions'. In fact, what evidence we have suggests that this was a ritual form characteristic of the area around Cithaeron, Plataea, and the Parasopia in southern Boeotia. We might therefore see the presence of the log in the Daphnephoria as an attempt to appropriate southern—particularly Plataean—elements in a Theban ritual.[26]

Finally, I would like to suggest that we might go even further, seeing in the Daphnephoria a hybrid or amalgam of different symbolic elements coded for marriage and for war, that thereby integrate aspects of both female and male initiation.[27] Thus scholars have noted that the κωπώ, adorned and dressed in its saffron robe (κροκωτός), represents a woman[28]—I would suggest, more specifically, a bride. For we have evidence, at least from Athens, of the κροκωτός having hymeneal associations.[29] Furthermore, we have a

[26] I am thus proposing a deliberate 'invention of tradition' along the lines analysed by Hobsbawm and Ranger (1983). For the geographic localization of the Daedala ritual and a fascinating analysis of the construction of regional identity through ongoing renovation and innovation in ritual forms, see Mackil (2003: 281–90).

[27] Cf. the classic formulation of Vernant (1988: 34): 'if for a boy the significance of the rites of passage was to mark his accession to the condition of a warrior, for the girl who took part alongside him in these same rites . . . the initiatory trials had the force of a preparation for marriage . . . Marriage is for the girl what war is for the boy . . .'

[28] Thus Schönberger (1942: 88–9); Schönberger also notes that a noun ending in −ώ is an especially common formation for female names. Cf. Schachter (1981: 84).

[29] Thus Perlman (1983: 125–6), citing A. *Ag.* 239 and Ar. *Lys.* 645. I would add to these passages also Ar. *Lys.* 219, where 'wearing the saffron-robe' is mentioned in the women's oath right after 'remaining unbulled within the house' (ἀταυρώτη, *Lys.* 217–18). Cf. also the formulation of Perlman (1989: 126): the *krokotos* is 'the garment

very suggestive parallel in the Daedala ritual dedicated to Hera in the neighbourhood of Cithaeron. Plutarch tells us, in an aetiological account of the origin of this festival, that a log was 'dressed as a bride' (καταστεῖλαι νυμφικῶς) and called Daedale, to enact a sham marriage with Zeus.[30] We might see in this staged *hieros gamos* a periodic renewal of the fertility of the land through the union of Zeus with a local version of Hera. In the Theban Daphnephoria, this *hieros gamos* has perhaps been transferred to Apollo in a union with the local nymph Melia in the Ismenion.[31] A marriage procession with the κωπώ as bride might also explain the presence of the maiden chorus, which is in fact anomalous from the point of view of an Apolline Daphnephoria.[32]

At the same time, the *aition* of the ritual and the other participants in the procession incorporate elements symbolic of war and male initiation. In this respect, the name of the legendary founder of the festival, Polematas, is significant, as is perhaps the participation of an adult male leading the maiden chorus.[33] Particularly striking is

appropriate for marriageable women and wives'. That is to say, the *krokotos* signifies a woman as opposed to a girl not yet ready for marriage. Upon reaching maturity, the woman dons the *krokotos* as her festival-wear—probably first and most memorably for her own marriage.

[30] Plu. fr. 157. For detailed discussion of the ritual and its close similarities to the 'kopophoria', see Schachter (1981: 245–50); Schachter (1981: 245) acknowledges that the *aition* itself explains the log procession as a form of sacred marriage.

[31] It must be acknowledged that the union of Apollo and Melia is itself a speculative reconstruction: Farnell long ago suggested the periodic celebration of a *hieros gamos* of Apollo and Melia based on Pi. *Pae.* 9.33–4 and *P.* 11.1–12 (1930: 318; 1932: 225, 414). Still, the coincidence of the names of Melia and the River Melas in the cults of Apollo Ismenios and Apollo Tegyraios, respectively, is intriguing, as is Plutarch's reference to the name 'Olive' (᾽Ελαίαν) for one of the two springs in the latter cult complex. Is there some connection between the name of this spring and the fact that the *kôpô* is said by Proclus to be made of 'olive wood' (ξύλον ἐλαίας)?

[32] Calame (1997: 58–9, 101–13) contends that a maiden chorus with a male leader is a standard by-form (modelled on the divine chorus of Muses led by Apollo Mousagetas), but contrast the Theban maiden chorus with the participants in the Delphic S(t)epteria, which consisted of a '*theoria* of young nobles' (Calame 1997: 101; cf. Brelich 1969: 387–438; Burkert 1983: 128–9). For maiden song as the proper accompaniment of a wedding, see e.g. Pi. *P.* 3.17–19.

[33] On the warlike significance of the name Polematas, see Severyns (1938: 2.217). According to the typological analysis of Calame (1997: 58–9), the male leader of a maiden chorus should be a youth of approximately the same age as the girl choreuts (since he plays the role of the youthful Apollo Mousagetas). In these terms, the adult

the *daphnêphoros*, whose attributes of long hair, flowing robe, and golden crown visually identify him with Apollo, while they also suggest a youth at the moment of transition to manhood.[34] The special footwear of the *daphnêphoros*, carefully detailed by Proclus, may also be significant. For the terms *epikratides* or *iphikratides* preserved by the two different manuscript traditions of Photius are associated in various late sources with the fourth-century Athenian general Iphicrates—so these may be, perhaps, some kind of military boot.[35]

In this artful intercalation of marriage and military symbolism in the rite, the *pais amphithalês* who leads the procession may do double duty. He is clearly associated with Apollo and rituals of male initiation, as is shown by his leadership of the enneateric Delphic

male *kôpô*-bearer in the Theban Daphnephoria is something of an anomaly. That is to say, Calame occludes the difference between the *daphnêphoros* and the *kôpô*-bearer as leaders of the maiden chorus.

[34] For the *daphnêphoros'* assimilation to Apollo, see Nilsson (1906: 164), Severyns (1938: 2.219), Burkert (1985: 97), Kowalzig (2002: 265–6). Angelos Chaniotis points out to me that the 'shining white garment' worn by the *daphnêphoros* in Proclus' account is particularly implausible from the perspective of classical ritual, in which ephebes are usually specifically forbidden to wear white. For Chaniotis, these kinds of incoherences in Proclus' account vitiate the whole and make it unusable as a source for reconstructing the ritual in any period. For the reasons stated above, I disagree. Indeed, Chaniotis goes further and contends that the various destructions of Thebes make any kind of ritual preservation and continuity impossible; but, as Lucia Prauscello points out to me, if we posit utter loss and disruption of ritual, that makes it *a fortiori* more likely that Proclus (whether an earlier *grammatikos* or the fifth-century CE Neoplatonic philosopher) is drawing on earlier *written* accounts for his narrative of the ritual.

[35] *Iphikratides* (reading of M): D.S. 15.44 and Ath. 11.471b (citing Clearchus) credit the fourth-century BCE Athenian general Iphicrates with the invention of light military boots called *iphikratides* (footwear also identified with Iphicrates by Pollux 7.89 and mentioned by Alciphr. 3.57, Dam. *Isid.* 89). *Epikratides* (reading of A): cf. Photius' *Lexicon* (ed. Porson 1822): Ἰφικρατίδες· αἱ Ἐπικρατίδες· ἔστι δὲ εἶδος ὑποδήματος. It is difficult to choose between these two readings. Even if we assume that the entry in Photius' *Lexicon* is derived from the text of Proclus, the structure of the *Lexicon*'s gloss implies that *epikratides* is the more familiar term, which is used to calque the less familiar term *iphikratides*. This in turn would suggest that *iphikratides* is the original reading, replaced in manuscripts of the A family by the more familiar term *epikratides*. Severyns (1938: 1.222–3) prefers to read *epikratides*, which he takes to be the precious preservation of a Boeotian dialect term; but he is forced to acknowledge the clear implication of the structure of the *Lexicon* entry and therefore proposes emending it to ἰφικρατίδες καὶ ἐπικρατίδες· ἔστιν εἶδος ὑποδημάτων.

S(t)epteria.[36] He is furthermore, as Louis Robert observed, very commonly involved in rites that require the cutting and bearing of sacred shoots or branches (Robert 1969). But the *pais amphithalês* is also (at least from what we know of Attic ritual) a key element in the marriage ceremony, in which he carries around among the participants a winnowing fan (λίκνον) filled with bread, intoning 'I have escaped the bad and found the better'.[37] Thus in the Theban Daphnephoria, the *pais amphithalês* himself may fuse in a single figure the Apolline military and matrimonial aspects of the rite.

This hybrid combination of elements also serves the multiple levels of community building I have posited for the rite. In these terms, the warlike Apolline elements (which alone figure in the Proclan aetiology) link Thebes to the rest of Boeotia—especially the Lake Copaïs region. At the same time, the elements associated with the *hieros gamos* may appropriate cult forms from southern Boeotia, while intimately connecting the city of Thebes with Apollo as civic god. And all these elements together enable the procession to represent symbolically all aspects of the Theban population: male and female, mature adult, and the young of both sexes making their passage to adulthood. And if, as appears to be the case in Pindar's poem, the *pais amphithalês*, the adult male *kôpô*-bearer, and the leader of the girls' chorus all derive from a single noble family, this family is given the opportunity on this occasion uniquely to represent all Thebes in its moment of radiant communion with the god.

III. READING FR. 94B: GENERIC MIXTURE AND RITUAL OCCASION

Thus I have identified three main features I regard as significant in Pausanias' and Proclus' accounts of the Daphnephoria ritual: 1. elite

---

[36] On this ritual and the participation of the *pais amphithalês* therein, see Nilsson (1906: 150–7), Severyns (1938: 2.212–13), Brelich (1969: 387–438), Burkert (1983: 127–30), Calame (1997: 101, 111).

[37] As reported by Zenobius (Leutsch–Schneidewin [1965: i, 82] = Zen. 3.98). For this function of the *pais amphithalês*, see Oepke (1934: 46), Severyns (1938: 2.222); for the significance of his actions and accoutrements in context, see Redfield (1982: 193).

competition within the Theban oligarchy and issues of *phthonos* (as reflected in Pausanias' comments on the tripod dedications); 2. the integration of Thebes with the broader territory of Boeotia; 3. the rite as a hybrid of symbolic elements associated with war and with marriage. At this point, I want to correlate these three aspects with distinctive features in what we have of Pindar's poem—features that have not always been noticed or accounted for. I want to suggest thereby that the fragmentary remains of Pindar's *partheneion* enact many of the same negotiations or reconciliations we have already detected in the rite, so that poem and rite can serve mutually to illuminate each other.[38]

I would further suggest that it is this process of negotiation that accounts for the fusion of *partheneion* and epinician elements, as the song in performance knits together praise of the family of Aeoladas and Pagondas with the civic role of the maiden chorus in the Daphnephoria.[39] This wedding of genres produces the effect of a fusion of interests between the entire civic community (for whom the chorus speaks) and the members of a single noble family (who lead the procession). At the same time, part of the apparently epinician praise of the family recapitulates their cultivation of connections and alliances within the broader Boeotian community. In order to track the complex interweaving of these multiple levels of negotiation, I will offer a sequential reading of the poem, attending particularly to these themes.

It is first worth noting how carefully the synthesis of civic ritual and familial praise is accomplished in what we have of the poem's

---

[38] It could be objected that the parallels detected here between rite and poem are simply the result of typological similarities of basic myth/ritual structures. It is to counter this kind of typological argument that I have emphasized (i) the need to focus on a structural system of distinctive features, and (ii) what is specifically *anomalous* about both rite and poem in typological terms (i.e. the hybridization of elements coded for male and female initiation, for war and marriage, within a single ritual structure). I would contend further that much of the discussion of Pindar's fragmentary *partheneion* in this section (both in relation to the socio-political negotiations posited and in relation to other Pindaric compositions) remains valid, even if the specific connections to the later accounts of the Daphnephoria ritual be rejected.

[39] Cf. Stehle (1997: 94–100) for a similar account of generic mixture in the poem (although her focus is exclusively on the complex gender politics of this combination).

opening triad. After what is probably an opening invocation, the chorus breathlessly sets the stage:[40]

ἥκε]ι γὰρ ὁ [Λοξ]ίας
π]ρ[ό]φρω[ν] ἀθανάταν χάριν
Θήβαις ἐπιμ⟨ε⟩ίξων.
ἀλλὰ ζωσαμένα τε πέπλον ὠκέως
χερσίν τ᾽ ἐν μαλακαῖσιν ὄρπακ᾽ ἀγλαόν
δάφνας ὀχέοισα πάν-
δοξον Αἰολάδα σταθμόν
υἱοῦ τε Παγώνδα
ὑμνήσω στεφάνοισι θάλ-
λοισα παρθένιον κάρα,
σειρῆνα δὲ κόμπον
αὐλίσκων ὑπὸ λωτίνων
μιμήσομ᾽ ἀοιδαῖς
κεῖνον. ὃς Ζεφύρου τε σιγάζει πνοὰς
αἰψηράς   (fr. 94b. 3–17)

For Loxias has come, kindly to mix immortal grace with Thebes. But swiftly having girt my peplos and bearing in my soft hands a shining branch of laurel, I shall hymn the all-glorious house of Aeoladas and his son Pagondas, blooming with crowns on my virgin head. And I shall imitate with songs, to the accompaniment of lotus pipes, that Siren boast which silences the swift blasts of Zephyr…

In response to the advent of Apollo, the chorus conjures up an image of its own hasty preparations, but at the moment the girls mention their festal task of 'bearing a shining branch of laurel', they splice to the 'all-glorious house of Aeoladas and his son Pagondas' as the topic of their celebratory song. Then, by a delicate interweaving, the chorus reverts to its festal self-description ('blooming as to my virgin head with crowns') immediately after mention of hymning the house of Aeoladas and Pagondas.[41]

---

[40] I follow the text of Maehler (2001), except where otherwise noted. I have, however, simplified the text; I have not reproduced sublinear dots indicating uncertainty about the papyrus reading of individual letters.

[41] Thus I diverge slightly from Eva Stehle, in her perceptive analysis of the complex self-construction of this maiden chorus, describing the chorus' 'erotic self-presentation (the fertility theme)' as '*interrupted* when they announce that they will sing of the family of Aiolidas' (Stehle 1997: 95; my italics). But this is not so much an interruption as an interweaving.

They proceed with the striking image of the 'siren boast'.[42] As scholars have noted, Pindar combines here aspects of Homer's Sirens (seductive virgins who promise Odysseus a heroized narrative of the Trojan War) and the Hesiodic Sirens who have the power to calm the wind.[43] After a few more lines whose meaning is obscured by corruption, the mention of the 'siren boast that silences' the winds is followed by a gap in the poem of either eight or twenty-three lines.[44] Eva Stehle speculates that this gap would have been filled with praises of the house of Aeoladas (Stehle 1997: 96). This may be, but I think it more likely that the image of the enchanting daemonic singers introduced a mythic narrative, since when the text resumes, we have what looks like a break-off from myth (cf. Lehnus 1984: 80 with n. 69):

> πολ]λὰ μὲν [τ]ὰ πάροιθ' [ἀείδοιμ' ἂν καλοῖς
> δαιδάλλοισ' ἔπεσιν, τὰ δ' ἀ[τρεκῆ μόνος
> Ζεὺς οἶδ', ἐμὲ δὲ πρέπει
> παρθενήϊα μὲν φρονεῖν
> γλώσσᾳ τε λέγεσθαι·   (fr. 94b. 31–5)

Many former things I would sing, ornamenting them with beautiful words, but Zeus alone knows these accurately. For me it is fitting to think maiden things and to speak them with my tongue.

I complete these lines *exempli gratia* with Snell's suggested supplements; Franco Ferrari has proposed an alternative version of line 31 that would construe δαιδάλλοισ' as a third-person plural indicative verb and thus sharpen the contrast between πολλὰ μέν and ἐμὲ δέ (Ferrari 1991: 393):[45]

---

[42] Scholars have identified this as a direct allusion to Alcman's *partheneia*, since in a couple of passages, Alcman seems to cast the Sirens in the role traditionally given to the Muses in other genres of song: see Lehnus (1984: 80), Stehle (1997: 95–6), citing Alcman frr. 1.96, 30 *PMG*.

[43] Thus Lehnus (1984: 80–2), Stehle (1997: 96–7), citing *Od.* 12.184–91, Hesiod frr. 27–8: Merkelbach–West.

[44] For these alternatives on the length of the lacuna, I follow Maehler (2001: ad loc.). But cf. D'Alessio (1991: 107–8): based on the layout of the papyrus, the gap between frr. 94a and 94b, and probable length of the epode of fr. 94a, D'Alessio contends that a lacuna of twenty-three lines is much more likely than one of eight lines.

[45] Ferrari (1991: 393). I cannot, however, agree with Ferrari's insistence that what 'poets adorn' must be stigmatized in the poem as 'false'—there is no language of falsehood (even in the text Ferrari himself proposes), nor is this a necessary

πολ]λὰ μὲν [τ]ὰ πάροιθ᾿ [ἀοιδοὶ ποικίλοις
δαιδάλλοισ᾿ ἔπεσιν, τὰ δ᾿ ἀ[τρεκῆ μόνος
Ζεὺς οἶδ᾿, ἐμὲ δὲ πρέπει κτλ.

Many former things singers ornament with variegated words, but Zeus alone
knows these things accurately. For me it is fitting…

But on either reading, the maiden chorus turns back from 'former
things' to their own proper sphere. I would suggest that the mythic
narrative here might even be something like the historical *aition* of
the Daphnephoria preserved in Proclus' account—a tale of war,
divine favour, and the beginnings of Boeotian control of the territory.[46] After all, the knowledge with which the Homeric Sirens
tantalize Odysseus is the Trojan War—'all that Argives and Trojans
toiled in broad Troy by the will of the gods' (*Od.* 12.189–90). On this
reconstruction, having offered a brief résumé of the military origins
of the festival, the maiden chorus would appropriately retreat to a
more suitable topic.

However that may be, the following lines again bear a striking
resemblance to a conventional epinician transition from myth to
praise of the victor and his house:

ἀνδρὸς δ᾿ οὔτε γυναικός, ὧν θάλεσσιν ἔγκειμαι, χρή μ[ε] λαθεῖν ἀοιδὰν πρόσφορον.
πιστὰ δ᾿ Ἀγασικλέει
μάρτυς ἤλυθον ἐς χορόν
ἐσλοῖς τε γονεῦσιν
ἀμφὶ προξενίαισι·   (fr. 94b. 36–41)

concomitant of δαιδάλλοισ᾿. A contrastive break-off from the myth does not
require the opposition of falsehood and truth, as is clear from Pindar's many mythic
break-offs.

[46] I am thus using 'myth' in the sense in which it is used in epinician scholarship,
to denote the past narrative portion of the poem. For examples of 'historical'
narrative filling the structural slot of myth in epinician, see Pi. *I.* 7 and B. 3. For a
parallel for a festival poem narrating a decisive historical battle, see Pi. *Pae.* 2.59–70;
for a maiden chorus singing of war, see Alcm. fr. 1.1–35 *PMG*. D'Alessio's argument
that the lacuna is more likely to be twenty-three lines than eight (cited in n. 44 above)
would allow plenty of space for the narrative of the ritual's historical *aition*. And, of
course, if this *was* the poem's 'myth', this might be the ultimate source of Proclus'
account (mediated, perhaps, through a long commentary tradition on the poem);
intriguingly, Färber (1936: 40) had already proposed that the aetiological tale of
Polematas must have figured in some daphnephoric composition, whence Proclus
derived it.

I must not forget suitable song of man nor of woman, to whose shoots I am devoted. But I have come to the chorus as a trusty witness for Agasicles and for his noble parents, concerning their acts of proxeny.

This sounds very like a choral version of the familiar epinician 'arrival motif', in which the poet breaks off from the myth with the indication that he has come to render some service to the house of the victor.[47] In like manner, in the second *partheneion*, the chorus asserts that they have come to bear witness for Agasicles and his noble parents. These lines would thus articulate both a shift in temporal focus (τὰ πάροιθ' vs the present festival occasion) and a gendered shift in topic from heroic martial exploits to a properly maiden theme. At the same time, the role of witness represents a finessing of the status of the maiden chorus: as *parthenoi*, their topic is appropriately the 'blooming' children and parents within a house; but the chorus also serves a representative function, speaking for the entire Theban community, and this authorizes their role as μάρτυς in spite of their gender.[48]

It is further worth noting where the emphasis of this solemn juridical speech act falls (for at this point, the poem pivots to the level of Theban–Boeotian negotiation). What is singled out for praise initially is the family's *proxeniai*—their acts as official protectors and helpers of citizens of other cities in Thebes and abroad.[49] This theme then continues to play a prominent part in the lines that follow:

> τίμαθεν γὰρ τὰ πάλαι τὰ νῦν
> τ' ἀμφικτιόνεσσιν
> ἵππων τ' ὠκυπόδων πο[λυ-
> γνώτοις ἐπὶ νίκαις,

[47] Cf. *O.* 9.80–4, *O.* 13.96–7, *N.* 6.53–7b, *N.* 7.52–63, *N.* 8.13–16, *I.* 5.21–2, *I.* 6.57–8, and (for a slightly different version of the 'arrival motif' adapted to the genre of paean) *Pae.* 6.5–11.

[48] I am indebted to an unpublished paper by Boris Maslov, 'Pindar's Choral Subjects: Legal Language and Poetic Authority in Epinician', for calling my attention to the significance of the imagery of witnessing in this passage. In addition, Maslov notes the anomaly of girls bearing witness, given what we know of most Greek legal systems. See also Richard Martin's discussion (ch. 2 of this volume) of the theme of 'witnessing' in this passage.

[49] On the official status of *proxenos* and the duties it entailed, see Marek (1984; for Boeotia specifically 125–6). See also Mackil (2003: 178–80).

αἷς ἐν ἀϊόνεσσιν Ὀγχη[στοῦ κλυ]τᾶς,
ταῖς δὲ ναὸν Ἰτωνίας α[......]α
χαίταν στεφάνοις ἐκό-
σμηθεν ἔν τε Πίσᾳ περιπ[(fr. 94b. 41–9)

For they were honoured of old and also now by the dwellers-around, and for their famous victories with swift-footed horses, those on the banks of glorious Onchestos, and others [at the?] temple of Itonia... they had their hair adorned with crowns both at Pisa...

These verses make explicit the domain of the family's longstanding *proxeniai* among the Boeotian 'dwellers-around'; that is the point of γάρ in line 42. But even when the topic seems to shift to the Aeoladadae's athletic victories, the theme of Boeotian community is still prominent. For the victory catalogue of these lines is markedly anomalous from an epinician perspective: in an epinician, athletic victories are almost invariably catalogued in order of the prestige of the games, so that it would be unimaginable to mention victories at the local contests of Onchestos and Itone *before* mention of an Olympic crown. In general, this speaks to the more epichoric cast of maiden song in contrast to the Panhellenic purview of epinician, but there is more to it than that. For Onchestos and Itone later became the two most prominent religious centres for the Boeotian *koinon*.

We know from Pindar that there were athletic contests of Poseidon at Onchestos already in the fifth century (cf. *I.* 1.33, 52–4), while Strabo tells us that 'Onchestos is where the Amphictyonic Council used to convene' (Ὀγχηστὸς δ' ἐστὶν ὅπου τὸ Ἀμφικτυονικὸν συνήγετο, Strabo 9.2.33/412).[50] This suggests that, even in the first half of the fifth century, the religious shrine and games at Onchestos would have provided an unofficial but still important context for Boeotian community-building. The same applies to the shrine of Athena Itonia at Coronea. This was a prominent cult centre already in the archaic period, as we know from vase painting and a fragment of Alcaeus, and of course Pindar confirms the existence of athletic contests there in the first half of the fifth century.[51] Inscriptional

---

[50] On the meaning of τὸ Ἀμφικτυονικόν here, see Buck (1979: 102 n. 22); otherwise: Schachter (1986: 220–1).

[51] Cf. Alcaeus fr. 325 Lobel–Page. For the vase evidence, see Ure (1929), Schachter (1981: 117–19).

evidence from the Hellenistic period makes clear that at this point the shrine of Athena at Coronea was a Boeotian federal sanctuary, while Polybius mentions that the *panêgyris* held there was called the Pamboeotia.[52] There is one final fact about the shrine of Athena Itonia at Coronea that may be significant: Plutarch tells us that this was where the Boeotians set up a trophy to commemorate their victory over the Athenians in the battle of Coronea in 447 BCE (Plu. *Ages.* 19.2). This was thus the site where the Boeotians cele-brated their liberation from Athenian domination and (perhaps) the first constitution of an independent Boeotian *koinon*.[53] Thus, like the games held at the shrine of Poseidon at Onchestos, athletic contests at the shrine of Athena Itonia were probably already in the fifth century an important occasion for inter-Boeotian networking by the elite of various cities. And if we follow Emily Mackil's argument, this kind of inter-elite networking at regional shrines provided the substructure that enabled the eventual crystallization of the Boeotian *koinon*.[54]

At this point, in the midst of the victory catalogue, the text breaks off, again for eight or twenty-three lines. When it resumes, we have mention of 'seven-gated Th[ebes]' and then what is perhaps the most obscure passage in this fragmentary poem:

[52] *IG* 9².1.170, *SEG* 18.240, Plb. 4.3.5, 9.34.11. Historians debate the antiquity of the founding of the cult and games within Boeotia; see Ziehen (1949: coll. 288–9), Ducat (1973: 60–1), Buck (1979: 88–9), Schachter (1981: 117–27), Mackil (2003: 175–83).

[53] Cf. Mackil (2003: 181–2).

[54] To return to Pindar's strikingly Boeotian-centred victory catalogue, scholars have connected the Olympic victory mentioned in the *partheneion* with Pausanias' report that a Theban Pagondas won the Olympic chariot race in the twenty-fifth Olympiad—that is, in 680 BCE (Paus. 5.8.7; thus Wilamowitz 1922: 436, Sbordone 1940: 30–1, Buck 1994: 133 n. 40). If this was a victory by a member of the same family, the fact that this Olympic win had occurred more than two centuries before the era of the current Pagondas might well account for its deferred mention in the victory catalogue. It would not do, after all, to upstage the family's recent victories, limited to local contests, with a too-prominent mention of an ancient Olympic crown. But, in a sense, this rationalization simply pushes the need for explanation one step further back: why should a family of the prominence of Pagondas' not have more recent victories from any of the Panhellenic contests? This may well represent a considered strategy of Boeotian community-building and patriotism on the part of the family by focusing their athletic efforts exclusively on local contests—a strategy that is then carefully recapitulated in the structure of Pindar's victory catalogue.

ἐνῆκεν καὶ ἔπειτ[α δυσμενὴς χό]λος
τῶνδ' ἀνδρῶν ἕνε[κε]ν μερίμνας σώφρονος
ἐχθρὰν ἔριν οὐ παλίγ-
γλωσσον, ἀλλὰ δίκας [ὁ]δούς
πιστὰς ἐφίλη[σα]ν.
Δαμαίνας πά[τε]ρ, ἡσ[ύχ]ῳ νῦν μοι ποδὶ
στείχων ἀγέο· [τ]ὶν γὰρ ε[ὔ]φρων ἕψεται
πρώτα θυγάτηρ [ὁ]δοῦ
δάφνας εὐπετάλου σχεδ[ό]ν
βαίνοισα πεδίλοις,
Ἀνδαισιστρότα ἂν ἐπά-
σκησε μήδεσ[ι.] . [.]τ[.]. .[]   (fr. 94b. 61–72)

Then also [hostile anger] provoked hateful relentless quarrel on account of the moderate aspiration of these men, but [they] loved the trusty ways of justice. O father of Damaena, now lead me going with calm foot; for [your] daughter will be the first to follow you upon the way, rejoicing, going with her sandals near to the lovely-leafed laurel, [your daughter] whom Andaesistrota carefully prepared with... thoughts...

Different supplements have been proposed for line 61; I have provided that of Grenfell-Hunt, *exempli gratia*. But even in their fragmentary state, it is clear that these lines address the topic of hostility within the city; they are thus akin to the motif of citizen *phthonos* in the epinicia.[55] Given that recognizable theme, τῶνδ' ἀνδρῶν ('these men' in line 62) should be members of the house of Pagondas, and these and the following lines should serve to defuse—even as they acknowledge—tensions and resentments between the individual noble house spotlighted in the festival and other elite houses (those most likely to feel envy), as well as in the civic community at large. We find confirmation for this interpretation in the verbal and thematic parallels between this passage and Darius' negative characterization of oligarchy in Herodotus. Recall that in Herodotus, 'for those cultivating virtue or achievement in the public sphere, strong private animosities tend to develop' (ἐν δὲ ὀλιγαρχίῃ πολλοῖσι ἀρετὴν ἐπασκέουσι ἐς τὸ κοινὸν ἔχθεα ἴδια ἰσχυρὰ φιλέει

---

55 Thus Grenfell and Hunt (1904: 59). For the theme of citizen *phthonos* in epinician, see Kurke (1991: 195–218). It is intriguing that fr. 94a SM, a poem also devoted to the house of Aeoladas (whatever its genre), is much concerned with the theme of *phthonos*; see esp. lines 8–10.

ἐγγίνεσθαι). Herodotus' ἔχθεα ἴδια ἰσχύρα parallel Pindar's ἐχθρὰν ἔριν οὐ παλίγγλωσσον ('relentless hateful quarrel'), while Herodotus' ἀρετή cultivated in the public sphere thus corresponds to the *partheneion's* μέριμνα. This parallel is illuminating for the meaning of the latter term; as often in the epinicia, μέριμνα designates 'athletic ambition', but in this context it can be understood more broadly to comprehend any kind of public 'care' or aspiration on the part of the family of Pagondas—athletic, religious, and civic.[56] Thus, depending on what filled the preceding lacuna, these lines may refer to the family's competition at athletic contests, their *proxeniai* within the broader Boeotian community, and even their generous support for public festivals like the one in which they are currently involved (which we must assume represented a major liturgy for a noble household).

Any or all of these might be sources of resentment on the part of fellow citizens, but how do these lines work to allay or defuse that resentment? The key is the epithet assigned to μερίμνας, σώφρονος—which asserts that, by its public 'care', the family does not aspire to excessive political power and influence within the city. This message of the family's moderation is developed in the succeeding clause: 'he'—or perhaps better, 'they'—'loved the trusty ways of justice'.[57] This line implies a host of civic virtues: in spite of hostility coming from outside, the family of Pagondas has consistently exhibited civic *philia* and respect for justice as opposed to *hubris* (political overreaching).

The next lines continue this theme even as they turn to the present of the festival. Thus notice that καὶ ἔπειτα in line 61 is answered by νῦν in line 66: just as in the past, Pagondas' ancestors displayed moderate care and love for the city, so also now Pagondas evinces these same civic virtues. Indeed, his civic ἀρετή is made visible, bodied forth by his manner of participating in the current festival: this is conveyed by the road imagery of his ancestors' 'trusty ways of justice' picked up by the maiden chorus's immediately following

---

[56] For μέριμνα as 'athletic ambition', cf. *O.* 1.109–11, *O.* 2.54, *P.* 8.92, *N.* 3.69, fr. 227.1 SM; thus also Grenfell and Hunt (1904: 59–60).

[57] I would thus prefer to read Puech's ἐφίλη[σα]ν, rather than Grenfell and Hunt's ἐφίλη[σε]ν, understanding the plural to refer back to τῶνδ' ἀνδρῶν.

imperative to Pagondas himself to 'lead me now, going with calm foot'. ἡσ[ύχ]ῳ ... ποδί here is more than a simple stage direction, for ἡσυχία is a buzzword for the same civic restraint and contentment with one's status already articulated in the adjective σώφρων and the noun δική.[58] Pagondas thus follows the same road as his ancestors, while his calm bearing and dignified pace make the festival procession itself the physical enactment of his civic moderation.

We find a striking epinician parallel for many of the themes touched on in the *partheneion* clustered together in the opening lines of *Isthmian* 4, significantly also composed for a Theban athletic victor (tentatively dated 474/3):

> Ἔστι μοι θεῶν ἕκατι μυρία παντᾷ κέλευθος,
> ὦ Μέλισσ', εὐμαχανίαν γὰρ ἔφανας Ἰσθμίοις,
> ὑμετέρας ἀρετὰς ὕμνῳ διώκειν·
> αἷσι Κλεωνυμίδαι θάλλοντες αἰεί
> σὺν θεῷ θνατὸν διέρχον-
>   ται βιότου τέλος. ἄλλοτε δ' ἀλλοῖος οὖρος
> πάντας ἀνθρώπους ἐπαΐσσων ἐλαύνει.
> τοὶ μὲν ὦν Θήβαισι τιμάεντες ἀρχᾶθεν λέγονται
> πρόξενοί τ' ἀμφικτιόνων κελαδεννᾶς τ' ὀρφανοί
> ὕβριος·   (I. 4.1–9)

Thanks to the gods I have ten thousand roads of song in every direction, o Melissus, to pursue your achievements with hymn, for you showed forth abundance of poetic material at the Isthmian Games. [Achievements] with which the Cleonymidae, blooming always with the god's favour, go through to the mortal end of life. And different sorts of winds, gusting at different times, drive all men. They [the Cleonymidae] indeed in Thebes are said from the beginning to be both honourable *proxenoi* of the dwellers-around and free from sounding *hubris*.

Road imagery here informs the entire sequence, while ὑμετέρας ἀρετὰς morphs in meaning over the course of these lines from reference to Melissus' Isthmian victory to the family's long-standing civic virtues: they are 'said from the beginning to be honourable

---

[58] The reading ἡσ[ύχ]ῳ was originally proposed by Lehnus (1977: 230 n. 7; 1984: 91 n. 101) and has been forcefully defended by Ferrari (1991: 394–5). For ἡσ[ύχ]ῳ ... ποδί as a stage direction, see Ferrari (1991: 395): 'un' interessante didascalia interna'. For the political significance of ἡσυχία in Pindar, see Young (1968: 21), Slater (1981), Kurke (1991: 217–18).

proxenoi of the dwellers-around and free from sounding *hubris*'. The latter expression provides the negative complement to the 'trusty ways of justice' dear to the ancestors of Pagondas in the *partheneion*: *hubris* is opposed to *dikê*, while the clamour of κελαδεννᾶς contrasts with Pagondas' own calm and moderate gait. Thus the two themes and levels of negotiation that are disposed around the victory catalogue in fr. 94b—the family's Boeotian community-building and their civic moderation within Thebes—are here closely conjoined, prominently articulated at the very beginning of the poem.[59]

Even more telling, perhaps, are the parallels with Pindar's eleventh *Pythian* ode, since this poem makes clear that the celebration of the Theban Thrasydaeus' athletic victory was conjoined with some kind of civic festival at the Ismenion. Thus the opening triad of *Pythian* 11 summons the heroines of Thebes—Semele, Ino, and Alcmene—to Melia in the Ismenion, where, we are told, '[Apollo] calls the native throng of heroines gathered together, to celebrate in song holy Themis and Pytho and the navel of the earth, straight in justice, together with the edge of evening, as a grace (χάριν) for seven-gated Thebes and for the contest of Cirrha...' (*P.* 11.7–12). Indeed, in this case Paola Angeli Bernardini has suggested that the epinician was performed on the occasion of the Daphnephoria, with the victor Thrasydaeus himself playing the role of *daphnêphoros*.[60] On her reconstruction, the choir of Theban cult heroines summoned in the poem's first triad represents the 'mythic projection' of the actual maiden chorus which would have performed a song weaving together honour for Apollo with celebration of Thrasydaeus' Pythian

---

[59] We might also note that both passages make a point of 'bearing witness' to the family's combination of virtues; but, where in the *partheneion*, the maiden chorus explicitly takes the role of witness (μάρτυς), in *I.* 4 the witnessing function (μαρτύρια, line 10) hovers impersonally, not attached to any human agency though still given breath by the singing chorus.

[60] Bernardini (1989), following Boeckh and Dissen (1821: 338), Pavese (1975: 246). Thus, like many other scholars, Bernardini collapses the roles of *pais amphithalês* and *daphnêphoros* in order to reconcile Proclus' account of the rite with Pausanias and the details of Pindar's poems. Bernardini also assumes a date of 474 for *P.* 11, which therefore makes Thrasydaeus a boy victor. Of the two possible dates offered by the scholiasts, I prefer 454 (for reasons stated in Kurke 1998): in that case, Thrasydaeus would be an adult victor and would have to play a different role in the Daphnephoria (if this is indeed the ritual to which the epinician performance is sutured; he could, e.g., be *kôpô*-bearer).

victory.[61] The eleventh *Pythian* and fr. 94b would thus represent similar cultic fusions along a generic spectrum: one poem in which epinician elements predominate and the choral speaker is gendered male; the other more predominantly daphnephoric, whose speaking *ego* is gendered female.

If we assume some such Theban performance context, it is striking how prominently the theme of citizen *phthonos* figures in *Pythian* 11. Indeed, it takes over much of the last triad, in which the poet affirms the value of civic virtues in a 'generalized first person' statement:

> θεόθεν ἐραίμαν καλῶν,
> δυνατὰ μαιόμενος ἐν ἁλικίᾳ.
>   τῶν γὰρ ἀνὰ πόλιν εὑρίσκων τὰ μέσα μακροτέρῳ
> {σὺν} ὄλβῳ τεθαλότα, μέμφομ᾽ αἶσαν τυραννίδων·
> ξυναῖσι δ᾽ ἀμφ᾽ ἀρεταῖς τέταμαι· φθονεροὶ δ᾽ ἀμύνονται,
>   ⟨ἀλλ᾽⟩ εἴ τις ἄκρον ἑλὼν
>   ἡσυχᾷ τε νεμόμενος αἰνὰν ὕβριν
> ἀπέφυγεν, μέλανος {δ᾽} ἂν ἐσχατιὰν
> καλλίονα θανάτου ⟨στείχοι⟩ γλυκυτάτᾳ γενεᾷ
> εὐώνυμον κτεάνων κρατίσταν χάριν πορών·   (P. 11.50–8)

I would desire good things from the god, striving after things that are possible according to my age. For of things in the city I find the middle flourishing with longer good fortune and I blame the lot of tyrannies. But I am strained over common virtues. And the envious are fended off, if someone, having taken the peak [of achievement] and conducting himself peaceably, has avoided dread *hubris*, and he would go to a better end of black death, granting to his sweetest offspring the grace of a good name as the best of possessions.

As has been recognized, this validation of middling status within the city and rejection of tyranny, while voiced by the poet's first person, actually affirms the political moderation of the victor and his house. Their achievement of prominent athletic victories at Olympia and Delphi do not aim at excessive political power and influence within Thebes.[62] But for the moment, I would like to focus especially on lines 54–6, because they offer close parallels of thought and diction with fr. 94b. 61–7. Thus the 'common achievements' espoused by the speaker (ξυναῖσι . . . ἀρεταῖς) recall both the 'moderate care' (μερίμνας

---

61 Thus Bernardini (1989: 43) 'proiezione mitica'.
62 Thus Young (1968: 10–19), Kurke (1991: 214–18; 1998).

σώφρονος) and 'trusty ways of justice' (δίκας ὁδούς/π[ισ]τάς) of the Aeoladadae. At the same time, ἡσυχᾷ . . . νεμόμενος of *P.* 11.55 corresponds almost exactly to the *partheneion's* ἡσύχῳ . . . ποδί, while making explicit the symbolic resonance of that phrase in its mention of *hubris* avoided. In this environment, it is worth pausing a moment over the epinician formulation ἄκρον ἑλών ('having taken the height'). Given the characteristically generalizing cast of Pindar's language, this phrase is usually read as a reference to athletic victory.[63] That it certainly is, but at the same time we might connect it with the formula ἐπ' ἄκρου χοροῦ ἱστάμενος/ἵστασθαι found in late sources to designate the *chorêgos* or chorus leader.[64] If indeed the victor Thrasydaeus fulfilled some ritual function within the Daphnephoria (whether as *pais amphithalês*, *daphnêphoros*, or *kôpô*-bearer), this secondary resonance for ἄκρον ἑλών would be very apposite, implying the same identification of proper choral and civic leadership within an oligarchic regime we have already noted in the use of κορυφαῖος by Herodotus.[65]

Finally (and most tentatively), I would suggest that we may find support for the bridal/matrimonial element I have proposed for the rite in several details of Pindar's fragmentary poem. First, the *partheneion* almost certainly began with an invocation, of which only χρυσόπ[επλ- remains in the poem's opening line: scholars have imagined that the chorus here summons either a Muse or 'golden-robed' Thebe herself.[66] I would suggest that a third possibility would be Melia, the Oceanid nymph whose *hieros gamos* seems to figure in Pindar's ninth *Paean*.[67] The epithet χρυσόπεπλε would then visually identify her with the saffron-robed κωπώ, borne in procession to represent a bride. Some sort of opening address like 'Golden-robed Melia, we summon you' would also make sense of lines 3–4 with their

[63] Thus Young (1968: 21): 'ἄκρον ἑλών is definitely, although not exclusively, a description of athletic victory'. Cf. Bernardini (1989: 46).

[64] Thus Suda s.v. ψιλεύς (ψ 101 Adler): ἐπ' ἄκρου χοροῦ ἱστάμενος, ὅθεν καὶ φιλόψιλος παρὰ Ἀλκμᾶνι, ἡ φιλοῦσα ἐπ' ἄκρου χοροῦ ἵστασθαι. Cf. Photius, *Lexicon* s.v. ψιλεύς; I owe these references to Calame (1997: 62 n. 160). Admittedly, the formula ἐπ' ἄκρου χοροῦ is not attested for the chorus leader in earlier sources.

[65] Notice that the term κορυφαῖος, which can mean 'chorus leader', is semantically very close to ἄκρος, since it is derived from the noun κορυφή, 'head, top, highest point'.

[66] Thus Sbordone (1940: 27), Lehnus (1984: 78 with n. 31), Snell ad loc. in Snell and Maehler (1975).

[67] See Farnell (1930: 318; 1932: 225, 414) and n. 31 above.

connective γάρ: 'for Loxias has come, kindly to mix immortal grace
with Thebes'. For, as Eva Stehle notes, the imagery of these lines is
sexual: this is true not just of ἐπιμείξων, but also of χάρις.[68]

A procession with wedding elements might also explain the oddly
concrete σταθμόν of line 9. σταθμός in Pindar never designates
a 'house' in the abstract sense of lineage, but always a physical
'dwelling'.[69] The chorus' self-described activity of hymning the 'dwelling of Aeoladas and his son Pagondas' in the song's first antistrophe
perhaps suggests that this was the spot at which the procession
originated, advancing from there to the shrines of Apollo Ismenios
and Chalazios (or Galaxios; the first of these three just outside the
Electran Gates). This processional route perhaps evoked a wedding
pompê, which would normally go from the house of the bride to that
of the groom. Indeed, we might even go a step further and imagine
that Damaena, prominently featured as daughter of Pagondas the
kôpô-bearer, doubled the role of the bride in the procession, for this
might explain the reference to the care and thoughtful preparation
of (her mother?) Andaesistrota.[70] In that case, we might see the *kôpô*-
bearer Pagondas symbolically playing the role of father of the bride.[71]
If all this is correct, it suggests that every time the festival occurred, the

---

68 Stehle (1997: 95). For χάρις in a sexual context, cf. A. *Ag.* 1206.

69 Cf. *O.* 5.10, *O.* 10.72, *P.* 4.76, *I.* 7.45.

70 Calame (1997: 61–2, 229) insists that there is no evidence that Andaesistrota is
in any way related to Pagondas and Damaena, citing Alcm. fr. 1.73 *PMG* for a parallel
of a female figure who seems to have filled the 'function of the educator who prepares
the chorus' (quotation from p. 62). But in contrast to Alcm. fr. 1, where the reference
seems to be to a tutor or trainer of all the girls of the chorus, here Andaesistrota
apparently concerns herself *only* with Damaena. Notice also the way in which the
echo of χρυσόπεπλος in the girl singer's reference to her own peplos (line 6) may link
the maiden chorus to the 'golden-robed' [Melia?] of the poem's first line and to the
yellow-robed *kôpô* of the ritual.

71 Wedding symbolism in the rite and poem might also suggest a new interpretation for the *partheneion*'s fragmentary lines 76–8. The presumed reference to 'my
spring' (κρά]νας ἐμᾶς) in line 76 is usually assumed to be metapoetic (which is
something of a problem, given the choral *ego* of this poem; see Lehnus 1984: 79,
D'Alessio 1994: 119–20), while the dual form of the verb οἴχεσθον in line 78 is very
mysterious. We might instead imagine that these lines contained a literal reference to
some part of the *hieros gamos* ritual, since (as we know from the Pindar scholia ad
P. 11.6, Drachmann 2.255), Melia was also the name of a 'spring' (πηγή) at or near the
Ismenion. We might then imagine that the dual signifies the divine couple Apollo and
Melia (which might account for their imbibing 'nectar'), or perhaps the father–son
pair of *kôpô*-bearer and *pais amphithalês*.

procession would start from a different noble house in Thebes; this in turn may account for the fact that Proclus does not tell us where the procession originated, only that 'they used to convey the Daphne-phoria along (παρέπεμπον) to [the shrines] of Apollo Ismenios and Chalazios (or Galaxios)'.[72]

As such, this would represent the extraordinary ritual spotlighting of a single family (which might well inspire envy among other leading families not chosen for this prestigious *chorêgia*). At the same time, the poem's own language affirms that this is not merely a matter of initiatory ritual for Damaena and the other girls of the chorus: we need to take seriously the first preserved lines of the *partheneion*, which tell us that Apollo 'has come to mingle immortal grace with *Thebes*'. In these terms, the god's periodic *hieros gamos* with a local nymph functions symbolically to confer his divine favour on the entire city of Thebes, instantiated each time by one of its noble families.

Thus, in this respect, I would diverge from the interpretation of the ritual offered by Claude Calame, who focuses exclusively on the level of individual initiation. And, as a parallel for this, we might think of the annual wedding of Venice and the sea celebrated in the Middle Ages and the Renaissance, in which the Doge, elected for life by a narrow oligarchy of families, instantiated Venice and enacted the marriage (symbolic of Venice's imperial control over the sea) by casting his ring into the Adriatic. In like manner, I would suggest, the Theban Daphnephoria ritual, by a potent act of embodiment, used its individual human participants to conjure the unity and prosperity of Thebes and of Boeotia. Conversely, it thereby also endowed the members of a single leading house (and through them, the entire ruling oligarchy) with a charismatic aura of legitimacy: their leadership of the city, as of the procession, thus came to seem cosmically right and proper.[73]

---

[72] To pick up the theme of Richard Martin's paper in this volume, this suggests another way in which a chorus is a *horos*, for the processional route of the chorus defines the ritually significant space of the city.

[73] Contra Calame (1997: 103–4). For this χάρις bestowed on all Thebes, cf. *P.* 11.8–12 and esp. *Pae.* 9.37. And note that in *Paean* 9 as a whole, Apollo's union with Melia is spotlighted in order to persuade the 'beam of the sun' to turn 'the prodigy common to all' of an eclipse 'to some untroubled blessedness *for Thebes*': that is, Apollo's union with the nymph is assumed to confer special benefit on the whole city. For discussion of the wedding of Venice and the sea and its political symbolism, see Muir (1981: 119–34).

So much for Thebes. To return to the question I posed at the outset: how does Athenian tragedy look different when set against the background of these epichoric ritual and choral forms? Specifically, what was distinctive about the tragic chorus in its relation to ritual, in contrast to what we can reconstruct for Thebes? This is obviously an immense topic; let me make two preliminary suggestions by way of conclusion.

1. Athenian choral forms (dithyramb, tragedy, and comedy) strikingly plucked the *chorêgos* out of the chorus. The comparison with Thebes allows us to see just how anomalous this was. For by transforming the *chorêgos* into the producer or money-man, the Athenian system seemed to be trying to short-circuit the potent effects of physical embodiment for its elite citizens—to mediate the charisma they might otherwise have derived from direct ritual participation. We might read this as a democratizing move in Athenian choral culture, although, as Peter Wilson (2000) has persuasively argued, it had the effect of simply displacing the sites of elite competition, display, and self-theatricalization. As a symptom of democratization in Athenian choral culture, it conformed to the extreme popularity of the dithyramb in Athens, for, as Richard Martin observes, the characteristic circular dance of the dithyrambic chorus meant that it was endless and boundless—it had no head or leader.[74]

---

[74] It is perhaps not emphasized enough how odd it is that the Athenian festival calendar of the fifth century staged dithyrambs for every possible ritual occasion—including rituals for Apollo, who was normally honoured outside Athens with the (often processional) *paean*. For this anomaly in the Athenian system, see Rutherford (2001: 32–3), Kowalzig (2004: 60 with n. 35). One could, in fact, elaborate a whole taxonomy of different choral forms and levels of choregic participation therein corresponding to—and supporting in turn—different socio-political systems in the different cities. Thus, e.g., as mentioned at the outset, many scholars argue that the names of the chorus leaders in Alcman's *partheneia* fragments strongly suggest their affiliation with the two royal houses of Sparta; so here, choral leadership perfectly corresponds or maps on to royal political leadership (see Calame 1977: 2.140–2 with full references to older scholarship; Nagy 1990: 347–9). Thus there is no rotation of leadership among elite families, but also no mention of *phthonos* in Alcman's *partheneia*; in Thebes, choral leadership rotates among elite families and *phthonos* is a very prominent topic; in Athens, the (amateur) chorus seems to speak for middling citizens onstage, while *phthonos* is displaced on to the mythic protagonists within the drama. Or contrast the relation of ritual choral performance to tripod dedication in Thebes and Athens: in Thebes, an individual elite family commemorates its embodied leadership of the Daphnephoria procession by dedicating a tripod

2. If Thebes could absorb rituals from Plataea to signify and cement her claims to territorial hegemony, what does it mean that Attic tragedy could absorb rituals from all over the Greek world? Or, in more general terms: if we accept that epichoric rituals and their choral instantiations served an important function in constituting political communities all over Greece, Athenian drama's characteristic mode of 'playing the other' must have had significant political implications. Modern scholars tend to insist on the close interimplication of Athenian drama and Athenian democracy (as indeed, in the Introduction to this volume). But tragedy's apparently effortless appropriation of the rituals and choral forms native to other cities suggests an equally important connection between tragic drama and Athenian *imperialism*.[75] This is the choral corollary of political imperialism and, in so far as this absorption of everybody else's ritual and choral forms contributed to tragedy's universalizing appeal, Athenian political hegemony in the fifth century is what enabled the cultural hegemony of tragedy in the succeeding centuries.[76]

in the Ismenion, thereby identifying elite father and son with their mythic precursors Amphitryon and Heracles; in Athens, the *chorêgos* as producer dedicates his victory tripod on the public street leading to the theatre, but is allowed to do so only by the grace and sufferance of the Athenian *dêmos* (thus Ober 1989: 243–5).

[75] For further development of this argument, see Kurke (1998). For a different way of posing the same issue, we might start from the important discussions of Henrichs (1995; 1996) and ask, in what ways is tragic 'choral projection' distinctive and different from that found in archaic choral lyric, and what are the *political* implications of those differences? For suggestive answers to these and related questions, see Kowalzig (2004: 60–5 and 2006).

[76] Thanks to Andrew Garrett, Deborah Kamen, Emily Mackil, Boris Maslov, Donald Mastronarde, and Peter Wilson for reading and commenting on earlier drafts of this paper. A shorter version was delivered at the Conference 'Poeti Vaganti: Wandering Poets in Ancient Greece' (Cambridge University, April 20–23, 2005). I am grateful to the conference organizers, Richard Hunter and Ian Rutherford, for their invitation, and to all the conference participants for exceptionally lively and stimulating discussion (which I have tried to reproduce, however inadequately, in the notes to the current version). I am especially grateful to Alan Cameron, Angelos Chaniotis, G. B. D'Alessio, Barbara Kowalzig, Simon Hornblower, Richard Hunter, Richard Martin, and Lucia Prauscello for helpful suggestions and engaged criticism. Thanks also to this volume's editors for their detailed suggestions on an earlier version, and their forbearance in the face of authorial intransigence.

II

Drama on Drama

4

Euripides and Aristophanes: What does Tragedy Teach?

Pietro Pucci

In Aristophanes' *Frogs* 1008–12, a short dialogue unfolds between two poets. Aeschylus asks Euripides for what qualities a poet should be admired, and Euripides answers without hesitation:

> δεξιότητος καὶ νουθεσίας, ὅτι βελτίους τε ποιοῦμεν
> τοὺς ἀνθρώπους ἐν ταῖς πόλεσιν.

Skill and good counsel and because we make people better in their cities.[1]

Aeschylus immediately takes advantage of this avowal and addresses the following question to his rival:

> ταῦτ' οὖν εἰ μὴ πεπόηκας,
> ἀλλ' ἐκ χρηστῶν καὶ γενναίων μοχθηροτάτους ἀπέδειξας,
> τί παθεῖν φήσεις ἄξιος εἶναι;

Therefore, if you haven't done this, but rather turned good upstanding people into evident scoundrels, what punishment would you say you deserve?

We wait with some curiosity for Euripides' answer, but Aristophanes has Dionysus intervene: τεθνάναι· μὴ τοῦτον ἐρώτα, 'Death: you needn't ask him'.

---

[1] See Dover (1993a: 12), who sees the close connection between *nouthesia* and the next clause: this last 'can hardly be separated from *nouthesia*, "admonition"'. Taplin (1993: 5–6) shows the 'ambitious claim' in this expression: the two poets agree on a 'universal, or at least, a pan-Hellenic, value'. For it is not in Athens alone, but in the plural 'cities' that the poets make citizens better.

With this comic reply (both Euripides and Aeschylus are dead and talking in Hades), the question of what Euripides believed he had produced to make people better citizens is truncated. It is a pity, because his statement 'we [poets] make people better citizens' has every reason to excite our curiosity and disbelief. It is, as we will see, a comic ploy: as Euripides is made to assert the didactic purpose and the political concern of his poetry, Aristophanes gains a legitimate and forceful position from which to ridicule the amorality and the nothingness of this teaching. Aristophanes knows Euripides very well and we should recognize and interpret his comic exaggerations, displacements, and disfigurations. Therefore there are serious reasons for agreeing with the scholars who have doubted that the historical Euripides would have agreed with this statement.[2] To doubt Aristophanes' objectivity in his rendition of Euripides' didactic and political purposes implies first of all suspending the question of Euripides' didactic 'intentions', which are certainly absent as such in his plays.[3] Secondly, it implies asking what specific stances Euripides actually took on the ethical, political, religious, and existential issues that were at the centre of what Croally calls the 'ideology' of Athens.[4] I think that he did not propose any precise teaching on these matters. Yet many critics today are inclined to emphasize the tight connections of tragedy to the political reality and the religious issues and the ritual practices of Athens. As such, Greek tragedy would constitute a powerful means of consolidating the polis' religious and political unity.[5]

The open question lies precisely in this notion of 'consolidation' and in the specific nature of this interaction and correspondence between civic ideology and Greek tragedy. Especially when tragedy is presented,

---

[2] Stanford (1962); Del Corno (1985) realizes that Aristophanes thereby displaces Euripides into the territory of Euripides' adversary; Heath (1987*a*: 47 and *passim*) has strongly argued against the historical validity of the Aristophanic statement.

[3] Heath (1987*b*). Of course ancient philosophers and critics have made didactic use of the poets' statements in order to accuse them: Xenophanes and Heraclitus, for instance, initiated the great quarrel (*megalê diaphorâ*) between poetry and philosophy. But that use has suited the polemical stance and the didactic 'intentions' of these critics. The reading of the poetic 'intentions', as we know, is a critical mire.

[4] Croally (1994: 44–7).

[5] See Bierl (1991); Winkler and Zeitlin (1990); Goldhill (1987); Connor (1989); etc.

as by Croally, among others, as the discourse that questions and desta-
bilizes, in a Dionysiac perspective, the image (the ideology) that the city
has of itself,[6] it is not clear how this questioning and this destabilizing
consolidate the unity of the polis. Nor is it clear how political or
antipolitical this destabilizing is. The critical trouble increases when
the full correspondences between the discourse of tragedy and the
political practices of the polis are legitimately suspected, as by Nicole
Loraux and others.[7] Tragedy opens up a sort of extra-political discourse, one that evades the strictures of the polis' confined ideology,
and gazes at a sort of elsewhere. Whether the outlines of this evasion
can be exactly delineated and the effects defined remains a difficult
question. On the one hand, 'the political' itself is a realm of indefinable
vastness, incorporating the whole life of a community, even whatever
tries to evade it; on the other, poetry, because of its iterability,[8] is
capable of producing its semantic and emotional effects even when
the original social and historical coordinates are completely lost and no
longer alive. Between these two almost immeasurable phenomena, it
would seem impossible for the critic to trace the precise political and
ideological outlines of a complex discourse such as that of Greek
tragedy.

However, we may perhaps begin by better defining the realm of the
political and of its ideology if we follow the distinctions that Nicole
Loraux (2002*a*) has elaborated. She realizes that in the aspects
in which Greek tragedy can be termed 'political', it is often 'antipolitical', i.e. as we say, 'questioning' the ideology of the city. She develops
a productive analysis of the 'antipolitical' by attributing two meanings
to this notion. If we consider 'the political' as the practice of consensus, then an attitude that exceeds the civic consensus and order is
'antipolitical' in the sense that it goes beyond and transgresses the

---

[6] Croally (1994: 39–43).

[7] Loraux (2002*a*: 20): 'the tragic universe is everything but a replica of the city—
which Vidal-Naquet characterizes as being "in its very structure an anti-tragic
machine"'. Loraux quotes some statements by Vidal-Naquet that emphasize the
disjunction between tragedy and the political life of Athens and in a note she observes
'these statements are all the more interesting considering that Vidal-Naquet has also
been known to state that "Tragedy is politics"' (99 n. 34).

[8] For an elaborated discussion on the iterability of poetry as source of its
trans-historical life, see Derrida (1992: 33–75).

political: it is the 'political other', as she calls it. Thus, for instance, the excess of mourning that theatre so often represents goes beyond not only the established laws, but even beyond the meaning of mourning as conceived by the city. If, on the other hand, we consider conflict, in the controlled and repressed status in which the city holds it, as the essence of the political, then a behaviour that differs from the customary one is authentically antipolitical in the sense of implying a policy that antagonizes another.[9] It is simply, as Loraux defines it, 'another politics'. This last, I assume, is the ' political' and 'antipolitical' of the politicians, orators, etc.

For Nicole Loraux[10] we may unavoidably confuse these two meanings of the antipolitical, since it is not simple to draw the distinction in the complex reality of the political universe and in the texts that speak about it; but what essentially and primordially characterizes tragedy, for her, is the 'antipolitical' in the former sense, in the sense of what exceeds the political, that is, 'the political other' (I will call it, to shorten the definition, the 'transgressing' antipolitical, or 'the political other'). Thus, for instance, the pity and compassion that the last part of the *Persians* exudes for the destroyed Persians 'taught' the spectators 'to recognize something that touched them above and beyond their identity as Athenians'.[11] It taught them the brotherhood of all mortals, even of enemies, before pain and death.

In what follows I will identify the different shades of the antipolitical in some instances of Euripides' tragedy and then of Aristophanes' comedy, starting from the issue of tragedy's didacticism. We will discover some surprising parallelisms between the two poets: both explicitly or implicitly avoid, through different strategies, dramatizing any positive response to any issue that could have some didactic or exemplary purpose.

In Euripides' tragedy, moral and political issues are debated through the plots and the diatribes of the *agônes*. As concerns the

---

   9 Loraux (2002*a*: 46, 24).
   10 Loraux (2002*a*: 47, 27).
   11 Loraux (2002*a*: 48 and 76). For a different and not necessarily contradictory interpretation of this 'pity' see Foley (2001: 27–9). Another act that Loraux elaborates is the female mourning lament and ritual that tragedy never ceases to represent: as, for instance, in Sophocles' *Electra* or Euripides' *Trojan Women*.

plots, from the *Alcestis* to the *Bacchae*, readers are baffled by the almost perfect reversal of ethical and political stances that occurs during the development of the tragic action. This reversal forecloses the emergence of any paradigmatic value: the two parties switch roles; the victim takes over the tactics of the oppressor and implements them with the same ferocity. For example, Foley writes of Medea: 'by pursuing her heroic code, she ends by imitating even her despised immediate oppressor and harming herself.'[12] Even in the plots of plays like the *Suppliant Women* and the *Children of Heracles* that appear to elaborate unrestricted praise of Athens, critics emphasize the many controversial and negative features that nullify or suspend the positive picture. A fragment of ancient literary criticism defines the *Suppliant Women* as 'an *enkômion* of the Athenians.'[13] Now it is true that Athens is generally sympathetically portrayed;[14] it is also true that Theseus here embodies the generosity of Athens, and that his heroism on behalf of the laws of the gods is rightly rewarded by success. But the precise analysis of the play by Croally and others shows how these positive features are overwhelmed by many scandalous and contradictory elements.[15] Kovacs adds that Theseus' first refusal of help is certainly 'out of character for the Athenian myth'.[16] In the *agônes*, almost never do the debates end with one argument overpowering the other: there are no victors nor losers. Croally agrees with Michael Lloyd (1992) that in most Euripidean *agônes* (with perhaps the exception of *Children of Heracles* and *Hecuba*), 'no character gains a meaningful victory'. If the meaning of this constant failure of the debates to produce a winning argument lies, as Croally suggests, in the fact that 'talking will not resolve tragic conflicts', how can it be said that Euripides teaches anything? Isn't tragedy a staging of long discussions connected to actions?

[12] Foley (2001: 268).
[13] *Suppliant Women*, Hypothesis.
[14] On the sympathy of tragedians toward Athens and the elaborated play of contrasts that ensues between Athens and cities of perversions like Thebes, and between self and other, see the illuminating work of Zeitlin (1990*b*).
[15] Croally (1994: 207–15) and Foley (2001: 38–44).
[16] Kovacs (1998: 4).

In effect, all the mastery Euripides displays in developing persuasive arguments and in sustaining with rhetorical force two opposite views is only a sort of lure through which to show the vanity of reasonable explanations. For nothing, neither the mythical stories, nor the sophistic elaborations, explains evil in the world. One paradigmatic example, among many, of the impotence of any *logos* to justify the works of evil occurs in the *Heracles*. Maddened by Hera, when Heracles regains his reason, he declares that god, if he is really god (*orthôs theos*), needs nothing and that the violent acts of the gods are 'the wretched stories (*dustênoi logoi*) of the poets' (1341–6). As the audience has just witnessed Hera's will, Iris' message, and Lyssa's action, they must conclude that these divine beings, though powerful, though identical to the traditional gods, are not really gods, and that their interventions are indeed the wretched stories of the poets. But, then, why would the poet, Euripides, present false gods on stage? And who would be the real god (*orthôs theos*)? Is Heracles uttering the utopian view that gods should be good? Does he not know that his misery comes from Hera? Euripides' writing raises undecidability to the level of the tragic issue. His *logos* has no straight *logoi*: even if Heracles' philosophizing was intended for the *sophoi*, it would still leave the mythical action unexplained. For, who are, then, these beings generated by the wretched stories of the poets?

The audience is left with contradictory evidence and explanations: neither myth nor philosophy attacking myth could offer any legitimation, and in their sterile opposition they create a void. The same void occurs when the great debate between Helen and Hecuba about divine and human responsibility ends with a tie: 'From the substance of the arguments themselves, it would have been difficult for the audience to decide whom to favour as a winner of the debate'.[17]

In the void created by the sterile conflict of mythical and philosophical explanations and of opposing divine forces, Euripides'

---

[17] Croally (1994: 157). Even the interpreters who believe in Euripides' idea of a universal order and justice have trouble sustaining it without all sorts of qualifying and paradoxical statements. Lloyd-Jones (1971: 155) closes his arguments on Euripides with the following words: 'as the one wise is willing and unwilling to be called Zeus, so Dike is unwilling and willing to be called Justice.'

drama proposes the dubious consolation provided by pity, by utopian desires and hopes. As Karl Reinhardt writes on late Euripides: 'Euripidean lyric no longer concentrates on the tragic events, it intensifies, it no longer interprets, it breaks out, flies over land and sea, raves, dances among the gods, wishes the world were otherwise, becomes escapist, longs to be elsewhere, generalizes.'[18] Indeed, Euripides' characters often uncover hidden horizons of escape and hope (e.g. *Hipp.* 191–7)[19] in the exhilarating company of beauty,[20] express desires of being elsewhere (e.g. *Or.* 982–6),[21] risk strange utopian ideas (e.g. *HF* 655–72), and dream of minor deities who feel pity for men (like Thetis in the *Andromache*).

These are the features of the antipolitical that Loraux calls 'the political other' and among them what dominates is the emotion of pity that Euripides' writing elicits from the audience. In the void of the nothing that justifies the *kakon* of life, Euripides offers the consoling song of pity. Pity, as Nicole Loraux reminds us in *The Mourning Voice*, 'is not and cannot be a political affect. Thucydides' Cleon distrusted pity: from the Athenian imperialist perspective, to see the other as one's fellow man was extremely threatening'.[22]

---

[18] Reinhardt (2003: 30). Padel (1974: 227–41) modifies Reinhardt's statement towards a more supple and imaginative relationship between choral odes and the action of the plays.

[19] *Hipp.* 191–7: 'But about something else that may be dearer than this life, darkness conceals it, embracing it with clouds, and we appear to be wrongly in love with the light that shines on earth, because of our ignorance of another life and because there is no evidence of a world below; and we are aimlessly carried along by myths.' See also *Ion* 1067, *Med.* 1039, and especially *IA* 1505–8.

[20] See the charming song at *HF* 674–86. Pericles in the Funeral Oration (Th. 2.41) asserts boldly that the Athenians do not need Homer to celebrate their city; and later he says that with his discourse 'I have celebrated our city' (2.42 *tên polin humnêsa*) using the verb the poets use for the praising of their subjects.

[21] *Or.* 982–6: (Electra speaking) 'Would that I could reach the stone hanging between heaven and earth [...] in order to speak to the old father Tantalus.' Here the escapist longing, expressed by the simple optative *moloimi*, creates pathos for the impossibility, even the foolishness, of the desire. For many other escapist passages (*metoikêsis*), see Willink (1986: 246).

[22] Loraux (2002*b*: 50). Pity does not occur in the idealized vision of the city presented by Pericles in Th. 2.35–46: Pericles praises the laws in defence of the victims of injustice (2.37), but he refuses to weep for the parents of the dead soldiers (2.44 *tous tônde nun tokeas* [...] *ouk olophuromai*) though he realizes that they will weep for their fallen sons (2.46).

This pity turns easily into self-pity[23] of which Euripides often acknowledges the therapeutic power,[24] as I have shown in my book on the *Medea*.[25] The specular effect of pity works in Euripides' repeated representations of human sacrifices: the young victims, girls and boys, accept their sacrificial death with a sublime and heroic poise. They are described as pitiful examples of an arbitrary and savage brutality, confirming the inexplicability of evil and eliciting the audience' pity. Yet on deeper-seated poetic grounds, as these girls and boys offer themselves somehow freely to the sacrificial knife, they become the incarnation of an analogous, but imaginary wound that the wise audience would agree to receive. For they would be offering themselves to the suffering produced by their pity for these sacrificed victims and would build on it a sort of existential preparedness that will fortify them against the evils, losses, exiles, and deaths to come. The sacrifice of the innocent victims (even the children of Heracles and those of Medea) is the pitiful image by which the wise audience will freely and beautifully—because through the beauty of the text—offer themselves to be touched and pained.[26] They would receive the analogous benefit of the sharing in a sacrifice, of a sacrifice, however,

---

[23] Konstan (2001: 64–71) shows that self-pity is an emotion rarely acknowledged in ancient Greece. This rare mention of self-pity is a supplementary evidence that the male civic ideology refused to grant citizenship especially to self-commiseration. But of course Greeks felt self-pity, even collectively, as X. *Ap.* 18 witnesses (*oiktirein heautous*). In Sophocles' late tragedies and in Euripides' plays, self-pity is often a dominating emotion. Heracles, in Euripides' play, indulges in crying for his own disgraces in 1351–7, lamenting that he has become slave of *tukhê* and in 1408–17 where he is taken by an irresistible desire to weep over his own misfortunes. Theseus finally becomes impatient and blames him for behaving like a woman (1412), offering us another luminous evidence of the civic male resistance to accepting this emotion.

[24] See Euripides frg. 964.1–6 N² where Theseus (the founder of the Athenian state!) says: 'I learned the following from a wise man: I was imagining in my mind cares, calamities, inflicting on myself exile from my fatherland and premature death and other ways of evil, so that if I had to suffer some of the things that I was imagining in my mind I would not be stung more sharply by the novelty of the event.'

[25] Pucci (1981).

[26] Mossman (1995: 145 and 152) underlines the pathos and the pity of the scene of Polyxena's sacrifice and correctly emphasizes the claim the young victim publicly asserts of dying free, as death is preferable to the life of a slave. In my paper (Pucci 1999: 231) I write: 'Vivre libre s'identifie ici avec la liberté de s'offrir à la mort.' The image of the virgin's statuesque beauty intimates the exemplary beauty of this gesture of hers, while simultaneously throwing a veil upon the non-sense and brutality of putting her to death.

invented and elaborated by poetic writing and experienced by the audience as the effect of a poetic artefact. In this sense, these representations of human sacrifices function as the 'supplement' of Euripides' writing, since they produce a remedy in the form of a poison, indulge in a brutality that is simultaneously an edification, and transform the wound of the sacrificial knife into the incision of a smart rhetorical *stilum*.[27]

This powerful representation and invention of the effects of pity sustain the transgressive antipolitical stance of Euripides' writing, while creating, in Aristotle's view, its strongest tragic asset. This transgressive discourse proper of the 'political other' discourse does not necessarily reach a more genuine expression of poetry than the other political, antipolitical speeches. This discourse too, like all discourses, gestures towards a deferred signified and fails to engage the full presence of the referent. It remains, as we have seen, ambivalent and produces dubious effects. The difference is that its area is identifiable with men's experience of anxiety before the inexplicable *kakon* of life and with their ceaseless elaboration of discourses to overcome that anxiety. Accordingly, in comparison with the simply antagonistic political discourse, this 'political other' elaboration touches upon a critical sense of humanity and intimates a stronger sympathy for the pains of individual consciousness.

It is time to return to Aristophanes' *Frogs* and try to investigate the same issues concerning the political and the antipolitical issues in his comedies. I focus on his dramatization of the debate between the poets, concerning tragedy's teaching purpose. On the one hand, this issue was debated in the cultural milieu of the polis; on the other, it is a theme dear to Aristophanes himself, as he incessantly attributes this purpose to his own plays. He even gives it an emphatic prominence in the *Frogs*, when his chorus says 'it is just for the holy chorus to give good advice and to instruct our city' (686–7).[28] Accordingly the debate between the two poets is a mirror of the play's own purpose, a *mise en abyme* of the play's avowed didactic function.

---

[27] These undecidable effects of pity are compounded with the disseminating roles of pity in the self, for pity throws us outside ourselves toward the other, and simultaneously consolidates the self in several ways.

[28] See Goldhill (1991: 186).

However, notwithstanding what seems to be a promising match between the two poets, notwithstanding Aeschylus' impetuous didacticism, the debate ends in a tie: no winner and no loser. Many arguments whirl through but all fall into derision and mockery.

A bit of background on the liberating and suppressing effects of comic laughter might be useful. For Kant in his *Critique of Judgment*, 'laughter is an affection arising from the sudden transformation of a strained expectation into nothing.'[29] No need to stress the close contact of this definition with Freud's interpretation of laughter as annulment of a disquieting expectation, return to familiarity, breaking of inhibition, breaking of the law of mechanical repetition, etc.[30] All these types of sudden relief generate comic laughter when they are produced by specific rhetorical manipulations. Comic laughter in fact arises only in a determined context, i.e. within comic boundaries[31] and through a specific form of language, acting, or other modes of representation. The grounding feature of comic laughter is the licence it has of playing with the signifier. The comic release flashes when the signifying chain with its rules and constraints is suddenly twisted, suspended in semantic displacements, in non-sense, in figural meanings that are turned backward to literality, and so on. The superposition, or simultaneity of this linguistic toying with a serious, substantial expression, as in a wordplay, produces the collapse of all seriousness. Suddenly it is derided.[32]

It is comic laughter that ridicules Aeschylus and the whole teaching function of tragedy, emptying the seriousness, the substance of the issue and showing the seriousness of this emptiness, of this

---

[29] See Genette (2002) who quotes this definition, but criticizes it by saying that 'death' could fit this definition and death is not at all laughable. But death, mine or that of my people, is hardly nothing, and in general does not succeed at all after a strained expectation.

[30] Freud (1963).

[31] A comic context (or the 'comic boundaries' to use Goldhill's term [1991: 194]) implies a series of structural, semantic premises, such as the right theatrical or social occasion, the explicit assertion that the performance is comic (see the various jokes at the outset of most Aristophanic comedies), the exclusion of any other genre or rhetoric, etc.

[32] I am summarizing here some of the points brilliantly elaborated by Gregory W. Dobrov in his work on Aristophanes, see for instance Dobrov (1997*b*: esp. 96–108). On the literalization of the metaphor, on its comic and tragic use, see Goldhill (1991: 189) and see further below.

nothing.[33] A nothing that of course reflects on the avowed purpose of the play itself, the *Frogs*: the purpose, as we have seen, of instructing the city. Let us analyse a few examples of this mockery.

After Aeschylus has shown how useful (1031 ὠφέλιμοι) was the teaching of the old poets (Musaeus taught the oracles, Orpheus the mysteries, Hesiod farming, Homer the techniques of war), Dionysus comments that no Homer taught Pantacles how to fasten the helmet on his head: καὶ μὴν οὐ Παντακλέα γε ἐδίδαξεν ὅμως τὸν σκαιότατον 1036–8). Dario Del Corno appropriately defines this remark 'a grotesque aside that breaks the spell of Aeschylus' committed preaching'. Dionysus' comment also makes the humorous point that there are too many things in this world to be taught and too many idiots who will never learn. The usefulness of the poets has unavoidable and banal limitations. How painful for such great masters!

Five lines are devoted to the four archaic Greek teacher–poets and three lines to the failure of these teachers to instruct the simpleton Pantacles whom everyone in the audience knew much better than Musaeus. It is easy to imagine the burst of laughter.[34] Aristophanes is poking fun at Aeschylus' idea of the poet–teacher. Certainly Aristophanes is mocking also when he has Aeschylus accuse Euripides of the representation of such immoral characters as the Stheneboeas and Phaedras.

After Aeschylus has asked what Euripides would deserve for corrupting the citizens, Dionysus' answer, 'Death' (1012 τεθνάναι· μὴ τοῦτον ἐρώτα), collapses or complicates the seriousness of the issue. On the one hand, the answer seems to correspond to what the Aristophanic Aeschylus would have answered, and therefore it seems to agree with Aeschylus; but on the other, since the characters are dead, Dionysus' answer is the equivalent of saying 'nothing! He does not deserve anything.' There is a semantic displacement that is the

---

[33] I use the synonyms of serious and unserious as suggested by Silk (2000: 315). For this scholar, Aristophanes is generally serious, even when comic, for comedy suspends but does not obliterate an issue, and accordingly Aristotle would be wrong to oppose *spoudaion* to *geloion*.

[34] Plato too (*R.* 600a) nullifies Homer's didactic knowledge and, as the speaker asks whether at the time of Homer any war was waged under the leadership or the advice of the poet, Glaucon of course answers: 'None'. In 589a ff. Plato again denies that Homer transmits any piece of real, useful knowledge.

source of the laughter: the normal expression here implied is that 'death is the deserved punishment for a crime', but since Euripides is already dead—and he died naturally, for no committed crime—the whole expression ('to deserve death') is absurdly resemanticized, i.e. voided, and 'death', the ultimate evil, turns out to mean a pleasant 'nothing'. Laughter arises from the voiding of the expected semantic value, i.e. from the dropping into nothing of the strained expectation produced by Aeschylus' heavy question. Of course, Dionysus came to resuscitate one of the poets, but this decision is still far away and will not be made on the ground of their poetic morality. Yet the audience may hear the joke as a sort of foretelling.

With 'you needn't ask him' (1012), Dionysus continues to be funny: he means, I believe, that Aeschylus cannot really expect a dead man to answer. But, while meaning this, Dionysus has a double comic focus: of course Euripides is dead and a dead person cannot speak, but, on another level already touched upon by Aeschylus (868–71), Dionysus intimates that Euripides' poetry is dead, since it is no longer performed, while that of Aeschylus is alive, because it is still performed in Athens.[35] Here the contrasting connotations of 'being dead' evoke man's death as he lies in a world other than ours, but the survival of his work in our world carries the consequence of a not-full death even in the other world: *non omnis moriar*.

This ambivalence rests with the linguistic play that is inherent in the metaphor 'to go to Hades', whose vehicle (the going to a place as a living person can do) replaces the tenor 'to die'. While for Dionysus the expression 'to go to Hades' (69, 118, etc.) has his real *katabasis* as a referent and no implied death, for the dead and for the two poets 'to go to Hades'(172, 771) or 'to be in Hades' (774) are metaphors that, though themselves half 'dead', are here revitalized by the contrast, and by their constant activation and deactivation. There ensues a sort of macabre playfulness.

Laughter certainly weakens or even nullifies Aeschylus' aggressive question, as we have seen, and by so doing it diffuses Euripides' assertion that 'we poets make people better citizens' into vagueness, leaving the audience still expecting the exposition of his teachings.

---

[35] For the revival of Aeschylus' plays see Wilamowitz (1914: 5–6), scholia to Ar. *Ach.* 10 (cf. scholia to *Frogs* 868), Philostr. *VA* 6.11 (p. 113.I Kayser).

But laughter also accompanies Euripides' extolling of his literary instructions and inventions, that of having both the slave and the girl speaking in his dramas like the master, or that of having taught the Athenians to λαλεῖν (954): ἔπειτα τουτουσὶ λαλεῖν ἐδίδαξα ('Then I taught these people [indicating the spectators] to talk').

Of course, since λαλεῖν means both 'to talk' and 'to chat', Euripides is presented as unintentionally making fun of himself. What can be more ridiculous than someone who pretends to be smart and makes a fool of himself? Furthermore Euripides directs his line to the actual audience, gesturing to them; he therefore breaks the dramatic illusion: he is no longer speaking from Hades but from the stage of the Athenian theatre.[36] He is alive and teaches once again to his Athenian audience more babbling and more chatter. Imperishable, unbeatable Euripides!

When Aeschylus hears this Euripidean teaching, he launches into a grave indictment that is completely absurd:

> εἶτ' αὖ λαλιὰν ἐπιτηδεῦσαι καὶ στωμυλίαν ἐδίδαξας,
> ἣ 'ξεκένωσεν τάς τε παλαίστρας καὶ τὰς πυγὰς ἐνέτριψεν
> τῶν μειρακίων στωμυλλομένων   (1069–71)

Then you taught people to cultivate chatter (λαλιὰν) and babbling which has emptied the wrestling schools and worn down the butts of the young men as they keep on babbling.

Even without quoting Dionysus' scatological comments—which follow the Aeschylean fixation with male bodies—this passage is sufficient to indicate the festive aura of ridicule and non-sense in which the teaching of the poets is set.

This suppression of seriousness and substance in the question of the educational purpose of tragedy must affect the claim the chorus makes for the educational goal of the *Frogs*, since the *mise en abyme* scene mirrors the great design of the play. Accordingly the numerous assertions that Aristophanes trumpets in his plays (e.g. *Ach.* 641–5) to the effect that he is the instructor of the city and its teacher of justice might fall under the same aura of ridicule that voids the assertions of the tragic poets in the *Frogs*. For instance, when Aristophanes defends himself against Cleon (*Ach.* 502–8), he is speaking dressed in the costume and using the language of a Euripidean character!

---

[36] Dobrov (2001: 14) calls this comic metatheatrical device 'surface play', like parody, quotations, reference to the theatre, etc.

The double and contradictory meaning of *lalia* that Aristophanes attributes to Euripides' teaching parallels, on a different level and perspective, the double sterile *logoi* of Euripides' debates.

At the end of the debate between the two tragic poets Aristophanes is forced to have Dionysus choose the 'best' poet (!) on grounds other than the literary and *poetic* ones that have been debated.[37] Just as in the Euripidean *agônes*, where proponents of two contrasting issues unfold brilliant arguments but are unable to overcome the other, here too each poet is made to raise his own arguments in contrast with the other but both fail to win the debate: the arguments are brought into the foreground as important and substantial and are yet simultaneously repressed by laughter.

The dramatization of polemical issues takes a large place in a scene of the *Acharnians*, where Aristophanes mocks Euripides' tendency to stage pitiful characters, deprived of traditional dignity. The theatrical genius of Aristophanes caught unmistakably the strength of Euripides' tragic writing. This theme of Euripides' pitiful representations, touched upon in the *Frogs* (1062–8), is oddly combined with that of Euripides' didacticism, in fact, with his teaching of justice. We are still in the area of the political and antipolitical in the sense of antagonistic views. I pursue the analysis in the *Acharnians* because it opens up a revealing, unnoticed aspect of the Euripides–Aristophanes relation, and because it will allow us to observe some traits of Aristophanes' escapist discourse.

At line 496 Dicaeopolis, disguised as Telephus, begins his *rhêsis makra* before the chorus and addressing the Athenian spectators:

> μή μοι φθονήσητ᾽, ἄνδρες οἱ θεώμενοι,
> εἰ πτωχὸς ὢν ἔπειτ᾽ ἐν Ἀθηναίοις λέγειν
> μέλλω περὶ τῆς πόλεως, τρυγῳδίαν ποιῶν.
> τὸ γὰρ δίκαιον οἶδε καὶ τρυγῳδία.
> ἐγὼ δὲ λέξω δεινὰ μέν δίκαια δέ.

Be not indignant with me, men of the audience if, though a beggar, I speak before the Athenians about (the affairs of) the city in a comedy. For even comedy is acquainted with justice; and what I will say is dreadful [shocking, heart-rending] but just. (*Ach.* 496–501).

---

[37] See 1411–13. The same inconclusive result occurs in other plays, but not in the *Clouds*: there both the Stronger Logos' and Pheidippides' arguments are victorious and Strepsiades, unable to answer them, decides to act instead of arguing.

The word *trugôidia* is a comic formation modelled on *tragôidia*. The pun holds in its grip simultaneously tragedy and comedy, and perfectly describes the paratragic recycling of some tragic scenes of the Euripidean *Telephus*. By having Dicaeopolis say that 'even (*kai*) comedy' deals with justice, Aristophanes has him imply that tragedy does so too. The comedian again likes to present Euripides' tragedy as having a political and ethical purpose.[38]

The tragedy Dicaeopolis is alluding to in the paratragic scene is Euripides' *Telephus* of which he misquotes some lines,[39] while wearing the hero's pitiful outfit.[40] Though in one fragment (23 Preiser, 706 N²) Telephus proclaims that he will uphold justice at any price,

---

[38] See Olson (2002: 201); Taplin (1983: 31–3). Besides this passage, Aristophanes suggests that the play *Telephus* is concerned with justice when at lines 317–18 he makes a clear reference to some lines spoken by the hero Telephus (23 Preiser, 706 N²) where Telephus says that he will speak out for justice even if threatened by an axe on his neck. For *trugôidia*, see the suggestive analysis by Edmunds (1980: 11) who drowns the serious ethical purposes of the comedy in its wine: '*trygôidia* comes from "trux", "raw wine" or "lees of wine" and *ôidê*, "song" [...] In asserting comedy's knowledge of justice (500), Aristophanes has this special understanding of comedy in mind: comedy as wine-song. Paradoxically, the political function of comedy rests on its association with wine. This conclusion appears less paradoxical, however, when one remembers that Aristophanes has already dramatized the same point. Dicaeopolis, "Just city" makes peace with Sparta. Peace is wine.' Edmunds is of course referring to the word for peace, *spondai*, which also means libations of wine. We will come back to this point.

[39] Euripides' text (12 Preiser, 723 N²) reads:

> μή μοι φθονήσητ᾽, ἄνδρες Ἑλλήνων ἄκροι,
> εἰ πτωχὸς ὢν τέτληκ᾽ ἐν ἐσθλοῖσιν λέγειν

Be not indignant with me, foremost men of the Greeks,
if though a beggar I dare to speak among the betters.

With these words Telephus begins the defence of the king of the Mysians and of the Mysians who had aggressively repelled the invading Achaeans. The second line has a *caesura mediana*, rare in tragedy and rarer in Euripides: Aristophanes preserves it probably to exhibit it. The many long syllables in the first line give solemnity and power to the *captatio benevolentiae*.

[40] As in my *Aristofane ed Euripide: Ricerche stilistiche e metriche* (1961), by 'para-tragedy', I mean the comic recycling of tragic plots, stage features (such as the *enkuklêma*) and lines that, though not built on a specific model, are yet reminiscent of tragedy. Recently Dobrov (2001: 16) has suggested the word 'contrafact' for this type of comic allusion. By 'parody' I mean a caricature of specific lines and traits of individual tragic style; the purpose of parody is not alone to produce a tragicomic action, but to mock a precise style and to contribute eventually to a paratragic scene. Of course the two forms of tragic allusion can be combined, and sometimes are difficult to distinguish.

Pietro Pucci

we do not know to what extent the play dealt with the issues of justice. Some known details, such as Telephus' snatching of the baby Orestes, the imposture of the pitiful disguise,[41] and Telephus' final collaboration with the Achaeans may raise some doubts: at any rate we can surmise a complex and odd series of events, a contradictory and unorthodox characterization, and final reconciliation or compromise.

Since, as I have shown, it is problematic to trace the *nouthesia* and the teaching contribution of the Euripidean play to the cause of justice, I move to the *Acharnians* scene where Dicaeopolis prepares himself for the 'great speech' of instruction in favour of justice.[42] My point will be that this comic scene in preparation for that serious and vital discourse gives us also a key to understand a bit of Aristophanes' obsession with Euripides. I am referring to *Acharnians* 393–479, where Dicaeopolis visits Euripides in order to obtain the costume of Telephus. This scene has no immediate dramatic role, is played outside the cognizance of the chorus, and replaces a typical agon:[43] it has essentially comic, satirical, and parodic purposes.[44]

---

41 Even without fully agreeing with Guido Paduano's view that Telephus' disguise as a beggar was a 'scandalous and subversive' novelty (Paduano 1967), one has to recognize that, indeed, Telephus *chooses* this disguise in order to promote his cause, and is not brought to this condition by external events (as is often the case). The unceasing reference by Aristophanes to this disguise ought to mean that the stage of the *Telephus* was, if not subversive, certainly shocking. Cavallone (1980) emphasizes the obvious hyperbolic distortion by Aristophanes, but agrees on the shocking effect that this self-humiliating disguise must have produced on the audience at the time of the drama's first performance.

42 For Aristophanes' political commitment in this paratragic *rhêsis makra*, see Kannicht (1996); Foley (1988); Goldhill (1991). The political assessment of the rhesis is made problematic also by the plural subject that Dicaeopolis represents: Goldhill defines exactly the peculiar effect of the confusion between Dicaeopolis and Aristophanes when he writes: 'The logic of Aristophanic self-reflexivity [. . .] reaches a bizarre limit-case, when the separation of character and the author's self-representation becomes difficult to determine with any security' (Goldhill 1991: 193).

43 Edmunds (1980: 9).

44 Comic, in the specific sense that the scene recycles Euripides and his slave into comic types, the former a sort of *alazôn*, the latter the conventional erudite slave of comic philosophers. We know the slaves of the *Knights* (16–18), who while trying to invent a stratagem think of course of Euripides, the slave of Agathon (in *Th.*) and of Hyperbolus (Pl. com. fr. 166, 3: 'Even if you did not get it, you got it, if you understand').

The parodist *qua* parodist is to some extent a parasitic author, one afflicted by some lack of authorial mastery, one indeed naively or obsessively prisoner of the Other's authorship and creativity.[45] Aristophanes is not simply a parodist, he is a comedian of extraordinary poetic creativity, so that, when he indulges in the parodic game as he does in *Acharnians* 393–479, he induces us to look attentively for his implicit reasons.

After the interview with Euripides' slave, Dicaeopolis enters Euripides' working place through the machinery of the *enkuklêma*[46] and asks the tragedian for the props of the most pitiful character in Euripides' theatre, the props of Telephus. Dicaeopolis occasionally quotes Euripides who does not seem to be aware of it:[47] the author is deprived of the awareness of being the author. Initially Euripides is agreeable and gives Dicaeopolis the pieces of the outfit, but soon the poet realizes that he will be completely robbed of his tragic props. He gives Dicaeopolis the stick of the beggar, and then commands the visitor to leave: 'Take this, and leave this marble hall' (449).

But the commands to leave, though repeated until line 479, have no effect: Dicaeopolis, acting in a paratragic scene of supplication, keeps pillaging Euripides' props and poking fun at him. In this sequence, with a typically Euripidean gesture, Dicaeopolis speaks to his own heart (450–3):

My heart, you see that I have been expelled from this house when I still need so many props. More than ever, be clinging, obsessing, and pressing. Euripides, give me a basket burned by the lamp.

---

[45] See the remarks by Deguy (1984: 4): 'La parodie est parasite. Elle exploite quelqu'un qu'elle fait connaitre en le défigurant, et dont elle détourne, grâce à la reconnaissance vers autre chose, vers quoi? Vers le projet de faire passer le modèle du coté de la copie [...] La parodie réussit, si elle réussit, à faire passer l'original pour une réplique de sa contrefaçon, ou, nuançons, au moins pour un exemplaire de la série que la parodie démultiplie.'

[46] The *enkuklêma* is a tool of the tragic stage and in comedy is often allusive to tragedy, see Rau (1967), who quotes *Ach.* 407 ff., *Clouds* 181 ff., *Th.* 96 ff. Foley (2001: 43) underlines the fact that through this mechanical way of entering backstage, comedy reveals 'the unglamorous, but important truth that tragedy (drama that depends on allusion) hides behind the stage.'

[47] See especially *Ach.* 441–2 δεῖ γάρ με δόξαι πτωχὸν εἶναι τήμερον, εἶναι μὲν ὅσπερ εἰμί, φαίνεσθαι δὲ μή· Here is the opportunity to notice the strange and upsetting asymmetrical relation between comedy and tragedy. Comedy mocks and parodies tragedy, but tragedy can never respond. In this scene, the fact that Euripides is mocked through his own lines and by a character who becomes one of Euripides' own characters adds endless irony to the play.

When Euripides reminds him that this basket can be of no use to him, Dicaeopolis answers: χρέος μὲν ουδέν, βούλομαι δ᾽ ὅμως λαβεῖν, 'I have no use for it, but I want it nevertheless.' (455)[48]

This is an extraordinary line. It tells us in the most explicit way that the whole parodic business, the pillaging of Euripides' tragic words, lines, props, ideas, etc. rests on no use, no necessity: it rests only on a sort of gratuitous desire.[49] It rests on a sort of *erôs* for a signified which eludes him, that sort of *erôs* that in the *Birds* pushes the two Athenian citizens to pursue their journey out of the city walls in the absence of any motivation whatever. It is the same as the passionate love (*pothos*) that Dionysus feels for Euripides (*Frogs* 66–7), a love that turns into erotic craziness about Euripides' phrases (μαίνομαι, *Frogs* 103). This erotic passion is comic because of its inappropriate object, a phrase of Euripides; and yet it is this sort of phrase that prods the god to go outside the world of men into Hades to resurrect a dead voice. In all these cases the desire, as Dobrov correctly notes, is the gap, the fundamental lack of an absent (deferred) signified.[50]

The line 'I have no use for it, but I want it nevertheless' analogously intimates, even with its comic playfulness, the paradoxical

---

[48] χρέος is used in the sense of χρεία: see LSJ and Olson (2002: ad loc.). For this sort of opposition see Euripides *El.* 900: αἰσχύνομαι μέν, βούλομαι δ᾽ εἰπεῖν ὅμως᾽ 'I feel ashamed, but I want to tell it nevertheless.' *Ach.* 455 'I have no use for it, but I want it nevertheless' belongs to the comic absurd: it dissolves the previous question by an unexpected light non-sense. As for the crucial interest of this line, we should avoid making one line the privileged clone of the whole critical enterprise, but, as the reader is aware, the meaning of this line is coherent with my whole critical analysis, beside being particularly eloquent.

[49] In reality, Telephus' tragic props, during Dicaeopolis' long speech, are intended to, and succeed in, deceiving the chorus (see Compton-Engle 2003: 510–15). But a few props would have been sufficient for that dramatic purpose, whereas the comic excess in piling up all the different props has no real dramatic usage, and immediately serves only to amuse the audience. Cavallone (1980) and others have shown that Aristophanes wildly exaggerates the lists of the props that Euripidean Telephus really used, making an absurd and farcical list of useless objects. An undifferentiated hoard of objects put together as in the comic lists of a *pnigos* thus results, where the meaning of each object is suspended or repressed by the nonsensical accumulation. There is also a histrionic feature that indirectly derives from the *Telephus*: Dicaeopolis speaks before a chopping block, his head ready to be put on it, literalizing a metaphor from the *Telephus*: see Kannicht (1996: 135).

[50] Dobrov (1997b: 105–6). I take it that in all these examples, we hear the voice of the poet filling the gap by different comic plays of images and metaphors in their non-sense, in their illusion, and nothingness.

love of Aristophanes for Euripides, his ironical and obsessional hunger for the tragedian's work, his mocking and perplexed block before Euripides' search into the spiritual features and tendencies that characterized their 'modernity'.[51] This unresolved love for Euripides gestures towards a common perception of, or sensibility for, the metaphysical temper and the spiritual crisis of the time that are placed beyond any positive cultural affinity. This common sensibility is an aspect of the transgressive, antipolitical work of the comedian.

Because of his oxymoronic *erôs*, parodic Aristophanes behaves like the pressing beggar who has no real need for what he gets, no reason for remaining, like a lover, in the house of the tragic poet, no real need to be instilled with that poetic discourse (447, 484), and yet he longs to remain: importunate, irksome, annoying. What he seeks, the signified that would stop his want, eludes him and what he gets remains a roar of laughter, because of the mechanical repetition of asking for those props, whose comic excess is an end in itself.[52] Why does this unsatisfied desire unfurl in the comic and ambiguous relation with Euripides? We can only guess: the desire to probe and fully appropriate Euripides' mastering voice of modernity (its fearsome aspects), the voice which, like Aristophanes' own, searches for a content beyond the threatened walls of the city. And simultaneously that desire to appropriate Euripides' restless, pained voice of modernity turns toward mockery, intimating the vanity (*lalia*), the arrogance even, of that restlessness and searching. For comedy is more

[51] See the fine judgement by Silk (2000: 52): 'Aristophanes is never hostile to Euripides *tout court*, but is content to seem ambivalent about the great tragedian's experiments. For even if Euripides *has* "stripped tragic art of its greatness" (*Frogs* 1494–5), he is still among "the true artists" (*Frogs* 896) [...] Euripides, the great experimenter, holds a special interest for Aristophanes, beyond all other tragedians, precisely because he is an experimenter.'

[52] I do not imply that the disguise has no dramatic function, but that the props' comic excess has significance for the scene I am analysing. Dobrov (2001: 19–20 and 39–41) terms the 'great speech' a *mise en abyme*, and Heath (1987a: 278) reconstructs for this same speech a parallel logical scheme for Dicaeopolis' and Telephus' arguments. The points of contact are certainly there and are emphasized by parody. The audience, being no dupe of Dicaeopolis' disguise, have no perplexity when he speaks with Aristophanes' voice and laments his troubles with Cleon. On this dramatization and re-enactment of Aristophanes' 'transgression', see the analysis of Goldhill (1991: 193–4).

alert than tragedy to the elusive force of language, to the fraudulent manipulation of language by its practitioners, and realizes that something forever eludes Euripides' search: the rescue coming from a special discourse is constantly drifting away. These two targets of desire, appropriation and mockery, are only superficially opposed: in reality they are the two Janus faces of the same phenomenon, of Aristophanes' love for Euripides.

The obsessive satire against Euripides' miserable props opens up contradictory significations. On the one hand, we face a gratuitous, pleasurable, polemical game leading into no opposition, into nothing. For Dicaeopolis is more than a disguised Telephus: he is Euripides himself. In line 447 Dicaeopolis is filled up with Euripidean phrases (those phrases with which Dionysus has fallen in love, in *Frogs* 100–3) and in line 484 he has swallowed Euripides.[53] Therefore, in accordance with this metaphorical representation, it is Euripides himself who finally parodies and satirizes Euripides: it is Euripides/Telephus/Dicaeopolis who pillages Euripides/Telephus; it is Euripides/Telephus/Dicaeopolis who will uphold the just cause of Aristophanes. The 'enemy brothers',[54] a cloned Telephus,[55] a mocked Euripides/Aristophanes, and laughter explodes...

But, on the other hand, beyond the rags of Euripidean tragedy lies a signifying space full of possible meanings that we can only surmise. Indeed these useless props gesture toward their metonymical meanings, drifting substitutes, symbolic allusions: for instance, they can allude to Euripides' dismissal of the solemnity of the royal costumes;

---

[53] At line 484 Dicaeopolis, fearing to speak to the Acharnians, addresses his soul in tragic fashion—namely himself—and says: ἔστηκας; οὐκ εἶ καταπιὼν Εὐριπίδην; 'What, you stand still? Will you not go, now that you have swallowed Euripides?'. Dicaeopolis has swallowed Euripides just as Zeus swallowed (with the same verb, κάππιεν) Metis in Hes. fr. 343.10. Dicaeopolis now masters the whole art of Euripides. But to what purpose? To cheat the chorus? Does he need such an art for those simpletons (443–4)? Or rather to speak like Euripides/Aristophanes to the alert audience (499–508)? This is the paradoxical result of the whole parodic operation, that Aristophanes defends his work through Euripides' recycled tragic art.

[54] Deguy (1984: 6): 'La parodie, en tant que structure du double, et donc de frères ennemis, fait passer la version de l'autre en dessous. L'écho est ce qu'il y a de plus réducteur.'

[55] Not only do Telephus and Euripides appear to be identical but also Telephus and Dicaeopolis, through Euripides, become identical.

the misery of the great heroes; the Odyssean source of the disguise motif and of the concern for endurance, survival, and pity;[56] the inability of the god of the theatre to reinvent the old greatness; the enigmas that theatre as representational machine produces; the trivial manipulation of props, language, and gestures that however create enduring works; the mysterious effect of the mask; and so on. These and other suspended issues are intimated as lying beyond those miserable metonymies: they gesture toward undecidable signifieds, political questions that are, in part at least, limitless questions on the side of the antipolitical that we call transgressive and the 'political other'.

Let us glance at some of Aristophanes' large antipolitical transgressive representations, real escapes from the world of the polis: Dicaeopolis who decides to make a separate peace with the Spartans, Lysistrata and her women who fight against the males and win the battle, Dionysus who plans to bring back to Athens a poet to be saviour of his theatre, Peisetaerus founding a new city nowhere,[57] on a simple linguistic and stage construct—and others that belong to the imaginary world that exceeds the boundaries of the polis. In Aristophanes', as in Euripides' plays, the two types of the antipolitical cannot be kept always neatly separated, each reciprocally invading the other's realm.

The whole action of the *Acharnians* depends on the initial jump into a comic utopia, the invention of a strange, unknown god,

---

[56] The self-humiliating and freely chosen disguise is an Odyssean theme, and not the only one in Euripides' drama: a study should be devoted to the massive presence of the *Odyssey* in his work. Suffice it to think of Odysseus' crying after Demodocus' song about the fall of Troy (8.521–31): 'Odysseus melted into tears [...] And as a woman cries and throws herself upon her dear husband who has fallen before his city and people trying to shield homes and children from the pitiless day, and at the sight of her dying and gasping man she flings herself on him with a piercing scream, while men behind her, smiting her back and shoulders with the spears drag her away as a slave to toil and misery, and her cheeks are wasted by the most pitiful agony, in the same way Odysseus poured out pitiful tears.' Some of the sensibility of the poetry of the *Trojan Women* is, *mutatis mutandis*, already there.

[57] See Konstan (1997). In order to define different forms of utopia in Aristophanes' *Birds*, Konstan has elaborated a classification of forms of utopia, grounding them on the norm of the *nomoi*. He attributes four shades of utopia (the anomian, antinomian, etc.) to the society described in the *Birds*. See also at p. 15 'the city of the birds can be the subject of inconsistent or contradictory political allegories.'

Amphitheos,[58] who can miraculously provide the *spondai*, treaties of peace with Sparta and bring them to Dicaeopolis as libation and therefore as wine[59] in flasks or bowls.[60] The whole play is made possible by this miracle/manipulation that allows the *spondai* to function simultaneously as treaties of peace, as libation, and then as wine: five-year-old wine, ten-year-old wine, and an even more improbable thirty-year-old wine.[61] The whole representation of the festivities of peace, of the violence of Lamachus, of the wounds of war rests on this wordplay, the unexpected and reversed transformation of a metaphor to its tenor and then to the tenor's metonymic meanings. Comedy is more aware than tragedy of the fictitious force of language and can count on it to produce a more pleasurable 'real' utopia. Euripides would have been able to represent the utopia on which the *Acharnians* lies by an optative verb, e.g.: 'Would that peace be as affordable as wine is in the market', but this longing would have brought into the foreground its impossibility and absurdity, its pathos. Not with Aristophanes: peace really is a bottle of wine that can be drunk and enjoyed. What an immense feat can be produced by a trivial prop, a bottle of wine! We are reminded of the *trugôidia*, the song of wine. Laughter follows and it is on the razor edge of the *double entendre* that we can perceive both despair and relief, cynical manipulation and miracle, nightmare and dream. This is what we learn.

---

[58] Should we not remember Aristophanes' mocking allegation against Euripides that he invents new gods (*Frogs* 888–91)? On the ambiguous meaning inherent in the etymology of the name 'thoroughly divine' or 'of dubious divinity', see Dobrov (1997*a*: 45).

[59] The play implies the use of *spondai* both in its figural meaning (vehicle) 'treaties' and in its literal/etymological meaning 'libation' and then in the metonymical meaning that 'libation' can of course take as 'wine'. It is however improper to speak of literalization, since the figural meaning never fully effaces the other shades, as it is evident in this case. See Lacan (1966: 507): 'The creative spark of metaphor flashes between two signifiers, one of which has taken the place of the other in the signifying chain, the occulted signifier remaining present through its (metonymic) connection with the rest of the chain.'

[60] For the use of bowls, see Olson (2002: ad loc.).

[61] On the habitual age of wine in Greece see Olson (2002: ad loc.). The nature of the *spondai* as wine becomes insisted in the joke at 188–90 where the five-year-old wine/treaty tastes over-resinated; at 198 where their smell/flavour speaks to the mouth; and so on.

5

What's in a Wall?

Simon Goldhill

'You can never bring in a wall. What say you, Bottom?'
...
'It is the wittiest partition that ever I heard discourse, my lord.'

Shakespeare, *A Midsummer Night's Dream*

There are few images as powerful in contemporary political consciousness as the fall of the Berlin Wall. The image is deeply evocative not merely because it heralded an extraordinary change in political order in Germany and in Europe in general, but also because it required a realignment of self-definition. Without the Cold War, without communism to fight, America and NATO needed new enemies against whom home values could be defined. Germans needed to rethink what national unity might mean in practical and ideological terms. European countries needed to articulate a new set of relations, marked still by the inheritance of the Second World War as much as by the years of the communist regimes. The remarkable scenes of joy and liberation at the dismantling of the wall (which for those outside Berlin appeared, so surprisingly, on television) developed also into political and social anxiety, as the work of finding a new sense of self in the integrated Germany proved more difficult and prolonged than had been hoped at the outset of the brave new world. Wolfgang Becker's delightful and poignant film 'Good Bye Lenin!' was a huge hit in Europe (and especially in Germany) in part at least precisely because it expressed these momentous political changes not just in familial terms but also in terms of deception

and self-deception, self-construction and the fragility of social identity. When the wall came down, the map of the self also changed.

The Berlin Wall remains a potent symbol of man's ability—or
desperate need—to construct boundaries that organize the world
into self-defining antitheses. Language may be a machine for organ-
izing reality, as Plato put it, but walls give an immediate and physical
instantiation of that organization. The Wall stood as an expression of
East against West, Communism against Capitalism, along with the
polarized values that structured those grand oppositions: individualism and community (whether troped as frontier can-do spirit against
the crushing machine of collectivism, or the strength of community
versus the selfish greed of bourgeois individualism), freedom/degen-
eracy versus compulsion/duty, wealth/oppression versus poverty/
equality, and so on.

There was also a history to this construction, however. Of course,
walls have always been used to defend oneself against the outside (in
all senses). But this is never a merely physical construction. So for
Thucydides, walled cities are the sign of man's emergence into political civilization from nomadic barbarism.[1] Our investment in the
myth of the wall as a triumph of civilization against the nomadic is
nowhere clearer than with the Great Wall of China.[2] It is still a myth
devoutly upheld that this wondrous construction was first built in
the third century BCE by Shih Huang Ti, the great ruler who brought
together the warring kingdoms of China into a single, centralized
Empire. The Wall he established, the myth insists, continued to be
repaired and extended, and acted as a military barrier that prevented
the barbarians of the north from coming into contact with the
civilization of China. The Wall we see today is a monument of
an unbroken tradition that defines the conceptual and physical
boundaries of China over the centuries, stretching back in time as
it stretches over the mountains. So, we are repeatedly told, it is the
one man-made object that can be seen from space.

In fact, there is almost nothing of the third-century wall to be seen.
The wall we see today was built largely in the sixteenth century by the

---

[1] See Garlan (1968: 255) 'la notion d'enceinte est inseparable du concept de cité'.
[2] My remarks on the Great Wall follow in particular Waldron (1990). For a
particularly charming collection of the myths, see the travelogue of Geil (1909).

Ming dynasty, and follows a significantly different route from earlier walls; there were several walls built over the centuries, each following different routes; the fragments of the Great Wall are not continuous; the Monguls who ruled before the Ming, and the Manchu who ruled after the Ming, were both dynasties of 'northern barbarians', which shows what a precarious defence work it proved; for many years in China it signified the failure of the Chinese to defend themselves, much as the Maginot line is a sign of collapsed policy in Europe. And it is certainly not possible to see the Great Wall from space (except by satellite images, by which one can see almost anything). The story that the Great Wall can be seen from the moon was started at the beginning of the twentieth century, when it could have been only a rhetorical exaggeration. Since the wall is only the width of a two-lane highway, and no higher than a single story house, a moment's thought will reveal the incredibility of the story of its immense visibility. That the myth continues to be believed so strongly is a perfect example of our investment in the powerful imagery of man's ability to construct barriers—barriers against each other, barriers over and against nature itself.

But in Germany in particular the Wall had a more specific history. The building of ghetto walls (especially in the major cities of what would be the Eastern block) was a repeated brutal strategy in the Nazi programme for the extermination of the Jews. Ghetto walls were designed by the Nazis to dehumanize their victims and separate them from what they declared to be true Germans. The language of pollution, corruption, and filth, which dehumanized those to be destroyed, was fulfilled in the horrific physical conditions enforced by the walls. To build a Wall between Germans, across Berlin, the capital city of Germany, brought with it grim echoes of Nazi building, and provoked painful questions of what it meant to divide Germans from Germans in such a way—of what the true German(y) was (to be). It is for this reason that however successful any Israeli Security Fence were to be in restricting suicide bombers, it must bring extremely unpleasant political associations with it.

The Berlin Wall is a uniquely evocative image also because in the modern nation state, obsessiveness about boundaries is not usually focused on the city, but on the state itself (for all that cities have a developed topography of centre and margins and 'zoning'). The patrolled and defended limits are between countries rather than towns, and these state boundaries are very rarely walls in a physical sense (though in the modern cityscape, houses and buildings are increasingly policed, as the mean streets are feared and celebrated in opposition to the safety or secrecy of the home or the order, corrupt or supportive, of the office). Athens of the classical period, however, was protected by its city walls, and its maritime strength was maintained by the Long Walls which connected Athens to the Piraeus.

These walls play a significant role in the conceptualization of Athens as a polis. The Long Walls turned Athens into an 'island', turning it towards the sea. The treaty which ended the Peloponnesian War was designedly humiliating to Athens because the walls were pulled down (and the fleet reduced to only twelve ships). Xenophon describes how Lysander, the Spartan commander who directed the operation, together with formerly exiled Athenians who had now returned, pulled down the walls 'to the sound of flutes and with enthusiasm, because they reckoned this day was the beginning of freedom for Greece' (*HG* 2.2.23), as if the walls were the precondition of Athenian imperialism. Whether this meant that the Athenian people generally rejoiced at the dismantling is less clear than some commentators have believed.[3] Spartans and their sympathizers are more likely to be quick to take Athens' defeat as a triumph of freedom than the Athenians themselves. The walls indeed were promptly rebuilt with the restoration of democracy, and they stood till Sulla's destruction of them in 86 BCE, when Athens became part of the Roman Empire. Yet the most famous military triumph of Athens— over the invading Persians—was won by re-imagining walls. 'Trust to the wooden walls' was the injunction of Apollo's oracle at Delphi, which was interpreted to mean that the city should be deserted, walls and all, and the future of Athens entrusted to the fleet.[4] The ideal security of walls in Athens was accompanied by the celebrated democratic boast that 'the city is the men'. The story of the Athenian citizen is constantly interwoven with the normative construction of the insider and the outsider, and the myth or ideology of the polis inevitably makes walls a charged space of definition.

---

[3] e.g. Ehrenberg (1967: 324): 'A large majority of the Athenian Assembly accepted these terms, probably with relief'.

[4] Hdt. 7.140–4, esp. 141.3 'Only the wooden wall is destined by Zeus to be undestroyed'.

This chapter looks at the use of walls as part of the discursive world of Athenian tragedy, and specifically at how two particular plays, Aeschylus' *Seven Against Thebes* and Euripides' *Phoenician Women* represent the city walls of Thebes in an interrelated but highly contrasting manner. These two plays are regularly compared because they deal with the same mythic scenario and because the Euripidean text clearly refers back to its Aeschylean predecessor. But I also choose these plays because they are works on which the honorand of this volume, Froma Zeitlin, has written so perceptively. This piece could not have been written in particular without her fine book-length treatment of the *Seven Against Thebes*, not least because *Under the Sign of the Shield*, more than any other study of this 'twice-orphaned' play,[5] brings into vivid clarity the largest questions of identity, self-definition, and social representation at work in Aeschylus' drama. As we will see, the representation of the walls of Thebes in these two plays raises questions which go well beyond any notion of 'background description' (though anyone who has studied topography in tragedy and other literature would find it hard to know what 'background description' would look like), and well beyond what might be thought an inevitable focus on walls in plays that take siege warfare as their topic. For both plays are concerned not merely with siege warfare but with fratricidal violence, with conflict between the city and the family, with tension between men and women, with the intergenerational horrors of incest and parricide—in short, as Zeitlin puts it, with the battle for stable antithesis to set against the fear of miscegenation and violence. It is in this context that walls take on their specific significance: in the Oedipal city, the boundary between inside and outside is always going to be especially charged. What is more, both plays develop their ideas against a literary tradition where Homer holds a privileged place, and where the walls of Troy provide a model for rethinking the oppositions that are so important for Greek identity.[6]

---

[5] Zeitlin (1982*b*: 15): 'an orphan twice over, for it has lost both of its predecessors in Aeschylus' Theban trilogy'—and probably its ending too.

[6] The questions I approach here are influenced by Zeitlin's work over many years. Thebes: Zeitlin (1985*a*); identity: Zeitlin (1985*b*; 1989; 1990*a*); gender: Zeitlin (1978; 1981; 1985*a*); literary tradition: Zeitlin (1981; 2001).

The action of the *Seven Against Thebes* is famously verbal. Its central scene is the description of the shield blazons of the champions of the invaders and the defenders, which takes the place of a battle narrative, or rather, which is a battle in and of representation.[7] The most hectic physical action takes place when the chorus rush in, hysterically crying in their fear, and are confronted by the city ruler, Eteocles. Presumably too his arming—usually imagined to take place on stage—and the chorus's attempt to dissuade him from his decision to fight his brother are moments of dramatically intense physical action. My concern, however, is with the topography of the play's action. For the family of Oedipus, '*where* you are' is an insistent question: οὐδ' ὁρᾶν ἵν' εἶ κακοῦ, 'Nor do you see where you are in your misery', as Sophocles' Teiresias taunts the king (*OT* 367). The crossroads in Sophocles' play is the most haunting image of the fated misrecognition of where you are and where you are going in your life—the trauma that dominates the family of Laius.

I take as my starting point this finely lapidary statement: 'Eteocles' defensive strategy, one might say, is dedicated both to preserving the integrity of the walls that protect the besieged city of Thebes and to preserving his unique singular identity'.[8] I want to follow the invitation of the 'and' in this sentence to consider the relation between the two projects of Eteocles. At one level, the relation seems clear enough. On the one hand, Eteocles does not preserve his 'unique singular identity': he lives out his father's curse and meets his doom, killing and killed by his brother. Brother to brother, warrior to warrior, killer to killer, victim to victim, they share a fate, a common end. The enemy, Polyneices, is not a monstrous, boastful giant but a member of the same family; not a foreigner but a rightful citizen; not an outsider but all too familiar. On the other hand, Eteocles' setting of champions for each gate is successful. The city is saved, and the walls are not breached at any point. The chorus's fears that the *purgoi* will not hold (234, 295, 313, 761–5; cf. 467, 797) are unfounded. It might seem, as Richard Seaford has argued, that the representative of the royal family must die in order for the polis to survive and continue.[9]

At another level, however, the relation between Eteocles' two desires is more complex. 'Preserving the integrity of the walls' is a

---

[7] See also Lissarrague in this volume (ch. 6).   [8] Zeitlin (1982*b*: 37).

[9] Seaford (1994).

happy metaphor for Eteocles' (failing) attempt to maintain his social and political identity, and the play's representation of the *purgoi* reflects this. First, it is important to note that there is no *staging* of the walls in the play: the *purgoi* and *pulai* are offstage. They are referred to repeatedly by the chorus and by other characters, and in particular the spy comes back with news of which champion is drawn up at which gate, while the messenger returns from the battlefield with news of the death of Eteocles. But there is no scene of observation from the walls and no scene of conversation on the walls. The wall is somewhere else.

This is in striking and, I think, significant contrast with the *Iliad* and the walls of Troy. The walls of Troy have a rich mythic history, which Euripides in particular exploits. The second stasimon of *Trojan Women*, a play set in the shadow of the sacked city, is sung after the harrowing scene in which Andromache discovers that her grief has not yet plumbed the depths because her son, Astyanax, is to be taken from her and thrown to his death from the walls of defeated Troy. The chorus reflect on the long history of the city and the difficult relation between its king and the gods. The great walls of the city were built by Poseidon and Apollo for king Laomedon. But he cheated them of their reward, and so they sent Telamon and Heracles to attack the city, and destroy its walls with fire. Heracles saved Hesione, Laomedon's daughter, from the flames, but was also cheated of his reward and so led a Greek expedition against the city itself and sacked it—the first destruction of Troy by Greece (*Tr.* 814–18):

> κανόνων δὲ τυκίσματα Φοίβου
> πυρὸς—πυρὸς φοίνικι πνοᾷ καθελὼν
> Τροίας ἐπόρθησε χθόνα.
> δὶς δὲ δυοῖν πιτύλοιν τείχη πέρι
> Δαρδανίδας φονία κατέλυσεν αἰχμά.

With the red blast of fire, of fire,
he destroyed the hewn stone workings of Apollo
 and sacked the land of Troy.
Twice in two battering attacks the bloody spear destroyed
the Dardanians around their walls.[10]

---

[10] This is basically the translation of Barlow (1986), who has good comments on the difficulty of this dense language.

The walls stand and fall under the protection of the gods, and the city stands and falls under the protection of its walls. A failure of reciprocity, a breach of trust, destroys the city (and we will see how important this association of trust and city walls is when we turn to Thucydides and Aeneas Tacticus later). It is not by chance that the chorus rehearses this mythic history not merely in a play which will end with another burning of the city, but also and more precisely as the hope of the city, Astyanax, Hector's son, is being thrown from the walls. His tumbling death from the city's defence images the fall of the city's future, just as the destruction of Hector and the city embodies for Hecuba the fragility of human achievements in the face of the gods' power (*Tr.* 612–13):

> ὁρῶ τὰ τῶν θεῶν, ὡς τὰ μὲν πυργοῦσ' ἄνω
> τὸ μηδὲν ὄντα, τὰ δὲ δοκοῦντ' ἀπώλεσαν.
>
> I see the work of the gods, how they build tower-high
> that which is nothing and destroy what seems strong.

The verb πυργοῦσ', 'build tower-high', designedly draws together the city walls as setting and the narrative of their rulers' collapse. The stasimon's evocation of place—Salamis, Athens, the lost baths and *gymnasia* of Troy—helps stress this pointed image. Reversal—that victors become losers—is one aggressive message of this play, which has often been taken as a telling address to the audience of imperial Athens. The focus on walls as the appearance of strength and their fall as sign of defeat may indeed be taken as prophetic for Athens.

The Sack of Troy (*Ilioupersis*)—as depicted in epic and in art in particular—is a constant background to any story of siege in the ancient world, but it is the walls of Troy as represented in the *Iliad* which form the essential intertext for Aeschylus' *Seven*. In book 3 of Homer's epic, Helen appears on the walls of Troy above the Scaean Gates (the combination of the language of *purgoi* and *pulai* is constant in each of the works I am discussing). The old men, no longer fit for war, are there gathered around Priam, 'good talkers all, like cicadas'. Priam invites Helen over to them, and at his request she gives a description of the Greek warriors ranged on the plain below (the scene usually known as the *teichoscopia*). Helen is always a disruptive force, whenever she appears, but there is no suggestion that this conversation between the woman and the man, between the brought-in

Greek and the Trojan, is a danger or a problem. Similarly, after Paris has lost the duel with Menelaus, and Aphrodite, his saviour, comes looking for Helen, the goddess finds her again πύργῳ ἐφ᾽ ὑψηλῷ, 'on a high wall-tower', this time surrounded by Trojan women (3.384). Helen appears on the walls with men or with women and without reproach. In the fifth century, it is a commonplace of male rhetoric that 'a woman should be on the inside' and not seen talking with men. But even with Helen, this moralism is not evident in the *Iliad*.

The scene between Andromache and Hector at the Scaean gate in book 6 is more spiky, and Andromache's military advice to her husband and his sharp rejoinder to her have given rise to comment since the scholia.[11] This is a highly emotive scene of husband, wife, and child, in doom-laden anticipation of the disaster of war, in a heady atmosphere of laughter through tears. Hector had gone to look for Andromache inside his house, and failed to find her there. The servants directed him to the walls, where, they say, she had rushed 'like a mad woman', because she had heard that the Trojans were suffering and the Greeks were doing well on the battlefield (382–9). Hector rushes after her and meets her as she comes down from the tower on the wall to the gate through the wall. In Euripides' *Bacchae* when the maddened women rush 'to the mountains', the very fact that they go to the wild space outside the house and the city is seen as part of their lack of control; but there is no such comment in the language of the maidservants who tell Hector where Andromache is or in his response to their information. 'Going to the walls' is not in itself a sign of improper behaviour in the *Iliad* (as it will be in Euripides' *Phoenician Women*). At the end of their long conversation, Hector does send Andromache back to the house, to take up her work at the loom inside (490–2), as 'war is a man's concern', thus reinforcing archetypal ancient gender roles. But there is no suggestion of reproof either in his search for her or in what he says: he speaks, says the narrator, 'with pity because he noticed his wife's tears mixed in her laughter', and he 'strokes her with his hand' (483–5). It is an emotionally tender conclusion.

[11] See Katz (1981). On Helen/Andromache in general see Redfield (1975), Worman (2002).

This affection will be pathetically recalled at Hector's death. Andromache sits working at the loom (where he had sent her) and when the sounds of grief come, she runs again to the wall-tower, again like a mad woman, only to see her dear husband dragged around the city (22.437–64). She throws her headdress far from her, and as many commentators have noted, the word κρήδεμνον (470) means both 'headdress' and 'battlement'. It was a gift from Aphrodite to Andromache on the day she married Hector (470–2). It is typical of Homer to invest material objects with layers of significance: the falling headdress is both the end of her marriage and, because of the death of Hector, the end of the city's chances too. (This image probably lies behind Euripides' lament for Troy in the second stasimon of *Hecuba* [910–11]: ἀπὸ δὲ στεφάναν κέκαρσαι πύργων, 'You have been shorn of your crown of towers'. 'Shorn' also invokes the cutting of women's hair and faces, during mourning, as the 'crown' recalls the headdress: again the lives of the Trojans and the standing walls are closely interwoven in densely layered imagistic language). Although *Iliad* 6 as a whole gives a picture of Hector with the different women of Troy that is absolutely central to understanding the gender discourse of the epic, there is no suggestion that the exchanges between men and women on the walls are somehow unseemly, or that the presence of the women watching the battle is morally dubious.

Eteocles in the *Seven Against Thebes*, however, does not have a wife, and his treatment of the chorus is a classic statement of male extreme dismissiveness of women. This has been particularly well analysed by Zeitlin in its mythic and political dimensions. She writes: 'Eteocles' flight from women, a refusal both of genealogy and generation, substitutes asexual autochthony for hypersexual incest, and replaces the biological mother with the symbolic mother of the collective city'[12]—though this politicized rhetoric will be undermined finally by such familial, incestuous blood ties. Above all, Eteocles sees the women as 'the enemy within', αὐτοὶ δ' ὑπ' αὐτῶν ἔνδοθεν πορθούμεθα, 'We are destroyed from within by ourselves' (194): the exclusionary boundaries are threatened with collapse by the chorus's behaviour. He wants indeed to have a separate life, to put

---

[12] Zeitlin (1982*b*: 34). This should be read alongside her fine discussion of *Hippolytus* in Zeitlin (1985*b*), and the seminal discussion of 'the race of women' in Loraux (1993: 72–110).

a wall between himself and the whole female sex: 'May I never share
an *oikos* with race of women, either in bad times or in domestic
peace!' (187–8). And he clearly echoes Hector's response to Andromache as he concludes his tirade (200–1):

μέλει γὰρ ἀνδρί, μὴ γυνὴ βουλευέτω,
τἄξωθεν· ἔνδον δ' οὖσα μὴ βλάβην τίθει.

For it is a man's concern—let no woman counsel!—
The outside. Inside is where you should be, and do no harm.

The attempt to hold the normative antithesis as a stable and rigid
polarization is clear in the verbal juxtaposition of *andri*, 'man'/ *gunê*,
'woman', and *exôthen*, 'outside'/ *endon*, 'inside', as well as in the desire
to keep the women silent on the inside while the men concern
themselves with the outside world. The rewriting of Homer also
highlights the particular extremism of Eteocles' sense of gender
relations. Not only is there no sense of familial affection and duty
in Eteocles' words, but also where Hector sent Andromache in to the
proper work of a woman in the household, Eteocles can at best hope
only that inside a woman will do no harm. Where Hector's words
were constantly infused with the longing for generational continuity,
Eteocles dismisses the very idea of shared family life. The distortions
of Eteocles are revealed in the mirror of Hector.

It is, then, a significant gesture of representational politics in this
play that there is no staging of any scene on the walls themselves.
Eteocles wants to keep the integrity of (his) boundaries, and yet is
constantly undermined by 'the enemy within'—his familial inheritance as much as the women of the chorus—much as he is challenged
(φεῦ ... 597) by the image of the 'good man' on the outside as enemy.
The extreme stance of Eteocles is matched by the refusal of the play to
let there be any exchange *on* the boundary. The wall is out there, an
object of imagination for the audience as it is an object of desire and
anxiety in the language of the characters of the play. There is no
possibility in this play of an exchange like that of Hector and
Andromache: at the wall. 'Mediation', writes Zeitlin, 'is the sustaining
fiction of the play',[13] and the representation of the wall is an integral
part of the failure of the promise of mediation. A wall of a city must,

---

[13] Zeitlin (1982*b*: 17). Bacon (1964) is important for the discussion of inside and
outside in the *Seven*, and as an influence for both Zeitlin (1982*b*) and Foley (1985).

of course, both be a defensive barrier, and allow transition for its citizens. But for Eteocles, so avid in the construction and defence of his walls, a liminal space for exchange on the walls is an especially difficult arena. It is as if Eteocles' failing desperation to keep the outside and the inside apart makes the wall itself a no-go area.

This strategy of representation both illumines and is illumined by Euripides' *Phoenician Women*, a play which works through the *Seven Against Thebes* at so many levels.[14] The *Phoenician Women*, typically for later Euripides, plays intricate and varied games with literary tradition. The walls of Thebes become part of this rewriting from the first scene. Following from Jocasta's blithely direct opening account of incest (from Homer to Sophocles her suicide becomes an expectation, apparently refused here), the old servant enters above the house on the walkway, preparing the way for Antigone's entrance. Here, immediately, we have a representation of the walls on stage, and a scene take place on them.

The servant stresses that Antigone is a *parthenos*, a young girl of marriageable age, and that her appearance needs careful overseeing. He points out that her mother has given permission for her to leave the confines of the house (89–90), and that he must check to see that no citizen is on the wall there (92–3), because if she were seen in public it would lead to reproach both for him as a servant and for her as a noble woman (94–5). In the same spirit he will return her inside at the end of the scene (193–201), as he hears the chorus approach. He has also been to the enemy camp itself, he tells us, as an intermediary between the brothers: 'from here to there, and to here in turn from him', ἐνθένδ' ἐκεῖσε δεῦρό τ' αὖ κείνου πάρα, a line strikingly made almost entirely of pronominal adverbs and prepositions, all relative motion. Not only is the scene set on the wall, but also the boundary is one criss-crossed by transition.

Where in the *Seven Against Thebes*, the spy brought essential information from the enemies' camp to his general, here we have a casual remark from an old man to a young girl. And as Foley nicely puts it: 'Eteocles' stress on the internal safety of the city and the proper role of women in time of war is reduced to a fussy concern over the

---

[14] See especially Foley (1985), Goff (1988), Zeitlin (1994).

niceties of Athenian morality'.[15] Indeed, where Eteocles had been deeply vexed by the threat of 'the enemy within', the old servant responds to Antigone's worry about whether the gates are properly secured[16] with, 'Don't worry. The city is safe on inside matters at any rate' (117 τά γ' ἔνδον), a line invested with irony by the unfolding events of the family and especially by the conclusion of the play. Where Homer had old Priam and Helen look out over the enemy and name the opposition leaders, Euripides has a young and inexperienced girl who cannot evaluate what she sees, or name it, and an old man who gives the identification of these heroes of myth. (As in Euripides' *Electra*, it is an old man who speaks for the inherited weight of literary tradition, as Euripides the modernist plays with it.) This is a very Euripidean image, designed to engage and disconcert an audience (and it would certainly vex the Aeschylean Eteocles!): looking over the wall, and all around for stray citizens, careful about being seen and about seeing, the young girl and old man, free and slave, chatting 'inconsequentially' (as the hypothesis worries), not quite like Andromache and Hector, nor quite like Priam and Helen. It is, I would suggest, not by chance that this scene takes place on the wall, the boundary and place of crossing and protection.

The first scene also drastically redrafts our expectations from the *Seven*. In Aeschylus' version Polyneices had on his shield the figure of Justice who promised that she would lead him home and that he would hold the city once again (647–8), but Eteocles keeps him outside the city. In Euripides' drama, Polyneices enters, under truce, and, as his opening words emphasize, he is doing precisely what his literary predecessor could not (261–2):

> τὰ μὲν πυλωρῶν κλῇθρά μ' εἰσεδέξατο
> δι' εὐπετείας τειχέων ἔσω μολεῖν.

> The bolts of the gatekeepers have admitted me
> With ease to come inside the walls.

The walls and gates allow transition. Polyneices is inside, and 'brings within the walls the *dikê* he claimed on his shield in the *Seven*'.[17] For

---

[15] Foley (1985: 117). On characters such as the old man see further Taplin in this volume (ch. 8).

[16] The text of line 114 is unclear, though not the general sense.

[17] Foley (1985: 120).

Euripides, the enemy within brings an *agôn* about justice. Remarkably, Polyneices has a good case. Eteocles' self-defence marks him as a power-hungry tyrant, who simply reneged on the deal with his brother to share the throne. The Aeschylean Eteocles spoke as the representative of the city and honoured king; Eteocles in Euripides is rash, aggressive, and committed to his own self-aggrandizement. It is far from clear who the enemy of the city is, who its rightful protector.

The second scene also distances Euripides' Eteocles from his Aeschylean counterpart: he has to be told by Creon to set seven champions at the gates; he does not name them, because it would take too long; he asks Creon to make sure Antigone marries Haemon (bypassing Oedipus, her father, but perhaps also cuing Sophocles); he suggests that Creon meet with the prophet Teiresias (because he had previously insulted the skill of prophecy). Most importantly, he will not take up a gate himself, and therefore resists the opportunity for an Aeschylean showdown with his brother.[18] The logic that tied Eteocles to the seventh gate and to the protection of the wall is here fragmented.

The third scene, however, is perhaps the most surprising of all. Teiresias informs Creon and Menoeceus, his son, that the city can be saved only if the boy is sacrificed for it. Creon is shocked and despairing and hurries to smuggle Menoeceus out of the city. Menoeceus agrees to the plan, but, when his father leaves, indicates to the chorus that he actually is all too prepared to die for the state—and at the beginning of the next scene the messenger describes his self-sacrifice. This episode appears to be an invention of Euripides and it has prompted some fine discussion of its 'ritual irony'.[19] It clearly goes to the heart of the issue of how the values of the family and the values of the polis can come into conflict. Creon's immediate disregard for the survival of the city, after his urgent advice to the king in the previous scene, stands in painful tension with the clarity of Menoeceus' idealism, which states in bald terms the ideology of a citizen's commitment to the polis.

For the sake of my argument here, I have only two brief interrelated points that I want to make on what is a complex scene.

---

[18] This is well discussed by Foley (1985: 123–6) and I will not rehearse her analysis here.

[19] Especially Foley (1985).

The first is familiar but needs mention as a starting point. Teiresias indicates that the sacrifice of Menoeceus is necessary for the safety of the city—but where does this leave the battle between the troops and the fratricidal duel that follow Menoeceus' death? With prophecy, neither clarity nor Aristotelian logic is a requirement, but the introduction of the Menoeceus story by Euripides opens a gap between the actions of the brothers and the outcome for Thebes. Who preserves the integrity of the walls and how? Whose death saves the city? The strange detail, revealed by Menoeceus himself, that he was suckled by Jocasta (987), draws the three sons together in an uneasy parallelism. Which child is to count?

From what I have said so far, it should be no surprise—and this is my second point—that this confusing gesture of Menoeceus should take place on the walls. Here is how he announces his decision to the chorus (1009–12):

> ἀλλ' εἶμι καὶ στὰς ἐξ ἐπαλξέων ἄκρων
> σφάξας ἐμαυτὸν σηκὸν ἐς μελαμβαθῆ
> δράκοντος, ἔνθ' ὁ μάντις ἐξηγήσατο,
> ἐλευθερώσω γαῖαν.

> Rather, I shall go and stand on the topmost battlement,
> And sacrifice myself, into the black-depthed lair
> Of the dragon, at the spot which the seer expounded,
> And thus free the land.

The short announcement by the messenger of Menoeceus' self-slaughter echoes this plan, and also emphasizes the spot (1090–2):

> ἐπεὶ Κρέοντος παῖς ὁ γῆς ὑπερθανὼν
> πύργων ἐπ' ἄκρων στὰς μελάνδετον ξίφος
> λαιμῶν διῆκε τῇδε γῇ σωτήριον . . .

> When Creon's son, who died for the land, stood
> On the topmost tower and plunged the black-bound sword
> Into his throat, and became the saviour of this land . . .

The repetitions (στάς, ἄκρων, μελαν-, γῆ, γαῖα) and the parallel terms (ἐπαλξέων/πύργων, ἐλευθερώσω/σωτήριον) link the two passages closely. The act which is to save the city according to Teiresias, is not fratricidal murder but a self-sacrifice. The vocabulary of murder in Greek, which overlaps killing kin and killing oneself (e.g. αὐτόχειρ), further complicates the difficult parallelism between Polyneices/Eteocles and Menoeceus as fighters for Thebes.[20] Where Aeschylus' *Seven Against Thebes* neither staged the wall nor allowed any exchange to take place on it, Euripides' *Phoenician Women* offers an act of saving the city that takes place *on the wall*. The city's saviour turns out to be neither brother (individually or collectively) but their mother's brother's son. As with Antigone's *teichoscopia*, or Polyneices' entrance into the city, the wall is the site for the scenes which fit least comfortably into the literary tradition.

The response of Jocasta to the news of the first battle and the impending duel is to call out Antigone. The girl is again nervous of leaving the maidens' quarters (1275), and ashamed to appear before the army (1276). But Jocasta insists: they must take up the space between the two brothers, they must go immediately ἐς μεταίχμιον, 'to the space between the armies' to stop the duel. This is indeed the space where the two brothers will fight, μέσον μεταίχμιον, 'the middle of the space between the two armies' (1361). Μεταίχμιον is a word which also has a metaphorical usage for anything that falls between two polarities, the grey space between black and white, the problematic overlap of categories.[21] Eteocles in Aeschylus' *Seven Against Thebes* used the word in a phrase that has bothered commentators, when he called for obedience from 'men, women and whatever is in between', ἀνὴρ γυνή τε χὤ τι τῶν μεταιχμίων (197). The scholiast suggests that he speaks in this apparently illogical way because of his anger; Rose warns us against thinking in a 'literal minded' way of 'hermaphrodites or eunuchs'; but Lupas and Petre suggest that although anger may be a good enough reason to explain the apparent difficulty, the crimes of Laius against Chrysippus or the 'virile' Jocasta may also be hinted at.[22] The 'in between', however, as we have seen, is the threat to the strong polarity of inside and outside that the Aeschylean Eteocles struggles to maintain. In Euripides, however, 'the middle space' is where the action is hottest.

---

[20] I have learnt here greatly from my graduate student Matthew Hiscock and his work on suicide.

[21] See e.g. A. *Ch.* 63 (with Garvie [1986] ad loc.); Arist. *PA* 3.1426. Later, see *AP* 9.597.3; [Lucian] 49.21, and cf. the discussion of Martin in this volume.

[22] Rose (1957: 1.177 ad loc.); Lupas and Petre (1981: 76 ad loc.).

Jocasta in the *Phoenician Women* arrives too late in the middle space. Her sons have already mortally wounded each other. She will come not between them, but kills herself over them. The mess of bodies does not allow separation: the two armies both claim victory, and it is only the fact that the Thebans are still sitting on their shields that allows them to rout the Argives and remove the threat of siege from the city. Yet even with this third fight over Thebes this most challenging of plays is not over. In the final scenes, Oedipus, previously shut up inside his house inside the city, comes out, only to be banished from the city—to save it—by Creon. This figure from inside the city walls must be expelled, and it is his *exodos* with which the play closes. He is accompanied by Antigone, who has refused marriage with Creon's son and who has expressed her outrage at Creon's treatment of Polyneices' corpse. The play ends by opening out beyond the walls of Thebes towards Cithairon, and farther still towards Colonus, where Oedipus will die in another *purgos* ('What tower of Attica will receive you?' 'Holy Colonus...' [1706–7]). Oedipus' place remains to be found.[23]

The *Phoenician Women* is an extraordinary play, full of 'redundancies and inconsistencies' which appear 'to be part of a deliberate and comprehensive iconoclastic strategy'.[24] It is generically challenging, 'a bold experiment in crossing theatrical forms with epic techniques'.[25] Its narrative resists simple ordering: its 'structural equipoise' is undercut by 'suspense', 'surprise', 'challenging piquancy', 'horror', 'ambivalence', and the 'hackneyed'.[26] It brings together the narratives of the family of Oedipus and the family of Creon in a novel mythic melange. The representation of the walls of Thebes is a crucial part of

[23] One might very tentatively suggest that the decision to bury Eteocles and not to bury Polyneices may resonate against a ritual practice noted by Pausanias and explored briefly by modern archaeologists (though it is not a practice attested in Athens). Aetolus, son of Oxylus, was buried in Elis right in the gate that led to Olympia and the shrine of Zeus. This was because an oracle told his parents (before whom he died) to bury him 'neither inside nor outside the city' (Paus. 5.4.4). He received offerings there as a hero. Similarly, Bérard says that there is a series of *hêrôa* (hero shrines) set in the walls of towns to provide supernatural defence for the gates in particular (Bérard 1970: 70). The hero as defender of the wall, living on the boundary, is an idea which may at any rate help focus the representation of Eteocles and the wall in both plays.

[24] Foley (1985: 132).   [25] Zeitlin (1994: 172).

[26] Craik (1988: 43, 41, 42).

the staging of this strange and wonderful play. The walls are constructed through both Homer's Troy and Aeschylus' Thebes. In contrast to Aeschylus, where the absent wall stands as an image for the strong drive towards separation, the boundary between inside and outside, the walls in Euripides are the stage for exchange, discussion, and heroic displays. Where the firm boundary of the wall in Aeschylus' drama was integral to Eteocles' rhetoric of inside and outside, with its worry of the 'enemy within' and the 'good man' (Amphiaraus) outside, Euripides' walls let the enemy from outside in, and send the women outside, to a 'middle place' between the armies. The heroism of Menoeceus—so difficult to place in the play's ideological ironies—takes place neither inside nor outside but on the walls; a gesture aimed not at the enemy outside, but, like so many actions of the Oedipal family, at oneself, but with huge implications for the safety of the whole polis. Even at the end of the play, the action turns to look for another *purgos* and to expel a former saving king beyond the walls. For Euripides, his different sense of social and political identity, his ironic articulation of the clash of mythic tradition and political rhetoric, find a significant expression in his different representation of the walls of the city. In each drama, the play's discursive work and its setting are mutually implicative.

At the same time, this game of boundaries is set against the Homeric paradigm. Eteocles in Aeschylus cannot be Hector, and Hector's remarks on gender roles turn into a passionate and extreme statement of separation. In Euripides, the Homeric resource is fragmented and disseminated: Polyneices has a wife, but before death speaks yearningly with his mother; Eteocles although taking part in the *agôn* with his brother and mother, barely addresses a word to the chorus and has no farewell scene. The *teichoscopia* inverts and plays with its Homeric model. The great walls of Troy are echoed, but in distant and fractured sounds.

Thucydides, great historian of war and the destruction of cities, may help us understand the context for Euripides' writing. Walls are 'a preoccupation' of Thucydides'.[27] In the Archaeology, they are seen first as a sign of the emergence of the civilization of the polis. But at the same time, the fact that Sparta did not have walls (it did not go

---

[27] Hornblower (1996: 127).

through the process of *sunoikismos* which made Athens a polis) does not seem to be negatively represented. It is perhaps a sign of the special status of Sparta, its 'unusualness' (as well as part of the contrast between Sparta and Athens).[28] But it is the representation of the walls of Athens which is especially striking. Thucydides spends five long chapters describing the construction of the city walls (1.89–93) and a further chapter on the Long Walls (1.107). The very length of such a description is emphatic in itself, but his narrative also lets us see vividly the politics of the construction.

The Spartans got wind of the plan to construct the walls and, fearing Athens' growing power, sent an embassy to suggest not only that the Athenians should not build their walls, but also that they should join the Spartans in destroying all such fortifications outside the Peloponnese. Their express reasoning was that such fortified cities would give the invading Persians strong bases for their operations (as they had used Thebes the last time). The Peloponnese would suffice as a place of refuge and a place from which to attack. But, Thucydides makes explicit, they did not make clear their real intention and their suspicion (τὸ βουλόμενον καὶ ὕποπτον, 1.90.2). Themistocles, ever resourceful, had the Athenians send them home with the promise of an immediate delegation to discuss the points raised. He then persuaded the Athenians to send him to Sparta as an ambassador while they quickly started to build the walls. He delayed the Spartans until it was too late and the walls were built. The walls were fully a city project (1.90.3):

τειχίζειν δὲ πάντας πανδημεὶ τοὺς ἐν τῇ πόλει [καὶ αὐτοὺς καὶ γυναῖκας καὶ παῖδας], φειδομένους μήτε ἰδίου μήτε δημοσίου οἰκοδομήματος ὅθεν τις ὠφελία ἔσται ἐς τὸ ἔργον, ἀλλὰ καθαιροῦντας πάντα.

Everybody in the city, the whole community, built the walls, sparing neither private nor public dwelling which might be of some use for the project; they demolished everything.

Thucydides strongly underlines the collective desire and the collective work of the city to build its walls: personal property and the property of the state were together put to a unified aim. The walls remain a memorial of that moment of zeal: 'In this way the Athenians

---

[28] Hornblower (1991: 35).

built their walls for the city in a short time. And still even today it is clear that the building was completed with real speed (κατὰ σπουδήν): the foundations are made of different sorts of stone, sometimes ill-fitting, but laid just as each came; there are many *stelai* from tombs, and sculpted stones built in' (1.93.1–2). The walls become a monument to Athens' collective effort and Themistocles' cunning leadership: the phrase ἔτι καὶ νῦν, 'still even today', the sign of aetiology and cultural inheritance, makes these fortifications, like so much in Thucydides' account of Athens' fall, a sign of potential, shadowed by destruction to come. As in the case of Berlin, a wall comes to mean much more than a divide or a defence.

This collective zeal is rapidly contrasted with the politics of building the Long Walls. In the early skirmishes of the war, Spartan military plans were influenced, Thucydides notes, because 'some Athenian men were secretly negotiating with them, in the hope both of destroying the democracy and of stopping the Long Walls from being built', ἐλπίσαντες δῆμόν τε καταπαύσειν καὶ τὰ μακρὰ τείχη οἰκοδομούμενα (1.107.4). This telling expression on the one hand indicates the presence of dissent within Athens, a non-democratic party aimed at the destruction of the *politeia* and its project of the Long Walls; on the other hand, it also connects the Long Walls with democracy. This is the background with which to read Xenophon's brief description of the destruction of the Long Walls after Athens' final defeat (which I cited at the beginning of this chapter). The Athenians in their turn send out their troops to battle because 'they also had some suspicion of the plot to overthrow democracy', καί τι καὶ τοῦ δήμου καταλύσεως ὑποψίᾳ (1.107.6). If building the walls of the city needed the stratagems of Themistocles and a collective effort, building the Long Walls is marked by internal division and suspicion.

Suspicion is a key note of Aeneas Tacticus' fourth-century discussion of city walls. As he sums up the worry of watching citizens with lights at night, διὸ δεῖ πάντα τὰ τοιαῦτα ὑποπτεύειν, 'Accordingly, everything like this must be a source of suspicion' (10.26). Loyal men who are happy with the current state of things are πρὸς τὰς τῶν ἄλλων ἐπιβουλὰς ... ἀντ' ἀκροπόλεως, 'the equivalent of an acropolis against the plots of others' (1.6). He instructs a commander what to do if citizens 'suspect one another', ἐν ὑποψίᾳ πρὸς ἀλλήλους (3.3), and how to organize his troops accordingly. Similarly (17.1) he describes the city which lacks *homonoia*, 'unity', and is full of 'mutual suspicions', and how one must keep a careful eye on possible plots (11) and how proclamations can be used (10.3) to deter plotters. He lists tricks to get into a besieged city (4) and devices of untrustworthy gatekeepers (18). Gates and doors and walls are where the greatest caution about trickery and plotting is to be exercised. Exiles are a particular fear (10.5–7), and no private citizen should be allowed up on to the walls for fear of treachery (3.3; 22.19)—remarks which may be left to echo with Euripides' *Phoenician Women*. Where Thucydides shows us a symbolic politics of Athens' walls, Aeneas provides a textbook for protecting city walls, which shows why suspicion, exile, secret entrance to the city, concealed negotiations, and violent plots join political idealism in the thematic texture of Euripides' writing—and why walls are the proper theatrical space for such a drama.

Euripides' walls, then, are certainly built on literary foundations. As ever, he works back through Aeschylus and Homer in the construction of a meaningful setting for his drama. In so doing, he makes the city walls part of his discussion of identity and the relation between tradition and political behaviour. Just as *Trojan Women* makes the transit camp a significant setting for a play about reversal of fortune and shifting commitments, or *Electra* makes the rural farm part of its discursive world, so here the walls of Thebes become a significant landscape for action. Euripides (like Froma Zeitlin) loves to explore boundaries and boundary-crossing. In the *Phoenician Women*, walls make a good setting for that exploration. This representation speaks closely to the symbolic politics of Athens, much as the language of self-sacrifice and autochthony speaks to the political rhetoric of Athens. For Athens, like Berlin, the building, crossing, and destruction of city walls establishes the political self. In the divided world of Athens at war, Euripides' dramatic work is, as ever, exploring and animating the political imagination.

III

Drama and Visualization: The Images of Tragedy and Myth

6

Looking at Shield Devices: Tragedy and Vase Painting

François Lissarrague

The great shield scene in Aeschylus' *Seven against Thebes* constitutes an extraordinary interpretative system, between riddle and oracle, whose rich complexity and semantic depth have been shown by Froma Zeitlin in her seminal book on the subject.[1]

The play, first performed in 467 BCE, won first prize and the long central shield scene must have made a great impression. Euripides recalls it in order to negate it in the *Phoenician Women*; it is also exploited by Aristophanes in the *Frogs*, to make fun of Aeschylus and his taste for compound words and devices on shields.[2]

Froma has given a masterly analysis of the way in which these shield descriptions constituted a system and corresponded with each other on many different levels, showing the relationship between the shield and its bearer, between the attacker and the defender, and between the shields themselves, on an increasing scale, in groups of two or three. She has also demonstrated a remarkable poetic system, predictive and interpretative at the same time, with no counterpart elsewhere in the tragic corpus as we know it, resting on the verbal descriptions given to Eteocles by the Messenger, and the former's successive interpretations of them. In this long scene the spectator does not see these shields; only the power of ecphrasis permits such a set of images.

---

[1] Zeitlin (1982*b*).   [2] E. *Ph.* 751; Ar. *Frogs* 928–30.

Pierre Vidal-Naquet has clearly seen that this shield system was
organized like a temple pediment and that recognition of such a
structure was linked to the plastic and visual experience drawn on
in archaic sculpture, with its effects of accretion, splitting, and
symmetry.[3]

I should like here to honour Froma, with whom I have so often
had the pleasure of discussing images, in particular on Attic vases, by
pursuing this type of comparison. I wish to analyse a small group of
portrayals of shields and attempt to show that Aeschylus did not
start from scratch, but that his experience and visual education
supplement—and surpass—the potters' work at the beginning of
the fifth century BCE.[4]

Let us begin with a psykter attributed to Oltos, *c*.510 BCE
(Fig. 6.1a and b).[5] Six hoplites in helmet and breastplate, with
spear and greaves, are riding dolphins; in front of each face we read
the same inscription *ΕΠΙ ΔΕΛΦΙΝΟΣ*, describing their posture;
the repetition suggests a chorus, even though there is no musician in
the image. Together, they form an unending circle of horsemen. This
circle is perfectly adapted to the shape of the vessel, but also matches
the circle of drinkers grouped round this psykter, which would be
plunged into a crater in order to cool the wine for the symposium.
The motifs on the shields are all different and belong to two distinct
systems. Three are circular motifs of traditional type: a threefold
animal with wings (griffin, lion, horse), a threefold leg, a wheel
(made of four dolphins). The other three are vessels and relate to
the symposium: a volute crater, a cup, a kantharos. Each series of
devices express a specific dimension: either the circularity of their
ride and speed, symbolized by the legs, the wheel, and the wings;
or the symposiastic circle, symbolized by the banquet vessels. These
self-referential signs constitute a system on a double plane, of

---

[3] Vidal-Naquet (1988: 273–300).

[4] This brief essay is part of a work in progress on the aesthetics of armour, in
particular of shield devices. The large number of representations of these has probably held back a general study. Beyond the little book by Chase (1979), there is an
unpublished dissertation by Vaerst (1980). See Phillip (2004: esp. ch. 2, 62–157). See
too, on the specific theme of satyrs, Paleothodoros (2001).

[5] New York, Schimmel donation; cf. Lissarrague (1987: fig. 88, pp. 112–13).

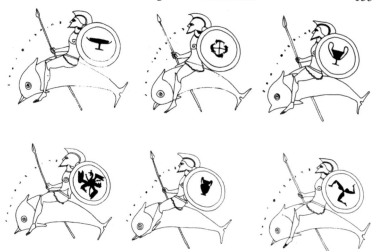

Fig. 6.1a and b Drawings after a red-figure psykter attributed to Oltos, showing hoplites with shields. Attic, *c.*510 BCE.

battle and banquet, switching between them so as to enliven the passage from war to feasting. Amusingly, and with undeniably skilled draughtsmanship, Oltos inserts into the image a *mise en abyme* repeating the semantic content of the knights on dolphins. The change of scale and pictorial technique on the shields—from red-figure to silhouette—produces, as it were, a comment in miniature on the overall scene.

There is an analogous effect on an unfortunately fragmentary cup attributed to Macron (Fig. 6.2).[6] On the front (the worse-preserved side) Ajax and Achilles, squatting before a pedestal, are intent on a board game, under the eyes of Athena.[7] The goddess's shield is adorned with a wide gorgoneion of traditional type, repeating the small gorgoneion on her aegis. The more interesting scene for our purpose is on the back. Round the two heroes absorbed in their game, a series of hoplites throw themselves into battle in answer to the signal given by the hoplite with a trumpet standing behind Ajax.

---

[6] Florence 3929 (Appendix no. 17); Beazley *ARV*² 460/15; Hartwig (1893: pl. 28); Kunisch (1997: pl. 53).

[7] On this theme see Mommsen (1980) and *LIMC* s.v. 'Achilleus'.

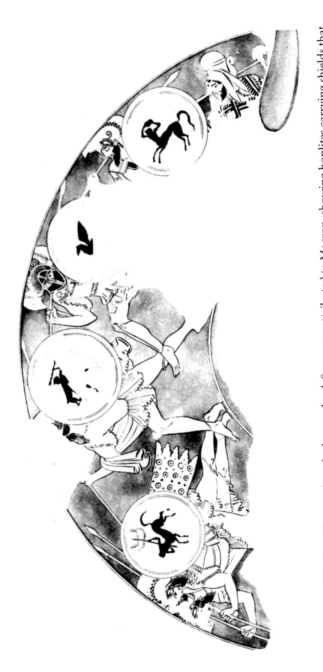

Fig. 6.2 Drawing from the exterior of a damaged red-figure cup attributed to Macron, showing hoplites carrying shields that together depict a black-figure centauromachy with Heracles. Attic, c.490 BCE.

These warriors carry shields with matching devices: from right to left a centaur, a Pegasus,[8] a Heracles brandishing his club, and another centaur. The four shields together display Heracles in a centauromachy superimposed on the war for Troy. The third shield, with Pegasus, seems incongruous from the narrative point of view, as does its bearer's face, which is seen front-on. However, from the formal point of view this device is perfectly in place: Pegasus the winged horse echoes the image of the centaur.[9] The frontal view of the warrior and the Pegasus on his shield in their turn echo the Gorgon, which gave birth to Pegasus and is nearly always seen frontally. Thus the interplay of the shields splits the image and matches up the signs. On one plane, in silhouette, a centauromachy spreading from shield to shield, like an additional episode on the Achaeans' path to Troy.

The shield motifs to be found on Attic vases are not always matched by archaeologically attested real devices. They are possible and plausible, in conformity with the logic of 'traditional devices' (to adopt an expression of Plutarch[10]), but sometimes go beyond those themes—especially in red-figure—to exploit visual strategies appropriate to the pictorial context of drinking vessels, as we have seen in the case of Oltos' psykter. Just as we cannot take the shields described by Aeschylus at face value, so we cannot see in every shield on a vase direct evidence documenting the archaeology of shields. Very early painters exploited the graphic possibilities made available by images framed within the image. This is not the place to multiply examples; I shall confine myself to the centaur motif, which has limited distribution but suffices to give a good idea of the wealth of this repertoire.[11]

---

[8] Completed by a fragment in New York, MMA 1972.70.1.

[9] There is a similar echo on a London crater attributed to Myson (Appendix no. 9): Acamas has a shield with a red-figure Pegasus making a pendant to Demophon, which has a centaur in black silhouette. To the interplay of hybrids is added the colour contrast of black and red.

[10] Plu. *Alc.* 16, on Alcibiades' eccentricity in commissioning a shield with Eros as its device, thus changing register from war to love. Cf. Ath. 12.534e, which emphasizes his wish to pass for καλός.

[11] See Appendix for the (probably incomplete) list of centaur devices I have been able to collect.

The oldest example is on an amphora by the Amasis Painter that on one side shows Poseidon, Ares, and Hermes.[12] Ares' shield has an incised image of a centaur brandishing a tree; perhaps the violence of this hybrid seemed to match that of the warrior god. In any case the motif is taken up by the Cleophrades Painter[13] on a fragmentary cup featuring Heracles defeating the Amazons (Fig. 6.3).[14] Against the hero, who is preparing to finish off his fallen adversary, another Amazon advances, brandishing a lance. On her shield, the motif of the centaur brandishing a tree repeats her movement. But at the same time there is interference between the two figurative planes, that of the encompassing image and that of the image encompassed, for the impression is given that Heracles is also fighting against the centaur. Two temporally separated episodes are thus presented simultaneously to the viewer: if the Amazon takes on the centaur's violence,[15] she will suffer the same fate. The painter has chosen a motif that functions at the same time as a pictorial echo and as a badge of identity that places the Amazon on the side of savagery.

More violence on a cup attributed to Macron (Fig. 6.4),[16] showing the youthful Troilus put to death by Achilles. To the right, a Trojan in oriental costume departs in terror. Troilus' horse has fallen and the young man is facing us. Achilles leans forward in order to drive his spear more forcefully into his victim's neck. Achilles' rage is echoed by the movement of the centaur on his shield, just as in a sense Troilus and his horse, brought down like his master, together suggest a centaur. The enclosed and receiving images thus correspond to each other across planes, but we can never foresee automatically the form this interplay of images within images will take, or establish

[12] London B 191; Beazley *ABV* 152/24; Von Bothmer (1985: no. 22, p. 123).

[13] We do not know the Cleophrades Painter's identity; he owes his name to the potter Cleophrades, son of Amasis. This suggests a possible route for transmission of the motif, as Von Bothmer (1985: 124) notes.

[14] Paris, Bibliothèque Nationale, Cabinet des Médailles 535 (Appendix no. 7); Beazley *ARV*^{2} 191/103; I use the drawing at Pfuhl (1923: fig. 371), based on the 'tolerable' drawing made for the duc de Luynes). For more detail on the state of the vase, see Beazley (1974: pls. 11–12 and pp. 9–10).

[15] Another Amazon, by the same painter, bears a shield also featuring a centaur: Louvre crater, G 166 (Appendix no. 6).

[16] Palermo V 659 (Appendix no. 18). I use the drawing by Hartwig (1893: 539, fig. 63b): the shield motif is completed from that on the medallion of the same cup (good photograph in Kunisch 1997: pl. 3).

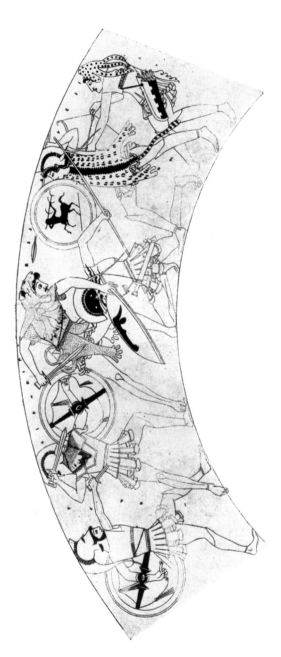

Fig. 6.3 Drawing from the exterior of a damaged red-figure cup attributed to the Cleophrades Painter, showing Heracles fighting the Amazons. Attic, c.500 BCE.

Fig. 6.4 Drawing from the exterior of a red-figure cup attributed to Macron, showing Achilles killing Troilus. Attic, *c.*490 BCE.

mechanically which device matches which figure. The list (given in the Appendix) of all shields bearing a centaur device clearly shows the range of persons with whom it is associated: Athena or Ares, Cycnus or Achilles, Demophon, Amazons, and (more often) anonymous hoplites. There is no necessary connection that imposes one personage rather than another. That is probably the charm of these devices on vases: the varied and open character of combinations that offer surprises at every turn.

On a pelike attributed to the Harrow Painter (Fig. 6.5)[17] a warrior stands before an altar flanked by a palm tree. There is no inscription to identify him, but the device on his shield is a centaur playing a *barbiton*. This musical figure is in contrast with the other centaurs' usual violence; it is probably Chiron, which at once invites us to name the hoplite. It might be Achilles, who as everyone knows was educated by the good centaur Chiron. Here the device refers to the bearer's previous history and constructs as it were a biography of the hero.

---

17 London, market; Appendix no. 12. Cf. *LIMC* s.v. Achilleus 832, pl. 138.

Fig. 6.5 Red-figure pelike attributed to the Harrow Painter, showing a warrior with a shield whose device is a centaur playing a barbiton. Attic, *c*.470 BCE.

Another remarkable case of a centaur appears on a column crater attributed to the Cleveland Painter (Fig. 6.6)[18]. This time the subject is a battle against centaurs. The hero Caeneus, who is almost invulnerable, can be killed only if he is forced into the earth, which is what the three centaurs attacking him with trees and rocks attempt to do. On his shield, in silhouette, can be seen a centaur brandishing a tree, a mirror image of the left-hand centaur's posture. Caeneus neither is a centaur—far from it—nor has a centaur's violence. The centaur's presence on his shield is explained rather by the visual effect produced than by a relation of identity between device and bearer. Nevertheless, somewhat as in the preceding example, we may see in this centaur device the presage of Caeneus' fate. The image does not recall the past but points to the future, the unlucky end of Caeneus, victim of the centaurs.

[18] Harrow T 50 (Appendix no. 19).

Fig. 6.6 Drawing from a red-figure column crater attributed to the Cleveland Painter, showing Caeneus fighting the centaurs. Attic, c.470 BCE.

Some years earlier, portraying the same theme on a vase of the same shape, the Pan Painter, to whom this crater is attributed (Fig. 6.7),[19] chose different motifs. Caeneus' shield is seen in profile and the tripod depicted on it, since the body is buried up to the waist, gives the appearance of resting on the ground. Other similar effects may be observed: to the left of the scene a naked warrior, turned left in attack towards the continuation on the other side of the vase, carries a shield seen in profile. Only half the device is visible: the hindquarters of a quadruped that might equally well be a horse or a centaur; the warrior himself is positioned in front of a centaur, so that the superimposition of their two bodies also produces an effect of hybridity, as if, on the first plane, he were himself a centaur. In this complex superimposition of mingled planes, bodies and categories are both conflated: Caeneus' bisexuality, the centaurs' hybridity are on a par with the half-horse on the shield.

Fig. 6.7 Red-figure column crater attributed to the Pan Painter, showing Caeneus fighting the centaurs. Attic, *c*.470 BCE.

[19] London E 473, Appendix no. 21.

These few examples of the centaur motif are far from exhausting the question as a whole, but reveal some of the main lines of a semantic logic that remains open and has a great poetic potential.

I should like to conclude by suggesting that Aeschylus, in his visual experience, may have encountered one or other of the *formulae* analysed above on banqueting vessels. In a certain way, with all due reservations, pottery may have inspired the tragic stage. The aim is not to draw up a classification and award the prize to the poet rather than the painter, any more than to prove the tragedy older than the painting, as has often been done—or even to reverse the relationship, as I suggest here. It is above all to underline the inter-action between these different modes of expression, these different visual experiences, theatrical and pictorial, the better to grasp the poetical and interpretative riches of Athens in the first half of the fifth century BCE.

Appendix

Centaur devices on Attic vases, all red-figure except nos. 1 and 2, which are black-figure. This list is probably not complete. I give in square brackets at the end of each entry the identity of the shield bearer.

1. Warsaw 198605. Panathenaic amphora. Painter of the Warsaw panathenaic; Para 127/2 [Athena].
2. London, British Museum B 19. Amphora. Amasis Painter; *ABV* 152/24 [Ares].
3. London, market. Cup. Ambrosius Painter. Sotheby 14/12/1995 no. 84 [Cycnus].
4. Basle, market. Cup. Unattributed. Münzen und Medaillen, auction 51, no. 151 [Hoplitodromos].
5. Basle, Antikenmuseum KA 424. Amphora. Cleophrades Painter; *ARV²* 183/8 [Warrior, possibly Achilles].
6. Paris, Louvre G 166 and Malibu, J. Paul Getty Museum 77.AE.11. Volute crater. Cleophrades Painter; *ARV²* 186/51 and 206/130 [Amazon].
7. Paris; BNF Cabinet des Médailles 535, 699. Cup. Cleophrades Painter; *ARV²* 191/103 [Amazon].
8. Cambridge GR 37.18. Cup. Eucharides Painter; *ARV²* 231/76 [Warrior].
9. London, British Museum E 458. Calix crater. Myson; *ARV²* 239/16 [Demophon].
10. Rome, Vatican, Astarita 428. Psykter. Myson *ARV²* 242/77 [Amazon].
11. Rome, market (Castellani). Hydria. Compared with class of Cabinet des Médailles 390; *ARV²* 255 [Giant].
12. London, market. Pelike. Harrow Painter; Sotheby's London 18/7/1985 no. 212. *LIMC* s.v. Cheiron 8, pl. 186 [Warrior, possibly Achilles].
13. London, ex Embirikos. Cup. Foundry Painter; *ARV²* 1650. Basel, Münzen und Medaillen, auction xxii, no. 159, pl. 51 [Hoplite].
14. Rome, Vatican 16583. Cup. Brygos Painter; *ARV²* 373/48 [Warrior].
15. Boston 10.195. Cup. Foundry Painter; *ARV²* 402/15 [Hoplite].
16. Münich 2640. Cup. Foundry Painter; *ARV²* 402/22 [Hoplite].
17. Florence 3929. Cup. Macron; *ARV²* 460/15 [Warrior].
18. Palermo 1480. Cup. Macron; *ARV²* 480/2 [Achilles].

19. Harrow T 50 (GW26). Column crater. Cleveland Painter; ARV^2 516/5 [Caeneus].
20. Cleveland 1978. 59. Lekythos. Painter of the Boston *Lykos kalos*; *CVA* 2 pl. 70 [Enceladus].
21. London, British Museum E 473. Column crater. Pan Painter; ARV^2 551/ 13 [Lapith (half horse)].
22. Malibu, J. Paul Getty Museum 76.AE.44. Kalpis fragment. Providence Painter; *Getty Journal* 11 (1983), 124, figs. 1–2; *LIMC* s.v. 'Helene' 245, pl. 335 [Menelas].
23. Brussels A 2317. Oinochoe. Painter of the Yale Lekythos; ARV^2 658/25 [Hoplite].
24. Berlin inv. 4498. Neck amphora. Epimedes Painter, Polygnotus Group; ARV^2 1044/3 [Theseus].

7

The Invention of the Erinyes

Françoise Frontisi-Ducroux

The story is well known: at the first performance of the *Eumenides*, the entry of the chorus of Erinyes allegedly aroused panic amongst the spectators. That is what we learn from a passage of the *Vita Aeschyli*: 'Some say that, on the appearance of the Eumenides, the scattered entry of the chorus so frightened the audience that children fainted (τὰ μὲν νήπια ἐκψῦξαι) and miscarriages took place (τὰ δὲ ἔμβρυα ἐξαμβλωθῆναι)'.

This anecdote is reported in a late work.[1] Its truth may be doubted: the presence of women, pregnant at that, in the Athenian theatre, in the middle of fifth century, gives rise to scepticism. But the authenticity of the event hardly matters. The essential feature is the conceivable and plausible part: the Erinyes' appearance on stage inspiring terror in the audience. The story's author explains that it was the chorus's movements that aroused panic and a number of spontaneous abortions.[2] According to Pollux (4.110), it was their number that frightened the audience: for the chorus comprised fifty *choreutai*, whereas traditionally the Erinyes numbered no more than three, as the Furies would later on, Megaera, Allecto, and Tisiphone.

At the very least, this detail indicates that an explanation was required, for after all, in 458 BCE, the date of the *Oresteia*, Athenian spectators were no longer novices in theatrical matters. They had

---

[1] The text of the *Vita Aeschyli* was attached to some manuscripts.

[2] Perhaps this detail was inspired by the word λόχος, used by the Pythia of the band of Erinyes (*Eum.* 46). As Nicole Loraux (1989) has well shown, this may mean either 'ambush', 'band of soldiers', or 'childbirth'.

seen other plays! In particular, they had been at the *Persians*, in 472,
when King Darius was summoned from the grave: a dead barbarian
ruler wrenched from his tomb and brought back to life by a ritual
whose staging must have taken on a terrifying quality (just as in
modern performances of this play). Yet tradition does not record any
panic on that occasion.

What *is* likely is that Aeschylus was the first tragedian to bring the
Erinyes on stage. To be sure, Pausanias' comment is not quite explicit
enough to serve as evidence; he says, 'It was Aeschylus who first
represented them with snakes in their hair'.[3] The priority he refers to
may indeed be only in placing snakes in their hair. However, portrayals
of the Erinyes are all but absent from Attic vase painting before the mid-
fifth century,[4] and specialists have considered that the influence of
Aeschylus' play was decisive.[5] This implies that the Athenian audience
had not previously had the opportunity of seeing these beings represented.[6] And that is just the impression that, as we shall see, emerges
from the statements made by the Pythia, the first to see them in reality.

This non-portrayal is not in the least surprising; are they not
described as creatures 'without a face'? The *Suda* explains the expression Ἐρινύων ἀπορρώξ, 'scion of the Erinyes', as ἐπὶ τῶν ἀπροσώπων
καὶ δυσειδῶν: 'it is said of persons without a face and painful to look
at'. This definition, admittedly late, posits an equivalence between a
revolting sight and ἀπροσωπία, the absence of face. The point is that
the Erinyes are among those deadly powers whose relation to death
places them in the field of the barely envisageable, or rather the
invisible—such as Hades (Ἀίδης), or such as the Gorgon, on whose
face and eyes none can bear to gaze: divinities and powers whose

---

[3] Pausanias 1.28.6.

[4] A possible exception: an Attic black-figure lekythos, Athens MN 19765, dated
470 (*LIMC* s.v. Erinys 7) may represent the Erinyes surrounding a partly dog-shaped
Hecate. The Erinyes are portrayed as 'normal' women.

[5] So Haiganuch Sarian (*LIMC* s.v. Erinys and 1986), who discounts the theory of
a prior representation in snake form; cf. the summary of theories in Lebeck
(1971: 345).

[6] And when they start to be portrayed, it is as beautiful women holding snakes in
their hands; there is nothing comparable with the fearsome creatures of Aeschylus'
text. Moreover, he brings them on stage only so that he can transform them into
Eumenides. Pausanias (above, n. 3) observes that the images of the *Semnai* have
nothing frightening about them.

representation, the rendering visible of the invisible, is not without its problems.[7]

At the same time, however, Pollux's *Onomasticon* (4.141) records the existence of a tragic mask for an Erinys. It features in the section on special masks, mentioned after the series of standard tragic masks (the fair-haired man, the old man, the servant, and so on). These ἔκσκευα πρόσωπα, 'off-list' accessories, include amongst others the horned mask of Actaeon, the mask of Phineus when blind, and those of Gorgo, Dikê, Thanatos, Lyssa, and the Erinys. This evidence confirms that Aeschylus, in opening the tragic stage to the Erinyes, those repulsive creatures without a human face whom it is painful, even unbearable, to look at, endowed them with a theatrical countenance.

The contradiction goes beyond the problem of rendering the invisible visible: in a theatrical context it involves material representation, for the sake of spectacle, of beings at whom it is thought impossible to look. That in itself may indeed serve to explain the spectators' panic. But reading Aeschylus' text reveals a gradual build-up for the terror that supposedly gripped the Athenians. The Erinyes are present long before they are seen on stage. We can follow the process by which they are constructed as characters,[8] that is to say as πρόσωπα, even though they have no πρόσωπον, no visible face. It is this process that we shall attempt to follow through its stages and to reconstruct.

The Erinyes begin to show themselves at the end of *The Libation Bearers*, where their arrival is put into words by Orestes addressing the chorus. This is made up of female prisoners from Troy in the service of Clytaemnestra, on whose orders they have accompanied Electra to Agamemnon's tomb, wearing mourning veils, to pour libations to the deceased—whence their name, χοηφόροι—and to make sacrifices to him. That is where Orestes is reunited with his sister and prepares vengeance with her. Once he has killed his mother, Orestes promptly feels the symptoms of madness and informs the chorus of what he sees or thinks he sees:

---

[7] No more terrifying than the ἀγάλματα of the Erinyes, as Pausanias likewise observes in the same passage (above no. 3), are those of the underworld deities (as might have been expected).

[8] Even though they make up the chorus, they are none the less the chief characters in the play named after them, in which they are recreated as Eumenides.

δμωαὶ γυναῖκες, αἵδε Γοργόνων δίκην
φαιοχίτωνες καὶ πεπλεκτανημέναι
πυκνοῖς δράκουσιν· (1048–50)

Captive women, these Gorgon-like creatures,
in dark robes interwoven with close-packed snakes.

This vision, laid before the audience by Orestes' words, has been
instigated by the chorus's preceding phrase 'you have delivered the
city of Argos'. Twenty lines earlier he had already evoked the first
signs of his disturbance: 'Phobos is ready to sing beside my heart', πρὸς
δὲ καρδίᾳ (1024–5). The preposition indicates that the phenomenon
comes from without, as already suggested in lines 1022–4: 'as if,
racing with a team of horses, I were holding the reins away from
the course; my φρένες, hard to control, bear me off in defeat.'[9]
Although the φρένες are internal organs, the seat of the feelings,
Orestes feels himself governed by an external force: Phobos, Terror,
which the editor of the text may choose to personify—a capital letter
will suffice.[10] In the following lines, however, he attempts to justify
himself, and 'still master of my reason', states his intention of going
to purify himself at Delphi.

To these troubled words the chorus replies, as if to free him from
guilt, reminding him that he has just freed Argos from tyranny 'by
cutting off with a well-struck blow, the heads of two serpents' (δυοῖν
δρακόντοιν εὐπετῶς τεμὼν κάρα, 1047).

The image of these two serpents, replacing the 'two tyrants' of line
973, in its reference to Clytaemnestra and Aegisthus[11] and severed
heads, seem to act as triggers for Orestes' vision.[12] It is the chorus's
words, with their highly allusive images, that act on him from
without, calling forth a hallucination. It is just as if δμωαὶ γυναῖκες,
'captive women',[13] apparently a vocative addressed to the chorus of

---

[9] Cf. Io in [A.] Pr. 883 and Heracles in E. HF.

[10] Phobos features on Athena's aegis along with other creatures surrounding
Gorgo's head, in Il. 5.739 and on Agamemnon's shield in Il. 11.37.

[11] Cf. line 994, Clytaemnestra as Echidna, and see Dupont (2001) on 'famille
serpent'.

[12] Zeitlin (1996a: 97) interprets the chorus's assertion as 'an ironic cue for Orestes'
first glimpse of the serpentine Furies'.

[13] The phrase δμωαὶ γυναῖκες often has negative connotations in Homer, e.g. Il.
6.323, of Helen's entourage; 9.477, Phoenix's account of his escape, in which he
evaded the vigilance of the φύλακες, the servants set to watch him, when his father

Clytaemnestra's slaves, served to reinforce the vision. It may equally well be understood as a nominative forming part of Orestes' description: 'Captive women, these Gorgon-like creatures, in dark robes interwoven with close-packed snakes'.[14] Indeed, this troop of women in dark clothes (*Lib.* 11) will again comprise the chorus in the next play, taking on the role of these creatures that must not be named. Naturally we are not to choose between these two interpretations of the same grammatical construction, but retain the semantic ambivalence the Greek permits. This ambivalence is essential for constructing Orestes' hallucinatory delirium as he oscillates between lucidity and delusion, and proves to be an element in the nature of the Erinyes, who are at once the driving force and the content of his visions.[15]

What Orestes sees and points out to the prisoners is Γοργόνων δίκην: '(something) in the manner of the Gorgons'. This mode of expression—an adverbial accusative—represents an attempt on Orestes' part to get up closer and delineate what he sees. At the beginning of *Eumenides*, as we shall see, the Pythia will employ similar approximations. However, the word δίκη is also employed here in its legal sense, recalling δίκην at the end of line 990, which referred to Orestes' just claim and the fundamental problem of the trilogy, that of δίκη: 'case' and 'justice'. The syntagm Γοργόνων δίκην also suggests 'Gorgon justice, Gorgon case', or 'the right of these quasi-Gorgons'.

The apparition becomes more precise with φαιοχίτωνες, 'in dark robes', a compound in which the element φαιός, 'grey', belongs to the vocabulary of light and manifestation.[16] The final qualifier, 'interwoven with close-packed snakes', brings us back to the Gorgons and to the serpent couple, Clytaemnestra and Aegisthus. The sight is

---

called down on him the vengeance of the Erinyes, στυγερὰς ᾿Ερινύς. In *Od.* 16.108, 22.396, 421, the δμωαὶ γυναῖκες are the maidservants on Ithaca, twelve of whom were hanged as traitors.

[14] So Verrall (1893). Cf. Lebeck (1971: 194 n. 5 and discussion p. 344).

[15] Thus in this passage of Aeschylus we cannot distinguish between illusion based on a real but misinterpreted vision and hallucination, as we apparently can in E. *Or.* 264–5, where the hero takes his sister for an Erinys, and 255, 'Here they are: they come leaping at me', a distinction made by the Stoics in their analysis of φαντασία: cf. Pigeaud (1987: 94 ff.).

[16] Cf. φαίνω. Is it from appearing colourless?

unbearable, and Orestes declares that he cannot stay. His dialogue with the chorus turns on the status of his visions: 'they are δόξαι, appearances,[17] that are spinning you round', says the chorus. 'No,' replies Orestes, they are not δόξαι.'

The Erinyes' status is thus depicted between φαίνειν and δοκεῖν, between visibility and semblance, and Orestes' reply gradually makes them material: σαφῶς γὰρ αἵδε 'they are there clearly, my mother's raging hounds', μητρὸς ἔγκοτοι κύνες (1054). Animal sounds, and in particular the barks of dogs, are a manifestation in sound of the Erinyes, as the Euripidean Orestes would later explain.[18] Orestes' words, which evoke the sound of barking, execute a verbal materialization of the Erinyes, before the chorus's reply renews the vision: that is the effect of blood, αἷμα, say the libation bearers, as if in an attempt at positivistic explanation. But this, on the contrary, elicits from Orestes a new visual detail: 'from their eyes drips a disgusting gore'.

'You see nothing, I do' (ὑμεῖς μὲν οὐχ ὁρᾶτε τάσδ', ἐγὼ δ' ὁρῶ), says Orestes at the end of the play as he leaves the stage. These final words set two kinds of vision against each other, the hero's and that of the others, chorus and audience. But the chorus occupies an intermediate position: it has taken part, through its dialogue with Orestes, with the steady progress of the Erinyes' apparition. Its hesitant reactions to Orestes' first exclamations have led him to make his hallucination more specific and to describe it in words, enabling his hearers to begin visualizing the Erinyes. But the chorus's role is not confined to that of the mere interlocutor. The physical presence of this group of women in mourning, as we have pointed out, was a factor in the onset of Orestes' madness, as if they were anticipating their part in the following play. They oscillate, then, in accordance with the fluctuations of Orestes' reason, between their present status as libation bearers and their future status as Erinyes.

To this progressive fashioning of the Erinyes, their verbal fabrication (ποίησις) by means of words heavy with textual, oral,

---

[17] At [E.] *Rh.* 780, the word is used of a dream; cf. Pl. *Tht.* 161e δόξαι καὶ φαντασίαι.

[18] At E. *IT* 294, the Erinyes imitate the sound of dogs (μιμήματα). One thinks too of Hecate.

and mythic references that conjure up images for Orestes and the spectators, must be added the character's gestures. Corporeal manifestations of Orestes' disturbed state—starts, jerky gesticulation, spinning round—must have accompanied the text and contributed physically to the tragic contagion.

The process of rendering the Erinyes visible continues in the following play, *Eumenides*. The scene opens at Delphi, before Apollo's temple, at which the Pythia arrives. Calmly she utters her prayer, then goes into the temple. Her reaction of horror takes the form both of gestures visible to the audience and of words: 'Oh! horrible to speak of, horrible for the eyes to see', ἦ δεινὰ λέξαι, δεινὰ δ' ὀφθαλμοῖς δρακεῖν (34). Her exclamation describes a passage from speaking to seeing: it adopts the spectator's standpoint and not her own, for she, conversely, has seen before she speaks. Her words prepare and induct the audience. The verb of seeing is not anodyne: it is δρακεῖν, the verb of the darted glance; it is a signal: 'Warning, snake ahead, δράκων'. There follows a somewhat chatty speech that leads the spectators gently with it, mingling suspense and circumspection.

First she describes Orestes, without naming him: 'a man cursed with pollution, crouching like a suppliant, his hands dripping blood, with a sword newly drawn from the wound, and a long branch of olive'; then: 'In front of the man, an astonishing troop (θαυμαστὸς λόχος)'. The troop sleeps (εὕδει); it consists of women (γυναικῶν) sitting on chairs: a relaxed, even calm observation that ought to reassure. Then she resumes, cleverly dispensing her description in small doses: 'not at all, they are not women, it is Gorgons that I mean', making the spectators recall the end of *The Libation Bearers*. We may imagine the audience shudders. But then, a fresh correction: 'No, not that either! It is not to Gorgon shapes that I shall compare them.' The Pythia seeks an appropriate comparison, but her language, εἰκάσω τύποις, belongs to the register of figurative art: the words εἰκών and τύπος—'fashioning'—place her effort at mental and verbal representation at the level of production for the eye.

The first approximation employed by the Pythia, Gorgons, echoes Orestes' comparison at the end of *The Libation Bearers* and situates what is seen in the order of what cannot be seen but which has not only been made visible but also made familiar to the audience by artistic representations, notoriously abundant in the case of the

Gorgons.[19] This is confirmed in the continuation of her staccato speech, as if hesitant and representing her mental exploration: 'I saw once, in the past—of Phineus—painted—the females who seized the dinner'. This evocation appeals to the audience's memories, and explicitly draws them to the plane of images—the harpies were γεγραμμένας, in drawing and painting. However, the name 'Harpies' is not spoken. These nameless creatures (whom, be it emphasized, their victim, the blind Phineus, is in no position to see) are thus furtively glimpsed through the recollection of a painting, halfway between their invisibility—for the blind man they torment—and the material rendering of a visible representation which the Pythia fleetingly recalls: a memory of an image.[20] But their hideous shape is evoked only to be immediately rejected and repudiated by the Pythia, who returns to the thing she is trying to describe feature by feature: 'no wings to see, these females, and black, and all disgusting to look at'.[21] The verb βδελύσσω 'inspire with disgust', is often used in relation to food, meaning, 'make (someone) wish to vomit', which suggests that the image of the Harpies and the meal that Phineus could not eat, sketched and discarded a moment ago, is still floating in the background. Next she passes to the plane first of sound: 'they snore', then of smell: 'they exhale repulsively'.[22] And the vision is given a specific focus on the face: 'from their eyes there runs a loathsome drip'. Does this repellent fluid still echo the libations of *The Libation Bearers*, which themselves had served as a euphemistic metaphor for spilt blood (*Libation Bearers* 1058)? As to their jewellery—καὶ κόσμος—a fresh euphemism: it is made up of serpents.

The Pythia concludes that she is faced with an unknown species: 'their race, I have never seen it, that of this crew'. All she can do is appeal to Apollo: 'Loxias almighty'. She leaves the stage, which is immediately occupied by Apollo; he promises to take the matter in hand, reassuring Orestes and the audience. After the god's brief

---

[19] I have more than once analysed the paradox of the superabundant portrayals of the Gorgon, a power on which (it is believed) none can gaze: Frontisi-Ducroux (1995: 65–75; 2003: 202–20).

[20] The Gorgons' problematic status of visibility recalls the 'blind man's memories' of Derrida (1990).

[21] Note that the Erinyes are usually portrayed with wings.

[22] The epithet ἄπλατος is often applied to the Gorgons.

intervention, the εἴδωλον, Clytaemnestra's ghost, will wake up the chorus, not without trouble and very much in stages. To her reproaches and complaints the creatures, still asleep, reply with inarticulate grunts and groans—μυγμοί and ὠγμοί—which she notes and remarks on even as she attempts to rouse them from their torpor. These first manifestations, in sound, are gradually transformed into distinct words: 'seize, seize', λαβέ, λαβέ, alternating with the musical cry ἰοὺ ἰού. The dead queen rightly interprets these exclamations as the outward expression of their dreams. In their sleep, the Erinyes dream that they are still pursuing their victim, as hunting hounds may do. For they are Clytaemnestra's hounds, those raging hounds with which the queen threatened Orestes just before the matricide and which the slayer clearly identified at the onset of his madness (*Libation Bearers* 924 and 1054). This breathless dialogue between the shade of the deceased and the piled-up sleepers dreaming aloud, whom the ghost tries to awaken—'kick sleep away' (*Eum.* 141)— forms the framework within which the Erinyes emerge. It is a dream space, bloodied with sufferings and hatreds, which affords an intermediate level between the invisible Beyond, home of these beings and the dead queen's ghost, and the reality of the stage where they will materialize before the spectators.[23] The voice of Clytaemnestra's ghost, in its brief appearance, tears them out of the depths of their dreams—glimpsed by the audience through their cries—to hoist them into daylight and set them in action. They probably arise at the moment when they begin to sing. And it was when they had stood up to form the chorus that the audience, so the tradition has it, also rose to its feet, in prey to panic.

One can now understand that, true or fictitious, this anecdote is inscribed in the logic of the performance and its effect. The audience, on seeing creatures that cannot be looked at, ought to react like Orestes and the Pythia. Or at least like Athena, who in due course will declare: 'at the sight of this strange crew, though my heart does not tremble, my eyes are astounded'.[24] To see Erinyes, who are at

---

[23] At the beginning of *The Libation Bearers* Clytaemnestra's nightmare, interpreted by the seers as a manifestation of the dead and narrated by the chorus, had played a similar intermediary role (*Ch.* 32–42, 925).

[24] *Eum.* 406–7. The goddess is in the grip of θαῦμα.

once the cause of Orestes' madness and the subject of his delusion, can be felt and experienced only as a participation in *Phobos*, Fear or Panic, which up till then had been acting only on Orestes. In bringing on stage creatures that neither gods nor men have ever seen, Aeschylus gives shape to powers belonging to the mental and verbal universe of religious beliefs that could reveal themselves in hallucinations or dreams, but up to then had not even been represented in art.[25] In rendering the Erinyes the tragic poet achieves a threefold result: externalization, materialization, and spreading of madness by contagion.

To recapitulate: the process by which Aeschylus constructs the Erinyes, creatures from an unseen world, proceeds by successive approximations, at first verbal, with sounds and words conveying mythical images and references that, accompanied by gestures, work on the mind's eye; then, once the audience has been prepared by this means, through a more concrete, visual invention: a material creation that uses costumes and masks. A pile of black rags heaped up on the ground, growling and rising to end up showing a terrifying face.

Aeschylus thus realizes his *mise en scène* by giving body to the void—the extreme case of scenic epiphany. Let us recall that the actor, in restoring to life a hero from the past—a being far more substantial than the Erinyes, envisaged as having lived under the gaze of former generations—is no more than his spokesman and his clothes horse, and must efface himself behind that character to the point where nothing else exists but the figure thus revived. The *choreutai* who flesh out the Erinyes efface themselves no less, but to give body and presence to invisible and impalpable powers.

To make the Erinyes materialize, finally, Aeschylus gives them black or grey *peploi*, equivalents of the shroud worn by a modern ghost, *not* necessarily the burial garment of a ghost in the traditional bed sheet that lifts up and inflates to a mysterious and disturbing bulk; instead, linen like the clothes that the Invisible Man must wear

---

[25] This explains the horrified surprise of Orestes and the Pythia, and their hesitant approximations. To describe what they see they have recourse to the Gorgon, a parallel case, but familiar as being something already seen, albeit invisible, whereas the Erinyes up to then have been both invisible and unseen.

in order to be seen. No less do their masks operate like the bandages clinging to the head of the same Invisible Man, mimicking a non-face, frightening by its strangeness. Hence the need for woven fabrics to bestow an appearance on the invisible by laying upon it the finest, supplest, and most pliable material. The woven cloth made to cling to the body, whose production is for the Greeks one of the signs of civilization, plays a fundamental part in that culmination of Greek culture that is the theatre. It is the material of a πλάσμα, of a moulding over a void. Masks, too, are made of rags and plaster, as one is reminded by a joke of Aristophanes' about the ragged face of one of his characters, an aged coquette made up to the nines.[26] It is, therefore, the Erinyes' clothing, their costume, that weaves together the φαινόμενα into the fabric of these spectres. The carefully staged progression seems even more calculated to manipulate suspense than to manipulate the spectators.

If we try to list the ingredients in Aeschylus' recipe for making Erinyes, we find: two decapitated serpents, captive women, dark grey fabrics, serpent tracery, Gorgons, bitches, wriggling, blood, tears of repugnant gore. Blood is the basic element, recurring in Aeschylus' trilogy and in the other poets, Sophocles and Euripides, since it is the central theme of the *Oresteia*. The Erinyes born of Clytaemnestra's blood and greedy for that of Orestes are hungry, and thirst for blood. Blood is their food, their substance. They are presented as receptacles to be filled with blood, as bloodsuckers, monstrous ticks, or rather vampires. At Delphi they are made up of Gorgons, Harpies, grey-blackness (want of colour, darkness, a hue of death), snores, repulsive breath, dripping eyes, growls, grunts, strident cries, and lamentations, and on top of all that the fabrics of costumes and masks—and we must not, of course, forget the musical accompaniment, now completely lost, about which we can only speculate. This recipe for a stage manifestation seems, all in all, simple enough in comparison to those of ancient and modern witches.

The masks,--an accessory specific to the dramatic epiphany, thanks to which Aeschylus confers a countenance on the Erinyes,

---

[26] Ar. *Wealth* 1051–65. The suggestive power of a rag—worn-out garment, tatters, even cleaning cloths—and its allegorical role as the double hinge between form and non-form has been well analysed by Didi-Huberman (2002).

are mentioned by Athena at the end of the play: 'From these fearsome faces I see emerging a great advantage for the citizens present here', ἐκ τῶν φοβερῶν τῶνδε προσώπων | μέγα κέρδος ὁρῶ τοῖσδε πολίταις' (990–1). The word πρόσωπον denotes the stage mask worn by the *choreutai*, the mask that for the first time gives a visible face to these creatures never seen before. The benefit for the Athenians will be the conversion of the Erinyes into tutelary goddesses, guarantors of prosperity, Eumenides. The advantage will be both political and legal: the creation of the Areopagus court, which puts an end to the murderous chain of private vengeance.

The masks of the Erinyes, pointed out by Athena when they are already on the way to becoming the Kindly Ones, whom one *may* look and gaze upon, thus appear as working two successive transformations: that from the invisible to the visible, and that from the terrifying—φοβερόν—to the beneficent. The former was the *sine qua non* of the latter: the manifestation of the Erinyes, who up till then could not be seen, transmutes them into divinities whose presence one may enter, better still, which are good to see, 'Kindly Ones'.

Aeschylus' achievement in bringing the Erinyes on stage, undoubtedly for the first time, exemplifies the tragic process towards the catharsis of fear. Tradition will have it that his treatment of them aroused a violent reaction. But for him to have succeeded the audience needed to regain its nerve and come back to sit on the steps of the theatre.[27]

---

[27] His success is further shown by the Attic iconography said to have been inspired by this performance, which retains no trace of Aeschylus' hideous and horrible creations.

8

A New Pair of Pairs: Tragic Witnesses in Western Greek Vase Painting?

Oliver Taplin

I

The most strikingly 'theatrical' of Greek mythological vase paintings are those from the high period of red-figure painting in the Greek West (or Magna Graecia), known as 'ornate Apulian'. We would be lost in this territory, had not the thousands of very varied pieces been sorted out and listed with amazing expertise by A. D. Trendall in his monumental *Red-Figured Vases of Apulia*. In addition to those in the big initial collection of 1982, there were literally hundreds of additions in the *Supplements* published in 1983 and 1991,[1] most of them vases which had come on the antiquities market without any recorded provenance in the 1970s and 1980s. To locate them in place, these 'ornate' vases were mostly painted in or around the cultured and prosperous city of Taras, although they have been found in settlements throughout that part of Italy. Set in time, this phase of ostentatious ceramics lasted between about 350 and 310 BCE. The most striking and unusual of all, many of them very large and highly crowded with figures, are those collected in Trendall's chapter 18; and dominating this chapter is the master hand of the Darius Painter. It is

---

[1] Trendall and Cambitoglou (1982; 1983; 1992). I shall refer to these simply as *RVAp*, *RVAp, Suppl.* 1, and *RVAp, Suppl.* 2. All three collections are organized by the same chapter numbers, and the best way to refer to an entry is by chapter/number, as, for example, *RVAp, Suppl. 2,* 18/47b (p. 148). The chapters which cover 'ornate' Apulian are (more or less) 8, 13, 16, 17, 18, 25, 27, and 29.

two recently published vases of his maturity that I am hoping Froma Zeitlin will find especially interesting.[2]

These vases are 'theatrical' in an associative sense, but not necessarily in a literal sense. The mythical narratives they show are usually melodramatic, often scenes of violence, danger, distress; and in these scenes heroic figures, many in richly decorated outfits, supplicate, threaten, look in amazement, face dilemmas. Modern viewers who are soaked in the texts will immediately think of the tragedies they know and love. But it is, in fact, much disputed how and how far, if at all, these paintings are related to tragedy, whether in texts or performances. The question of whether or not the picture on any particular vase should be related to a play depends ultimately on much larger questions about the relationships between the place of tragedy and the place of these funerary paintings within the lives of the Western Greeks who viewed them both—complex and contested questions which I have attempted to explore in a full-length study.[3]

There is at present a stand-off between conflicting views, rooted ultimately in the ancient struggle for superiority between the visual arts and literature. The conflict is between what has come to be regarded as the 'old' view—that the paintings are inspired by or are dependent upon the tragedies, are even 'illustrations' of them[4]—and the 'new' view that the artistic tradition is fully self-explanatory with no need of any reference to any literature;[5] or that the public for these vases would not even have directly known the plays.[6] I hope to break out of this deadlocked polarization by asking the questions that viewers bring to the pictures: what does this picture evoke, what does it point towards, what does it signal? I am coming to realize that there is a whole array of signals that may suggest that the recollection of a tragedy in performance will inform the appreciation of any particular mythological narrative. The viewer who does not recognize the signals, or does not know the play, will still have an

---

[2] The concerns of this article are related to, for example, Zeitlin (1994).

[3] Taplin (2007).

[4] This attitude is to be found in, for example, many entries in Webster and Trendall (1971), and in some though by no means all of the articles in *LIMC*.

[5] Most articulately argued by Moret (1975); see also, most recently, Giuliani (2003).

[6] Most articulately argued by Giuliani (1995) and elsewhere.

adequate and self-sufficient response to the painting—the picture does not *need* the play—but the response will be less rich and complex without the connection.

It is essential to understand that the vase paintings do not show the myths *as* tragedy; they are not set in the theatre. The crucial point was established, in my view, by Green (1991a): tragedy-related vases do not have to display any overt sign that the myth is being enacted in the theatre; not only that, but, on the contrary and in polarized contrast with comedy-related vases, they do not declare their own theatricality. To put the point another way, the vase paintings do not show tragedy, they show the myths in a form that is enriched and made more potent by tragedy. So the questions become a matter of identifying the signals: what are they, how prominent are they, how do they reinforce each other? In the case of any particular painting, do they or do they not amount to an evocation of a tragedy?

In this offering I shall be considering just one such, relatively marginal, signal: the presence of anonymous figures. I shall do this, though, with special reference to two vases that have not yet received any significant attention beyond their original publication. One was first fully published in the excellent Boston Museum of Fine Arts catalogue *Vase-Painting in Italy* as number 42.[7] The other, now in the Musée d'Art et Histoire in Geneva (formerly in a private collection), was first published in *Antike Kunst* for 1995—so it first came on the scene too late for inclusion in Trendall's *Second Supplement*.[8] These two pieces are remarkably similar amphoras of the form known as 'Apulian Panathenaic', and were almost certainly made originally as markers for male burials.[9] Both stand at just under 90 centimetres in height (very tall, in other words!), and have two bands of decorative figures on the main body. The upper band is divided beneath the handles between a very unusual mythological scene on one side, fortunately glossed with inscriptions of identification, and on the other varied figures of the type typically found in these funerary paintings. These figures include youths, women, *erôtes* and maenads; they often have Dionysiac

---

[7] Boston 1991.437 = Padgett et al. (1993: 115–18, with colour plate XI = *RVAp, Suppl. 2,* 18/47b [p. 148], with plate XXXVI,1); also reported at Green (1995: 117).

[8] Birchler and Chamay (1995); reported at Green (1995: 117–18). It scraped into the final volume of *LIMC* as 'Hesione' (S) 1*.

[9] See Green (1991b: 53).

associations, and may well be associated with a blessed afterlife. On both vases the lower frieze is continuous all the way round and is also populated by figures of this sort. So these amphorae differ in layout from the more familiar volute craters, which often have divinities above and the human narrative scene below.

Now to turn to the two mythological scenes in detail. The Boston amphora has a melodramatic and violent central image: Atreus (labelled *ATPEYΣ*), with a deadly wound to his breast, is violently turned upside-down on his throne (looking like some victim discovered in a Tarantino movie!) There are three figures to his left and three to his right (Fig. 8.1). On the left are the assassins, Thyestes (*ΘYEΣTHΣ*) and his son Aegisthus (*AΓIΣΘOΣ*), both with their swords in their hands; and lastly the unhappy Pelopeia (*ΠEΛOΠEIA*) turning away from them, her hands held up in horror. The relatively little-known story, which has to be patched together from various and mostly late sources, is not a nice one. Thyestes received an oracle that he would be revenged on Atreus for the notorious child-pie only through the agency of an incestuous son. So, concealing his identity, he raped his own daughter Pelopeia; their son—Aegisthus—was rescued from exposure and brought up by Atreus himself, who had in the meantime married Pelopeia. A sword proves to be the recognition token that reveals Thyestes as Aegisthus' true father; and with the help of his son he takes his long-delayed revenge on Atreus. Pelopeia will seize the sword from her son/brother and kill herself. So there is no shortage of reasons why in the painting the winged Erinys-figure of Revenge (*ΠOINH*) approaches swiftly behind the dead man's throne: all three male figures are in one way or another agents of vengeance, who themselves meet with revenge. Lastly on the right (Fig. 8.2), completing the symmetry of the scene, are two women, signalled by an inscription as being 'Maids' (*ΔMΩIAI*). They both look towards the main scene with alarm. The Boston catalogue notes their shared inscription as 'unique'—as indeed it was in 1993.[10]

---

[10] Padgett et al. (1993: 118). The nearest thing to an exception is a couple of Erinyes in an Orpheus-in-the-Underworld scene, who are labelled *EY]MENIΔEΣ*. These are on some mid-century Apulian fragments in Ruvo, formerly in the Fenicia Collection, and known only through an old drawing. This is Aellen (1994: no. 6, plate 9). But a sample of a group of divinities is rather a different matter.

Fig. 8.1 Detail from red-figure amphora attributed to the Darius Painter. Obverse, showing the death of Atreus. South Italian, c.340–330 BCE.

Fig. 8.2 Red-figure amphora attributed to the Darius Painter. Obverse, detail showing a winged figure labelled *ΠΟΙΝΗ* (Revenge) and two females labelled *ΔΜΩΙΑΙ* (Maids). South Italian, c.340–330 BCE.

There is no known tragedy, to the best of my knowledge, to which this story can be connected with any probability. But it can be said with some confidence that, if there are connections at all between these ornate Apulian mythological paintings and tragedies, then this vase must be a likely candidate. The family violence, the gender tension, the centrality of vengeance—all are highly characteristic of tragedy. And Aegisthus, with his incestuous life story, might well be regarded as an archetypal figure of a certain kind of tragedy of unnatural family relations.[11] By a strange coincidence, his presence in fourth-century vase painting has been recently increased. The beginning of his life story as a baby is narrated on a calyx crater also by the Darius Painter, also recently acquired by the Boston Museum of Fine Arts, and also evocative of tragedy.[12] And Aegisthus is the one and only fully fledged tragic figure ever to have been found in a vase painting set on a comic stage—the extraordinary '*Chorêgos* vase', now in the Getty Museum.[13]

The Geneva composition, while less shocking, narrates another little-known chapter of myth. And it is similarly redolent of tragedy. Again there are seven main figures, again helpfully labelled, but this time with the addition of a hovering Eros, who is to some degree balanced compositionally by a pillar surmounted by a hydria (Fig. 8.3). The central figure this time, contrasting with the distorted Atreus, is a rather statuesque and noble Heracles (*hHPAKΛHΣ*). He has a kneeling suppliant figure on either side: to the left is the aged king Laomedon (*ΛΑΟΜΕΔΩΝ*), matched on the other by his young son Priam (*ΠΡΙΑΜΟΣ*).[14] Heracles looks towards the Eros and the pensive princess Hesione (*HΣΙΟΝΗ*), evidently suggesting an erotic interest between them. Behind her on the far left is a maid with a fan, not given any label.

---

[11] Aegisthus is cited by And. *Mys.* 129 as a mythical *exemplum* of perverted family relations. After talking about the various women with whom Callias' father had children, Andocides asks, 'What should he be called? Oedipus or Aegisthus or what?'

[12] Boston 1987.53; this is Padgett et al. (1993 no. 41) = *RVAp, Suppl.* 2, 18/65c. If there is a tragedy related, it might possibly have been Sophocles' *Thyestes in Sicyon*. The Boston catalogue (118) speaks of the Death of Atreus amphora as its 'sequel'; but their close sequence in acquisition by Boston is presumably a coincidence?

[13] *RVAp, Suppl.* 2 1/124 (p. 7–8); they are the 'comic angels', discussed in Taplin (1993: esp. 55–9).

[14] Birchler and Chamay (1995: 53) are not unreasonably baffled by the bag lying by Priam's feet.

Fig. 8.3 Detail from red-figure amphora attributed to the Darius Painter. Obverse, showing Heracles being supplicated by

Once again the story has to be patched together from various sources. King Laomedon refused to compensate Poseidon for his part in building the walls of Troy; the offended god sent a sea monster which would be satisfied only by Laomedon's daughter Hesione. Like Perseus in the Andromeda story, Heracles turns up, kills the monster, and rescues the maiden. But Laomedon reneges again on the promised reward; Heracles kills him and all his sons except Priam; and he gives Hesione to Telamon. The erotic interest shown by Heracles in this painting was previously unattested; so was the element of contest between Laomedon and Priam, if that is what their balanced supplications imply.

To complete the picture, the two female figures on the left of the row are balanced on the right by two Trojan men with spears and oriental caps and outfits, one standing and one sitting, and both looking calmly towards the central scene (Fig. 8.4). They are labelled 'Phrygians' (*ΦΡΥΓΕΣ*), evidently meaning 'Trojans'. In poetic usage from the early fifth century onwards 'Phrygian' does not seem to have had any precise geographical association with Phrygia proper, which was some distance away from Troy. The earliest known use of *Phryges* to signify Trojans is probably the title of the third play in Aeschylus' *Achilles* trilogy.[15] But again, however much the narrative may make us think of tragedy, it does not match any tragedy of which we have previous knowledge.

But before coming to tragedy as such, I want to turn the spotlight on those anonymous figures, in preparation for a survey of all the anonymous labelled figures in Apulian mythological vase paintings in Section III below. Although rare outside Apulia, it is not unprecedented for anonymous figures to be labelled in Greek vase paintings. Occasionally groups of collective divinities such as the Charites or the Muses are identified.[16] And there is a single anonymous individual as early as the François Vase (*c*.560s) where, amidst 123 labels, there is a 'nurse' marked out as *ΤΡΟΦΟΣ*.[17] What is previously unheard of, to the best of my knowledge, whether in

[15] See Hall (1989: 38–9), who rightly questions the introduction of the usage by conjecture in Alcaeus 42.15.

[16] See Wachter (2001: 283 §401). Wachter stops his record at 400 BCE. See n. 10 above for an Apulian example.

[17] This is the only anonymous label recorded in Immerwahr (1990).

Fig. 8.4 Red-figure amphora attributed to the Darius Painter. Obverse, detail showing two Trojan spearmen labelled *ΦΡΥΓΕΣ* (Phrygians) observing the main action. South Italian, *c.*340–330 BCE.

Apulian vase painting or in Attic or in any of the other earlier fabrics, is a labelled anonymous *pair* of human figures.[18] The two maids on the Boston Atreus murder scene and the two Trojan soldiers on the Geneva Heracles/Hesione scene are, then, my 'new pair of pairs'.

II

The anonymous figures of Greek tragedy are all too easily neglected. Yet they are present in more than one guise in every single tragedy without exception. It is important to remember the sight of them when attempting to visualize tragedy in performance. But they are also important to visualizing in a less concrete sense: they are fellow watchers of the great catastrophic events. While caught up in them and moved by them, they are nonetheless not the central agents; and they do not, generally speaking, suffer overwhelming changes to their lives. They are tragic witnesses.

There are at least three differentiable categories of anonymous tragic figures on stage. The least important never speak: they are the attendants, soldiers, spear carriers, maids, and others who always used to accompany figures of high status. Here and there throughout tragedy the major characters turn to attendants of one sort or another with instructions—evidently they were always there, ready when needed.[19] The notable exceptions, which in effect prove the rule, are when a high-status character explicitly does not have attendants, such as Aegisthus (him again!) in *The Libation Bearers* (766–70), or Pentheus in *Bacchae* once dressed as a maenad (961–2). Assiduous attendants of this kind also inhabit the world of Homeric epic, of course, where they are usually but not always anonymous. They may not have been so ubiquitous in the realities of fifth-century Athens—nor even the Taras of the fourth century—but they were far from unknown there as well. In general, however, they add

---

[18] Wachter (2001: 114–15) records a peculiar late-sixth-century Corinthian cup, whose authenticity is not certain, which has two boxers and a label *ΠΥΚΤΑ*, which looks like a dual, 'pair of Boxers'.

[19] Cf. Taplin (1977: 79–80).

grandeur and social distinction to the great and powerful, often royal, figures of the world of tragedy. They wait upon that world, but do not fully share in it.

A second category emerges from these servants: the anonymous figures who actually deliver spoken lines. It is noteworthy that there is at least one such character in every single surviving tragedy. Many tend to be covered under the blanket term of 'messenger', although the eyewitness figure who brings the message may well be particularized as a manservant, a maid, a soldier, a shepherd, and so forth.[20] Sometimes they have no role to play within the story except to report; but often they can also be essential agents in the main story like, for example, the two old former shepherds in *Oedipus the King*, the Nurse in *Hippolytus*, or the loyal old slave in *Iphigenia at Aulis*. They are always, however, only links in the story, and are not themselves the central figures of it.[21] And they are always anonymous, with the single exception (at least in surviving texts) of the Nurse in *The Libation Bearers* (called Cilissa at line 732). And these nameless speaking characters are always socially subordinate, many explicitly slaves. Very rarely are they freeborn—the notable exception, who again proves the rule, is the impoverished yeoman farmer who is Electra's token husband in Euripides' *Electra*.

Thirdly, and most important—though significantly different from the previous two categories—are the choruses of tragedy. Their social status is not fixed and by no means uniform. They can be freeborn; they can be highly respected, for example the elders of a community; they can even be divinities, though it seems that greater variability of choruses was a feature of earlier tragedy.[22] The majority are, on the contrary, of inferior social status: they are often women, often slaves, sometimes non-Greek foreigners; and sometimes two or all three of these inferior classes of humanity. Whatever their status, they are never personally named; they are part of a group that never splinters into differentiated individuals. They may occasionally take part in the plot, but in a rather minor way, with the exceptional centrality of

---

[20] See, for example, de Jong (1991: esp. 65–73), Stephanis (1997).

[21] See, however, Hall (1997: 112–18), who makes a case for a more sociologically informed centrality for at least some of these slave roles.

[22] Aeschylean titles include *Eumenides*, *Heliades*, *Hiereiai*, *Kabeiroi*, *Nereides*.

two choruses of Aeschylus (*Suppliants* and *Eumenides*). It is (to cut a long story short) their normal and typical role to witness and to react, above all responding in lyric song and dance. And they survive without disaster.[23]

Although they differ in many ways, all these categories of anonymous folk are what I am calling the 'witness figures' of tragedy. They are onlookers and survivors. They are unlike the audience, because they belong to the world of the play which is distant in time and usually distant in place also: but they also have affinities with the audience who, like them, submerge their named existences into the communal experience of watching, hearing, and vicariously experiencing the tragic catastrophes. They are deeply affected by the tragic events that have unfolded before them, but they outlive them with their futures intact. Both the anonymous bystanders of the events there within the world of the play, and the audience in the theatre alike, live to tell the tale. So the witness figures are important intermediaries or mediators between that distant world and the present world of the citizens watching in the theatre.

III

It is time now to return to the vases and to consider the anonymous witness figures we see on them. The earlier archaic and classical vases with mythological scenes display a good scatter of attendants, soldiers, etc. who are not identifiable participants in the story—the painted equivalents, then, of the first category of nameless figures in tragedy. They are even thicker on the ground on our monumental Apulian pieces, where they serve not only as attendants but as marginal figures who fill out crowded tableaux, sometimes including more than twenty figures. Quite frequently they serve to complete the symmetry of the composition, as, for example, the maid with the fan at the left-hand side of the Hesione amphora. While they are often

---

[23] Well mapped out by Gould (1996); cf. also Taplin (1997: 172–3, with bibliography at 222 n. 6). See also, however, Foley (2003), who makes a good case against an overemphasis on the homogeneity and passivity of the tragic chorus.

clearly attached to one of the main participants, they are not always connected to the narrative; and, while they are usually portrayed as witnessing the main events, even with a degree of interest, they are not always even looking in the right direction. So, while these figures add to the overall visualization, rather like the minor attendants of tragedy, there is no good reason to regard them as any particular signal of a connection with a tragic version of the myth story in question. On the other hand, since such figures are also ubiquitous in tragedy, there is no reason to regard their equivalent on vases as in any way contraindicating a connection with tragedy. And, as the witness figures in tragedy act as intermediaries for the audience, so these fringe figures on the vases have the function of intermediaries for the viewers: they are concerned with the narrative in the picture, unnoticed presences at the edges, but they are not centrally part of it.

The second category in tragedy was the anonymous figures who have speaking roles within the play. These can, necessarily, have no direct equivalent in paintings. But some of the attendant figures on the vases are indicated in one way or another as being participants in the story, and more than decorative bystanders. Two types of servant are probably the most distinctly recurrent: male and female carers, that is nurses and tutors, or *trophoi* and *paidagôgoi*. 'Nurses' are often quite easy to identify, as they have white hair and are physically close to an important female figure. In a spectacular painting which tells the story of Melanippe and her newborn twins this figure is explicitly labelled 'nurse', *TPOΦOΣ*.[24] The old 'tutor' is even more distinctive. He is represented as white-haired and bent, with a short chiton which reveals surprisingly ornate boots, a crooked stick and a simple cloak. No fewer than 53 such figures have been invaluably collected and discussed by Green (1999).[25] As he brings out, the great majority of the relevant vases are Apulian, and no fewer than 14 of them are by the Darius Painter himself. Many of these so-called *paidagôgoi* (male child-carers) are clearly attached to a youthful figure within the myth, and are thus *paidagôgoi* in the strict sense of the word. One,

---

[24] Emory University Museum 1994.1 = *RVAp, Suppl.* 2, 18/283 = Cambitoglou et al. (1986: 190 ff.). This is by the other main artist of *RVAp* chapter 18, the Underworld Painter.

[25] His Catalogue (55–60) gives full bibliography. See also Goldhill, ch. 5 of this volume.

who laments over the dead Opheltes/Archemorus in the Hypsipyle story is actually labelled *ΠΑΙΔΑΓΩΓΟΣ*.[26] Another within the story of Phrixus and the golden ram is labelled *ΤΡΟΦΕΥΣ* ('male nurse').[27]

There is not always, however, a youthful person to whom this bent old man can be attached. He sometimes appears in his own right or as someone who brings news, a 'messenger'. This is clearest on the name painting of the Darius Painter: he stands on a plinth, actually inscribed *ΠΕΡΣΑΙ* ('Persians'), and speaks to King Darius, presumably telling of events in Greece.[28] And on the vase just mentioned with the Melanippe story, it is clearly signalled that he is neither a *paidagôgos* nor a messenger: he is the *ΒΟΤΗΡ*, the 'cowherd' who brings the infant twins discovered in the cowsheds to the attention of Aeolus and Hellen. Whether or not this vase reflects Euripides' *Melanippê Sophê*, this '*botêr*' is an active link in the story.[29]

Green makes the case for holding that this figure in a vase painting is *always* the signal of a connection with a tragic dramatization of the story represented. While it might be going too far to claim him as an invariable signal, the case for maintaining that he has a strong theatrical link is cogent. One particular element in the case might have been put even more strongly:[30] the two exceptional examples of this figure on vases painted in Sicily, both attributed by Trendall to an artist he dubs the Capodarso Painter. The characters on one of these (in Caltanisetta) are quite explicitly put upon a stage of the kind which is familiar from the comic vases, but is uniquely explicit among vases which might be claimed to show tragedy on a stage.[31]

---

[26] Naples 81934 (H3255) = *RVAp* 18/42 (Darius Painter) = Green (1999: no. 27, with plates 11 and 12). It has to be acknowledged that there is no trace of a speaking *paidagôgos* in the quite extensive surviving fragments of Euripides' *Hypsipyle*.

[27] Berlin 1984.41 = *RVAp* 18/41b (Darius Painter) = Green (1999: no. 7, with plates 24 and 25).

[28] Naples 81947 (H3253) = *RVAp* 18/38 = Green (1999: no. 29) = Webster and Trendall (1971: III. 5,6).

[29] The hypothesis to the Euripidean play (see Collard et al. 1995: 248) says that some of the *boukoloi* (herdsmen) saw the twins being suckled by a cow and, taking them to be monstrosities, took them to the king. The hypothesis also specifies that it was the Nurse (*trophos*)—see above—who first took the twins to the stables.

[30] Green (1991a: 44).

[31] Caltanisetta Museum = Trendall (1967: 601/98, with plate 235) = Webster and Trendall (1971: III. 6,1) = Taplin (1993: 6.111) = Green (1999: no. 51).

The four figures on this stage are all striking dramatic postures, and the one on the right is, sure enough, the little old man. The scene portrayed here has not yet been plausibly connected with any particular play—and there is indeed no reason why it should represent a scene that happens to be from one of the relatively small number of plays that happen to be known to us. The other closely related painting, the well-known 'Oedipus' vase in Syracuse, is apparently also set on a stage, but not so clearly.[32] It also has four figures, this time with the little old man on the left. Following Trendall, this is usually taken as reflecting the scene from Sophocles' *Oedipus the King* where Jocasta first recognizes the truth. If that is right, as seems to me very likely, then the little old man is not a *paidagôgos* nor really a messenger (although in most texts he is rather lazily called *angelos*): he is the Corinthian who comes to tell Oedipus that he has been proclaimed as the new king of Corinth, the same man who turns out to have taken the baby Oedipus down from Cithaeron to his foster home in Corinth. The fact that in both of these exceptionally direct theatrical paintings, the figure of the little old man is included surely clinches his conventional association with the tragic stage.

I would suggest, then, that all these anonymous figures with labels are muted 'signals' of a theatrical association—in other words the viewer who connects them to a particular tragedy will make more of the picture and its power. They are marked out as more than merely an attendant; each is someone who is sufficiently individualized in their participation to earn a label, while too humble to have a name. On the other hand these anonymous labels do not occur all that frequently, and the absence of a label would certainly not prove that an anonymous figure in a tragedy-related picture did not have a speaking part in the tragedy in question.

I have so far collected four of these figures (*ΤΡΟΦΟΣ, ΤΡΟΦΕΥΣ, ΠΑΙΔΑΓΩΓΟΣ, ΒΟΤΗΡ*), and I am in fact aware of only three others. One is an oriental attendant on the Lydian Pelops in a scene with Oenomaus: he is labelled *ΦΡΥΞ* ('Phrygian').[33] The other two

---

[32] Siracusa 66557 = Trendall (1983: 105/98a) = Webster and Trendall (1971: III. 2,8) = Taplin (1993: 6.112) = Green (1999: no. 50).

[33] Rome, Villa Giulia 18003, Apulian situla = *RVAp* 8/149.

might possibly, though not probably, be held against a theatrical connection as much as in favour of it. On the huge volute crater in Boston (125 centimetres in height) by a forerunner of the Darius Painter, which shows the aftermath of Achilles' decapitation of Thersites, there are towards the bottom right-hand corner of the picture a young soldier labelled *AITΩΛOΣ*, presumably an anonymous 'Aetolian' rather than a proper name, and a young attendant labelled *ΔMΩΣ* ('servant').[34] This *dmôs* looks back in horror at the corpse of Thersites and appears to be attached to him in some sense—perhaps he reported the violent killing of his master in a play? That play, if so, has often been speculated to have been the *Achilleus Thersitoktonos* by the mid-fourth-century Chaeremon.[35] If this connection with the tragedy of Chaeremon is to be maintained, then there is a feature of this painting which is more strange than has been properly given attention: most of the inscriptions which are susceptible to being put in Doric dialect are in Doric spellings: *ΘΕΡΣΙΤΑΣ, AΘANA, EPMAΣ* ('Thersitas', 'Athana', 'Hermas'), and *ΠOINA* ('Revenge'). Contrast her Doric spelling here with the *ΠOINH* on the new Boston Death of Atreus vase (see §1 above). *ΔIOMHΔHΣ* ('Diomedes') is not an exception since this would be his spelling in Doric also. Perhaps this painter (probably himself Doric-speaking, if he came from Taras) is simply not as careful as the Darius Painter to remember to write tragedy-related labels in Attic dialect. Or could this be evidence of a tragedy in Doric dialect? An intriguing thought, but without any supporting evidence. Or might the Doric spellings indicate some connection with choral lyric rather than tragedy? Whatever the case with this peculiar vase, the Attic dialect of all the other labels on these ornate Apulian mythological scenes is, I propose, a pointer—not conspicuous, but there for those who have eyes for it—towards a connection with tragedy. And another feature of diction which may point towards a tragic connection—and certainly does not militate against it—is the use of poetic words such as *dmôs* and *botêr*.

---

[34] *RVAp* 17/75 (p. 472) = Boston 1900.03.804 = Padgett et al. (1993: no. 39, with full bibliography on p. 106) = Webster and Trendall (1971: III. 4,2).

[35] Playwright 71 in *TrGF* vol. 1. This play and this vase are the subject of Morelli (2001), fully and interestingly reviewed by Green (2002).

Are there, finally, any equivalents of the tragic chorus in these Western Greek vase paintings?[36] The first point to make quite clear is that there are no clear instances of the inclusion of a chorus. There is nothing remotely like the well-known early-fifth-century Attic painting in Basel with six young men identically costumed as soldiers and dancing in unison before what is probably a tomb.[37] At first glance this might seem a serious argument against supposing any connection at all between these paintings and tragedy. But that would be to forget the fundamental point that the serious vases (unlike the comic) avoid the explicit declaration of theatricality. And so it is not to be expected that there would be any representation of the chorus as such.

There are paintings which have several similar bystanders, but they are never in formation and never clearly represented as dancing. So it is not really possible to say whether these groups are there for primarily compositional reasons, or whether they are a gesture—an inexplicit gesture—towards the chorus. It is perhaps in the reflection of tragic scenes whose texts survive that the case for a distant allusion to the chorus seems most likely. There are two such scenes which are especially frequent, and especially plausible in this respect. Both are from the *Oresteia*, one the iconography of Electra and Orestes at the tomb of Agamemnon, where there are sometimes several maids with Electra; and the other that of Orestes at Delphi, where there are usually at least two Furies.[38]

These two common scenes do not, however, appear among the monumental vases of 'Trendall chapter 18'. The painting of that kind which most readily brings a chorus to mind, at least at first sight, is the name painting of the Darius Painter (see text to n. 28 above). In the middle of the three registers (which include 22 figures in all!), on either side of the central figures around Darius, there are councillors,

---

[36] There is no reason to doubt that performances of tragedy throughout the Greek world in the fourth century always included a chorus, though it may have been smaller than in Athens. It would be interesting to know if its members travelled with the actors, or whether (more likely?) they were recruited and trained locally.

[37] For recent discussion see Green (1994: 18 with bibliography at 177 n. 5).

[38] There are full listings in *LIMC* s.v. Elektra 1, nos. 2–65, and Orestes 7–35; for a small selection see Webster and Trendall (1971: II. 1,2–6 and 9–12); for a fuller sample Knoepfler (1993).

four sitting and one standing. They might make one think of the elders in Aeschylus' *Persians*, or of the triple title attributed to Phrynichus, *Dikaioi* or *Persai* or *Synthokoi*.[39] But there are objections to seeing these five figures as reflections of the chorus. It is not one that they are sitting, since that might be seen as all part of avoiding explicit theatricality. But only three of the five are in Oriental costume, like Darius himself, while two of them are not; and, while this might be regarded as merely a matter of variety, that variety must count as a contraindication against a chorus.[40] It is a further point against that they are not all facing in the same direction, and so not all paying attention to the central scene. What is missing is any signal that these seated councillors—or any of the other comparable clusters—are to be thought of as having a group identity, since that is the essence of chorality.

IV

This group identity is what *is* indicated, I suggest (at last!), by the new pair of pairs at the right-hand side of the Boston Atreus amphora and the Geneva Hesione amphora. The two *dmôiai*, Maids, are not identical, either in stance or in details of costume, but they do clutch each other in horror and both gesture towards the scene of slaughter (and—though a small detail—they have both dropped their spindles). Above all, they both stare at the dreadful central spectacle; they are both responsive witnesses. And why does *Poinê* glance towards them? Were they complicit in the plot? Or perhaps vengeance was the theme of one of their choral lyrics?

The two *Phryges*, Trojans, on the Geneva vase are more relaxed, but then the scene that they are witnessing is less horrific. They both have spears and are costumed similarly though not identically—the

---

[39] 3 F 4a in *TrGF*—this title seems to fit Phrynichus' precedent for Aeschylus' *Persians*, as related in its Hypothesis, better than what we know of his *Phoenician Women*.

[40] Margot Schmidt (1982) even put forward a fascinating theory that the councillors are identifiable historical individuals from the Herodotean account of the Ionian Revolt.

left-hand one has a cloak and his sleeves and trousers are darker, for example. One stands while the other sits. But, at the same time, they are both looking together at the central rather sensational events: they are unified as witnesses. They make me wonder whether their rather sombre reflectiveness might have been suggested by the contents of a choral song.

The idea that these two pairs are painterly transformations of the tragic chorus prompts me, finally, to some musings about what a chorus might have meant in relation to a theatre audience. While the maids and the Trojans are not identical, and while they each have their own individual accoutrements, they are united by what they witness and by what they appear to be experiencing in response to it. This shared experience is specifically signalled by the joint label of identification. So, in a way, these witness figures are even more analogous to the theatre audience than either of the other two categories.

For the duration of the play the public in the theatre collectively lose their individual names and identities; they submerge their individuality into the shared experience. Together they witness and respond with thought and emotion. Yet this is far from saying that they become mental or physical clones. It is important that after the play they will find that they have come away with multitudinously varying thoughts and recollections. But those constructive shades of difference would not be interesting if they had not been reached through an experience of temporarily shared witnessing. Like the two pairs on the new vases they remain individuals, and yet at the same time they relinquish their names, their unique identities, in order to be identified with each other. To adapt Plato's claim that someone who has not participated in a chorus has not been educated, someone who has not participated in the communality of belonging to a theatre audience has not known the benefit of tragedy.[41]

[41] I am most grateful to the editors of this volume, especially Jaś Elsner, and to Edith Hall for their constructive suggestions.

9

Medea in Eleusis, in Princeton

Luca Giuliani and Glenn W. Most

A large Apulian volute crater of the late fourth century in the Art Museum of Princeton University (Fig. 9.1)[1] has on its obverse an elaborate scene with many figures but very little visible action; on the reverse of the vase is a Dionysiac scene. The setting of the obverse is a sanctuary, and most of the twelve figures are engaged in dialogues with one another. In the middle of the scene there is a small Ionic temple decorated with a festoon from which small tablets are hanging. Inside the building a lady is explaining something to an elderly servant who is listening attentively: he looks like a messenger or a *paidagôgos*. Right in front of the two, directly below the temple, two boys[2] of slightly different ages are sitting peacefully on an altar, looking (and perhaps talking) to each other; these children strongly suggest that the elderly servant is a *paidagôgos* and not a messenger. In the upper left corner of the image Nikê is flying to the right to crown Athena with a wreath; the goddess is seated on her shield, holding her helmet. In the opposite upper right corner, two goddesses both holding crossbar torches are involved in conversation, one sitting and one standing. The sitting one, who is speaking to her partner and addressing her with a gesture of the right hand, is wearing a wheaten wreath and must be Demeter; the other one,

[1] Princeton University, Art Museum, Inv. 83–13. Trendall and Cambitoglou (1983: 78, 18/41a). The crater was first published by Trendall (1984). Cf. also Schefold and Jung (1989: 45 Abb. 27 *bis*).

[2] Schefold and Jung (1989: 46) suggest that the children are to be understood as a boy and a girl; Trendall (1984: 8) as well as Schmidt (1986: 169) see them as two boys.

Fig. 9.1 Red-figure volute crater attributed to the Darius Painter, showing Medea at Eleusis. South Italian, *c.*340–330 BCE.

wearing a crown, can be no one else but her daughter Korê. Below the temple on the right stands Heracles with his club and lionskin, a fillet around his head, carrying in both hands myrtle boughs decorated with more fillets. He listens closely to a winged goddess holding a *kerykeion*: she has her right hand raised with two fingers outstretched in the same gesture as Demeter's. In the bottom left corner there are two virtually naked youths. The upper one is leaning on a stick, holding a crossbar torch with fillets in his right hand, a strigil and an *aryballos* in his left hand. The other one is seated below him, wearing a *petasos*; he holds a stick and a strigil in his left hand and a ribbon in his right hand; at his side there is a small table with three more crossbar torches. The attributes of these two men are very general: they indicate only the athletic activities typical of the palaestra, and the sanctuary of Demeter. As they lack any other more specific attribute, they could be anybody; iconographically speaking, they *are* just anybody. They are structurally anonymous visitors of the sanctuary.[3]

The sanctuary itself, on the contrary, bears a name: an inscription on the architrave of the temple reads *ΕΛΕΥΣΙΣ · ΤΟ ΙΕΡΟΝ*. Given the presence of Demeter and Korê (and of the many crossbar torches), this specification does not come as a surprise. Much more surprising is the name of the lady inside the temple; an inscription on the stylobate identifies her as *ΜΗΔΕΙΑ*. This is definitely not a name one would have expected in such a surrounding—indeed, without this inscription it would never have occurred to anyone to identify her as Medea.

Representations of the myth of Medea in fourth-century South Italian red-figure vases are relatively numerous and striking, but with the sole exception of the Princeton crater they all show a completely different situation: Medea has just murdered her two children and is fleeing in a magical chariot drawn by flying snakes, pursued in vain by Jason[4]—so for example on an amphora in Naples (Figs. 9.2 and 9.3)[5] which is ascribed to the same artist, the Darius

---

[3] Trendall (1984: 94) suggested they be identified as the Dioscuri; the identification is accepted without discussion by Schmidt (1986: 169) as well as by Schefold and Jung (1989: 46). But they lack every conventional attribute of the Dioscuri. To name them as such, or indeed as any other identifiable individuals, is entirely arbitrary.

[4] *LIMC* 6, 391 f. s.v. Medeia nr. 29.35–8.

[5] Naples, Museo Nazionale Inv. 81954, H 3221: Trendall and Cambitoglou (1982: 497, 18/43); *LIMC* 6, 392 s.v. Medeia nr. 37; Aellen (1994: 207, cat. 42, fig. 52).

Fig. 9.2 Red-figure amphora, ascribed to the Darius Painter, showing Medea fleeing from Corinth in a chariot pulled by serpents with a dead child behind her and Jason in pursuit. South Italian, *c.*340–330 BCE.

Painter, as the Princeton crater. It is not surprising that this should be the scene which is represented so often, given that it corresponds to the bloody and spectacular climax of the events in Corinth as they are presented most memorably in Euripides' *Medea*. The fame of Euripides' tragedy and the psychological and artistic fascination of images of the murderous mother ensured that they dominate in the iconography of Medea in all media and all periods of ancient and modern art.[6] By contrast, the Princeton volute crater shows a peaceful scene set at the temple of Eleusis—a place not connected with Medea in any surviving literary text or in any other pictorial representation. What is Medea doing in Eleusis? Not surprisingly, finding a satisfactory answer to this question has proved very difficult.

A highly sophisticated attempt to overcome the difficulties in interpreting this image was undertaken almost twenty years ago by the late Margot Schmidt.[7] The question from which she began was very simple: is there any literary source that tells us of an encounter between Medea and Heracles? The information Schmidt was looking for is provided by two passages in Diodorus Siculus (4.54.7 and 55.4). According to the first passage, Medea, after slaying her children in Corinth, fled 'and made her way safely to Heracles in Thebes. Her reason for doing so was that Heracles had acted as a mediator in Colchis in connection with the agreements [*sc.* between Jason and Medea] and had sworn an oath that he would come to her aid if she should ever find that they had been violated.' The second passage reports that when Medea arrived in Thebes she found 'that Heracles, possessed by a mad frenzy, had just slain his own sons; Medea restored him to health by means of drugs. But since Eurystheus was pressing Heracles with his commands, she despaired of receiving any aid from him at the moment and sought refuge in Athens with Aegeus, the son of Pandion,' whom she then married. In Schmidt's interpretation this literary tradition gives us all the clues we need in order to understand what is represented on the Princeton crater. In the lower register the children of Heracles have sought refuge on the altar; Heracles himself

---

[6] A convenient survey is provided by Mastronarde (2002: 64–70).

[7] Schmidt (1986: 169–74). Cf. also *LIMC* 4, 726 s.v. Herakleidai nr. 9* (M. Schmidt); 806 s.v. Herakles Nr. 1409* (J. Boardman); *LIMC* 5, 755 s.v. Iris I nr. 153 (A. Kossatz-Deissmann); *LIMC* 6, 394 s.v. Medeia 68 (M. Schmidt); Harten 1999: 138–41 (with a criticism of Schmidt's interpretation).

is not yet possessed by his murderous insanity, but Iris is already there, announcing to Heracles (and indicating to us) what is about to happen according to the decision of the gods. Later—after the children have been killed—Medea will succeed in healing the hero. In Diodorus' version, Medea is not so much the mother who murders her own children as rather a healing sorceress; paradoxically it is Heracles, the strongest of all heroes, who himself stands in dire need of help, and it is he who kills his own children.

Obviously the fascination of this variant of the myth has to do with unexpected reversals of roles: Medea's murder of her children, famous from Euripides' tragedy, seems to have been displaced on to and conflated with Heracles' murder of his children, famous from another tragedy by the same playwright. But is all this really compatible with what we see on the Princeton crater? In the first place, the Diodorus version does not provide any answer to the question with which we began: what is Medea doing in Eleusis? There are only two inscriptions in the painting, one naming Eleusis and one naming Medea: it is inconvenient that an interpretative hypothesis does not explain their connection. But there are other and more serious objections. If Schmidt were right, the action in the lower register would have to take place in Thebes. We would therefore have to separate the altar, on which the children are sitting, from the temple in Eleusis, in which Medea and the *paidagôgos* are conversing. The temple and the altar, which seem so close to one another in the image, would be separated by a wide distance in the story: the result of this separation would be, in Eleusis, a temple without an altar and a *paidagôgos* without children and, in Thebes, an altar without a temple and two children without a *paidagôgos*. But there is more: for how are we to know on the basis of the image that any part of it is to be understood as taking place in Thebes? The painting is full of Eleusinian elements and names Eleusis prominently in the inscription on the architrave of the temple: it gives us not the slightest hint concerning Thebes.

The central point of the story as reported by Diodorus is obviously the madness of Heracles. Now frenzy is not an unusual topic in Apulian vase paintings. If a hero is overcome by insanity, then the vase painters show him being attacked by a personification, usually female, often winged and in violent action. This figure wears a standard outfit, a short chiton and boots; it is armed with torches

and/or snakes, with which it menaces its victim. Its name is sometimes indicated by an inscription (*Mania, Lyssa, Apatê, Poinê,* or
Oistros), but often there is no inscription: the beholder is evidently
supposed to be able to recognize easily who the personification is and
to know that its attack has devastating consequences.[8] On the
Princeton crater, by contrast, no fury is to be seen. The conversa-
tional partner to whom Heracles is listening is indeed a winged
creature wearing a short chiton and boots, but her characteristic
attribute is the messenger's *kerykeion*. She bears neither torches nor
snakes and she obviously has no evil effect: she is simply speaking.
From an iconographical as well as from a mythological point of view,
she is the exact opposite of a fury: she can only be Iris. As for
Heracles, he is listening attentively, but his whole attitude is perfectly
relaxed: the fillet around his head and the decorated branches in his
hands imply that he has been performing or is about to perform
some kind of sacred, peaceful ceremony. Are these the attitude and
the attributes of a man who in the very next moment is going to be
overcome by frenzy and kill his own children? Any attack from him
would come as a complete surprise—not only to the figures on the
vase (and first of all to the children on the altar), but also to the
beholder: the image gives us not the slightest hint of it.

In short, Schmidt starts out with the characters of Medea and
Heracles as though they figured in a list of names and then seeks
some mythical situation to which they could be applied. But what she
ignores by proceeding in this way is the visual logic of the image.
Methodologically, the proper procedure would instead be the opposite. First we ought to try to understand this visual logic, that is, the
narrative situation the painter is indicating by using the specifically
artistic means at his disposal; only afterwards can we try to identify
that situation with other evidence concerning Greek myths.

This is in general a sound methodological principle; but it seems to
be especially valid in the case of the Darius Painter. His subjects often
show a high degree of mythological learning, and he sometimes does
indeed choose to depict a very specific and less well known variant of
a myth: but when he does so, he makes this evident by visible clues.
A good example for such clues and for the way in which the composition of an image can be used in order to highlight the narrative

8 Aellen (1994: 24–81).

Fig. 9.3 Red-figure amphora, ascribed to the Darius Painter. Detail of Fig. 9.2, showing Medea fleeing from Corinth in a

structure of a story is offered by the Darius Painter's amphora in Naples (Figs. 9.2 and 9.3). There the narrative content is perfectly clear. In the middle of the scene Medea is fleeing in a chariot drawn by two serpents: it is the flying chariot given to her by her father Helius, with which she escapes from Corinth at the end of Euripides' tragedy. She is leaving behind her a dead child and a sword: the weapon has done its duty, she does not need it any more and has let it fall. Jason on horseback and two armed men on foot are pursuing Medea, but she is beyond their reach—not even on horseback can Jason catch up with her, not even supported by soldiers will he be able to punish her. This is clearly shown by the feeble attitude with which Jason is holding his spear, and by the goddess of the moon, Selene, riding on a horse at the right end of the image:[9] in the next moment the magical serpent-chariot, preceded by the moon goddess, is going to rise up into the sky. Between Selene and the chariot the painter has placed a fury: she wears her typical outfit, boots and a short chiton, with an animal skin around her shoulders. She is holding a torch in her left hand and a sword in her right hand—the same weapon with which Medea has just killed her own child. Untypical for the conventional fury is the nimbus she has around her head: a very similar nimbus is shining around the head of Selene. The nimbus characterizes both figures as heavenly beings and links them both closely to Medea: Selene is also the goddess of darkness and magic, and the fury obviously embodies the murderous forces of evil by which Medea is driven.[10] All this corresponds very closely to Euripides' tragedy.

The scene on the Naples amphora is arranged in two complementary halves, the left one male, the right one female: on the left we see Jason and his attendants, engaged in a fruitless pursuit; on the right Medea flees with her superhuman companions, a dark trio of magic and fury. The Medea scene on the Princeton crater is of a much higher degree of formal complexity. The composition has a rhyming structure, determined by two horizontal registers and by two diagonal axes. In the upper register we see exclusively goddesses, in the

---

[9] *LIMC* 2, 911 s.v. Astra nr. 28; Aellen (1994: 124 f.).

[10] Aellen (1994: 41 f., 54, 124 f.). Medea's association with the moon here is strengthened by her link with Hecate (E. *Med*. 395–7), also identified by the end of the fifth century with Artemis as the moon goddess and patroness of sorcery; this becomes a standard feature in such later treatments of the Medea myth as those of Apollonius Rhodius, Ovid, and Seneca.

lower register a mixture of mortal, divine, and semi-divine beings. Of the diagonal axes one (stressed by the multitude of cross bar torches) goes from top right to bottom left: it emphasizes Eleusis, with the two clearly identified goddesses Demeter and Korê and two anonymous human worshippers of them—these worshippers are two in number for no other reason than that all the other figures, in the other three corners as well as in the central panel and below it, come in pairs. This axis indicates the specific character of the Eleusinian sanctuary: pure, tranquil, free of violence and miasma. It requires no specific explanation: it gives the locale, the background. On the other axis from top left to bottom right (stressed by the presence of winged creatures: Nikê and Iris) we find Athena and Heracles. Both are outsiders to the sanctuary; this is shown most clearly by Athena, who—in opposition to Demeter—is not facing the Eleusinian temple: she is looking away from the centre of the image, her attention is obviously not concentrated on the sanctuary. Both Athena and Heracles seem to be involved in a specific dramatic situation that we shall have to try to explain.

But let us first establish what is plainly evident. In the middle of the picture Medea is standing inside the temple, at the epicentre of purity and holiness. It is impossible to stand there without the approval of Demeter and Korê. But such an approval would be unthinkable if Medea had murdered her children; were she a murderer of her own kin, she would bear the abhorrent stigma of religious pollution and could never be standing where she is. In fact, the children are not dead: they are alive, and are sitting on the altar below the temple. Again, by purely compositional means the painter has made perfectly clear to whom the children belong: they are related to Medea as the altar on which they sit is related to the temple; just as the altar belongs to the temple, so too the children belong to Medea. They are Medea's children, not someone else's. Medea and the children are mediated by the *paidagôgos* whose staff points to the children. Medea is speaking with the *paidagôgos*: what about, if not about her children? But why is she speaking with the *paidagôgos* about her children rather than dealing with them directly herself? It must be because what she is saying to the *paidagôgos* about her children is a set of instructions for him to take care of them in a situation in which she will not be able to do so herself. This must mean that she is about to go away; why and where, we cannot tell. But so much is clear: in this scene Medea does not appear as a murderous mother but as a good and caring one: she has brought her children to the Eleusinian sanctuary as the safest of all possible places, putting them under the protection of the Eleusinian goddesses. Now she has to leave again, continuing her journey: before she does so, she is giving her instructions to the *paidagôgos*, making sure that he will take care of them.

But these are not the only instructions that are being given: just as Medea is instructing the *paidagôgos*, Iris is making an announcement to Heracles. Iris of course is a messenger from the gods. On whose behalf is she acting in this case? The painting offers only two possibilities: either the Eleusinian goddesses or Athena. Demeter, to be sure, is shown speaking: but why would she need Iris to send a message to Heracles in her own sanctuary at Eleusis? Much more likely is a diagonal connection. As the two worshippers at the bottom left are connected with the Eleusinian goddesses at the top right, Iris at the bottom right is connected with Athena at the top left. It is hard to say what the narrative background of this connection might be. On the one hand Athena is sitting on her shield and receives a victory wreath from a winged Nikê, evidently in response to something that Athena has done. On the other hand another winged creature, Iris, is transmitting instructions to Heracles. Most likely she has been sent by Athena: in any case it is difficult to imagine what Iris' announcement might concern if not—once again—the two children sitting on the altar. Under these circumstances Heracles can hardly have any other function than to act as a protector: he is after all the strongest of all possible human protectors. And he has all the more reason to come to the aid of Eleusis—was he not famously initiated into the Eleusinian mysteries himself,[11] as his attributes here suggest? Even if we do not understand all the details, the general sense of the image is clear: the children are going to be saved, the joint forces of Athena, the Eleusinian goddesses and Heracles will be crowned by success— just as Athena is already being crowned by Nikê.

Comparing one more painting by the Darius Painter, on a volute crater in Berlin (Fig. 9.4),[12] will confirm our suggestions regarding

[11] See Lloyd-Jones (1967).
[12] Antikensammlungen, Inv. 1984.41: Giuliani (1995: 26–31, 88–94).

Fig. 9.4 Red-figure volute crater attributed to the Darius Painter, showing Phrixus and Athamas before an altar. South Italian, *c.*340–330 BCE.

the narrative strategies this particular artist favoured. Here again, as in the Princeton crater, the setting is in a sanctuary, as the altar indicates; in the upper zone of the picture an assembly of gods is witnessing what the humans are doing—although in fact there is very little action to be seen. Beside the altar, a young man (identified by an inscription as Phrixus) is winding a knotted *taenia* around the head of a ram; next to him on the right, a bearded king identified as Athamas is holding up the sacrificial knife. At first glance, everything seems to be perfectly clear: the ram is about to be sacrificed. But when we look closer we find some disturbing details. Why is Phrixus too wearing on his head a *taenia* identical to the one with which he is adorning the ram? What is the function of the lady at the left (named in an inscription as Ino) to whom the king is demonstratively pointing with his finger, and why is Phrixus turning his head towards her? Directly above the group with the ram, Zeus is sitting in conversation with Athena: but why are his brows contracted and his look so gloomy? He seems to disapprove of what he sees or hears: but why should he disapprove of a sacrifice in his honour? At the right end of the gods' assembly there is a lady between Apollo and Hermes who is named in an inscription as Nephelê. Although she seems to be listening to Hermes, everything about her—her arms, her dress, her feet—is in motion. As this motion has no evident functional purpose, it can only have a psychological meaning: Nephelê is violently distressed by what is happening at the altar, towards which she is pointing with an expressive gesture of her right hand. But again, what is the cause of her distress? Why should the harmless sacrifice of a ram provoke such violent reactions?

The answer to all these questions is provided by the myth.[13] Athamas, king of Boeotia, married Nephelê ('Cloud'), from whom he had two children, Phrixus and Helle (the latter is standing directly below Nephelê, listening to a *paidagôgos*). After Nephelê's early death, Athamas married again; Ino, his second wife, turned out to be a typically malevolent stepmother and attempted to destroy Nephelê's children. She convinced the Boeotian women to roast the corn before sowing it: as a result, the corn did not sprout, there was no harvest, and a famine followed. Athamas sent a messenger to the oracle in Delphi to inquire how to appease the gods. The messenger had been corrupted by Ino, and he reported that the gods required the sacrifice of the king's son, Phrixus. For what happens next in the story, two different variants are reported. According to one,[14] Athamas gives in to the pressure of the Boeotian people and consents to the sacrifice. Phrixus, who is the only person who has no idea what is going on, is asked to choose the best ram in the herd and to bring it to the altar. At the very last moment a divine wonder takes place: the ram begins to speak and tells Phrixus who is really supposed to be the victim; then the ram takes both of Nephelê's children on to its back and flies up into the air, rescuing them from danger. During the subsequent flight Helle falls into the sea and drowns, giving the Hellespont its name; Phrixus is carried by the flying ram to a faraway

---

[13] Apollod. 1.9.1.   [14] *Σ. Il.* 7.86 = *FHG* 3,34 fr. 37 (Philostephanus).

country, where he will finally sacrifice the ram to Zeus and marry the daughter of the king. According to the other variant,[15] Athamas refuses to obey the alleged oracle but, against the will of his father, Phrixus volunteers himself as victim in order to preserve his people from starvation—whereupon the corrupted messenger, impressed by so much heroism, denounces Ino's intrigue.

Now we can understand the *taenia* around the head of Phrixus: it characterizes him as a sacrificial victim. We also understand Athamas' finger pointing to Ino, Zeus' frown, and Nephelê's excitement: what is about to take place in this sanctuary is a human sacrifice, the result of an impious, murderous intrigue. We see Phrixus adorning the ram for the sacrifice: his gesture would be absurd if he did not still believe that the ram was going to be the victim. But at the same time Phrixus is turning his head away from the ram, back to his stepmother, following the hint of his father's finger, as if he had finally begun to understand that Ino was the real cause of all his trouble. The painter gives the viewer precise visual clues in order to make perfectly clear which variant of the story he is depicting: he is obviously not representing Phrixus as a heroic volunteer offering to be sacrificed but as an unconscious victim. Phrixus is shown in the precise moment in which he comes to a full understanding of the action in which he is involved. In this regard there is a peculiar affinity between Phrixus and the viewer: for at first glance the viewer too will interpret what he sees as the preparation for an ordinary sacrifice; only when he looks closer will he begin to realize that the ram is only a pretext and that Phrixus himself is the designated victim.

Of course, in the case of the Berlin crater the reason that we are able to supply a satisfactory meaning to the visual clues is that we know from literary sources the version of the story the painter had in mind. If we did not happen to have these sources, many details of the picture would remain incomprehensible. But even then we would not have to give up altogether the attempt at interpretation—so long as we were willing to rely on what we see. In that case, we would say that a king is about to sacrifice a ram in a sanctuary; but we would suspect

---

[15] Hygin. *Fab.* 2; this variant of the story was probably invented by Euripides: Webster (1967*b*: 131–6); Aigner (1982: 148–51).

that this was unlikely to be the whole meaning. For there is definitely something strange about this sacrifice. The king himself seems to be hinting at something with his outstretched finger, and his principal attendant is turning his eyes away from the victim, distracted from the holy action by something of the utmost importance. The gods have assembled in the upper zone of the picture: but Zeus—probably the god to whom the sacrifice is directed—is obviously displeased by what is happening, and a goddess named Nephelê seems to be in a state of great excitement and anxiety. Even if we knew nothing from the surviving literary evidence, we could be sure on the basis of the visual signals alone that the whole picture is hinting at some kind of hidden evil.

Let us now return to the Princeton crater to see what relation ought to obtain between our understanding of it and the mythographic traditions. The differences between the representations of Medea on the Princeton crater and on the amphora in Naples are so drastic that the two images must evidently refer to two completely different variants of the myth. In the one case (Naples) we see the furious, murderous mother we know from Euripides' tragedy; in the other case (Princeton) we see Medea as a completely different character, as a mother taking care of her children and acting in agreement with Athena and the Eleusinian goddesses. Up to now we have examined only the possible connection between the Princeton crater and the story reported by Diodorus: but the image on the crater and the Diodorus story are in fact not at all compatible with each other. We are left with only one set of alternatives: either to try to find some (inevitably very complicated) explanation for why the painter, although he had Diodorus' story in mind, decided to show it in such an enigmatic way; or else to trust the picture in its visual logic. But in the latter case we shall be obliged to set aside Diodorus' story altogether.

And yet there is no other attested version of any myth involving Medea which fits the image on the Princeton crater any better. Hence we must give up the attempt to identify that image with any attested version of a Medea myth. But does that entail refusing to identify the image with any version of such a myth whatsoever? Of course not: on the one hand we can be certain on principle that not all versions of Medea myths which the Greek imagination ever invented have survived;[16] and on the other hand a number of elements in the image—the names, the apparent relations between the figures, the specific location—make no sense whatsoever unless they are intended to communicate to us a specific narrative situation. Hence we must conclude that the painter of the vase must have been dealing with some other version of the myth: a version not preserved in any extant literary source.

This is exactly the line of interpretation proposed by Arthur Dale Trendall when he first published the Princeton vase. He pointed to the fact that in some versions of the story 'Medea did *not* murder her children, but put them as suppliants on an altar in the sanctuary of Hera Akraia at Perachora, near Corinth, in the hope that they would be looked after by Jason'.[17] Put in these terms, the image of the children on an altar makes perfectly good sense, even if in the present case the sanctuary is not the one at Perachora but in Eleusis. To be sure, there is no literary evidence that Medea chose Eleusis as a refuge for her children, but in fact this

would be an appropriate place for the purpose, since it is in Attica and near to Athens where she herself will find asylum with Aigeus, as we are reminded by the presence of Athena on the Princeton vase. It would also give the children the protection not only of a particularly holy spot but also of [. . .] Herakles, a protector par excellence, who may well have been sent there under divine instruction for this purpose, as the presence of Iris might indicate. Medea looks to be explaining the situation to the slightly puzzled *paidagogos*; if her look is rather worried, it is nonetheless comparatively tranquil, as if she wishes to do the right thing for her children and secure for them all the religious support that can be had.[18]

So far the interpretation proposed by Trendall. He is certainly on the right track. But maybe we can go a few steps further.

Let us begin with the question of where Medea is going. The various myths of Medea indicate locations for her activities stretching from Asia through most of Greece; her story begins in remote Colchis and it returns there again at the end. But the Princeton image offers only one

---

[16] For example, the Index of *TrGF* vol. 2 lists the following lost *Medea* tragedies by minor and unknown tragedians: 15 F 1–3; 17 T 1; 23 F ?; 29 F 1; 52 F 1a; 70 F 1e; 78 A T 1; 88 F 1e; 205 F 1; ad. 6a; *701.

[17] Trendall (1984: 13).   [18] Trendall (1984: 14).

figure who signifies any city other than Eleusis, i.e. Athena, who regularly signifies Athens (Heracles is of course connected with Thebes in myth, but his presence in images never indicates the city). So presumably Medea is going to Athens; Eleusis is on her way there. According to various accounts, she plays an important role in Athenian mythology—she is the wife of Aegeus and the mother by him of Medus; stepmother as she is, she tries to murder Theseus, Aegeus' son by Aethra, but fails, and flees home to Colchis together with Medus.[19] In none of these accounts do any children of hers by Jason make any appearance at all in Athens (where at the very least they would certainly have been rather inconvenient for her). Hence any myth that tells of Medea's escape to Athens has to account for the failure of her children by Jason to arrive there with her. Although the version of the story of Medea represented on the Princeton crater is unique, we can understand the dramatic situation it depicts by considering its parallels with and its differences from extant versions. Here Medea does not kill her children but instead saves them by assigning them to a temple. Elsewhere she uses the temple of Hera Acraia near Corinth;[20] here she evidently uses Eleusis. The crucial point is that in Athenian mythology Medea plays a role but her children with Jason do not; hence they cannot be brought with her from Corinth to Athens but must be discarded somewhere along the way. The various outcomes for these children—Medea kills them intentionally, she kills them unintentionally, the Corinthians kill them, they are rescued in a temple—differ enormously in their emotional impact, but in regard to the narrative economy they are functionally identical.

In the version depicted on the Princeton crater, Medea is leaving the children in the temple of Eleusis under the protective care of a *paidagôgos*. The choice and gestures of the figures who surround them on the vase indicate clearly that they have protected Eleusis from attack and will always do so. Who is likely to have attacked Eleusis in order to kill Medea's children? The likeliest candidates

---

[19] Hdt. 7.62.1; Apollod. 1.9.28; E. *Aigeus* fr. 1 ff. *TrGF*. Already E. *Med.* 663–758 refers to her Athenian future.

[20] Apollod. 1.9.28; Σ. E. *Med.* 264 (Parmeniscus); Σ. Pind. *O.* 13.74g; Eumelus fr. 5 Bernabé. Mastronarde (2002: 50–3) provides a helpful survey of the various mythical traditions regarding Medea's children.

are the Corinthians, who would have attacked the temple in order to avenge themselves upon Medea's children for the death of their king's child; and the sanctuary (and presumably Medea's children) would have been successfully defended by Athena (i.e. the Athenians) and Heracles. So we can be sure that Eleusis was not destroyed by the Corinthians—indeed, no Greek poet who had claimed that it was would have been believed.

And yet a problem remains, for even though Eleusis is successfully protected against attack, Medea's children do not come with her to Athens. Do they survive and remain in Eleusis as priests or functionaries in the temple (perhaps like Ion at Delphi)? Do they offer themselves as sacrificial victims in order to save Eleusis? Are they killed treacherously by the Corinthians? In any case, why does Nikê crown Athena? Has there been an actual military conflict in which the Athenians have defeated the Corinthians? Has a Corinthian attack been threatened but averted, perhaps by a quick and impressive Athenian reaction? Or is Athena always victorious?[21] It must be recognized that the measures invoked in this painting in order to protect Medea's children are particularly massive; Iris' message to Heracles doubles Medea's message to the *paidagôgos* and provides the children with enormous divine protection; and yet they end up never coming to Athens. If this is because they die, then what good was Heracles? So all in all it is perhaps likeliest that they stay on in Eleusis in the temple. Yet in the present state of the evidence this problem remains unsolvable.

In this version, why does Medea leave the children in Eleusis rather than in Corinth? In Euripides' play, Medea kills the children in Corinth herself and says that she will convey their dead bodies to the temple of Hera Acraia at Perachora near Corinth (1378–83). In another version, she is a good mother who wishes to save them and brings them to the same temple, but nevertheless they are killed there. In the Princeton version, she takes them to a different place, Eleusis, once again because she wants to save them; and the choice of this new place may perhaps provide further evidence for our suggestion that this time they do not die but are rescued after all. To be sure, Eleusis is geographically a quite plausible place for Medea

---

21 See further, on Athens and *Nikê*, Wilson in this volume.

to stop at on the way from Corinth to Athens. But Medea could have stopped anywhere during her trip: why then at Eleusis and not elsewhere? Obviously, because Eleusis was the most important extra-urban cult centre of Athens; the children could not have been left anywhere else that would have provided them with a protection reinforced by such strong religious sanctions (one more reason to think that they survive). But perhaps there is even more. Eleusis is a sanctuary full of myths and rituals involving death and immortality and telling of failed and successful rescues.[22] Hence it is a perfect place for Medea to leave her endangered children in the hope that they will thereby be rescued—and it is a perfect place for a clever poet to have her leave them, so as to create suspense among his audience about whether the rescue will end up being a failure or a success.

***

All we have is this vase. No surviving text elucidates it completely. Can we nonetheless make some sort of informed guess about the literary version of the myth which seems to lie behind it and to which it seems to refer? That such a literary version must have existed does indeed seem to be presupposed by the visual signals in this painting; and the same signals make it probable that this version was dramatic, and hence, given the subject matter, a tragedy. We have no evidence about who the author is to whose play this vase seems to make reference. But presumably that play was post-Euripidean. If so, perhaps it not only was influenced by Euripides but also ventured to improve upon Euripides by trying to provide an answer for one question which he had left open: why can Medea not simply take the children with her when she leaves Corinth?[23] In Euripides' tragedy, Medea does indeed raise the possibility of taking them away with her (1045, 1058), but after a certain point she irrationally suppresses that option and is only any longer capable of recognizing two others: either to leave them to be killed in Corinth by her enemies, or to

---

[22] Burkert (1985: 285–90); and, in general, Burkert (1987). Mastronarde (2002: 51–2) points out a connection between the *Homeric Hymn to Demeter* and the myth of Medea.

[23] Aristotle criticized what he considered to be a different flaw in the construction of the play, Aegeus' arrival: *Po.* 25.1461^b 20–1.

kill them herself (1060–1, 1236–41).[24] Given these alternatives, she decides to kill them herself.

But a later author might well have wondered why she could not simply save them by taking them along with her to Athens. Besides leaving them behind and killing them herself, was there really no other option open to Medea? This vase might be evidence for a correction along these lines. Presumably Medea cannot take the children with her to Athens because she knows that she is going to marry Aegeus there. As we know from Euripides' *Medea*, Aegeus is urgently interested in having children of his own, and it does not seem an excess of caution to suppose that he would not be likely to look with much favour on a wife who brought with her into marriage with him the children she had had by some other man. Perhaps Medea thinks she will eventually win over Aegeus: loving her, and with children now of his own, perhaps he will some day come to accept her children by Jason. In the *Ion*, Xuthus proposes a similarly optimistic and self-serving line of reasoning (654–60). Medea might have thought that her children would not have to stay at Eleusis forever. But as it happens, matters turn out very differently from what she had expected. She will have to leave Athens in a hurry, and her children will never be able to join her there.

Hypothetically, we might even try to reconstruct how the plot of such a tragedy could conceivably have been organized. We can easily imagine a prologue, spoken most probably by Athena (or perhaps by Medea herself), which explained the past premises of the immediate situation; if the speaker was divine, it could also have hinted at the eventual outcome. Whoever the prologue was entrusted to, Medea herself will have had to enter the stage at or very near the beginning of the play, if not in its first lines then immediately after the prologue. The astonishing presence of the notorious barbarian sorceress at Eleusis, this holiest of sanctuaries, will surely have come as a shock to the audience of the play and might well have had the same effect upon a chorus (of Eleusinians? or of Athenian visitors to the sanctuary, as in Euripides' *Ion*?) within it too; but the general horror could have been

---

[24] This apparent incoherence is one of the reasons Medea's celebrated monologue (1056–80) has so often been suspected by textual critics; for a recent analysis of the problems and solutions, see Mastronarde (2002: 388–97).

placated by a speech by Medea in which she explained the events in Corinth from her own point of view and thereby created sufficient sympathy for herself, among her audience inside and outside of the play, to make it clear that this tragedian's Medea was a very different woman from Euripides'. Such a scene could have been modelled upon the meeting between Oedipus and the chorus of pious Colonians in Sophocles' *Oedipus at Colonus*. The scene with the *paidagôgos* which is represented on the vase could well have followed shortly thereafter: Medea will have given him her instructions, warned him to be careful, and then left for Athens. She will never have reappeared upon the stage in this play. Instead, there will have been the grave menace of a Corinthian attack. Perhaps a herald or envoys will have arrived to announce the Corinthians' demand that the children be given up to them; if so, this will have been rejected proudly by the Eleusinians. In any case there was probably an extended messenger's speech which recounted in vivid detail how the Corinthian attack was either defeated or thwarted by the Athenians and Heracles. Athens will once again have demonstrated her piety and strength in the protection of suppliants against cruel foreigners (as for example in Sophocles' *Oedipus at Colonus* and in Euripides' *Children of Heracles* and *Suppliant Women*).[25] A final divine or heroic figure (Demeter? Heracles?) could have revealed the future destinies of Medea and her children and prepared the way for a triumphal general exit.

No doubt, if the play depicted on the Princeton crater was anything like this tentative hypothesis, it was very far from being a great tragedy. But we are not professional dramatists, and we have little doubt that a professional tragedian, even a mediocre one, could have come up with a dramatic version that would have worked well enough on the stage to inspire audiences that included a first-rate Apulian artist. What we offer here is not great theatre: at best it would have been nothing more than possible theatre. But for our argument this is all that matters.

---

[25] Loraux (1981: 67–9); and see now in general Grethlein (2003).

IV

Visualizing Drama: The Divinities
of Tragedy and Comedy

10

Tragedy Personified

Edith Hall

1. VISUALIZING TRAGEDY

In a volume celebrating a scholar esteemed for illuminating the relationship between ancient Greek tragic drama and the visual imagination, the personification of Tragedy itself is an appropriate issue to raise. Ancient historians described events as if they were episodes in tragic drama; novelists and poets composed ecphraseis of scenes derived from tragic theatre; sculptors and potters carved and painted figures from individual tragedies. But what did Tragedy actually *look like*? There were never many attempts to personify Tragedy: just as the Muses were in general less important in literature than the self-awareness of individual poets,[1] so allegorical figures representing genres of poetry and theatre appeared less frequently than images of their composers or performers. From the late fourth century onwards most attempts to visualize Tragedy will probably have owed something to the painting *Dionysus with Tragedy and Comedy* by the influential artist Aetion (Pliny, *NH* 35.78). An approximate contemporary of Apelles, Aetion was most famous for his painting of the marriage of Alexander to Roxana (327 BCE), a work which legend held had been displayed at the Olympic Games (Lucian, *Aetion* 4–6). The motif Aetion there devised of winged Erotes playing with Alexander's armour was imitated in Roman wall paintings of Hercules and Mars. And Aetion's conception of

---

[1] Spentzou (2002: 21).

Tragedy and Comedy, as mediated through later ancient artworks, still underlies most modern answers to the question of what Tragedy looks like (see section 5 below).

By the late fifth century, however, there were already word pictures of the art of Tragedy—the *technê* which, according to Aristophanes, Euripides had inherited from Aeschylus so overweight that she needed to be treated with a purgative diet, walks, and monodies (*Frogs* 939–44).[2] By the mid-fourth century Aristotle could describe Tragedy in language suggesting an organic being who physically matures and reaches her *telos* (*Po.* 4.1449ᵃ 9–15).[3] Both these personifications of Tragedy as a woman are technically non-mimetic, and yet still function visually by making the abstraction appear concrete before the mind's eye.[4] Such literary personifications, assembled from words rather than stone or paint, are especially rich in societies such as ancient Greece in which systematic anthropomorphism determines the conception of gods. Literary personifications accompany developed symbolic codes of visual representation in painting, sculpture, coins, and the theatre of the kind which Zeitlin has suggested typified the culture of classical Athens.[5] Personification in written discourse fascinated twentieth-century literary theorists: it was defined as a form of textually constituted anthropomorphism, which, since it posits as given 'an identification at the level of substance', is the most extreme form of figurative language.[6] But what were the substantive images of Tragedy in the cultural repertoire of Aristophanes' spectators or Aristotle's students?

Some of the earliest personifications of genres appeared on the dramatic stage itself, for example the character Iambê who may have participated in the satyr play by Sophocles named after her: in the *Homeric Hymn to Demeter* Iambê cheered the mourning Demeter

---

  ² See Newiger (1957: 130–3).

  ³ See Webster (1956: 7).

  ⁴ Warner (1987: 82).

  ⁵ See Zeitlin (1994). Useful bibliography includes Aellen (1994) on personification in fourth-century vase painting, Petersen (1939: 67–72) on Hellenistic personifications, and Paxson (1994: 13) on drama and rhetorical *prosôpopoeia*. There is an excellent overview of personification in Greek art and literature offered by Stafford (2000), especially her theoretical first chapter, although none of her subsequent case studies deals with the personification of literary genres.

  ⁶ See de Man (1984: 241).

by telling her jokes (202–5). Iambê was an aetiological figure personifying *iambos* through her association with the obscene jesting of women celebrating the Thesmophoria (Apollod. 1.5.1).[7] Although the date of the Sophoclean *Iambê* is unknown, the other metapoetic personifications that appeared in the Athenian theatre belong to the last three decades of the fifth century, a period which 'witnessed an unparalleled burst of intensely aggressive metapoetic debate inside poetry produced in Athens'.[8] The most remarkable was the figure of *Kômôidia* who appeared in Cratinus' comedy *Pytinê* (*Wine-Flask*) in 423 BCE; this uproarious play triumphed over the first version of Aristophanes' *Clouds*. In *Pytinê* Comedy was the embittered wife of Cratinus himself. She wanted to divorce him because he was consorting with another woman, Pytinê—i.e. with drinking.[9] The comedy presented Cratinus' fondness for drink as impeding his dramatic creativity. In a comparable play by Pherecrates, entitled *Cheirôn*, Mousikê herself appeared as a plaintiff; she listed the outrages inflicted upon her by poets including Timotheus, the arch-apostle of the New Music.[10] There were also two lost plays by Aristophanes (*Gêrytades* and *Poiêsis*) in which Poetry may have appeared on stage.[11] In the fourth century Antiphanes followed suit with a comedy entitled *Poiêsis*.

Yet no known playwright made an actor dress up as *Tragôidia*. The sole candidate is Euripides' slovenly, dancing Muse in Aristophanes' *Frogs*, but she is no personification of Tragedy generically. Her castanets (see 1305) are reminiscent of those played by Euripides' Hypsipyle to the baby Opheltes in the lowly office of his nurse in the play named after her.[12] The Aristophanic *mousa Euripidou* is also associated with Lesbos, implying fellatio and the music of Terpander (1308); she is neither young nor attractive and her social status is low.[13] A subversive personification of an aesthetic evaluation, she

---

[7] The sole fragment of Sophocles' *Iambê* (Sophocles fr. inc. 731 *TrGF*) has also been attributed to his *Triptolemus*: see Pearson (1917: 3.1). On Iambê see Foley (1994: 45–6).

[8] Wilson (1999–2000: 431).

[9] See *Pytinê* T i and ii and Cratinus fragments 193–6 *PCG*, with Hall (2000: 410–11); Rosen (2000).

[10] See Pherecrates fr. 155 *PCG*; Hall (2000: 414–15); Dobrov and Urios-Aparisi (1995).

[11] See Hall (2000: 413–14).

[12] Fr. I ii 9–16 in Cockle (1987: 59).   [13] Dover (1993a: 351–2).

is Euripides' Muse only as conceived from the biased perspective of Aristophanes' reactionary Aeschylus. She physically manifests a prejudicial judgement on an individual dramatist, rather than personifying what the classical Athenians in general imagined Tragedy looked like. The only other candidate for a staged personification of tragedy is the muse who appears in the *Rhesus* attributed to Euripides and laments *ex machina* the death of her Thracian son (890–982). But the ancient scholar who identified her as Calliope was probably correct; she is an intertextual figure, marking the relationship between the *Iliad* and her play.[14]

Perhaps *Tragôidia*'s non-appearance on stage expresses one significant generic difference between tragic and comic theatre. *Tragôidia* could scarcely appear in tragedy herself, since the poets were evoking a heroic world where drama had not yet existed; they avoided using the terminology of the theatre, its spectators, the acting profession, and the dramatic genres.[15] Although overt metatheatre has recently been sought with great enthusiasm in Athenian tragedy, it remains undeniable that the playwrights erased the anachronistic notion of theatre from their vision of Bronze Age entertainments, defined in the language of choral dancing, *epos* and *melê*.[16] But Tragedy does not seem to have appeared in comedy, either. Perhaps this is because one definitive difference between fifth-century tragedy and comedy is that tragedy virtually never breaks what used to be called 'the dramatic illusion' in order directly to apostrophize its audience.[17] The comic poets could not even conceive, perhaps, of making a personification of Tragedy address the comic audience, because the closed-off characters in Tragedy's genre hardly ever do themselves.

[14] The text of the play does not give the Muse a name. The author of the first hypothesis identifies her as Calliope; in the third hypothesis Aristophanes of Byzantium anachronistically suggested that she might be Terpsichore. See further Hall (1999: 97 and nn. 4–7); Ebener (1966: 114). On the Homeric echoes in the Muse scene in *Rhesus*, see Bond (1996: 263–4).

[15] Easterling (1985).

[16] I argue this in greater detail in Hall (2006: ch. 4), a discussion which depends more than I can express on Froma's work.

[17] See e.g. Taplin (1986). There are isolated rule-proving exceptions, above all Electra's use of the second person plural at E. *Or.* 128. But there are other ways in which that drama plays dangerously with subverting conventional distinctions between comedy and tragedy.

2. VASE PAINTINGS OF *TRAGÔIDIA*

The fine *LIMC* article on 'Tragoedia' by Annelise Kossatz-Deissman reveals that the earliest answer to the question 'what did Tragedy look like?' is provided by a red-figure vase dated to about 440 BCE and now in The Vivenel Museum in Compiègne, France (Fig. 10.1). *Tragôidia* enters the history of the visual imagination as one of the female figures—usually maenads—named after genres who appear in Dionysiac scenes on mid-fifth-century Athenian red-figure vases. The image, painted by the unnamed hand of a member of the group of Polygnotus, is undistinguished in either conception or execution. Yet one feature is unexpected: the earliest identifiable visualization of Tragedy in the art of the world holds, in addition to a thyrsus, a crouching leveret (see detail, Fig. 10.2).

Fig. 10.1 Red-figure crater painted by a member of the Polygnotus Group. Athenian *c.*440–430 BCE.

Fig. 10.2 Red-figure crater painted by a member of the Polygnotus Group. Detail of Fig. 10.1, showing a personification of Tragedy, with a thyrsus and crouching leveret. Athenian, *c.*440 BCE.

Dionysiac imagery involving maenads was an Athenian sixth-century invention; the maenads joined the *thiasos* relatively late, at around the time when Peisistratus was encouraging the development of the Dionysia, and indeed when tragedy first began (its official inauguration is dated to 534). Subsequently, the visual experience of theatre had a crucial if unquantifiable effect on the depiction of the Dionysiac *thiasos*.[18] The scenes with maenads specifically named *Tragôidia*, however, do not appear until a century after the maenads joined the Dionysiac revel. They are preceded by satyrs named for dances, such as *Sikinnos*;[19] *Kômôidia* is first

[18] Schöne (1987: 190).
[19] Fränkel (1912: 54). On genre labels in vase painting in the late fifth century see Couëlle (1991), some of which is reprised in Couëlle (1998). On the evolution of personified abstractions more generally, see Shapiro (1993).

identified as a thyrsus-bearing attendant on the mid-fifth-century bell crater in the Louvre (G 421) depicting Dionysus leading Hephaestus back to Olympus, accompanied by an aulos-playing Marsyas. Although on the reverse of the Compiègne crater a certain energy characterizes the satyr's pursuit of a maenad, *Tragôidia* herself appears in a much calmer, domestic tableau, one of the images of the family life of satyrs analysed by François Lissarrague.[20]

Tragôidia stands to the left, behind the seated Dionysus. He offers wine to an infant satyr named *Kômos*, and Ariadne, on the right, replenishes the cup from an oinochoe. *Tragôidia* apparently intends the leveret, into whose eyes she smiles playfully, to be a gift for *Kômos*. Her presence seems to link Dionysus and Ariadne with *theatre*. Each side of the vase thus represents a different perspective on Dionysiac festivals and the dramatic competitions: the name of the satyr child, indeed, recalls both the processional revels before the plays began, and the celebrations of the victorious performers that followed them.[21] In a study of Polygnotus, Matheson calls this *Tragôidia* a 'maenad-like figure' rather than a maenad,[22] but she certainly carries a thyrsus. She also wears a distinctive round, peaked headdress (*sakkos*), of soft fabric, worn by maenads in *thiasos* scenes on other vases.[23]

The other obvious accoutrement of the Compiègne *Tragôidia* is the leveret. A fully grown hare, like a cock, can often connote a sexual advance in the form of a gift bestowed by an *erastês* on an *erômenos*, and a mildly flirtatious implication may be intended here. In non-Dionysiac scenes hares can bear other meanings: they can communicate a rural setting, or the speed of the running Boreads, or hunting (Cheiron regularly carries a fox and a hare on a stick in his role as hunter). Since hares were known to come out of their forms to feed

---

[20] Lissarrague (2003).

[21] Lissarrague (2003: 182–3).

[22] Matheson (1995: 192).

[23] See Galoin (2001: 151). This is also worn by a maenad on a pointed amphora by the Achilles Painter, in the Cabinet des Médailles (357 = *ARV*² 987.2), published by Shefton (1967). This scene portrays a night-time revel, with satyrs and maenads in different attitudes; the maenad in question holds a torch. She is the figure on the far left of the photograph reproduced in Robertson (1992: 196, fig. 206). Thanks to Oliver Dickinson for this reference.

only under cover of darkness, when hare hunts therefore took place, their presence in art might suggest a nocturnal scene. In black-figure vases, youths wearing fillets and carrying wineskins sometimes also carry hares, apparently intended as offerings.[24] When it comes to Dionysiac scenes, adult hares sometimes appear hanging dead from pegs behind the god (e.g. *ABV* 63.2). Women bring hares to Dionysus on two vases by the Amasis Painter.[25] One of these, dated to the 530s, is the earliest vase on which females attend Dionysus alone without satyrs, and on which a female wears a leopard skin. Dionysus stands to the left holding his kantharos and waving as two women approach. They wear ivy wreaths and hold sprigs of ivy; one holds a hare and the other a small stag. As Carpenter says, by the time of this vase 'women have become central to the meaning of a Dionysian scene'; it is 'likely they had a specific inspiration' and may represent changes, connected with theatre, in the Athenian understanding of Dionysus' women.[26] Does this archaic hare-bearing maenad illuminate *Tragôidia*'s leveret? The Compiègne painter is aware that the hare is a traditional maenadic accoutrement, and an erotic gift, but has scaled the animal down to fit the playful, familial tone of his domestic *thiasos*. The earliest parallel actually occurs in a *thiasos* scene on a cup by Lydus in which a small satyr leans down to pat a hare.[27] But there is no parallel to the tiny leveret sitting on an outstretched palm.

The hare-bearing *Tragôidia* is not a personification in the modern sense of that term. Yet her materiality does articulate something of the relation she bears to other phenomena connected with her vase. Tragedy is part of theatre, and theatre is part of the collective ritual process of worshipping Dionysus at Athens. From this perspective the closest parallel is another cute, quasi-familial scene represented on a fragmentary vase dated to about 430 BCE; a satyr leans over

---

[24] See Carpenter (1986: 51–2); Koch-Harnack (1983: 63–79).

[25] *ABV* 151.21 and 152.25.

[26] Carpenter (1986: 90). Beazley (1951: 57) calls the animals borne by the women their 'pets', but the way in which they are carried suggests more violent associations, and that the women are 'sisters of the hunter-maenads described by Euripides in *Bacchae* 734–48' (Carpenter 1986: 90 n. 65).

[27] London B 148, *ABV* 109.29; Tiverios (1976: pls. 51a and 52a).

the small satyr boy, between maenads who seem likely to have represented Tragedy and Comedy.[28]

The Compiègne scene also resembles two mid-fifth-century vase paintings in which nymphs attend the infant Dionysus and his father Zeus.[29] Perhaps the Compiègne artist, when wishing to incorporate Dionysus, Tragedy, and the *kômos* into a visual design, saw the relationships between these phenomena as intergenerational, and analogous to the parental and nurturing roles played in the instance of the child Dionysus by Zeus and the nymphs respectively. Yet the *Tragôidia* scene provides neither a direct allegory nor a genealogically conceived narrative of origins: it crystallizes, through the use of a conventional mythical framework, a set of symbiotic and interdependent relationships operating within the drama festivals. *Tragôidia* is configured as older and more dignified than the bibulous *Kômos*, even if her gift to him has a coy connotation.[30]

On two slightly later vases, emanating from a period when Csapo has argued that there was a strong rise in the self-conscious notion of tragedy as a performance,[31] *Tragôidia* is a wilder maenad, and her primary relationship is with an adult male in her *thiasos*, a sexually excited satyr. The earlier occurs on the neck of a volute crater from Gela of about 430 BCE, now in New York (MMA 1924.97.250). On both of the images on the neck there are *thiasos* scenes; on the side without Dionysus two satyrs, both named Simos, approach maenads named *Kômôidia* and *Tragôidia* (with thyrsus) respectively (Fig. 10.3). This scene of pursuit, with its whirling clothes, speed, and excitement, is related psychologically to the experience of the dancing chorus central and ancestral to all genres of drama. It is quite different from the static rural tableau of the Compiègne scene, which evokes an atmosphere nearer to that of a spoken episode separating the choruses of a satyr play, such as the hillside dialogue in the

---

[28] Fragments in Florence and Leipzig: *ARV*[2] 1258, 2.

[29] See Fuhrmann (1950–1: 116–20). Both these 'Birth of Dionysus' vases are in Ferrara.

[30] Olympio in Plautus' *Casina* fantasizes about the words of affection the lovely eponymous heroine Casina will bestow on him (46–50), which he hopes will conclude 'my sparrow chick, my dove, my hare!' (*mi lepus*).

[31] Csapo (2004*a*).

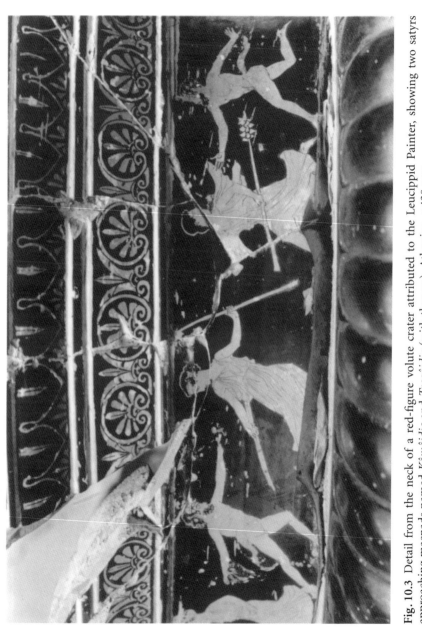

Fig. 10.3 Detail from the neck of a red-figure volute crater attributed to the Leucippid Painter, showing two satyrs approaching maenads named *Kōmōidia* and *Tragōidia* (with thyrsos). Athenian, c.430 BCE.

Trackers of Sophocles in which the nymph Cyllene hushes the satyrs and describes Hermes' birth to them.[32]

Of slightly later date is the famous vase in Oxford (Ashmolean 534), which depicts a satyr named Kissos priapically creeping up to a sleeping maenad named *Tragôidia*, thus configuring the relationship of satyrdom to Tragedy as one of covert sexual assault (Fig. 10.4). This is a revealing way of looking at the dialectical interdependence of the two types of drama enacted sequentially at the Dionysia; it can be argued that satyr drama functioned to 'ambush' the foregoing serious drama, and reorient the tragic audiences in a collective identity founded in uproarious masculinity: as the dialogue between Agathon and Euripides' In-Law in Aristophanes' *Women at the Thesmophoria* comically suggests (148–58), the appropriate frame of mind in which to compose satyr drama was while enjoying penetrative sexual intercourse with another man.[33] The jolly celebration of masculinity in satyr drama was psychosocially desirable given the intense emotional identification, often with women and always with emotions socially constructed as feminine (the process Zeitlin calls 'playing the other'), which the audience had experienced in the three preceding tragedies.[34] The presentation of the relationship between the satyr and the maenad here approaches an 'allegorical' reading of the relationships between tragedy and satyr drama; indeed, the Ashmolean maenad has been regarded as an early example of the personification which was to become such a habitual mark of fourth-century Athenian thought; on this argument she provides a parallel with the personified Philosophy in Isocrates' *Panegyric*, and with the personified dramatic poetry whom Plato drove from his ideal state.[35]

Tragôidia begins to appear in different guises on late-fifth-century vases. The contexts, still Dionysiac, are more explicit about their status as representations of the 'real world' of the drama competitions. The relationship between *Tragôidia* and the Dionysiac *thiasos* becomes less abstract, less remote from the experience of the

---

[32] See Sophocles *TrGF* fr. 314, especially 221–404, with Hall (1998: 16–17). The rustic setting of satyr-drama was one of the most important ways in which it differed from the usual polis-context of tragedy: see Vitruvius 5.6.9.

[33] See Hall (1998).   [34] Zeitlin (1985a).

[35] Webster (1956: 40–1 with n. 1).

Fig. 10.4 Red-figure oinochoe, showing a satyr approaching the sleeping figure of Tragedy. Athenian, *c*.430 BCE.

spectators, and signifies the agonistic structures and performance conventions within which drama was enjoyed. Thus on an (extremely) fragmentary Barcelona pelike (Mus. Arch. 33), Apollo and Dionysus, with his *thiasos*, are depicted at a victory tripod. On the left flies a Nikê-like figure securely named *Kômôidia* (see the reconstruction of the painting in Fig. 10.5a); the other (largely lost) winged figure, in a low position second from the right and between a satyr holding a jug and *Paidia* (a personification of the playful element in the satyric revel), is probably *Tragôidia* (see Fig. 10.5b).[36] She is certainly preparing to bestow a tragic mask on the tripod. The explicit choregic context emphasizes the liturgical dimension of theatre; it also shows that Tragedy herself is becoming a figure capable—like one of her actors—of changes in costume and appearance. From serene, pursued, or naked maenad she has transmuted into a triumphant winged Nikê, in elaborately patterned robes. But it is also noteworthy that, for the first time, the convention of depicting Tragedy as holding an actor's mask has slipped into the iconography. *Tragôidia*'s journey from maenad to figure tied to histrionic practice is significantly advanced on this pelike.

One of the recurrent elements in the personification of Tragedy subsequently became patterned robes and accessories signifying her variegated nature. The Byzantine Michael Psellus, for example, visualizes Tragedy (*tragikê poiêsis*) as 'adorned (*kosmoumenê*) with a variety of rhythms, and encompassing variegated (*poikila*) metres'.[37] These decorated robes first appear at the time of the late-fifth-century metamorphosis of Tragedy which began to figure her as an actor in her own genre of theatre, a beautiful woman in an embroidered gown, presiding over a choregic revel. For the 'mystery lady' on the Pronomos vase in Naples, sitting on the couch to the right of Dionysus and Ariadne at the centre of the upper level, turning towards Himeros and holding a mask, is in my view none other than *Tragôidia* herself (Fig. 10.6). This possibility, long ago envisaged by Ludwig Curtius, has not found recent support.[38] Yet the vase painter must have been aware that *Tragôidia* could conventionally appear as an attendant of Dionysus—indeed, of Dionysus with Ariadne, as on the Compiègne vase; perhaps he could assume that viewers would identify

[36] See the remarks of Shapiro (1993: 185), who discusses this vase in the course of his analysis of *Paidia* in vases generally.

[37] *Essay on Euripides and George of Pisidia*, Dyck (1986: 21–4).

[38] Curtius (1929: 16 n. 1). The details of the vase painting (Museo Nazionale Archeologico, 3240) can conveniently be studied in the drawing published by Bieber (1961), reproduced in one of Zeitlin's most important collaborative volumes (Winkler and Zeitlin 1990: pl. 1).

Fig. 10.5a Drawing of a red-figure pelike now in Barcelona, with Apollo, Dionysus, and personifications of Tragedy (?) and Comedy. Athenian, late fifth century.

Fig. 10.5b Detail of Fig. 10.5a, showing the fragment with a satyr holding a jug and the now largely lost figure probably to be identified as Tragedy.

his mysterious female as *Tragôidia*. It is most unlikely that she is the actor who played Hesione, since she inhabits the divine sphere. But it has been suggested that she is a maenad, a nymph, a personification of satyr drama, or of the training required by performing in a chorus (i.e. a form of *Paideia*).[39] Bieber was surely nearer the mark in suggesting that the woman is not exactly personified satyr drama, but rather *Paidia*, personified (and slightly sexy) play.[40] But even this interpretation misses the point that satyr drama had not yet been separated

[39] For discussions and bibliography see Arias and Shefton (1962: 377–80) and the remarks (of Krumeich) in the archaeological section of the introduction to Krumeich et al. (1999: 62–5).

[40] Bieber (1961: 10), followed by Froning (1971: 10).

Fig. 10.6 Detail from a red-figure volute crater, known as the Pronomos vase, showing Dionysus, Ariadne, Himeros, and figures here identified as Tragedy. Found in Ruvo, Apulia, c.400 BCE.

from the tragic tetralogy at all; that step did not come until the mid-
fourth century (see below). The Pronomos vase may portray its chorus
in the costumes that they wore for the *final* drama in the victorious
group, but they had performed beforehand, in less boisterous guises, in
no fewer than three successive tragedies. Satyr drama itself acquired no
name with a suffix *-ôidia*, along the lines of *Tragôidia* or *Kômôidia*, but
was always called instead just 'the satyrs' or 'satyric drama' (see e.g. Ar.
Th. 157). This was because it had developed as an integral and
inseparable part of the *tragic* performance. The Pronomos *Tragôidia*
therefore presides appropriately over the company of actors and *choreutai* who have just achieved their splendid victory, in what else but the
tragic competition. She may be, as Demetrius was later to call satyr
drama, tragedy at play, *Tragôidia paizousa* (*Eloc.* 169), but she is still
Tragôidia.

Yet she was about to undergo the most important revolution in her
history. By the late fourth century she severed the primordial cord
that had always bound her to satyr drama. By 341 the satyr play
had even been dropped from the tragic tetralogy at the Athenian
Dionysia, creating a tragic group of three tragedies, with an entirely
separate satyr play performed at the *beginning* of the festival
programme. This crucial piece of information is recorded by the
Didaskaliai, the series of fragmentary inscriptions from the south
slope of the Acropolis which documented the history of drama.[41]

In fifth-century Athenian vase painting *Tragôidia* had invariably
been envisaged in a Dionysiac group including satyrs. Although
paired with Comedy several times, and iconographically similar
to her, the satyric ethos was ever present. It was, however, about
to disappear. New possibilities for representing tragedy generically began to be explored, perhaps including the figure labelled
ΑΙΓΙΣΘΟΣ (AIGISTHOS) on the '*Chorêgos* vase'.[42] This character,
in his tragic costume, forms a contrast with the other, comic figures.
Indeed, scenes on several South Italian vases of the fourth century
combine comic and tragic images, sometimes giving them labels
which draw more explicitly generic distinctions of tone and manner.

[41] *IG* II² 2319–23. The implications of the detachment of the satyr play are well
brought out in Easterling (1997*b*: 214–16).
[42] The suggestion of Taplin (1993: 62).

These include the so-called New York Goose Play vase.[43] In another example, a single naked youth labelled *tragôdos* is painted on a late Apulian crater, the reverse of which portrays a comic mask,[44] thus opposing the two major dramatic genres. Tragedy and Comedy, as equivalent presences within the sphere of Dionysus, have here transmuted into the binary, antithetical pair which is still so familiar today.

3. TRAGEDY'S ESCAPE FROM ATHENS

By the mid-fourth century Aristotle's *Poetics* had developed a theoretical view of important disparities between tragedy and comedy: these distinguished, for example, the origins of the two types of theatre, the social class and morals of the characters, and the invented characters of comedy from the well-known families of tragic myth. Tragedy's appearance for the rest of antiquity may have been determined by whatever transformation she underwent in Aetion's famous painting of Dionysus with Tragedy and Comedy (Pliny, *NH* 35.78). It would be good to know whether it was on differences between the two handmaids of Dionysus that Aetion played, or on their similarities. Both Aristotle and Aetion were reacting to epochal shifts in the conditions under which tragedy was performed, and both reflect the divorce of tragedy from its context at the Athenian festivals of Dionysus.[45] But this process had already begun long before. The internationalization of tragedy, which became marked towards

---

[43] New York, MMA 24.98.104. Taplin (1993: 62 and fig. 10.2) argued that the label *tragôidos* was attached to the small, half-naked boy, painted on a higher plane than the figures in comic costume; he may have represented a jibe at tragedy from the perspective of those keen to promote comedy. But Schmidt (1998: 26–8) has pointed out that the label cannot refer to this boy, who is of a type which on vases conventionally represents the attendants of naked men at the palaestra such as the man on the bottom left of the painting. Whom or what the label 'tragode' designates therefore remains a mystery, although Schmidt recognizes that the scene must nevertheless juxtapose tragedy and comedy in a fairly sophisticated manner. Thanks to Oliver Taplin for help on this point.

[44] Trendall and Cambitoglou (1983: 122. 22/563d, with pl. 22.6); see Taplin (1993: 62 n. 19).

[45] Xanthakis-Karamanos (1993: 121); Hall (1996).

the end of the fifth century, was facilitated by the fact that tragedy had never been quite as Athenian as other competitive choral events at Athens;[46] tragic competitions, unlike dithyrambic ones, were never organized on a tribal basis (except for the selection of judges). In this they also differed from the comic competitions, which transferred the responsibility of selecting *chorêgoi* from the *archôn basileus* to the tribes, thus lending comedy a greater sense of tribal competition.

Wealthy tyrants had long been able to commission new works from Athenian playwrights, such as the *Women of Etna* which Aeschylus wrote for Hieron of Syracuse. Hieron also solicited the reperformance of works such as *Persians*, which the *Life of Aeschylus* 18 reports was revived in Sicily.[47] But the situation was transformed by the end of the fifth century. Vases with scenes related to theatre found in Megale Hellas imply that plays by Euripides were being produced regularly around Heracleia in southern Italy.[48] Macedon, from the accession of Archelaus in 413 onwards, had systematically set about attracting tragedians away from Athens; when it emerged as a world power it spread drama throughout the polis culture of the Balkans and the newly conquered areas of Asia.[49] Other cities and islands, including Rhodes, became centres of theatrical activity during the first half of the fourth century.[50]

This picture of the wholesale export of tragic drama from Athens does not tally with the narrative of terminal decline after the deaths of Euripides and Sophocles, a narrative extracted from Aristophanes' *Frogs* and widely believed until recently. Emphasis is now rightly laid on the evidence for the massive amount of tragic theatre being enjoyed in the fourth century, and in many more venues.[51] When Plato was citing tragedy, 'he was not attacking something which was dead and out of date'.[52] Tragic theatre was evolving rapidly, especially in terms of the increasing prominence of the actors. This process had started with the addition of a prize for a tragic actor to the Dionysia programme as early as 449 (or 447).[53] An actor's prize was subsequently instituted at

---

[46] Osborne (1993).   [47] Taplin (1999).   [48] Taplin (1993: 19).
[49] Revermann (1999–2000: 456); Maloney (2003).
[50] Stephanis (1988: nos. 139, 363); Csapo (2004*a*).
[51] Easterling (1993).   [52] Webster (1956: 31).
[53] In 449 or 447 the name of the victorious actor is added to the notice of the tragic competition in the inscription known as the *Fasti* (*IG* II² 2318).

the Lenaea, probably in 432, but certainly by 423.[54] It is symptomatic that the first tragic actor whom we can name in connection with a specific first performance of an extant tragedy is Hegelochus, the protagonist in Euripides' *Orestes* in 408 (*Σ* Ar. *Frogs* 303). And the earliest evidence for actors touring outside Attica comes from around the turn of the century.[55]

The raised status of the *tragic* actor is reflected in the revivals of old tragedies institutionalized at Athens in 387/6; the same practice was not initiated for comic drama until four decades later.[56] Reperformance, which swiftly resulted in the emergence of a repertoire, had a major impact on the relative importance of the actor. Not only did it remove the poet from competition for a prize altogether, but it gave the actor independence. He could develop a touring repertoire, play at short notice, and travel freely.[57] The institution of the revival of old tragedies inevitably produced the first generation of truly international acting stars, men like the peerless *tragôidos* Theodorus (see further below), who won prizes at Athens but also performed for enormous fees in theatres across increasingly extensive areas of the Greek-speaking world.[58] The phenomenon of the itinerant star professional consolidated the inexorable trend, documented by the musical papyri, towards the performance of tragedy in the form of excerpted highlights.[59] Excerpts also could also be enjoyed in contexts, such as the symposium, removed from festival drama.[60] Reperformance also led to new plays becoming increasingly imitative of the canonical masterpieces; in the second

---

[54] The precise date depends on reconciling the evidence from several inscriptions; see Csapo and Slater (1995: 227–8).

[55] The Demosthenic *Against Euboulides* (13), delivered *c*.345 BCE, refers to the actor Cleandrus' presence in Leucas (on the route to Italy) some years subsequent to the Decelean War of 413 BCE.

[56] *IG* II² 2318, cols. viii and xii.

[57] Csapo and Slater (1995: 40).

[58] See Sifakis (1967: esp. 75–7); Gentili (1979: 22–7); Hall (2002*b*).

[59] See Hall (2002*b*: 13–14).

[60] For further anecdotes of this nature see Hall (1999). There were already signs of tragic excerpts in venues quite other than the theatre in the 420s; Philocleon envisages the performance of speeches by the actor Oiagros in the law courts (Ar. *Wasps* 579–80), and Strepsiades says his son wants to perform speeches from Euripides at a symposium (Ar. *Clouds* 1371–2).

quarter of the fourth century BCE, for example, the tragic actor Androsthenes performed two plays by Theodorides called *Medea* and *Phaethon*, the titles of two famous Euripidean plays. This process is confirmed by Aristotle's observation that most of the tragedies in his day are written about just a handful of families (*Po.* 13.1453ª18–22).[61]

These developments were accompanied by the emergence of a much greater awareness of what Tragedy might be as a generic entity. In the fifth century BCE there had been talk about the art of rhetoric, discussion of something called Poetry, and the first inklings of a need to classify sub-species of the genus Poetry according to what we call categories of genre. This period, for example, saw tragedy become central to Old Comedy, and some, at least, of its stylistic and visual effects explored in the new fashion of paratragedy.[62] But there were few signs of any attempt to define Tragedy according to the analytical, tonal, and qualitative aesthetic criteria which were to emerge in the fourth century. Most's excellent article on the idea of the tragic in antiquity argues that tragedy received the 'poetological prerogative' of being theorized earlier and more intensively than any other genre.[63] He is correct when it comes to Plato onwards, but what is his evidence for specific prose discussions of the tragic as early as the fifth century? The only candidates are Sophocles in his apocryphal prose treatise on the chorus (attested by so dubious a source as the *Suda*), and Gorgias' *Encomium of Helen*. This contains nothing which could not apply equally to the effect of Homeric epic; its points of contact with the Helen scene in Euripides' *Trojan Women* are the persuasive force of verbal rhetoric and physical beauty (8–19), rather than with anything exclusive to tragic theatre. Moreover, Ford has recently argued cogently that, far from an embryonic model of tragedy, Gorgias' *Helen* develops a scientific understanding of language which attempts to synthesize the perspectives of natural philosophy, including Democritean materialism and Anaxagorean theory of Mind.[64] Although Gorgias did famously say that Tragedy entails deceit (82 B 23 DK), a superior witness in Most's defence would be the anonymous author of the somewhat later *Dissoi*

---

[61] Stephanis (1988: no. 182); Hall (2006).
[62] Silk (1993).　　[63] Most (2000: 18–19).　　[64] Ford (2002: 176–80).

Logoi, who draws a parallel between the fictive power of painting and tragedy.[65]

It is truer to the evidence to stress how remarkably *late* it was that there arose discussions of any depth or complexity of what we would call 'literature'.[66] Nightingale has argued that it took Plato's agonistic conception of the relationship between types of discourse to elicit embryonic notions of genre.[67] Certainly, although the names of the nine muses listed in Hesiod's *Theogony* 77–9 include Thalia and Melpomene, the individual muses are given no generic specifications.[68] Indeed, the idea that each muse was responsible for a separate province of art is a later, Hellenistic development. Plato's *Phaedrus* includes a suggestive account of the function and structure of tragedy—its capacity to arouse pity and fear, and the need for the speeches in a tragedy to be fitted together so as to form a whole (268c). Yet the myth of the cicadas in the same dialogue (259b5–d8), which was probably the inspiration behind the later classification of the muses,[69] fails even to mention Melpomene, who became the Hellenistic muse of tragedy; this development was connected with the old Athenian cult title of Dionysus *Melpomenos* (see Pausanias 1.2.5), under which his *technîtai*, the Hellenistic guild of actors, worshipped him.[70] Theorizing Tragedy as a genre begins with Plato, at the time that Tragedy had begun to be exported from its original performance context. In discussing Hellenistic poetry, Nagy once observed that 'the very concept of *genre* only becomes necessary when the *occasion* for a given speech-act, that is, for a given poem or song, is lost'.[71] This observation has become celebrated in discussions of genre, for example the Introduction to Depew and Obbink's col-

---

[65] 90 B 3.10 DK. On the relationship between these embryonic attempts to theorize tragedy and the experience of the contemporary audience, see Finkelberg (1998: 176–81).

[66] Stressed by Trimpi (1983: 5).

[67] Nightingale (1995: 193–5).

[68] Murray (2002: 40). See Nancy (1996: ch. 1), which asks why are there several arts—and therefore eventually several muses—and not just one?

[69] Murray (2002: 40), following Grube (1965: 5–6 and n. 3).

[70] See the supplemented line 28 of the Amphictyonic decree confirming the privileges of the Athenian *technîtai* in le Guen (2001: i. 92–8 [no. 11]; see also ii. 74 n. 2; 97 n. 468); Lightfoot (2002: 210–11), and further below.

[71] Nagy (1990: 362 n. 127).

lection, *Matrices of Genre*.[72] It can also illuminate the relationship between the transformations in the performance conditions of tragedy and in personifications of the genre.

4. FROM THE *THIASOS* TO THASOS

Generic discussions of Tragedy were therefore delayed until Tragedy became detached from the context in which she had originated and in which her nature and function had been self-evident. To paraphrase Nagy, the very concept of the tragic genre only became necessary when the occasion for her given nature became subject to radical change. This argument corresponds with the findings in section 2 above that in late-fifth-century visualizations of Tragedy she mutated from a maenad into a range of slightly different figures. She became a winged Nikê, similar to a flying creature in a tragedy; in holding a tragic mask (as she does on the Barcelona pelike and on the Pronomos vase), she became more closely identified with the figure who, by the act of assuming a mask, mediated the boundary between fictive mimetic world and the real world of the spectator. That figure was of course the actor. During the rest of antiquity the ways in which Tragedy was personified become dissociated altogether from the dancer of the chorus mythically represented by satyrs and maenads, and identified with the expert professional vocalist—the *tragôidos* who represented kings and queens and mighty heroes.

The most remarkable ancient configuration of *Tragôidia* is a marble statue in a sanctuary on the northern Aegean island of Thasos.[73] Here *Tragôidia* was personified as an imposing female holding a tragic mask. It is not, however, the conventionally lovely female mask which *Tragôidia* was holding on the Pronomos vase, but an extraordinary *prosôpon* imitating a blind male character. Beneath the statue were inscribed the words 'Tragedy, Theodorus acted (*hupekrî-neto*)'; the identification of Tragedy with her actor has here, for the first time, become almost complete. The statue belongs to a

---

[72] Depew and Obbink (2000: 3).
[73] The date is a matter of controversy: see below.

monument in the Thasian Dionysion. Thasos had been part of the Athenian empire, but Spartan rule lasted from 405 until 389, when the Thasians reverted to their pro-Athenian stance. From 356 onwards they became pro-Macedonian. Their interest in theatre seems to have remained consistent throughout their affiliation with both Athens and Macedon: fourth-century Thasian *amphorai* sometimes bear stamps decorated with theatrical masks.[74] The view that Thasos enjoyed a vigorous performance tradition is confirmed by the beauty of its theatre, which in its present form however dates from the early third century.

The monument within which the personification of *Tragôidia* stood has been compared with the choregic monuments in Athens: beyond a Doric portico, on a semicircular arc, stood a statue representing Dionysus, alongside allegorical figures representing Tragedy, Comedy, Dithyramb, and a musical piece entitled *Nykterinos*, or 'Nocturne'.[75] Beneath the statues were the accompanying inscriptions: 'Dionysus'; 'Tragedy, Theodorus acted (*hupekrineto*)'; 'Comedy, Philemon acted'; 'Dithyramb, Ariston of Miletus played the aulos (*êulei*)'; '*Nykterinos*, Batalus played the aulos'.[76]

The three substantial surviving statue pieces are the long-haired head of Dionysus (now the centrepiece of the Thasos museum), a headless torso of *Kômôidia* (see Fig. 10.7), who was tall, dignified, and elaborately draped, and the mask of a blind man, part of the equipment of *Tragôidia*. The head depicted on this mask is bald, with sunken cheeks, bags under the eyes, and lines on its forehead (see Fig. 10.8); the sculptor is thinking beyond the manufactured *prosôpon* worn by the actor to the acted *prosôpon* or 'role'; the effect is more that of a blind old man than a conventional mask of one. The role was probably determined by the play Theodorus performed at the festival being commemorated: he may have worn the mask of Oedipus at Colonus, Phineus, or possibly Tiresias.

Theodorus of Athens was arguably the most famous actor in antiquity. His tomb on the Sacred Way near the Cephisus could still be visited in Pausanias' day (1.37.3). He won at least four

---

[74] Webster (1967a: 47).

[75] See the photographs in Devambez (1941: esp. 94–5 figs. 1 and 2), and the diagrams in Grandjean and Salviat (2000: 92–3).

[76] *IG* xii Suppl. 400; see the discussion in Salviat (1979).

Fig. 10.7 Figure of Comedy from a statue group dedicated in the Dionysion in Thasos. Marble. Mid to late fourth century BCE.

Fig. 10.8 Head of Tragedy as the mask of a blind old man, from the Dionysion in Thasos. Marble. Mid to late fourth century BCE.

victories at the Athenian Lenaea, and almost certainly also at the Dionysia.[77] In the 360s BCE, he performed in the theatre in Pherae in Thessaly, and reduced the vicious local tyrant Alexander

[77] *IG* II² 2325.262; *IG* II² 2325.31. See Stephanis (1988: no. 1157).

to tears by his performance as a Euripidean heroine (Aerope, Merope, or Hecuba, depending on which source is to be credited); his performances in Sophocles' *Antigone* and *Electra* were also the stuff of legend.[78] Aristotle regards him as the first actor to have spoken in a convincingly 'realistic' way (*Rh.* 3.2.4). He was determined to be given the prologue in any tragedy he was to perform, on the ground that the prologist inevitably won the audience's sympathy (Arist. *Pol.* 6.1336^b 27–31). This *nonpareil* had by 361 BCE already amassed a sufficient fortune to subscribe no less a sum than seventy drachmas to the rebuilding of the temple of Apollo at Delphi, a donation testifying to his sense of the importance, as an international celebrity, of courting public opinion.[79]

Theodorus' epigraphic presence in the Thasos monument is testimony to his visit to that island, perhaps mid-century, by which date his reputation alone would have made him a remarkably important visitor. Theodorus' fame was directly related to the establishment of the old tragedies as a regular event at the Athenian Dionysia in 387/6. The appearance of his name, along with those of Philemon, a famous comic actor of the same generation, and Batalus, an illustrious Ephesian aulete, suggests that the first editor of the inscriptions, Georges Daux, had arrived at too late a date in proposing that they originated at the beginning of the third century BCE.[80] The Dionysion on Thasos was a familiar landmark in the fifth century, mentioned in the Hippocratic *Epidemics I* (2.13), but the choregic monument is probably mid-fourth-century.[81] The statues seem to have celebrated 'a particular performance at which tragedy, comedy and two kinds of choral song…were performed in honour of Dionysos';[82] they

---

[78] On Theodorus in Euripides see Plu. *Pel.* 29.4–6; Ael. *VH* 14.40; Lada-Richards (2002: 414–15); Hall (2002*a*: 421–3). For his Sophoclean roles see Pl. *Symp.* 737b; D. 19.246.

[79] *SIG* 239 B. On actors' consciousness of celebrity, see Artem. 2.30: dreaming about making public donations bodes ill for most people, but 'actors and thymelic musicians' are among the exceptions, since they win praise by making financial contributions to the public weal.

[80] Daux (1926: 34–6).

[81] Salviat (1979: 157); Lambin (1982); Wilson (2000: 295). Stephanis (1988), dates both Theodorus and Philemon to 375–325 BCE (nos. 1157, 2485).

[82] Webster (1967*a*: 49–50), although his caption to fig. 6 suggests uncertainty about the chronology.

were probably commissioned by the local *chorêgos* who organized the occasion at which these famous actors and auletes performed alongside choruses consisting of Thasian amateurs.

The statue of Tragedy herself has disappeared, although the archaeological remains imply that she was similar to her counterpart, Comedy. The mask was not new in *Tragôidia's* iconography, but, amongst the available evidence, the specificity of the blind male role, and the naming of the individual actor Theodorus, are unprecedented. Tragedy stands proud in a new island home, a dignified companion of Dionysus and Comedy, attended by other, non-theatrical genres of *mousikê*. She proves that Tragedy has achieved both independence from satyr drama, and the generic autonomy insisted upon by the *Poetics* of Aristotle, an admirer of Theodorus from nearby Stagira, a short boat ride away from Thasos on the easternmost promontory of Chalcidice.

5. THE FUTURE OF *TRAGÔIDIA*

The Thasos monument represents a turning point in the iconography of *Tragôidia* for several reasons besides its negotiation, through identification with a specific actor, of the distinction between the represented world of the stage and the world external to it. The monument is material proof of Tragedy's escape from Athens to every corner of the Hellenistic world where theatre might be enjoyed; it also represents Tragedy's escape from the specific ritual context of the Athenian Dionysia. Above all it represents Tragedy's divorce from satyr drama. In leaving the *thiasos*, Tragedy began consorting with other genres of literature, and she is to be found during the rest of antiquity in quite different company.

With the exception of Aristotle, the ancients struggled to analyse what they meant by tragedy or the tragic. But one of the ways in which they could generate meaning was by placing tragedy in a relationship with other literary genres. Homeric epic is the important 'other' in two Hellenistic visualizations of *Tragôidia*. A curious anecdote records how the grammarian Dionysius Thrax, a student at Alexandria of the great Iliadic scholar Aristarchus, painted a picture of his teacher: because Aristarchus knew all tragedy by heart, Dionysius painted *Tragôidia* on his master's breast.[83] Tragedy is also seen as an art subsidiary to (and derivative of) Homeric epic in the so-called *Apotheosis of Homer* which Archelaus of Priene sculpted in the second century BCE. This marble relief, found at Bovillae near Rome (London BM 2191), depicts a soaring *Tragôidia* in a procession of allegorical figures saluting the supreme poet, Homer, in the presence of Time: she stands between the more diminutive *Poiêsis* and *Kômôidia*. Like a Hellenistic tragic actor, she wears an imposing headdress, built up over her forehead, and shoes with very thick soles.[84] By the first century BCE, and the building of elaborate stone theatres with complicated staging arrangements in every corner of the Hellenistic world, the notion of the theatrical stage, the *skênê*, even threatened to oust *Tragôidia* from visually encoded representations of the tragedian's art altogether: a remarkable marble relief sculpture from Smyrna represents Euripides seated between Dionysus on his right, and a female figure labelled *ΣΚΗΝΗ* (SKÊNÊ) on his left, who hands him a mask of Heracles.[85]

Although Tragedy's primordial relationship with the *thiasos* briefly re-emerges in Horace's *Ars Poetica*, where she is a stately matron coerced into dancing by satyrs on festal days (231–3), Horace is the only Latin author to visualize Tragedy in relationship to Satyr Play. Far more elaborate is the personification of Tragedy who appears in an elegy by Ovid (*Amores* 3.1), the only exponent of that genre

---

[83] D. T. T 6 b in the edition of Linke (1977). Thanks to Francesca Schironi for help on this.

[84] Watzinger (1903: pl. I); Webster (1967a: Appendix, pl. 10). The shoes give her even more height than the elevated sole on the right foot of a statue in clothing suggestive of an actor's costume, who may represent Tragedy, dating from the second century BCE on the northern periphery of the Pergamon altar. She originally held a sword, and on her preserved right foot, protruding from her long chiton, is a beautiful shoe, richly decorated with leaves and a palmette, and elevated on an unusually high sole (3.5 centimetres). See the drawing in Winter (1908: 77), who however believes she is probably Melpomene rather than Tragedy. For a fascinating discussion of the other figures on Archelaus' sculpture see Zeitlin (2001: 197–200).

[85] See the photograph reproduced in Moraw (2002: 123 fig. 157) and Hall (2006: 41). On Heracles as the archetypal theatrical hero, see below and n. 105.

known to have attempted a tragedy.[86] In a sacred grove, Ovid is visited by Tragedy and Elegy, appropriately costumed. They each woo him with a dramatic speech. Elegy appears first, her hair scented and elegantly dressed, clad in the sheerest of dresses, flashing seductive glances; she carries Venus's myrtle branch, and suffers from the elegiac malady of having one foot slightly shorter than the other (7, 9–10, 33–4). The first epithet used for Tragedy, on the other hand, is *violenta* (11), referring both to the content of tragic drama and to the imposing gait of her actors; she storms in with large strides (*ingenti ... passu*, 11), a detail suggesting both buskins and the male actor beneath the costume. She is histrionically equipped with imposing hair, trailing robe, and royal sceptre (12–14).[87] Her key gesture is a regal shaking of her head—which perhaps bears Homeric rather than tragic overtones.

Ovid's *Tragoedia* is the only surviving ancient personification of Tragedy to speak; she delivers elegiac couplets (a rare but not unprecedented metre in tragedy—see E. *Andr.* 103–16), but her diction is parodically elevated. This is evident in the striking apostrophe, *O argumenti lente poeta tui* (16), in which the hiatus between the *O* and *argumenti*, the rare instance of the adjective *lentus* with a genitive, and of course the apostrophaic *O* itself, combine to determine unmistakeably the lofty register of her speech.[88] Ovid chooses Elegy over Tragedy, but only after accumulating Callimachean technical distinctions between the two, presented in anthropomorphic guise: Elegy's style, like her dress, is *tenuissima* (3.9), while *Tragoedia's* language is *gravis* (3.35); other key terms in ancient poetics—*sublimis, exiguus, levis, fortis*—are also implicated in the scene. And even though Ovid chooses Elegy, it is no permanent rejection of Tragedy's call that he intends. 'Allow your priest a little time', he pleads (3.1.67–70).[89]

---

86 Perhaps by that time the tragic Muse had indeed appeared on the ancient stage: Pollux's list of characters requiring special masks includes an unelaborated mention of 'Muses' (see Stafford 2000: 13 on this list).

87 See Davis (1989: 109 n. 11). Brandt (1911: 141) compares the term *violenta* with Horace's word for tragedy, *severe* (*Odes* 2.1.9). For a discussion of the terminology in Ovid's description of Tragedy, and its parallels in other Ovidian texts, see Schrijvers (1976: 416–18); Wyke (2002: 124–5).

88 See the detailed analysis in Schrijvers (1976: 418–19).

89 On the presence of Ovid's *Medea* in his other works, see Hinds (1993).

Lee long ago saw that the power of this episode ('quite the best piece of narrative in the *Amores*') rested on the device of treating these two personifications simultaneously as human beings and as genres.[90] Yet scholarship on the poem was long dominated by the question of its allegorical antecedents, whether Prodicus' allegory of Heracles at the Crossroads (X. *Mem.* 2.1.21–34), or the Judgement of Paris.[91] Other scholars focused on the poem's function as 'the most complex of all Ovid's programmatic poems', and sought its ancestry in Hesiod's visitation by the Muses (*Th.* 26), the Callimachean tradition of the *recusatio*, and above all in Propertius 3.3, where both Apollo and Calliope insist that the poet should avoid epic and stick to elegy.[92] The most sensitive interpretations have appreciated the theatricality of the scene: Ovid, the actor for much of the *Amores*, here turns into the spectator, and there is a scenic contrast between elegy's backdrop (the door of the beloved) and tragedy's kingly, palatial setting (*regia*).[93] But the poem has never been read against the full tradition of personified literary genres, above all personifications of *Tragôidia*. Furthermore, given Ovid's interest in comedy, he may well be influenced by the juxtaposition of Tragedy and Comedy in the visual art of the fourth century, above all in Aetion's painting, a suggestion made many decades ago by Bartholomé;[94] for Ovid's personification of Elegy as erotic and light-hearted also resembles his conception of Thalia, Muse of Comedy, in the *Ars Amatoria* (1.264) and in Sappho's epistle to Phaon (*Heroides* 15.84).[95]

---

[90] Lee (1962: 169).

[91] For bibliography see Davis (1989: 108–9 n. 6). Wyke (2002), a revised version of an article first published in 1989, explores the implications of the correspondence between Ovid's scene and the 'Choice of Heracles' 'for reading elegy's female forms as playful signifiers of a moral or political position' (p. 131): writing tragedy becomes equated with an Augustan version of Prodicus' vision of the pursuit of virtue.

[92] Morgan (1977: 17–19). Recent scholars have intelligently discussed Ovid's personification of Elegy in *Amores* 3.1, but with less reference to her partner Tragedy, for example Sharrock (2002: 225–7).

[93] Davis (1989); Brandt (1911: 143).

[94] Bartholomé (1935: 45–6).

[95] Elegy's affinity with Comedy in Ovid was to have later artistic repercussions: *Amores* 3.1 was probably one of the sources, supplementing Pliny's account of Aetion's *Dionysus with Tragedy and Comedy*, for Joshua Reynolds' famous painting *Garrick between Tragedy and Comedy* (1761). See Postle (1995: 25); Wyke (2002: 120–1).

A similarly theatrical and antithetical repudiation of Tragedy occurs in a passage of Plutarch. In his epideictic oration clumsily titled *Are the Athenians More Famous for War or for Wisdom?* (= *Moralia* 345c–51b) Plutarch proposes—apparently for the sake of argument—that the Athenians' wars constituted a greater achievement than their literary culture. This text will always be important to the visualization of the tragic, if only for Plutarch's remarks on the means by which the historiographer Thucydides makes his narrative 'like a painting' by 'vivid representation of emotions and characters' (347a).[96]

Emotions and characters—*pathê* and *prosôpa*—belong quite as much to tragic theatre as to tragic history, and in the following chapters Plutarch challenges the achievement of Athenian tragedy. He first points out that there was no non-dramatic genre of poetry associated with that city, and dismisses comedy as too plebeian to matter (he alleges that Areopagites were banned from writing comedy). Plutarch then proposes that he and his readers imagine that they are staging a theatrical competition between Athenian tragedy and Athenian military prowess, with figures representing the adversarial parties entering from opposite sides of the theatre. Tragedy is represented by her poets, chanting and bearing her equipment; the tragic authors are to be accompanied by the tragic actors (including the famous Theodorus commemorated in the Dionysion at Thasos):

men like Nicostratus and Callipides, Mynniscus, Theodorus, and Polus, who robe Tragedy and bear her stool, as though she were some woman of wealth; or rather, let them follow on as though they were painters and gilders and dyers of statues. Let there be provided also a bounteous outlay for stage furnishings, supernumeraries, sea-purple robes, stage machinery, as well as dancing masters and bodyguards, an intractable crowd.' (348e–f).[97]

Plutarch rhetorically paints an imposing but decadent scene—Tragedy resembles an unadorned statue waiting to be decorated, a woman rich enough to hire numerous attendants, costumiers, and beauty therapists. In an elaborate gesture to the iconographic tradition (and perhaps to the distinctly tragic trope of the analogy

---

[96] On this passage in Plutarch see Meijering (1987: 37).
[97] Translated by Babbitt (1936: 512–13), slightly adapted.

between an artwork and a beautiful woman),[98] *Tragôidia* herself mutates into an ecphrastic work of visual art, clothed and ornamented by her performers. The individual poets (Aeschylus, Sophocles, and Euripides) are studiously not named, which allows the less august names of the actors—albeit the most celebrated actors of the classical period—to dominate.[99] Plutarch here exploits the lower status of actors in the Roman Empire relative to their high reputation in the fourth and third centuries BCE. He also invokes misogynist prejudices, as ancient as Hesiod's Pandora, against the female as an economic drain and an artificial surface, in addition to the Platonic reaction against the sophists' fascination with the power of artistic mimesis.[100] The traditional association of femininity with despotism is insinuated by the stool-bearers and bodyguards. This gaudy, extravagant, specious *Tragôidia*, with her army of lackeys, is unlikely to be preferred to the impressive opponents Plutarch marshals against her: these are Persian Wars generals, along with personifications of their victories. Marathon leads forward the Victory of Miltiades, Salamis the Victory of Themistocles, Cimon's Nikê leads Phoenician ships from Eurymedon, and so on. Against the victors in the canonical victories won by the Athenian democracy over the barbarians, *Tragôidia* stands no chance at all.[101]

After the classical period *Tragôidia* was therefore seen as subordinate to epic, as the rival of Elegy, or as a flashy and trivial pursuit in comparison with the serious business of military history. Her meaning is everywhere constituted as the 'other' of the art form or achievement which is primarily under scrutiny. This tendency probably reflects the relative unimportance, by the Roman imperial period, of staged, spoken tragedy in comparison with the more fashionable ways of consuming tragic material. Tragedy was mostly enjoyed in the new medium of pantomime.[102] Pantomimes were danced versions of

---

[98] Zeitlin (1996*a*: 53–86); Hall (2006: 99–141).

[99] On this ancient 'canon' of iconic actors, see Easterling (2002).

[100] At 348c Plutarch has already actually drawn attention to Gorgias 82 B 23 DK on the deceiver and the deceived (see above, section 3).

[101] The discussion of Vasunia (2003: 371–5) brings out well how Plutarch's polemical agenda, and in particular his fixation on the loss of the classical Athenian Empire, entail subordinating her artistic achievements to her military exploits.

[102] See Kelly (1979); Jory (1996); Hall and Wyles (forthcoming).

tragic myth, a type of musical theatre that emerged in Asia in the first century BCE before taking the Roman Empire by storm. Its popularity is reflected in the reallocation of the Muse Pol(h)ymnia to the department of Pantomime (as on the better preserved of the two 'Muses mosaics' in Trier [Augusta Treverorum]).[103] This development ran parallel to the continuing passion for sung recitals of tragic arias, and the concomitant understanding of the name of the Muse of Tragedy, Melpomene, as the singing Muse in charge of sung—rather than fully staged—performances. The singing Melpomene who sometimes appears from Hellenistic times on coins and in statuary is identified less with star actors than with the *nonpareil* amongst canonical mythical figures of international tragedy and their props—Heracles/Hercules, complete with lionskin and club.[104] Heracles was certainly one of the characters in the repertoire of the expert singers, for Lucian remarks on the unfortunate effect when a *tragôidos* with a small, feminine voice attempts to sing in the persona of the mighty Heracles (*Nigrinus* 11). By Lucian's day, Heracles had become a favourite role in every type of theatre; his props were synonymous with the acting profession generally.[105] But *Tragôidia*, as the fourth century BCE had understood her, had reached her acme in the age of the great actors catalogued by Plutarch, and was rarely to dominate either public entertainment or literary culture to the same extent again. One exception may have been in court circles during the reign of the Emperor Hadrian (117–38 CE), a patron of Greek culture, entitled 'the new Dionysus' by the Artists of Dionysus. His villa at Tivoli demonstrates his interest in the promotion of theatre: the undercroft of the stage and the cavea bowl of the North ('Greek') Theatre, built with maximum afternoon sunlight in mind, are preserved.[106] The South Theatre (often called the 'Odeion'), with its six stairways leading to underground tunnels, may have been used for

---

[103] See Hoffmann (1999: 37–8 with fig. 38). The other Trier mosaic with Muses preserves an attractive Melpomene, holding a mask with high *onkos* (Hoffmann 1999: 34–6 with fig. 41).

[104] See Webster (1967a: 59–60).

[105] *AP* 11.169, an epigram dedicated to the tragic actor Apollophanes, gives primacy amongst his props to the club of Heracles. See also Suetonius, *Nero* 21 on Heracles in sung tragedy; Macrobius 2.4 on pantomime.

[106] MacDonald and Pinto (1995: 42). On Hadrian's revival of tragedy see Jones (1993).

more private theatricals.[107] In the design of the villa's grounds, with their vast landscapes, terraces, and fountains, thought was put to the selection and placement of statues, about 250 of which survive (there will originally have been far more); Hadrian wanted to populate his villa with innumerable 'symbolic recollections of society's foundations',[108] including figures representative of myth, divinity, history, architectural achievements (caryatids), and imperial territories (a crocodile). This was an eclectic High Empire project expressing the cultural aspirations of the era.

Consideration was given to the arrangement of statues in pairs (for example, twinned animals), often in facing niches.[109] Perhaps the most influential of all ancient personifications of Tragedy and Comedy are the twin busts, probably of Greek provenance, discovered in 1735 by the Count Giuseppe Fede at the entrance of the North Theatre; it was however Bartolomeo Cavaceppi, the sculptor, who identified them as personifications of these genres. Cavaceppi restored ancient statues for the Pope at his Museo Pio Clementino, which still houses these two busts.[110] Cavaceppi publicized the statues in his three-volume collection of plates illustrating the artefacts he had restored,[111] which stimulated the taste for artistic representations of Tragedy and Comedy from the late eighteenth century; one beautiful pair of stipple engravings by Heinrich Sintzenich, from drawings which may have been by Angelica Kauffman, was issued in mid-1777.[112] The fashion also arose for leading ladies, such as Madame Rachel, to be depicted as the Tragic Muse. The most well known is Joshua Reynolds' *Sarah Siddons as the Tragic Muse* (1784), although a stronger sense of tragic emotion emanates from Richard Cosway's *Sarah Siddons as Tragedy* (*c.*1785).

Such iconic images have conditioned the form still taken by Tragedy in contemporary culture. In most of our imaginations Tragedy is still a tall, straight-featured, doleful, dark-robed female. She has long hair, either flowing in disorder or monumentally coiffed. She may wear or hold a theatrical mask; she may raise

---

[107] MacDonald and Pinto (1995: 135).
[108] MacDonald and Pinto (1995: 141).
[109] MacDonald and Pinto (1995: 148).
[110] Inv. nr. 262, 285 (South Rotunda). See Raeder (1983: 100).
[111] Cavaceppi (1768–72).
[112] See Alexander (1992: 162 with figs. 136 and 137).

one arm in a grand histrionic gesture. She is not in the first flush of youth, and has experienced motherhood. She may be contrasted with other art forms, or intellectual abstractions. Indeed, *fin de siècle* Viennese stole, choker, and hairstyle apart, she would resemble Gustav Klimt's fierce-eyed *Tragödie* of 1897, an allegorical figure he created in black crayon, pencil and wash, heightened with white and gold, as one of a set including personifications of Sculpture and Love.[113]

Yet this type of iconography originally evolved in tandem with ancient theatre practice. Surveying ancient personifications of Tragedy has shown how their evolution related subtly to shifts in the experience of theatre *in performance*. The cheerful Polygnotan maenad, with her baby hare, has little in common with the solemn statue in the Thasian Dionysion, with her ugly mask; equally, the mid-fifth-century Athenian festival of Dionysus would have been almost unrecognizable to the Tivoli spectator enjoying the Hadrianic elite revival of the classical repertoire. The stately matron of late antique sculpture herself emerged from ancient identifications of Tragedy with her actors and their elaborate costumes, masks, and accoutrements. But all these figures—member of the rustic *thiasos*, victim of sexual assault, winged Nikê, statuesque allegory, and cosmetically enhanced society lady—attest to a continuing ancient interest not only in visualizing scenes that were by one definition or another tragic, but in visually personifying *Tragôidia*.[114]

[113] Whitford (1990: 40–1, with fig. 21). It is in the Vienna Historisches Museum. It adorns the jacket of a recent book on Greek tragedy by one of Froma's former research students, Daniel Mendelsohn (2002).

[114] This research for this paper has been generously supported by a grant at the Archive of Performances of Greek and Roman Drama, funded at Oxford and Durham by the AHRB. The argument has benefited from presentation at the Durham Classics Department's Research Seminar, the Istituto Umanistico in Florence, and the Oxford Philological Society. In addition to those named in individual notes, thanks for helpful comments and advice are also due to the editors of this volume, Peter Brown, François Lissarrague, Carine Weicherding, Victoria Amengual, Pat Easterling, and especially Oliver Taplin and Eric Csapo.

11

Nikê's Cosmetics: Dramatic Victory, the End of Comedy, and Beyond[1]

Peter Wilson

1. VISUALIZING VICTORY

Greek Victory—*Nikê*—is a young woman from a very rough background. But she is extremely beautiful. A child of the old regime, daughter of Styx and the Titan Pallas, at first glance she gives the appearance of being the odd one out among her siblings, those 'glorious children,' as the authoritative Hesiodic *Theogony* puts it.[2] An only daughter, she has three brothers: *Kratos*—supremacy over others; *Bia*—violence; and *Zêlos*—a term whose meaning is difficult to capture but which describes the complex feelings evoked in onlookers by witnessing the success of others, and which they feel they merit themselves—perhaps 'competitive ambition' or 'spur to emulation.'[3] Only *Nikê* is singled out for particularizing description: she has 'beautiful ankles' (καλλίσφυρον, 384). What her brothers looked like, we are not told (and this willingness to visualize the beautiful daughter and not her brothers is not confined to Hesiod).[4]

[1] Thanks to the editors, Claude Calame, Martin Revermann, Ian Ruffell, Frances Muecke, Andrew Hartwig. I am also indebted to an as yet unpublished lecture on the imagery of *Eros* and *Nikê* by François Lissarrague.

[2] *Th.* 383–403; cf. also B. *Epigr.* 1 M. (= fr. 48 Bgk) for *Nikê* as the daughter of Pallas, though Page (1981: 151) regards this as 'plainly a product of the Alexandrian era'. The *Homeric Hymn to Ares* (8.4) names Ares as father of *Nikê*, but this probably dates from the first century CE: Càssola (1975: 297).

[3] See the various studies in Konstan and Rutter (2003).

[4] In contrast with the thousands of images available for the *LIMC* entry s.v. *Nikê*, the joint entry 'Bia et Kratos' has only three; there are none identified of *Zêlos*.

There is, however, no mistaking the relation between these siblings. They all, as a group, made the timely change of allegiance from the old order to the new, taking advantage of Zeus' assurance that any Titan who fought for him would not be cast from their rights, 'but each would have the same honours which he had before amongst the immortal gods' (*Th.* 393–4). And so Victory, Supremacy, Violence, and the 'Spur to Emulation' are forever thereafter in Zeus' company (401); they legitimize his rule all the more effectively by providing a continuity with what preceded it, and by having changed sides altogether of their own volition.

After his victory over the Titans, Zeus did something he usually leaves to others—he *danced*.[5] Having deserted her own kind in this very struggle at the opportune moment, beautiful *Nikê* was there to celebrate Zeus' victory and sanctify the new order by establishing the first choral dance in her new master's honour. The cult statue of Zeus at Olympia showed *Nikê* on Zeus' right palm. It also had a chorus of *Nikai* winding around the feet of the great throne, fulfilling a practical function of physical, as well as aesthetic and ideological, support.[6] Zeus' victory dance with *Nikai* expresses the assertion of order after violence and was to serve in its turn as the model, in the generation of heroes, for Heracles, who was also to dance after his final labour and be hailed as *kallinikos*. And, *via* Heracles, later still this dance was the ultimate model for Olympic victors, whose *agônes* were likewise crowned with the beauty of choral celebration (the *epinikion*).[7] In fact, in the rhetoric of its practitioners at least, the victory song and dance is itself what brings fulfilment and finality to the victory. *Nikê* is the arbiter of the end in achievement (B. 11.6–7 κρίνεις τέλος ἀθανάτοισίν τε καὶ θνατοῖς ἀρετᾶς).[8]

Nikê's good looks thus work very hard for Zeus and his worshippers. Her principle task, put simply, is to bring a vision of beauty and transcendence to those areas of mortal life—and there are many in the Greek world—where her brothers are active: Violence, Supremacy,

⁵ Ath. 1.22c; Wilamowitz (1909: 258), on E. *HF* 180.

⁶ Paus. 5.11.1–2 with Maddoli and Saladino (1995: 238–9); cf. 5.14.8, altar of Zeus Catharsios and *Nikê*; Nonn. 2.709.

⁷ Cf. esp. the account of Heracles' founding of the Olympic games in Pi. *O.* 10, esp. 76–7.

⁸ On *Nikê* in B. 11 see Maehler (1982: 207–8); cf. Barchiesi (1997: 207).

and 'Spur to Emulation'. Hers is work that conceals itself. And *Nikê* thus comes to serve as a master closural device in Greek culture. 'Victory' in Greek is not simply a description of the end of conflict; she is an integral part of the process of making conflict seem reassuringly final and 'clean', asserting a transcendence and authority in the face of the reprisals and recriminations which inevitably follow in a culture fuelled by 'zero-sum' competition and to which war was endemic.

2. ATHENIAN *NIKÊ*

Nikê is omnipresent in classical Athens, a city perhaps more than any other addicted to the aestheticization of supremacy, and certainly to aggressive competition in all its forms.[9] Her services are particularly put to the aid of Zeus' favourite daughter, Athena—and so of her worshippers. In fact, Athena's relationship to *Nikê* becomes so close as to result in the goddess sharing the Titan's name.[10] Such infuriatingly minimal evidence as there is for an entirely *independent* Athenian cult of *Nikê* herself points, intriguingly, to an association with the theatre.[11] But the important polis cult of Athena *Nikê* was prominent by the middle of the fifth century, and had its own priestess.[12] There was also a festival named *Nikêtêria*—almost certainly not for *Nikê* herself, but to memorialize the victory of Athena over Poseidon for possession of the territory, and so probably in honour of Athena *Nikê* and her defeated male rival. This intriguing and ill-attested event embedded the very useful political myth according to which the curse of the defeated Poseidon—the curse of eternal poor deliberation for the Athenians—was corrected by Athena so that no matter how

[9] Osborne (1993) on the proliferation of festival competition. Classical Athens' radical intensification of military conflict is well known.

[10] Baudrillart (1894: 7) describes the relation as 'une sorte de lien mystique.' Cf. *Suda* s.v. Athena Hygieia: Νίκη is ἐπώνυμος of Athena, rather than an epithet. The cultic association between Athena and *Nikê* is also found in Erythrai, Megara, and Rhodes: Thöne (1999: 26, 57).

[11] *Proedria* for priest of (Olympian) *Nikê* in the theatre: *IG* II²5027, probably of the Hadrianic era: Maass (1972: 106); Baudrillart (1894: 16).

[12] *IG* I³35, 36.

poor Athenian deliberation, it resulted all the same in successful outcomes.[13]

To judge from the surviving evidence, Athenians were especially keen to have *Nikê* in their names: the Attic volume of the *Lexicon of Greek Personal Names* gives close to a hundred different entries that seek to involve her in the fortunes of their bearers (male and female): 'Bringer of Victory', 'Possessor of Victory', 'Better Victory', 'Choral Victory', 'Beautiful Victory', 'Lover of Victory'... the list goes on. They could also be notoriously hard on those, like Nikias, who were felt not to have lived up to their name.[14]

Perhaps the single most frequently represented of all divine beings in Attic red-figure vases, *Nikê*'s career in Athenian pictures starts after the Persian wars and really takes off about the time of Cimon's success at Eurymedon.[15] Thereafter she is omnipresent; and her prominence in the visual register stands in contrast with her relatively fleeting appearances as an independent entity in the literary record.[16] In images, she is the winged, delicately robed young female figure endlessly on the move between the world of gods and the earthly realm of mortal struggles. At libations and sacrifices, at scenes of military, athletic, erotic, or musical victory, she is there to beautify the culmination of human conflict—to mark out the victorious with ribbons, with wine, by displaying the instrument of their success (in the case of a *kithara* held aloft by a flying *Nikê* over an altar), or their prize tripod, or merely by her presence.[17] She herself invariably stands clear of the actual conflicts, of which there is scarcely ever any trace in her imagery.[18]

---

[13] Σ Ar. *Ec.*. 472; Procl. *in Tim.* 53d; Plu. 'On brotherly love' 18; cf. Hdt. 8.55; Plu. *Them.* 19; Paus. 1.24.5, 1.26.5; Apollod. 3.14.1. This myth is important in Aristophanes' *Women at the Assembly*: cf. 473 ff.

[14] See e.g. Ar. *Birds* 640 (μελλονικᾶν) with Dunbar (1995: 414); cf. Plu. *Nic.* 1.3.

[15] Webster (1972: 152–78); Thöne (1999: 32) stresses the very probable impulse from the Persian wars, but also notes that 'Die Bildthemen aber machen einen derart direkten Zusammenhang nicht evident'—another important case, I would suggest, of *Nikê* concealing the nature of the work she accomplishes.

[16] Thöne (1999: 16): '*Nike* wird vor allem innerhalb der bildenden Kunst faßbar'. On *Nikê* outside Athens see Giuliani and Most (ch. 9 of this volume).

[17] For images see *LIMC* s.v. *Nikê* and Thöne (1999: Tafel 9.2a) for *Nikê* with *kithara* and altar, a neck amphora from Gela of *c.*475 (Oxford Ashmolean Museum 274, *ARV*² 203, 100). Froning (1971) for images and relief sculpture of *Nikê* with tripods, many plausibly related to dithyrambic *agônes*.

[18] Baudrillart (1894: 21).

Nikê's wings do not simply signify that she, unlike other gods, can fly. They signify rather that mobility and transition are essential to her identity, that her role is to move between this world and that, between before and after. Hence her presence on the heights of temples and stoas everywhere, as the favoured form of the classical acroterion, forever on the point of enacting the flight between earth and heaven.[19] *Nikê* is the visual marker of the authorizing contact with the divine after conflict that beautifies the actions of (successful) men and cities. Or rather, *Nikê* does the work of beautifying after conflict, without showing any sign of the effort involved. The operation of what we might call '*Nikê*'s cosmetics' is most forcefully seen in the military sphere. The large revenues raised by victors from the sale or ransom of prisoners of war generated tithes that became votive offerings which often themselves took the form of *Nikê*— and in the case of the famous *Nikê* of Paeonius at Olympia, the design of the *Nikê* was itself decided by an *agôn*.[20] As Walter Burkert has put it: 'Some of the most renowned artistic monuments of Greece came into existence in this way... the Sacred Way at Delphi is lined with monuments to the victories with which the Greeks destroyed themselves in the fifth and fourth centuries.'[21] With its increasingly intense and absorbing dedication to military conflict (as well as cultural contest) over the course of the fifth century, the city of Athens stood in need of *Nikai*. The victories of the sixth and seventh years of the Archidamian war (426–425), for instance, generated a tithe that was converted into an Athena *Nikê*, and at least two major *Nikai* of solid gold are known from the same period.[22]

The most famous example of Athenian visualization of *Nikê* at this time is also the most contentious of interpretation—and that is on the rich sculptural programme of the balustrade of the temple of Athena *Nikê* on the Acropolis. The contentiousness is integral to the imagery, for this is the most startling exception to the rule that *Nikê* keeps clear of any act of violence. And it may demonstrate that, for all

[19] The basic notion is confirmed rather than contradicted by the idea of a *Nikê* made wingless so as to ensure her unfailing presence among a people: Paus. 3.15.7.
[20] M–L no. 74.
[21] Burkert (1985: 69).
[22] Athena *Nikê*: *IG* II²403 with Mark (1993: 123); gold *Nikai*: *IG* I³468. See further below.

their addiction to *Nikê*'s cosmetic powers, the Athenians of this age did not suspend their critical faculties when representing *Nikê* in the central cultic spaces of their city. For that reason it will serve particularly well as a preface to my principle concern—the operations of *Nikê* in the more spectacularly critical idiom of contemporary drama, especially comedy.

The shrine of Athena that had stood on the Mycenean bastion at the entrance of the Acropolis from at least the archaic age was destroyed by the Persians and replaced by a modest structure, until some (disputed) time in the mid fifth century, when a much more ambitious replacement was planned. A consensus is emerging that dates the relief sculpture on the balustrade of this new shrine to *c.*415 BCE.[23] Each of the (extremely fragmentary) three main faces of the balustrade is crowded with winged *Nikai*, some of them apparently setting up trophies to commemorate victories over Persians and Greeks. A seated Athena appears on each side; a sacrifice of a bull is central to each. The many contested details of interpretation lie well beyond my concerns here. I would simply point to one aspect that has dominated the art-historical discussion of the monument: the numerous *Nikai* are represented here with an altogether unprecedented sensuousness and flowing gracefulness—in their bodily forms, their poses, and their dress. At the same time, perhaps uniquely in the vast portfolio of her imagery, *Nikê* is shown here as directly engaged in the act of slaughter, and although it is sacrificial slaughter, it is in its stark form of *sphagia*, most familiar to Athenian men from its pre-battle form in which 'prayer for success, the taking of signs, and the prefiguring of the result of battle are combined in a single powerful act.'[24] It is as though this unprecedented degree of calm grace and sensuous beauty in *Nikê* were needed, in the nervous Athens of the last quarter of the century, in order to perform her usual operation of aestheticizing conflict, just as there is a need for her direct involvement in the act of ritual slaughter that makes Athenian victory secure. It may seem as though *Nikê* is more relaxed and elegant than ever on this monument; but that merely masks the fact that she is working harder than ever. Art historians debate as to whether

---

[23] Mark (1993: 137); Thöne (1999: 64–73).
[24] Jameson (1994: 317) with further bibliography.

this novel combination of violence and extreme grace implies Athenian supremacist confidence or neurotic insecurity, or perhaps an escapist attempt to beguile.[25] A combination of all such responses is likely in this work's viewers: what they share is an increased awareness of the work of *Nikê* as the imperial city's master scheme of closure, a hint that the normative association—even identification— between beauty and victory was being picked apart.[26] Things were to get worse for Athenian *Nikê*. By 406, the Athenians were reduced to melting down a number of gold *Nikai*—a difficult experience, surely, and one that may have generated a direct comic response in Plato's comedy entitled *Nikai*.[27]

3. DRAMATIC *NIKÊ*

If an anxiety or self-consciousness over *Nikê*'s work seeps through these Athenian images of the teens of the fifth century, it was in the theatre, and not on temple walls, that the Athenians had already for many years been energetically exploring their fears and hopes for *Nikê*'s cosmetics.[28] For tragedy and comedy are—it is almost a

---

[25] Cf. Stewart (1985: 70) who thinks of a neurotic Athenian need for constant reassertion of *nikê*; Jameson (1994: 319) by contrast senses the 'reckless confidence' that lured the Athenians to Sicily 'in the combination of insouciant mannerism and blunt celebration of power.'

[26] The most recent full-scale interpretation of the images, that of Thöne (1999), sees them as honouring tribal victory in the 'home' competitions of the Panathenaea in a generalized manner. The attempt (to my mind unsuccessful, especially given the presence of Persian shields) to remove the images from a military context has the effect of making the novel combination of grace and violence less eccentric and insistent. Thöne's general interpretation of *Nikê* in this period as essentially 'private', the marker of individual (democratic) *aretê*, is largely based on the absence of explicit markers of a military or political context in her images. But in the case of *Nikê* such absence may be integral to the creative representation of the aftermath of conflict.

[27] The melting down: *IG* I³ 379, 469, with Samons (2000: 281–5, 323–4). Plato's *Nikai*: *PCG* 7, 468–9; Meineke *FCG* 1. 175; Geissler (1969: 44) proposed a chorus of *Nikai* for the play, and saw the influence of the newly gracious images from the Athena *Nikê* balustrade.

[28] This is not to suggest that the 'world' outside the theatre can be regarded as a stable evaluative 'backdrop' against which the problematizing dynamics of tragic and comic drama can be simply calibrated. On this see Gellrich (1995); Pelling (1997).

banality to say it—symbolic and performative forms to which conflict, and the question of its resolution in victory and defeat, are utterly central. Quite apart from the profoundly agonistic formal structures of drama (with its rhetorical *agônes*, the combative potential of *stichomythia* and of the basic formal opposition between chorus and actor), as poetic genres and social performances they explore the practices and mentalities which were the realm of *Nikê* and her siblings, and do so under the extreme conditions of heroic myth and fantasy that are media of true experimentation.[29] The elusive goddess herself is even the recipient of tragic and comic prayer, as we shall see.

That there is no unambiguously 'clean' victory in tragedy I take as read. Tragedy lives as a genre by exposing as problematic the logic, rhetoric, and practices of victory. Tragic conflict is so often—particularly in Thebes, as Zeitlin has shown—that unholy form of violence against one's own that the Greeks named *stasis*, rather than the righteous form of war (*polemos*) against outsiders. And even the security of that divide, between a good victory against foreigners and a bad one against one's own kind, is often undermined by the representation of the divide between enemy and friend, between same and other, as an unstable one, as in much Trojan tragic myth—or even, to some extent, in Aeschylus' representation of the iconic Greek victory over barbarian in the *Persians*. At the episodic level of the set debate, or *agôn* of words, these never produce an entirely stable ground for judgement of the issues they have raised, and their 'victors' carry away hollow prizes, or worse. Victory in tragedy is shown to cast a moral shadow that renders impossible any unambiguous celebratory sweep from the stage into the city. And whether or not we regard Euripides' plays with 'happy endings' as deliberate attempts to subvert the genre by inverting one of its most characteristic elements, in general terms, the narrative movement of tragic closure is—unlike comedy—hardly one of triumphalism.[30]

---

[29] Lloyd (1992) on tragic *agôn*; Dunn (1996), Roberts (1987; 1988) on tragic ends, including the victory 'coda'; Gellrich (1988) on tragic conflict. Griffith (1990) is an excellent exploration of the psychology of *nikê* in relation to mythic and poetic forms, including drama; cf. Wilson (2000: esp. 194–7).

[30] One strand of recent interpretation of the aetiologies with which many tragedies close argues that they in effect represent the triumphal victory of integrative

The much-vaunted exception, the end of the *Eumenides*, is to my mind no true exception at all. The entire trilogy is a profound meditation on the perilous logic of *nikê*.[31] The acts of revenge which provide the motor of the narrative are hailed by their perpetrators as victories, yet in the same moment, they are shown to be a form of domestic *stasis* (cf. especially A. *A*. 1117) which, in accordance with a long tradition of Greek thought, could only ever be termed an 'evil' or 'ugly' victory.[32] In the *Eumenides*, Athena seeks to turn *nikê* into a righteous and 'beautiful' form, with the polis as its agent and beneficiary rather than any individual or partisan group (915 ἀστύνικον πόλιν, cf. 1009). After their 'conversion', the Erinyes are thus to sing for 'the kind of things that look to a victory that is not ugly' (903 ὁποῖα νίκης μὴ κακῆς ἐπίσκοπα)—a divine, choral song that does indeed seem far from the triumphal acclamation reported of Zeus in the *Agamemnon*, ἐπινίκια κλάζων (174), and a hymn that we are presumably to imagine will form part of the blessings provided by their future cult under the Acropolis. In short, Athena would establish a firm distinction and secure polarity between *polemos* and *stasis* in the religious and civic order of the polis, so as to distinguish between 'ugly' and 'beautiful' *Nikê*.

(Dionysiac) rituals of the democratic city state at the cost (or perhaps, with the benefit) of the destruction of an (elite, royal) hero or heroic family: esp. Seaford (1994). For criticisms of such a view, which must largely disregard the genre's emphasis on the human experience of suffering and conflict of its characters, as well as the ambiguity inherent to its form, see e.g. Segal (1998; also 1993; 1997). The view that such aetiologies are (in Euripides at least) literary fictions (Scullion 1999–2000) is no more satisfactory.

On Euripidean 'happy endings' see Burnett (1971); Michelini (1987). Euripides' use of short closing choral prayers to *Nikê* that are divorced from their dramatic context seems to be a development under comedy's influence and the poet's generic experimentalism. See *IT* 1490–9, esp. 1497–9, bracketed by Diggle = *Ph.* 1764–6 = *Or.* 1691–3 and §4 below on the comic material. *Rh.* 993–6 is interestingly different for its greater dramatic integration. A tradition preserved by Pollux (4.111) claims that Euripides introduced into many of his tragedies (including the *Danae*) the comic practice of a choral parabasis in which the chorus sings 'on his behalf' (ὑπὲρ αὐτοῦ). If true this brings Euripides' tragic practice another step closer to comedy in its self-conscious agonistic rhetoric.

[31] In a vast bibliography, cf. esp. the work of Goldhill, who long ago analysed the troubling homophonies of *nikê*, *dikê*, and related terms (1984; 1986); cf. Wilson (2006).

[32] Cf. Democr. fr. 249 D-K. On *stasis* see esp. Loraux (2002a).

Without dwelling for too long on a text that continues to generate voluminous and antagonistic responses, I would suggest that, amid all the celebratory show of unity in the finale of the trilogy, there remains both a sense in which Athena's persuasion is working energetically and optimistically to restore the purity of *Nikê*'s cosmetics; *and* at the same time, a sense in which the effort of that work is foregrounded, and remains dangerously exposed, in all its artificiality and with its thinly veiled threat of force.

The success of the conclusion is for instance made to depend on the absence of *nikê*, on the belief that in the trial the Erinyes 'have not been defeated' (795 οὐ γὰρ νενίκησθ'). Yet Athena proclaims that 'our *eris* for good is victorious for all time'—νικᾶι δ' ἀγαθῶν ἔρις ἡμετέρα διὰ παντός (974–5). Victory within the city has thus been elided, and however convinced we may be by that operation,[33] this first attempt to project it out beyond the city produces a curious idea and very awkward language to express it, in the use here of *eris*. Against the grain of regular linguistic usage and all the associations it has accrued, as a partner of *stasis* throughout the trilogy, *eris* changes its meaning from competitive 'strife' to cooperative 'striving'. The rhetorical coerciveness here—the 'violent persuasion'—might be deemed justified under the circumstances; but the maintenance of such distinctions, difficult enough in language, is all the more difficult in reality. A stark reminder of the risks of victory, and of the impossibility of distinguishing between the twin *Erides* of the Hesiodic tradition,[34] is as important to the end of this play and trilogy as any note of final triumph.

The end of the *Eumenides* has long been regarded as having affinities with the ends of (Aristophanic) comedy.[35] The successful resolution of conflict, a torchlit procession, choral prayers, a 'victorious', celebratory departure into a civic space that is perceived as more or less directly continuous with the space of the drama[36]—these are some features identified as shared between the two. While certain of

---

[33] Athena's elision of the 'defeat' of the Erinyes in the trial is all the more coercive if, as I believe, her own vote to acquit Orestes turned a condemnation (a victory of the Erinyes) into an acquittal (defeat of the Erinyes): *contra* Seaford (1995).

[34] *Works and Days* 11–26. Cf. Pucci (1977).

[35] Herington (1963); Taplin (1996: 198).

[36] The final procession of the *Eumenides* is not exactly a victory parade but a procession of incorporation that may draw on the ritual resources of the Panathenaic

these formal parallels are indisputable, I would argue that what comedy in fact shares with the *Eumenides* is what I have identified as its more critical and cautionary approach to *nikê*, and this is something that also brings it closer to the generic mainstream of tragic reflection on and through *nikê*.

4. COMIC *NIKÊ*

In the most general terms, Old Comedy has an overtly triumphal narrative shape.[37] Although needing many qualifications of detail in each case, a typical schema sees the comic hero (or heroine), in the face of a dilemma, coming up with a 'Grande Idée'[38] to overcome it. The narrative of the drama enacts the attempts, and the opposition to them, to make this idea real. In the end, the hero and his idea triumph, and he goes off in 'comastic' triumph, sometimes to be married or at least to enjoy a range of pleasures of his victory.[39] (This schema applies strictly to *Acharnians*, *Birds*, and *Peace* only, but the inherently agonistic and triumphal shape of comedy is also evident in *Knights*, *Frogs*, *Lysistrata*, *Wasps*, and *Women at the Assembly*.)[40] Much of Old Comedy thus builds towards a victorious and highly

procession. Yet the closing refrain evokes the ὀλολυγή and its associations of joy at victory both within and beyond the trilogy. Within the trilogy these associations are for victories where joy is at best a dubious response (*A.* 28, 587, 595, 1118, 1236–7, *Ch.* 942). Haldane (1965: 38): 'Not until the exodos of the *Eumenides* does the ὀλολυγή signify true and lasting victory'. One could as readily argue that the closing phrase of this victory cry carries the contamination of its earlier usages.

[37] Carrière (1979); cf. Whittaker (1935: 184–7). Taplin (1996: 196–9) is an important contribution to the issue of generic differentiation in this respect. Gelzer (1993) on 'festival structures' in comedy.

[38] Carrière (1979: 86) uses the expression.

[39] Celebrations at marriages could in fact be termed ἐπινίκια: Lucian *Dearum Iudicium*; and the presence of *Nikê* in the iconography of marriage is common: Oakley and Sinos (1993). For the 'komastic' processional exodos as a traditional form of comic ending, old and new, see Arnott (1965); cf. Green (1994: 91–2).

[40] While in *Women at the Thesmophoria* after the *agôn* the emphasis is rather on reconciliation, reflected in the choral finale's reference to 'moderation in play' πέπαισται μετρίως (1227) rather than on *nikê*; and the chorus in fact disperse to their individual homes.

mobile finale, with an emphasis on direct movement ('offstage') into a world where the vision will be realized, or its realization enjoyed.

A common and crucial element of this movement towards victory involves the creation of a sense of the victory of the *comedy* itself in its festival *agón* as the 'natural' concomitant of—or indeed, as virtually equivalent to—the victory of the comic hero and his Idea. The rhetoric of comic *nikê* thus links comedy powerfully to the city through its festival structures. A successful comic hero (and chorus—and poet, and sponsor) marches out of the theatre as if into a city newly remade for him. Much of the work of the drama has been to make that movement seem natural, but the reality of the theatrical judgement must intervene at some point, determining victors and vanquished, and who may legitimately celebrate their victory with the god's favour—and possibly even who had the right to dedicate their masks in or near his sanctuary.[41] Comic victory's appropriation of the city in this way is the grandest 'metatheatrical' gesture possible, and produces some characteristically megalomaniacal claims. For instance, the victory of the chorus within the narrative of the *Women at the Thesmophoria*—and this chorus actually delivers a prayer to *Nikê*—becomes not only the assumed victory of the *Women at the Thesmophoria* as a drama, but will result in nothing less than victory for Athens in the Peloponnesian war.[42] Yet comedy's sophistication, in part driven by its agonistic structure—and in company with deeper concerns of the age with the practices and mentality of *nikê*—ensures that such naturalized and easy triumphalism rarely escapes exposing its own work to scrutiny. In fact, in some cases, comedy turns the 'ugliness' that is central to its generic identity to the end of exposing and questioning the assumption that *nikê* is 'naturally' *kalê*.[43]

There are many means by which the victory of the comic vision is welded on to the persuasive sense of the 'rightness' of the victory of the comedy in the festival *agôn*—or what we might term, in order to distinguish what Aristophanes and others seek to assimilate, 'comedic' victory. A full study would include the calls made by the chorus

[41] Green (1994: 78–84, 91).

[42] Cf. *Th.* 972, with Sommerstein (1994: 219).

[43] For the importance of comedy's use of physical ugliness see Taplin (1996) and Winkler (1989).

and characters for victory throughout, as well as their 'advice' to, and abuse of, the judges;[44] the whole parabatic (or 'quasi-parabatic') discourse of poetic self-presentation by the poet, where the palimpsestic persona of the chorus shapes the identity of the great comic poet who stands far above all his rivals and who, no matter how fickle his audience (or segments of it), will continue to produce his elevated form of *kômôidia* that is so good for the city;[45] and the more direct closing calls for victory made by a departing chorus.[46]

A passage from the *Frogs* provides an instance of the way other elements of comedy (in this case the parodos) can be deployed to mould a sense of the 'rightness' of the victory of the comedy in its competition on to a sense of the 'rightness' of the vision of the comedy itself. Given that the *Frogs* is a comedy with no 'archetypal' mortal comic hero, it is no surprise that this metatheatrical anticipation of victory comes from the mouths of its chorus of Initiates. It is from their invocation of Demeter in anapaestic tetrameters, but it forms a unit with the preceding quasi-parabatic passage of anapaests calling for political and poetic rectitude, and keeping out of the way of 'our choruses' (354) those who do not appreciate (Aristophanic) comedy along with those guilty of political misconduct—particularly fomenters of *stasis* (359–68). Demeter is asked to 'save your own chorus' (388), and leave us 'to sport all day in safety and to be a chorus' (387–8 ἀσφαλῶς πανήμερον | παῖσαί τε καὶ χορεῦσαι) 'and to say many funny things, and many serious, and having sported and joked in a way worthy of your festival, to get the victory and be tied with ribbons' (391–95 νικήσαντα ταινιοῦσθαι). The shift here between the Eleusinian and Lenaean identities of this chorus is made easier, as Dover notes, by the fact that the Eleusinian deities had a

[44] See below, text to n. 81.

[45] See esp. Hubbard (1991); Goldhill (1991: 167–222); Bremer (1993); Biles (2001).

[46] This is so traditional a motif as to preserve a chorocentric victory orientation long after the chorus had ceased to be central to the dramatic action of comedy: see esp. the closing lines of Men. *Sam.* (736–7), which may have a deliberately nostalgic or archaizing feel: ἡ δὲ κα]λλίστων ἀγώνων πάρεδρος ἄφθιτος θεὰ/[εὐμε]νὴς ἔποιτο Νίκη τοῖς ἐμοῖς ἀεὶ χοροῖς. Cf. also *Mis.* 996; *Dysk.* 968–9; *Sik.* 422–3; Posidipp. fr. 6.11–13 *PCG* We might compare the two reliefs found in the Agora, dating to the late fourth century, which seem to memorialize comedy through its chorus: Wilson (2000: 241–2).

foothold in the Lenaea.[47] As far as we can tell, however, the Mysteries did not involve choral contest. The call for victory that forms the climax of their prayer thus stresses their identity as a comic chorus in a clear if fairly subtle manner.[48] The audience is drawn into the Initiates' view of their blessed activities and the success they derive from them in a more gentle way, and so are led to identify the comedy's agonistic success as the natural concomitant of the Initiates' 'successful' way of life—or rather, of life and death—a view that many of them will of course have shared as Initiates at Eleusis. The effect is resumed with greater force at the end of the comedy, where in the final 'tragic' *agôn* in Hades, the Eleusinian associations of Aeschylus make that poet's victory rather less unexpected than it might have otherwise appeared, given Dionysus' original expressed intention of going to Hades to bring back Euripides. Moreover Aeschylus' procession, victorious, offstage, and into the upper world draws on the procession offstage and below ground of the *Semnai Theai* in the *Eumenides*,[49] and so adds to the *Frogs'* powerful palimpsest of *nikê* the illustrious precedent of the victorious trilogy that so imprinted itself on Athenian theatrical memory.

Such 'seeds' are, in the general schema, preparations for the closing and closural moments, where the comic hero leaves the stage, with or without the chorus, for a victory procession that welds a fictive and often fantastic event of victorious celebration (marriage to Opora or Basilinna, winning the Choes *agôn*, and so on) with the anticipated victory celebrations of the comedic *agôn*. In this way comic *nikê* claims comedic *nikê*, and seems to strive to make the two indistinguishable.

What I want to suggest however, is that for all the efforts of *nikê* to perform her usual task of bridging, and to naturalize the transition from comic vision to comedic prize, in some important cases the

---

[47] Dover (1993*b*: 179): a ritual formula of the Lenaea identifies Dionysus with Iacchus, and the managers of the Mysteries also helped manage the Lenaea. See also lines 356–7, 366–8 with Dover (1993*a*: 239) for other places where the chorus' identity as Eleusinian-Lenaean is established.

[48] On musical performance in mystery cult see Hardie (2004). When the chorus of *Knights* pray to Pallas Athena to bring victory to the Sausage-Seller and themselves over Paphlagon, they ask her to take *Nikê* with her, describing her as ἦ χορικῶν ἐστιν ἑταίρα (589). This is another quite subtle case of assimilation of victory within the drama with the victory of the drama.

[49] See esp. *Frogs* 1530 with A. *Eu.* 1011–12.

thrust of comic self-consciousness is deliberately to undermine those efforts and to expose their mechanics.[50] We need glance only at the bizarre and wonderful close of the *Wasps*, with its comic contest of tragic dancing between the sons of Carcinus and Philocleon— expressly flagged as an entirely novel way to close a comedy (especially 1536–7)—to see that drawing attention to ending comedy became a comic end in itself.

The *Acharnians* (Lenaea, 425) offers a very clear example of the triumphalist contours of comic narrative. Through his 'Grande Idée' of a private peace, Dicaeopolis wins a victory over his bellicose fellow demesmen (cf. 626); over the representative of Athenian militarism, the general Lamachus; over the bellicose and—far worse—politically corrupt polis as a whole—as well as, along the way, over the generic rival of tragedy. The victory of the hero's vision is dramatized spectacularly in the closing scenes which elaborately contrast his fate, as he prepares a feast enriched by goods from his newly opened private market, with that of Lamachus, called up for border patrol on the wintry passes of the Boeotian frontier and who, in the midst of Dicaeopolis' preparations returns, wounded and in great pain.

Dicaeopolis' march off at the end has usually been seen as marking the natural and deserved triumph of his eirenic vision, and as the just deserts of a bravely independent 'ordinary' man of the land. As Henderson puts it, 'even when [the hero's] achievement rescues only the hero (as in *Acharnians*), the spectators are encouraged to feel admiration and envy rather than alienation and resentment.'[51] More recently, however, some have argued that Dicaeopolis' radically self-interested victory may have alienated rather than attracted.[52] A close examination of the mechanics of metatheatrical *nikê* further supports this position.

The feast to celebrate his personal victory that Dicaeopolis is having prepared in the closing scenes is to be held in the context of

---

[50] See now the important discussion of choral *exodoi* in comedy and the ambivalence of the chorus' authority in delivering them by Calame (2004). Cf. Dobrov (2001: 5) on 'ancient metatheatrics as an important accomplice of the Athenian theatre in its transgressive dimension'.

[51] Henderson (1993: 310); cf. Taplin (1996: 196): 'there is, as far as I can see, no encouragement to resist his final victory-parade.'

[52] Esp. Foley (1988); Bowie (1993: 32–9); Macleod (1983); cf. the balanced assessment of Olson (2002: esp. pp. xliii–lii).

the Anthesteria, at which he has apparently just won—or at least he anticipates winning—the drinking contest of the Choes (cf. 1202–3, 1227). With these already multiple victory celebrations the anticipated victory of the *Acharnians* itself is powerfully 'merged'. His call at 1224–5 'Take me to the judges! Where is the *Basileus*? Give me the wineskin!' is the clearest instance of this merging, since the *Basileus* was the official in charge of both Anthesteria and Lenaea. Dicaeopolis' march off under the sign of *Nikê*, with the most explicit of all markers of victory, the refrain of τήνελλα καλλίνικος, thus seems to effect an easy slide across the end of the comedy.

And yet no Athenian needed to be reminded (as we do) of the very particular quality of the contest and victory won at the Choes that distinguishes it sharply from a Lenaean victory.[53] Victory at the Choes was an unusually solitary affair, and the relevant mythology and ritual of the festival speak of the isolation of the difficult and socially threatening individual, and how to respond to it. Furthermore, the metatheatrical merging of Dicaeopolis' celebrations and those anticipated for the *Acharnians* itself begins much earlier and goes rather deeper than is usually noted. In fact, it begins as early as 883 (see below), and thus involves much of the open market scene and all of the preparation of food that follows it. And it goes deeper in the sense that a parallel is established (again, by 883) between Dicaeopolis' victory feast and the special feast expected of its *chorêgos* by a winning choral troupe, which was known as an *epinikia*.[54] The little we know about this practice (and among that little, that which is not derived solely from comedy), shows that it was not simply a sympotic occasion but involved a sacrifice of thanksgiving and a meal—and one whose meat was, unlike the equivalent for the dithyrambic *agônes*, apparently provided 'privately' by the *chorêgos*. It appears to have been designed for the chorus only, not the actors.[55]

---

[53] Hamilton (1992: esp. 12–13); Bowie (1993: 34–8); Olson (2002: 31).

[54] On this see Wilson (2000: 102–3).

[55] Cf. esp. Pl. *Smp.* 173a: τὰ ἐπινίκια ἔθυεν αὐτός [sc. Agathon] τε καὶ οἱ χορευταί. Doubtless things were not so clear-cut, with actors, friends, and other associates of the production—even aulos-players—often involved. By the fictional date of the *Symposium* (416) the separate prize for actors had long since existed, and so too a degree of separation between (victorious) actor and any particular choral troupe, including the successful one.

The dramatic *epinikia* was thus a somewhat exclusive affair,[56] but it was also, importantly, validated by a judgment of the polis as a whole, in the persons of the democratically appointed panel of festival judges, the empowered arbiters of theatrical *nikê*.[57]

If it is reasonable to explain away Dicaeopolis' failure to involve the Acharnian chorus fully in his own final victory and drinking celebrations (see below), it is surely much more difficult to do the same when the feast from which they are excluded actively triggers in the audience thoughts of an event in the immediate festival context, the comic *epinicia* of the Lenaea. And, what is more, this chorus has experienced such exclusion before, as it goes to some trouble to make clear.

The Theban who was blown into Dicaeopolis' market on the blasts of the ethnically stereotyped *aulos* (860) provides, among his wares, eels from lake Copaïs, and a fine piece of paratragedy to go with them (883–6):[58]

> Theban: Come, thou chief of fifty Copaïc maidens,
>   come out here and do the gentleman a favour.
> Dik.:   O dearest one, long yearned for, thou
>   hast come—the heart's desire of trugic choruses.

The Copaïc eels which are to grace Dicaeopolis' feast are eels that come, metatheatrically, much-longed-for by comic choruses. In other words, this delicacy is the stuff of celebratory *epinicia*, what comic choruses hope for as part of the return for their success.[59] Dicaeopolis' victories and the comedic victory of the chorus are thus merged through the flesh of Copaïc eels. This metatheatrical move was further strengthened by the fact that Boeotian *aulos*-players were famous as musical professionals, so the players who accompany the Theban trader with these eels probably also evoke the world of theatrical music.[60]

---

[56] That notwithstanding Plato's Socrates' deliberately charged use of the term *okhlos* (*Smp.* 174a) to describe the 'mob' at Agathon's *epinicia*. Exclusivity is relative.

[57] To judge from (e.g.) *Ec.* 1141–3 judges—and spectators!—could be invited to the *epinicia*. Such hyperbolic generosity is clearly part of the rhetoric of persuasion.

[58] Translations from Sommerstein, with modifications.

[59] Sommerstein (1980: 201); Olson (2002: 294–5, 349).

[60] Boeotian *aulos*-players: Roesch (1989). Lake Copais was also renowned as the source of the best reeds for manufacturing *auloi*: Thphr. *HP* 4.2.1–7; cf. Pi. *P.* 12.27.

Diacaeopolis and his slave carry off the array of newly acquired delicacies into his house (969–70), and the chorus comments shortly after—perhaps as he briefly opens the door to dispose of a load of feathers and other unwanted bird parts (987–8):[61]

> He is in a flutter for his dinner
> and his pride is great indeed,
> and as evidence of his lifestyle
> he cast these feathers out before his doors.

From being a sign of his triumphal peace, with its reopening of the avenues of exchange, the delicacies of Dicaeopolis' dining—or rather, their unwanted refuse—have become an oppressive sign of his lifestyle to those outside his *oikos* who are not so lucky, a group which happens to consist of the comic chorus made up of fellow demesmen. The attitude is a comic variant on the familiar theme of the hybristic and status-hungry member of the elite who lords his socio-economic superiority over others—one who, as the chorus says of Dicaeopolis, μέγα φρονεῖ. Such 'big thinking' is a familiar fault in tragic figures before their fall.[62]

And so, despite its being assimilated to choral *epinicia*, there is no guarantee that the chorus will be invited to the sympotic victors' feast with the *Basileus* to which Dicaeopolis eventually departs. They certainly receive no direct invitation, as he does (1085–94). And he makes no effort to include them in his company. On the contrary, during the elaborate kitchen scene, as they watch Dicaeopolis give orders for the careful boiling, roasting, and spitting of hare, and the skewering of thrush that he is to take with him to this feast, the chorus comments (1008–10):

> I envy you your good policy,
> or rather your good fare,
> sir, which is here before us

That Dicaeopolis calls the players Χαιριδῆς βομβαύλιοι at 866 clinches the point, since whatever his critics claimed (see *Ach.* 16), Chairis was a theatrical performer of some note: Stephanis (1988: 455–6). At *Peace* 1005–15 Trygaeus prays to Peace and adds Copaic eels to the list of things longed for, to be enjoyed by an army of (?) epinician gluttons that *excludes* the tragic poet Melanthius.

[61] Thus Olson (2002: 315).   [62] Bowie (1993: 35).

and later (1044–6):

> You'll starve me to death,
> me and the neighbours, what with the aroma
> and the words, if you shout out things like that.

('that' being an instruction to broil the eels.) After the chorus has bade the two 'campaigners' farewell on their very different courses, they turn to a choral 'interlude' (1150–61) whose relevance to the work as a whole has in the past been much doubted. Starkie called it 'a satiric chanson, entirely outside the action of the piece;'[63] and Dale, 'an irrelevant lampoon'.[64] This is Sommerstein's translation:[65]

> As for Antimachus, son of Showers, the draftsman,
> the composer of wretched lyrics,
> to put it bluntly, may Zeus destroy him utterly!
> For when he sponsored a Lenaean
> chorus, he dismissed poor me without a dinner.
> May I yet live to see him longing
> for squid; and may it lie, well cooked
> and sizzling, shipshape on the table,
> and make land safely; and then, when
> he is about to take it, may a dog
> snatch it and make off with it.

There are many interesting issues raised by this metafestive abuse of Antimachus, wretched draftsman (of decrees—or prose author?),[66] poet, *and chorêgos*. Whether the reference here is to a real comic chorus deprived of its feast by an Antimachus serving as *chorêgos*; whether the Acharnian chorus thus speaks for themselves as that same earlier chorus, or for all Aristophanic choruses—or indeed for all comic choruses; whether the poet for the deprived chorus was Aristophanes, Cratinus, or another; whether the meal was not forthcoming because the comedy did not win first prize—all of these are intriguing, much-discussed but unanswerable questions.[67] I would

[63] Starkie (1909: 223).

[64] Dale (1969: 292). However see now Bowie (1993: 35) for a defence of its relevance.

[65] There are textual problems with 1151, and Olson (2002) is probably right to obelize.

[66] Olson (2002: 348).

[67] See now Olson (2002: 349) with earlier bibliography.

stress the ways in which this passage of metachorality is in fact linked intimately with what goes before and after. For the chorus is moved to this choral abuse by what it has witnessed onstage—the misery of Lamachus' exclusion from the feast of the Choes, in extended contrast to the pleasures awaiting Dicaeopolis. As the voice of 'comic *choreutai* in general' (to my mind the most likely interpretation on that issue),[68] the Acharnians respond to the action onstage with memories of their own—of deprivation of or exclusion from celebratory feasts.[69] This was not due to war, but (in their minds at least) to the appalling failure in generosity on the part of a member of the theatrical world, a poet and *chorêgos*.[70]

The chorus' predicament thus brings them much closer to Lamachus than Dicaeopolis at this crucial point. We should recall that the latter has already begun his feasting as they start to sing this piece. And the metafestival step backwards and out of the comic present to the close of another theatrical festival taken in this song also sets up more forcefully the question as to what lies ahead, beyond the end of *this* drama, for *this* chorus. It is much more common for comic choruses at this point in a drama to be anticipating, preparing for or asserting imminent victory rather than recalling past failure. When the moment arrives, Dicaeopolis stage-manages their final exit himself. Having emptied his pitcher—full of neat wine, the drink of barbarians—he raises the victory cry for himself: τήνελλα καλλίνικος (1227); to which the chorus responds with τήνελλα δῆτ᾽, εἴπερ καλεῖς γ᾽, ὦ πρέσβυ, καλλίνικος—a response whose exact tone is

---

[68] Dover (1987: 303).

[69] At 1155 most editors print ἀπέλυσ᾽ ἄδειπνον ('he dismissed me without a dinner') rather than the reading of the oldest codex (Ravenna)—ἀπέκλεισε δείπνων ('he excluded me from the feasts')—with its emphasis on exclusion. The original may have included some form of ἀποκλῄω, which, as Olson (2002: 349) notes, is a common Aristophanic verb.

[70] The various explanations offered by the scholia on 1150 look like free invention from the text, especially the claim that a decree authored by Antimachus against κωμῳδεῖν ἐξ ὀνόματος had the effect of reducing comic production and so increasing choral hunger. That of Σ *vet.* 1150c has an air of slightly greater plausibility: it says that Antimachus authored a decree 'so that the choruses received nothing from the *chorêgoi*.' A control on expenditure permitted by the elite on their choruses is more plausible, given the potential for personal patronage that the relationship allowed (Wilson 2000: 123–30), the hints of such control elsewhere in comic scholia, and known examples of Athenian sumptuary laws.

extremely hard to gauge, but which seems to imply some degree of diffidence: 'Well, since you call for it, old man, hurrah for the victor!' (1228).[71] The play—or at least our text—ends with Dicaeopolis ordering the chorus to follow him, singing the victory hymn over him for his achievement. And they dutifully do so; at least, their closing iambs declare (1232–3):

> Follow we will, for your sake,
> singing 'hurrah for the victor!',
> for you and your wineskin.

—an expression which hardly conceals the fact that there is an enormous gulf between them as celebrants and the subject of their song. This is of course in order, for the victor has by his achievements put himself beyond the circle of ordinary mortals. But the choral performance that follows a victory should also serve to integrate the victor back into his community, not isolate him forever in the transcendent and dangerous moment of his glory. Moreover, this chorus is made up of fellow demesmen who continue to suffer from the very predicament over which Dicaeopolis has triumphed. And the τήνελλα καλλίνικος ought surely arise rather more spontaneously than this. The charm of victory's beauty depends on such spontaneity— or at least on its appearance.

I say that our text (rather than the play) ends here not simply because of the (perhaps considerable) remaining action involved in clearing the stage, but because it is often stated as a fact that—to quote Sommerstein—'The words [of the victory song], as not having been composed by the dramatist but taken over ready-made, will have been omitted from the texts of the play that went into circulation.'[72] This seems an especially dangerous argument from silence, and I think we ought to take this particular aposiopesis seriously: having discharged in a minimal way their promise to raise the *kallinikos*, the chorus leaves with no further song. The assumption that they carry Dicaeopolis off on their shoulders in procession is no more than an assumption. It is equally possible that Dicaeopolis left

---

[71] Bowie (1993: 38) takes the expression as an invitation, but one of ambiguous sincerity: 'if you really do invite us'; cf. Macleod (1983: 50); Olson (2002: 364) *contra* sees the expression as one 'not of doubt but of a confident eagerness to cooperate'.

[72] Sommerstein (1980: 215); cf. similarly Henderson (1987: 214) on *Lys.* 1316–17.

the stage by entering the *skênê*, his own house and site of celebrations with the *Basileus*, leaving the chorus, excluded, to depart in silence.

The extensive treatment of Dicaeopolis as victor with which the *Acharnians* closes shows little sign of that communal involvement crucial to a society's—especially a democratic society's—integration of the victor. But that very representation in turn serves the useful (democratic) function of exploring the logic and practice of *Nikê* itself as it operated across a range of social practices—in rhetorical contest, in war, poetry, and, more broadly, in the competitive pursuit of individual advantage in a democratic society. But what of the marked assimilation of Dicaeopolis' victory with that of the *Acharnians* itself that I discussed earlier? It is surely the most impressive token of Aristophanes' seriousness that he risks, or indeed courts, any degree of disjunction between his comic hero's victory and his comedy's victory in this way.

And yet there is an intriguing possibility that the formal structure of the festival enabled this disjunction and limited its risk: the separate prize for protagonists (as distinct from whole productions) had very probably existed at the Lenaea from *c*.442.[73] If it had, the *Acharnians* may work with this structural dynamic. Dicaeopolis *qua* protagonist can win a victory distinct from that to which the play (and its chorus) as a whole aspires. This separation in agonistic objectives between protagonist and chorus will have made available such exploration, through formal structures, of ideas of individual and collective *nikê*.

Not all comedies take such risks. But the importance of such critique to a play of the early fourth century (Lenaea, 391) about which Zeitlin has taught us so much, the *Women at the Assembly*, has not been fully recognized. Before turning to the spectacularly self-conscious close of that work, I shall make some brief remarks about the way another 'anti-war' comedy, the *Peace* (Great Dionysia, 421), uses its own agonistic context to the end of undermining the aggressive logic of *nikê*.

In the parabasis, the chorus' extended praise for their *kômôidodidaskalos* as a man who has defended the integrity of a noble ideal of the comic *tekhnê* (738–50) and courageously protected the

---

[73] Pickard-Cambridge (1988: 125).

city against the predations of Cleon and his like (754–60) passes seamlessly to their call for the comedic victory of the *Peace*. In the *pnigos*, three groups are called upon 'to join in agitating for victory with us' (768 ξυσπουδάζειν περὶ τῆς νίκης): men, boys and—the third term comes as the comic surprise—*baldies*. Quite apart from feeling naturally predisposed to favour the bald poet, the bald are as a group deemed most likely to concur with the deconstruction of the accepted equation of beauty and worth (καλλινίκη), and so most likely to want this work and its decidedly eirenic hero to achieve victory. For it more than any other of Aristophanes' surviving comedies undoes that equation. By redefining what constitutes victory in war and poetry, the *Peace*, a comedy by a bald poet with the most noble brow, shows that *Nikê*'s traditional good looks mask an inner ugliness.[74]

The same thematic is effectively explored in the (non-)sacrifice scene that immediately follows the parabasis. At 1017 Trygaeus tells his slave to take the knife and slaughter the sheep μαγειρικῶς, 'like a butcher'. The use of this unusual adverb heightens the sense of mimetic action at this point—the slave is to 'act like a butcher'. His objection that it is not *themis* to sacrifice a sheep for Peace, because she takes no pleasure in blood sacrifice (1018–19) results in the order from Trygaeus that he take it inside, sacrifice it there, remove the thigh bones and bring them out here: 'That way the sheep is saved for the *chorêgos*' (1020–2 χοὔτω τὸ πρόβατον τῶι χορηγῶι σώιζεται). We should see in this comic business more than a practical need to avoid engaging in sacrificial slaughter on stage.[75] The reference to choregic convenience is also a reference to the anticipated victory of the comedy (*via* the epinician feast sponsored by the *chorêgos*), and so prepares the way for the assimilation of Trygaeus' victory and the play's victory—an assimilation that seems entirely unproblematic in

---

[74] Baldness may be a generic marker of comedy more generally, given the indications that adult male comic masks could portray a degree of hair loss.

[75] Olson (1998: 265). It is fascinating that what is kept from the view of the audience (and from the altar of Peace) is the act of bloody slaughter itself. The comic poet occludes from view the moment that is also routinely avoided in visual representation, while making of the occlusion both a prohibition in keeping with Peace's rituals and an anticipation of the *Peace*'s victory. The scene may thus even expose the 'staginess' of the conventions surrounding that central drama of Greek religious life, the *thysia*.

this play, and that comes to fullest fruit at the close, with its inclusive invitation from the chorus to the (?) audience[76] to follow their hymeneal procession and join in eating cakes (1355–7):

> ὦ χαίρετε χαίρετ', ἄν-
> δρες· κἂν ξυνέπησθέ μοι,
> πλακοῦντας ἔδεσθε

And yet a slight disjunction does remain. For a play that secures victory for the bloodless ways of Peace anticipates its own celebratory victory party with the slaughter of the animal whose blood so displeased Peace. The message is clear: blood sacrifice may trouble Peace, but *Nikê*—including the *Nikê* that oversees this comic *agon*—is not so troubled.[77]

The closing lines of the *Women at the Assembly* have long been recognized as among the most overt of all metatheatrical calls to epinician success, gliding on the back of the triumphal achievement of the play's own vision (1180–2):

> αἴρεσθ' ἄνω, ἰαὶ εὐαί.
> δειπνήσομεν, εὐοῖ εὐαί.
> εὐαί, ὡς ἐπὶ νίκηι·
> εὐαί, εὐαί, εὐαί, εὐαί.

> Raise it high, iai, evai!
> We're going to feast, evoi, evai,
> evai, a feast of victory!
> Evai, evai, evai, evai!

The Dionysian resonances of the cries εὐοῖ, εὐαί are especially appropriate to an anticipated epinician feast, presumably offered in thanks to Dionysus Lenaeus.[78] But the feast is both that of the play's desired victory and that of the victory of Praxagora's new regime, her great communistic feeding of the city, from which apparently none is to be

---

[76] Thus Olson (1998: 318).

[77] Sommerstein (1985) believes that the *chorêgos* is simply saved the cost of a sheep which he would have had to provide if it were killed onstage. We do not hear of *chorêgoi* supplying stage properties (even if it is not inherently improbable), and it is at least as likely that this is meant to be a way of anticipating a 'cost saving' for the *chorêgos*, by virtue of the fact that he will have this beast for his *epinikia*. This seems to suit the use of σώιζω somewhat better, with the common sense of 'kept back from death'.

[78] Ussher (1973: 237); cf. *Lys.* 1291–4.

excluded—its very inclusiveness also makes these Dionysian cries apposite. Here comic utopian largesse spills over abundantly into the city. And yet here too as in *Acharnians*, this passage of *Nikê* opens a reflective prism of critique.

Most of the second half of the play is devoted to the new means of distribution of the two essential elements in Praxagora's system—food and sex.[79] At 1112 Praxagora's maid arrives to escort her mistress's husband to the *deipnon* at which apparently he alone of 'more than thirty thousand citizens' has not yet attended (1132–3). The entire 'blessed' *dêmos*, with its new female political agents and their husbands, their male and female children—even, it seems, with their slaves—has been enjoying the largesse of Praxagora, and it is now at last the turn of Blepyrus to go off to the feast.

In issuing her invitation, Praxagora's maid further includes (1141–2):

> anyone among the spectators who is well disposed,
> and any of the judges who isn't looking elsewhere.

In other words, the invitation opens on to the world of the city, in so far as it is a city with the power to translate the play's comic vision into a comedic victory. But given the sequence of events, this invitation is in fact an overt bribe, an offer to share the fruits of the success that they can produce—'for we shall provide everything' (1143). Such dramatized bribery of the festival judges, along with flattery, cajoling, and threats, was not uncommon in Old Comedy. But it should not be regarded as a stale *topos* for that.[80] Bribery in the political sphere is one of the evils against which Aristophanic comedy frequently rages, and in all other contexts of civic discourse outside comedy, it is far from being a joking matter. Which is, of course, part of the very reason it is such good matter for joking here. But the city also took the practice of empanelling its *theatrical* juries seriously enough to control it with extremely elaborate precautions against

---

[79] Zeitlin (1999); see also Said (1996).

[80] Cf. Cratin. *Pl.* fr. 171 *PCG*; Ar. *Birds* 1102–15., *Clouds* 1115–30; Pherecr. *Krap.* fr. 102 *PCG* At *Birds* 444–5 the very continuation of the comedy is deftly made conditional on the foreclosure of the comedic *agôn*. Pisthetaerus extracts an oath that the birds will not harm him, on condition (imposed by the choral birds) that all the *kritai* vote for them. They add: 'And if I break my oath, may I win by only one *kritês*'. See Calame (2004: 176–81).

partiality, prescribing death for anyone who dared tamper with the jars containing the names of potential judges preselected by the tribes, which were sealed by the prytaneis and guarded by the Treasurers of Athena on the Acropolis.[81] The judges of the dramatic festival were deemed to be performing no less serious a duty than their fellows elsewhere. It is equally clear, however, that these precautions were taken in the face of manifest partiality, intimidation, and the not very democratic sentiment of 'doing a *chorêgos* a favour' ([Andocid.] 4.21).

The important point here, it seems to me, is not simply the fact that a democratic institution is being represented in *precisely* the manner its protocols were designed to prevent. It is more significant that the course the judges are being coerced into taking, and which represents the victorious vision of the comedy, involves a complete abandonment of the political altogether. For to vote for Praxagora's play and to take part in her and its celebrations is to be involved in a full-scale displacement of the political. In her earlier exchange with Blepyrus, Praxagora made it abundantly clear that her feeding of the city is an act of depoliticization. When he asks where they are to eat their meals, she replies 'I shall turn all the *dikastêria* and *stoai* into dining rooms.' 'And what will you use the *bêma* for?' 'I'll make it a stand for the mixing bowls and pitchers...' (676–8) Likewise, the ballot booths are to be used to allot tickets to indicate to diners in which building they are to eat.

Praxagora's politics have removed the need for politics, given that a fundamental rationale behind political life—sustaining the community as a whole—has been removed at a blow by her fantastic largesse. Yet there is much more (and less) than a vision of *eutopia* here. The wholesale abandonment of political agency facilitated through the actions of a 'nurturing' woman treads a fine line between dream and nightmare.[82] The implications of abutting this depoliticized city of food so sharply against civic reality—as a result of its success—are worth considering.

---

[81] Isoc. *Trapez.* 33–4; Csapo and Slater (1995: 157–65); Wilson (2000: 98–102); Marshall and Van Willigenburg (2004).

[82] Schmitt-Pantel (1992: 222–31, esp. 230–1). Cf. Wilkins (1997).

As the chorus hurry Blepyrus on, they announce they will sing a song—'a sort of pre-dining celebration song' (in Sommerstein's translation of μέλος τι μελλοδειπνικόν 1153: 1154–62).

> But I want to give a little bit of advice to the judges:
> to those who are intellectual, to remember the intellectual bits and vote for me;
> to those who enjoy a laugh, to think of the laughs they've had and vote for me;
> in other words, I'm telling just about *everyone* to vote for me.
> And don't let the lottery and the fact that our play was produced first
> act to our disadvantage at all: you must remember all these things,
> and not break your oath, but always judge the choruses fairly
> and not behave in the same way as those wretched supertarts,
> who never have a place in their memory for any man but their latest one!

This is not a bribe, but a warning, and forthright orders about how to vote. It is of course entirely in keeping with comedy's unashamedly aggressive 'advice' about the rights and wrongs of the *dêmos*' exercise of its central power, that of *krisis*, judgement. But likening recalcitrant judges—men seated directly before them—to bad *hetairai* as they exercise their powers of *krisis* is a more brutal use of metatheatrical confrontation than has generally been recognized. The appeal works with that postulated divided audience, the 'clever' and those who just like a good laugh, with which Aristophanes negotiated all throughout his career.[83] Elsewhere, however, he is very keen to distinguish his work as appealing only to the former and abjuring the tastes of the latter. Here, what are usually offered as the grounds for making the sharpest possible discriminations in the judgement of *kômôidia* are presented as indistinguishable alternatives which lead to the same conclusion, and can thus be viewed as a resignation of advanced critical powers entirely fitting to the outcome it will produce—the abandonment of the political. It virtually amounts to an order to suspend those critical faculties which Aristotle saw as defining the democratic citizen (*Pol.* 3.1275ᵃ22–3), as though, if they were to exercise their vote in favour of this comic vision, it may be the last time they do so. However, as with other instances of the closing metatheatrical critique of *nikê*, this is not to turn into a reaction against the Praxagorean vision, and hence the Aristophanic play. On the contrary, amid the laughter and the surface inclination towards

---

[83] Bremer (1993: 143).

embracing the victory's apparent charms, the political sensibilities of the audience will have been all the more sharpened by this critique of and through *nikê*.

5. BEYOND THE END

Those interested in reconstructing the dramaturgy of the classical comic theatre appear to have overlooked what must be one of the safest hypotheses regarding the dramatic and symbolic use of (final) exits from the comic stage: the likelihood that the triumphal, comastic comic exits of Blepyrus, Trygaeus, & co. made their way east, and down the parodos of the theatre of Dionysus that led uninterrupted into the Street of Tripods (*Tripodes*).[84] This street was not only the principal route of access into and from the theatre, but a street of choral *Nikê*—substantially lined, even by 415, with a forest of monuments celebrating victories won in the theatre of Dionysus. And *Tripodes* was also quite physically the link between the theatre and the political heart of Athens, joining the Prytaneion (whence the Archon sent the *pompê* of the Dionysia) directly to the theatre and sanctuary of Dionysus. An exit by the eastern parodos would thus place a comic troupe instantly in the company of victors—and it may well be that theatre audiences watched many a comic chorus make their *exodos* down that parodos and some way beyond the monuments that lined the south-western corner of the adjacent Odeion, until they disappeared out of view around the bend at the corner of that building. It would be entirely in keeping with what we know of Aristophanic practice not to respect any sharp boundary between 'theatrical space' (as defined by the limit of the eastern parodos) and the civic world beyond (the start of *Tripodes*).[85]

[84] The forthcoming work of Martin Revermann promises to offer an important corrective to this neglect. The topography of the region prior to the 'Lycurgan' rebuilding of the theatre is unclear, but *Tripodes* has remains of choregic monuments that date from the fifth century, so a parallel relationship between the eastern parodos and the street to that which existed in the better-known later fourth century is very likely: See Goette (2007) and Wilson (2000: 209–35).

[85] In 307/6 an extraordinary gate was built at the eastern entrance to the theatre by Xenocles of Sphettos, as *agônothetês*. This may have served to demarcate the

The dramaturgical potential of such an exit for the rampantly triumphal comic close is clear. And so it is surprising that, alongside the many monuments commemorating dithyrambic victories that we know lined *Tripodes* (and whose prize awarded by the city—the bronze tripod—was its most distinguishing feature), no single monument to comedic victory has been identified.[86] (Many of these tripod dedications, it might be noted, were erected on bases with elegant *Nikai* carved in relief on their sides).[87] This may be due to no more than the vagaries of survival, but it is worth asking whether there is something about comedic victory that made such final and permanent commemoration under *Nikê*'s care a less straightforward affair. We could point to the fact (also true of tragedy), that comedy was contested by individuals (poets, *chorêgoi*) and a group (chorus) who represented no subdivision of the Athenian polis, unlike the tribal affiliation of dithyramb. As a result, there may have been a certain ideological restraint upon the manner in which theatrical victory was memorialized, since such a victory—even in a purely 'cultural' contest—may have carried connotations of victory over one's own kind, or of renegade individualism.

A glance at such evidence for comedic victory dedication of any kind that we have is revealing: it suggests (a degree of) impermanence (the dedication of masks and other σκευή in the sanctuary) and, moreover, generic continuity—in the sense that comedy's own idiom infiltrates the final conceptualization of comedic *nikê*, without the full mediating and transforming effects of *Nikê* that we have seen elsewhere. Consider, in conclusion, our best piece of evidence for such memorialization in Attic, a fourth-century inscription from a monument erected in the deme of Anagyrous, a long way from the urban centre and *Tripodes*.[88]

---

boundary more clearly. See Goette (2007: 141), who points out that this is the first known example of a 'triumphal' arch in the Greek world.

[86] However, a number of substantial qualifications should be noted: not all of *Tripodes* has been excavated; some bases on the street have no identifying inscriptions or related design of any sort to identify the genre they commemorate; the same absence of dedication in this region applies to tragedy: full discussion in Wilson (2000: 236–44).

[87] Goette (2007); Froning (1971).

[88] *IG* II²3101; Wilson (2000: 246–8).

ἡδυγέλωτι χορῶι Διονύσια σύμ ποτε ἐν[ίκων],
μνημόσυνον δὲ θεῶι νίκης τόδε δῶρον [ἔθηκα],
δήμωι μὲν κόσμον, ζῆλον πατρὶ κισσοφο[ροῦντι]·
τοῦδε δὲ ἔτι πρότερος στεφανηφόρον ε[ἷλον ἀγῶνα].

I was once victorious at the Dionysia with a chorus of sweet laughter,
and I have set up this gift to the god as a memorial of the victory—
an adornment to the deme, and a spur to emulation for my
    father, crowned in ivy.
Even before him did I [take] the crown-bearing [contest].

Whether the victory that gave rise to this monument was won at the local deme Dionysia of Anagyrous, or represents an example of an urban victory won by a proud Anagyrasius who has chosen to 'export' its prestige back to his home deme by building a substantial monument there, this epinician epigram is intriguing for a number of reasons. In the first place, we might notice the prominent presence of *Nikê*'s less attractive brother, *Zêlos*, in the same emphatic place in his line as his sister is in hers above, after the caesura. It is especially striking too that there is not a whisper of a *poet* here, whom we might expect to merit a mention in the lasting record of the victory. This *chorêgos*, whoever he was, has managed to appropriate the victory to himself so efficiently as to sideline the *kômôidodidaskalos* altogether— no mean feat in itself. The monument—with its two bronze statues (of comic chorus members?) presents itself as a gift to the god and, quite explicitly, a 'reminder of the victory'.

And just how does it 'remind' us of comedic victory? It deploys the language and *topoi* of comedy to do so: the opening words ἡδυγέλωτι χορῶι are part of comic discourse's own language of self-description. As the passage of metatheatrical comic advice from the end of the *Women at the Assembly* (1156) which I discussed above shows, the stylization of comedy's function as to produce sweet laughter was an acknowledged part of comedy's own self-description, even if it was not Aristophanes' own preferred model.

What is more, the epigram implies a narrative for the victory that comes straight out of Old Comedy. Here we have a son winning a victory as comic *chorêgos* and that victory acts as a spur to his father to try to do the same. The inscription goes to some trouble to underline the sequence of events, precisely because they are not in accordance with the norm that sees sons emulating fathers. Instead we have a standard theme of comedy, best exploited for us in the *Wasps*—the inversion of the norms expected of the generations.

This however is a monument very far from the urban centre where the heat of agonistic struggles in the theatre was most intense. We are left wondering about the absence of such victory monuments there. Perhaps, ultimately, comedy and lovely *Nikê* were in fact an incompatible pair, their tasks inimical—hers, to aestheticize a widely permeated ideology of glamorous supremacy; comedy's, relentlessly to unpick such confidence at the seams.

12

Everything to do with Dionysus? (Medelhavsmuseet, Stockholm, inv. MM 1962:7/*ABV* 374 no. 197)

John Henderson

Dionysos est à la fois ici et ailleurs
(Frontisi-Ducroux 1991: 177)

Theatre reposes on crisis through duplicities of presence within representation; it's a cultural affair: 'here, this is? father?—here, this is vengeance/horror/humanity/another me', and so forth (the authenti-city principle of appellation). Dionysus presides over the ambience and tropology of Athenian Tragedy, so divinity and masquerade superimpose there insufferably.[1] In their diagrammatic 2-D medium, Attic pot painters had long explored graphic terms for conceiving mimetic baffle, proposing schematic operators of dramatic oscillation in-between sign and token, their stock-in-trade and staple commission to develop a powerful visual semiotics for Dionysiac mimesis. In devising a striking transcription for the irruption of 'How you see' in 'What you see', enterprising artists already, generations 'before Tragedy', probed the potential of their medium to find designs that would reach beyond the bounds of normalcy

---

[1] 'We are plunged into the heart of the tragic drama along with the lord of theater himself, the god Dionysos, who presides over those theatrical activities of role-playing, reenactment, doubling, repetition, and reversal, and who sets the stage for probing the mysteries of identity and designs of the self': Zeitlin (1996*a*: 315), as ever setting the stage for probing the mysteries and masteries of Hellenic culture and designs of Greek art. Cf. discussion in Friedrich (1996). For light shone by pots straight on *Bacchae*, see March (1989).

towards signifying experience under the influence of outside-in power to disturb the senses. Extemporizing on the proto-language of imagery developed within their craft,[2] a painter could so warp the semiotic field as to gesture towards an untenable co-presence of legible elements of mimesis at odds with marked features of distortion. This staging has plenty to do with evoking Dionysus, master signified of the Greek winejar. Put the city in/on his pot.[3]

Two one-offs. This essay plays off one of the most feted images on all Attic clay against an under-appreciated *coup de théâtre* in Greek ceramics. Between Paris and Stockholm. Together (and you will soon *see* their connection) these *jeux* back the claim that this genre of craftwork was out to ring the changes on schematized pieces of traditional scopic stock, so as to move beyond registration of formulaic labelling and off toward psychotropic optical equivocation— putting a trained eye out for catching the shock mutation of visual arrest. Beyond, not least, *words*. The best that Euripides can write for Dionysiac para-visuality—'two suns, a fourteen-gated Thebes—and you, a bull-god, horns on head'—scarcely begins to script the othering of the play into space available to this culture's graphic image repertoire (E. *Ba.* 918–21):[4]

> καὶ μὴν ὁρᾶν μοι δύο μὲν ἡλίους δοκῶ,
> δισσὰς δὲ Θήβας καὶ πόλισμ' ἑπτάστομον·
> καὶ ταῦρος ἡμῖν πρόσθεν ἡγεῖσθαι δοκεῖς
> καὶ σῷ κέρατα κρατὶ προσπεφυκέναι…

This essay suggests that vase-painterly special effects have attracted too little interest in apprehending the cultural discourse of Greek space—spatiality through fantasized visualization.[5] Both containers counterpose *obverse* schemata of regular semiosis with improvised *lusus* on *reverse*.

---

[2] Iteration structures graphic language: Ferrari (2002). Thus providing the platform for launching into the surreal.

[3] Frontisi-Ducroux (1991: 182).

[4] Seaford (1987), Scott (1975) on these motifs; Foley (1980: 123 n. 26): 'It is unclear precisely what Pentheus sees here—the stranger and his double with horns (Dodds), a stranger who is part man, part bull, or a bull whom he realizes is also the stranger'. Cf. Segal (1982: 229–32, 236), Gregory (1985) on the whole play of vision.

[5] Written differently, see the difference(s) (cf. Henderson 1994). Or the Amasis pot stays wrapped in its pack of descriptivist labelling, and the Stockholm jar is held to the margins (dulled as variant; binned as botchery).

1

The name-piece of the Amasis Painter is so treasured an icon, you must just feel its massive scholarship hold back from blurting what there is to see (Figs. 12.1 and 12.2).⁶ On the *obverse*, diplomatic negotiations are under way between the majestic divinities Athene and Poseidon. Perilously adjacent toes and threateningly invasive finger-pointing jut past her uncle's still securely grounded trident missile to annul its spatial function of demarcation line between this pair of heavily militarized zones. But these hulking superpowers make equal fists of it, massing equivalent might on either side of a stout second line of defence provided by the artist, in the form of the verbal cordon sanitaire of the lettering

ΑΜΑΣΙΣ ΜΕΠΟΙΗΣΕΝ

which, beneath the horizontal captions counterposing the showdown at eyeline:

[ATHENE] v. ΠΟΣΕΙΔΟΝ

bisects the field of this straight-up image. The stand-off holds. Just. For her part, unbiddable Athene stands her ground, her upheld palm playing 'paper' to her opponent's 'scissors'. She coolly absorbs the affront of that intrusive finger salient, for all that it already rouses her chain-mail shield of venomous sidewinders into red-alert offensive mode. In reserve, but poised at the ready for immediate strike without warning, that white-knuckled grip on the heavy artillery backs up her unbudging stance of flexible response to any conceivable compromise of her autonomous territory. Make no mistake, what she has she holds.⁷

---

⁶ Extensive bibliography and exemplary description in Von Bothmer (1985: 125–9, no. 23). Cf. Carpenter (1991: fig. 9). It must always be *wrong* to put these things into words. Verbal visualizing: *pecco uolens*.

⁷ On the band running around the shoulder of the vase, ant-like rows of duelling heavy-armed spearmen lock shields and shove. Dionysus' hemisphere laces together a necklace of five pairs in 'M'-shape patterns (in just one pair, behind the god, a warrior turns—feinting or turned?). On the 'Athens' panel, the pairs do not interlace, but stand proud; and they are one man light, for behind Poseidon, a man is floored for the kill, sandwiched in a murderous trio: advantage Athene—discreetly? (Von Bothmer 1985: 127).

Fig. 12.1 Black-figure neck amphora signed by Amasis as potter, showing Athene and Poseidon. Athenian, late sixth century BCE. Obverse *ABV* 64.28. Cabinet des Médailles (1863, Luynes Collection), Bibliothèque Nationale de France 222, Paris.

Fig. 12.2 Black-figure neck amphora signed by Amasis as potter, showing Dionysus with two maenads. Athenian, late sixth century BCE. Reverse *ABV* 64.28. Cabinet des Médailles (1863, Luynes Collection), Bibliothèque Nationale de France 222, Paris.

All Athenians knew these two deserve each other, for this wave-happy city needs at all costs to bear with the sea: mutual respect is the only diplomacy in town; and their heavily armed virago is a match for any pushy elder. No visual schema could present so united a front of well-oiled iconography, functioning smooth and solid as seal and counter-signature for the freight of wine herewith labelled 'Export of Athens'. For more on this organized promo campaign,[8] see the *reverse*, where divine power is presented more dramatically, as Come-to-Daddy Alcohol works his magic. Calm wizz Dionysus combines in one posture the reversed profile of Poseidon with identical fore-grounded hand signals half-inched from Athena, spear-heading the marketing campaign.[9] Thereby vacating a space to fill with out-of-body self-imagery.[10] Rapprochement, then—and—look, disturbance to the visual field.

Two maenads dance Dionysus' way, as one bringing him gifts of hare and staglet, summoned to (mirror him, and personify) his hypnotic *kantharos*.[11] Both waft ivy fronds; the nearer points our way the panther skin she wears for the pair of 'em. They are at one; but their bodily getting together, and redoubled sight-line, behind the proffered hare's returned eyeballing with Dionysus, s(up)port the killer pun which hexes the frontal panther-stare of immobilizing death into doubling up as the rear end of that trailer, the ~~double-headed~~ stag trophy.[12] Effortless, the god presences his overall controlling power (here *is* Dionysus) by finger-tip acceptance of the tribute and by toe-to-toe touching. Signalled by the central caption

[8] Aimed at Corinthian product, economy, ascendancy: an early government-backed advertising drive toward engulfing a global market (Henderson 1999).

[9] Her snakes pun with his beard, and with his handle. Everything to the right of the proffered hare 'for' that prodding index finger doubles up otherwheres excitation: just so, everything to the left doubles for the two stern antithetical powers squaring up diametrically opposite on the far side of the vase.

'Dionysus, kantharos, satyrs, vines in grape' brand the Attic amphora wine-vat, whether literally in the instance of the individual pot or in its type, and marketing talk makes an apter discourse than art for these containers, for all their designer nous (hence my insistence on the 'sticker' of ad-land, and other arch vulgarities in what follows—'wizz', 'half-inched', 'overdub', etc.).

[10] Piratized away in his primal *Homeric Hymn*, provoked Dionysus forever *throws* a visual self forward into the prow at the instant he turns to morph on the spot: bear *plus* lion.

[11] The *kantharos* as Dionysus' monopoly: Frontisi-Ducroux (1991: 86).

[12] Frontality as disorientation, e.g. Steiner (2001: 177).

ΑΜΑΣΙΣ

that links

ΔΙΟΝΥΣΟΣ

with his reduplicative creation(s) slotting into place beneath

ΜΕΠΟΙΗΣΕΝ.

The females realize the energy dissimulated in the god's serene pose of casual reception and graphically contained in the strength of that classic one-handed horizontal grip on his *ar*tillery piece, the two-handled *kantharos*. See, it takes a twosome to handle this strong stuff extended in promise of ecstasy. The One who doesn't have to try too hard *is* the stimulant held *here*, within this trademark flagon super-imposed on his full-bodied figure. No you cannot merely *see* it, only watch it happen. As his creatures enfold themselves at the neck and waist into a crazed monsterpiece of double-girdled wrap-around volume, they play as the prospective potency of the uncorked con-tents of our full-bodied neck amphora. The image takes the lid off the way it feels. Beside yourself, excitation awaits.[13] Welcome to Athens' secret army, as vital as any top brass. Getting on famously.

2

Pride of the collection of classical ceramics in the Swedish Museum of Mediterranean Antiquities is an excellently well-preserved Attic black-figure neck amphora, currently exhibited as the compelling centrepiece in a glass-case installation of Dionysiaca and classical vinosity. Preserved whole and in great nick, this late sixth-century vase turned up without provenance on the market at Rome, and was presented to the Museum by the King of Sweden in 1961.[14] Tullia

---

[13] Maenadic psych-out: Schlesier (1993).

[14] Technical imperfections include black paint smearing on one handle ornament and on the vine, plus a blob below the reins; and 'the black glaze has misfired and turned into red on the right-hand satyr, as well as on Hermes, and in a large area on and around the other handle': Rönne-Linders (1963: 58).

None of this need make the pot 'not the work of any of the great artists'. That 'Hermes conceals part of [the paintwork scroll]' and 'the palmette, on the other side

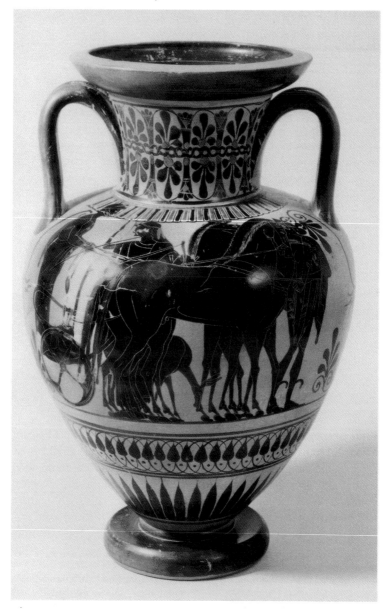

Fig. 12.3 Black-figure neck amphora of the Leagros Group. Late sixth century BCE. Obverse, showing a male mounting a chariot.

Rönne-Linders presented exemplary description and scholarly analysis in the *Museum Bulletin* for 1963. She recognized it as none other than *ABV* 374 no. 197, in time for Sir John Beazley to confirm the identification. Together with a cluster of its close relatives, a fine set of photographs of the vase are included: whence Figures 12.3–5.

This pot got me, on sight; it requires a double take.

One side (*obverse*) shows a male mounting a chariot; he is seen on board, and is to be given a background send-off by a saluting female figure positioned the far side of the yoked team of horses led by the nose by Hermes;[15] a deer by her side, and alongside theirs. The ultra-traditional scheme of harnessed muscle configured as maximum horsepower rings the changes on staple indicators of ascendancy: the charioteer's head (superior being) uniquely piercing the ceiling of the heavens through the tongue-patterned panel-frame tells us how the controlling mind bosses eye–hand coordination of (t)his promotional scenario. In this version, featuring (shall we say?) Apollo and Artemis, the set piece emblazons cooperative majesty so apportioned between twin divinities as to polarize but harmonize their gendered power roles. She doubles as both admiring audience, saluting her racing-driver's parade of sangfroid, and as formula for his preternatural match in terms of sheer speed. Manufactured velocity, *wheels!* The attribute of nonchalantly grazing deer foregrounds its cultural equivalent, the massively rippling team of four-deep steeds pacing ready for the thunderous charge across the field, the instant they are given their head by the fleet-footed squire as yet tending those restraining reins at the business end. This chariot of glory parades its potential, *wild!* One of many more all set to explode into aggression, it visibly pledges maximized impetus in hand. Express delivery, controlled... *vin extraordinaire!*[16] The *schema* conveys excitation, defers exclamation.

of the vase, makes allowances for the wheel of the chariot', while 'the upper right-hand palmette shows only the tip of a tendril, above the shoulder of the charioteer, as if the rest were hidden from him', all goes to show that these 'very competent and skilful craftsmen' knew to leave their trademark of self-promotionally sported mimetics on this latest *coup d'oeil*: for full revaluation, see Neer (2002: *passim*).

[15] A standard Hermes: see esp. Rönne-Linders (1963: 58, 61 and fig. 13).

[16] Designs ring the changes on these charioteers: Dionysus and Ariadne appear side-by-side on the same sportsmobile led by our Hermes on Panathenaic neck-amphora, Royal Toronto Museum of Archaeology 927.39.3 (*ABV* 373 no. 180): Rönne-Linders (1963: 58 and fig. 11).

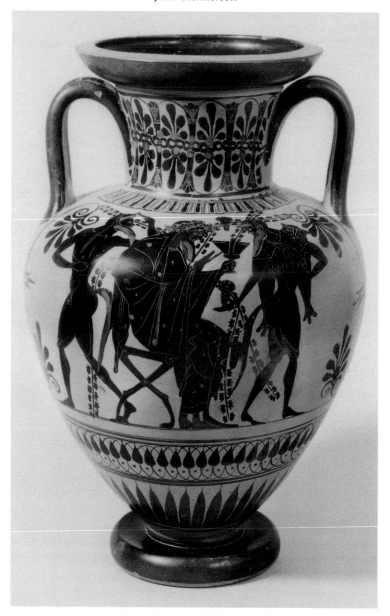

Fig. 12.4 Black-figure neck amphora of the Leagros Group. Late sixth century BCE. Reverse, showing Dionysos with a consort and satyrs.

Expect to sample putative rivalry, equipollence, even inter-convertibility between the two mutually obscured picture panels of such showpiece amphorae. Rotate the vase, and the *reverse* shows up (Fig. 12.4), at centre, Dionysus and consort (Ariadne, we shall say), sat easy side by side on folding chair, the god powerfully grasping his attribute, the *kantharos*, and concentrating the image's four intent eye-lines down upon this sticker guarantee of knock-out neat wine sealed within the real clay vat. Who could doubt it, when these waves of energy reticulate the picture plane, in the form of vine tendrils tracking the god's command of vine and wine-cup?

Round behind the royal couple poses one reassuringly formulaic prancing, gesticulating satyr, wheeling helically about the vine that issues, like him, from the arching ensemble of god and consort. Her crooked elbow is poised beneath the tarpaulin of her robe, where the rhyming nudity of satyr's flailing arm choreographs a rhythm that unpacks the dynamite stored here under wraps. His master's horse-goat-android-ape person-beast-thing[17] contorts at the waist, so that his head and snowy beard echo and reinforce Dionysus' visual and mental concentration; but his tail twists athletically so that he dances tail to fabric appendage dangling down back of the chair; and his emergence from behind the sedate hulk of godhead runs, down the vine-trail flight path, top-to-toe from his half-obscured elbow through said tail to ankle-high cross-over with the folding chair's own paw, aligned below the knee in parallel reduplication of the chair-legs' crosswise jointing. He is the wildness[18] summoned to android males by Dionysus—the physical embodiment of excitation. The dancing loosens limbs.[19] And this flexi-pirouette makes him the figural animation of the double curvature of the container surface, too, as his bare torso sites the visual twist of this expertly customized design: body rotation at the turn of the amphora shoulder, where the view from above must merge unstably into any side-on view, also holds him magnetically secured to his Dionysus fixation, against the centrifugal lateral pull of the vase surface toward vanishing point off at the handle. So this cliché satyr is a volumetric centring device. Basic background.[20]

---

[17] Satyr/ape: Lissarrague (1997).   [18] Esp. Lissarrague (1993).

[19] Greeks dance: Naerebout (1997), Lissarrague (1990: index s.v.).

[20] Similar satyrs: esp. Rönne-Linders (1963: 61).

But his rhyming opposite number, caught busy cavorting, to right, before the central couple, does more than close the ring for symmetry. Between them, the mirrored bodies of the satyr pair counterpose the plain contours of a coherent physique against surreal body-doubling. For as he dances out of his own profile, the Other is left behind in the Dionysiac wake. In the form of the panther skin that marks his otherness to self. The viewer is halted by those dead eyes that sit where someone's head *would* top their torso; while, in the scene, and in the instant, the satyr's wheeling superstructure stills— to stare down the vine from grape bunch through wine goblet, to the second grape bunch at waist level, then on to the third, knee-high, along the vertical that stakes out the adjacency of creature and divinity. Instead of a left arm raised in jiving salutation, this acolyte's left palm cups both beneath that poised *kantharos*, and *as if* beneath the grapes ripening on the vine. His braking stance draws feet closer as you inspect them.

And yet, those tendrils track a *one-two* storyline of crossing and forking. While we never do lose sight of the persistence of that unitary contortionist prancing in his spin, the addition of an extra pair of dangling panther 'arms' emphasizes the *impossible* transform- ation of this satyr's own right arm, matching the crooked elbow of his mate, into a *left* arm appropriated by the shadow self with panther head. All of which stresses the crucial centrality of his other, correctly lowered, left arm gesture that underscores the eternal miracle of soft fruit converted into the meed of exhilaration. And, of course, the work of representation travels both ways, as the dance freezes to catch that juice, but the story of wine itself materializes into the familiar shape of its capering genie from the bottle.[21] Inside this proffered goblet, brags this come-on label, is the arrest/release stuff presently

[21] Cf. Lissarrague (1990: 14) (on a red-figure cup by Epictetus): 'a satyr...is guzzling from a huge amphora. Here all the rules of decorous drinking are ignored: there is no mixture, no sharing with other guests; not even a drinking-cup, but pure wine taken straight from the amphora used to store it. These are the manners of a satyr, a reckless, untamed drinker, always lured by the aroma of wine'; (18) (on a black-figure amphora): 'A satyr dances...and turns back to the god....Dionysos holds a...kantharos. The image is focussed around this unusually shaped vase, typical of the god, which...visually draws the connection between the grape and the wine, without there being a depiction of the technical processes—harvesting, pressing, vinification—that make possible the passage from one state to the other'.

Fig. 12.5 Detail of Fig. 12.4.

tanked within the amphora we hold and behold. Finish the process: get decanting, you hoofing, purring, beast, and dance. At the double, dance to it.

Now this aberrant thaumaturgy unpacks the godhead immanent in the god's gift. So does the embodied centrepiece of the divine pair, visually fused into the single entity of a conjugality realized beyond sexual dissymmetry.[22] The two-as-one togetherness of myth's Dionysiac erotics. For this god uniquely took a mortal bride for his official wife, and without erotic violence.[23] And that's his bag, too, the chilled-out approach to power play: for Dionysus fuels, rather than fools with, mayhem. And understated dominance here takes the form of play on a primeval visual schema within 'the ideology of ways of sitting'.[24] When enthroned rulers renounce vertical assertiveness for Olympian nonchalance (generally on high), they have often elevated their household above the realm by lifting spouse above all other subjects to join them. In the process, no doubt they vindicate their masculine potency, but risk and court power-sharing with their female visual equivalent. Intimate gestures and attributes generally readjust the balance, but what you see in such tableaux still depends on how you see it. Where you, not they, are coming from.

In 3-D sculptural installations such as the colossal granite Egyptian Pharaohs, frontality was built into physical access routes for worship.[25] But when flat designs show statues receiving cult, all

---

[22] Dionysus and Ariadne share their folding chair again, as dancing satyrs and maenads wheel around them, on Panathenaic neck amphora, British Museum, London B 206 (*ABV* 369 no. 120): Rönne-Linders (1963: 58, 61 and fig. 13).

[23] Cf. Lyons (1997: 104–33, 'The heroine in Dionysiac context', esp. 124–8, 'Ariadne').

[24] Hodge and Kress (1988: 61–4). Cf. esp. (below) Cook (1940: 1048–50): '*Appendix R, The Hieròs Gámos*, (a) Zeus with Hera behind him; (b) Zeus with Hera beside him; (g) Zeus with Hera facing him'.

[25] Cf. esp. 'the two pyramids crowned by colossal seated statues of the Pharaoh Amenemhet III and his queen set in the centre of Lake Moeris in the Fayum' (Ling and Ling (2000: 19). When Pharaoh Horemheb, right hand holding sceptre across chest and left holding an amulet flat to his thigh, shares a throne with his queen Mutnodme (on left, same height, in black granite), her right arm coils around his waist, and his left hand lies flat on his thigh: Scamuzzi (1965: pl. 32). When 'A husband and wife' on a late-fourteenth-century tempera mural sit together, *she* sits the nearer, the same height as him, left arm around his waist, right hand resting on his right arm. His right hand rests on her lap, grasping a knot of linen robe, his left arm fully extended. But ... they are in 3/4 profile, so she does not block him out: Scamuzzi (1965: pl. L, from the Der-el-Medìna excavations [1905: cat. 1379, Drovetti Collection]).

Fig. 12.6 Marble hero relief from Chrysapha (Laconia). Mid sixth century BCE. Staatliche Museen, Berlin 731.

participants must be shown side-on. This will mean that a shared throne must not only risk effacing all marks of relative superiority, but also mask one partner behind the profile of the other. Greek examples (often with 'Egyptianizing' traits)[26] will generally superimpose Zeus upon Hera,[27] and man upon backgrounded wife,[28] thus cancelling her upgrading from appendage to quasi-equal, as in a mid-sixth-century sculpted 'hero relief' where the couple sits besides each other, punning tresses and knees-to-toes, but (bearded, eye-balling) male demands, and seizes, priority over (ear-ringed, in profile) female (Fig. 12.6).[29] Accordingly, marked *insistence* will inhere in any schema breaking this norm.[30]

One power-packed ceramic image transcribed from a black-figure hydria makes its point from just such transgression (Fig. 12.7).[31] Here, Athene's right fist grips her mighty spear aslant, extending a left palm in greeting to a pair of female offerers. All we can see of her father [ ] is his left hand clasping the bolt, and the full-bearded face aligned precisely to shadow his daughter's extravagantly slant-eyed profile. *This* design 'promotes Athene to the place of honour—a

[26] e.g. on a fragmentary hydria from Clazomenae, found at Athens (mid-fifth century National Museum 5610, Athens), a herald leads in a team of horses, approaching the enthroned couple to right. He is nearer, half-obscuring her rhyming pose of right hand raised in salutation and open left palm offered flat. A *sphinx* ornament sits between the chair legs: Charbonneaux, Martin, and Villard (1968: 93, fig. 102). Cf. fig. 12.6 (n. 29 below).

[27] On a red-figure amphora by the Nicephorus Painter, at Munich, Zeus sits nearer, clutching bolt (r.) and eagle-mounted staff (l.); empty-handed, Hera is poured a bowl by an angel: Cook (1940: 1048, fig. 841).

[28] As Robin Osborne reminded me, Bérard and Durand (1984: 18, fig. 21a) enter their *Cité des Images* with the scenario of twin cult statues sat in their shrine: he the nearer, both their right hands extending bowls as the worshippers approach, and left hands gripping staffs, on a crater in Museo Nazionale, Ferrara T 128 (*ARV*² 1052.25).

[29] From Chrysapha (Laconia): Charbonneaux, Martin, and Villard (1968: 149, fig. 183). Cf. Boardman (1978: fig. 253), 'The man holds a kantharos, the woman a pomegranate... The throne type, with lion legs, is *Egyptian*'. The couple of worshippers approaching the throne station male (with cock; no tresses) *before* female (with flower; and with tresses) in marked antithesis to the giant royalty (sat still as statues? statues come alive?).

[30] A mid-fifth-century votive relief from Locri shows (why?) an enthroned couple with her the nearer, holding a cock and ears of corn, while he clutches a shell and sprig of foliage. They match in size, with a cock between chair legs that end in pawed feet: Charbonneaux, Martin, and Villard (1969: 122, fig. 129): Museo Nazionale, Reggio di Calabria.

[31] From Vulci, at Berlin: Cook (1940: 1049, fig. 842).

Fig. 12.7   Transcription of image from black-figure hydria from Vulci, at Berlin: Cook (1940) 1049, fig. 842.

novelty pardonable on the part of an Athenian painter. With a spear that length she can hardly be Hera...'[32] A double spatial baffle marks the spot of spatial usurpation here: 1. Hermes' oblique sceptre and that javelin introduce recession into the field, so that Hermes is both this side of Athene's spear butt, but behind both his companion Dionysus and Athene's elbow and throne; 2. Zeus' left arm and draping sleeve is the far side of Athene's left hand and rhyming sleeve, but in front of her knees to toes. Moreover, her left thumb is in front of the spear which is before the bolt, and her fingers are in front of the bolt which is before the offerer's sleeve; yet the offerer's left arm sports a peculiar-looking *right* hand toward the goddess. At all events, all this cumulative disjunctivity powerfully compacts these paired superpowers into one melded compound of cosmic serenity. Athene's mimetic coup is to take over the throne—more than displacing Hera—by sitting tight with Zeus alongside. In her penumbra, because she's worth it.

Ariadne, by contrast, does not force Dionysus' field. He *lets* her take his light. Even before most of her (white-painted) face fell off, this semiotic overdub unit shared three feet, one vine-trailer facial, and, you have no other way to see it, the chance that, for once, *she gets to hold his kantharos*. None of which obscurantist visual by-play lessens in the least the unchallenged control of this entire theatre by the laid-back god who sloshes, liquid, within. Designers and customers, take heed, alike.

This vascular programme thus orchestrates movement as design creates visual illusion through the employment of clothing and posture, utilizing graphic principles of stark symmetry and slick volumetric deception.[33] The challenge of the wine-jar to test interarticulation

---

[32] Cook (1940: 1049).

[33] Black-figure pioneered miscegenate multi-corporeality through superpositioning that would luxuriate into extravaganzas such as the Satyr-fawn-Hermes on the name-piece red-figure amphora by the Berlin Painter (early fifth century *ARV*² 196.1. Staatliche Museen Berlin 2160). See Neer (2002: 68, fig. 30, with discussion at 69–70); cf. Kurz and Beazley (1983: fig. 5, with fig. 6), ecorché drawing of the satyr, showing how the triple arc described through the swing of wine-jar, plectrum, and tail to left blurs into the single outline of many-legged but twin-headed torso, while the hidden arm supporting the lyre (erection) allows its satyr shoulder to be precisely positioned so as to extend *into* the god's arm stretching the wand out to right aligned with the questing animal nose beneath. A vision not merely of complexity, but *with* it.

between obverse and reverse has taken the form of a syncrisis between chariot and chair, team and dancers, twins and partners, lateral depart-ure and centred stasis. Both these bold jar stickers harness insistent energy to representational tradition in fashioning their counterposed slogans of epiphany: celebrate right-on Apollo (wave), exacerbate the visual theatricality of Dionysus in-the-round (not a flicker). See obvi-ous power (on its way); watch power (power you can't see). Here is a shot at 'the what ∼ the how' basis of theatralization (see power hallucinate from the other side of vision).[34] The Greek cultural reper-toire, visualizing visualizing.

[34] See Corrigan (1988).

V

The History of Tragic Vision

13

Philostratus Visualizes the Tragic: Some Ecphrastic and Pictorial Receptions of Greek Tragedy in the Roman Era*

Jaś Elsner

The Elder Philostratus plays many games in the course of his series of ecphraseis of paintings purportedly on display in an elegant private gallery in early-third-century CE Naples.[1] Among these is a wickedly ironic engagement with pictures illustrating (well-known) Greek tragedies. Ecphrasis within tragedy (as well as within epic and the prose novel) generally has an interventive role, disrupting the larger narrative structure of the text, pausing or varying the pace, supplying a different kind of (descriptive) narrative.[2] As has frequently been suggested, this role—and especially when the ecphrasis is of a material object, most characteristically a work of art—offers a self-reflexive and metatextual reflection on the poem, play, or novel as a whole while ostensibly discussing the object within the text.[3] The poetics of the fashioning or reception of a described object thus has the potential to become a meditation on the larger literary poetics of

* My thanks are due to Chris Kraus for her very incisive comments, and to Froma Zeitlin for inspiration over the long term.

[1] On Philostratus, see e.g. Anderson (1986); Billault (2000) and the essays in Bowie and Elsner (forthcoming). I use (and often adapt) Fairbanks's Loeb translation (1931).

[2] Needless to say, in thinking about ecphrasis and Greek tragedy I am above all indebted to the work of Froma Zeitlin. See especially Zeitlin (1994; 1996a). Generally on interventive ecphrasis, with bibliography, see Elsner (2002: esp. 3–9).

[3] See e.g. Becker (1995: 4–5).

the authorship and reading of the text where the ecphrasis occurs. With his customary panache, Philostratus inverts this pattern in his *Imagines*. Instead of the ecphrasis being contained as a brief interlude in the play, Philostratus' picture (and the description it generates) comes to encompass the entire play, indeed to constitute its only reality within the world of the *Imagines*. Effectively, if the pre-Philostratean norms of ecphrasis have description as the hand and the containing text as the glove, Philostratus conducts a virtuoso act of invagination whereby the hand now turns out to contain the glove.

One might say that Philostratus' tragic ecphraseis move the address of ecphrasis as a literary trope from the epistemological sphere of a reflection on how art (usually literary art figured as visual art) works, to an ontological arena whereby the *Bacchae*, *Hippolytus*, or *Madness of Heracles* come to be dramatized solely as a visual *painted* experience. The diachronic flow of dramatic narrative is caught in the single synchronic frame of a panel picture, only for that to be 'translated' into the new descriptive movement of Philostratean literary ecphrasis. Philostratus' own performance of ecphrasis becomes a narrative encompassing a picture which itself has frozen in a single frame an earlier dramatic or mythological story. This is a brilliant and self-conscious move in many respects. It turns poetic drama into prose description; it simultaneously disrupts and reconstitutes narrative flow; it enables a novel form of the miniaturization and transformation of traditional themes in a way that highlights innovative sophistic display.[4] From the specific angle of visuality, this procedure emphasizes both the visualization of written drama *as* picture and the occlusion of the visual (the purported original painting) in competition with the Philostratean ecphrastic text. These problems are hardly irrelevant to tragedy—with its concerns about how to enact fully and convincingly its dramatic action, how to achieve naturalistic stage scenery most successfully and so forth. In Philostratus, these issues receive what might be called a playful and highly literary critical commentary.

---

[4] It is worth noting that Philostratus is quite explicit in his allusions to the Callimachean aesthetics of weaving and *leptotês* in 2.28. See esp. McCombie (2002: esp. 148–50).

As always in the *Imagines*, the discursive scope of Philostratus' attention is directed at least in two ways at once. First, he is concerned with a textual recension in which his own descriptions allude to, syncopate, and quote much larger and canonical literary masterpieces. Second, he is conducting a competition (a *paragone*) with the purported painting, the ur-image, by which his description is ostensibly inspired.[5] In both cases we are offered complex and sophisticated acts of translation: the ancient verse forms of tragic drama are made accessible as modern prose; the visual content of a panel picture is made verbal as description. Both these moves might be characterized as the transmutation of earlier genres (tragedy, poetry, painting) into something new—the hypervisual literary performance of display ecphrasis,[6] which for the first time in antiquity comes to constitute a self-standing text (or set of texts) valid in its own right. In both cases, as in other instances in the *Imagines*, there is a significant self-awareness about the partial nature of the Philostratean 'take'—the fact that (for all their performative authority) Philostratus' ecphraseis are effectively the articulation of a particular view. This resonates with the attempt to transform ecphrasis itself from a discrete and relatively brief metareflection on a text's poetics within that text (both a privileged view in being the author's own production and a kind of overview) to a summary of an acknowledged masterpiece in another genre, itself refracted through the fiction of a non-literary intermediary (namely, a painting).

The range of Philostratus' pictorial interventions in tragedy is wide and varied, as one might expect. A specific, and of course ironic, strategy is the persistent choice to make a picture from the tragic climax of a play that happens—in the dynamics of Greek tragedy— not to be performed on stage but recited to the audience *via* a

---

[5] The literature on the *paragone*, the contest of art and literature, is rich and governs some of the principal discussions of ecphrasis outside antiquity. However, the agonistic mode is by no means the only one characteristic of ancient ecphrasis: see the excellent discussion of Becker (2003) with extensive bibliography.

[6] It is not clear whether the Elder Philostratus' ecphraseis are written for oral performance—as he presents his sophist offering them to an audience of young men in a gallery (1. Proem 4–5)—or only as written evocations of such an event. The Younger Philostratus does seem to have composed his ecphraseis only to be read, and asks his reader to assume the presence of 'a person to whom the details are to be described' (Proem 7).

messenger speech.[7] Philostratean ecphrasis thus genuflects (especially) to Euripidean ecphrasis (in so far as Euripides' messenger speeches bring to mind descriptively events, including objects, not seen directly on stage), while simultaneously surpassing Euripides' failure to enact the deaths of Pentheus, Hippolytus, or the children of Heracles by offering a painting that fills the absence.[8] At the same time—by the same stroke one might say—Philostratus surpasses the purported picture he describes since what he offers is not a picture but an ecphrasis, displaying significant *literary* rather than painterly skills. An alternative strategy, as we shall see, is to create a new picture, a kind of composite tragedy, out of the plays of several playwrights, as in 'Cassandra' 2.10—where the comparison of pictorial and dramatic modes of representation is most explicit.

It might be argued that I have been outrageously textual in my general reflections on the Philostratean *tragica*: after all, his descriptions purport to relate to real paintings and there can be no doubt (at least to my mind) that Philostratus' text as a whole takes genuine account of contemporary pictorial culture. However, it is interesting that the tragic climaxes seized upon by Philostatus are relatively rare in Graeco-Roman art in general and particularly so in the period in which Philostratus was writing (so far as we can tell from the surviving material). With the exception of the death of Pentheus, where it does seem that Philostratus takes account of available iconographic traditions, the other tragic ecphraseis (the death of Hippolytus, the madness of Heracles, the murder of Cassandra and Agamemnon) appear to be far more deeply engaged in a play with literary than with pictorial culture (unlike, say, the image of Seasons at 2.34, which I would claim does play upon certain patterns of visual imagery).[9] In a sense this is not surprising. The *Imagines* is a text with a double enterprise: it both addresses the literary heritage of Greek *paideia* that was central to the Second Sophistic, rendering it as a

---

[7] On messenger speeches and the verbal evocation of the visual, see Heath (1987*b*) and de Jong (1991: 8–12 and 183–4).

[8] So 'Bacchae' 1.18 draws especially on the messenger speech at E. *Ba.* 1043–52; 'Hippolytus' 2.4 draws especially on the messenger speech at E. *Hipp.* 1173–1254; the 'Madness of Heracles' 2.23 draws especially on the messenger speech at E. *HF* 922–1015.

[9] See Elsner (2000: esp. 266–76).

series of described pictures, and it confronts the ancient problem of mimesis using the motif of naturalistic representation in painting. Partly, the interest in naturalism as mimesis relates to specific issues in both ancient aesthetics and philosophical discussion since Plato, but partly it is a self-reflexive means of examining Philostratus' own strategy of the textual imitation of pictures through ecphrasis. The tragic pictures, within the economy of the *Imagines* as a whole, represent (along with the ecphraseis that explore the epic tradition and especially Homer)[10] the apogee of Philostratus' literary theme.

Let us put some more precise flesh on these general reflections by turning to some of Philostratus' descriptions of pictures from tragedy. 'Bacchae' (1.18) opens in classic Philostratean style with γέγραπται—the wonderful word (with which Philostratus ends his entire enterprise of the *Imagines* at 2.34.3) meaning both 'here are painted' and 'here are written'. Given that he is purportedly describing a picture, both these meanings are apposite. The topic painted or written is Βακχῶν χοροί, 'choruses of Bacchae'—a specific reference to Euripides' play whose chorus indeed comprised Bacchantes. The first sentences drop a parade of references and quotations from the play, using Euripidean language and word choice as the building blocks of Philostratean ecphrastic construction.[11] The pigments of Philostratus' verbal picture reflect a *sparagmos* of Euripides' text and its reconsititution as ecphrasis—just as the women tear Pentheus to pieces at 1.18.1 (cf. E. *Ba.* 1114–52) and as Pentheus' relatives try to fit the bits back together again before burying the corpse at 1.18.2 (cf. E. *Ba.* 1299–300). Where Euripides takes the bulk of his play to build up to the climactic scene of Pentheus' death, Philostratus opens

---

[10] e.g. 1.1 (Scamander), 1.7 (Memnon), 1.27 (Amphiaraus), 2.7 (Antilochus), 2.13 (the death of Ajax son of Oileus).

[11] So: πέτραι: cf. E. *Ba.* 38, 306, 704, 982, 1097, 1138; νέκταρ: cf. E. *Ba.* 143; γάλακτι: cf. E. *Ba.* 142, 700, 710; βοτρύων: cf. E. *Ba.* 12, 261, 279, 382, 534; ὄεις: cf. E. *Ba.* 698, 1331; θύρσου: cf. E. *Ba.* 25, 80, 176, 188, 240, 254, 495, 554, 557, 704, 711, 724, 733, 799, 835, 941, 1054, 1099, 1141; μέλι: cf. E. *Ba.* 711; στάζοντα: cf. E. *Ba.* 1163 (ironically used by Philostratus since here it means 'dripping with honey' while Euripides uses it for 'dripping with blood'); ἐλάτη: cf. E. *Ba.*: 684, 1062, 1064, 1095. One could continue but this demonstration is sufficient to show the fine and persistent detail of Philostratus' use of Euripides, although it could be argued that a number of these terms are to be expected in a Bacchic context. For further correspondences see the commentary of Schönberger and Kalinka (1968: 335–8).

with it. Euripides enacts his ghastly climax not directly on stage but by means of a lengthy messenger speech (*Ba.* 1043–52)[12]—itself an extended ecphrasis (though not of a work of art) that renders visual and vivid in the audience's minds' eye the death of Pentheus purely through description and not performance.[13] Philostratus' picture, however, surpasses its source in portraying the death visually (as a purported painting), thus allowing the description to glory in vivid evocation—not least a riot of present tenses and sensual suggestions.[14] This ecphrastic vividness is of course a wicked game with the fact that Euripides' play (in principle more vivid than any description of its action, and as a ritual dramatic process more immediate than any pictorial version)[15] has itself to resort to ecphrasis to perform its dramatic crisis.

At 1.18.2, using the excuse of the picture's foreground (τὰ δὲ ἐγγύς), Philostratus changes scene in a way that threatens to play havoc with the presumed synchronic unity of his original supposed picture. Whereas Euripides moves swiftly beyond the death of Pentheus to the fates of Cadmus and Agave and to Dionysus' judgment (sadly incomplete in our surviving text), Philostratus dwells on the pathos of Pentheus' corpse (1.18.2):

There lies the head of Pentheus, no longer a dubious thing, but such as to excite the pity even of Dionysus—very youthful, with delicate chin and locks of reddish hue, not wreathed with ivy or bryony or sprays of vine, nor are they tossed in wild disorder by flute or Bacchic frenzy. From those locks he derived his vigour, and he imparted vigour to them.

The pity of post-mortem trauma is here highlighted by the eroticized description of the dead youth—a favourite Philostratean

---

[12] On this speech see de Jong (1991: 10 n. 21 and 36–7).

[13] On Euripides' concern in *Bacchae* with issues of vision and illusion, see e.g. Goldhill (1986: 277–84).

[14] For the senses: wine, nectar, grapes, milk, and honey all suggest taste and perhaps also smell; the rending, tearing, and dragging of Pentheus evokes touch; the Bacchic shout of victory and the Bacchantes' saying that they hear a lion's roar suggests sound; Dionysus watches. All this at 1.18.1. Further on the senses in Philostratus, see Mathieu-Castellani (1996: esp. 94–5); Manieri (1999); Leach (2000: esp. 248–50).

[15] On issues of ritual in relation to *Bacchae* see Seaford (1994: 254–5, 288–91, 318–19, 402–5).

trope.[16] The movement from climactic event to pity at its effects extends at 1.18.3 beyond Pentheus to the Bacchae, now collapsed and self-aware, and to Agave eager to embrace the son she slew but stained on hands, cheeks, and her naked breast by his blood. All this might conceivably have been extrapolated from the play, but the ending of the ecphrasis, with Harmonia and Cadmus as snakes from the thighs down breaks with the literary source by fulfilling in the dramatic (or pictorial) present of the here and now what in Euripides is Dionysus' prophecy at *Ba.* 1330–9. Again, the ecphrasis fulfils in painted actuality what Euripides could only report as dramatic speech rather than show as performative action. But, like the very first ecphrasis in the *Imagines*—of the battle between Hephaestus and Scamander, which follows *Iliad* 21.342–76 but specifically marks where it differs from the ur-text at the end ('In this Homer is no longer followed', 1.1.2)—Philostratus' 'Bacchae' signals its pictorial difference from Euripides at its conclusion.[17] Here the problem of literary dependence (the anxiety of influence, one might say) is diffracted as painterly transmutation (the shift from Euripides' textual medium to the painting's visual medium). This shift indeed appears to give painting the edge in its *paragone* with literature: it can after all portray so much more than Euripides can only describe. At the same time the panel's integrity as a painted surface is put under some stress (or one might say is wickedly exploited in Philostratus' overweening textual dispensation) as the ecphrasis moves to yet a fourth episode (that is, Cadmus and Harmonia in addition to the exhausted Bacchantes, the relatives fitting together the pieces of the corpse and the scene of tearing Pentheus apart) which must be imagined as accommodated in the pictorial space.[18] Where Euripides' play can narrate its drama only sequentially, Philostratus is able to represent sequence and simultaneity. He might be said here to be commenting on drama's invitation to its audience to respond

[16] Cf. Menoeceus: 1.4.3–4; Memnon: 1.7.2; Hyacinthus: 1.24.3; Hippolytus: 2.4.3–4; Arrichion: 2.6.5; Antilochus: 2.7.5; Abderus: 2.25.1.

[17] On *Im.* 1.1, see Cämmerer (1967: 73–4); Blanchard (1980: esp. 130–5); Conan (1987: esp. 165–7); Bartsch (1989); Elsner (1995: 30–1; 2000: 258–9).

[18] Generally here one has to disagree with Blanchard (1980: 132) who claims that Philostratus' *Imagines* are 'totally descriptive and nonnarrative…they never contribute to the development of a story in progress'.

and interpret: in the case of his ecphrasis, Philostratus appears to be putting pressure on his reader/viewer to act as interpreter of the picture, sorting out and introducing temporal sequence.

Part of the explanation for the narrative excess in filling the pictorial frame in 'Bacchae' may be put down to a deliberate decision to conflate more than one iconographic theme for the Pentheus myth, current in Graeco-Roman art of the imperial period. The pictorial tradition offers significant examples of the scene where Pentheus is torn to pieces—most famously in the fresco from *triclinium* n of the Casa dei Vettii in Pompeii, painted in about 70 CE (vi.15.1: Fig. 13.1).[19] Here, occupying the central pictorial space of the room's east wall, with images of the baby Heracles strangling snakes and the death of Dirce in the same position on the north and south walls, a nude kneeling Pentheus is represented being attacked by the maenads. Later versions of this iconography survive in sculptural relief on urns and sarcophagi—for instance on the marble urn now in Boston from about 200 CE (roughly when Philostratus was writing) whose kneeling Pentheus between bacchantes is strikingly parallel iconographically to the Vettii fresco over a hundred years earlier (Fig. 13.2).[20] Philostratus borrows this theme for the opening of his ecphrasis, although all the pictorial examples keep Pentheus whole (effectively rendering the moment just before the *sparagmos*) while Philostratus makes much of the dismemberment at 1.18.1 in order to generate the pieces that can be fitted together again at 1.18.2. His Dionysus watching the scene might even be said to emulate a possible model like the Dionysus on the left of the Boston urn in Fig. 13.2. But at 1.18.3, as he turns to Agave wanting to embrace her son, Philostratus appears to be evoking for his readers a different iconographic theme of the Roman period, where Agave appears with the head of Pentheus.[21] Although it is attested in a lost Pompeian wall painting,[22] this subject survives now mainly in gems and reliefs

[19] See Sampaolo (1994: esp. 529–30, with a bibliography at 470). For this iconographic tradition, see Bazant and Berger-Doer (1994: 310–11).

[20] See Comstock and Vermeule (1976: 151–2, no. 243); Sinn (1987: 259, no. 691). Interestingly this iconography of the kneeling Pentheus between Bacchants looks back to Apulian painted pottery—e.g. Trendall and Cambitoglou (1982: i. 180, no. 111 and 198, no. 52); see Bazant and Berger-Doer (1994: 308–9, nos. 6, 7, 12).

[21] See Bazant and Berger-Doer (1994: 312–13).

[22] See Mau (1890: esp. 250–1).

Fig. 13.1 The death of Pentheus, wall painting from the House of the Vettii, Pompeii (vi.15.1, triclinium n). About 70 CE.

(e.g. Fig. 13.3). Typically these images represent a maenad in ecstasy carrying a severed head—emphasizing both Agave's bacchic rapture in which Pentheus is killed (described by Philostratus at 1.18.1) and the loneliness of Agave when self-knowledge comes (implied by Philostratus at 1.18.3, and effectively contrasted by him with the image of the loneliness of Pentheus in death at 1.18.2). None of the surviving images offers as complex a mix of subjects as Philostratus' purported picture, but the specific focalizations of the pictorial

Fig. 13.2 The death of Pentheus, carved relief front of the marble funerary urn of Cassius, now in the Museum of Fine Arts, Boston (Benjamin and Lucy Rowland Fund). About 200 CE.

tradition do provide a visual frame that informs Philostratus' radical simplification of the unfolding of drama and his emphasis on key features essential to the narrative, whether conceived as literary or pictorial.

By contrast with the intimacy with which Philostratus' 'Bacchae' hugs the verbal patterns of Euripides' play, his 'Hippolytus' (2.4) is

Fig. 13.3 Agave with the head of Pentheus, bas-relief from a marble candelabrum base now in the Museo Archeologico, Venice. Perhaps first quarter of the second century CE.

much more oblique. The key terms of the narrative—Theseus' curse, the bull from the sea, Hippolytus' chariot and horses—these are of course repeated from Euripides, but with specific variations. The bull—an ἄγριον τέρας, 'savage marvel', in the play (lines 1214, 1247)—is a θηρίον, 'wild beast', at the opening of the ecphrasis (2.4.1, cf. 2.4.2); the bull is white (λευκοῶ, 2.4.1) in Philostratus, but the colour is never specified in Euripides; its emergence from the sea is compared with (perhaps in the imagined picture even accompanied by) dolphins (κατὰ τοὺς δελφῖνας, 2.4.1) again adding a detail conspicuously absent from the play (but typical of Graeco-

Roman marine scenes).²³ This opening to the description, followed by a very bald summary of the play's plot in a sentence (2.4.1), signals a series of significant gaps between picture and play, the Philostratean ecphrastic dispensation and the Euripidean. In Euripides, the messenger was one of Hippolytus' entourage—not an observer or even an 'attendant lord' but rather a full participant in the nightmare chase of chariot and bull.²⁴ He insistently uses the first person plural,²⁵ reliving a personal tragedy as he speaks and by integrating the audience imaginatively into its action through the 'we' he shares with them, he moves them emotionally. Philostratus, by contrast, employs the second person singular—addressing the boy (to whom he claims to deliver all his descriptions at 1. Proem 5) at the opening of the second paragraph: 'The horses, as you see...' (2.4.2).

Instead of the immediacy of personal tragedy and the anguish of memory whose passion intrudes beyond the messenger's listeners within the play (Theseus and the Chorus) to move the audience watching the play, Philostratus offers a distancing, a looking into and at a pictorial space of horses all in a muddle (2.4.2):

The horses, as you see, scorning the yoke toss their manes unchecked, not stamping their feet like well-bred and intelligent creatures, but overcome with panic and terror, and spattering the plain with foam, one while fleeing has turned its head toward the beast, another has leaped up at it, another looks at it askance, while the onrush of the fourth carries him into the sea as though he had forgotten both himself and dry land; and with erect nostrils they neigh shrilly, unless you fail to hear the painting (εἰ μὴ παρακούεις τῆς γραφῆς).

While a panic of the horses (δεινὸς ... φόβος, E. *Hipp*. 1218) is clearly essential to the Euripidean narrative, here all the tragic and personal distress of heroic death appears displaced onto an aesthetics of horses failing to show their good breeding. The repetition of the second person ('unless you fail to hear the painting') seems to underscore

---

²³ For further parallels see Schönberger and Kalinka (1968: 386).

²⁴ On this speech in Euripides, see de Jong (1991: 106, 127, 146–7, 152).

²⁵ ἐκτενίζομεν ('we combed the horses' coats', E. *Hipp*. 1174); εἰπόμεσθα ('we accompanied our master', E. *Hipp*. 1196); εἰσεβάλλομεν ('we struck deserted country', E. *Hipp*. 1198); εἴδομεν ('we saw', E. *Hipp*. 1206); ἐλειπόμεσθα ('we were left behind', E. *Hipp*. 1244).

the problem that the picture or its viewers or its describer appear to miss the point altogether: how absurd, how mannered to play with the decorum of horses and the oddities of 'hearing a picture' when its poetic substance and content (at least in the Euripidean ur-text) are so heart-rending.

In the third paragraph, Philostratus continues his use of the second person singular: 'And you, O youth...' (*Σὺ δὲ μειράκιον*, 2.4.3). But he shifts addressee from the boy to Hippolytus himself, from the (fictional?) child outside the picture to the mythological youth within it. The movement from third person definition of the painted subject (2.4.1) via the aesthetics of chaos specifically described to the boy (2.4.2) becomes an immersion in the picture (2.4.3):

And you, O youth, that loved chastity, you have suffered injustice at the hands of your stepmother and worse injustice at the hands of your father, so that the painting itself (*καὶ ἡ γραφή*—perhaps also meaning 'this text') mourns for you, having composed a sort of poetic lament in your honour.

Instead of tragedy—the agonies of Hippolytus and Theseus with which Euripides' play ends—Philostratus offers an eroticized elegy in which speaker, viewer, and picture unite in a poetic lament addressed directly to the picture's subject. The painted mountains take the form of mourning women in tears, the meadows the form of beautiful youths (*μειρακίων*, like Hippolytus himself, 2.4.3). In a kind of paroxysm of homoerotic wish-fulfilment fantasy and iden-tification, Philostratus climaxes with the image of Hippolytus—his limbs crushed and in pieces but his breast still breathing—looking at his own wounds, and comments (shifting finally back to the third person, 2.4.4.):

Ah, his beauty (*φεῦ τῆς ὥρας*)! How proof it is against wounds no one would have dreamed. Not even now does it quit the boy, but a charm lingers even on the wounds.[26]

In the 'Hippolytus', the shift in media from tragedy to painting is simultaneously a radical change in emotive register and a significant

---

[26] Note my translation here is some distance from Fairbanks's Loeb, which mis-takenly misprints 'body' for 'boy' (*μειράκιον*) and keeps the second person from the previous sentence. But the shift to 'objectivity' is normal in the final sentence or two at the end of descriptions in the *Imagines*—e.g. 1.1.2, 1.2.5, 1.4.4, and so on.

shift in subject matter. The narrative may remain broadly the same, but Philostratus has no interest in Theseus or Phaedra,[27] or indeed in the Euripidean tragic movement of Hippolytus from the scorner of Aphrodite to the hearer of Artemis' cool judgement at the end.[28] His focus is entirely on Hippolytus as an exquisite pastoral tragedy of youth unjustly cut off, and as an erotic tableau—the oxymoron of beauty lingering on wrecked and defiled limbs.[29] Implicit here is a meditation on different kinds of audience response with Philostratus specifically staging a play of identification. In part this is a proposal about the reception of pictorial as opposed to performative and dramatic art. In part it emphasizes a Second Sophistic homoeroticism as relationship of viewer and viewed frequent in Philostratus' work—not only in the *Imagines* but also in the *Letters*.[30] Most disturbingly the shift from 'you' meaning the boy outside the picture to 'you' meaning the broken boy painted on the (virtual) canvas elides the boundaries of 'real' and 'pictorial' space in ways emulated elsewhere in the *Imagines*.[31] Here that movement is what allows the viewer to enter the world of a two-dimensional picture whose temporality and narrativity must be constructed in the imagination, by contrast with the performative movement of drama where the audience lives through the unfolding of a sequence of events. In his 'Hippolytus', Philostratus not only narrates a process from the general story via the chaos of the horses to the focus on mourning for the dying youth, but he focalizes this by means of shifting the persons of his address and the figures addressed. The result is that he emulates the way tragedy can move its viewers by taking us inside a picture whose very landscape responds with what would later be called 'pathetic fallacy' to the emotive demands his interpretation has made. But the price (if that be a fair term here) is that the effect is high camp melodrama in place of catharsis.

In so far as Hippolytus is a μειράκιον, he echoes Narcissus (at 1.23.2) and the boy who is object of erotic pursuit by the hunters

[27] See Blanchard (1986: esp. 146).

[28] On this in Euripides see Zeitlin (1996*a*: 219–84).

[29] Froma Zeitlin has suggested that sexualization in *sparagmos* is already present in the Euripidean ur-text: Zeitlin (1996*a*: 249).

[30] On the letters, see now Rosenmeyer (2001: 322–38) and Goldhill (forthcoming *a*).

[31] See Elsner (1995: 33–7).

(in 1.28.1 and 8). This term is not used of the boy to whom Philostratus addresses his descriptions (a παῖς, 1 Proem 5), but it is specifically employed for the other youths who urge Philostratus to speak and who come to hear his addresses (1 Proem 4 and 5). If the erotics of Philostratus' relations with the μειράκιον in the picture are in any sense to be extended to the μειράκια outside the picture in Philostratus' narrative frame (for whose benefit the *Imagines* have been delivered), then the pedagogic enterprise of this text stands at risk of proving pederastic.[32]

While paintings of the death of Hippolytus are attested in the literary tradition (e.g. Plin. *HN* 35.114, Prudent. *C. Symm.* 54–6), none survive from antiquity save on Apulian vases.[33] All that remains from the Roman imperial period are a few sarcophagus ends and one back, showing the horses in disarray, the chariot wheels (both favoured Philostratean motifs for this theme at 2.4.2), the fallen hero, and the bull from the sea (Fig. 13.4). These are frankly the least important and most sketchily carved sections of Roman sarcophagi, and it is telling that the death of Hippolytus never appears on a sarcophagus front, despite the general popularity of Hippolytus subjects (not only on sarcophagi but also in mosaic and painting).[34] What the visual tradition offers is a formal frame within which Philostratus' ecphrastic imagination can take off, using the Euripidean narrative as a counterpoint. While one might see Philostratus' attempts at erotic identification as bathetic by contrast with the cathartic intensity of Euripides' drama, they make much more sense as critical engagements with the given pictorial frame of a discrete scene like the sarcophagus end from Agrigento. Interestingly, given the popularity of Hippolytus as a subject in Roman art, Philostratus chooses a subject relatively rare in the pictorial repertoire, but of course ideal for his literary reprise of Euripides.

---

[32] So, at greater length and in relation to other examples, see Elsner (2004).

[33] See Linant de Bellefonds (1994: esp. 457–9). On the Apulian vases, see Oakley (1991).

[34] Generally see Linant de Bellefonds (1994). For sarcophagi, see Koch and Sichtermann, (1982: 150–3, 393–8); Lewerentz (1995); Rogge (1995: 73–92, 112–18); Zanker (1999).

Fig. 13.4 The death of Hippolytus, carved relief from the left end of a marble sarcophagus, now in San Nicola, Agrigento. Perhaps second quarter of the third century CE.

In the 'Madness of Heracles', the third of Philostratus' explicitly Euripidean messenger-speech pictures, and the one where Euripides' original play is openly referred to (2.23.1), the ecphrasis ends by specifically distancing his picture from its ur-text (2.23.4)[35]:

---

[35] For textual parallels between Eurpides and Philostratus, see Schönberger and Kalinka (1968: 451–2).

To this point the painting goes, but poets go on to add humiliating details, and they even tell of the binding of Heracles, and that though they say that Prometheus was freed from bonds by him.

The binding of Heracles, after his murderous burst of madness in which he killed his wife and children, is told by the messenger at the end of his speech in the play (E. *HF* 1009–11) and repeated by the chorus, Amphytrion, and Heracles himself (1035–8, 1055, 1094–7, 1123–4).[36] Apparently, this ending of the ecphrasis is an articulation of what painting can do by contrast with poetic drama. Here, instead of going beyond the Euripidean original (as he does in different ways in both his 'Bacchae' and his 'Hippolytus'), Philostratus affirms the limits of painting, justified as decency—a careful avoidance of the unseemly indignities (προσπαροινοῦσι) heaped on by Euripides. The turn to an emphasis on painting *as painting*, on painterliness as such, is marked early in the description: 'as for you (addressing the boy outside the picture again), it is high time for you to occupy yourself with the painting' (2.23.2), and is motivated by the subject of the picture—that is, the *deceptions* of madness as represented in the pictorial regime of (deceptive) naturalism.

Twice Philostratus goes out of his way to emphasize Heracles' madness as a 'deceptive thing':

...for madness is a deceptive thing (ἀπατηλὸν γάρ τι ἡ μανία) and prone to draw one away from things that are to things that are not (δεινὸν ἐκ τῶν πάροντων ἀγαγεῖν εἰς τὰ μὴ παρόντα). (2.23.1)

He (Heracles) however has no consciousness of what he is doing (τῷ δὲ αἴσθησις μὲν αὐτῶν οὐδεμία)...letting the thought behind his glance stray away to fancies that deceive him (τὴν δὲ τοῦ βλέμματος ἔννοιαν ἀπάγων εἰς ἃ ἐξηπάτηται). (2.23.3)

Heracles' gaze betrays him—although at Thebes, his eyes (or, rather, his fancies) tell him he is in Argos (Ἄργος βλέπων, 2.23.1) and although his eyes are fixed on his actions (τοῖς ὀφθαλμοῖς ἀτενίζων εἰς αὐτά, 2.23.3), the mental command behind his glance leads away to deception (τοῦ βλέμματος ἔννοιαν ἀπάγων εἰς ἃ ἐξηπάτηται). The act of viewing and being deceived is itself a central figure of several other pictures in the *Imagines*. Narcissus (1.23) turns on the gaze of

---

[36] On the messenger speech in E. *HF* see de Jong (1991: 128–9, 162, 165–71).

the youth into the pool—deceived (ἐξηπάτησεν, 1.23.3) not by a painting in pigments and wax but by nature itself in the form of water and by his own desire or longing (ἵμερον) for his own beauty.[37] That deceived gaze is parallel to the deception of a real bee by the painted flowers in the picture or of us, its viewers, in thinking that a painted bee is real (1.23.2):

The painting has such regard for realism (ἀλήθειαν) that it even shows drops of dew dripping from the flowers and a bee settling on the flowers—whether a real bee has been deceived (ἐξαπατηθεῖσα) by the painted flowers or whether we are to be deceived (ἐξαπατῆσθαι χρή) into thinking that a painted bee is real, I do not know.

The figure of the boy and the pool becomes inextricable from the deceptions of naturalistic art, its uncanny concern with the real (ἀλήθεια, technically meaning 'truth') and its deceptive need to persuade us that what is realistically painted *is* true.[38] The problem of looking at naturalistic art and being deceived is specifically drama-tized in the conjunction of 1.27 and 1.28. *Imagines* 1.27—a descrip-tion of the death of the oracular prophet Amphiaraus—ends with the image of Truth (Ἀλήθεια) dressed in white standing by the gate of dreams where those who consult the oracle must come and where true dreams emerge (1.27.3). This emphasis on truth (twice repeated in one paragraph), bolstered by its divine associations with oracular revelation, gives way in 1.28.1 to a description of hunters chasing a boar who turn out (in Philostratus' dominant authorial view—ἐγὼ μέντοι οἶμαι) to be in pursuit of a boy. Actual hunting becomes a figure for erotic pursuit in a brilliant piece of psychological interpretation that renders the visual subject a sublimation for a deeper theme.[39] This structure collapses at 1.28.2 in the author's professed shock at his own delusion in being taken in by the deceit (τῆς ἀπάτης) of the picture into believing that its world was real and not painted.[40]

[37] See Thein (2002: esp. 139–40 with bibliography).

[38] Note that the first sentence of the proem opens with ἀλήθεια as realism: cf. also 1.13.5; 1.23.2; 2.28.3.

[39] Further on the hermeneutics of interpretation in *Imagines* see Graziani (1990: esp. 13–20); also Mathieu-Castellani (1996: 92–4).

[40] See at greater length, Elsner (1995: 33–6).

The text of the opening of 2.23 ('Madness of Heracles') is unfortunately corrupt, so the thrust of its address is not wholly clear. But it might seem the partner of 1.28 ('Hunters') if the call to 'fight, brave youths, surround Heracles and advance' is to be trusted. The issue is whether this address is to the attendants in the picture (as the address in 1.28 is to the hunters in the painting) or to the group of young men to whom Philostratus is speaking. After a humorous comparison of the task of the youths in restraining Heracles with the hero's own labours before his madness (2.23.1), Philostratus urges 'fear not at all; he is gone from you, for his eyes are directed towards Argos and he thinks he is slaying the children of Eurystheus' (2.23.1). Is this address to his audience in the Neapolitan art gallery, turning their act of viewing into a Herculean task tinged with fear? Or is it to the attendants in the picture? And if so, what is the status of his second-person plural address to a world within the canvas? Given the reference to Euripides' play at 2.23.1, the urge to 'fear not at all' (ἀλλὰ δείσητε μηδέν) is deeply problematic. The child whom the youths are charged to defend is indeed saved briefly in Euripides' play when Heracles' wife, Megara, shuts herself and the child in a room and bolts the doors (E. *HF* 996–7), only for Heracles to uproot the door and force out the doorposts before putting them both to death (E. *HF* 998–1000). When Philostratus calls to the youths to fight and enjoins them to 'fear not', he conspicuously undermines his own authority in appearing to reveal a lack of command of the Euripidean ur-narrative, in so far as the child *will* be killed. Or does his urgency to intervene, as it were, between the consecutive lines of Euripides' messenger speech reveal the immediacy and vividness of his ecphrastic response (or the painting's pictorial response) to the terrible story he tells? Does he perform a desperate and doomed intervention (motivated by a laudable suspension of disbelief and memory of the authoritative narrative) within the ecphrastic intervention that constitutes the climax of Euripides' play?

Certainly, at 2.23.2, Philostratus' attention shifts from the plural youths (within or without the picture: 'enough for these youths!', 2.23.2) to the boy (the παῖς of 1 Proem 5 and 1.1.1)—'it is high time for you to occupy yourself with the painting'. This brutally cuts through the orgy of wish-fulfilment fantasy and imagination that had narrated us into the world of the picture in the preceding paragraph (in ways echoed elsewhere in the *Imagines*)[41] but it also disturbingly aligns the boy outside the picture with the παῖς within it—the one surviving child whom Heracles has not yet killed (2.23.2), whom Philostratus was urging the youths to save ('Heaven grant that he spare the remaining boy', 2.23.1) and whom a reading of the play will reveal to be about to die. Even as this description attempts to affirm the boundary of real and imaginary, of picture and world, Philostratus pulls off a brilliant obfuscation of our certainties as readers that mirrors not only the deceptions of madness and realism but also of viewing and imagination that are effectively the subject of this ecphrasis.

In relation to the structure of deceit and naturalism both within pictures and in the viewing of them, the 'Madness of Heracles' is a dramatic meditation on the tragic effects of deluded viewing. In this it is heavily indebted to the profound self-referentiality and concern with artifice in the messenger speech of its Euripidean ur-text.[42] Where in Euripides Heracles' madness is portrayed as a series of terrible and misguided acts—the one reference to the hero's eyes being to their gorgon-like glare (E. *HF* 990)[43]—Philostratus insistently performs the disjunction between what Heracles *sees* and what he *thinks* he sees as governing the catastrophe of his actions. The picture becomes a disturbing meditation on the dangers of the gaze—a gaze that even Philostratus cannot always guarantee he will get right (as at 1.28.1–2)—in the context of naturalistic deceptivity. But it also sets up a contrast between literature as the narrative of action and painting (or, rather, its ecphrasis) as a narrative of the gaze—notwithstanding the fact that tragedy is in fact a form of literature performed under the gaze.[44] We are told (2.23.4) that:

The Fury which has gained mastery over him you have seen many times on the stage, but you cannot see her here; for she has entered into Heracles himself and she dances through his breast and leaps up inside him and muddles his mind.

---

[41] Notably at 1.28.2: 'It really is a painting before which we stand'.

[42] See Kraus (1998: esp. 152–6).

[43] As Bond's commentary points out ad loc., this is the culmination of a series of references to Gorgons in the play (330, 868, 883).

[44] See Taplin (1978: 1–8); Zeitlin (1994); Goldhill (2000*b*).

It turns out that we too cannot see everything that is going on, everything that Philostratus' superior command (authorial authority?) allows him to name. Even as Heracles' madness turns on a gaze that misconstrues, so our reception of that subject cannot wholly construe what we look at. The narrativity of performative drama can indeed play out the process of the Fury coming and entering the hero, while the painting gives us rather the intense moment of frenzy.

In the case of the 'Madness of Heracles', where Philostratus' interest is at least as much in the problem of the misguided gaze as in the mythic/tragic theme in itself, it is not surprising that again there are almost no visual prototypes.[45] Despite a reference by Pliny to a lost picture by Nearchus (*HN* 35.141), it appears that this theme excited little demand from Greek and Roman patrons. One might argue that the absence of a pictorial tradition was in this case an advantage, since Philostratus' aim is to focus on naturalistic pictorialism as such and the way it may be differentiated from Euripides' tragic treatment to which he refers explicitly.

The question of what painting can do better than tragedy when dealing with tragedy's most climactic actions is effectively implicit in all these descriptions and explicitly so in the 'Heracles' with its allusion to Euripides and the stage in the first paragraph and its closing comment about the humiliating extras added by poets. But it is at 2.10 that Philostratus makes his most direct case for a pictorial dimension to the representation of tragic narrative that exceeds what tragedy itself can do. This is the 'Cassandra', which seizes a moment twice described in the ur-texts but never enacted directly—the murder of Agamemnon and Cassandra by Clytaemnestra and Aegisthus.[46] In the *Odyssey*, the narrative is told in the third person and the past tense to Odysseus by the ghost of Agamemnon in the underworld (*Od.* 11.405–34); in Aeschylus' *Agamemnon*, the action takes place off stage while the chorus listens (*A.* 1343–7), although it is prophetically foretold by Cassandra at lines 1107–29 and then described by Clytaemnestra in what is less a messenger speech than a first-person song of triumph at lines 1372–98, 1431–47. Breaking away

---

[45] See Boardman (1988: esp. 835–6) for the few examples.
[46] On this ecphrasis, see Blanchard (1986: 148–51) and Beall (1993: esp. 352–3).

from these past- and future-tense versions, Philostratus' picture leaps *in medias res*—Agamemnon's drunken entourage lies slaughtered in the present tense, blood mixed with wine, bringing to life *Od.* 11.412–20 and explicitly referring to items in Homer's account such as the mixing bowl (κρατήρ: 2.10.1, cf. *Od.* 11.419 and *A.* 1397) and the tables (τραπεζῶν: 2.10.1, cf. *Od.* 11.419: the following is all from 2.10.1):[47]

The men who lie here and there in the men's great hall, the blood commingled with the wine, the men sprawling on the tables breathe out their life, and yonder mixing bowl that has been kicked aside by the man who lies there gasping beside it, a maiden in the garb of a prophetess who gazes at the axe which is about to descend upon her—thus Clytaemnestra welcomes Agamemnon on his return from Troy. And while others are slaying Agamemnon's followers, who are so drunken as to embolden even Aegisthus for the deed, Clytaemnestra, enveloping Agamemnon in a device of a mantle from which there is no escape, brings down upon him this two-edged axe by which even great trees are laid low, and the daughter of Priam, esteemed by Agamemnon as of surpassing beauty, who chanted prophecies that were not believed, she slays with the still warm axe.

The vividness of Philostratus' account stretches to uniting references to all three classic playwrights, as well as Homer, reconstituting elements from the *Odyssey*, the *Oresteia* of Aeschylus, the *Electra* of Sophocles and the *Orestes* and *Electra* of Euripides. And yet the specific theme depicted here, never seen in any surviving tragedy, is the one which Philostratus most consciously and deliberately compares with drama: 'If we examine this scene as a drama, my boy, a great tragedy has been enacted in a brief space (2.10.1, καὶ εἰ μὲν ὡς δρᾶμα ἐξετάζομεν, ὦ παῖ, ταῦτα, τετραγῴδηται μεγάλα ἐν σμικρῷ).[48] This deliberate encapsulation of tragedy in one of its defining moments (the death of Agamemnon) is at once contrasted with Philostratus' own *pictorial* medium: 'but if [we examine it] as a painting, you will see more in it (2.10.1, εἰ δ' ὡς γραφήν, πλείω ἐν αὐτοῖς ὄψει).

Here we have a kind of crunch case in relation to how pictorial and ecphrastic media might surpass their ur-texts—not only tragic and

---

47 More on these genuflections to earlier literature in Schönberger and Kalinka (1968: 407–9).

48 Fairbanks's Loeb translates 'a brief space of time' (p. 173), but Philostratus must encompass also the brief space of the pictorial frame and of his own ecphrasis in σμικρῷ.

epic, but by implication pastoral and mythological as well. But much is at stake in the comparative: more than what? Fairbanks's Loeb edition, transgressing strict accuracy in translation, glosses 'more than a drama' (i.e. that it is also a picture, obeying pictorial rules?).[49] But there are numerous other options—more than you would see in a drama? more than a drama could ever render visible? more than tragedy? more still in a brief frame than even the essence of a great classic tragedy? and so forth. When he needs to be, Philostratus is the master of studied ambiguity. The rest of the ecphrasis might be taken as his typically elliptical way of glossing this ambivalent proposition.

After the challenge that 'you will see more' if you examine the scene as a picture, Philostratus continues playfully: 'for look! Here are torches to provide light—evidently these events are taking place at night' (2.10.2, σκόπει γὰρ· λαμπτῆρες οὗτοι χορηγοὶ φωτός—ἐν νυκτὶ γὰρ ταῦτά που). 'You will see more' leads to 'look!' (a classic hyper-realist Philostratean trope[50]), an injunction upon which humorous light is cast by the reference to torches, a more ludic way of eliding the line between viewer and picture than in 2.23, for example, with the immediate explanation that the painted scene is set at night-time, confirming at once the barrier between painting and beholder: here the light firmly belongs in the canvas. Yet even as the account promises to shift away from drama, the lamps turn out to be *chorêgoi*—chorus leaders or theatre producers of the picture's light. What Philostratus goes on to describe is the substance of what he mentioned before, much of it borrowed from Homer and the tragedians: mixing bowls, bowls of gold brighter than the torches' flames, tables laden with food, all in disorder and so forth (2.10.2–3). This puzzling repetition of the tropes from which the disjunction at the end of 2.10.1 between tragedy and picture was meant to release us, is still more emphasized by the sophist's insistence on carrying on his strategy of deliberate quotation from Homer and the tragedians in the second half of the ecphrasis.[51] Where the poetics of Philostratus' ecphrasis most differ from the thrust of 'a great tragedy enacted' is at its ending.

[49] See Fairbanks (1931: 173).
[50] See Maffei (1991: esp. 617–18) and Bryson (1994: esp. 266–7, 270, 280, 282).
[51] Critics have seen quotations from or references to *Od.* 22.19–20 at 2.10.1; to *Od.* 22.329 and *Il.* 5.585 at 2.10.2; to A. *Ch.* 364–5, *Od.* 11.411 and 421–2, A. *A.* 1265 and E. *Tr.* 451–2 at 2.10.4. See Schönberger and Kalinka (1968: 408–9) and the notes of Fairbanks (1931: 171–7).

Here Philostratus takes us to 'the most prominent place in the scene' (τὸ δὲ κυριώτατον τῆς σκηνῆς, 2.10.4)—a charged piece of phrasing since σκηνή may be taken to imply not only the dramatic setting of the picture he describes, but also the tragic stage and therefore all the plays from which he insists his painting differs, if you look carefully enough at it. Agamemnon lies stricken, but (2.10.4):

Even more striking in its pathos is the figure of Cassandra—the way Clytaemnestra, her eyes crazed, her hair flying, her arm savagely raised, stands over her with the axe, and the way Cassandra herself, tenderly and in a state of inspiration, has tried to throw herself upon Agamemnon as she hurls her fillets from her and as it were casts about him the protection of her prophetic art; and as the axe is now posed above her, she turns her eyes towards it and utters so pathetic a cry that even Agamemnon, with the remnants of life that is in him, pities her, hearing her cry; for he will recount it to Odysseus in Hades at the concourse of souls.

Here, at the climax of the ecphrasis, Philostratus shifts from an emphasis on the gaze (Clytaemnestra's eyes and Cassandra's eyes) to the medium of sound in Cassandra's cry which Agamemnon, poised between life and death, hears and which he retells to Odysseus in the *Odyssey* (11.421). Playing upon both the visual and the oral dimensions of tragedy, Philostratus' picture effectively enters a meta-level of representation in which his characters can speak across texts, their cries echoing between tragedy and epic. His intertextuality of cries—picking up Cassandra's choric wails which introduce most of her speeches in the *Agamemnon* (1072–3, 1076–7, 1100, 1107, 1114, 1125, 1136, 1146, 1156–7, 1167–8. 1214, 1256–7, 1305, 1307) and Clytaemnestra's dismissal of Cassandra's death cry (1444–6),[52] as well as Agamemnon's speech in the *Odyssey*—allows Philostratus' ecphrastic performance to outclass the use of sound in the classic exemplars of the genre of ecphrasis, whose sounds certainly fail to penetrate the ears of characters in other books.[53]

---

[52] Note that Philostratus effectively supplies Cassandra's actual death cry which is not heard in Aeschylus' *Agamemnon*, although Agamemnon himself is heard offstage.

[53] On sound in ecphrasis, see Laird (1993: esp. 20–4). For sound in Homer's Shield of Achilles, see *Il.* 18.493, 502, 570, 579–80; for sound in the Pseudo-Hesiodic Shield of Heracles, see *Aspis* 205–6, 231–3, 242–3, 278–83.

In Cassandra's 'tender inspiration' (ἁβρῶς τε καὶ ἐνθέως) for Agamemnon, Philostratus shifts to the erotic register which we have already noted in his pictures of Pentheus and Hippolytus. This time, what is spotlit is not a homoerotic anthem for a doomed youth but a heterosexual vignette of passionate affection at the moment of tragic immolation. This is a fundamental reversal of the *Agamemnon* in several ways.[54] First, on the Philostratean painted stage (σκηνή), we see the act of death as it happens—Clytaemnestra wielding the axe and the specific acts of affection between the dying Agamemnon and the doomed Cassandra even as the axe falls on her. This is in marked distinction from the way the bodies of the dead Agamemnon and Cassandra are revealed by Aeschylus (*A.* 1372 ff.)[55] with the action of killing recorded only in the highly partial voice of Clytaemnestra herself. The image of Cassandra flinging off her fillets and throwing herself on to Agamemnon refers specifically to *A.* 1264–8 but reverses the thrust of Cassandra's prophecy there (since she talks only of fillets and not of Agamemnon). The erotic but also plainly sympathetic affection of the murdered lovers in Philostratus contrasts with the emotional register of Clytaemnestra's brutal speech at *A.* 1440–3 (tr. Lloyd-Jones):

> bedfellow for him, the trusty prophetess
> who shared his couch, the public harlot
> of the sailors' benches.

So one might say that the Cassandra picture at 2.10 is the peak of a pattern in the Philostratean tragic ecphraseis leading from 'Bacchae' (1.18) via 'Hippolytus' (2.4) in which tragic drama is intensely experienced as painting but its cathartic thrust is transformed in Philostratus' retelling to become an eroticized dwelling on youths or lovers at their moment of disaster. Each of these pictures culminates on a kind of snapshot or pause at the 'most prominent place in

---

[54] If one assumes Aeschylus to be Philostratus' prime source here and one follows Fraenkel's argument that Aeschylus had Clytaemnestra conduct the murders with a sword (see Fraenkel 1950: App. B, ii. 806–9), then Philostratus' choice of murder weapon (following S. *El.* 99, E. *Hec.* 1279, *Tr.* 361–2, and *El.* 279) is a further reversal. But Fraenkel's suggestion is anyway controversial: see Davies (1987) and Prag (1991).

[55] There is of course no stage direction, but see Fraenkel (1950: ii. 644) and Taplin (1977: 325–7).

the scene' (2.10.4), where Philostratus dwells on the pathos of dying
with an eroticized strategy of identification radically at odds with the
spirit of tragedy as such.[56] Is this the 'more' that we see in painting,
by contrast with drama? The last of the tragic pictures (in the
sequence of the *Imagines*) is 2.23 (the 'Madness of Heracles') whose
theme turns not on erotics but on the betrayals of the gaze and hence
on the naturalistic painted medium against which and with which
Philostratus' writing is so engaged. If these four pictures may be
taken as a thematic group across the *Imagines*, then 2.23 picks up not
only the explicit contrast of painting and drama signalled at 2.10.1,
but also on the eyes of 2.10.4—those of Cassandra turned to the axe
poised above her and the crazed eyes of Clytaemnestra (μανικὸν
βλέπουσα) which prefigure the misdirected eyes of the mad Heracles
at 2.23. In the sequence of the tragic pictures, 'Bacchae' (1.18) and
'Hippolytus' (2.4) may be said to state the case, to demonstrate a
transformation of themes (from tragic to erotic) that accompanies
a transformation of media (from drama to picture) that itself parallels Philostratus' own transformation of media (from image to
ecphrasis). 'Cassandra' (2.10) then makes explicit the problem of
difference between drama and picture, while stating that the picture
may potentially offer 'more' than tragedy. This 'more' is of course
also a claim about representation itself in which imitation (the
picture's copying of the original tragedy, Philostratus' verbal reworking of the original picture) can be seen to offer more than its
prototype. That claim about imitations and prototypes is of course
well grounded in the world of Roman art practice, with its rich
diversity of visual replications and emulations of earlier models.[57]
The 'Madness of Heracles' (2.23) turns to the specific problems
implicit in this 'more' in the world of pictures and viewing, by
showing the difficulties of the gaze under the regime of naturalistic
deception (brilliantly exemplified in the gaze of the mad Heracles).
But it also directly addresses the problems of viewer absorption and
identification in the world of an image whose internal dynamics

---

[56] Perhaps what Blanchard (1986: 151) means when he writes of the 'effet de
trivialiser la mort du héros' (of Agamemnon).

[57] This is a large subject in the study of Roman art. For a recent summary of the
state of the field, see the essays in Gazda (2002).

cannot be entirely separated from the external dynamics of the viewer's gaze that apprehends it.[58] Where 'Bacchae' and 'Hippolytus' can genuinely claim to draw upon some currents in Graeco-Roman iconographic representations of their themes, both the Cassandra and the Heracles images (more directly concerned with secondary or philosophical questions about what 'more' there is to pictures and how their viewing might work) deal with themes very little attested in surviving pictorial tradition—in the case of the death of Agamemnon not at all in surviving imagery from the Roman era.[59]

The disjunction of the prior narrative and its visual representation articulated at 2.10.1 has a parallel shortly after in the linear reading of the *Imagines* at 2.13.2. Here, in a picture that relates the death of Ajax the son of Oileus, Philostratus enters firmly epic territory recounting a story from *Odyssey* 4.499–511, and borrowing some quotations from the *Iliad* (e.g. *Il.* 13.59).[60]

ὁ μὲν δὴ λόγος τῆς γραφῆς οὗτος· τόδε δ' ἐναργές·

Such is the story of the painting; but what is shown to the eye is this.[61]

As in the Cassandra description, one might initially wonder how great the distinction really is between what is described before and after this significant differentiating statement. Here we have an epic hero, not mad like Heracles, but hubristic (a term used twice in the last sentence of 2.13.1). At the opening of the ecphrasis Ajax is defined by his gaze—glaring fiercely (δεινὸν βλέπων, 2.13.1) but in 2.13.2 his gaze is much closer to that of Heracles in 2.23: 'Ajax gazes out (περιαθρεῖ) over the sea like a man emerging from a drunken sleep, seeing neither ship nor land'. His hubris, like Heracles' madness, within the dispensation of (the description of) naturalistic painting turns on the deceptions of the gaze.

---

[58] See on this issue Newby (forthcoming). The classic art historical discussion of absorption and theatricality is Fried (1980).

[59] See for imagery of the murder, Touchefu and Kraukopf (1981: esp. 271–2); Morizot, (1992: esp. 74); Paoletti (1994: esp. 967).

[60] See Schönberger and Kalinka (1968: 413–15). Generally on Philostratus and Homer, see Lesky (1940).

[61] So Fairbanks's translation. But one might also translate the last clause (τόδε δ' ἐναργές) by 'what is rendered vivid [*sc.* as much by Philostratus' rhetoric as by the picture] is this'...

Philostratus' need to differentiate his enterprise from the classic exemplars, tragic and epic, out of which he constructs his verbal versions of pictures marks more than his self-awareness about being secondary.[62] In other texts, notably the *Life of Apollonius* and the *Heroicus*, Philostratus' obsession with the sacred and Homeric past entails the claim that the Homeric age can be made to live again in the present in figures like Apollonius or the Vine Dresser with his personal relationship with the hero Protesilaus.[63] *Heroicus* in particular turns on the vivid *phantasia* by which the Homeric heroes can be made present in the Severan age. In *Imagines*, with its specific remit to worry about truth and wisdom (ἀλήθεια and σοφία—terms prominent at the opening of the first sentence of the proem)[64] and its focus on the strategies of naturalism, Philostratus is less optimistic. Homer and the classic tragedians are summoned, but the limits of their relevance for modern concerns are made explicit. At the opening of the very last ecphrasis of the *Imagines* (2.34.1), Homer is evoked as an intimate of the *Horae* in heaven, but rapidly dismissed since the picture is about men and the earth.[65]

In relation to the art history implicit in the *Imagines* this is very significant. Unlike the heroic Plinian account of naturalistic representation (aptly described as the passage from winter to spring),[66] Philostratus is more subtle. His antiquarianism, which includes a very profound veneration for the things of the past, is—like that of Pausanias—acutely aware of what the present may have lost. Just as Pausanias is sensitive to the divine effects of non-naturalistic images, their archaic power, one may say,[67] so Philostratus' exploration of naturalism is keenly aware of its limitations. The tragic pictures, in

[62] I mean this not only in the sense of Philostratus' invention of the 'Second Sophistic' as a defining term for the culture he stood for, but also in the sense of the 'secondariness' of the *persona* of the ecphrasist, discussed by Bryson (1994: 273–83), and its dialectic with the reading of Karl Lehmann which dominated studies of the *Imagines* for much of the second half of the twentieth century: Lehmann-Hartleben (1941).

[63] See esp. Zeitlin (2001: esp. 246–66).

[64] The principal discussion remains Maffei (1991).

[65] See Elsner (2000: 256, 259).

[66] The analogy is by Bryson (1984: 7). Recently on Pliny's art history (with bibliography), see Carey (2003: 102–111).

[67] See e.g. Paus. 2.4.5 on the uncouthness of Daedalus' statues but their 'having something divine about them', with Morris (1992: 248) and Arafat (1996: 68).

replacing Euripidean catharsis with erotic identification and pathetic fallacy, in turning from tragic immediacy to iconographic convention rephrased as scintillating rhetorical erudition, chart the limitations of the idioms of naturalistic painting in Philostratus' time no less perceptively than the Impressionists' critique of Academic painting by the likes of Cabanel and Bouguereau.[68] In general, the *Imagines* is an extraordinary and sympathetic celebration of the wonders, techniques, and effects of naturalism—taking in painterly skills, the mastery of artists, the variety of viewer investments, the psychology of identification. But, within this scheme, the tragic pictures demonstrate the text's sensitivity to the limitations of the mimetic regime of representation—limitations marked by Pausanias, for example, in his interest in the ritual and religious functions of images alongside their aesthetic and connoisseurial value.[69] Philostratus' reworking of tragedy (and epic) as briefly described, framed pictures both makes the masterpieces of the past new again and accessible for a contemporary readership, and keenly marks the gap with the present. What Philostratus' pictures can achieve, given their double nature as image and text and the limitations of a regime of representation dependent on the tricks of deceptive naturalism, is not the same as the tragic exemplars he cites and evokes. That he advertises his awareness of this—explicitly indeed in so regularly bringing up the models of Homer and Tragedy—is a mark of the thoughtful self-awareness of Philostratus' remarkable enterprise in the critical reception of naturalism, couched as it is in so playful and creative a form as the ecphrasis of pictures.

[68] See for instance Clark (1986: 79–146).

[69] On Pausanias and the ritual appreciation of art, see Elsner (1996); on Pausanias and connoisseurship, see Elsner (1998: esp. 419–28).

14

Pulling the Other? Longus on Tragedy

Ewen Bowie

The five 'ideal' Greek novels that have been transmitted complete in a continuous manuscript tradition present as their major theme heterosexual desire, one sense of the term 'pulling the other' which my title (unashamedly intertextual) exploits. All five novels also include Attic tragedies of the classical period among the canonical texts that they evoke to achieve their own literary goals: this is most insistent and self-conscious in Heliodorus' *Theagenes and Charicleia*,[1] but the technique is already visible in our earliest novel, Chariton's *Chaereas and Callirhoe*. This paper explores to what extent and with what possible purpose Attic tragedy is exploited by Longus in his miniature and pastoral novel, *Daphnis and Chloe*, and argues that a major objective is to stress how different is the presentation of ἔρως in *Daphnis and Chloe* and in its novelistic predecessors from that in Attic tragedy. I contribute it in the hope that its focus on generic boundaries, on tragedy, and on the novel will match our honorand's interests.

At first glance tragedy is not the most prominent among the archaic and classical genres evoked by *Daphnis and Chloe*. That work's resonances are much more with historiography, Attic comedy, pastoral poetry, and archaic lyric poetry.[2]

---

[1] Cf. Paulsen (1992).

[2] The discussion of Hunter (1983: 59–83) remains fundamental; for further work Morgan's excellent commentary (2004) is now the essential point of departure. See too Pattoni (2005).

After Thucydides' claims for his work have been teased in the preface (pr. 3), and a typically historiographic description of a city has been fleetingly displayed in the opening lines of the narrative itself (1.1.1), historiography fades into the background until the war between Mytilene and Methymna that Chloe's abduction has provoked allows the writer to indulge in a 23-line vignette flecked with Thucydidean detail (3.1.1–3.1).[3] Chloe's abduction itself gives Longus the opportunity for a reworking of the striking Herodotean passage in which Philippides conveys to the Athenians Pan's message that they had hitherto been neglecting him: the Nymphs point out to the distraught Daphnis that he and Chloe had hitherto failed to honour, even with garlands, the statue of Pan erected beneath their pine tree.[4]

Attic New Comedy also makes its debut in the preface. The cave of the Nymphs is immediately revealed to be connected with Pan (pr. 3), a *mise en scène* that to many readers would evoke Menander's *Bad-tempered Man* (*Dyskolos*). A New Comedy motif is immediately presented in the exposure of the two babies of city families (1.2–4). New Comedy characters emerge first with the pleasure cruise of the rich young Methymnans (2.12–18), then in greater strength in book 4, both with the elite parents of the exposed couple and with the son of one of these families, playing a role that matches his name Astylus, and his loathsome parasite, Gnathon.

The constant backcloth is, of course, a pastoral world meticulously constructed from the hexameter poetry of the hellenistic poet Theocritus. Detail after evocative detail takes readers back to Theocritus; some lead them further back to Sappho and Alcaeus, palmary intertexts for a novel exploring desire, ἔρως, and set on Lesbos. Thus archaic Aeolic lyric poetry becomes the fourth genre to make an important contribution to the texture of *Daphnis and Chloe*.

It is only after these four genres that tragedy can be claimed as an intertext. Given that there are other poetic genres also occasionally exploited—for example, early hexameter epic and hellenistic

---

[3] Thucydidean vocabulary also marks the opening of the cruise by rich νέοι which precipitates the abduction, i.e. προσκώπους at 2.12.1, cf. Th. 1.10.3, and Hunter (1983: 85 with n. 6).

[4] 2.23.4, cf. Hdt. 6.105.3, Paus. 1.28.4.

epigram—the relatively low profile of tragic intertextuality is remarkable. In what follows I first set out cases where a tragic intertext might be argued for on grounds of language or (less often) content; then I offer a possible explanation of the phenomenon.

TRAGIC INTERTEXTS?

(a) Language that may evoke two or more tragedians

1.9.2 τοσαύτης δὴ πάντα κατεχούσης εὐωρίας 'with everything in the spell of so fine a spring.' εὐωρία appears only here in extant literature (though it is also found in a document, *Sammelbuch* 4324.7) but its existence is perhaps implied by the verb εὐωριάζειν, S. fr. 561 Radt and conjectured by Porson at [A.] *Pr.* 17 (Longus will have imagined the *Prometheus* to be by Aeschylus); note too εὔωρος γάμος, S. fr. 200 Radt.

1.20.2 The stately phrase ἀνδρὸς ὁπλίτου (instead of simply ὁπλίτου) is poetical (A. *Th.* 717, E. *Supp.* 585). It is never used by Thucydides and only once, for effect, by Herodotus, writing of the phantom at Marathon (6.117.3). κράνος is also poetical, e.g. A. *Th.* 385. Of claimed prose usages X. *Cyr.* 6.1.51 is interpolated, Plu. *an seni* 10 (= *Mor.* 789d) is perhaps consciously poetical. It may be relevant that ἀνδρὸς ὁπλίτου κράνος could form the second limb of an iambic trimeter.

1.23.2 θαλπόμενος τούτοις ἅπασιν: 'heated up by all these things'. The metaphorical sense of θάλπειν is only found here in the novelists, although other metaphorical terms from the language of fire are common. Almost all earlier metaphorical uses in the context of passion are in tragedy: [A.] *Pr.* 590, 650, S. *Tr.* 102, *El.* 888, fr. 474 Radt. Herodas' use at *Mimiambi* 2.81 is formally an exception, but can be argued itself to be allusive; Alciphron's use at 2.2, probably later than Longus, is in a related but not identical context.

2.1.2 κατεξασμένης (from καταξαίνω) 'pounded to shreds' is a word whose classical attestations are chiefly in tragedy, e.g. A. *A.* 197, fr. 132c Radt, S. *Aj.* 728, E. *Med.* 1030, *Hipp.* 274, *HF* 285, *Ion*

1267, *Tr.* 509, *Ph.* 1145, *Supp.* 503. Aristophanes' use at *Ach.* 320 is arguably paratragic. Its use by Longus elevates the humble function of the *agnus castus* that has been shredded to make a rustic torch.

2.14.1 κλυδώνιον of (slightly) rough water is chiefly tragic, whether literally in Euripides (*Hec.* 48, *Hel.* 1209), or metaphorically in Aeschylus (*Th.* 795, *Ch.* 183). Although it also appears as a *varia lectio* at Th. 2.84.3 and in Arr. *Peripl. M. Eux.* 3, it seems most likely that for Longus it had a tragic resonance.

3.4.1 In classical Greek the noun οἰκουρία is found only in Euripides (*HF* 1373) and most cognate words (οἰκουρεῖν, οἰκούρημα, οἰκουρίος) are found only in tragedy (although οἰκουρός is more widely attested). However οἰκουρία is common in imperial prose (e.g. Plu. *Qu. Rom.* 30 = *Mor.* 271e, *Cor.* 35.2, Ael. *NA.* 1.15, Alciphr. 3.22.2) so it is unclear whether for Longus it had a tragic ring.

3.12.4 τὸν Ἴτυν . . . ἠκρίβουν. Explanation of the nightingale's song as a lament for Itys is found as early as *Od.* 19.522, but there the form of his name is Ἴτυλον, and it is chiefly in tragedy that Ἴτυν is the name form that signals the myth: A. *A.* 1144, S. *El.* 148–9, E. fr. 773 Nauck. Although there are of course other places Longus could find the name Itys used to evoke the whole myth (e.g. Ar. *Birds* 212), and although his predecessor Achilles Tatius tells the myth twice (but without using the name Itys: 5.3.4–8, 5.5.1–9) the link here with a story of family violence might support a claim that Longus draws Itys from tragedy.

4.21.2 πόρπην χρυσήλατον: at 1.2.3 this clasp was simply termed χρυσῆ, but the higher emotional register of this scene may have induced Longus to choose a grand compound adjective which may evoke Attic tragedy. It is found at A. *Th.* 644 and S. *OT* 1268, and most strikingly it is used of πόρπαι by Euripides at *Ph.* 62 (χρυσήλατοις πόρπαισιν). Though it also found in some other imperial Greek texts (e.g. Plu. *Demetr.* 53.2, Luc. *Sat.* 8) a tragic and especially Euripidean intertextuality seems likely.

4.24.3 κρεῖττον γὰρ τοῖς εὖ φρονοῦσιν ἀδελφοῦ κτῆμα οὐδέν: this high value set on brothers might recall S. *Ant.* 905–20.[5] The intertextuality

---

[5] So Morgan (2004: 240 ad loc.). The notoriously related passage at Hdt. 3.119.6 is less likely to be evoked here by Longus.

is made more probable by the formulation, which is reminiscent of tragic *gnomai*, e.g. E. *Andr.* 896 οὔκ ἐστιν οὐδὲν κρεῖσσον οἰκείου φίλου, *Or.* 1155 οὔκ ἐστιν οὐδὲν κρεῖσσον ἢ φίλος σαφής. There are of course similar formulations in other gnomic poetry, e.g. Thgn., though in that collection all are positive and lack οὐδέν e.g. *Theognidea* 1074 κρεῖσσόν τοι σοφίη καὶ μεγάλης ἀρετῆς (cf. 218, 618, 1173).

(b) Aeschylus

2.22.3 λειπεργάτης ἐσόμενος, 'destined to abandon my work'. In λειπεργάτης Longus uses a word otherwise unattested to convey Daphnis' tragic vision of himself. The model is perhaps Agamemnon imagining himself as λιπόναυς at A. *A.* 212, picked up by λιποναύταν at Theoc. 13.73.

2.27.1 μαινομέναις φρεσίν maintains the high poetic style of the preceding superlatives and seems to recall A. *Th.* 484 μαινομένᾳ φρενί. The context—intervention by a wrathful divinity—is as near as Longus' main narrative ever comes to the mad, bad world of Attic tragedy.

2.27.3 βορὰν ἰχθύων 'a meal for the fish' might recall the self-imprecation of Io at [A.] *Pr.* 582–3 ἢ ποντίοις δάκεσι δὸς βοράν, but the threat of being a βορά for fish is already in Ach. Tat. 3.5.4 εἰ δὲ καὶ θηρίων ἡμᾶς βορὰν πέπρωται γενέσθαι, εἰς ἡμᾶς ἰχθὺς ἀναλωσάτω, and the idea goes right back to *Il.* 19.268 where βόσιν ἰχθύων characterizes a sacrifice thrown into the sea.

(c) Sophocles

pr. 4 πάντως γὰρ οὐδεὶς Ἔρωτα ἔφυγεν ἢ φεύξεται. Morgan (2004: 150) persuasively suggests that this alludes to the well-known song in S. *Ant.* 787 where it is said of Eros καί σ' οὔτ' ἀθανάτων φύξιμος οὐδεὶς οὔθ' ἀμερίων σέ γ' ἀνθρώπων. As he goes on to observe: 'The allusion points Longus's innovation: Love in this novel is wholly positive, if properly conducted'.

2.22 ποίοις ποσὶν ἄπειμι παρὰ τὸν πατέρα καὶ τὴν μητέρα has been convincingly argued by Maria Pia Pattoni[6] to recall Ajax's words in S. *Aj.* 462–4:

> καὶ ποῖον ὄμμα πατρὶ δηλώσω φανεὶς
> Τελαμῶνι; πῶς με τλήσεται ποτ' εἰσιδεῖν
> γυμνὸν φανέντα τῶν ἀριστείων ἄτερ . . .

Pattoni shows how a number of details in Longus' phraseology remodel this passage with what she argues to be parodic intent (e.g. the replacement of the high-style ὄμμα with the down-to-earth ποσίν) though she misses the possible Aeschylean allusion in λειπεργάτης (cf. above). It seems to me that the contrast Pattoni observes between the expected response of Ajax's father Telamon (adducing also 1010–21) and the sympathetic distress of Daphnis' parents (οἳ καὶ αὐτοὶ κεῖνται χαμαί, 2.23.5) offer less support to an explanation in terms of parody than to the insistence on generic difference for which I am arguing.

3.6.2 ὡς οὐκ αἰσίοις ὄρνισιν ἐλθών: Di Virgilio (1991: ad loc.) suggests that these words allude to S. *OT* 52 ὄρνιθι αἰσίῳ. If there is such an allusion it is hard to gauge its effect in a context where, as is seen by Morgan (2004: 203), the reference to augury in connection with a bird hunt is playful; but the collocation is not rare enough to support an allusion (cf. e.g. Pi. *N.* 9.18).

3.28.2 μυδῶν 'rotting' or 'clammy' describes the body of Polyneices at S. *Ant.* 410, and its use in that play again at 1008 and *OT* 1298 might mark it as a particularly Sophoclean word. But it is also found in Polybius and medical writers (e.g. Hp. *VC* 15, *Ulc.* 10, Diosc. 1.71, 72. Evocation here of Polyneices in *Antigone* might be thought far-fetched, were it not that in his preface (see above on pr. 4) Longus had given readers such a clear pointer to the play.

(d) Euripides

pr. 4 The prayer ἡμῖν δὲ ὁ θεὸς παράσχοι σωφρονοῦσι τὰ τῶν ἄλλων γράφειν, 'but to us may the god grant that we write the deeds of others

---

[6] Pattoni (2004: 84–9).

with self-control'[7] may recall the prayer to Ἔρως of the chorus in E. *Hipp.* 528–9: μή μοί ποτε σὺν κακῷ φανείης μηδ' ἄρρυθμος ἔλθοις.

1.9.1 κατῆδον: the verb appears only twice in classical texts, at E. *IT* 1337 and Hdt. 7.191.2. Longus could have known the word from either passage, but his phraseology is also influenced by Ar. *Frogs* 224 οἷον κατεμελίτωσε τὴν λόχμην ὅλην.

1.13.5 ἄση, 'heartache', appears first in Sappho's prayer to Aphrodite, fr. 1.3 Voigt, perhaps also at fr. 96.17 Voigt, then at E. *Med.* 245. Although found in medical writing its rarity, and the influence of Sappho fr. 31 Voigt elsewhere in this passage, together suggest that Longus draws directly on Sappho, and that the word's appearance at *Med.* 245 is not enough to support a claim that this is a Euripidean intertext.

1.13.6 Chloe's inability to eat (cf. 1.17.4, 2.7.4) may be drawn from that of Phaedra in E. *Hipp.* 135–7, 275, her restlessness from *Hipp.* 181–5, the term οἶστρος from *Hipp.* 1300.

1.14.1 for love as a νόσος cf. E. *Hipp.* 131–40. Prima facie this is too widespread a perception of ἔρως to allow us to infer a Euripidean intertext, cf. Pl. *Phdr.* 255d, Theoc. 2.85, X. *Eph.* 1.5, 6, Ach. Tat. 1.6. However its appearance close to the metaphor ἕλκος, for which cf. E. *Hipp.* 530, greatly strengthens the case: ἕλκος is found only here in Longus, and indeed only here in the novelists for the metaphorical wound of love (Achilles Tatius uses ἕλκος metaphorically, but not of love, at 2.29.3, 5, 5.8.2). Longus could, admittedly, have drawn it from Call. *AP* 12.134 (=*HE* 1103–8) or (more probably) from Theoc. 11.15, a poem he certainly reworks shortly after this passage (1.17.3), or from Theoc. 30.10.

1.15.2: the νεβρίδα βακχικήν that Dorcon gives to Chloe may be known to readers from E. *Ba.* 676, but there could be many other literary sources e.g. *AP* 6.172 (= Page [1981: 1124–9], possibly hellenistic), [Theoc.] *AP* 6.177 (= *HE* 3398–401) and indeed artistic representations, cf. Merkelbach (1988).

1.20.2 Dorcon's trick of dressing himself in a wolfskin could recall its wearing in the Doloneia, *Il.* 10.334, or its use for disguise at [E.]

---

[7] For the (as often) complex connotations of *sôphrosynê* here and its implications for our reading of Longus' text see the very perceptive discussion by Morgan (2004: 148).

Rh. 208–9. The way his donning it is described (κατανωτισάμενος. . . χάσμα) recalls the description of Heracles at E. *HF* 361–3: πυρσῷ δ' ἀμφεκαλύφθη | ξανθὸν κρᾶτ' ἐπινωτίσας | δεινοῦ χάσματι θηρός.

1.20.3 The verb ἐκθηριόω occurs only once in a classical author, E. *Ba.* 1331 (of Agave's fate).

1.21.5 τολμημάτων is here used of 'lovers' reckless acts'. τόλμημα is common (especially in the plural) in Euripides, but so too in Josephus and Plutarch, and occurs twice elsewhere in the novelists (Chariton 4.2.9, Hld. 6.13.5).

1.22.3 φάρμακον is a well-established metaphor for 'cure' in an erotic context, cf. Morgan (2004: 183) on 2.7.7. Its earliest such use is at E. *Hipp.* 516, but Longus may know it chiefly from Theoc. 11.1 and 17 (where, as here, amelioration and not cure is meant): this is a poem that Longus has already evoked in his use of νόσος (1.14.1, see above).

1.27.1 τὰ θρυλούμενα, cf. τὸ θρυλούμενον E. fr. 285.1 Nauck, but θρυλεῖσθαι is also used of stories at Pl. *Phd.* 65b, Isoc. 12.237.

2.5.1 κύκνος ὁμοίως ἐμοὶ γέρων γενόμενος: the legend that the swan sings shortly before death first appears at A. *A.* 1444 (cf. Fraenkel 1950: ad loc.). The chorus of the *Heracles* compares itself to a swan at 110–11, γέρων ἀοιδὸς ὥστε πολιὸς ὄρνις, and commentators dispute whether this is an allusion to the legend (see Bond 1988: ad loc.). Again, the chorus figures itself later as a γέρων ἀοιδὸς (678, 692), and at 692 the comparison is explicitly with a swan, κύκνος ὡς γέρων ἀοιδός. Although the legend is known from later texts (the next being Pl. *Phd.* 84e) the collocation κύκνος . . . γέρων seems very likely to have come to Longus from Euripides' *Heracles*.

2.7.7 οὐδὲν φάρμακον, οὐ πινόμενον, οὐκ ἐσθιόμενον might perhaps recall E. *Hipp.* 516 πότερα δὲ χριστὸν ἢ ποτὸν τὸ φάρμακον;—but as for φάρμακον at 1.22.3 (cf. above), the immediate inspiration is most likely Theoc. 11.1–2: οὐδὲν πὸτ τὸν ἔρωτα πεφύκει φάρμακον ἄλλο, Νικία, οὔτ' ἔγχριστον, ἐμοὶ δοκεῖ, οὔτ' ἐπίπαστον, cf. Hunter (1999) on 11.1–6.

2.11.1 κατὰ τὴν τῶν χειλῶν προσβολήν: προσβολαί of kisses is found at E. *Supp.* 138, προσβολαὶ προσώπων, and προσβολαί is used on its own to mean 'embraces' at *Med.* 1074. Achilles Tatius had already adapted the first of these phrases in τὰς προσβολὰς τῶν ἀσπασμάτων, 5.8.3.

2.25.3 ff. The combination of fire and noise in these portents is also found at E. *Ba.* 622–3, and that may be one, but only one, of many sources drawn upon by Longus for his depiction of Pan's miracles (others include Dionysus' capture by Tyrrhenian pirates in *h. Hom. Bacch.*, esp. 38–41, and *h. Hom. Ap.* 399–441).

3.4.5 ἀμήχανος is found only here in Longus, and here alone of persons in the novelists. It picks out women's 'helplessness' at E. *Med.* 408 and *Hipp.* 643, but the word itself is not uncommon, and the sense 'helpless' is also used by Eurycleia to describe herself at *Od.* 19.363.

3.20.2 ἀρτιμαθής is used of Daphnis' recent acquisition of sexual experience. The word appears only once in classical poetry, at E. *Hec.* 687, βακχεῖον ἐξ ἀλάστορος ἀρτιμαθῆ νόμον, of Hecuba's response to recent acquaintance with misfortune. It reappears in second-century medical and philosophical contexts that might be thought closer to the situation of Daphnis here (Sor. 1.4, Gal. 11.466, Clem. Al. 6.20) and Longus might know it from these.

3.21.2 The sense of ἀμέλεια in ἐς καμάτων ἀμέλειαν, 'distraction' i.e. 'to divert their attention from their labours' is hard to parallel. Valley (1926: 69) compared ἀμελίᾳ δός in the sense 'apportion to what does not cause you concern' at E. *IA* 850 (where L and P read, unmetrically, ἀμελείᾳ), but the sense is not close enough to suggest that Longus had Euripides in mind.

κελευστὴς ναυτικὰς ᾖδεν ᾠδάς: the κελευστής, 'time-caller', important to keeping the rowers of a classical trireme in time, could be known to Longus from E. *Hel.* 1576, but it is just as likely he knew the term from one of the several prose texts in which it is found, e.g. Th. 2.84.3.

4.17.2 μυσάττεσθαι is not common in classical writing, and E. *Med.* 1149 (μυσαχθεῖσ') is one place Longus might have found it. But he could also know it (in the participial form μυσαττόμενον) from X. *Cyr.* 1.3.5 and he is not the only Second Sophistic writer to use it, cf. Luc. *Somn.* 8, *Prom. Es.* 4, *DMeretr.* 11.3.

4.18.1 μεγάλους ὁ Ἔρως ποιεῖ σοφιστάς. The speaker Astylos here surely alludes to the well-known line from Euripides' *Stheneboea* (fr. 663 Nauck): ποιητὴν δ' ἄρα | Ἔρως διδάσκει, κἂν ἄμουσος ᾖ τὸ πρίν ('Love instructs a man to be a poet, even if he did not know the Muse before'). The lines are much quoted by Plutarch and picked up in two hexameters (*SH* 566) which the scholiast on Theocritus claims to be a response by Nicias of Miletus to Theocritus 11: ἦν ἄρ' ἀληθὲς τοῦτο, Θεόκριτε· οἱ γὰρ Ἔρωτες | ποιητὰς πολλοὺς ἐδίδαξαν τοὺς πρὶν ἀμούσους.[8] Assessment of Longus' strategy is complicated by a further probable intertext, X. *Cyr.* 6.1.41, where the words νῦν τοῦτο πεφιλοσόφηκα μετὰ τοῦ ἀδίκου σοφιστοῦ τοῦ Ἔρωτος are spoken by Araspas in Xenophon's famous tale of his love for Pantheia (a story reworked in the second century CE, whether by the sophist Dionysius of Miletus or by the imperial secretary Celer, cf. Philostr. *VS* 1.22.524).

Given the other Euripidean intertexts that have seemed possible or even probable it should be allowed that here Longus does indeed evoke Euripides, especially since the *gnome* was clearly well known.

4.35.4 πλοῦτος ἐπέρρει: the phrase may recall E. *Med.* 1229 ὄλβου ἐπρρέοντος, though X. *Ap.* 27 has ἀγαθῶν ἐπιρρεόντων, and Chariton had already written πλοῦτος ... βασιλικὸς ... ἐπιρρέων (1.11.7). Longus himself a little earlier (4.23.1) had used ἐπίρρει of a πλῆθος θεραπόντων (cf. X. *Cyr.* 7.5.39, Pl. *Phdr.* 229d7, Theoc. 15.59). *Non liquet.*

AN EXPLANATION?

As I have already said, the above set of possible intertexts seems to me remarkably small in an author so richly intertextual as Longus. But it is not negligible. Two different sorts of explanation might be offered for the presence of tragic intertexts:

1. Longus might be using words that he saw as classical, poetic, or elevated but that he did not associate either with the genre tragedy in general or with tragic poets or any of their individual plays in particular. This explanation might indeed be correct for some cases

[8] See Hunter (1999: 221 on Theoc. 11).

(e.g. the phrase ἀνδρὸς ὁπλίτου at 1.20.2) and it must be borne in mind that some tragic vocabulary appears in most of the ambitious writers of the period and that a word's appearance in tragedy is cited by some lexicographers as a support for its Attic pedigree.[9] Even if this were how the phenomenon in Longus should be understood, it can still be argued that some tragic colour is bound to remain attached to words chosen as both high style and Attic if the guarantee of those registers is their presence in an Attic tragedy. But in fact the apparent verbal intertextuality with one or two particular passages in tragedy together with arguable intertextuality of content (e.g. the combination of fire and noise in the portents at 2.25.3, also found at E. *Ba.* 622–3) suggests that a more purposeful game is being played.

2. Longus' game may be to highlight important features of his own work by contrast with tragedy. The opening intertexts with Sopho-cles' *Antigone* and Euripides' *Hippolytus* are crucial for this effect.

The penultimate sentence of the preface 4, πάντως γὰρ οὐδεὶς Ἔρωτα ἔφυγεν ἢ φεύξεται, takes readers to a hymn to Ἔρως in a play (and in a genre) in which fraternal conflict destroys a whole family and where a young couple's ἔρως simply draws in yet another victim. Longus' own story, we shall discover, is of fruitful, not destructive, ἔρως, and is one in which the relations between Astylus and Daphnis are marked not by any fraternal conflict or jealousy but by solicitude and harmony. If we learn this lesson from the preface, it may be to remind us of it that Longus' use of μυδῶν at 3.28.2 to describe the 'rotting' body of the dolphin takes us to S. *Ant.* 410 and 1008. The lesson is hammered home by the evocation of *Ant.* 905–20 in Astylus' words at 4.24.3: κρεῖττον γὰρ τοῖς εὖ φρονοῦσιν ἀδελφοῦ κτῆμα οὐδέν.

The preface's next and final sentence takes readers to another hymn to Ἔρως, that of E. *Hipp.* 525–64, where the young women of Trozen pray for the *sôphrosynê* that is denied in different ways to Hippolytus and Phaedra. It focuses our attention on the issue of how ἔρως can be appropriately managed, and prepares us to see differences in its handling by Longus and by tragedians.

When the symptoms of desire are first described (1.13.5–14.1), a cluster of terms seems to evoke Euripides' *Medea* and *Hippolytus*:

---

[9] Though not by Moeris, as Claudia Strobel has pointed out to me.

other intertexts may also be claimed at 2.1.1, 3.4.5, 4.17.2 (see further below), and 4.35.4. That the principle point of contrast in the latter play is the chain of destructive consequences of Phaedra's ἔρως seems likely if my reading of the preface is correct: note the destructive power of Ἔρως which the chorus of *Hippolytus* picks out at 541–3 and which greatly outweighs its gentler qualities in the stasimon as a whole. It might be confirmed by the *Hippolytus* intertext of φάρμακον at 1.22.3 and 2.7.7. The contrast is again brought out in the virtually certain intertext with the *Stheneboea* at 4.18.1, where Astylus' comment on Gnathon's speech also invites us to compare different genres' application of the motif. But *Hippolytus* also displays brutal and uncaring treatment of a child by a parent: that too is a story pattern which is developed by *Daphnis and Chloe* (as it is by Comedy), in such a way that fathers make potentially destructive decisions, but that these decisions are not irreversible, and a happy reunion of parent and child is somehow achieved. The destruction of children by a divinely maddened parent is of course a central theme of Euripides' *Heracles* and *Bacchae*: the contrast with the judicious and (by and large) controlled behaviour of the parents of Daphnis and Chloe in Book 4 may then be one of the reasons for the certain intertexts with *Heracles* at 2.5.1 and *Bacchae* at 2.25.3 and for those that can be argued for at 1.20.2 (*Heracles*) and 1.15.2, 20.3 (*Bacchae*).

What can be adduced in favour of this line of interpretation? In a piece written a decade ago but only recently published I argued for an analogous function for the three inset tales (at 1.27, 2.34, and 3.23). I was to some extent concerned to challenge the view of Jack Winkler[10] that the sexual violence perpetrated by Pan against Nymphs in the second and third of the inset tales (and alluded to in a song sung by the cowgirl in the first) is in some way a warning of violence that Chloe will herself experience when she loses her virginity: instead I proposed that the inset tales' pattern of domination of females by males contrasted with the behaviour of Daphnis and Chloe at all stages in Longus' story, and at no point is imitated by them.[11] This argument can now be taken further. The mythological world of the inset tales—divine lust leading to destruction or metamorphosis of a girl who is not herself immortal—is part of a nexus of tales drawn

---

[10] Winkler (1990).   [11] Bowie (2003: esp. 372).

upon by Attic tragedy (e.g. the story of Semele) and more generally
by archaic, classical, and hellenistic narrative poetry, even if the
particular myths of Syrinx and Echo were probably first developed
in hellenistic poetry,[12] while the origins of the Pitys story are uncer-
tain. In confining destructive consequences of sexual attraction to his
inset tales, firmly described as μῦθοι,[13] Longus contrasts the characteristic actions of gods and sufferings of mortals in traditional Greek
mythology with their handling in his own sort of story.

This is not to say that Longus does not also engage in other intertextual games. For example, the use of *Stheneboea* fr. 663 Nauck (see
above) has been seen to draw in—by its change of ποιητὴν to
σοφιστάς—one of the novel's classical models, Xenophon's *Cyropai-
deia*. We are thus invited to speculate whether the writer of our text is
himself a practising σοφιστής, and even whether he too owes his
sophistic skill to his subject Eros. Our readerly reaction to the words
may be further modulated by our awareness of their relation to the
opening and theme of Theocritus 11, a poem which has been evoked
repeatedly throughout *Daphnis and Chloe*. On this assessment,
the exploitation of Euripidean tragedy in Longus' work can on
occasion significantly modify its impact by fusing it with other,
more novelistic genres.

A further detail in Longus' narrative might seem to confirm the
above nexus of hypotheses—that a number of intertexts with Attic
tragedy function as pointers to contrasts between the texture of tragedy
and that of Longus' narrative, and that the inset tales likewise point up a
contrast between novelistic narrative and traditional mythological narrative. When the parasite Gnathon pleads with his young master
Astylus to be given Daphnis, his two highly emotional, over-the-top
speeches are broken by Astylus' response to the first: Astylus promises
to ask his father to give Daphnis to Gnathon, but then 'asked with
a smile if he felt no embarrassment kissing Lamon's son, but was
actually keen to lie down with a lad who tended goats' (ἐπυνθάνετο
μειδιῶν εἰ οὐκ αἰσχύνεται Λάμωνος υἱὸν φιλῶν ἀλλὰ καὶ σπουδάζει
συγκατακλιθῆναι νέμοντι αἶγας μειρακίῳ, 4.17.2). Longus then gives a
stage direction: καὶ ἅμα ὑπεκρίνετο τὴν τραγικὴν δυσωδίαν
μυσάττεσθαι. How should this be understood? On the surface it seems

----

[12] So persuasively Morgan (2004: 196, 215).   [13] See Bowie (2003: 365).

to mean what all translators have decided it must mean: 'and at the same time he acted out revulsion at the foul smell of goats'. But the term ὑπεκρίνετο should give us pause. It is of course the regular term for an actor playing a stage role (cf. LSJ s.v. ὑπεκρίνω B.II.1), and once we are taken on stage our reading of τραγικὴν has to be re-examined. In by far the greatest number of cases τραγικός means 'tragic' (cf. LSJ s.v. τραγικός II). Among the very few instances where it means 'goatish' is a passage in Plato's *Cratylus* (408c7) where it seems at the same time to mean 'tragic' *and* 'goatish'. Here too, in Longus, I suggest we are invited to read on two levels: alongside revulsion at the foul smell of goats Astylus is 'acting out' revulsion at tragedy. The revulsion is occasioned by the rhetoric of Gnathon's total domination by ἔρως, culminating in his threat to seize a dagger and kill himself (4.16.4)— rhetoric which reworks, albeit in a parodic and comic register, the despair of a tragic lover. It is perhaps a deliberate tactic by Longus to have held back this ambiguous adjective τραγικός for use in this *coup de théâtre*: it is surely surprising that in a novel heavily populated by goats the writer has somehow had no occasion to use the adjective earlier.[14]

That such a reading is appropriate may be supported by further points.

First, the register of Gnathon's emotional and exaggerated outburst is what some writers of the second and third centuries CE call τραγῳδία,[15] or for which they use the verb τραγῳδεῖν.[16] The use is one which can be traced back to a passage in Plato's *Cratylus* (414c4) a few pages after that which offers the punning senses 'tragic' and 'goatish' for τραγικός. It is true that a male lover is rare in tragedy and very common in New Comedy,[17] and that as I noted in my introduction Gnathon is very much a character evocative of New Comedy. But it is not beyond Longus' skill in fusing intertextualities to offer us a character who both recalls a comic stereotype and reminds us of tragedy by his flowery, paratragic rhetoric.[18]

---

[14] This point was made to me (along with other helpful points) in a discussion following delivery of a version of this paper at a Kyknos conference at Gregynog on 19 May 2005.

[15] Plu. *On the Pythian Oracles* 400c, *Against Colotes* 1119c.

[16] Plu. *Dem.* 21.2, Arr. *Epict.* 4.7.15, Hld. 2.11.2 (and ἐπιτραγῳδεῖν 1.3).

[17] I am grateful to Helene Foley for drawing my attention to this point.

[18] We should recall that a male comic version of female tragic ἔρως goes back as far as Aristophanes' *Wasps*.

Secondly, Astylus' reaction to Gnathon's second speech suggests that he hears in it the tones of τραγῳδία: it is precisely in this reaction (4.18.1) that he unambiguously evokes Euripides' *Stheneboea* in his exclamation μεγάλους ὁ Ἔρως ποιεῖ σοφιστάς.

Thirdly, there may also be a pun lurking in δυσωδίαν. The element -ῳδία is one that in this period would be chiefly familiar from the artistic technical terms αὐλῳδία, ἱλαρῳδία, κιθαρῳδία, κωμῳδία, and, of course, the granny of them all, τραγῳδία. In these compounds the sense of -ῳδία is 'singing'. So τὴν τραγικὴν δυσωδίαν might be read as 'the foul singing of tragedy' as well as 'the foul smell of goats'. It is important to bear in mind that in most documents of this period, as in not a few literary papyri,[19] *iota* adscript is not written.

CONCLUSIONS

Astylus' response to Gnathon's emoting matches the game the narrator plays with tragic intertexts and with the destructive erotic myths of the inset tales. Longus wants us to contrast the type of story about desire, ἔρως, that he and his novelistic predecessors tell from that preponderant in classical mythology in general and in tragedy in particular. As far as we can tell Attic tragedy never explores stories of mutual and symmetrical desire nor does it present a positive image of female desire (i.e. one that does not lead to destruction). Both symmetrical desire and a positive image of female ἔρως are crucial to the discourse of the novel. The clue that Longus plants in Astylus' speech of course stretches our readerly credulity: is he pulling our leg? When we recall the 'learned' and internally inconsistent digressions of 1.30.6 and 2.1.4, parodying the recurrent exploitation of this trope by Achilles Tatius, we can see that there Longus is surely pulling our leg. Why not concede, then, that at 4.17.2 he is pulling the other?

[19] e.g. *P. Oxy.* 2301 fr. 4(b) (Alcaeus) line 8.

15

Envisioning the Tragic Chorus on the
Modern Stage

Helene P. Foley

Many contemporary performances of Greek tragedy include a chorus
of one to three actors that neither sings nor dances and, for an
audience accustomed to realistic theatre, often appears to impede
the action and awkwardly clutter the set. For example, in a 1998
Broadway production of Sophocles' *Electra* starring Zoe Wanamaker
and directed by David Leveaux that stressed psychological realism, a
maternal chorus of three had little to do but prosaically underline the
heroine's heavily Freudian neuroses. By contrast, Sophocles' chorus
originally created an initially resistant but ultimately dynamic and
politically engaged community of fellow lamenters and avengers. The
style, movement, and language of larger tragic choruses can also
appear painfully artificial and unfamiliar. Productions in contemporary Greece typically include large, well-rehearsed choruses that
both sing and dance choral odes and often take advantage of familiar
native music and dance traditions; but outside Greece twentieth- and
twenty-first-century directors rarely present tragedies in which the
chorus comes close to competing with or even upstaging the actors
dramatically. When the French director Ariane Mnouchkine used
large, spectacularly costumed choruses to international acclaim in
her 1990 *Les Atrides* (Euripides' *Iphigeneia at Aulis* plus Aeschylus'
Oresteia) at the Théâtre du Soleil in Paris, their electrifying inter-
cultural music and dance eclipsed the chorus's dense and complex

words, which were spoken exclusively by the chorus leader in a fashion that made it difficult to engage with them.

Productions of Greek tragedy that attempt to include some version of the full range of song and dance, on the part of both actors and chorus, found in the originals are remarkably rare. Given the recent successful collaborations between dance groups and singers in opera performances and important developments in dance theatre, it is surprising, despite a growing interest in the production of Greek tragedy on the modern stage, how rarely directors of Greek tragedy have even gestured in this direction. Indeed, many modern adaptations or new versions of Greek tragedy even eliminate the chorus altogether. The expense and the rehearsal time involved in mounting a large chorus that can sing and dance as it did in the original plays is and was at the time a critical factor. Yet there are many other reasons why a chorus has stood in the way of or occasionally enhanced a successful modern revival or adaptation. Among the major factors to be discussed below, it is impossible to reproduce the complex original relation between audience and performance on the modern stage; familiar choral traditions associated with opera and musicals can distort an audience's reception of the very different Greek tragic chorus; above all, creating any undifferentiated collectivity on stage runs counter to modern ideas about the individual's complex and ambivalent relation to social groups and the representation of this relation in performance. Nevertheless, in this essay I am more interested in what kinds of approaches have been most interesting and/or successful in revitalizing choral performance on the contemporary stage. Before moving on to recent modern productions and adaptations, however, I shall review some of the major features of the chorus in Greek tragedy that will be critical for thinking about choral performance and the general difficulties and opportunities that the chorus has posed for twentieth-century artists.

First, the role and reception of the Greek tragic chorus originally depended very much on performance.[1] A masked chorus of twelve or later fifteen occupied the orchestra or dancing space close to the audience; it usually entered from outside the stage building and

---

[1] On the ancient evidence, see Pickard-Cambridge (1988), Csapo and Slater (1995), Wilson (2000).

rarely went into it. The audience to the performance could not avoid its highly visible and largely continuous presence and although actors could sing and dance, song and dance were the defining activities of the chorus. Choral costumes were lavish, and choral training in voice and movement extensive (about six months). Tragedy as a genre is thought to have grown out of choral performance, and in the early fifth century BCE at least, the choral tradition was likely to have been far more developed than the acting tradition that ultimately eclipsed it in later centuries. Indeed, much ancient evidence shows that the success of each poet's set of three tragedies and a satyr play depended critically on choral performance and that the judges of the dramatic contests, who had all participated in choruses from boyhood, were connoisseurs of choral practice.[2]

The chorus mediated not only spatially, but temporally and formally between audience and actors. Its act-dividing songs could mark a lapse of time between episodes, serve to anticipate or to link episodes thematically and through repeated images, and to intensify dramatic tension or to provide release from it. It could help to direct or channel the emotional response or expectations of the audience. When it referred to its own or other choral performance in its songs, it could draw attention both to its own performance and to its ritual function.[3] Its use of religious invocation, prayer, and hymnic forms, to say nothing of its meditations on the role of the divine in human action, also drew the audience's attention more often than the characters did to the religious dimensions or implications of tragic performance.

The chorus was a repository of cultural memory, largely in the form of traditional myth. It tried to make sense of past, present, and future events through these myths, and through the citation of traditional wisdom, although it rarely succeeded in doing so. Hence the audience could not rely on the chorus's judgement to interpret the action, although it could relate to the choral struggle to do so.

Although its social status within the plays was lower than that of the royal figures represented by the actors, the language and performance of the tragic chorus, at least when it was singing, drew from

---

[2] Foley (2003: 2–12) with earlier bibliography.
[3] See especially Henrichs (1995) and (1996).

an archaic tradition that put it on a higher level, stylistically, than the actors, at least when the actors spoke. Shared songs by chorus and actors moved them both to another plane. The chorus's shifts from speech to recitative to song also gave it a wide range of different 'voices' in performance.[4] Choral language is often difficult, at least to us. To a culture that grew up with these traditions and experienced them through performance they may have been far more accessible; Aristophanes' parody of Aeschylus' lyrics in his *Frogs* suggests, however, that choral language could be obscure even for his near contemporaries. Nevertheless, the complexity, metaphorical density, and at times distanced quality of choral language may be precisely what permitted it to resonate and generalize meaning on many levels.

The choral role was also formally limited, especially in relation to actors, in a number of dimensions. It could engage in dialogue with the actors, but rarely made speeches of any length. Only once in extant tragedy, in Aeschylus' *Agamemnon*, did it break into twelve separate voices. In extant tragedy the chorus represented a particular, often marginal group within a community, never the political community of Athens itself, which consisted above all of male citizens of Athens of various ages.[5] Most choruses represented women and old men, largely from cities other than Athens, foreigners, slaves, or, more rarely, soldiers.[6] Choruses, like the actors, were often far more ignorant of the outcome of myths and less able to interpret the action than the audience itself, and hence ironically divided from that audience in this respect. Choruses are said to be incapable of initiating or taking action, and hence morally inferior to the actors. They reputedly survive unscathed while the actors often meet with major changes of fortune. I have recently argued that there are major flaws in these last two generalizations; choruses can act and be put at risk, even to the same degree as characters, even if this occurs relatively rarely. What I think we can say is that choruses tend to have or display far less capacity for leadership than many principals,

---

[4] Silk (1998a).

[5] On the composition of the audience, see especially Henderson (1991) and Goldhill (1994*b*).

[6] On choral identity, see especially Goldhill (1996), Gould (1996), and Foley (2003).

and can often be dependent on or acolytes of a particular character.[7] Choruses whose primary loyalty is to the city (most often old men) differ from those whose primary focus is on the fate of a particular household or a particular hero or heroine (above all, some female and military choruses).[8]

The choruses of the three major poets differed in many ways in terms of their degree of involvement in the action, the length of their songs and the amount of sung engagement with the actors, and in the content of their meditations. Some choral odes were far more free-floating and detached from the action than others. Choruses could increase their engagement in the action as the play proceeded and/or become gradually silenced. For the modern reader or viewer of tragedy these many variations in choral role make it harder to grasp; so does the tendency of many translations not to indicate to the modern artist or reader which parts of the original were sung, danced, recited, spoken, or accompanied by music.

Before we go any further then, a number of general problems for modern performance of the chorus have emerged. First, problems relating to production, including expense and difficulties for choral performance posed by an indoor proscenium as opposed to an outdoor arena stage, which changes the chorus's theatrical relation to the audience, remain critical. (Modern outdoor performances or reconfigured indoor spaces by no means recreate the original relation between audience and performance, however.) The apparent lack of familiarity with choral and tragic form and non-naturalistic theatre sometimes said to impede its reception by a modern audience is in my view something of a red herring. Contemporary theatre in both East and West has by now experimented for some time with theatrically eclectic and non-naturalistic performances. The chorus of Greek tragedy helps to make family drama a public matter, and contemporary playwrights and directors have often seized on this opportunity because of the frequent absence of comparable public contexts in other central artistic forms of the culture (such as film or television drama).[9] Some playwrights, such as the American

---

[7] Foley (2003: 14–19).

[8] See Foley (2003: 19–25), which cites earlier bibliography.

[9] Exceptions, such as Woody Allen's *Mighty Aphrodite*, turned to Greek drama to produce a humorous version of choral comment.

playwright Peter Morris, have even included choruses in contemporary plays not based on Greek drama to create a public or communal setting as well; a staged reading of his *The Salivation Army* took place at New York City's Soho Rep in 2004. Moreover, the most popular theatrical form in the United States, for example, remains the musical. However different the choral roles in musicals (or in opera and dance) are from those in Greek tragedy, the artifices involved in deploying choruses are in principle familiar and many high-school students have come of age performing in such roles. I could even go so far as to argue that some plots of musicals deliberately adapt Greek tragedy; *The Music Man*, for example, is in many ways the *Bacchae* moved to the mid-West. Here a travelling con-artist mesmerizes a frontier town with the promise of music and dance. Though he is nearly run out of town, his scheme eventually wins enough converts to become an unexpected reality. Nevertheless, the expectations generated by an audience's familiarity with musicals or opera can also interfere with its reception of the very different Greek tragic chorus.

The chorus's religious and ritual dimension and its complex political relation to its original community cannot be recreated for an eclectic modern audience that does not have the shared historical and cultural experience of the Attic polis. Once again, however, some comparable if different performance contexts can be exploited to reproduce some of the energy generated by the Attic context. Church services have increasingly imported and created new rituals by drawing on contemporary music and performance and theatrical techniques (see my discussion of Breuer's *Gospel at Colonus* below). Choral reactions of the kind represented in tragedy are also not unknown in modern contexts and performances can explore these possibilities. Interviews with survivors of the 9/11 disaster by the Columbia University oral history program, for example, show a consistent effort to understand each miraculous survival in terms of divine causes, luck, or sheer human ingenuity.[10] At their best, the media or journalists also create from similar interviews a kind of choral reaction to current events that preserves the integrity of

---

[10] I am grateful to Jessica Wiederhorn of the Columbia Oral History project for sharing some of this unpublished material with me.

individual voices. Some recent remakings of Greek tragedy have played on the role of the media to create a 'choral' perspective on the action. For example, in Theater Faction's 2004 eclectic new version of the *Oresteia* in New York, Erik Nelson's *Agamemnon* began with Clytaemnestra chalking up logical syllogisms and ethical queries about good effects of bad actions on blackboards while passers-by on Eighth Avenue became a chorus on video by replying to questions about whether a wife could justly kill her husband if he had killed one of her daughters.

The chorus's language and its often condensed mythological references create another set of barriers, even in translations adapted for the stage. Certain Greek myths are, however, at least partially familiar to audiences in countries ranging from the US and Europe to Japan and formerly colonial Africa and the importance of recovering, preserving, and re-evaluating cultural memories is now pervasive in an increasingly diverse world. Programme notes, prologues, relatively minor revisions in translations, or supertitles for choral songs, can go a long way towards making a chorus engaging in cases where a director wishes to pursue this option. Robert Woodruff's chorus in a 2004 production of Sophocles' *Oedipus Rex* at the American Repertory Theatre in Cambridge, Mass. arrestingly sang their odes in ancient Greek (with English supertitles) to music by Evan Ziporyn and the performance included some speeches from the actors delivered in Greek that were sung in the original (for example, the blinded Oedipus' first words to the chorus). The alienation produced by the incomprehensible language served to underline for the audience the different mode represented by a tragic chorus and its complex relation to the action; at the same time, the supertitles permitted it to focus on the meaning of the words without being diverted from the power of the music and movement.

The chorus's unified group personality and the supposed limitations on its engagement in the action have raised complex class and other ideological and theatrical issues for Western audiences. Nineteenth-century European critics of the chorus, for example, began to find the chorus's group identity problematic in a world where the individual had apparently become paramount and communal consciousness on all issues, whether religious, social, or political, was thought to be divided or non-existent. In Wagner's view, for example, the putatively conservative and cautious choral voice could impede the revolutionary thrust of art. For these reasons he came to reject the chorus even in opera, where it was a fixture, and proposed to replace it with the relation between singer and orchestra. Others, such as the Irish poet Yeats, turned to the chorus in the late nineteenth–early twentieth century to revive a vaguely defined communal identity, but did not in fact follow through effectively on these ideas in his plays. For Friedrich von Schiller (see his 1803 *Die Braut von Messina*) the chorus served as a tool to counter the growing naturalism of the contemporary stage, but his experiment did not generate followers until the twentieth century.[11] In my view, many of these nineteenth-century views are based on partial misapprehensions about choral function, identity, and performance in Greek tragedy, (e.g. interpreting the chorus as an ideal spectator or representative of the whole community), but were nevertheless influential. The ambivalence of nineteenth-century critics about choral performance left an unfortunate legacy to twentieth- and twenty-first-century artists; at the same time, the problem of producing a viable collective voice on the modern stage remains compelling and problematic.

Nevertheless, late nineteenth- and early-twentieth-century Germany left another more provocative heritage that has recently been exploited in new attempts to revitalize the chorus. Wagner's aesthetic writings celebrating the creation of 'total artworks' (*Gesamtkunstwerke*) that drew on all the performance arts, above all on the vital mixture of poetry, dance, and song that defined theatrical performance in antiquity, proved highly infectious. For example, the famous productions of *Oedipus Rex* by the Austrian-born director Max Reinhardt aimed to exploit theatre as the form of community ritual it originally was. These productions, which took place throughout Europe and later in the US (perhaps most famously in the Circus Schumann in Berlin in 1910, and in 1912 at Covent Garden in London), planted the chorus and crowds of suppliants to Oedipus between the audience and the stage in large, reconfigured public spaces. Actors entered from and exited into the larger audience. Dramatic lighting, music, colourful costume, movement, and non- or even anti-naturalistic staging appealed to and nearly overwhelmed

---

[11] Silk (1998*b*).

the senses in a fashion that proportionally reduced the contribution of words and the speaking voice if not the importance of the actor.[12] This attempt to recreate an albeit temporary 'community' through the power of multidimensional performance itself has been revived in various new forms by directors such as André Serban, Lee Breuer, and Richard Schechner in their remakings of Greek tragedy to be discussed below.

Recent twentieth-century performances and adaptations or re-makings of tragedy have sometimes developed a new interest in and rationale for the chorus nevertheless; in different ways, each of the performances discussed below directly confronts the problem of staging a collective voice/identity in an era firmly attached to pre-serving individual ones. A significant range of artists, for example, has been attracted to the chorus, especially if not exclusively to Euripidean choruses, either to express group suffering in the wake of twentieth-century wars or group complicity in historical events. Performances of Euripides' *Trojan Women* in multiple contexts have most typically served the former impulse. In the wake of World War II and twentieth-century communist and fascist movements, play-wrights and directors have used the chorus to explore historical attempts to generate new collectivities. Bertolt Brecht's adaptation of *Antigone*, first performed in Switzerland in 1948, is an example of the latter impulse earlier in the century, that has been followed by later artists in various forms. Although Greek tragic choruses (such as that of Euripides' *Iphigeneia among the Taurians*) can become complicit with the actors and participate in their plots and decep-tions, twentieth-century versions of the plays can considerably en-hance, draw attention to, as well as call into question this aspect of the plays. Brecht's chorus of old men is deeply complicit with his Creon throughout. In this play, the tyrant Creon has engaged in an imperialistic war of aggression to acquire wealth in the form of metal from the mountains of Argos. In its first speech, the chorus does not celebrate peace, as does Sophocles' chorus, but greedily anticipates the returning spoils of war. Sophocles' famous choral ode on man (*Antigone* 332–75) becomes in Brecht's version a meditation on human greed and monstrosity. Soon the chorus, instead of giving

---

[12] For a useful summary of these aspects of Reinhardt's theatre, see Styan (1982).

up its festal celebration of peace at Creon's first entrance as in Sophocles, begins to enter into a celebratory orgy in honor of the god Dionysus that distracts them from loss, mourning, and the absence of the young men, who have not yet returned from battle. After hearing predictions by Antigone and Tiresias about the city's fate, the chorus discovers from Creon that the war is in fact not going as well as it had thought. The elders face the fact that tyrants, as Brecht's Antigone had warned, eventually begin to treat their own countrymen as enemies. But this revelation is too late; a messenger arrives to announce a disastrous defeat of the army and the death of Creon's son Menoeceus; Creon soon returns with the bloody shirt of his dead son Haimon. Despite its disillusionment with Creon, however, the chorus closes the play by vowing to follow their leader, even if from now on the city's course will be all downhill. In this adaptation, whose relevance to recent events in Nazi Germany hardly needs elaborating, the chorus is critical to Brecht's exploration of cultural responsibility for historical disasters and the role of collaborators and those who passively tolerate imperialistic policies.

The Japanese director Suzuki Tadashi's 1981 version of the *Bacchae* shifted the focus more pointedly to nationalism and religion. He had his chorus, wrapped in the red and white Japanese naval flag, follow the god Dionysus like puppets. In their mesmerized resistance to the tyrant Pentheus, they apparently suggested Japanese subservience to authority in World War II, or, because the chorus included both Japanese and Western actors and the production emphasized the problems of East–West communication, adherents of Hitler or American flag-worshippers as well. The choral implication in the action was grimly underlined when one of the bacchic followers of the god accompanied the returning Agave with an arm that she dropped during her dazed wanderings on the stage.[13]

Peter Stein's 1980 *Oresteia* in Berlin used the relation between chorus, characters, and audience to suggest a different kind of ominous collective urge to silence the past still lingering in post-war Germany. At the close of *Agamemnon* the chorus of old men took off

---

[13] For further interpretation and detail, see the discussion of Suzuki's *Bacchae* by McDonald (1992: esp. 64–8 and 70). Suzuki has in fact produced many versions of his *Bacchae* over a period of years.

their jackets and, as actors, began to remove from the stage the traces of the violence that had just occurred during the play. But, the production insisted, such terrible acts and memories are not so easily erased. In *Eumenides* the Furies lurked between audience and raised stage in genderless dark costumes that clearly defined their inhuman character. Their divine anger over the outcome of the trial took the form of a terrifying collective sound that blasted the jurors from their seats and set them in conflict with each other. A persuasive Athena gradually brought each pacified Fury on to the stage by hand; there they received purple cloaks and were led down from the stage again by the goddess and the jury, who settled them in a bound row at the bottom of the stage. The trilogy closed with the suggestion that the insect-like Furies, who may well have been illegitimately tricked into submission, would hatch from their chrysalis at another time in the very theatre where the performance took place.[14]

Alternatively, collective identities generated in response to gender issues became increasingly specific in the 1990s and later. The 2003 version of *Medea* directed by Satoshi Miyagi for the Ku na'uka Theatre Company in Tokyo created a 'chorus' of pointedly male narrators of Euripides' text. The play opened as the men selected a group of women, who were standing with paper bags over their heads imprinted with their photographs, to play the parts. The men's offhand remarks clearly indicated their traditional attitudes to the women who went on, in Bunraku style, to enact silently the text recited by men, who were seated on a low platform around the stage. In this production, however, the female 'puppets' eventually broke out of the text and killed the narrators as a rain of books fell from the top of the stage. Miyagi's challenge to both Euripides' version of the myth and the conventions of male-dominated theatrical traditions was broadened through creating a collective male responsibility for the performance that was ultimately resisted collectively by the exploited women.

Other directors or adapters of tragedy, especially those who are interested in cultural memory, have given a prominent role to the chorus that can play off individual voices against a collective one created by war and suffering. A 2004 performance of *Agamemnon* by the Aquila

[14] On Stein's production, see esp. Fischer-Lichte (2004: 344–52) and Bierl (1996).

Theater Company at the John Jay Theatre in New York City gave the
choral lines to seven individuals in an unbroken sequence. Each
chorus member had a characteristic 'voice' or perspective on the
action and spoke lines or adopted a tone and set of movements
that fitted his particular character. The chorus remained a group
with a consistent set of tensions between its members and the royal
family (above all Clytaemnestra), yet preserved throughout a sense of
different individual interpretations of the evolving action. Both performances and remakings of Greek tragedy in this category sometimes break down a group sharing in collective suffering into
individualized voices with a range of specific stories that substitute
contemporary memories for mythical ones.[15] Among various recent
performances of Euripides' *Trojan Women*, the Classical Theater of
Harlem's 2004 performance interwove excerpts taken from the experiences of African refugees with Euripides' choral stasima. Charles
Mee's more radical revision of Euripides, *The Trojan Women: A Love
Story,* repeatedly orchestrated a movement from individual story to
shared catastrophe. Here is a brief excerpt that weaves together
different experiences by chorus members of moments during the
'fall of Troy'. Significantly, the scene reverses choral and principal
roles, as Hecuba and Andromache cannot in this scene understand
the choral stories or speak their own. Those familiar with the choral
ode from Euripides' *Hecuba* (905–51) that offers a vignette of a
Trojan wife's experience of the fall that begins in her bedroom and
moves to disaster will recognize its influence on this passage.[16] In the
original ode, one wife's last night momentarily stands in for all. In
Mee's version each chorus member's experience of and relation to
catastrophe is not only deliberately different, but contradicts that of
others. Yet in other scenes, this same group has no choice but to face
captivity and their lot as victims of war collectively, and their shared
circumstances make this compelling.

[15] For performances that challenged the possibility of creating a unified community either of chorus members or spectators, see Fischer-Lichte (2004: 337–59) on
Klaus Michael Grüber's 1974 *Bacchae* and Einar Schleff's 1986 *The Mothers*.

[16] Mee 1998: 164–6. The earliest productions were done in 1996 at University of
Washington in Seattle and by En Garde Arts (directed by Tina Landau) in New York
City.

CHORUS MEMBER 2, SEI:
I had just come into the room and said 'good morning',
and suddenly it turned bright red.
I felt hot on my cheeks,
and when I came to,
I realized everyone was lying
on one side to the room.
No one was standing.
The chairs were all blown to one side.
There was no window glass.
My white shirt was red all over.
I thought it was funny because
I wasn't hurt.
I looked around
And then I realized
That the girl lying next to me had pieces
Of broken glass stuck all over her body.
Her blood had splashed onto my shirt.
And she had bits of wood stuck into her.

SEI: I had been holding my son in my arms,
when a young woman in front of me said, 'Please
take this seat.'
We were just changing places
when suddenly there was a strange sound.
All at once it was dark
And before I knew it,
I had jumped outside.
Fragments of glass had lodged in my son's head.
But he looked at my face and smiled.
He did not understand what had happened.
I had plenty of milk
which he drank all that day.
I think my child sucked the poison right out of my body.
And soon after that
he died.

HECUBA: Why was this done?

   [ANDROMACHE rushes down front again and picks
up a microphone, tries to speak. She still cannot. Puts down
the microphone and retreats upstage.]

ELSA: I was sitting in a box at the opera,
dressed in a new gown.
My hair was done up so beautifully.
And when it came to the line,
'There is the devil',
a company of enemy soldiers ran in,
stomping their feet,
and came right up to me.
They had a secret machine
that had told them
that when I heard the word devil I thought of their general.
I looked around for help,
but everyone in the audience was staring straight ahead,
not even showing pity for what I'd got myself into.
An elderly gentleman in the box next to mine
looked over at me,
but when I started to speak to him,
he spit in my face.

AIMABLE: I was at a movie,
a very large theater, very dark,
a downtown theater,
and I knew it was wrong for me to be there.
Only enemy soldiers were allowed there.
And their general came in and sat next to me.
And I was more scared than ever.
But he put his arm around me.
[Tears come to her eyes.]
And I felt comforted.
He put his hand on me.
Inside my thigh.
And I liked it.

Recent performances look beyond politically created collectivities to more symbolic ones as well. Choruses in other productions, building on the close identity between, for example, tragic female or military choruses with their same sex protagonist in the original plays, can become visible extensions of the hero or heroine's psyche. The sixteen-man chorus of Yukio Ninagawa's Japanese *Medea* (performed in various venues from 1978 to 1999) which did not sing, but played music on the Tsugaru shamisen and used considerable choreographed movement, was particularly interesting for the way in which it echoed the heroine's divided self. After Medea first decided to take revenge on Jason for his betrayal of her, the chorus recited its famous ode about how Medea's story has inverted a female reputation for inconstancy that was falsely claimed in songs and stories written by men (*Medea* 410–45). Medea and her complicit chorus borrowed a Kabuki/Bunraku tradition by drawing red ribbons from their mouths to the accompaniment of music similar to Handel's 'Lascia ch'io pianga' ('Leave me to anguish') from *Rinaldo* or Corelli's *La Follia*. These ribbons represented blood but also, as Mae Smethurst has pointed out, the gesture violently inverts another Japanese tradition in which girls put ribbons attached to their hats into their mouths to exhibit love coyly.[17] Here Medea and the chorus together spat out love and took up revenge. The chorus shared the heroine's growing sense of empowerment, as Ninagawa intended the women in his audience to do as well.[18]

Similarly, Suzuki Tadashi's various versions of Sophocles' *Electra* set the play in a psychiatric hospital.[19] The chorus of patients are thus visibly implicated in the heroine's madness/confinement/abasement. The brilliant choreography includes a choral dance in wheelchairs that mesmerizingly captures a collective confinement to 'spinning their wheels' by Clytaemnestra.[20] Finally, the American director Peter Sellars cast a deaf actor as the hero in his version of Sophocles' *Ajax* (translated and adapted by Robert Auletta, 1986): the actor, Howie Seago, used sign language, but his lines were largely spoken by members of the chorus (or at one point, by his wife, Tecmessa.) This device expressed both the painful dependence on and implication in the fate of Ajax felt by his family and followers and the hero's alienation from them, his different language and sensibility. Each of these choruses, by writing the protagonist's psychological conflicts large, in a sense functioned in a (nevertheless not naturalistic) mode that does not conflict with a modern audience's expectations about dramatic representations of individual psyches.

---

[17] Smethurst (2000: 198) and (2002: 13).
[18] Smethurst (2000: 191–2, 202–3) and (2002: 1, 4, 15, and 32).
[19] I viewed a performance at Japan Society in New York in 2001.
[20] The wheelchair motif is inspired by Beckett's *Endgame*.

Some theatre groups that have begun to experiment with aspects of choral performance have found new and different potential in its sound and movement. In general, various theatre groups and directors in this category are interested in drawing on a mix of various world theatre traditions or on a range of folk traditions to produce theatre that communicates non-verbally across cultural boundaries. Sound, music, movement, and invented rituals are used to communicate tragic ideas, often at the expense of comprehensible words and sometimes even at the expense of narrative. In this kind of context, the newly defined chorus becomes the centre of theatrical energy out of which actors with individual stories can emerge and disappear. These plays take the impulse of Max Reinhardt mentioned earlier to create a ritual context or collectivity through multidimensional performances in new directions.[21] They also recreate in a new context the choral group of singers and dancers out of which Greek drama is thought originally to have emerged; at the same time, their deliberate eclecticism liberates the plays from any particular cultural context.

For example, a Polish experimental theatre group Gardzienice developed a piece called *Metamorphoses* (*Metamophozy*) that it presented at La Mama ETC in New York in 2001.[22] The piece was based on fragments of ancient Greek music reconstructed from inscriptions and papyrus fragments. The performance developed these musical fragments using both instrumental and vocal inspiration from Eastern European and Balkan folk traditions. The group's movement was also developed from dance steps and poses in Greek art. The resulting piece had no real narrative, but aimed to recuperate the Dionysiac energy of earlier pagan traditions repressed and distorted over the centuries in the view of the director by a moralizing Christianity.

Others have developed new versions of Greek tragedies through the use of music and movement. In the early 1970s (1972–4), the Romanian Director André Serban produced with composer Elizabeth Swados a set of three remakings of Greek tragedy, *Fragments of a Greek Trilogy*. The plays were performed with new casts at various

---

[21] Reinhardt is by no means the only influence. Serban, for example, was directly inspired by Peter Brook's 1970–1 *Orghast*.

[22] A CD, Gardzienice, *Metamorphozy, Music of Ancient Greece*, is available from Altmaster sp. Z o. o. 5423692 (2000).

intervals in the next twenty years at La Mama ETC in New York City (four times, including spring 2004) and in a number of other countries. All three of the plays presented, new versions of Euripides' *Medea* and *Trojan Women* and Sophocles' *Electra,* used language incomprehensible to the audience—ancient Greek, Latin with a smattering of African and Amerindian languages—in performances that closely echoed the shape of the original plots but reduced them to a skeleton of the original. The actors and chorus tried to capitalize on the phonetic force of ancient tongues to create a 'ballet for the mouth' and to 'inhabit their bodies' with the sound of ancient texts, using every possible human body cavity as a resonator to discover what enabled Greek actors to project and produce intense communication with an audience and its gods in a huge open space.[23] Techniques of integrating voice, body, and movement borrowed from Noh, Kathakali, Kabuki, and Balinese theatrical traditions were used to tap what Serban called the 'energy' that produced the ideas of the texts. The music was deliberately drawn from a mix of world traditions and the varied movement often became a form of invented ritual.

Serban avoided settings with a proscenium stage, which at times brought the audience into the play or challenged its relation to it. For example, the audience for *Trojan Women* was led in a festal procession into a large rectangular space framed by scaffolding on all four sides, with a platform at the back from which a ramp and stairs could be lowered. In the first performance the theatre was initially pitch black, and members of the audience were soon separated from their friends by soldiers who pushed through the crowd with groups of Trojan prisoners. Scenes—some only partially visible depending on where one was standing—were played on or around carts pushed through the audience, by groups of actors moving through the crowd, or on the scaffolding on the sides of the theater. Later, the lights went up and the audience (now redefined through performance) was ushered to sit on the sides of the theatre on both levels (floor and scaffolding) to observe scenes played on the upper platform with the ramp, in the central space, or on a lower front

[23] Elizabeth Swados, quoted in a WNYC-TV documentary on Ellen Stewart, 21 September 1990 (A. S. Green 1994: 48, n. 21). Barstow (1988: 294), and Menta (1995: 16).

platform. The play moved to a close with a gathering of the women on the front platform in a group that began to sway as if in an imaginary ship to the music of a sorrowful song. If one knew the plot of *Trojan Women*, versions of Euripidean scenes involving Cassandra, Andromache and Astyanax, Hecuba, Helen, or Polyxena could be made out, but the distinction between chorus and actor was considerably reduced by the lack of comprehensible language, the brevity of the scenes, the return of actors to the chorus after playing individual roles, and the nearly continuous sounds of voice and music that accompanied the action. The performance itself emphasized with visceral clarity collective over individual suffering. The choral role in each scene was expanded and more active than in the original. For example, the anger of Euripides' chorus at Helen was graphically enacted for the audience. When a triumphant Helen was wheeled in on a cart, the Trojan women tore off her clothes and smeared her naked body with mud and straw before she was humiliatingly raped by a man dressed as a bear and killed.[24]

Reginald Burton's book on Sophoclean choruses already pronounced Sophocles' *Oedipus at Colonus* to be the oratorio it in essence became in Lee Breuer's and Bob Telson's *Gospel at Colonus*,[25] where the play was represented as a sermon on fate and death from 'The Book of Oedipus' performed at a pentecostal service by African-American singers and actors before an African-American gospel choir (Brooklyn's Institutional Radio Choir accompanied by Telson's band). Here the Choir served as the congregation and responded throughout. Sophocles' original already contained an exceptional degree of choral engagement apparently typical of his later plays. The chorus of *Oedipus at Colonus* not only sings four choral odes and five lyric dialogues with actors, but engages in rapid stichomythia (dialogue) and initiates and repeatedly tries to participate in the action. Both the play's rapid and fluid movement from event to event and song to song and the gradual transformation of the

---

[24] A bowdlerized version of this scene is available on a video that includes excerpts from the trilogy from Insight Media. A full tape is available at the Library for Performing Arts at Lincoln Center in New York City.

[25] Burton (1980: 240), Breuer (1989). A tape of *Gospel at Colonus* made for PBS television was purchased by some universities and an audio tape and CD are available from Nonesuch.

suffering Oedipus to heroic status made it more adaptable in terms of both form and content than other Greek tragedy to the Christian context of *Gospel*. The play's roles were performed by multiple characters, some singers or groups of singers and some speakers. For example, Oedipus was played by both a gospel group, Clarence Fountain and the Five Blind Boys of Alabama, and the actor Morgan Freeman, who also served as preacher. The choral role itself was divided between a large seated choir and smaller choral groups who represented it in direct engagement with the actors and used a mixture of solo and group song. Breuer's adaptation deliberately exploited theatrical elements of the African-American religious tradition: gospel musicals, as well as elements of pentecostal church services such as chanted sermons, call-and-response, active engagement of the congregation in the service, and the participation of a range of music and musical groups throughout.

Let me give as an example the first meeting between chorus, Oedipus, and Antigone. In Sophocles, the blind Oedipus and Antigone arrive at the sacred grove of the Eumenides in Colonus and encounter a local man, who then summons the chorus as guardians of the religious site. The chorus insists that Oedipus and Antigone move from sacred ground, and they do so. In *Gospel*, after the announcement of the sermon from 'the book of Oedipus' and the opening phases of a church service have set the scene, Oedipus (Fountain and the Five Blind Boys) and Antigone (Isabell Monk) arrive and ask where they have come. A solo voice (Willie Rogers) sings in falsetto part of the choral ode about Colonus that appears much later in Sophocles' play (668–719) in reply to this query. A small male chorus (J. J. Farley and the Original Soul Stirrers) tries to block the forward movement of the collective Oedipus and Antigone to the sanctuary (a white piano), singing a song with the repeated refrain 'Stop, do not go on'. Oedipus then sings in response a plea to give him shelter. Neither the text nor the alternation of music and speech of *Gospel* corresponds directly to Sophocles' play, yet *Gospel* uses the alternation of song and speech found in the original to capture its basic action and to adapt its meaning.

This is the only adaptation of Greek tragedy known to me that attempted to make the choral engagement in the story grow logically out of a contemporary ritual setting and which contained a version of the full mixture of speech, act-dividing song, and shared lyrics between actor and chorus contained in the originals. Although many critics questioned the play's amalgamation of pagan tragedy and pentecostal service, the performance itself demonstrated that contemporary collective settings with a vibrant musical and rhetorical dimension can enact a narrative that unites a group and those who emerge to perform roles from within it on the modern stage.[26] At the same time, this version retained the power of a ritualized performance that did not reproduce the more familiar relation between actor and choral singers in the musical. The performance invited both its internal audience, the members of the church service, and its theatrical one to respond to events as they unfolded and *Gospel* typically ended with audience members dancing or singing in the aisles. After its opening at Brooklyn Academy of Music in 1983, the performance toured the country and was performed a second time in Broadway's Lunt-Fontanne Theatre in New York in 1988 and a third time at New York's Apollo Theater in 2004.

A number of modern adaptations restructured the chorus/actor/ audience relation to make it the central if often unstable dramatic point. Richard Schechner's *Dionysus in 69*, like Serban's *Fragments*, relied on a particular performance space to structure such relations. His New York Performance Group built a series of platforms along the periphery of the large open space of a former garage. In the centre a set of three black rubber mats defined a sacred performance space (twelve feet by eight feet rectangle) for the actors. The audience, as potential Dionysiac initiates, was brought into the space individually and each person chose where he or she wanted to sit. During the performance, both actors and chorus members constantly moved into the spaces occupied by the audience, and audience members were free to join in and were specifically invited to share in the performance of Dionysiac ecstasy. Froma Zeitlin has written eloquently on the performance from the perspective of an audience member.[27]

The performance of *Dionysus in 69* grew out of improvisational work between cast and director. All members of the cast performed

---

[26] For critical reactions to the play, see most recently, with extensive bibliography, Wetmore (2003: 102–18).

[27] See Zeitlin (2004) with further bibliography.

in the chorus throughout its run and different cast members played different principal roles on different nights with important variations in the lines spoken by each or in the interpretation of characters and their relations. Chorus members also improvised lines or spoke different lines (which were selected by each actor) simultaneously and at different tempos and pitches as they engaged directly with different sections of the audience. On some nights the assignment of roles was not determined in advance. Sometimes two cast members played one role, such as Agave. As Schechner put it: 'Scenes come from the chorus and dissolve back into it. Everyone is part of the chorus, emerging from it to play specific roles. Thus the chorus is the underground that gives birth to the entire play. As such it is indestructible.'[28]

The performance changed significantly over time and the ever-changing audience (some of whom attended many times) ensured that no one performance was ever the same. In the climactic scene leading to the death of Pentheus, for example, Dionysus and Pentheus temporarily left the stage and went into a closed pit in the stage. In the earliest version of this scene the cast brought members of the audience to the centre of the performance space and massaged, kissed, and stroked them on the ground. A low hum accompanied the caressing. When Pentheus emerged from the pit, the future Agaves did the same to Pentheus, and their caresses gradually became more violent. Animal cries filled the air. In later performances a dance accompanied by various spoken lines was substituted for the caressing, which became hard to maintain. Pentheus was finally destroyed in a symbolic death ritual. In an early scene, the chorus gave symbolic birth to Dionysus as he emerged from a womb made of naked men lying below and naked women standing above. At the death the women swallowed Pentheus back into a destructive womb of women and killed him with a violence described as 'American as cherry pie.' Each woman in the cast (the women were given their real names) killed each man in the cast. All dripped with stage blood. The doubling of Agave in

---

[28] Schechner (1970) has no page numbers. A video tape by Brian de Palma drawn from two performances can be purchased from Richard Schechner, who teaches performance studies at New York University.

the recognition scene reflected the collective complicity of the cast as did the closing scene where the whole group except Dionysus cleaned the stage before departing. Distinctions among chorus, actor, and audience became as blurred as did all such distinctions under the influence of 'Dionysus', who, in this very 1960s play, embodied the fantasies of self and political liberation so central to the era. Dionysiac religion itself became in this play an artefact both produced by the performance and questioned by it. In many ways this made the punitive turning of Dionysus at the end on all members of the cast and the audience, and his sudden, final demand for 'real' recognition as a god after so much metatheatricality, a far greater shock. In Schechner's view, his audience could be counted on to disbelieve the *Bacchae's* myths. Yet the 'visible breaking down of the performance' and its display of the actors' private lives could capitalize on the audience's investment in the performance itself and in the power of modern ecstasy. Here the generation of the play from the chorus became a self-conscious modern analogue to the putative birth of tragedy from choruses in honour of Dionysus in Athens.

In my last example, the playwright takes an entirely new tack by making the chorus and its role the critical frame for the entire performance. John Barton's epic cycle of ten plays, *Tantalus*, is an original work that attempts to fill in gaps in the Trojan War saga left by the loss of the Greek epic cycle poems. It draws heavily as well on Euripides, but always transforms the poet's originals into new dramatic forms that respond to but do not directly reproduce tragedy. Later performed in Britain, it had its premiere at the Denver Performing Arts Center in Colorado in 2001. The Directors Peter and Edward Hall fell out with playwright Barton and called on Colin Teevan to cut and rewrite his text. My own discussion will stick with one exception to the published script, because the performance radically changed both the choral role and the major point of the whole cycle. While the performance dwelt largely on the futility of war and human action, the script is ultimately about storytelling. It uses the chorus to engage the audience in the mythmaking process, the power of storytelling, and the elusive truth of stories. 'If you want to know the future/you must go into the past' (Barton 2000: 511).

Tantalus opens with a group of twelve 'girls' (Barton's term) sleeping on barren ground. Nine of the girls become a chorus, and three play various female parts throughout the cycle of plays. The group begins to tell each other conflicting myths about the origin of the world. The chorus, which claims to know all the traditional Greek myths, wants to know which version is true. It debates whether to drink from the nearby oracular streams of Trophonius. One stream makes one forget the present moment, the other makes one remember even things one does not consciously know. A poet enters with a wine bag; he tells the chorus that he stitches together stories. The sceptical chorus, who at first prefers its own stories and one truth, is lured into testing out the poet's bag of masks and engaging with multiple conflicting stories. The poet and three women begin to don new roles and reenact story fragments for an increasingly engaged chorus. The chorus women toss stones over their shoulders in imitation of Deucalion and Pyrra and three men emerge. Creative power begins to overtake them. 'We made you', they say to the men, 'so you'll do exactly what we tell you' (2000: 33). They become upset when the men that they made do not enact the judgement of Paris correctly, but want to change or reinterpret things (2000: 138). Throughout the cycle the chorus is torn between a desire to pin down the story and a compulsion to watch it regardless of the consequences (2000: 68):

> (CHORUS): Who is to blame?
> POET: All, but all are innocent.
> (CHORUS): Could it have been otherwise?
> —Is that how it really happened?
> —Why did it have to happen?
> POET: Because that is the story. (2000: 174)

In the course of the remaining plays, the chorus moves from trying to make sense of the myths and different versions of them to playing an actual role in the plays. At first they retain their original identity when they take on roles. Gradually, the choral involvement makes it forget its knowledge of the myths (2000: 130, 146). Mistrusting the poet, they no longer want to hear about stories they cannot enter (2000: 179). The chorus finally engages in the action as participants in hopes of changing the story like the poet and preserving Troy from the Trojan horse. They drink of the two streams of Trophonius (2000: 220–1). Of course, the choral plan fails. In their newly donned ignorance as chorus members within a play, the women become the eager perpetrators of the error with the Trojan Horse and suffer branding and hard labour as enslaved Trojan women. No longer innocent spectators, they kill the helpless child of the Thracian Polymestor (2000: 338), and turn repeatedly on members of their own sex (Cassandra, Hecuba [2000: 340], Ilione [344], and Helen). Finally, liberated from slavery by the loss of their masters, they proceed in a new role as women of the West to a trial of Helen at Delphi. There, as Helen's accusers, they witness her exoneration from guilt in a new version of Euripides' play, *Helen*, in which not Helen, but her image, went to Troy, while the innocent original sat out the war in Egypt. This episode represents the climax to the choral desire to assign blame for the war correctly; the chorus finally accepts Helen's innocence and is left without the answer that it wanted, an ending to the story, the presence of their poet, or even the setting at Delphi with its promise of truth, since the shrine has burned (2000: 452–3). The choral transformation into erring and suffering players was powerfully dramatized in the production as each chorus member deliberately put on a mask that resembled her own face.

At the end of the cycle, however, the chorus is transformed into the nine Muses, each one becoming herself representative of history, tragedy, and so forth. The chorus then reassesses the errors made by both men and women in the Trojan myths. The Delphic Pythoness tells them that although men have lost their way in the fifth age, women have not. The chorus begins to become myth makers and, reluctant to leave the play, becomes increasingly intoxicated from wine and the two streams of Trophonius. Finally, however, the chorus takes off its masks (in Barton's version the chorus receives masks only as they become Muses) and departs as a group of still foolish girls, leaving the three female actors to begin telling stories to a child, the son of Orestes and Erigone, a daughter of Aegisthus and Clytaemnestra whose birth had earlier marked a temporary hiatus of disaster in the Trojan saga.

In *Tantalus*, the poet who stands in for Barton finally gives over story-making power to his internal audience, the young female chorus. The play's persistent and highly self-conscious metatheatricality, which is often shared by characters as well, becomes a vehicle for a re-examination of the role of myths and stories in our lives.

Barton's chorus moves from interested observer, to endangered and ignorant actor barely rescued by the poet's narrative, to storyteller, each with the voice of her own Muse. In this sense, Barton has confronted many earlier modern objections to the chorus. His chorus members, as poets-initiate, are not a group that necessarily excludes individual identity and perspectives in principle, even if they are not fully characterized at any point. They belong to no specific place and time. The community that they represent is one of storytellers and hearers of stories who try to make sense of their world/human history, and hence in the broadest sense, all human-kind. The pagan perspective on divine and human action becomes so merged with Barton's own post-modern perspective on action in *Tantalus* that the play in part erases the problematic religious dis-tance between the Greeks and ourselves.

Yet Tantalus also represents the story-telling power as ambivalent and even dangerous. Clytaemnestra criticizes the chorus for its prurient imagination. 'Curses are not bred by what is done in palaces/But by what is told afterwards/by women like you' (2000: 85; see also 102, 116). Many characters warn of the dangerous effects of stories of fame or war on men (2000: 126, 384). Achilles is destroyed by hearing his destiny from his mother Thetis; he spends his life looking death in the face. His truth-loving son Neoptole-mus is destroyed by Odysseus' lies. At the same time, the women of the chorus argue, their own lives would be unbearable without knowing the secrets of kings and queens (2000: 140). Many of the views on myth and its effects in *Tantalus* are in fact adapted from Euripides. Yet the persistent focus on these issues and the effort to live out the questions from so many perspectives give them a new vitality here.

I close with Barton's cycle of plays because it is the only adaptation I know that tries to explore and reconsider the choral role in Greek tragedy so extensively and self-consciously. In the end, I cannot offer a conclusion for a topic that this essay has only begun to explore. We can say for now at least that the following developments have gener-ated new interest in the Greek chorus. 1. Engagement with multi-cultural world theatre traditions and techniques that communicate across cultural boundaries. This shift has gradually made audiences open to engaging with unfamiliar elements in theatre such as the Greek chorus and generated new possibilities for performing them. 2. A shift away from naturalistic and heavily psychologized performance on the modern stage, often toward various post-modern alternatives. 3. The use of new kinds of spaces and settings for performance that dovetails with an interest in breaking down and exploring the audience/actor/chorus relation and in creating the chorus as the focal point of theatrical energy that makes this work, especially when speaking voices emerge in a non-naturalistic way from a simmering and exciting pool of choral energy and performance. 4. The desire to explore shared stories and collective memories as well as broad cultural responsibility for historical events, but without necessarily excluding the many single voices that create this convergence of ordinary people's experience, and sometimes highlighting them. The growth of oral history in the academy and its influence on popular journalism and on documentary film and theatre may have fomented these developments. 5. The growing popularity of performance and adaptation of Greek tragedy worldwide has encouraged those producing the plays to invest in more ambitious productions. Finally, we are often brought up to believe in ourselves above all as 'individuals'; yet the twentieth century has once again taught us that the ways in which we are or become part of collectivities may often be at least as engaging and fascinating.[29]

[29] I would like to thank the other editors of this volume and Christian Wolff for their helpful comments on an earlier draft of this paper.

VI

Coda

16

Rencontre avec Froma

† Jean-Pierre Vernant

J'aurais aimé apporter à ce volume, comme contribution personnelle, un article original digne de figurer dans l'ouvrage et de témoigner valablement par sa qualité de mon admiration pour l'œuvre et la personne de Froma Zeitlin. Je ne suis malheureusement plus en état de le faire. Me fallait-il dans ces conditions renoncer à être présent dans l'hommage collectif qui lui est rendu? L'idée m'en est apparu insupportable. J'ai donc choisi, au dernier moment, faute de pouvoir inventer et écrire du neuf, de puiser dans ma mémoire et de raconter, tels que me les présentent aujourd'hui mes souvenirs, les circonstances de ma première rencontre avec Froma, les hasards qui ont en quelque sorte agencé cette réunion, et la façon dont cet événement fortuit a inauguré l'entrecroisement ultérieur de nos vies et de nos cheminements intellectuels.

C'était, me semble-t-il, en 1970. Nous nous trouvions, ma femme Lida et moi, au Canada, où j'enseignais pour un trimestre à l'université de Montréal. Lida était venue m'y rejoindre pendant une courte période de vacances universitaires. Elle comptait bien profiter de ce bref séjour outre Atlantique pour faire un saut jusqu'au Etats Unis où elle n'avait encore jamais mis les pieds. L'occasion était d'autant plus favorable que le gîte, à New York, nous était assuré et qu'on nous y attendait, nous le savions, les bras ouverts. Lida avait en effet une petite cousine, Marousia, qui avait dû, tout enfant, en 1940, fuir la France avec ses parents, pour gagner les Etats-Unis et s'y installer pour toujours. Elle s'était mariée et demeurait avec ses enfants et son mari, Sidney Klein, à New York, dans un appartement où elle m'avait déjà accueilli lors de précédents voyages. Nous avons donc décidé de débarquer un peu à l'improviste chez Marousia pour y passer quelques jours. La seule difficulté était pour moi d'obtenir, du consulat américain à Montréal, un visa qu'on me refusait sous prétexte qu'en raison de mes opinions politiques j'étais interdit de séjour aux USA. Finalement, après un échange multiplié de télex entre Montréal et Paris, on m'accorda une autorisation minimale de fin de semaine.

Nous voilà donc à New York chez Marousia qui nous embarque presque aussitôt pour nous emmener en voiture dans sa maison de campagne dans le Vermont. A peine installé, le téléphone sonne. C'est une amie d'enfance de Marousia; elles ont été à l'école ensemble et sont restées liées par la suite. Elle s'appelle Froma, Froma Zeitlin. Elle demande des nouvelles de la famille. Marousia lui explique que si elle se trouve dans le Vermont c'est parce qu'ils ont reçu visite d'une cousine française plus âgée, nommée Lida, qui a débarqué avec son mari nommé Vernant. Vernant, observe Froma, est-ce qu'il ne s'occupe pas des Grecs? Marousia me transmet la question. J'opine du bonnet. Silence. Marousia raccroche. Je l'interroge: qu'est-ce qu'elle t'a dit? 'Rien. Elle a dit seulement: j'arrive'.

De fait nous rejoignent très vite par la route une jeune femme et son mari. J'ignore tout de cette Froma sauf que, petite fille, elle formait, avec la cousine de mon épouse, un couple de bonnes copines. La conversation que j'eu ce jour là avec elle fut chaleureuse mais difficile. Froma baragouinait un peu le français, moi, beaucoup plus mal encore qu'elle, l'anglais. Mais les Grecs anciens trouvèrent quand même le moyen de pointer le bout de leur nez dans cet échange. Les Zeitlin nous ramenèrent en auto à New York. Le contact était établi, pas encore ou pas tout à fait le lien. Je suppose que Froma connaissait certains de mes textes déjà publiés sur la tragédie. Je n'avais encore rien lu d'elle. Je savais seulement qu'elle était une jeune helléniste, je veux dire qu'elle appartenait à une autre génération que la mienne.

Quand j'y réfléchis, aujourd'hui, je comprends pourquoi, dans cette entrevue inopinée, en dehors même des difficultés de langue, je n'étais pas dans de bonnes dispositions pour découvrir d'emblée à qui j'avais à faire et qui était Froma. Un double obstacle—dont j'assume avec honte la responsabilité—a joué pour fausser au départ les conditions d'un vrai dialogue. D'un côté une très jeune dame, à une époque où les femmes n'avaient pas encore conquis, dans les études classiques, le statut d'égalité avec les hommes qui leur est maintenant reconnu. De l'autre, un homme 'dans la force de l'âge'. J'ai 56 ans, déjà publié, fondé et dirigé le Centre de recherches comparées sur les sociétés anciennes. Je n'ai pas su, comme j'aurai dû, faire en sorte que nous nous retrouvions d'emblée sur la même longueur d'ondes.

Le déclic n'eut lieu que plus tard. Dans la matinée du lendemain, avant de prendre l'avion pour le retour, en furetant dans la bibliothèque des Klein, je mis la main sur un petit opuscule dont son auteur, Froma Zeitlin, avait fait cadeau à son amie Marousia. Il s'agissait d'une étude sur Iphigénie et le sacrifice corrompu dans *l'Orestie* d'Eschyle. La curiosité l'emporta sur mes scrupules. Je mis le texte dans ma poche, me persuadant que je le rendrai à son propriétaire dès que j'y aurai jeté un œil.

C'est alors que tout s'est joué. Dans l'avion qui me ramenait en France, j'ai sorti le texte de cette Froma; je l'ai lu d'un trait, médusé, et relu, tout au long du trajet page après page. Je ne vois pas d'autre façon de dire ce qui s'est alors passé sinon de parler d'un coup de foudre intellectuel. Je ne fus pas le seul à être frappé. Rentré à Paris je passais le livre à Vidal-Naquet, en pleine écriture de ce qui sera plus tard le *Chasseur noir*. Il réagit comme moi et fit aussitôt circuler le texte chez tous les membres de l'équipe du Centre qui l'adoptèrent avec enthousiasme comme un texte de référence. En quelques mois, son auteur avait subi à mes yeux une véritable métamorphose. Cette jeune demoiselle, qu'avec une bienveillance un peu hautaine j'avais imaginée, dans le Vermont, frappant timidement à la porte d'entrée des études classiques, était maintenant un savant d'élite, rigoureux et inventif, qui marchait du même pas que les meilleurs d'entre nous, nous tirant au besoin en avant, en nous montrant, à l'occasion des œuvres tragiques, comment il était possible, dans la pratique, sur le terrain même des textes, de mettre en oeuvre cette interprétation anthropologique que nous tentions nous mêmes de définir et d'appliquer.

Par la suite, Froma s'intégra plus intimement au Centre que nous avons un peu plus tard rebaptisé Centre Louis Gernet. Elle en a suivi tous les travaux de recherches dont elle connaissait à l'avance les projets. Elle savait tout sur cette équipe, sur son orientation générale et sur le parcours de chacun des chercheurs à la façon dont un habitant d'un petit village n'ignore rien de ses voisins, depuis les secrets de famille jusqu'aux grandes entreprises communes.

Parmi tous les savants étrangers, avec qui nous avions à la même époque établi d'étroits rapports de collaboration, je ne vois que Riccardo di Donato, qui se soit aussi parfaitement inclus dans l'aventure intellectuelle collective du Centre parisien, et qui ait su, comme Froma, tout en gardant sa pleine originalité, figurer comme partie prenante à part entière dans ce que Bernard Knox, avec une sympathie un peu ironique, a appelé, dans l'article qu'il nous consacrait dans le *NYRB*, 'une Grèce à la française'.

En retour, la Grèce à l'américaine, ou, pour parler plus sérieusement, la Grèce tout court, telle que contribuent à la découvrir nos collègues des USA, c'est Froma qui a su nous la rendre plus familière. Tous, les uns après les autres, et parfois les uns et les autres ensemble, nous sommes passés par Princeton, c'est à dire, par Froma et chez Froma, dans nos itinéraires américains. Dois-je ajouter que toujours, ou qu'elle se trouva dans ses pérégrinations, elle accouru auprès de moi, ou d'autres membres de l'équipe, lorsque les coups et les douleurs de l'existence ne nous furent pas épargnés.

Au miroir de l'amitié comme dans l'œil de son vis à vis, si l'on en croit Platon, c'est lui-même que chacun voit et que son regard fasciné découvre. L'amitié affectueuse qui nous a liés, Froma et moi, n'a pas seulement rapproché, des deux côtés de l'Atlantique, nos vies personnelles. Elle a facilité, dans notre travail de recherche la convergence d'orientation, le partage et le maintien, jusque dans les divergences, d'un même univers intellectuel, de convictions scientifiques communes, de telle sorte qu'en lisant l'autre chacun se sent aussi bien chez soi.

Dans le recueil de textes qu'elle a publié sous le titre *Mortals and Immortals,* Froma a su, dans une longue introduction, présenter l'analyse la plus complète et la plus perspicace de ce que j'ai tenté de faire dans mon itinéraire de recherche, en particulier dans le domaine de la tragédie. Aujourd'hui encore, au terme de l'âge, quand regardant en arrière je m'interroge sur le sens de tous ces livres que j'ai écrits, sur la portée de ce long effort poursuivi, c'est en relisant son texte que j'ai le sentiment de me découvrir et de me comprendre mieux que je ne le fais moi-même.

Translation, by Leofranc Holford-Strevens:

I should have liked to bring to this volume, as my personal contribution, an original article worthy to appear in it and of a quality to offer valid testimony of my admiration for Froma Zeitlin as a scholar and a human being. Unfortunately I am no longer in a position to do so. Should I therefore have declined to play my part in the collective homage paid to her? I could not bear the thought. At the last minute, therefore, not being able to devise something new to write, I have decided to draw upon the well of memory and relate, according to my present recollection, the circumstances in which I first met Froma, the accidents that in a sense brought this meeting about, and the way in which this chance event led to the subsequent intertwining of our lives and intellectual paths.

I think it was in 1970. My wife Lida and I were in Canada, where I was teaching for a term at McGill. Lida had come to join me briefly there during the university vacation. She meant to profit from this short trip across the Atlantic to go as far as the USA, where she had never set foot. The occasion was all the more auspicious in that we already had somewhere to stay, in New York, and that we knew we were awaited with open arms; for Lida had a younger cousin, Marousia, who as a child had had to flee France in 1940 with her parents, had reached the USA, and had settled there for good. She had married and was living with her children and her husband, Sidney Klein, in New York, in an apartment where she had already put me up on previous visits. We had therefore decided at short notice to stop over at Marousia's and spend some days there. The only difficulty was in getting me a visa from the American consulate in Montreal, which was refused on the grounds that owing to my political opinions I was forbidden to stay in the USA. Finally, after a prolonged exchange of telexes between Montreal and Paris, I was granted the minimum authorization for a weekend.

So there we were in New York at Marousia's; almost at once she put us in her car to drive to her country house in Vermont. Hardly were we there when the telephone rang. It was a childhood friend of Marousia's; they had been at school together and had maintained the connection ever since. She was called Froma, Froma Zeitlin. She asked for news of the family. Marousia explained that the reason she was in Vermont was that they had visitors, an older French cousin called Lida with her husband called Vernant. 'Vernant', Froma observed, 'doesn't he deal with the Greeks?' Marousia passed on the question to me. I nodded. Silence. Marousia hung up. I asked her, 'What did she say?' 'Nothing. She just said "I'm coming"'.

Indeed, very soon a young woman and her husband had driven down to join us. I knew nothing about this Froma except that she was a young woman who was great friends with my wife's cousin. My conversation with her that day was warm but difficult. Froma spoke a little halting French, my English was far worse. But even so the ancient Greeks managed to work their way in. The Zeitlins drove us to New York. Contact had been established, but not yet the bond, or not completely. I supposed that Froma knew some things I had already published on tragedy. I had not yet read anything of hers. I knew only that she was a young Hellenist, meaning that she belonged to a different generation from mine.

When I think about it today, I understand why in this unexpected encounter, I was ill placed to discover right away, even despite the language difficulties, whom I was dealing with and who Froma was. There was at the outset a twofold impediment to a true dialogue. On the one hand a very young lady at a time when women had not yet obtained the equal status in classical studies with men that is now accorded them. On the other, a man in the prime of life. I was 56, had already published, had founded and directed the Centre de Recherches Comparées sur les Sociétés Anciennes. I was unable, as I ought, to make the adjustments to get us at once on the same wavelength.

The catch was not released till later. Next morning, before leaving to catch my return flight, ferreting through the Kleins' library, I put my hand on a little work that its author, Froma Zeitlin, had presented to her friend Marousia. It was a study of Iphigenia and the corrupted sacrifice in Aeschylus' *Oresteia*. Curiosity overpowered my scruples. I put it in my pocket, persuading myself that I should return it to its owner once I had cast an eye over it.

That was when it all happened. In the aeroplane taking me home to France I took out this Froma's offprint; I read it straight through, transfixed, and reread it page by page the whole flight long. I can describe what happened only as an intellectual thunderbolt. I was not the only one to be struck. Back in Paris I passed it on to Vidal-Naquet, who was busy writing what would become *Le Chasseur noir*. He reacted as I had and immediately sent the piece round all the members of the Centre team, who enthusiastically adopted it as a reference text. Within a few months its author had undergone nothing short of a metamorphosis in my eyes. This young girl, whom with somewhat lofty goodwill I had imagined, in Vermont, knocking timidly on the entrance door to the classics, was now a top-flight scholar, rigorous and creative, who marched in step with the best of us, if necessary drawing us ahead by showing us in regard to tragedy how it was possible in practice, even at the textual level, to undertake the anthropological interpretation we ourselves were attempting to define and apply.

After that Froma became more intimately involved with the Centre, which soon afterwards we renamed the Centre Louis Gernet. She followed all its researches, and was aware of the projects in advance. She knew everything about this team, its general orientation and every researcher's progress in the way that an inhabitant of a small village knows everything about his neighbours from family secrets to great common undertakings.

Among all the foreign scholars with whom we had established a close collaboration during the same period, only Riccardo Di Donato became so perfectly part of the Centre's intellectual collective and, like Froma, could while maintaining his originality intact be a full participant in what Bernard Knox, with a slightly ironic sympathy, called, in his article about us in the *New York Review of Books* (3/3/1983), a 'Greece *à la française*'.

In return, it was Froma who managed to make us more familiar with Greece *à l'américaine*, or to be more serious, Greece *tout court* as our US colleagues help us discover it. We all, one after another and sometimes all together, have, on our American trips, been to Princeton, to see Froma and stay with her. Need I add that, wherever she was on her travels, she always hastened to see me, or other members of the *équipe*, when we could not escape the buffets and sorrows of existence.

In the mirror of friendship as in the other person's eye, if we believe Plato, it is ourselves that each of us sees and discovers with fascinated gaze. The friendship and affection that has linked Froma and me has not only brought our personal lives together on both sides of the Atlantic. It has made it easier for us to direct our research work to common goals, to share and, even in our disagreements, to maintain a common intellectual universe, common scholarly convictions, so that each on reading the other feels just as much at home.

In the collection of my essays that she published under the title *Mortals and Immortals,* Froma in her long introduction presented the fullest and most perspicacious analysis of what I had tried to do in the course of my research, in particular on tragedy. Even now, at the end of my days, when looking back I ask myself what all those books I have written mean, what that long-drawn-out effort comes to, rereading her introduction gives me the sense of discovering myself and understanding myself better than I had done on my own account.

17

Présence de Froma Zeitlin

†*Pierre Vidal-Naquet*

Au terme de ce long et—je me permets de le dire—magnifique volume, extraordinaire hommage à une personne tout à fait hors norme, il m'appartient, en concurrence amicale avec Jean-Pierre Vernant, d'écrire quelques mots de conclusion. Je le ferai en évoquant, comme le fait Vernant, les circonstances qui ont entraîné de proche en proche la rencontre avec Froma, rapprochement intellectuel, puis, à Paris, à Princeton, et à New York, suivi d'une amitié qui dure encore et dont je ne vois pas pourquoi elle pourrait s'interrompre.

En un sens, cette rencontre était nécessaire et inévitable. Notre monde d'hellénistes est un petit monde. C'est même un petit monde qui a tendance à se clore sur lui-même, ce que Paul Éluard appelait 'un petit monde meurtrier'. Relativement rares sont ceux qui refusent de s'enfermer dans leur spécialité pour faire un utile détour par d'autres disciplines et faire souffler un peu d'air frais. Jean-Pierre Vernant était, est toujours de ceux-là. A la génération précédente, c'était le cas de deux hommes très différents, Henri Jeanmaire, qui, avant d'enseigner à la section des sciences religieuses de l'École pratique des hautes études, avait soutenu une thèse révolutionnaire intitulée *Couroi et Courètes* (1939), qui posait dans toute son ampleur le problème des rites d'adolescence dans le monde grec et notamment à Sparte 'sous le masque de Lycurgue', utilisant largement la comparaison avec les sociétés africaines; et Louis Gernet, qui fut un éditeur et un commentateur des textes des orateurs attiques en même temps qu'un disciple de Durkheim, et pendant un temps un directeur de *L'Année sociologique.*

Gernet avait passé de longues années à la Faculté des Lettres d'Alger dont il fut le doyen, corrigeant des versions et des thèmes grecs tout en développant une oeuvre originale dont toute l'ampleur fut révélée à partir de 1968, grâce à Jean-Pierre Vernant et François Maspero, avec la publication de *l'Anthologie de la Grèce ancienne.* Depuis, c'est Riccardo Di Donato qui, à Pise, a consacré une large part de sa vie aux études gernétiennes. Beaucoup des travaux les plus originaux de Louis Gernet n'avaient pas été répertoriés dans *L'Année philologique* qui est censée nous mettre en relation les uns avec les autres. Il est caractéristique que j'aie fait la connaissance et de Gernet et d'ailleurs de Vernant à la fin de 1957, à l'occasion d'un épisode atroce de la guerre d'Algérie, la disparition sous la torture d'un jeune mathématicien de la Faculté des Sciences d'Alger, Maurice Audin. Gernet présida la conférence de presse à Paris et compara l'affaire Audin à l'affaire Dreyfus, avec laquelle il s'était familiarisé pendant sa jeunesse. Autour de Vernant et de Gernet, autour d'Ignace Meyerson, directeur du *Journal de Psychologie,* s'agrégèrent un certain nombre de 'classicistes' plus ou moins marginaux comme Marcel Detienne, Jean-Paul Brisson, Claude Mossé, Nicole Loraux et beaucoup d'autres qui ne restèrent, heureusement ou malheureusement, pas toute leur vie marginaux. Ils occupèrent des chaires dans les diverses sections de l'École pratique des hautes études, voire du Collège de France dans le cas de Vernant, rejoignant des personnalités plus 'orthodoxes' comme Jacqueline de Romilly, qui fut tout de même la première femme à occuper une chaire au Collège.

Et l'Amérique dans tout cela? Le premier natif de New York que je rencontrai fut Moses I. Finley; soupçonné de communisme au moment de la crise McCarthyste, il avait gagné à Cambridge, Jesus College, des eaux moins agitées, et je consacrai en 1965, dans les *Archives européennes de sociologie,* une grosse étude à l'ensemble de son oeuvre. L'amitié vint ensuite et dura jusqu'à sa mort, suivant de quelques heures celle de son épouse, Mary. À la guerre d'Algérie menée par la France succéda la guerre du Vietnam où les Américains prirent le relais de nos compatriotes, suscitant l'opposition de nombre d'universitaires et d'intellectuels. Parmi eux Maria Jolas, Américaine de Paris, ancienne exécutrice testamentaire, avec son mari, de James Joyce. Par elle, je connus Gabriel et Joyce Kolko, historiens du vingtième siècle, et Charles P. Segal, qui fut en somme le premier helléniste américain à s'affilier intellectuellement au Centre de recherches comparées sur les sociétés anciennes, qui fut successivement dirigé par Jean-Pierre Vernant, par moi, par François Hartog, et François Lissarrague, son directeur actuel.

Comme il était naturel c'est Jean-Pierre Vernant qui, de nous deux, rencontra le premier Froma, en 1970, et il le relate ici lui-même. Je travaillais alors à mon séminaire de l'École des hautes études (6ᵐᵉ section), où j'avais rejoint Vernant, sur l'*Orestie* d'Eschyle. En 1968 j'avais publié, en français et en anglais, mon article 'Le Chasseur noir et l'origine de l'éphébie athénienne', qui fut, quelques années plus tard, le titre éponyme de mon livre *Le Chasseur noir. Formes de pensée et formes de société dans le monde grec* (Paris, 1981), livre qui devait plus tard être traduit en anglais. J'essayai, dans une série de séminaires, de voir ce que signifiait chez Eschyle ce thème de la chasse. C'est alors que Vernant me donna à lire un tiré à part des *Transactions and Proceedings of the American Philological Society* (*TAPA*) de 1965, intitulé 'The Motif of the Corrupted Sacrifice in Aeschylus' *Oresteia*', ajoutant: il ne faut pas se limiter à la chasse, il faut associer à la chasse le 'sacrifice corrompu'.

Ce fut un trait de lumière. Si la chasse est un mode de communication avec la nature sauvage, le sacrifice est un mode de communication avec les dieux. Que l'un et l'autre se mélangent, et la catastrophe est là! En règle générale, l'animal sacrifié n'est pas un animal chassé. Or Oreste, éphèbe, homme de la montagne sauvage, vient à Argos sacrifier Clytemnestre, avant d'être à son tour traqué, chassé par les Erinyes destinées à devenir non sans ambiguïté les Euménides. Le mélange de la chasse et du sacrifice illumine l'ensemble de la trilogie et cela je devais à Froma, via Vernant, de le comprendre. L'éphèbe Oreste, 'chasseur noir' s'il en fut jamais, avait rejoint le monde des Indiens de Claude Lévi-Strauss, et c'était largement grâce à cet article d'une quarantaine de pages, le premier, je crois, qu'ait publié Froma.

Froma a mis au monde, depuis, les grands livres qu'elle a publiés ou dirigés, notamment, avec J. J. Winkler, *Nothing to do with Dionysos?* (Princeton, 1990), *Playing the Other. Gender and Society in Classical Greek Literature* (Chicago, 1996) et, dès 1982, à Rome, aux éditions de l'Ateneo, *Under the Sign of the Shield. Semiotics and*

Aeschylus' Seven against Thebes. Sur ce dernier terrain notamment nous nous sommes à nouveau rencontrés. Au milieu, si je me souviens bien, des années 1970, Froma vint à Paris, et suivit quelque temps mon séminaire. C'était l'époque où je m'étais plongé dans l'histoire de l'histoire, domaine dans lequel excelle entre tous—hélas, ce verbe est à mettre à l'imparfait—Arnaldo Momigliano, et où, avec Nicole Loraux, je préparais une étude sur 'La Formation de l'Athènes bourgeoise', publiée depuis dans mon recueil *La Démocratie grecque vue d'ailleurs* (Paris, 1993). J'entends encore Froma me dire: 'Qu'est-ce que je sais, moi, de Condorcet?'

Elle a rejoint alors dans mes amitiés américaines Arno J. Mayer, historien du contemporain et dont j'avais fait la connaissance à l'occasion de la crise de 1968. Cette crise avait une dimension étudiante et une dimension ouvrière. Grâce à Mayer et Kolko, je pus, lorsque je publiai avec Alain Schnapp un recueil intitulé *Journal de la Commune étudiante,* et qui devint en Amérique, traduit par Maria Jolas, *The French Student Uprising,* consacrer un large prélude aux soulèvements étudiants en Amérique, depuis la révolte de Berkeley en 1964 jusqu'à celle de Columbia en 1968. Je fus, à la fois comme antiquisant et comme contemporanéiste, invité à Princeton où Froma Zeitlin et Carl Schorske me donnèrent la parole en 1978. C'était pour moi découvrir l'Amérique et ses campus, au sens propre du terme. Contrairement à Vernant, je n'avais jamais franchi l'Atlantique. J'habitai chez Arno à Princeton, et, quand ma femme vint me rejoindre, chez les Zeitlin à New York. De campus en campus, nous fîmes un tour du pays via Chicago et la Californie.

Il était difficilement imaginable de trouver deux introducteurs à l'Amérique plus différents qu'Arno Mayer et Froma Zeitlin. Certes, tous deux étaient juifs, mais d'une façon très différente. Arno était luxembourgeois, d'extrême gauche quoique étranger au communisme et au marxisme. Froma avait une culture religieuse et sa famille venait de l'empire russe. Elle était proche du sionisme, ce qui n'était pas le cas d'Arno, peu préoccupé de religion et étranger au nationalisme. Froma était new-yorkaise et démocrate. Chez elle j'ai rencontré l'élite de l'hellénisme américain, Seth Benardete, Charles Segal (depuis disparus), Seth Schein. Grâce à elle je fis la connaissance à Washington de Bernard Knox, ancien combattant du régiment 'La Marseillaise' pendant la guerre d'Espagne, et de Jenny Strauss Clay, fille adoptive de Leo Strauss, et à San Francisco de Thomas Rosenmeyer, et, ce qui est mieux encore, je me familiarisai avec les rues de New York, avec Greenwich Village et Little Italy. Assurément les campus ne sont pas l'Amérique et New York n'est pas Little Rock, mais c'est quand même tout un monde qui s'ouvrait devant moi.

Mais arrêtons d'égrener des souvenirs, même heureux, et disons quelques mots de l'extraordinaire volume que j'ai l'honneur, avec Jean-Pierre Vernant, de conclure. Que le Centre, que j'ai dirigé pendant huit ans après Vernant, y soit abondamment représenté, c'est tout naturel, de même qu'il est naturel qu'un ami du centre comme Pietro Pucci y soit présent, et je n'insisterai pas là-dessus.

S'il est un thème qui m'a toujours fasciné depuis l'adolescence, c'est celui du double ou, mieux, du dédoublement. Je dis 'depuis l'adolescence' en pensant au poème de Musset où apparaît

> Un jeune homme vêtu de noir
> Qui me ressemblait comme un frère,

thème que l'on retrouve par exemple dans le film de Losey *Monsieur Klein,* et qui traverse les siècles depuis les temps de Castor et Pollux, d'Oreste et Électre et de tant d'autres. Rien de plus proche, rien de plus séparé que la fraternité ou, mieux, la gémellité. Pensons à Antigone et Ismène, qu'elles soient, ou non, accompagnées de Chrysothémis comme dans une pièce du poète grec d'aujourd'hui, Yiannis Ritsos; pensons aussi à Cassandre et Hector, en dépit de leur multitude de frères et de soeurs.

Tous les articles réunis dans ce volume abordent ce thème du double, directement ou indirectement. Ainsi Pietro Pucci nous montre Aristophane dédoublant Euripide qu'il fait profession de fustiger. Le thème du double apparaît jusque dans le titre de la contribution d'Oliver Taplin que nul n'accusera d'être un obsédé des structures: 'A New Pair of Pairs: Tragic Witnesses in Western Greek Vase Painting?'. Ce sont parfois les titres mêmes des oeuvres de Froma qui provoquent un dédoublement chargé d'humour. Ainsi Ewen Bowie appelant 'Pulling the Other' une étude sur Longus, et aussi bien John Henderson intitulant son hommage 'Everything to do with Dionysus'. J. Elsner montre comment, à l'apogée de l'Empire romain, Philostrate visualise la tragédie à travers la peinture. Helene Foley confronte le choeur antique et ses représentations modernes. Luca

Giuliani et Glenn W. Most jouent sur les deux faces d'un cratère apulien conservé au Musée de Princeton. Edith Hall, dans une contribution que je me permets de qualifier de magistrale, confronte la tragédie avec les représentations iconographiques non des tragédies mais de Madame Tragédie qui fait son apparition dès le milieu du cinquième siècle. Simon Goldhill enfin confronte le mur contemporain, tel celui qui fut détruit à Berlin, avec les murailles antiques, signes de l'apparition de la civilisation aux yeux de Thucydide. Je pense qu'un chercheur comme Yvon Garlan lira ces pages avec satisfaction.

Le même et l'autre, Sparte et Athènes, Athènes et Thèbes, la tragédie et la comédie (confrontées, ici, par Peter Wilson), le texte et l'image, fraternité ambiguë qui scande tout le volume... Je pense que Froma méritait plus et mieux qu'un choeur d'admirateurs, il lui fallait cette réflexion à plusieurs voix sur le thème du double. Au coeur de son oeuvre, n'y a-t-il pas une méditation sur le dédoublement fondamental, celui qui associe et oppose le masculin et le féminin?

Translation, by Leofranc Holford-Strevens:

At the end of this long and—I take the liberty of saying—magnificent volume, an extraordinary tribute to a quite exceptional person, it falls to me, in friendly rivalry with Jean-Pierre Vernant, to write some closing words. I shall do so by recalling, like him, the circumstances that gradually led to my meeting Froma: an intellectual sympathy, then personal contact in Paris, Princeton, and New York, followed by a friendship that has lasted to this day and so far as I can see is bound to continue.

In one sense, this meeting was necessary and inevitable. We Hellenists form a small world. It is even a small world with a tendency to close in upon itself, what Paul Éluard called a 'small murderous world' (*un petit monde meurtrier*). There are relatively few who refuse to shut themselves up in their speciality to make a useful detour through other disciplines and let in a little fresh air. Jean-Pierre Vernant was and still is one of them. In the previous generation, there were instances in two very different men, Henri Jeanmaire, who before going on to teach in the Section des Sciences Religieuses at the École Pratique des Hautes Études, had defended a revolutionary thesis entitled *Couroi et Courètes* (1939), which stated in all its breadth the problem of rites of adolescence in the Greek world and in particular at Sparta 'beneath the mask of Lycurgus', making large use of comparison with African societies; and Louis Gernet, who was at the same time an editor of and commentator on texts of Attic orators and a disciple of Durkheim, and for a while a director of *L'Année sociologique*.

Gernet had spent many years at the Faculté des Lettres in Algiers, of which he was the dean, correcting Greek proses and unseens even as he developed an original body of work whose full breadth was revealed from 1968 onwards, thanks to Jean-Pierre Vernant and François Maspero, with the publication of *Anthologie de la Grèce ancienne*. Then, at Pisa, Riccardo Di Donato devoted a large part of his life to Gernet studies. Many of Gernet's most original works had not been listed in *L'Année philologique*, which is supposed to put us in touch with each other. It is typical that I should have met both Gernet and indeed Vernant at the end of 1957, on the occasion of an atrocity committed during the Algerian war, the death under torture of a young mathematician at the Faculté des Sciences in Algiers, Maurice Audin. Gernet presided over the press conference in Paris and compared the *affaire Audin* to the *affaire Dreyfus*, with which he had made himself familiar in youth. Round Vernant and Gemet, and round Meyerson, the director of the *Journal de Psychologie*, gathered a certain number of more or less marginal 'classicists' like Marcel Detienne, Jean-Paul Brisson, Claude Mossé, Nicole Loraux, and many others who for good or ill did not remain marginal throughout their lives. They came to hold chairs in the various sections of the École Pratique des Hautes Études, even the Collège de France in the case of Vernant, reunited with more 'orthodox' personalities like Jacqueline de Romilly, who was all the same the first woman to hold a chair at the Collège.

And America in all that? The first native New Yorker I met was Moses I. Finley: suspected of communism during the McCarthy crisis, he had found calmer waters at Jesus College, Cambridge, and in the *Archives européennes de sociologie* for 1965 I devoted a major study to his work as a whole. Friendship followed and lasted till his death, which followed a few hours after that of his wife Mary. The Algerian war waged by France was followed by the Vietnam War, in which the Americans took up our compatriots' baton, arousing the opposition of a number of academics and intellectuals. Among them was Maria Jolas, an American living in Paris, the former executrix, along with her husband, of James Joyce's will. Through her I made the acquaintance of Gabriel and Joyce Kolko, twentieth-century historians, and of Charles P. Segal, who was essentially the first American Hellenist to align himself intellectually with the 'Centre de Recherches Comparées sur les Sociétés Anciennes' successively directed by Jean-Pierre Vernant, myself, François Hartog, and its current director François Lissarrague.

As was natural, of the two of us it was Vernant who first met Froma, in 1970; he tells the story himself in this book. At the time I was working in my seminar at l'École des Hautes Études (6me section), where I had met Vernant again, on Aeschylus' *Oresteia*. In 1968 I had published, in French and English, my article 'The Black Hunter and the Origin of the Athenian Ephebia', which a few years later yielded the title of my book *Le Chasseur noir: Formes de pensée et formes de société dans le monde grec* (Paris, 1981), later translated into English as *The Black Hunter: Forms of Thought and Forms of Society in the Greek World* (Baltimore, 1986). I attempted, in a series of seminars, to see what this theme of the hunt meant in Aeschylus. It was then that Vernant showed me an offprint from the *Transactions and Proceedings of the American Philological Society* (*TAPA*) for 1965, entitled 'The Motif of the Corrupted Sacrifice in Aeschylus' *Oresteia*', adding that I ought not to limit myself to the hunt, but associate the 'corrupted sacrifice' with it.

This was a flash of light. If hunting is a mode of communication with wild nature, sacrifice is a mode of communication with the gods. Let the two be conflated, and disaster is at hand! As a general rule, the sacrificed animal is not a hunted animal. Now Orestes, an ephebe, a man from the wild mountain, comes to Argos to sacrifice Clytaemnestra, before in his turn being tracked down and hunted by the Erinyes, who are destined to become, not unambiguously, the Eumenides. The conflation of hunt and sacrifice casts light on the entire trilogy and I owed my understanding of the fact to Froma, by way of Vernant. The ephebe Orestes, a 'black hunter' if ever there was one, had met the world of Claude Lévi-Strauss's Indians, and it was largely thanks to that article of forty-odd pages, the first, I think, that Froma published.

After that Froma brought out the great books that she published or edited, notably *Nothing to do with Dionysos?* (with J. J. Winkler, Princeton, 1990), *Playing the Other: Gender and Society in Classical Greek Literature* (Chicago, 1996) and, as early as 1982, at Rome, for l'Ateneo, *Under the Sign of the Shield: Semiotics and Aeschylus' Seven against Thebes*. Particularly on this last terrain we often met again. In the mid 1970s, if I recall aright, Froma came to Paris, and attended my seminar for a time. That was the time when I plunged into the history of history, a field in which the supreme figure is— alas, that should be a past tense—Arnaldo Momigliano, and in which, together with Nicole Loraux, I prepared a study on 'La Formation de l'Athènes bourgeoise', later published in my collection *La Démocratie grecque vue d'ailleurs* (Paris, 1993). I can still hear Froma saying to me, 'What do *I* know about Condorcet?'

It was at that time that she met another of my American friends, Arno J. Mayer, a contemporary historian whose acquaintance I had made during the crisis of 1968. That crisis had a student dimension and a working-class dimension. Thanks to Mayer and Kolko, I was able, when with Alain

Schnapp I published a collection called *Journal de la Commune étudiante*—translated in America by Maria Jolas as *The French Student Uprising*—to devote an extensive introduction to student rebellions in America from the Berkeley revolt of 1964 to that at Columbia in 1968. As an investigator of both ancient and modern times I was invited to Princeton, where Froma Zeitlin and Carl Schorske invited me to speak in 1978. For me it was a chance to discover America and its campuses, in the proper sense of the word. Unlike Vernant, I had never crossed the Atlantic. I lived with Arno at Princeton, and, when my wife came to join me, with the Zeitlins in New York. We toured the country from campus to campus by way of Chicago and California.

One could hardly conceive being introduced to America by two persons more different than Arno Mayer and Froma Zeitlin. True, both were Jews, but in a very different way. Arno was from Luxembourg, on the far left, though a stranger to Communism and Marxism. Froma had a religious background and her family came from the Russian empire. She was close to Zionism, which was not the case with Arno, who took little interest in religion and was a stranger to nationalism. Froma was a New Yorker and a Democrat. At her house I met the cream of American Hellenism, Seth Benardete, Charles Segal (both since deceased), Seth Schein. Thanks to her I made the acquaintance in Washington of Bernard Knox, a former soldier in the La Marseillaise Battalion during the Spanish Civil War, and Jenny Strauss Clay, the adoptive daughter of Leo Strauss, and in San Francisco of Thomas Rosenmeyer, and, what is still more, I became familiar with the streets of New York, with Greenwich Village and Little Italy. To be sure the campuses are not America and New York is not Little Rock, but all the same it was a whole world that opened up before me.

But let us cease peeling off memories, even happy ones, and say a few words about the extraordinary volume I have the honour, along with Jean-Pierre Vernant, of concluding. That the Centre I directed for eight years after him should be abundantly represented in it is entirely natural, just as it is natural that a friend of the Centre like Pietro Pucci should be there, and I shall say no more about that.

If there is a theme that has fascinated me ever since adolescence, it is that of the pair, or rather of pairing. I say 'from adolescence' having in mind Musset's poem featuring 'a young man dressed in black | who resembled me like a brother' ('Un jeune homme vêtu de noir | Qui me ressemblait comme un frère'), a theme that recurs for example in Losey's film *Monsieur Klein*, and has come down through the centuries from the time of Castor and Pollux, Orestes and Electra, and so many others. There is nothing closer, nothing more separate than being a sibling, or rather a twin. Think of

Antigone and Ismene, whether or not they have Chrysothemis with them as in a play by the contemporary Greek poet Yiannis Ritsos; think too of Cassandra and Hector, despite their multitude of brothers and sisters.

All the chapters in this collection broach this theme of pairing, directly or indirectly. Thus Pietro Pucci shows us Aristophanes mimicking the Euripides he professes to chastise. The theme appears even in the heading of Oliver Taplin's contribution, though no one will accuse him of being obsessed with structures: 'A New Pair of Pairs: Tragic Witnesses in Western Greek Vase Painting?'. Sometimes the very titles of Froma's work provoke humorous echoes. Thus Ewen Bowie's study of Longus, 'Pulling the Other'; likewise John Henderson calls his tribute 'Everything to do with Dionysus'. Jaś Elsner shows how, at the height of the Roman Empire, Philostratus visualizes tragedy through painting. Helene Foley compares the ancient chorus with its modern representations. Luca Giuliani and Glenn W. Most play off the two sides of an Apulian crater preserved in the Princeton University Art Museum. Edith Hall, in a contribution I take leave to call magisterial, discusses tragedy in the light of iconographical representations showing not particular tragedies but Lady Tragedy, who makes her appearance in the mid-fifth century. Finally, Simon Goldhill sets the modern wall, like the one destroyed in Berlin, with ancient city walls, seen by Thucydides as signs of emerging civilization. I think that a scholar like Yvon Garlan will read these pages with satisfaction.

The same and the other, Sparta and Athens, Athens and Thebes, tragedy and comedy (compared here by Peter Wilson), text and image, an ambiguous relation of brotherhood that pervades the whole volume... I think that Froma deserved something more and better than a chorus of admirers: she needed this polyphonic reflection on the theme of the pair. At the heart of her work, is there not a meditation on the fundamental pairing, that which brings together, and pits against each other, the masculine and the feminine?

References

1. ABBREVIATIONS

ABV   Beazley, J. D. (1956), *Attic Black-Figure Vase-Painters*. Oxford.

AP   Dübner, F. (1864–72), *Epigrammatum Anthologia Palatine*. Paris.

ARV²   Beazley, J. D. (1963), *Attic Red-Figure Vase-Painters*. 2nd edn. Oxford.

CVA   (1922–), *Corpus vasorum antiquorum*. Paris.

FCG   Meinecke, A. (1839–57) (ed.), *Fragmenta comicorum graecorum*. Berlin.

FHG   Müller, C. (1841–70) (ed.), *Fragmenta historicorum graecorum*, 5 vols. Paris.

HE   Gow, A. S. F. and Page, D. L. (1965) (eds.), *The Greek Anthology: Hellenistic Epigrams*. 2 vols. Cambridge.

IG   (1873–), *Inscriptiones graecae*. Berlin.

LIMC   (1981–97), *Lexicon iconographicum mythologiae classicae*. Zurich.

LSJ   Liddell, H. G. and Scott, R. (1968) (eds.), *A Greek–English Lexicon*. Rev. edn by H. S. Jones et al. Oxford.

M–L   Meiggs, R. and Lewis, D. (1989) (eds.), *A Selection of Greek Historical Inscriptions to the End of the Fifth Century* BC. Revised edition. Oxford.

PCG   Kassel, R. and Austin, C. (1983–2001) (eds.), *Poetae comici graeci*. Berlin.

PMG   Page, D. L. (1962) (ed.), *Poetae melici graeci*. Oxford.

RE   Pauly, A. F. von and Wissowa, G. (1894–1972) (eds.), *Paulys Realencyclopädie der classischen Altertumswissenschaft*. Stuttgart.

SEG   (1923–), *Supplementum epigraphicum graecum*. Amsterdam.

SH   Lloyd-Jones, H. and Parsons, P. 1983 (eds.), *Supplementum hellenisticum*. Berlin.

SM   SNELL, B. and MAEHLER, H. (1975) (eds.), *Pindarus*, pars 2, *Fragmenta*, Indices. 4th edn. Leipzig.

TrGF   SNELL, B., et al. (1971–2004) (eds.), *Tragicorum graecorum fragmenta*. Göttingen.

2. LIST OF WORKS CITED

AELLEN, C. (1994), *À la recherche de l'ordre cosmique: Forme et fonction des personifications dans la céramique Italiote*, vols. 1–2 (Kilchberg).

AIGNER, H. (1982), *Der Selbstmord im Mythos* (Graz).

ALEXANDER, D. (1992), 'Kauffman and the Print Market in Eighteenth-Century England', in W. Wassyng-Roworth (ed.), *Angelica Kauffman: A Continental Artist in Georgian England* (London), 141–78.

AMANDRY, P. (1976), 'Trépieds d'Athènes: Dionysies', *BCH* 100: 15–93.

ANDERSON, G. (1986), *Philostratus* (London).

ARAFAT, K. (1996), *Pausanias' Greece* (Cambridge).

ARIAS, P. E., and SHEFTON, B. B. (1962), *A History of Greek Vase Painting*, text and notes by P. E. Arias, tr. and rev. by B. B. Shefton (London).

ARNOTT, W. (1965), "Ὥσπερ λαμπάδιον δράματος", *Hermes* 93: 253–5.

BABBITT, F. C. (1936) (tr.), *Plutarch's Moralia*, vol. 4 (Cambridge, MA).

BACON, H. (1964), 'The Shield of Eteocles', *Arion* 3: 27–38.

BAKKER, E. (1999), 'Mimesis as Performance: Rereading Auerbach's First Chapter', *Poetics Today* 20: 11–26.

BARCHIESI, A. (1997), 'Endgames: Ovid's *Metamorphoses* 5 and *Fasti* 6', in D. Roberts, F. Dunn, and D. Fowler (eds.), *Classical Closure: Reading the End in Greek and Latin Literature* (Princeton), 181–208.

BARLOW, S. (1986) (ed. and tr.), *Euripides: Trojan Women* (Warminster).

BARTHOLOMÉ, H. (1935), *Ovid und die bildende Kunst* (Borna).

BARSTOW, A. (1988), *The Director's Voice: 21 Interviews* (New York).

BARTON, J. (2000), *Tantalus, an Ancient Myth for a New Millennium* (London).

BARTSCH, S. (1989), *Decoding the Ancient Novel* (Princeton).

BASSI, K. (1998), *Acting Like Men: Gender, Drama, and Nostalgia in Ancient Greece* (Ann Arbor).

BAUDRILLART, A. (1894), *Les divinités de la victoire en Grèce et en Italie* (Paris).

BAZANT, J., and BERGER-DOER, G. (1994), 'Pentheus', *LIMC*, vol. 7.1: 306–17.

BEALL, S. (1993), 'Word-Painting in the *Imagines* of the Elder Philostratus', *Hermes* 121: 350–63.

400   *References*

BEAZLEY, J. D. (1951), *The Development of Attic Black-Figure* (Berkeley).
—— (1974), *The Kleophrades Painter* (Mainz).
BECKER, A. (1995), *The Shield of Achilles and the Poetics of Ekphrasis* (Lanham).
—— (2003), 'Contest or Concert? A Speculative Essay on Ecphrasis and Rivalry Between the Arts', *CML* 23: 1–14.
BEISTER, H., and BUCKLER, J. (1989) (eds.), *Boiotika: Vorträge vom 5. internationalen Böotien-Kolloquium zu Ehren von Prof. Dr. S. Lauffer* (Munich).
BELL, C. (1992), *Ritual Theory, Ritual Practice* (Oxford).
BÉRARD, C. (1970), *Eretria III. L'Héroon à la porte de l'Ouest* (Berne).
—— and DURAND, J.-L. (1984), 'Entrer en imagerie', in C. Bérard (ed.), *La Cité des images* (Lausanne), 18–33.
BERGREN, A. (1979), 'Helen's Web: Time and Tableau in the *Iliad*', *Helios* 7: 19–34.
BERNARDINI, P. A. (1989), 'Il proemio della *Pitica* XI di Pindaro e culti tebani', in Beister and Buckler (1989), 39–47.
BEUTLER, R. (1957), 'Proklos [4]', *RE*, vol. 23.1, coll. 186–247.
BIEBER, M. (1961), *The History of the Greek and Roman Theater*, 2nd edn. (Princeton).
BIERL, A. (1996), *Die Orestie des Aischylos auf der modernen Bühne: Theoretische Konzeptionen und ihre szenische Realisierung* (Stuttgart and Weimar).
BIERL, H. A. F. (1991), *Dionysos und die griechische Tragödie* (Tübingen).
BILES, Z. (2001), 'Aristophanes' Victory Dance: Old Poets in the Parabasis of *Knights*', *ZPE* 136: 195–200.
BILLAULT, A. (2000), *L'Univers de Philostrate* (Brussels).
BIRCHLER, P., and CHAMAY, J. (1995), 'Hesione en Apulie: un chef-d'oeuvre de la peinture apulienne', *Antike Kunst* 38: 50–7.
BLANCHARD, M. (1980), *Description: Sign, Self, Desire* (The Hague).
—— (1986), 'Philostrate: Problèmes du texte et du tableau' in B. Cassin (ed.), *Les limites de l'imitation à l'époque hellénistique et sous l'Empire* (Paris), 131–54.
BLOK, J., and LARDINOIS, A. (2006), *Solon of Athens: New Historical and Philological Approaches* (Leiden).
BOARDMAN, J. (1978), *Greek Sculpture, The Archaic Period. A Handbook* (London).
—— (1988), 'Herakles', *LIMC*, vol 4.1: 728–838.
BOECKH, A., and DISSEN, L. (1821), *Pindari Epiniciorum interpretatio Latina cum commentario perpetuo*, vol. 3, *Fragmenta et Indices* (Leipzig).
BOND, G. (1988) (ed.), *Euripides, Heracles* (Oxford).
BOND, R. S. (1996), 'Homeric Echoes in *Rhesus*', *AJP* 117: 255–73.
BOTHMER, D. VON (1985), *The Amasis Painter and his World. Vase Painting in Sixth-Century B.C. Athens* (Malibu).

Bowie, A. (1993), *Aristophanes: Myth, Ritual and Comedy* (Cambridge).

Bowie, E. L. (2003), 'The Function of Mythology in Longus' *Daphnis and Chloe*' in J. A. López Férez (ed.), *Mitos en la literatura griega helenistica e imperial* (Madrid), 361–76.

—— and Elsner, J. (forthcoming) (eds.), *Philostratus* (Cambridge).

Bowra, C. M. (1961), *Greek Lyric Poetry from Alcman to Simonides*, 2nd edn. (Oxford).

Brandt, P. (1911) (ed.), *P. Ovidi Nasonis Amorum libri tres* (Leipzig).

Brecht, B. (1990), *Sophocles' Antigone*, adapted by Bertolt Brecht; based on the German translation by Friedrich Hölderlin and translated into English by Judith Malina (New York).

Brelich, A. (1969), *Paides e Parthenoi*, Incunabula Graeca vol. 36 (Rome).

Bremer, J. (1993), 'Aristophanes on his own Poetry', in Bremer and Handley (1993), 125–72.

—— and Handley, E. (1993) (eds.), *Aristophane: Entretiens sur l'Antiquité Classique*, vol. 38 (Geneva).

Breuer, L. (1989), *Gospel at Colonus* (New York).

Bryson, N. (1984), *Tradition and Desire* (Cambridge).

—— (1994), 'Philostratus and the Imaginary Museum', in Goldhill and Osborne (1994), 255–83.

Buck, R. J. (1972), 'The Formation of the Boeotian League', *CP* 68: 94–101.

—— (1979), *A History of Boeotia* (Edmonton).

—— (1994), *Boiotia and the Boiotian League, 423–371 BC* (Edmonton).

Burkert, W. (1983), *Homo Necans: The Anthropology of Ancient Greek Sacrificial Ritual and Myth*, tr. P. Bing (Berkeley).

—— (1985), *Greek Religion*, tr. J. Raffan (Cambridge, MA).

—— (1987), *Ancient Mystery Cults* (Cambridge, MA).

Burnett, A. (1971), *Catastrophe Survived: Euripides' Plays of Mixed Reversal* (Oxford).

Burton, R. W. B. (1980), *The Chorus in Sophocles' Tragedies* (Oxford).

Calame, C. (1977), *Les choeurs de jeunes filles en Grèce archaïque*, 2 vols. (Rome).

—— (1995), *The Craft of Poetic Speech in Greece* (Ithaca).

—— (1997), *Choruses of Young Women in Ancient Greece: Their Morphology, Religious Role, and Social Functions*, tr. D. Collins and J. Orion (Lanham).

—— (2004), 'Choral Forms in Aristophanic Comedy: Musical Mimesis and Dramatic Performance in Classical Athens', in Murray and Wilson (2004), 157–84.

Cambitoglou, A., Aellen, C., and Chamay, J. (1986), *Le Peintre de Darius et son milieu*, Hellas et Roma IV (Geneva).

CÄMMERER, B. (1967), *Beiträge zur Beurteilung der Glaubwurdigkeit der Gemäldebeschreibungen des älteren Philostrat* (Berlin).

CAREY, S. (2003), *Pliny's Catalogue of Culture* (Oxford).

CARPENTER, T. H. (1986), *Dionysian Imagery in Archaic Greek Art* (Oxford).

—— (1991), *Art and Myth in Ancient Greece. A Handbook* (London).

—— and FARAONE, C. A. (1993) (eds.), *Masks of Dionysus* (Ithaca).

CARRIÈRE, J.-C. (1979), *Le Carnaval et la politique* (Paris).

CÀSSOLA, F. (1975), *Inni Omerici* (Verona).

CAVACEPPI, B. (1768–72), *Raccolta d'antiche statue, busti, bassirilievi ed altre sculture*, 3 vols (Rome).

CAVALLONE, M. (1980), 'Il travestimento come espediente in Eschilo e Euripide', *BollClass* 1 (3rd ser.): 93–107.

CHANTRAINE, P. (1968–80), *Dictionnaire étymologique de la langue grecque*, 4 vols (Paris).

CHARBONNEAUX, J., MARTIN, R., and VILLARD, F. (1968), *Grèce archaïque* (Paris).

—— (1969), *Grèce classique* (Paris).

CHASE, G. H. (1979), *The Shield Devices of the Greeks in Art and Literature* (Cambridge, MA; orig. pub. Chicago, 1902).

CLARK, T. J. (1986), *The Painting of Modern Life* (London).

COCKLE, W. E. H. (1987) (ed.), *Euripides, Hypsipyle. Text and Annotation based on a Re-Examination of the Papyri* (Rome).

COLLARD, C., CROPP, M., and LEE, K. (1995) (eds. and trs.), *Euripides. Selected Fragmentary Plays*, vol. 1 (Warminster).

COMPTON-ENGLE, G. (2003), 'Control of Costume in Three Plays of Aristophanes', *AJP* 124: 510–15.

COMSTOCK, M. B., and VERMEULE, C. C. (1976), *Sculpture in Stone: The Greek, Roman and Etruscan Collections of the Museum of Fine Arts, Boston* (Boston).

CONAN, M. (1987), 'The *Imagines* of Philostratus', *Word and Image* 3: 162–71.

CONNOR, W. R. (1989), 'City Dionysia and Athenian Democracy', *C&M* 40: 7–32.

COOK, A. B. (1940), *Zeus. A Study in Ancient Religion*. Vol. 3, *Zeus of the Dark Sky (Earthquakes, Clouds, Wind, Dew, Rain, Meteorites)*. Part ii, Appendices and Notes (Cambridge).

CORRIGAN, P. (1988), ' "Innocent Stupidities": De-picturing (Human) Nature. On Hopeful Resistances and Possible Refusals: Celebrating Difference(s)— Again', in G. Fyfe and J. Law (eds.), *Picturing Power. Visual Depiction and Social Relations* (London), 255–81.

COUËLLE, C. (1991), 'Les noms de la gloire et du plaisir. Étude et fonctionnement des personnages inscrits dans la céramique attique de la fin du vème siècle av. J.-C.', Ph.D. Diss. (Montpellier).

—— (1998), 'Dire en toutes lettres? Allusions et sous-entendus chez le Peintre de Meidias', *Metis* 13: 135–54.

CRAIK, E. (1988) (ed. and tr.), *Euripides: Phoenician Women* (Warminster).

CROALLY, N. (1994), *Euripidean Polemic* (Cambridge).

CSAPO, E. (2004*a*), 'Some Social and Economic Conditions behind the Rise of the Acting Profession in the Fifth and Fourth Centuries BC', in C. Hugoniot, F. Hurlet, and S. Milanezi (eds.), *Le statut de l'acteur dans l'Antiquité grecque et romaine*, Collection Perspectives Historiques 9 (Tours), 53–76.

—— (2004*b*), 'The Politics of the New Music', in Murray and Wilson (2004), 207–48.

—— and SLATER, W. J. (1995), *The Context of Ancient Drama* (Ann Arbor).

CURTIUS, L. (1929), *Pentheus*, Winkelmanns-program der archäologischen Gesellschaft zu Berlin, 88 (Berlin).

DALE, A. M. (1969), *Collected Papers* (Cambridge).

D'ALESSIO, G. B. (1991), 'Osservazioni e paralipomeni ad una nuova edizione dei frammenti di Pindaro', *RFIC* 119: 91–117.

—— (1994), 'First-Person Problems in Pindar', *BICS* 39: 117–39.

—— (2000), ' "Tra gli dèi ad Apollo, e tra gli uomini ad Echecrate": P. Louvre E7734 + 7733 (Pind. fr. dub. 333S.-M.)', in M. Cannatà Fera and S. Grandolini (eds.), *Poesia e religione in Grecia. Studi in onore di G. Aurelio Privitera* (Naples), 233–62.

DAUX, G. (1926), 'Nouvelles inscriptions de Thasos (1921–1924)', *BCH* 50: 213–49.

DAVIES, M. (1987), 'Aeschylus' Clytaemnestra: Sword or Axe?', *CQ* 37: 65–71.

DAVIS, J. T. (1989), *Fictus Adulter: Poet as Actor in the Amores* (Amsterdam).

DAY, J. (1994), 'Interactive Offerings: Early Greek Dedicatory Epigrams and Ritual', *HSCP* 96: 37–74.

—— (2000), 'Epigram and Reader: Generic Force as (Re-)Activation of Ritual', in Depew and Obbink (2000), 37–57.

DEGUY, M. (1984), 'Limitations ou illimitations de l'imitation', in *Le singe à la porte. Vers une theorie de la parodie* (New York).

DEL CORNO, D. (1985) (ed. and tr.), *Aristofane: Le Rane* (Milano).

DEMAND, N. H. (1982), *Thebes in the Fifth Century: Heracles Resurgent* (London).

DEPEW, M. (1997), 'Reading Greek Prayers', *CA* 16: 229–58.

—— and OBBINK, D. (2000) (eds.), *Matrices of Genre: Authors, Canons, Society* (Cambridge, MA).

DERRIDA, J. (1990), *Mémoires d'aveugle* (Paris).

—— (1992), *Acts of Literature*, ed. D. Attridge (London).

DEVAMBEZ, P. (1941), 'Sculptures d'un monument chorégique à Thasos', *Monuments et mémoires publiés par l'Académie des inscriptions et belles-lettres* 38: 93–116.

DI VIRGILIO, R. (1991) (ed. and tr.), *Longo Sofista: Dafni e Cloe* (Milan).

DIDI-HUBERMAN, G. (2002), *Ninfa Moderna. Essai sur le drapé tombé* (Paris).

DOBROV, G. W. (1997a), *The City as Comedy* (Chapel Hill).

—— (1997b), 'Language, Fiction and Utopia', in Dobrov (1997a), 95–132.

—— (2001), *Figures of Play: Greek Drama and Metafictional Poetics* (Oxford).

—— and URIOS-APARISI, E. (1995), 'The Maculate Muse: Gender and Genre in the *Cheiron* of Pherecrates', in G. W. Dobrov (ed.), *Beyond Aristophanes* (Atlanta), 139–74.

DOVER, K. J. (1987), *Greek and the Greeks: Collected Papers* I (Oxford).

—— (1993a) (ed.), *Aristophanes: 'Frogs'* (Oxford).

—— (1993b), 'The Chorus of Initiates in Aristophanes' *Frogs*', in Bremer and Handley (1993), 173–201.

DUCAT, J. (1973), 'La Confédération Béotienne et l'expansion Thébaine à l'èpoque archaïque', *BCH* 97: 59–73.

DUNBAR, N. (1995) (ed.), *Aristophanes: 'Birds'* (Oxford).

DUNN, F. (1996), *Tragedy's End: Closure and Innovation in Euripidean Drama* (Oxford).

DUPONT, F. (2001), *L'Insignifiance tragique* (Paris).

DYCK, A. R. (1986) (ed.), *Michael Psellus. The Essays on Euripides and George of Pisidia and on Heliodorus and Achilles Tatius* (Vienna).

EASTERLING, P. E. (1985), 'Anachronism in Greek tragedy', *JHS* 105: 1–10.

—— (1993), 'The End of an Era? Tragedy in the Early Fourth Century', in Sommerstein et al. (1993), 559–69.

—— (1997a), (ed.), *The Cambridge Companion to Greek Tragedy* (Cambridge).

—— (1997b), 'From Repertoire to Canon', in Easterling 1997a, 211–27.

—— (2002), 'Actor as Icon', in Easterling and Hall (2002), 327–41.

—— and HALL, E. (2002) (eds.), *Greek and Roman Actors: Aspects of an Ancient Profession* (Cambridge).

EBENER, D. (1966) (ed.), *Rhesos. Tragödie eines unbekanntes Dichters* (Berlin).

EBERT, J. (1972), *Griechische Epigramme auf Sieger an gymnischen und hippischen Agonen* (Berlin).

EDMUNDS, A. L. (1980), 'Aristophanes' *Acharnians*', in J. Henderson (ed.), *Aristophanes, Essays in Interpretation*, YCS 36 (Cambridge): 1–41.

EHRENBERG, V. (1967), *From Solon to Socrates* (London).

ELSNER, J. (1995), *Art and the Roman Viewer* (Cambridge).

—— (1996), 'Image and Ritual: Reflections on the Graeco-Roman Appreciation of Art', *CQ* 46: 515–31.

—— (1998), 'Ancient Viewing and Modern Art History', *Metis* 13: 417–37.

—— (2000), 'Making Myth Visual: The Horae of Philostratus and the Dance of the Text', *Römische Mitteilungen* 107: 253–76.

—— (2002), 'The Genres of Ekphrasis', *Ramus* 31: 1–18.

—— (2004), 'Seeing and Saying: A Psycho-Analytic Account of Ekphrasis', in M. Buchan and J. Porter (eds.), *Before Subjectivity? Lacan and the Classics, Helios* 31: 1–2.

FAIRBANKS, A. (1931), *Philostratus: Imagines* (London).

FÄRBER, H. (1936), *Die Lyrik in der Kunsttheorie der Antike* (Munich).

FARNELL, L. R. (1930), *The Works of Pindar*, vol. 1, *Translation in Rhythmical Prose with Literary Comments* (London).

—— (1932), *The Works of Pindar*, vol. 2, *Critical Commentary* (London).

FENIK, B. (1968), *Typical Battle Scenes in the Iliad: Studies in the Narrative Technique of Homeric Battle Description* (Wiesbaden).

FERRARI, F. (1991), 'Tre papiri Pindarici', *RFIC* 119: 385–407.

FERRARI, G. (2002), *Figures of Speech: Men and Maidens in Ancient Greece* (Chicago).

FINKELBERG, M. (1998), *The Birth of Literary Fiction in Ancient Greece* (Oxford).

FINLEY, M. (1985), *Studies in Land and Credit in Ancient Athens, 500–200 BC*: The Horos Inscriptions, repr. with a new introduction by P. Millett (New Brunswick).

FISCHER-LICHTE, E. (2004), 'Thinking about the Origins of Theatre in the 1970s', in E. Hall, F. Macintosh, and A. Wrigley, eds., *Dionysus Since 69: Greek Tragedy at the Dawn of the Third Millennium* (Oxford), 329–60.

FOLEY, H. P. (1980), 'The Masque of Dionysos', *TAPA* 110: 107–33.

—— (1981) (ed.), *Reflections of Women in Antiquity* (London).

—— (1985), *Ritual Irony: Poetry and Sacrifice in Euripides* (Ithaca).

—— (1988), 'Tragedy and Politics in Aristophanes' *Acharnians*', *JHS* 108: 33–47.

—— (1994) (ed.), *The Homeric Hymn to Demeter* (Princeton).

—— (2001), *Female Acts in Greek Tragedy* (Princeton).

—— (2003), 'Choral Identity in Greek Tragedy', *CP* 98: 1–30.

FORD, A. (2002), *The Origins of Criticism: Literary Culture and Poetic Theory in Classical Greece* (Princeton).

FRAENKEL, E. (1950), *Aeschylus Agamemnon*, 3 vols. (Oxford).

FRÄNKEL, C. (1912), 'Satyr- und Bakchennamen auf Vasenbildern', Diss. Bonn.

FREUD, S. (1963), *Jokes and their Relation to the Unconscious*, tr. J. Strachey (New York).

FRIED, M. (1980), *Absorption and Theatricality: Painting and the Beholder in the Age of Diderot* (Chicago).

FRIEDLÄNDER, P. (1948), *Epigrammata. Greek Inscriptions in Verse*, repr. 1987 (Chicago).

FRIEDRICH, R. (1996), 'Everything to Do with Dionysos?', with R. Seaford's reply, in Silk (1996), 257–94.

FRONING, H. (1971), *Dithyrambos und Vasenmalerei in Athen* (Würzburg).

FRONTISI-DUCROUX, F. (1991), *Le Dieu-Masque. Une Figure du Dionysos d'Athènes* (Paris).

—— (1995), *Du masque au visage* (Paris).

—— (2003), *L'Homme-cerf et la femme-araignée* (Paris).

FUHRMANN, H. (1950–1), 'Athamas', *JDAI* 54–5: 103–34.

GALLAVOTTI, C. (1975), 'Letture epigrafiche', *QUCC* 20: 165–91.

GALOIN, A. (2001), *Vases Grecs: Collections des musées de Compiègne et de Laon*, Musée Antoine Vivenel Publications (Paris).

GARLAN, Y. (1968), 'Fortifications et histoire grecque', in Vernant, J.-P. (ed.), *Problèmes de la guerre en Grèce ancienne* (Paris), 245–60.

GARVIE, A. F. (1986) (ed.), *Aeschylus, Choephori* (Cambridge).

GAZDA, E. (2002) (ed.), *The Ancient Art of Emulation* (Ann Arbor).

GEERTZ, C. (1980), *Negara: The Theatre State in Nineteenth-Century Bali* (Princeton).

GEIL, W. E. (1909), *The Great Wall of China* (London).

GEISSLER, P. (1969), *Chronologie der altattischen Komödie*, 2nd edn. (Dublin).

GELLRICH, M. (1988), *Tragedy and Theory: The Problem of Conflict since Aristotle* (Princeton).

—— (1995), 'Interpreting Greek Tragedy: History, Theory, and the New Philology', in Goff (1995), 38–58.

GELZER, T. (1993), 'Feste Strukturen in der Komödie des Aristophanes', in Bremer and Handley (1993), 51–91.

GENETTE, G. (2002), *Figures V* (Paris).

GENTILI, B. (1979), *Theatrical Performances in the Ancient World: Hellenistic and Early Roman Theatre* (Amsterdam).

GERBER, D. E. (1999) (ed. and tr.), *Greek Elegiac Poetry* (Cambridge, MA).

GIULIANI, L. (1995), *Tragik, Trauer und Trost. Bildervasen für eine apulische Totenfeier* (Berlin).

—— (2003), *Bild und Mythos* (Munich).

GOETTE, H. (2007), 'Choregic Monuments and the Athenian Democracy' in P. Wilson (ed.), *The Greek Theatre and Festivals: Documentary Studies* (Oxford), 122–49.

GOFF, B. (1988), 'The Shields of *Phoenissae*', *GRBS* 25: 135–52.

—— (1995) (ed.), *History, Tragedy, Theory: Dialogues on Athenian Drama* (Austin).

GOLDHILL, S. (1984), *Language, Sexuality, Narrative: the 'Oresteia'* (Cambridge).

—— (1986), *Reading Greek Tragedy* (Cambridge).

—— (1987), 'The Great Dionysia and Civic Ideology', *JHS* 107: 58–76.

—— (1991), *The Poet's Voice* (Cambridge).

—— (1994*a*), 'The Naïve and Knowing Eye: Ecphrasis and the Culture of Viewing in the Hellenistic World', in Goldhill and Osborne (1994), 197–223.

—— (1994*b*), 'Representing Democracy: Women at the Great Dionysia', in R. Osborne and S. Hornblower (eds.), *Ritual, Finance, Politics. Athenian Democratic Accounts Presented to David Lewis* (Oxford), 347–69.

—— (1996), 'Collectivity and Otherness—The Authority of the Tragic Chorus: Response to Gould', in M. S. Silk (ed.), *Tragedy and the Tragic. Greek Theatre and Beyond* (Oxford), 244–56.

—— (2000*a*), 'Civic Ideology and the Problem of Difference: The Politics of Aeschylean Tragedy, Once Again', *JHS* 120: 34–56.

—— (2000*b*), 'Placing Theatre in the History of Vision', in N. K. Rutter and B. Sparkes (eds.), *Word and Image in Ancient Greece* (Edinburgh), 161–79.

—— (forthcoming *a*), ' "Drink to Me Only with Thine Eyes": Philostratus' *Letters*', in Bowie and Elsner (forthcoming).

—— (forthcoming *b*), 'What is Ecphrasis for?'.

—— and OSBORNE, R. (1994) (eds.), *Art and Text in Ancient Greek Culture* (Cambridge).

—— —— (1999) (eds.), *Performance Culture and Athenian Democracy* (Cambridge).

GOULD, J. (1996), 'Tragedy and Collective Experience', in Silk (1996), 217–43.

GRANDJEAN, Y., and SALVIAT, F. (2000), *Guide de Thasos*, 2nd edn., French School at Athens Publications (Athens).

GRAZIANI, F. (1990), ' "La Peinture parlante". Ecphrasis et herméneutique dans les *Images* de Philostrate et leur posterité en France au XVIIe siècle', *Saggi e ricerche di letteratura Francese* 29: 9–44.

GREEN, A. S. (1994), *The Revisionist Stage: American Directors Reinvent the Classics* (New York).

—— (1991), 'Women and the Dramatic Festivals', *TAPA* 121: 133–47.

GREEN, J. R. (1991*a*), 'On Seeing and Depicting the Theatre in Classical Athens', *GRBS* 32: 15–50.

—— (1991*b*), 'Notes on Phlyax Vases', *NAC* 20: 49–56.

—— (1994), *Theatre in Ancient Greek Society* (London).

—— (1995), 'Theatre Production: 1987–1995', *Lustrum* 37: 7–202.

—— (1999), 'Tragedy and the Spectacle of the Mind: Messenger Speeches, Actors, Narrative, and Audience Imagination in Fourth-Century BCE Vase Painting', in B. Bergmann and C. Kondoleon (eds.), *The Art of Ancient Spectacle* (New Haven), 37–63.

—— (2002), review of Morelli (2001), *BMCR* 2002.12.01.

GREGORY, J. (1985), 'Some Aspects of Seeing in Euripides *Bacchae*', *G&R* 32: 23–31.

GRENFELL, B. P., and HUNT, A. S. (1904) (eds.), *The Oxyrhynchus Papyri*, part 4 (London).

GRETHLEIN, J. (2003), *Asyl und Athen: die Konstruktion kollektiver Identität in der griechischen Tragödie* (Stuttgart).

GRIFFITH, M. (1990), 'Contest and Contradiction in Early Greek Poetry', in Griffith and Mastronarde (1990), 185–207.

—— and MASTRONARDE, D. (1990) (eds.), *Cabinet of the Muses: Essays on Classical and Comparative Literature in Honor of Thomas G. Rosenmeyer* (Atlanta).

GRUBE, G. M. A. (1965), *The Greek and Roman Critics* (London).

HABICHT, C. (1985), *Pausanias' Guide to Ancient Greece* (Berkeley).

HALDANE, J. (1965), 'Musical Themes and Imagery in Aeschylus', *JHS* 85: 33–41.

HALL, E. (1989), *Inventing the Barbarian* (Oxford).

—— (1996), 'Is there a Polis in Aristotle's *Poetics*?', in Silk (1996), 295–309.

—— (1997), 'The Sociology of Athenian Tragedy', in Easterling 1997a, 93–126.

—— (1998), 'Ithyphallic Males Behaving Badly: Satyr Drama as Gendered Tragic Ending', in M. Wyke (ed.), *Parchments of Gender: Deciphering the Bodies of Antiquity*, (Oxford) 13–37.

—— (1999), 'Actor's Song in Tragedy', in Goldhill and Osborne (1999), 96–122.

—— (2000), 'Female Figures and Metapoetry in Old Comedy', in Harvey and Wilkins (2000), 407–18.

—— (2002a), 'The Ancient Actor's Presence since the Renaissance', in Easterling and Hall (2002), 419–34.

—— (2002b), 'The Singing Actors of Antiquity', in Easterling and Hall (2002), 1–38.

—— (2006), 'The Theatrical Cast of Athens: Roles in Ancient Greek Drama and Society' Interactions between Ancient Greek Drama and Society (Oxford).

—— (forthcoming a), 'Greek Tragedy 431–380 BCE', in R. Osborne (ed.), *Anatomy of a Cultural Revolution* (Cambridge).

HALL, E. and WYLES, R. (forthcoming b) (eds.) New Directions in Ancient Pantomime (Oxford).

HALLERAN, M. (1988), *The Heracles of Euripides* (Cambridge, MA).

HALPERIN, D. M., WINKLER, J. J., and ZEITLIN, F. I. (1990) (eds.), *Before Sexuality: The Construction of Erotic Experience in the Ancient Greek World* (Princeton).

HAMILTON, R. (1992), *Choes and Anthesteria* (Ann Arbor).

HANSEN, M. H. (1995), 'Boiotian *Poleis*—a Test Case', in M. H. Hansen (ed.), *Sources for the Ancient Greek City-State*, Symposium August 24–27 1994, Acts of the Copenhagen Polis Centre vol. 2 (Copenhagen), 13–63.

HANSEN, P. (1983) (ed.), *Carmina Epigraphica Graeca*, vol. 1 (Berlin).

—— (1989) (ed.), *Carmina Epigraphica Graeca*, vol. 2 (Berlin).

HARDIE, A. (2004), 'Muses and Mysteries', in Murray and Wilson (2004), 11–37.

HARTEN, T. (1999), *Paidagogos. Der Pädagoge in der griechischen Kunst* (Kiel).

HARTWIG, P. (1893) (ed.), *Die griechischen Meisterschalen der Blüthezeit des strengen rothfigurigen Stiles, mit Unterstützung der Königlich Sächsischen Gesellschaft der Wissenschaften und aus privaten Mitteln* (Stuttgart).

HARVEY, D., and WILKINS, J. (2000) (eds.), *The Rivals of Aristophanes* (Exeter).

HEATH, M. (1987*a*), 'Euripides' *Telephus*' *CQ* 37: 272–80.

—— (1987*b*), *The Poetics of Greek Tragedy* (London).

HENDERSON, J. (1987) (ed.), *Aristophanes 'Lysistrata'* (Oxford).

—— (1991), 'Women and the Dramatic Festivals', *TAPA* 121: 133–47.

—— (1993), 'Comic Hero versus Political Elite', in Sommerstein et al. (1993), 307–19.

HENDERSON, J. G. W. (1994), '*Timeo Danaos*: Approaching Amazons in early Greek Art and Pottery', in Goldhill and Osborne (1994), 85–137.

—— (1999), 'Smashing Bodies: the Corinthian Tydeus-Ismene Vase', in J. I. Porter (ed.), *Constructions of the Classical Body* (Ann Arbor), 19–49.

HENRICHS, A. (1995), 'Why Should I Dance? Choral Self-Referentiality in Greek Tragedy', *Arion* 3: 56–111.

—— (1996), 'Dancing in Athens, Dancing on Delos: Some Patterns of Choral Projection in Euripides', *Philologus* 140: 48–62.

HERINGTON, C. (1963), 'The Influence of Old Comedy on Aeschylus' later Trilogies', *TAPA* 94: 113–23.

HINDS, S. (1993), 'Medea in Ovid: Scenes from the Life of an Intertextual Heroine', *MD* 30: 9–47.

HOBSBAWM, E., and RANGER T., (1983) (eds.), *The Invention of Tradition* (Cambridge).

HODGE, R., and KRESS, G. (1988), *Social Semiotics* (Cambridge).

HOFFMANN, P. (1999), *Römische Mosaike im rheinischen Landesmuseum Trier* (Trier).

HORNBLOWER, S. (1991), *A Commentary on Thucydides*, vol. 1, books *1–3* (Oxford).

—— (1996), *A Commentary on Thucydides*, vol. 2, books *4–5.24* (Oxford).

HUBBARD, T. (1991), *The Mask of Comedy: Aristophanes and the Intertextual Parabasis* (Ithaca).

HUNTER, R. L. (1983), *A Study of Daphnis and Chloe* (Cambridge).

—— (1999) (ed.), *Theocritus. A Selection* (Cambridge).

Hurwit, J. (1999), *The Athenian Acropolis: History, Mythology, and Archaeology from the Neolithic Era to the Present* (Cambridge).

Ieranò, G. (1997), *Il Ditirambo di Dioniso* (Rome).

Immerwahr, H. (1990), *Attic Script. A Survey* (Oxford).

Jameson, M. (1994), 'The Ritual of the Athena *Nike* Parapet', in R. Osborne and S. Hornblower (eds.), *Ritual, Finance, Politics: Athenian Democratic Accounts Presented to David Lewis* (Oxford), 307–24.

Jones, C. P. (1993), 'Greek Drama in the Roman Empire', in R. Scodel (ed.), *Theater and Society in the Classical World* (Ann Arbor), 39–52.

—— (2001), 'Pausanias and His Guides', in S. E. Alcock, J. F. Cherry, and J. Elsner (eds.), *Pausanias: Travel and Memory in Roman Greece* (Oxford), 33–9.

Jong, de I. (1991), *Narrative in Drama: The Art of the Euripidean Messenger Speech, Mnemosyne* Suppl. 116 (Leiden).

Jory, J. (1996), 'The Drama of the Dance: Prolegomena to an Iconography of Imperial Pantomime', in W. J. Slater (ed.), *Roman Theater and Society* (Ann Arbor), 1–27.

Kaibel, G. (1878), *Epigrammata Graeca,* repr. 1965, Hildesheim.

Kannicht, R. (1996), *Paradeigmata. Aufsätze zur Griechieschen Poesie,* eds. L. von Kappel and E. A. Schmidt (Heidelberg).

Katz, M. A. (1981), 'The Divided World of *Iliad* VI', in Foley (1981).

Kelly, H. A. (1979), 'Tragedy and the Performance of Tragedy in late Roman Antiquity', *Traditio* 35: 21–44.

Kim, J. (2000), *The Pity of Achilles* (Lanham).

Knoepfler, D. (1993), *Les imagiers de l'Orestie* (Zurich).

Koch, G., and Sichtermann, H. (1982), *Römische Sarkophage* (Munich).

Koch-Harnack, G. (1983), *Knabenliebe und Tiergeschenke: Ihre Bedeutung im päderastischen Erziehungssytem Athens* (Berlin).

Konstan, D. (1997), 'The Greek Polis and its Negations', in Dobrov 1997*a*, 3–22.

—— (2001), *Pity Transformed* (London).

—— and Rutter, N. K. (2003) (eds.), *Envy, Spite and Jealousy: The Rivalrous Emotions in Ancient Greece* (Edinburgh).

Kossatz-Deissmann, A. (1997), 'Tragodia', *LIMC* 8.1, 48–50.

Kovacs, D. (1998) (ed. and tr.), *Euripides,* vol. 3 (Cambridge, MA).

Kowalzig, B. (2002), 'Singing for the Gods: Aetiological Myth, Ritual and Locality in Greek Choral Poetry of the Late Archaic Period', D.Phil. Thesis, Oxford University.

—— (2004), 'Changing Choral Worlds: Song-Dance and Society in Athens and Beyond', in Murray and Wilson (2004), 39–65.

—— (2006), 'The Aetiology of Empire? Hero-cult and Athenian Tragedy', in J. Davidson, F. Muecke, and P. Wilson, (eds.), *Greek Drama III: Essays in Honour of Kevin Lee*, BICS Suppl. (London), 79–98.

KRAUS, C. S. (1998), 'Dangerous Supplements: Etymology and Genealogy in Euripides' *Heracles*', *PCPS* 44: 137–57.

KRUMEICH, R., PECHSTEIN, N., and SEIDENSTICKER, B. (1999) (eds.), *Das griechische Satyrspiel* (Darmstadt).

KUNISCH, N. (1997), *Makron* (Mainz am Rhein).

KURKE, L. (1991), *The Traffic in Praise: Pindar and the Poetics of Social Economy* (Ithaca).

—— (1998), 'The Cultural Impact of (on) Democracy: Decentering Tragedy', in I. Morris and K. A. Raaflaub (eds.), *Democracy 2500? Questions and Challenges*. AIA Colloquia and Conference Papers, No. 2 (Dubuque), 155–69.

—— (1999), *Coins, Bodies, Games, and Gold : The Politics of Meaning in Archaic Greece* (Princeton).

—— (2005), 'Choral Lyric as "Ritualization": Poetic Sacrifice and Poetic *Ego* in Pindar's Sixth Paian', *CA* 24: 81–130.

—— and DOUGHERTY, C. (1993) (eds.), *Cultural Poetics in Archaic Greece* (Cambridge).

—— —— (2003) (eds.), *The Cultures within Ancient Greek Culture* (Cambridge).

KURTZ, D. C., and BEAZLEY, J. (1983), *The Berlin Painter* (Oxford).

LACAN, J. (1966), *Écrits* (Paris).

LADA-RICHARDS, I. (2002), 'The Subjectivity of Greek Performance', in Easterling and Hall (2002), 395–418.

LAIRD, A. (1993), 'Sounding out Ecphrasis: Art and Text in Catullus 64', *JRS* 83: 18–30.

LAMBIN, G. (1982), 'Le surnom Βάταλος et les mots de cette famille', *RPH* 56: 249–63.

LARSEN, J. A. O. (1968), *Greek Federal States: Their Institutions and History* (Oxford).

LATTIMORE, R. (1961) (tr.), *Homer, The Iliad* (Chicago).

LE GUEN, B. (2001), *Les associations de technites dionysiaques à l'époque hellénistique*, 2 vols. (Nancy).

LEACH, E. W. (2000), 'Narrative Space and the Viewer in Philostratus' *Eikones*', *Römische Mitteilungen* 107: 237–51.

LEBECK, A. (1971), *The Oresteia: A Study in Language and Structure* (Cambridge, MA).

LEE, A. G. (1962), 'Tenerorum lusor amorum', in J. P. Sullivan (ed.), *Critical Essays on Roman Literature: Elegy and Lyric* (London), 149–79.

LEHMANN-HARTLEBEN, K. (1941), 'The *Imagines* of the Elder Philostratus', *ABull* 23: 16–44.

LEHNUS, L. (1977), 'Da una nuova ispezione di *P. Oxy.* IV 659', *MPhL* 2: 227–31.

—— (1984), 'Pindaro: Il Dafneforico per Agasicle (Fr. 94b Sn.-M.)', *BICS* 31: 61–92.

LEONARD, M. (2005), *Athens in Paris: Ancient Greece and the Political in Postwar French Thought* (Oxford).

LEONHARDT, J. (1991), *Phalloslied und Dithyrambos: Aristoteles über den Ursprung des griechischen Dramas*, Abh. Heid. Ak. Wiss. (phil-hist. Klasse) 4 (Heidelberg).

LESKY, A. (1940), 'Bildwerk und Deutung bei Philostrat und Homer', *Hermes* 75: 38–53.

LEUTSCH, E. L. von, and SCHNEIDEWIN, F. G. (1965) (eds.) *Corpus Paroemiographorum Graecorum*, 2 vols., (Hildesheim).

LEWERENTZ, A. (1995), 'Die Sepulkralsymbolik des Hippolytosmythos auf stadtrömischen Sarkophagen', *Boreas* 18: 111–30.

LEWIS, D., and JEFFERY, L. (1994) (eds.), *Inscriptiones Graecae*, vol. 1 (3rd edn.), fasc. 2, *Dedicationes, catalogi, termini, tituli sepulcrales, varia, tituli Attici extra Atticam reperti, addenda* (Berlin).

LIGHTFOOT, J. L. (2002), 'Nothing to Do with the *Technitai* of Dionysus?', in Easterling and Hall (2002), 209–24.

LINANT DE BELLEFONDS, P. (1994), 'Hippolytos I', *LIMC*, vol. 5, 445–64.

LING, R., and LING, L. (2000), 'Colossal Statues', in R. Ling (ed.), *Making Classical Art: Process and Practice* (Stroud), 108–23.

LINKE, K. (1977) (ed.), *Die Fragmente des Grammatikers Dionysios Thrax, Sammlung griechischer und lateinischer Grammatiker*, vol. 3 (Berlin).

LISSARRAGUE, F. (1987), *Un flot d'images, une esthétique du banquet grec* (Paris).

—— (1990), *The Aesthetics of the Greek Banquet: Images of Wine and Ritual* (Princeton).

—— (1993), 'On the Wildness of Satyrs', in Carpenter and Faraone (1993), 207–20.

LISSARRAGUE, F. (1997), 'L'homme, le singe et le satyre', in B. Cassin and J. L. Labarrière (eds.), *L'Animal dans l'Antiquité* (Paris), 455–72.

—— (2003), 'Satiri tra le donne', in P. Veyne, F. Lissarrague, and F. Frontisi-Ducroux (eds.), *I misteri del gineceo*, tr. B. Gregori (Rome), 171–90.

LLOYD, M. (1992), *The Agon in Euripides* (Oxford).

LLOYD-JONES, H. (1967), 'Heracles at Eleusis', *Maia* 19: 206–29.

—— (1971), *The Justice of Zeus* (Berkeley).

LORAUX, N. (1981), *L'invention d'Athènes. Histoire de l'oraison funèbre dans la cité classique* (Paris).

—— (1989), *'Le lit, la guerre'. Les expériences de Tirésias* (Paris).

—— (1993), *The Children of Athena: Athenian Ideas about Citizenship and the Division between the Sexes*, tr. C. Levine (Princeton).

—— (2002*a*), *The Divided City: On Memory and Forgetting in Ancient Athens*, tr. C. O. Pache (New York).

—— (2002*b*), *The Mourning Voice*, tr. E. T. Rawlings (Ithaca; orig. pub. Paris, 1999).

LUPAS, L., and PETRE, Z. (1981), *Commentaire aux Sept contre Thèbes d'Eschyle* (Paris).

LYONS, D. (1997), *Gender and Immortality: Heroines in Ancient Greek Myth and Cult* (Princeton).

MAASS, P. (1972), *Die Proedrie des Dionysostheaters in Athen* (Munich).

McDONALD, M. (1992), *Ancient Sun, Modern Light: Greek Drama on the Modern Stage* (New York).

MacDONALD, W. L., and PINTO, J. A. (1995), *Hadrian's Villa and its Legacy* (New Haven).

MacDOWELL, D. M. (1990) (ed.), *Demosthenes, 'Against Meidias' (Oration 21)* (Oxford).

MACKIL, E. (2003), '*Koinon* and *Koinonia*: Mechanisms and Structures of Political Collectivity in Classical and Hellenistic Greece.' Ph.D. Diss., Princeton University.

MACLEOD, C. (1983), *Collected Papers* (Oxford).

MADDOLI, G., and SALADINO, V. (1995) (eds. and trs.), *Pausania: Guida della Grecia. Libro V* (Milan).

MAEHLER, H. (1982) (ed.), *Die Lieder des Bakchylides*, vol. I (Leiden).

—— (2001) (ed.), *Pindarus. Pars II: Fragmenta, Indices* (Leipzig).

MAFFEI, S. (1991), 'La σοφία del pittore e del poeta nel proemio delle *Imagines* di Filostrato Maggiore', *ASNP* 21: 591–621.

MALONEY, E. P. (2003), 'Theatre for a New Age. Macedonia and Ancient Greek Drama', Ph.D. Diss., Cambridge.

MAN, P. DE (1984), *The Rhetoric of Romanticism* (New York).

MANIERI, A. (1999), 'Colori, suoni e profumi nelle *Imagines*: principi dell'estetica filostratea', *QUCC* 63: 111–21.

MARCH, J. (1989), 'Euripides' *Bakchai*: A Reconsideration in the Light of the Vase Paintings', *BICS* 36: 33–65.

MAREK, C. (1984), *Die Proxenie* (Frankfurt am Main).

MARK, I. (1993), *The Sanctuary of Athena Nike in Athens: Architectural Stages and Chronology*, *Hesperia* Suppl. 26 (Princeton).

MARSHALL, C., and VAN WILLIGENBURG, S. (2004), 'Judging Athenian Dramatic Competitions', *JHS* 124: 90–107.

MARTIN, R. (1989), *The Language of Heroes: Speech and Performance in The Iliad* (Ithaca).

—— (1993), 'The Seven Sages as Performers of Wisdom', in Kurke and Dougherty (1993), 108–28.

—— (2003), 'The Pipes are Brawling: Conceptualizing Musical Performance in Classical Athens', in Kurke and Dougherty (2003), 153–80.

—— (2006), 'Solon in No Man's Land', in Blok and Lardinois (2006), 157–72.

MASLOV, B. (2003), 'Pindar's Choral Subjects: Legal Language and Poetic Authority in Epinician', unpublished seminar paper.

MASTRONARDE, D. J. (2002) (ed.), *Euripides, Medea* (Cambridge).

MATHESON, S. (1995), *Polygnotus and Vase Painting in Classical Athens* (Madison).

MATHIEU-CASTELLANI, G. (1996), 'Les *Images* de Philostrate: Une histoire d'amour', *La Licorne* 35: 89–98.

MAU, A. (1890), 'Scavi in Pompei', *Römische Mitteilungen* 5: 228–84.

McCOMBIE, D. (2002), 'Philostratus, *Histoi, Imagines* 2.28: Ekphrasis and the Web of Illusion', *Ramus* 31: 146–57.

McDONALD, M. (1992), *Ancient Sun, Modern Light: Greek Drama on the Modern Stage* (New York).

MEE, C. L. (1998), *History Plays* (Baltimore and London).

MEIJERING, R. (1987), *Literary and Rhetorical Theories in Greek Scholia* (Groningen).

MENDELSOHN, D. (2002), *Gender and the City in Euripides' Political Plays* (Oxford).

MENTA, E. (1995), *The Magic World Behind the Curtain: Andrei Serban in American Theatre* (New York).

MERKELBACH, R. (1988), *Die Hirten des Dionysos: die Dionysos-Mysterien der römischen Kaiserzeit und der bukolische Roman des Longus* (Stuttgart).

—— and WEST, M. L. (1967) (eds.), *Fragmenta Hesiodea* (Oxford).

METTE, H. (1977), *Urkunden dramatischer Aufführungen in Griechenland* (Berlin).

MICHELINI, A. (1987), *Euripides and the Tragic Tradition* (Madison).

MOMMSEN, H. (1980), 'Achill und Aias pflichtvergessen?', in H. A. Cahn and E. Simon, eds., *Tainia: Roland Hampe zum 70. Geburtstag am 2. Dezember 1978. Dargebracht von Mitarbeitern, Schülern und Freunden* (Mainz am Rhein), 139–52.

MORAW, S. (2002), 'Die grossen Dramatiker', in S. Moraw and E. Nölle (eds.), *Die Geburt des Theaters in der griechischen Antike* (Mainz am Rhein), 119–27.

Morelli, G. (2001), *Teatro attico e pittura vascolare. Una tragedia di Cheremone nella ceramica italiota*, Spudasmata 84 (Hildesheim).

Moret, J-M. (1975), *L' Ilioupersis dans la céramique italiote* (Geneva).

Morgan, J. R. (2004) (ed. and tr.), *Longus: Daphnis and Chloe* (Oxford).

Morgan, K. (1977), *Ovid's Art of Imitation: Propertius in the Amores* (Leiden).

Morizot, Y. (1992), 'Klytaimnestra', *LIMC*, vol. 6.1, 72–81.

Morris, S. (1992), *Daidalos and the Origins of Greek Art* (Princeton).

Mossman, J. M. (1995), *Wild Justice: A Study of Euripides' Hecuba* (Oxford).

Most, G. W. (1986), 'Pindar, Fr. 94b.19–20 Sn.-M.', *ZPE* 64: 33–8.

—— (2000), 'Generating Genres: The Idea of the Tragic', in Depew and Obbink (2000), 15–35.

Muir, E. (1981), *Civic Ritual in Renaissance Venice* (Princeton).

Murray, P. (2002), 'Plato's Muses: The Goddesses that Endure', in Spentzou and Fowler (2002), 29–46.

—— and Wilson, P. (2004) (eds.), *Music and the Muses: The Culture of 'Mousikê' in the Classical Athenian City* (Oxford).

Naerebout, F. G. (1997), *Attractive Performances: Ancient Greek Dance, Three Preliminary Studies* (Amsterdam).

Nagy, G. (1983), 'Sema and Noesis: Some Illustrations', *Arethusa* 16: 35–55.

—— (1990), *Pindar's Homer: The Lyric Possession of an Epic Past* (Baltimore).

Nancy, J.-L. (1996), *The Muses*, tr. P. Kamuf (Stanford).

Neer, R. T. (2002), *Style and Politics in Athenian Vase-Painting: The Craft of Democracy, ca. 530–460 BCE.* (Cambridge).

Newby, Z. (forthcoming), 'Absorption and Erudition in Philostratus' *Imagines*' in Bowie and Elsner (forthcoming).

Newiger, H. J. (1957), *Metapher und Allegorie. Studien zu Aristophanes* (Munich).

Nightingale, A. W. (1995), *Genres in Dialogue: Plato and the Construct of Philosophy* (Cambridge).

—— (2004), *Spectacles of Truth in Classical Greek Philosophy: Theoria in its Cultural Context* (Cambridge).

Nilsson, M. (1906), *Griechische Feste mit Ausnahme der Attischen* (Leipzig).

Oakley, J. (1991), ' "The Death of Hippolytus" in South Italian Vase Painting', *Quaderni Ticinesi di Numismatica e Antichità Classiche* 20: 63–84.

—— and Sinos, R. (1993), *The Wedding in Ancient Athens* (Madison).

Ober, J. (1989), *Mass and Elite in Democratic Athens: Rhetoric, Ideology, and the Power of the People* (Princeton).

—— (1995), 'Greek Horoi: Artifactual Texts and the Contingency of Meaning', in D. B. Small (ed.), *Methods in the Mediterranean. Historical and Archeological Views on Texts and Archaeology* (Leiden), 91–123.

OBER, J. (2006), 'Solon and the Horoi: Facts on the Ground in Archaic Athens', in Blok and Lardinois (2006), 441–56.

OEPKE, A. (1934), '*ΑΜΦΙΘΑΛΕΙΣ* im griechischen und hellenistischen Kult', *Archiv für Religionswissenschaft* 31: 42–56.

OLSON, D. (1998) (ed.), *Aristophanes 'Peace'* (Oxford).

—— (2002) (ed.), *Aristophanes 'Acharnians'* (Oxford).

OSBORNE, R. (1993), 'Competitive Festivals and the Polis: The Emergence of the Dramatic Festivals at Athens', in Sommerstein et al. (1993), 21–37.

PADEL, R. (1974), 'Imagery of the Elsewhere. Two Choral Odes of Euripides', *CQ* 24: 227–41.

PADGETT, J. M., COMSTOCK, M., HERRMANN, J., and VERMEULE, C. (1993), *Vase-Painting in Italy: Red-Figure and Related Works in the Museum of Fine Arts* (Boston).

PADUANO, G. (1967), 'Il motivo del re mendicante e lo scandalo del Telefo', *SCO* 116: 330–42.

PAGE, D. L. (1968) (ed.), *Lyrica Graeca selecta* (Oxford).

—— (1975) (ed.), *Epigrammata Graeca* (Oxford).

—— (1981) (ed.), *Further Greek Epigrams* (Cambridge).

PALEOTHODOROS, D. (2001), 'Satyrs as Shield Devices in Vase Painting', *Eulimene* 2: 67–92.

PAOLETTI, O. (1994), 'Kassandra', *LIMC*, vol. 7.1, 956–70.

PATTONI, M. P. (2004), 'I Pastoralia di Longo e la contaminazione dei generi. Alcune proposte interpretative', *MD* 53: 83–123.

—— (2005) (ed. and tr.), *Longo sofista: Dafni e Cloe* (Milan).

PAULSEN, T. (1992), *Inszenierung des Schicksals: Tragödie und Komödie im Roman des Heliodor*, Bochumer Altertumswissenschafstscolloquium 10 (Trier).

PAVESE, C. (1975), 'La decima e la undecima Pitica di Pindaro', in *Studi triestini di antichità in onore di L. A. Stella* (Trieste), 235–53.

PAXSON, J. J. (1994), *The Poetics of Personification* (Cambridge).

PEARSON, A. C. (1917) (ed.), *The Fragments of Sophocles*, 3 vols. (Cambridge).

PEEK, W. (1974), 'Zu der Dreifussbasis IG I² 673', *ZPE* 13: 199–200.

PELLING, C. (1997), 'Conclusion', in *Greek Tragedy and the Historian* (Oxford), 213–35.

PEPONI, A.-E. (2004), 'Initiating the Viewer: Deixis and Visual Perception in Alcman's Lyric Drama', *Arethusa* 37: 295–316.

PEPPA-DELMOUSOU, D. (1971), 'Das Akropolis-Epigramm IG I² 673', *AM* 86: 55–66.

PERLMAN, P. (1983), 'Plato *Laws* 833C–834D and the Bears of Brauron', *GRBS* 24: 115–30.

—— (1989), 'Acting the She-Bear for Artemis', *Arethusa* 22: 111–33.

PETERSEN, L. (1939), *Zur geschichte der Personifikation in griechischer Dichtung und bildender Kunst* (Würzburg).

PFUHL, E. (1923), *Malerei und Zeichnung der Griechen* (Munich).

PHILLIP, H. (2004), *Archaische Silhouettenbleche und Schildzeichen in Olympia*, Olympische Forschungen 30 (Berlin).

PICKARD-CAMBRIDGE, A. (1962), *Dithyramb, Tragedy, and Comedy*, 2nd edn., rev. T. Webster (Oxford).

—— (1988), *The Dramatic Festivals of Athens*, 2nd edn., rev. J. Gould and D. Lewis (Oxford).

PIGEAUD, J. (1987), *Folie et cures de la folie* (Paris).

PODLECKI, A. (1981), 'Some Early Athenian Commemorations of Choral Victories', in G. Shrimpton and D. McCargar (eds.), *Classical Contributions: Studies in Honour of Malcolm Francis McGregor* (Locust Valley), 95–101.

POSTLE, M. (1995), *Sir Joshua Reynolds: The Subject Pictures* (Cambridge).

PRAG, A. J. N. W. (1991), 'Clytaemnestra's Weapon Yet Once More', *CQ* 41: 242–6.

PRIER, R. (1989), *Thauma Idesthai: The Phenomenology of Sight and Appearance in Archaic Greek* (Tallahassee).

PUCCI, P. (1961), *Aristofane ed Euripide: Ricerche stilistiche e metriche* (Roma).

—— (1977), *Hesiod and the Language of Poetry* (Baltimore).

—— (1981), *The Violence of Pity in Euripides' Medea* (Ithaca).

—— (1999), 'Écriture tragique et récit mythique', *Europe* 77: 209–41.

RACE, W. (1997*a*) (ed. and tr.), *Pindar. Olympian Odes, Pythian Odes* (Cambridge, MA).

—— (1997*b*) (ed. and tr,), *Pindar. Nemean Odes. Isthmian Odes. Fragments* (Cambridge, MA).

RAEDER, J. (1983), *Die statuarische Ausstattung der Villa Hadriana bei Tivoli* (Frankfurt am Main).

RAU, P. (1967), *Paratragoedia* (Munich).

RAUBITSCHEK, A. (1949), *Dedications from the Athenian Akropolis* (Cambridge, MA).

REDFIELD, J. (1975), *Nature and Culture in the Iliad: the Tragedy of Hector* (Chicago).

—— (1982), 'Notes on the Greek Wedding', *Arethusa* 15: 181–201.

REINHARDT, K. (2003), 'The Intellectual Crises in Euripides', in J. M. Mossman (ed.), *Euripides, Oxford Reading in Classical Studies* (Oxford; orig. pub. 1960).

REVERMANN, M. (1999–2000), 'Euripides, Tragedy and Macedon: Some Conditions of Reception', *ICS* 24–5: 451–67.

RHODES, P. (2003), 'Nothing to Do with Democracy: Athenian Drama and the *polis*', *JHS* 123: 104–19.

RIEMER, P. and ZIMMERMANN, B. (eds.) (1998), *Der Chor im antiken und modernen Drama* (Stuttgart and Weimar).

ROBERT, L. (1969), '*ΑΜΦΙΘΑΛΗΣ*', in *Opera minora selecta*, vol. 1 (Amsterdam), 633–43.

ROBERTS, D. (1987), 'Parting Words: Final Lines in Sophocles and Euripides', *CQ* 37: 51–64.

—— (1988), 'Sophoclean Endings: Another Story', *Arethusa* 21: 177–96.

ROBERTSON, M. (1992), *The Art of Vase-Painting in Classical Athens* (Cambridge).

ROBINSON, G. (1999), 'The Eyes of Achilleus: *Iliad* 1.200', *Phoenix* 53: 1–7.

ROESCH, P. (1989), 'L'aulos et les aulètes en Béotie,' in Beister and Buckler (1989), 203–14.

ROGGE, S. (1995), *Die attischen Sarkophage*, I: *Achill und Hippolytos* (Berlin).

RÖNNE-LINDERS, T. (1963), 'A Black-Figured Neck-Amphora of the Leagros Group', *Medelhavsmuseet Museum Bulletin* 3: 54–66.

ROSE, H. J. (1957), *A Commentary on The Surviving Plays of Aeschylus*, 2 vols. (Amsterdam).

ROSEN, R. (1999), 'Comedy and Confusion in Callias' Letter Tragedy', *CP* 94: 147–67.

—— (2000), 'Cratinus' *Pytine* and the Construction of the Comic Self', in Harvey and Wilkins (2000), 23–39.

ROSENMEYER, P. (2001), *Ancient Epistolary Fictions* (Cambridge).

RUCK, C. (1967), *IG II^2 2323. The List of the Victors in Comedies at the Dionysia* (Leiden).

RUTHERFORD, I. (2001), *Pindar's Paeans: A Reading of the Fragments with a Survey of the Genre* (Oxford).

SAID, S. (1996), 'The *Assemblywomen*: Women, Economy, and Politics', in E. Segal (ed.), *Oxford Readings in Aristophanes* (Oxford), 282–313 (orig. pub. 1979).

SALVIAT, F. (1979), 'Vedettes de la scène en province: signification et date des monuments chorégiques de Thasos', *Thasiaca, BCH* suppl. 5, 155–67.

SAMONS, L. (2000), *Empire of the Owl: Athenian Imperial Finance. Historia Einzelschriften* (Stuttgart).

SAMPAOLO, V. (1994), 'VI. 15, 1: Casa dei Vettii', in G. Pugliese Carratelli— I. Baldassarre (eds.), *Pompei. Pitture e Mosaici*, vol. 5 (Rome), 468–572.

SARIAN, H. (1986), 'Réflexions sur l'iconographie des Erinyes', *BCH* Suppl. 14, 25–35.

SBORDONE, F. (1940), 'Partenii Pindarici e Dafneforie Tebane', *Athenaeum* 18: 26–50.

SCAMUZZI, E. (1965), *Egyptian Art in the Egyptian Museum of Turin* (New York).

SCARRY, E. (1987), *The Body in Pain: the Making and Unmaking of the World* (Oxford).

SCHACHTER, A. (1967), 'A Boeotian Cult Type', *BICS* 14: 1–16.

—— (1981), *Cults of Boiotia*, vol. 1, *Acheloos to Hera*, *BICS* suppl. no. 38.1.

—— (1986). *Cults of Boiotia*, vol. 2, *Herakles to Poseidon*, *BICS* suppl. no. 38.2.

SCHECHNER, R. (ed.) (1970), *The Performance Group: Dionysus in 69* (New York).

SCHEFOLD, K., and JUNG, F. (1989), *Die Sagen von den Argonauten, von Theben und Troia in der klassischen und hellenistischen Kunst* (Munich).

SCHLESIER, R. (1993), 'Mixtures of Masks: Maenads as Tragic Models', in Carpenter and Faraone (1993), 89–114.

SCHMIDT, M. (1982), 'Asia und Apate', in L. Beschi, M. L. Gualandi, L. Massei, and S. Settis (eds.), *Aparchai: Nuove richerche e studi sulla Magna Graecia e la Sicilia antica in onore di Paolo Enrico Arias* (Pisa), 505–20.

—— (1986), 'Medea und Heracles—zwei tragische Kindermörder', in E. Böhr and W. Martini (eds.), *Studien zur Mythologie und Vasenmalerei. Konrad Schauenburg zum 65. Geburtstag am 16. April 1986* (Mainz), 169–74.

—— (1998), 'Komische arme Teufel und andere Gesellen auf der griechischen Komödienbühne', *AK* 41: 17–32.

SCHMITT-PANTEL, P. (1992), *La cité au banquet: Histoire des repas publics dans les cités grecques* (Rome).

SCHÖNBERGER, J. K. (1942), 'Κωπώ', *Glotta* 29: 87–9.

SCHÖNBERGER, O., and KALINKA, E. (1968) (eds.), *Philostratos: Die Bilder* (Munich).

SCHÖNE, A. (1987), *Der Thiasos: Eine Ikonographische Untersuchung über das Gefolge des Dionysos in der attischen Vasenmalerei des 6. und 5. Jhs v. Chr.* (Göteborg).

SCHRIJVERS, P. H. (1976), 'O Tragoedia tu labor aeternus: Étude sur l'élégie III,1 des *Amores* d'Ovide', in J. M. Bremer, S. L. Radt, C. J. Ruijgh (eds.), *Miscellanea tragica in honorem J. C. Kamerbeek* (Amsterdam), 405–24.

SCOTT, W. C. (1975), 'Two Suns over Thebes: Imagery and Stage-Effects in the *Bacchae*', *TAPA* 105: 333–46.

SCULLION, S. (1999–2000), 'Tradition and Innovation in Euripidean Aetiology', *ICS* 24–5: 217–33.

SEAFORD, R. (1987), 'Pentheus' Vision: Bacchae 918–22', *CQ* 37: 76–8.

—— (1994), *Reciprocity and Ritual: Homer and Tragedy in the Developing City State* (Oxford).

—— (1995), 'Historicizing Tragic Ambivalence: The Vote of Athena', in Goff (1995), 202–21.

References

Segal, C. P. (1981), *Tragedy and Civilization* (Cambridge).

—— (1982), *Dionysiac Poetics and Euripides' Bacchae* (Princeton).

—— (1993), *Euripides and the Poetics of Sorrow* (Durham).

—— (1997), *Dionysiac Poetics and Euripides' 'Bacchae'*, 2nd edn. (Princeton).

—— (1998), Reply to Richard Seaford's Review (*BMCR* 98.3.10) of Segal (1997), *BMCR* 98.5.26.

Severyns, A. (1938), *Recherches sur la Chrestomathie de Proclos*, Première Partie: *Le Codex 239 de Photius*, 2 vols, Bibliothèque de la Faculté de Philosophie et Lettres de l'Université de Liège, Fasc. LXXVIII–LXXIX, Paris.

Shapiro, H. A. (1993), *Personifications in Greek Art: The Representation of Abstract Concepts, 600–400 BC* (Zurich).

Sharrock, A. (2002), 'An A-musing Tale: Gender, Genre, and Ovid's Battle with Inspiration in the *Metamorphoses*,' in Spentzou and Fowler (2002), 207–27.

Shefton, B. B. (1967), 'Attisches Meisterwerk und etruskische Kopie', *WZUR* 16: 529–37.

Sifakis, G. M. (1967), *Studies in the History of Hellenistic Drama* (London).

Silk, M. S. (1993), 'Aristophanic paratragedy', in Sommerstein et al. (1993), 477–504.

—— (1996), (ed.), *Tragedy and the Tragic* (Oxford).

—— (1998a), 'Style, Voice, and Authority in the Choruses of Greek Drama', in P. Riemer and B. Zimmermann (1998) 1–26.

—— (1998b), ' "Das Urproblem der Tragödie": Notions of the Chorus in the Nineteenth Century', in Riemer and Zimmermann (1998), 195–226.

—— (2000), *Aristophanes and the Definition of Comedy* (Oxford).

Sinn, F. (1987), *Stadtrömische Marmorurnen* (Mainz).

Slater, W. J. (1981), 'Peace, the Symposium, and the Poet', *ICS* 4: 205–14.

—— (1997), 'L'hegemôn dans les fêtes hellénistiques', *Pallas* 47: 97–106.

Smethurst, M. (2000), 'The Japanese Presence in Ninagawa's Medea', in E. Hall, F. Macintosh, and O. Taplin (eds.), *Medea in Performance 1500–2000* (Oxford).

—— (2002), 'Ninagawa's Production and Euripides' *Medea*', *AJP* 123.1: 1–34.

Smyth, H. W. (1926) (ed. and tr.), *Aeschylus*, vol. 2 (Cambridge, MA).

—— (1956), *Greek Grammar*, rev. G. Messing (Cambridge, MA).

Snell, B., and Maehler, H. (1975) (eds.), *Pindarus*, pars 2, *Fragmenta, Indices* (Leipzig).

Sommerstein, A. (1980) (ed. and tr.), *The Comedies of Aristophanes*, vol. 1, *'Acharnians'* (Warminster).

—— (1985) (ed. and tr.), *The Comedies of Aristophanes*, vol. 5, *'Peace'* (Warminster).

—— (1994) (ed. and tr.), *The Comedies of Aristophanes*, vol. 8, '*Thesmo-phoriazusae*' (Warminster).

—— HALLIWELL, S., HENDERSON, J., and ZIMMERMANN, B. (1993) (eds.), *Tragedy, Comedy and the Polis: Papers from the Greek Drama Conference, Nottingham, 18–20 July 1990* (Bari).

SPENTZOU, E. (2002), 'Introduction: Secularizing the Muse', in Spentzou and Fowler (2002), 1–28.

—— and FOWLER, D. (2002) (eds.), *Cultivating the Muses: Struggles for Power and Inspiration in Classical Greek Literature* (Oxford).

STAFFORD, E. (2000), *Worshipping Virtues: Personification and the Divine in Ancient Greece* (London).

STANFORD, W. B. (1962) (ed.), *Aristophanes. The Frogs*, 2nd edn. (London).

STARKIE, W. (1909) (ed.), *The 'Acharnians' of Aristophanes* (London).

STEHLE, E. (1997), *Performance and Gender in Ancient Greece* (Princeton).

STEINER, D. T. (1994), *The Tyrant's Writ: Myths and Images of Writing in Ancient Greece* (Princeton).

—— (2001), *Images in Mind. Statues in Archaic and Classical Greek Literature and Thought* (Princeton).

STEINER, G. (1984), *Antigones* (Oxford).

STEPHANIS, A. (1997), *Le Messager dans la tragédie grecque* (Athens).

STEPHANIS, I. E. (1988), *Dionysiakoi technitai. Symboles sten prosopographia tou theatrou kai tes mousikes ton archaion ellenon* (Herakleion).

STEWART, A. (1985), 'History, Myth and Allegory in the Program of the Temple of Athena *Nike*, Athens', in H. Kessler and M. Simpson (eds.), *Pictorial Narrative in Antiquity and the Middle Ages*, Studies in the History of Art 16 (Washington).

STYAN, J. L. (1982), *Max Reinhardt* (Cambridge).

SVENBRO, J. (1993), *Phrasikleia: An Anthropology of Reading in Ancient Greece*, tr. J. Lloyd (Ithaca).

TAPLIN, O. (1977), *The Stagecraft of Aeschylus* (Oxford).

—— (1978), *Greek Tragedy in Action* (London).

—— (1983), 'Tragedy and Trugedy', *CQ* 33: 31–3.

—— (1986), 'Fifth-Century Tragedy and Comedy: A Synkrisis', *JHS* 106: 163–74.

—— (1993), *Comic Angels: and Other Approaches to Greek Drama through Vase-Paintings* (Oxford).

—— (1996), 'Tragedy and the Comic', in Silk (1996), 188–202.

—— (1997), 'The Chorus of Mams', in S. Byrne (1997) (ed.), *Tony Harrison. Loiner* (Oxford), 171–84.

—— (1999), 'Spreading the Word through Performance', in Goldhill and Osborne (1999), 33–57.

TAPLIN, O. (2007) *Pots and Plays. Interactions between Tragedy and Greek Vase-Painting of the Fourth Century* BCE (Los Angeles).

THEIN, K. (2002), 'Gods and Painters: Philostratus the Elder, Stoic Phantasia and the Strategy of Describing', *Ramus* 31: 136–45.

THÖNE, C. (1999), *Ikonografische Studien zu Nike im 5. Jahrhundert v. Chr* (Heidelberg).

TIVERIOS, M. A. (1976), *Ho Lydos Kai To Ergo tou* (Athens).

TOUCHEFU, O., and KRAUKOPF, I. (1981), 'Agamemnon', *LIMC*, vol. 1.1, 256–77.

TRENDALL, A. D. (1967), *The Red-Figured Vases of Lucania, Campania and Sicily* (Oxford).

—— (1983), *The Red-Figured Vases of Lucania, Campania and Sicily, Third Supplement (consolidated), BICS* suppl. 41 (London).

—— (1984), 'Medea at Eleusis on a Volute Krater by the Darius Painter', *Record of the Art Museum Princeton University* 43.1: 4–17.

—— and CAMBITOGLOU, A. (1982), *The Red-Figured Vases of Apulia* (Oxford).

—— (1983), *First Supplement to the Red-Figured Vases of Apulia, BICS* Suppl. 42 (London).

—— (1992), *Second Supplement to the Red-Figured Vases of Apulia, BICS* Suppl. 60 (London).

—— and WEBSTER, T. (1970), *Illustrations of Greek Drama* (London).

TRIMPI, W. (1983), *Muses of One Mind: The Literary Analysis of Experience and its Continuity* (Princeton).

URE, A. D. (1929), 'Boeotian Geometricising Vases', *JHS* 49: 160–71.

USSHER, S. (1973) (ed.), *Aristophanes 'Ecclesiazusae'* (Oxford).

VAERST, A. (1980), 'Griechische Schildzeichen vom 8. bis zum ausgehenden 6. Jh.', Diss. Salzburg.

VALLEY, G. (1926), *Über den Sprachgebrauch des Longus* (Uppsala).

VASUNIA, P. (2003), 'Plutarch and the Return of the Archaic', in A. J. Boyle and W. J. Domink (eds.), *Flavian Rome: Culture, Image, Text* (Leiden), 369–89.

VERNANT, J.-P. (1988), *Myth and Society in Ancient Greece*, tr. J. Lloyd (New York).

—— (1989), 'Dim Body, Dazzling Body', in M. Feher (ed.), *Fragments for a History of the Human Body* (New York), 18–47.

VERRALL, A. W. (1893) (ed. and tr.), *The 'Choephori' of Aeschylus* (London).

VIDAL-NAQUET, P. (1988), 'The Shields of the Heroes: Essay on the Central Theme of the Seven Against Thebes', in J.-P. Vernant and P. Vidal-Naquet, *Myth and Tragedy in Ancient Greece*, tr. J. Lloyd (New York), 273–300.

WACHTER, R. (2001), *Non-Attic Vase Inscriptions* (Oxford).

WAGNER, R. (1892–9), *Richard Wagner's Prose Works*, 8 vols., tr. William Ashton Ellis (London).

WALDRON, A. (1990), *The Great Wall of China: From History to Myth* (Cambridge).

WARNER, M. (1987), *Monuments and Maidens: The Allegory of the Female Form* (London).

WATZINGER, C. (1903), *Das Relief des Archelaos von Priene* (Berlin).

WEBB, R. (1997), 'Imagination and the Arousal of the Emotions', in S. Braund and C. Gill (eds.), *The Passions in Roman Literature and Thought* (Cambridge), 112–27.

—— (1999), '*Ekphrasis* Ancient and Modern: The Invention of a Genre', *Word and Image* 15: 7–18.

WEBSTER, T. B. L. (1956), *Art and Literature in Fourth Century Athens* (London).

WEBSTER, T. B. L. (1967*a*), *Hellenistic Art* (London).

—— (1967*b*), *The Tragedies of Euripides* (London).

—— (1972), *Potter and Patron in Classical Athens* (London).

—— and TRENDALL, A. D. (1971), *Illustrations of Greek Drama* (London).

WEST, M. L. (1993), *Greek Lyric Poetry: The Poems and Fragments of the Greek Iambic, Elegiac, and Melic Poets (Excluding Pindar and Bacchylides) down to 450 b.c.* (Oxford).

WETMORE, K. (2003), *Black Dionysus. Greek Tragedy and African American Theatre* (Jefferson, NC and London).

WHITFORD, F. (1990), *Klimt* (London).

WHITTAKER, M. (1935), 'The Comic Fragments in their Relation to the Structure of Old Attic Comedy', *CQ* 29: 181–91.

WILAMOWITZ-MOELLENDORFF, U. VON (1909) (ed.), *Euripides 'Herakles'*, 2nd edn. (Leipzig).

—— (1913), *Sappho und Simonides* (Berlin).

—— (1914), *Aischylos* (Berlin).

—— (1921), *Griechische Verskunst* (Berlin).

—— (1922), *Pindaros* (Berlin).

WILKINS, J. (1997), 'Comic Cuisine: Food and Eating in the Comic Polis', in Dobrov (1997*a*), 250–68.

WILLINK, C. W. (1986) (ed.), *Euripides: Orestes* (Oxford).

WILSON, N. G. (1996), *Scholars of Byzantium*, rev. edn. (London).

WILSON, P. (1999–2000), 'Euripides' Tragic Muse', *ICS* 24–5: 427–49.

WILSON, P. (2000), *The Athenian Institution of the Khoregia: The Chorus, the City and the Stage* (Cambridge).

—— (2002), 'The Musicians among the Actors', in Easterling and Hall (2002), 39–68.

WILSON, P. (2003), 'The Politics of Dance: Dithyrambic Contest and Social Order in Ancient Greece', in D. Phillips and D. Pritchard (eds.), *Sport and Festival in the Ancient Greek World*, Swansea, 163–96.

—— (2006), '*diken* in the *Oresteia*', in J. Davidson, F. Muecke, P. Wilson (eds.), Greek Drama III: Studies in Honour of Kevin Lee. BICS Supplement 87 (London), 187–201.

WINKLER, J. J. (1989), '*Phallos politikos*: Representing the Body Politic in Athens', *Differences* 2: 29–45.

—— (1990), *The Constraints of Desire: The Anthropology of Sex and Gender in Ancient Greece*, London.

—— and ZEITLIN, F. I. (1990) (eds.), *Nothing to Do with Dionysos? Athenian Drama in its Social Context* (Princeton).

WINTER, F. (1908), *Altertümer von Pergamon. Die Skulpturen mit Ausnahme der Altarreliefs* (Berlin).

WORMAN, N. (2002), *The Cast of Character: Style in Greek Literature* (Princeton).

WYCHERLEY, R. E. (1957), *The Athenian Agora*, vol. 3, *Literary and Epigraphical Testimonia* (Princeton).

WYKE, M. (2002), 'Reading Female Flesh: Ovid *Amores* 3.1', in *The Roman Mistress: Ancient and Modern Representations* (Oxford), 115–54.

XANTHAKIS-KARAMANOS, G. (1993), 'Hellenistic Drama: Studies in Form and Performance', *Platon* 45: 117–32.

YOUNG, D. C. (1968), *Three Odes of Pindar: A Literary Study of Pythian 11, Pythian 3, and Olympian 7*, *Mnemosyne* Supplement 9 (Leiden).

ZANKER, G. (1981), 'Enargeia in Ancient Criticism of Poetry', *RhM* 124: 297–311.

ZANKER, P. (1999), 'Phädras Trauer und Hippolytos' Bildung: Zu einem Sarkophag in Thermenmuseum', in F. de Angelis and S. Muth (eds.), *Im Spiegel der Mythos: Bilderwelt und Lebenswelt* (Wiesbaden), 131–42.

ZEITLIN, F. I. (1965), 'The Motif of the Corrupted Sacrifice in Aeschylus' *Oresteia*', *TAPA* 96: 463–508.

—— (1966), 'Postscript to the Sacrificial Imagery in the *Oresteia* (*Ag.* 1235–37)', *TAPA* 97: 645–53.

—— (1970), 'The Argive Festival of Hera and Euripides' *Electra*', *TAPA* 101: 645–69.

—— (1978), 'The Dynamics of Misogyny: Myth and Mythmaking in the *Oresteia* of Aeschylus', *Arethusa* 11: 149–84.

—— (1981), 'Travesties of Gender and Genre in Aristophanes' *Thesmophoriazusae*', in Foley (1981).

—— (1982*a*), 'Cultic Models of the Female: Rites of Dionysus and Demeter', *Arethusa* 15: 129–58.

—— (1982*b*), *Under the Sign of the Shield: Semiotics and Aeschylus'* Seven against Thebes (Rome).

—— (1985*a*), 'Playing the Other: Theater, Theatricality, and the Feminine in Greek Drama', *Representations* 11: 63–96.

—— (1985*b*), 'The Power of Aphrodite: Eros and the Boundaries of the Self in the *Hippolytus*', in Burian, P. (ed.), *Directions in Euripidean Criticism* (Durham), 52–111, 189–208.

—— (1989), 'Mysteries of Identity and Designs of the Self in Euripides' *Ion*', *PCPS* 35: 144–97.

—— (1990*a*), 'Patterns of Gender in Aeschylean Drama: the *Seven Against Thebes* and the Danaid Trilogy', in Griffith and Mastronarde (1990).

—— (1990*b*), 'Thebes: Theater of Self and Society in Athenian Drama', in Winkler and Zeitlin (1990), 130–67.

—— (1993), 'Staging Dionysus between Thebes and Athens', in Carpenter and Faraone (1993), 147–82.

—— (1994), 'The Artful Eye: Vision, Ecphrasis and Spectacle in the Euripidean Theatre', in Goldhill and Osborne (1994), 138–96.

ZEITLIN, F. I. (1996*a*), *Playing the Other. Gender and Society in Classical Greek Literature* (Chicago).

—— (1996*b*), 'The Body's Revenge: Dionysos and Tragic Action in Euripides' *Hekabe*', in Zeitlin (1996*a*), 172–216.

—— (1999), 'Aristophanes: The Performance of Utopia in the *Ecclesiazousae*', in Goldhill and Osborne (1999), 167–97.

—— (2001), 'Visions and Revisions of Homer', in S. Goldhill (ed.), *Being Greek Under Rome* (Cambridge), 195–266.

—— (2004), 'Dionysus in '69', in E. Hall, F. Macintosh, and A. Wrigley (eds.), *Dionysus since 69: Greek Tragedy at the Dawn of the Third Millennium* (Oxford), 49–76.

ZIEHEN, L. (1949), 'Pamboiotia', *RE*, vol. 18.3, coll. 288–9.

Index Locorum

ACHILLES TATIUS
1.6: 344
2.29.3: 344
2.29.5: 344
3.5.4: 342
5.3.4–8: 341
5.5.1–9: 341
5.8.3: 345–6

AELIAN
De natura animalium
1.15: 341
Varia Historia
14.40: 247 and n.78

AENEAS TACTICUS
1.6: 146
3.3: 146, 147
10.3: 147
10.4: 147
10.5–7: 147
10.18: 147
10.26: 146
17.1: 147
17.11: 147
22.19: 147

AESCHYLUS
Agamemnon
107–29: 329
174: 265
197: 340
212: 342
773–81: 57
779–80: 57
782–6: 57–8
1072–3: 332
1076–7: 332
1100: 332
1107: 332
1114: 332
1117: 265
1125: 332
1136: 332

1144: 341
1146: 332
1156–7: 332
1167–8: 332
1206: 98n.68
1214: 332
1256–7: 332
1264–8: 333
1265: 331 and n.51
1305: 332
1307: 332
1343–7: 329
1372ff.: 333
1372–98: 329
1397: 330
1431–47: 329
1440–3: 333
1444: 345
1444–6: 332
Libation Bearers
11: 169
63: 142n.21
72: 188
124–5: 168
148–50: 168
183: 341
364–5: 331 and n.51
406–7: 173
766–70: 187
924: 173
973: 168
994: 268n.11
1022–4: 168
1041: 173
1047: 168
1054: 170, 173
1058: 172
Eumenides
34: 171
95: 265
795: 266
903: 265
974–5: 266
990–1: 176

1009: 265
Prometheus Bound
17: 340
582–3: 342
590: 340
650: 340
883: 168n.9
Seven Against Thebes
187–8: 137
194: 136
197: 142
385: 340
484: 342
597: 137
644: 341
647–8: 139
717: 340
795: 341

fr. 132c Radt: 340

Vita Aeschyli
18: 239

ALCAEUS
42.15: 185n.37
fr. 325 LP: 90n.51

ALCIPHRON
2.2: 340
3.22.2: 341
3.57: 83n.35

ALCMAN
Partheneia 65: 87
1P: 39–43, 47–8

ALCMAEON
fr. 1: 98n.70

ANDOCIDES
Mysteriae
129: 183n.11

[ANDOC.]
4.21: 282

[ANON.]
Dissoi Logoi
90 B 3.10: 242 and n.65

APOLLODORUS
1.9.1: 209–10
1.9.28: 213 and nn.19, 20
3.14.1: 260 and n.13

ARISTOPHANES
Acharnians
Σ10: 116n.35
16: 274
320: 341
393–479: 120, 121
429: 271
441–2: 121n.47
443–4: 124n.53
447: 123, 124
449: 121
450–3: 121
455: 122
479: 121
484: 123, 124
496–501: 118
499–508: 124
500: 119n.38
502–8: 117
626: 271
641–5: 117
860: 273
866: 274n.60
883: 272
883–6: 273
969–70: 274
987–8: 274
1008–10: 274
1044–6: 275
1050–61: 275
1085–94: 274
1150: 276
Σ1150c: 276n.70
1202–3: 272
1224–5: 272
1227: 276
1227–34: 51
1228: 277
1232–3: 277
Birds
212: 341
640: 260 and n.14
748: 35n.1
1102–15: 281n.80

Clouds
115–30: 281n.80
371–2: 240n.60
Frogs
66–7: 122
69: 116
100–3: 124
103: 122
118: 116
172: 116
224: 344
*Σ*303: 240
354: 269
356–7: 270n.47
359–68: 269
366–8: 270
387–8: 269
388: 269
389–95: 269
686–7: 113
771: 116
774: 116
*Σ*868: 116n.35
868–71: 116
888–9: 126n.58
939–44: 222
1008–12: 105
1012: 115, 116
1031: 115
1036–8: 115
1062–8: 118
1069–71: 117
1305: 223
1308: 223
1411–13: 118n.37
Knights
16–18: 120n.44
589: 270n.48
Lysistrata
217–18: 81n.29
219: 81n.29
Peace
738–50: 278
754–60: 279
768: 279
1005–15: 274n.60
1017: 279
1018–19: 279
1020–2: 279

1355–7: 280
Wasps
220: 35n.1
579–80: 240n.60
1536–7: 271
Wealth
953: 78n.23
1051–65: 175
Women at the Assembly
*Σ*472: 260 and n.13
676–8: 282
1112: 281
1132–3: 281
1141–2: 281
1143: 281
1153: 283
1154–62: 283
1156: 286
1180–2: 280
Women at the Thesmophoria
148–58: 231
157: 237
473ff.: 260 and n.13
972: 268

ARISTOTLE
Constitution of Athens
12.5: 48–9
Parts of Animals
3.1426: 142n.21
Poetics
1275^{a}2–3: 283
1277^{a}11: 78n.23
1302^{b}27–30: 68
1336^{b}27–31: 247
Rhetoric
3.2.4: 247

ARRIAN
Epicteti Dissertationes
4.7.15: 351 and n.16
Periplus Maris Euxeni
3: 341

ATHENAEUS
1.22c: 258
11.471b: 76n.29
12.534e: 155n.10
12.543e: 45n.27

BACCHYLIDES
3.438–9: 43n.19
5.144: 48
11: 258 and n.8
Epigrammatum 1 M (=fr. 48 Bgk): 257
and n.2

CALLIAS
Grammatikê Theôria: 50

CALLIMACHUS
AP 12.134 = *HE* 1103–8: 344

CHAEREMON (?)
Achilleus Thersitoktonos: 193

CHARITON
1.11.7: 347
4.2.9: 345

CLEMENS ALEXANDRINUS
6.20: 346

CRATINUS
Pytinê
T i: 223
T ii: 223

fr. 171 K.-A.: 281n.80
fr. 193–6 *PCG*: 223

DEMOSTHENES
19.246: 247 and n.78
21.60: 78n.23

DAMASCIUS
Vita Isidori: 83n.35, 89

DEMETRIUS
De elocutione
169: 237

DEMOCRITUS
fr. 249 D-K: 265 and n.32

DIODORUS SICULUS
4.54.7: 201
15.44: 76.29
55.4: 201

DIONYSIUS THRAX
T 6: 248–9

DIOSCORIDES
1.71: 343
1.72: 343

EUMELUS
fr. 5 Bernabé: 213 and n.20

EURIPIDES
Aegeus
fr. 1ff. *TrGF*: 213 and n.19
Andromache
103–16: 250
896: 342
Bacchae
12: 313n.11
25: 313n.11
38: 313n.11
80: 313n.11
142: 313n.11
143: 313n.11
143–52: 312 and n.8
176: 313n.11
188: 313n.11
240: 313n.11
254: 313n.11
261: 313n.11
279: 313n.11
306: 313n.11
382: 313n.11
495: 313n.11
534: 313n.11
554: 313n.11
557: 313n.11
569–70: 56
622–3: 346, 348
676: 344
684: 313n.11
698: 313n.11
700: 313n.11
704: 313n.11
710: 313n.11
711: 313n.11
724: 313n.11
733: 313n.11
734–48: 228n.26
799: 313n.11

835: 313n.11
918–21: 289
918–24: 7
941: 313n.11
961–2: 187
982: 313n.11
1043–52: 314
1054: 313n.11
1062: 313n.11
1064: 313n.11
1095: 313n.11
1097: 313n.11
1099: 313n.11
1114–52: 313
1138: 313n.11
1141: 313n.11
1163: 313n.11
1299–1300: 313
1331: 313n.11, 345
Electra
279: 332 and n. 53
900: 122n.48
Hecuba
48: 341
687: 346
905–51: 364
910–11: 136
1279: 332 and n.53
Helen
1209: 341
1576: 346
Hippolytus
131–40: 344
135–7: 344
181–5: 344
191–7: 111 and n.19
274: 340
275: 344
516: 345
525–64: 348
528–9: 344
530: 344
541–3: 349
643: 346
1173–1254: 312 and n.8
1174: 320 and n.26
1196: 320 and n.26
1198: 320 and n.26
1206: 320 and n.26

1214: 319
1218: 320
1244: 320 and n.26
1247: 319
1300: 344
Hypsipyle
fr. 1 ii 9–16 Cockle (1987): 223
Ion
654–60: 216
1067: 111n.19
1267: 341
Iphigeneia at Aulis
850: 346
1054–7: 56
1505–8: 111n.19
*Iphigeneia among
    the Taurians*
294: 170n.18
1337: 344
1490–9: 264–5 and n.30
The Madness of Heracles
110–11: 345
285: 340
330: 328 and n.43
361–3: 345
655–72: 51–2, 111
656: 53
659: 52
669–72: 53
671–2: 53–4
673–7: 53–4
674–86: 111n.20
678: 345
692: 345
868: 328 and n.43
883: 328 and n.43
922–1015: 312 and n.8
990: 328
996–7: 327
998–1000: 327
1009–11: 325
1035–8: 325
1055: 325
1094–7: 325
1123–4: 325
1351–7: 112n.23
1373: 341
1408–17: 112n.23
1412: 112n.23

Medea
245: 344
Σ264 (Parmeniscus): 213 and n.20
395–7: 205n.10
408: 346
410–45: 367
663–758: 213 and n.19
1030: 340
1039: 111n.19
1045: 215
1056–80: 216 and n.24
1058: 215
1060–1: 216
1074: 345
1149: 346
1229: 347
1236–41: 216
Orestes
128: 224 and n.17
255: 169n.15
264–5: 169n.15
982–96: 111n.21
1155: 342
1691–3: 264–5 and n.30
Phoenician Women
62: 341
89–90: 138
92–3: 138
94–5: 138
117: 139
193–201: 138
234–8: 56
261–2: 139
987: 141
1009–12: 141
1090–2: 141
1145: 341
1275: 142
1276: 142
1361: 142
1706–7: 143
1764–6: 264–5 and n.30
Rhesus
208–9: 344–5
780: 170n.17
890–982: 224
993–6: 254–5 and n.30
Stheneboea
(fr. 663 Nauck): 346–7, 349

Suppliants
138: 345
503: 341
585: 340
Telephus
12 Preiser 723 N²: 317–18
23 Preiser 706 N²: 119n.38
Trojan Women
8–19: 241
361–2: 332 and n.53
451–2: 331 and n.51
509: 341

fr. 285.1 Nauck: 345
fr. 773 Nauck: 341
fr. 964.1–6 Nauck²: 112n.24

GALEN
466: 346

GORGIAS
82 B 23 DK: 241, 253

HELIODORUS
1.3: 351 and n.16
2.11.2: 351 and n.16
6.13.5: 345

HERODAS
Mimiambi
281: 340

HERODOTUS
3.82.3: 78
3.119.6: 341n.9
6.105.3: 339 and n.4
6.108.5: 69n.10
6.117.3: 340
7.62.1: 213 and n.19
7.140–4: 130n.4
7.191.2: 344
8.55: 260 and n.13
9.15.1: 69n.10
9.86–8: 68

HESIOD
[*Shield*]
205–6: 332 and n.53
231–3: 332 and n.53

242–3: 332 and n.53
247–83: 332 and n.53
Theogony
26: 251
77–9: 242
383–403: 257
393–4: 258
401: 258
Works and Days
11–26: 266
654–9: 44n.24
fr. 343.10: 124n.53

HIPPOCRATES
Epidemics I
2.13: 247
On Head Wounds
15: 343
On Wounds
10: 343

HOMER
Iliad
3.154–60: 26
3.384: 135
3.382–9: 135
3.483–5: 135
3.490–2: 135
5.127–8: 21
5.179–87: 22n.19
5.585: 331 and n.51
5.739: 168n.10
6: 29–30
6.123–43: 22n.19
6.323: 168n.13
6.357–8: 60
6.450–65: 30
Σ7.86: 209n.14
9.477: 168n.13
10.334: 344
11.37: 168n.10
11.248–53: 20n.4
11.419: 330
11.599: 20n.5
12.430–5: 20n.8
13.59: 335
13.99: 23n.13
15.285–91: 23n.13
16.342–4: 22

16.658: 23
17.645–7: 20
18.225–7: 25
18.493: 332 and n.53
18.502: 332 and n.53
18.570: 332 and n.53
18.579–80: 332 and n.53
19.268: 342
20.320–4: 22n.12
20.344: 23n.13
20.417: 27n.16
21.54: 23n.13
21.108–13: 25
21.342–76: 315
22.66–76: 32
22.168–70: 23n.13
23.309–10: 58
22.437–64: 136
22.470: 136
22.470–2: 136
23.329–33: 59
23.358–9: 59n.52
24.480–4: 27
Odyssey
4.499–511: 335
8.190–6: 58
11.405–34: 329
11.411: 331 and n.51
11.421: 332
11.421–2: 331 and n.51
12.189–90: 88
16.108: 169n.13
19.363: 346
19.522: 341
22.19–20: 31
22.329: 331 and n.51
22.396: 169n.13
22.421: 169n.13

Hymn to Apollo
174–5: 41
399–441: 346
Hymn to Demeter
2–5: 223
Hymn to Dionysus
38–41: 346

HORACE
Ars Poetica
231–3: 249

Odes
2.1.9: 250 and n.87

Hyginus
Fabula 2: 210

Inscriptiones Graecae
I³35: 259
I³36: 259
I³379: 263 and n.27
I³469: 263 and n.27
I³766: 40–1n.14
I³833: Fig. 1, 39–40
I³957–62: 36n.6
I³963–6: 36n.6
I³966: 37
II²2325.31: 245–6 and n.77
II²2325.262: 245–6 and n.77
II²3101: 285
II²5027: 259 and n.10
II²2318 (Fasti): 239 and n.52
II²2318 (Fasti), cols.viii and vii: 240 and n.56
II²2319–23: 237 and n.41
IX²1.170: 91n.52
XII Suppl. 400: 244 and n.76

Ion of Chios
Epidêmiai: 35n.1

Isocrates
12.237: 345
Trapez.
33–4: 282n.81

Longus
Daphnis and Chloe
pr. 3: 339
pr. 4: 342, 343, 343–4, 348
1.1.1: 339
1.2.3: 341
1.2–4: 339
1.9.1: 344
1.9.2: 340
1.13.5: 344
1.13.5–14: 348–9
1.13.6: 344
1.14.1: 344, 345
1.15.2: 349
1.17.3: 344

1.17.4: 344
1.20.2: 340, 344, 348, 349
1.20.3: 345, 349
1.22.3: 345, 349
1.23.2: 340
1.27: 349
1.27.1: 345
1.30.6: 352
2.1.1: 349
2.1.2: 340
2.1.4: 352
2.5.1: 345, 349
2.7.4: 344
2.7.7: 345, 349
2.11.1: 345
2.12.1: 339n.3
2.12–28: 339
2.13.1: 341
2.22.3: 342
2.23.4: 339 and n.4
2.23.5: 343
2.25.3: 348, 349
2.25.3ff.: 346
2.27.1: 342
2.27.3: 342
2.34: 349
3.1.1–3.1: 339
3.4.5: 346, 349
3.6.2: 343
3.12.4: 341
3.20.2: 346
3.21.2: 346
3.23: 349
3.28.2: 343, 348
4: 339, 349
4.16.4: 351
4.17.2: 346, 348, 350, 352
4.18.1: 346, 349, 352
4.21.2: 347
4.23.1: 347
4.24.3: 341–2, 348
4.35.3: 347
4.35.4: 349

Lucian
Aetion

4–6: 221
Dialogi Meretrici
11.3: 346
Nigrinus
11: 254
Prometheus Es in Verbis
4: 346
Saturnalia
8: 341
Somnium sive Vita Luciani
8: 346

[LUCIAN]
49.21: 142n.21

MACROBIUS
2.4: 254n.105

MENANDER
Dyskolos
968–9: 269n.46
Misoumenai
996: 269n.46
Samia
736–7: 269n.46
Sikyonioi
422–43: 269

OVID
Amores
3.1: 249–50
3.1.7: 250
3.1.9–10: 250
3.1.11: 250
3.1.12–14: 250
3.1.16: 250
3.1.33–4: 250
3.1.35: 250
3.1.67–70: 250
Ars amatoria
1.264: 251
Heroides
15.84: 251

MICHAEL PSELLUS
Essays on Euripides and George of Pidisia:
233 and n.27

Palatine Anthology
6.172: 344

6.177: 344
9.597.3: 142n.21
11.169: 254n.105
12.134: 344
13.28: 42–3

PAUSANIAS
1.2.5: 242
1.24.5: 260 and n.13
1.26.5: 260 and n.13
1.28.4: 339n.4
1.28.6: 166, 167n.7
1.37.3: 244
2.4.5: 336 and n.67
3.11.9: 49
3.15.7: 261 and n.19
5.4.4: 143n.23
5.11.1–2: 258 and n.6
9.10.4: 72

PHERECRATES
Cheiron
155 PCG: 223
Krapataloi
fr. 102 K.-A.: 281n.80

PHILOSTEPHANUS
3, 34 fr. 37 FHG: 209n.14

PHILOSTRATUS
Imagines
1. Proem 4–5: 311n.6, 323
1. Proem 5: 320, 323, 327
Proem 7: 311n.6
1.1 (Scamander): 313, 315
1.1.1: 327
1.1.2: 315, 321
1.2.5: 321
1.4.3–4 (Menoeceus): 315
    and n.16
1.4.4: 321
1.7 (Memnon):
1.7.2: 315 and n.16
1.13.5: 326
1.18 (Bacchae): 313, 333, 334
1.18.1: 313, 314n.14, 315, 316, 317
1.18.2: 313, 314, 316, 317
1.18.3: 316, 317
1.23 (Narcissus): 325

1.23.2: 322–3, 326
1.23.3: 326
1.24.3 (Hyacinthus): 315 and n.16
1.27 (Amphiareus): 313, 326
1.28: 327
1.28.1: 323, 326
1.28.1–2: 328
1.27.2: 326, 327, 328
1.28.8: 323
2.4 (Hippolytus): 318, 333, 334
2.4.1: 319, 320
2.4.2: 319, 320, 323
2.4.3: 321
2.4.3–4: 315 and n.16
2.4.4: 321
2.6.5 (Arrichion): 315 and n.16
2.7 (Antilochus):
2.7.5: 315 and n.16
2.10 (Cassandra): 312, 329, 332–4
2.10.1: 330, 333, 334, 335
2.10.2: 331
2.10.2–3: 331
2.10.4: 332, 334
2.13 (death of Aias Oileades): 313
2.13.1: 335
2.13.2: 335
2.23 (madness of Heracles): 312 and n.8,
327, 331, 334, 335
2.23.1: 324, 325, 327, 328
2.23.2: 325, 327, 328
2.23.3: 325
2.23.4: 324
2.25.1 (Abderus): 315 and n.16
2.28 (*leptotês*, etc.): 310n.4
2.28.3: 326
2.34 (Seasons): 312
2.34.1: 336
Vita Apollonii
6.11: 116n.35
Vita Sophistarum
1.22.524: 347

PHOTIUS
Lexicon: 76n.20, 83n.35, 97n.64
See also PROCLUS

PINDAR
Olympian
1.109–11: 93n.56

2.54: 93n.56
4.1–3: 47
7: 60
9.80–4: 89n.47
10.76–7: 258 and n.7
Σ13.74g: 213 and n.20
Nemean
3.69: 93n.56
6.53–7b: 89n.47
7.52–63: 89n.47
8.13–16: 89n.47
9.18: 343
Isthmian
1.33: 90
1.52–4: 90
4.1–9: 94
5.21–2: 89n.47
6.57–8: 89n.47
Pythian
3.17–19: 82n.32
8.92: 93n.56
9.111–13: 61
9.112: 61
9.117–20: 61
9.118: 61
11: 95, 96
11.1–12: 82n.31
Σ11.6 (Drachmann 119–20): 98n.71
11.7–12: 95–6
11.50–8: 96
11.54–6: 96
12.27: 273n.60
Paians
9.33–4: 82n.31
Partheneion 2 (= fr. 94b SM)
3–4: 97–8
3–17: 86
7–8: 65
8–10: 92n.55
9: 65, 98
10: 65
19–20: 65
31: 65, 87
36–41: 88
42: 90
42–9: 89–90
61: 92
61–7: 96
61–72: 92

67–70: 74
71: 65–6
76: 98n.71
78: 98n.71
fr. 227.1 SM: 93n.56

PLATO
Cratylus
408c7: 351
Phaedo
84e: 345
Phaedrus: 65b: 345
229d7: 347
255d: 344
295b5–d8: 242
268c: 242
Republic
589a ff.: 115n.34
600a: 115n.34
Symposium
173a: 272 and n.55
174a: 273n.56
416: 272 and n.55
737b: 247 and n.78
Theaetetus
161e: 170n.17

PLATO COMICUS
Nikai
Meinecke *FCG* 1.175: 263
and n.27
PCG 7: 263 and n.27, 468–9

PLAUTUS
Casina
46–50: 229n.30
com. fr. 166, 3c: 120n.44

PLINY
Natural History
35.78: 221, 238
35.114: 323
35.141: 329

PLUTARCH
Against Colotes
19c: 351
Alcibiades
16: 155n.10

Coriolanus
35.2: 341
Demetrius
21.2: 351
53.2: 341
Moralia
271e: 341
345c-51b: 252
347a: 252
348c: 253 and n.100
348e-r: 252
789d: 340
Nicias
29.2–3: 35n.1
On Brotherly Love
18: 260 and n.13
On the Pythian Oracles: 351
Pelopidas
16.3–4: 79
16.3–4: 76n.20
29.4–6: 247 and n.79
Quaestiones Romanae: 341
Themistocles
19: 260 and n.13
fr. 157: 76n.20, 82n.30

POLLUX
Onomasticon
4.110: 165
4.111: 264–5 and n.30
4.141: 167
7.89: 76n.20, 83n.35

POLYBIUS
4.3.5: 91n.52
9.34.11: 91n.52

POSIDIPPUS
fr. 6.11–13: 269n.46

P. Oxy.
659: 65 and n.2

PROCLUS
Chrest. Apud Photius *Bibliothêkê*
Cod. 239, pp. 321a35–b32 Bekker: 72–3,
74
In Platonis Timaeum commentarii
53d: 260 and n.13

PROPERTIUS
3.3: 251

PRUDENTIUS
Contra Symmachum
54–6: 323

SAPPHO
fr. 1.3 Voigt: 344
fr. 31 Voigt: 344
fr. 96.17 Voigt: 344

SEG
18.240: 91n.52

SH
566: 347

SIMONIDES
48 B: 43n.19

SOLON
36W²: 46
37W²: 7–10, 48–9

SOPHOCLES
Ajax
462–4: 343
728: 340
1010–21: 343
Antigone
332–75: 361
410: 343, 348
787: 342
905–20: 341, 348
1008: 343, 348
Electra
99: 332 and n.53
148–9: 341
888: 340
Oedipus at Colonus
668–719: 371
Oedipus the King
52: 343
234: 132
295: 132
313: 132
367: 132
467: 132
761–5: 132

797: 132
1186–97: 2
1268: 341
1298: 343
Women of Trachis
102: 340
498–530: 51
612–13: 134

fr. 200 Radt: 340
fr. 474 Radt: 340
fr. 561 Radt: 340

TrGF fr. 314: 231

SORANUS
1.4: 346

STRABO
9.2.33/412: 90

Suda
Ψ 101 Adler: 97n.64
s.v. Athena: 259n.10
s.v. Athena Hygieia: 259n.10

SUETONIUS
Nero
21: 254n.105

THEOCRITUS
2.85: 344
11: 350
Σ11: 347
11.1: 345
11.1–2: 345
11.1–6: 345
11.15: 344
11.17: 345
13.73: 342
15.59: 347
30.10: 344
AP 6.177: 344

THEOGNIS
Theognidae
39–52: 77n.22
216: 342
226–9: 53
237–47: 41–2

249–50: 42n.16
618: 342
1074: 342
1173: 342

THEOPHRASTUS
Historia Plantarum: 373n.60

THUCYDIDES
1.10.3: 339n.3
1.12.3: 70n.10
1.89–93: 145
1.90.2: 145
1.90.3: 145
1.93.1–2: 146
1.107: 145
1.107.4: 146
1.107.6: 146
2.34–46: 111n.22
2.37: 111n.22
2.41: 111n.20
2.42: 111n.20
2.44: 111n.22
2.46: 111n.22
2.84.3: 341, 346
3.62.3–4: 68
3.68.5: 69n.10
4.90–6: 66

*TrGF*²
15 F 1–3: 212n.16
17 T 1: 212n.16

23 F ?: 212n.16
29 F 1: 212n.16
52 F 1a: 212n.16
70 F e: 212n.16
78 A T: 212n.16
88 F 1e: 212n.16
205 F 1: 212n.16
ad. 6a: 212n.16
*701: 212n.16

VITRUVIUS
5.6.9: 231n.32

XENOPHON
Apologia Socratis
18: 112n.23
27: 347
Cyropaedia
1.3.5: 346
6.1.41: 347
6.1.51: 340
7.5.39: 347
History of Greece
2.2.23: 130
Memorabilia
2.1.21–34: 251

XENOPHON EPHESIUS
1.5, 6: 344

ZENOBIUS
1.3.98: 84n.37

Index of Artefacts

Athens, National Archaeological Museum
19765: 166n.4 (Erinyes?), 248
5610: 302n.26

Atlanta, Emory University Museum
1994.1, RVAp, Suppl. 2, 18/283: 190 and n.24 (nurse, tutor)

Barcelona, Archaeological Museum of Catalonia
33: 323–3; figs. 10.5a, b (Apollo, Dionysus, komôidia, paidia)

Berlin, Antikensammlung
Once 3210 (now lost) = Beazley Archive 310449, ABV 151.21: 228 and n.25 (Dionysus)
F2160 (2160) 201809, ARV² 196.1: 304n.33 (Satyr, fawn, and Hermes)

Berlin, Staatliche Museen
1984.41, RVAp, Suppl. 2, 18/41B: 191 and n.27 (Tropheus)
731: 302; fig. 12.6 (marble hero relief)

Boston, Museum of Fine Arts
1972.356 (carved funerary urn): 316 and n.20; fig 13.2 (death of Pentheus)
1900.03.804, RVAp, Suppl. 2, 17/75: 193 and n.34 (Aitolos et al.)
1991.437, RVAp, Suppl. 2, 18/47b [p. 148]: 180, 183, 193, 195–6; figs 8.1 and 8.2 (Atreids)
1987.53, RVAp, Suppl. 2, 18/65c: 183 and n.12 (baby Atreus)

Caltanisetta Museum
Trendall and Webster (1971: III.6,1), Taplin (1993: 6.111): 191–2 and n.31 (tragedy on a stage)

Ferrara, Museo Nazionale
2897 (T 128) 213655, ARV² 21052.25: 301n.28 (twin statues)

Florence, Museo Archeologico Etrusco
3929 204696, ARV² 460/15: 153–4; fig. 6.2 (centaur)
22 B 324, ARV² 1258.2: 229n.28 (satyr, maenads). *See also* **Leipzig, Antikenmuseum,** T 727 217070

Geneva, Musée d'art et histoire
LIMC, Hesione (S) 1*: 179 and n.8, 195–6; figs. 8.3, 8.4 (Heracles; Phrygians)

Heidelberg, Ruprecht-Karls-Universität
S61 300546, ABV 63.2: 228 (Dionysus, hares)

Izmir, Archaeological Museum
Marble relief: 249 (Dionysus between Euripides and *Skênê*)

Leipzig, Antikenmuseum
T 727 2107070, ARV² 1258.2: 229n.28 (satyr, maenads)

London, British Museum
B 148 310175, ABV 109.29: (satyr, hare)
B 191 (1839.10–25.13) 310448, ABV 152/24: 156 (centaur)
B 206 302115, ABV 369.120: 300 and n.22 (Dionysus and Ariadne)
E 458 202164, ARV² 239/16: 155n.9 (centaur)
2191, Apotheosis of Homer: 249 and n.84 (marble relief of Tragôidia)

London, Market, Sotheby's
17–18.7.1985, no.571 (A) 7166 = Sotheby's London 18/7/1985, n.12: 158; fig. 6.5
(centaur)

Los Angeles, Getty Museum
96.AE.29, RVAp, Suppl. 2, 1/124 [p. 7–8]: 183 and n.13 (comic Aegisthus)

Munich, Antikensammlungen
3296, *LIMC* 6, 391F., s.v. Medeia Nr. 29.35–8: 199 and n.4; figs. 9.2, 9.3 (Medea
pursued by Jason)

Naples, Museo Nazionale Archeologico
3240: 233–7; fig. 10.6 (Tragôidia?)
81947, RVAp, Suppl. 2, 18/38: 191 and n.28 (Persai)
81934, RVAp, Suppl. 2, 18/42: 190–1 and n. 26 (Paidagogos)
81954 H 3221, Trendall and Cambitoglou (1982: 497, 18/43): 199–207; fig. 9.2
(Medea)
Fresco vi.15.1, once Pompeii, House of the Vettii (vi.15.1), Pentheus Room: 316–17;
fig. 13.1 (Pentheus being torn asunder)

New York, Metropolitan Museum of Art
1924.97.250: 229; fig. 10.3 (Dionysus, Komôidia, Tragôidia)
1924.98.104: 238 and n.43 (tragôidos)

Olympia, Archaeological Museum
M-L n. 74: 261 (Nikê of Paeonius)

Oxford, Ashmolean Museum
534: 231–2; fig. 10.4 (Tragôidia, satyr)
274 (1890.30) 201908, ARV² 203/100: 260 and n.17 (Nikê)

Paris, Cabinet des Médailles, Bibliothèque Nationale de France
222 310452, ABV 152.25: 228 and n.25 (Dionysus)
535 201741, ARV² 191.03: 156; fig. 6.3 (centaur)
357 213822, ARV² 987.2: 227n.23 (night-time revel)
222, ABV 64.28: 288–93; figs 12.1 and 12.2 (Athena, Poseidon, Dionysus, maenads)

Paris, Musée du Louvre
G 421 213489: 227 (Dionysus)

Princeton, Princeton University Art Museum
83–13, Trendall and Cambitoglou (1983: 78, 18/41a): 197–9, 205–6, 217; fig. 9.1 (Medea, Eleusis)

Rome, Museo Archeologico Villa Giulia
18003, RVAp, Suppl. 2, 18/149: 192 and n.33 (Phrygian)

Stockholm, Medelhavsmuseet
302192, ABV 374/197: 293–305; figs. 12.3, 12.4, 12.5 (Dionysus, Apollo, and Artemis)

Syracusa, Museo Nazionale
66557, Trendall (1983: 105/98a) = Taplin (1993: 6.112): 191 and n.32 (Corinthian messenger)

Thasos, Dionysion; now, Thasos, Archaeological Museum
Marble sculptural group: 243–4; fig. 10.8 (Dionysus, Tragedy as a blind old man, Comedy, Dithyramb, and Nykterinos)

Toronto, Royal Ontario Museum
927.39.3 (306) 302175, ABV 373/180, 80: 294n.16 (Dionysus and Ariadne; Hermes)

Venice, Museo Archeologico
Marble relief: 316–17; fig. 13.3 (Agave with Pentheus' head)

General Index

Achilles 25, 156 and fig. 6.4, 158 and fig.
    6.5
  and Priam 28
  rapport with the gods 22–3
  on vase, 193
Achilles Tatius 5
ἀχλύς 21, 23, 27n.16, 30n.20
actor(s) 243
  advent of superstar 240 and n.60
  Batalus 247
  Chairis 274n.60
  and chorus 355–7, 373
  eclipse tragedians (Plutarch) 253
  in *Eumenides* 174
  guild of 242
  increasing prominence of 239–40
  merger with chorus 370
  Tragôidia 233, 243
  Philemon 247 and n.81
  prizes won 272n.56.
  see also Orestes; Theodorus; theatre;
    tragedy
Aegeus 201
Aegisthus 187
Aeneas Tacticus 146–7
Aeschylus 3
  Achilles trilogy, 185
  Agamemnon 57
  Libation Bearers 10, 167, 187, 194
  Erinyes 165–76
  Eumenides 10, 170–6, 194, 265–7
  intertextuality with Longus 342
  Oresteia (modernized) 362
  Persians 108, 166, 264
    on vase, 191 and n.28, 195
  Seven against Thebes 8, 13, 131–3, 151
    compared with *Phoenician
      Women* 142, 144
    great shield scene in 151
  Vita Aeschyli 165, 239
  Women of Aetna 239
  *See also Index Locorum; individual
    characters*

Aetion 221–2, 238
Agave 315, 316, 373–4
agôn 2, 37–8, 140, 261, 264
  in Aristophanes 113–18, 120, 268,
    270, 281n.80
  paragone 311 and n.5, 315
αἰδώς 33
Aiolidas 86, 92, 98
Ajax 20
  See also Index Locorum
ἄκρον ἑλών 97
Alcman 47–8, 87
ἀλήθεια 326 and n.38, 336
Allen, W.: *Mighty Aphrodite* 357
Amasis Painter 156, 228, 290, 293 and
    figs. 12.1 and 12.2
amazon: on vase 156 and fig. 3.
  See also Heracles
Amphiaraus 326
Amphitheus 126
ἀναγκαῖον, τό 34
anapests: in comedy 269
Andromache: parting scene with
    Hector 28–32, 33–4, 135–6
Androsthenes 241
animals in tragedy/vase painting/
    comedy 298, 373
  bear 370
  birds 281n.80
  bull (Dionysiac) 289n.4
  cicadas 242
  cock 301nn.29, 30
  dogs 170, 173
  deer 294
  eels 273, 275
  fawn 304n.33
  hare 227–9 and n.30, 274, 292
  goats 351
  horses 294, 320
  panther 299
  ram (sacrificial) 280
  snakes 166, 171, 172, 175
  sheep (sacrificial) 279, 280

animals in tragedy/vase painting/
    comedy (*cont'd.*)
  staglet 292
  thrush 274
anonymous figures ('witness figures'):
  botêr 191 and n.29
  chorus 188–9, 194, 195–6
  functions of 190–1
  in Greek tragedy 187–9
    with labels 190–3
    with lines 188
    silent 187–8
    messenger 191
    paidagôgos 190–1 and n. 26; 197
      and fig. 9.1, 202, 206–7, 209, 214,
      217
    trophos 190
  on vases 189–95
Antigone 138, 142
  See also Oedipus; Sophocles: *Antigone*
Antiphanes 223
'antipolitical', the: different shades
    of 108–26
Anthesteria 271–2
Apollo 72, 82, 83, 86, 99, 100n.74
  in *Eumenides* 172–3
  Homeric Hymn to 41
  temple at Delphi 247
  See also Daphnephoria; gods
Apollodorus: myth solves quandary on
    vase 209–10
Apollonius of Tyana 5
aposiopesis 277–8
Aquila Theater Company 364
ἀρετή 93, 94, 96
Ariadne: on vase (with Dionysus) 233,
    298, 304
Aristophanes:
  Acharnians 125, 271–8
  Birds 125n.57, 281n.80
  Clouds 223
  elevation of, 269
  Frogs 115–22, 151, 239, 356
  lost plays 223
  love for Euripides 123 and n.51, 124
  parodies Euripides and
    Aeschylus 105–6, 113–26
  Peace 278–80
  as parodist 121

Wasps 287, 351
Women at the Assembly, Eumenides
    compared with 266n.33
Women at the Thesmophoria 268
  See also Index Locorum
Aristotle 2, 6
  Poetics 238, 241, 248
art:
  deceptions of 326
  Roman as imitative 334
  See also painting; vases
Artemis: on vase 294
Astyanax 32–3, 133
Athamas: on vase and myth of 208–10
Athena 21, 173, 206, 207, 213, 216
  and Achilles 22
  Acropolis 261
  in Aristophanes 248
  and Eumenides 265
  and Hector 22
  Itonia, shrine at Coroneia 90, 91
  on vase 290–2 and fig. 12.1, n.7, 301,
    fig. 12.7, and 304
  See also gods; Nikê
Athena Nikê 259
  as coins 261, 263 and n.27
  temple on Acropolis 261–3
  See also Nikê; victory
Athens 3, 38–9, 213, 216, 217, 244
  Athenian Nikê 259–63
  hegemony of 101
  Long Walls 130, 145, 146
  Plutarch on military vs. tragedy
    in 252–3 and n.101
  praised in tragedy 109
  tragedy's escape from 238–43
athletics:
  and dance 59
  as metaphor 52, 56, 57, 58
Atreids:
  painted on Boston amphora 180–3
    and figs. 8.1, 8.2.
  See also myth
audience, tragic:
  actual viewers 196
  bribery of 281 and n.80
  analogous to readers 315–16
  drawn into action 320–1, 369, 372,
    373, 374

on-stage characters 187–9
real world recreated as 359
response, 322
See also actor(s); performance;
theatre; tragedy
aulos 273 and n.60

Bacchae 315
See also Euripides: *Bacchae;* Dionysus;
maenads
Bacchylides iii, 42–3, 46n.30, 48
See also Index Locorum
Banquet, *see* symposium
Barton, J. 374–8
Baudrillart, A. 259 and n.10
Beazley, Sir J. 294
Becker, W.: *Good Bye Lenin!* 127
Bell, C. 68
Berlin Painter 304n.33
Berlin Wall:
fall of 127, 128
symbolism of 128, 146
Bernardini, Angeli P. 95 and n.60
Blanchard, M. 316n.18, 334n.56
blood 175
See also war
Boiotians:
confused with Thebans 69–70
koinon of 69–70 n.10, 70–1
See also Thebes
Boston amphora 180–3 and
figs. 8.1, 8.2
boundary *see horos*
Bowie, E. 277n.71
Brandt, P. 250n.89
Brecht, B. 361–2
Breuer, L. 370–1
bride:
in Daphnephoria 82
Dionysus and Ariadne, 300
See also wedding
Burkert, W. 261
Burton, R. 370–1

Caeneus: depicted on vase, 159 and fig.
6.6, 161 and fig. 6.7
Calame, C. 82–3n.33, 98n.70, 99,
271n.50
Callias 50

Carpenter, T. H. 228 and n.26
Cassandra: shows that pictorial exceeds
tragic 329, 332–4
Cavaceppi, B. 255
centauromachy: on vase 155
centaurs: depicted on vases 63–4,
155–62
ceramics
and tragic themes 4, 7, 8, 9–10, 11,
151–62;
inspiration for 162
See also painting; vases
Chaniotis, A. 83n.34
chiasmus 49, 50; ring composition 54
Chiron, depicted on vase 158 and fig.
6.5
See also centaurs
Choes 272, 277
choral poetry, Theban, 63–101
See also chorus
Choregos vase 183 and n.13
choreutai 174
choros: wordplay with *horos* 49–50,
53–4, 99n.72
chorus:
and actors 355–7, 375–6
of *Acharnians* 273–8
of *Libation Bearers* 167–9, 170
composition of 356
exclusion of from feast 273–5, 278
exodoi of 271n.50
and Greek culture 55
fusion with political 78, 363–6
psyche 366–67
in *Madness of Heracles* 51–52, 53–55
inclusion of in feast 281
vs. individualism 359–61
individualized 363 and n.15
language of 356
lyric 47–8
metachorality 276
metafestival 276
in *Oedipus the King* 132
old men vs. young girls 55
opposes individualism 359–60
as origin of tragedy 374
as palimpsest 269
parallels with Broadway musicals 358
in Pindar fr. 94B 86–9

chorus (*cont'd.*)
　as prize 61–2
　Women of Trachis 134
　tragic (anonymity of) 10, 188–9, 194,
　　195–6
　major features of 354–7, 277
　on modern stage 353–78
　See also choral poetry; Erinyes
Christianity 368, 370–1
Cleophrades Painter 156 and n.13, fig.
　6.3
Cleveland Painter 159 and fig. 6.5
cicadas: myth of 242
city, *see* polis
Clytaemnestra: in *Eumenides* 173
Colonus 143
comedy 3, 118
　in Euripides 264–5 and n.30
　Old Comedy, 241
　opposed to Nikê? 287
　Plutarch dismisses 252
　purpose of 286
　vs. tragedy 9, 10–11, 13, 119,
　　121n.47, 123–4, 224, 237–8,
　　239, 251, 265n.30, 271
　　Aristotle on 238
　　conflict in both 263–4
　See also Aristophanes; New Comedy;
　　Old Comedy
Compiègne Artist/vase 227, 228, 233
Cook, A. B. 300n.24
Corinth 214–15
Corinthians 214, 217
Coroneia 90, 91
　See also Boiotia
Cosway R.: *Sarah Siddons as*
　　Tragedy 255
Cratinus, *Pytinê* 223
Croally, N. 109
Csapo, E. 229
Curtius, L. 233

Daidale 82
Danaus 61
dancing:
　choral 224, 258, 367
　tragedy dissociated from 243, 354
Daphnephoria, 67–8, 71, 95, 99
　as 'deliberate hybrid' 81

Pausanias on 72, 74, 76–7, 78
　politics in 78–81
　Proclus on 73, 74, 79
daphnêphorika 66–7
daphnêphoros 82–3 and n.34, 95 and
　n.60
　See also pais amphithalês
Darius 195
Darius Painter 177–8, fig. 8.2, 183, 190,
　191, 194, 197 and fig. 9.1, 199
　and figs. 9.2, 9.3, 203, 207 and
　fig. 9.4
Daux, G. 247
death: in Aristophanes 115–16
dedication: of tripods 37 and n.7, 39
　and n.9
Deguy, M. 124n.54
Del Corno, D. 115
Deliades 41, 55
Delphic Oracle 130, 209, 376
　See also Apollo
Demeter 199, 269
　and Korê 199, 206, 207
democracy 146
democratization: reflected in chorus,
　100
description: in Philostratus 314–15 and
　n.16
　See also ecphrasis
didacticism: in tragedy, ridiculed 114,
　114–15
Didaskaliai 237
Dikê *See* justice
Diodorus Siculus 202, 211
　See also Index Locorum
Diomedes: *aristeia* of 21
Dionysia 37, 231, 237, 244, 246, 247,
　286
　Great Dionysia, 278
　See also Dionysus; tragedy
Dionysus 7, 11, 55–6, 105, 115, 115–16,
　117, 118, 122, 124
　on vase fig. 12.2 and n.7, 298–300 and
　figs. 12.4, 12.5
　Lenaeus 280
　in modernized *Bacchae* 373–4
　relation with theatre 288–9
　theatricality of 288–305
　See also Ariadne; wine

Dionysus with Tragedy and Comedy 95
(painting by Aetion) 221–22,
238, 251n.
Dios apatê 26–7
dithyrambs 8, 35, 36, 37, 38–42, 45, 51,
60, 62, 100 and n.74
Di Virgilio, R. 343
Dobrov, G. W. 117n.36, 119n.40, 122,
123n.52, 271n.50
Dover, K. 269–70 and n.47
δρακεῖν/δράκων 171
duality: 143, 144, 328, 389
See also comedy: vs.
tragedy; gender
opposition
δυσωδίαν, 352
See also τραγῳδία

ecphrasis 7–8, 151, 221, 253, 329–33
ambivalence in 331
intertextuality in 332
language of 327, 330
narrative of gaze 328–9, 332
paralleled with tragedy and
epic 329–33
as photography 333–4
and pictorial legacy 335;
'secondariness' of 336 and n.62
sound in 332 and nn.52, 53
relation to tragedy 248–9, 309–37
transcends genre 332, 336
transformed 311
See also Index of Artefacts; Philostratus
Edmunds, E. L. 119n.38
Egyptian statues 300–1 and n.25
as influence 301 and n.26, figs. 12.6,
12.7
elegy: personified 250–1
in Philostratus 321
Eleusis 215
Initiates at 270
as refuge 212, 213–15, 216, 217
on vase 199 and fig. 9.1, 201, 202,
207, 213–14
elitism 74, 77
enargeia 7
enkuklêma 121 and n.46
ἐνόησε 19
epic: anticipates tragedy 30 and n.21, 34
ideology of 29

limits of 28–9, 30–1, 32–4
paralleled with tragedy
See also Homer; *Iliad; Odyssey*
Epictetus (vase painter) 299n.21
epinician: fusion with *partheneion* 85
and history/myth 88 and n.46, 89
hybrid with *partheneion* 66, 67
ἐπινίκια 272–3, 274–6, 280
Erinyes 10, 165–76, 363
become Eumenides 176, 265
clothing of 168, 174–5
described 172, 175
effect on audience at debut 165
painted on lekythos 166 and n.4
Boston amphora 180
See also Aeschylus; myth; tragedy
eris 266. *See also stasis*
erôs 11–12, 122, 123, 326, 344
in *Agamemnon*, 333
in Attic tragedy vs. in Longus 338,
339–49, 352
in Longus, *Daphnis and Chloe* 338–52
passim
See also Dios apatê; Helen of Troy
Eteocles: Aeschylus' vs. Euripides' 140
in *Phoenician Women* 138
in *Seven against Thebes* 132–3,
136–8, 142
Eumenides, *see* Erinyes
Euripides 3–4, 13
Bacchae 7, 55–6, 135, 187, 289, 358,
362, 373–4
Children of Heracles 217
comedy in 264–5 and n.30
compared with Philostratus 315–30
as Dicaeopolis 124
Electra 139, 147
Hecuba 136, 364
Helen 376
The Madness of Heracles 51–2, 53–4,
110
Hippolytus 188
Ion 216
intertextuality with Longus 343–7
Iphigenia at Aulis 188, 353
Iphigenia among the Taurians 361
Medea 197–211 and figs. 2.1, 2.2.,
2.3, 363, 366–7
Melanippê Sophê 191 and n.29

Euripides (*cont'd.*)
  Oresteia 353
  Orestes 240
  Philostratus emulates 313–30
  Phoenician Women 8, 138–44, 151
  quoted 5, 35n.1
  Stheneboea 352
  structure of plays 108–9
  Suppliant Women 217
  Telephus 119–25
  as Telephus 124 and n.54
  Trojan Women 147, 361, 364, 370
  *See also Index Locorum; individual
    characters*
  evil: inexplicability of 110, 113

family, vs. polis 140
Fede, Count G. 255
Ferrari, F. 87 and n.45
Foley, H. 138–9, 289n.4
food, *see* animals
Ford, A. 241
Foucault, M. 11
Fraenkel, E. 3, 333n.54
François vase 185
Frenzy, 329: depicted on vases, 203
Freud, S. 114
fury 205, 328–9
  See also Aeschylus: *Eumenides*; Erinyes

Gallavotti, C. 40
Gardzienice 368
Garlan, Y. 128n.1
gaze 332
  of madness 328, 334–5
  See also seeing; sight
Geertz, C. 68
γέγραπται: in Philostratus 313
gender opposition 90, 96, 112n.23, 135,
    136, 137, 142, 144, 363, 367, 376
  See also marriage
Genette, G. 114n.29
genitive 59–60
genres:
  categorization of 24
  crossover among 51, 85, 221, 334
  evolve into one another 337
  Nagy on 242–3
  in Ovid 249–51

tragedy defined 264, 355
  See also ecphrasis; painting;
    personification; theatre; tragedy
Gesamtkunstwerke 360
ghetto walls 129
gnômai, tragic 342
gods 198–9
  Euripides on 109–10
  and humans 22, 27, 52–3, 350
  and human vision 21
  (collectively) on vase 208 and fig. 9.4,
    209
Goette, H. 284–5n.85
Goldhill, S. 120n.42, 123n.52
Gorgias 241
'Gorgon' faces 166, 171–2, 174, 328n.43
  See also sight
'Grande Idée' 267, 271
Great Wall of China 128–9
Green, J. R. 191

Hadrian: as 'new Dionysus' 254–5
Harpies 172
Harrow Painter 158 and fig. 6.5
Heath, M. 123n.52
Hector 22, 23
  and Andromache 28–32, 33–4, 135–6
  vs. Eteocles 137
Hegel, G. W. F.: *Antigone* 5
Hegelochus 240
Helen of Troy:
  abused 370
  Encomium of Helen 241
  visual effect on gods and
    mortals 25–6, 134–5
  See also erôs
  helissô 55–6
Helle 209
Hellenica Oxyrhynchia 70
Hellespont 209
Henderson, J. 271
Hera 82
  Dios apatê 26–7
  as oppressor 110
Heracles 54, 183, 185, 206, 207, 213, 214
  dance origin of Olympics 258
  fights Amazons 162 fig. 3
  infanticide of, 201–2
  madness of 324–30

role favored by actors 254
tragedy of 110, 168n.9, 201–2
  See also Euripides: *Madness of Heracles*
Hermes, on vase 304 and fig. 12.7
Herodotus 339
  See also Index Locorum
Hesiod 87
  on Nikê 257–8
  Theogony 242
  See also Index Locorum
Hesione 183, 185
Hesione amphora 183–5 and figs. 8.3, 8.4
  See also vases
hieros gamos 81–2 and n.31, 97, 99, 300n.24
  See also marriage; wedding
Hippolytus: in Philostratus vs.
  Euripides 318–23 and fig. 13.4
historiography 339
Homer 2, 8, 136, 144
  See also Iliad; Odyssey
Homeric Hymn to Apollo 41
Homeric Hymn to Demeter 222
Homeric Hymn to Dionysus 292
homonoia 147
hoplites: painted on sixth-century psykter 152–3
  cup 153–5
Horace 249–51
  non omnis moriar 116
horos (boundary) 43–5, 58
  absence of 53
  as *martus* 46–8
  Ober on 44 and n.22
  and *terma* 56–9
  wordplay with *khoros* 49–50, 50–4, 58, 60–1
hubris, in tragedy ridiculed 274
hunting 387
  as erotic pursuit 326

Iambê 222–23
idein / eidenai 7
Iliad: basis for tragedies 133–6
  tragic visualizing in 19–34
  See also Homer; *Index Locorum; individual characters;* Troy
imperialism 101
  See also democratization

incest 138, 180, 183 and n.11
infanticide, *see* Heracles; Medea
initiation (male/female) 81–2
  See also gender opposition
Ino:
  on vase 208–9 and fig. 9.4
  as evil stepmother 209, 210
intertextuality:
  in ecphrasis 332
  among genres 334, 350, 352
  in Longus 340–50
  See also ecphrasis; epic; Philostratus; tragedy
invented ritual 369
'invention of tradition' 81n.26
iphikratides / epikratides 76n.20, 83n.35
Iphikratides 83n.35
Iris 202, 206, 207, 214
Ismenion 72, 75, 77, 78
Isocrates: *Panegyric* 231

Jason 212
  pursuing Medea on amphora figs. 9.1, 9.2, 9.3, 205
Jocasta 138, 141, 142
judges:
  of festivals 282, 355
  Aristophanes' characters address 283–4
justice (Dikê / δίκη) 120
  and boundary language 57–8
  in *Libation Bearers* 169
  comedy and 119n.38
  on shield 139

kanêphoroi 77
Kant, E.:
  Critique of Judgment 114
Kauffman, A. 255
kharaktêr 52
kharis 55, 58
khorêgos 37 and n.6, 46, 97 and n.64, 100, 239, 246–7, 272, 275, 276, 279–80 and n.77, 286
khorodidaskaloi 37, 40, 41
  as *Paideia*, 235
κλέος 41–2, 60, 62
  excludes women, children, in *Iliad*, 28
Klimt, G.: *Tragödie* (1897) 256

koinon / koina 70–1, 90, 91
  See also Boiotians
Kômôidia 229, fig. 10.5a
  statue of fig. 10.7
  See also comedy; tragedy; Tragôidia
komôidodidaskalos 278–9, 286
Kômos 229
  See also tragedy; Tragôidia
Konstan, D. 125n.57
kôpô 74, 76 and n.29, 80, 82n.31, 82–3n.33, 84, 95n.60, 97, 98 and n.70
κορυφαῖος 78, 97
  See also chorus
kosmos 55
Kossatz-Deissman, A. 225
κροκωτός 81–2 and n.29
Kowalzig, Barbara 71n.11

Lacan, J. 126n.59
Lake Copais 80, 81, 84, 273 and n.60
λαλεῖν (double entendre) 117
lalia 123
  and *logoi* 118
language 50, 117, 118
  'ballet for the mouth' 369
Laomedon 183, 185
Larsen, J. A. O. 71
laughter: comic 114–15 and n.31
  at death 115–16
  Kant on 114
  as purpose of comedy 286
  tragic 135
Lehnus, L. 65 and n.3, 67 and n.6
Lenaea 244, 246, 270, 271, 273, 278
Leucippid Painter fig. 10.3
Leveaux, D. 353
Lexicon of Greek Personal Names 260
light: in *Iliad* 20
Lloyd-Jones, Sir H. 110n.17
Longus 11–12
  tragic intertextuality in 340–7
  on tragedy 338–52
Long Walls, *see* Athens
Loraux, N. 107–8 and n.7, 111
  and n.22
Lycaon 24–5, 27

Mackil, Emily 69–70 and nn.9, 10, 70, 79, 80, 91

Macron: vases attributed to 153–5 and fig. 6.2, 156–7 and fig. 6.4
madness:
  deceptions of 325
  and the gaze 328–9
  of Orestes 167–8, 169–70, 174
  See also Euripides: *Madness of Heracles*; Heracles; seeing; sight
maenads 187, 235, 243, 256, 292–3, 316, 317
  Ashmolean Maenad 231
  depicted on vases 227, and n.23, 228, 229–30 and fig. 10.3; 231 and fig. 10.4
  See also Bacchae; Dionysus; Euripides: *Bacchae*; Pentheus
marriage 97, 98
  Daphnephoria as hybrid of, with war 80–4
  Nikê and 267n.39
  See also hieros gamos
martus (witness): as *horos* 46–8, 89, 95n.59
masks, tragic 167, 175–6, 248, 285
  in iconography 233, 243
Maslov, B. 89n.48
Medea 4, 10
  on fourth-century south Italian red-figure vases, 198–207 and figs. 9.1, 9.2, and 9.3, 211
  with children 206–7
  as healing sorceress 202–3
  infanticide of 199–201 and figs. 9.2, 9.3, 203–5 and fig. 9.3
  versions of children's fate 213–14 and n.20
  myth 212–13 and n.16, 217
Mee, C. 364
megalê diaphora 106n.3
Melpomene 242, 254 and n.103
Men, *see* gender opposition
Menander: *Dyskolos* 339
men / de 54–5
Menoeceus:
  in *Antigone* 362
  in *Phoenician Women* 140–2, 144
μέριμνα 93 and n.56, 96
'messenger speech' 311–12 and n.8, 327
  as ecphrasis 314
  language of 320

μεταίχμιον 142
metaphor 43, 50, 56
    See also horos; khoros; martus;
    personification; simile
mimesis 4, 7, 63–4, 313
    limits of 337
misogyny 13
    of Eteocles 136–7
    in Plutarch 253
    See also gender opposition;
    wom(a)(e)n
Mist, see ἀχλύς
Miyagi, S. 363
Mnouchkine, A. 353
moderation 93–4, 95, 96
Morgan, J. R. 342
Morris, P. 358
Mortals, see gods
Mossman, J. M. 112n.26
mourning: in tragedy 107–8
Mousikê 223
'Muse', Euripides' 224
Muses 224 and n.14, 242, 250n.86, 376
music 273 and n.60
    in modernized tragedy 368, 370–2
    See also choral song; chorus; dancing
Music Man, The: parallels with
    Euripides' Bacchae 358
μῦθοι 350
myth 3–4, 61, 110, 377
    Apollodorus and 209–10
    of cicadas 242
    painted onto vases 178–217 passim
    and tragic chorus 355, 356, 374–6
    versions of Medea myth 212n.16
    children's fate, 213 and n.20
    widely familiar, 359
    See also Daphnephoria; individual
    names; ritual; tragedy

Nagy, G. 64
Narcissus: in Philostratus 325
Nephelê: on vase fig. 9.4, 209–10, 211
New Comedy: in Longus 339, 351
Nightingale, A. W. 242
Nikê 197 and fig. 9.1, 206, 207, 214, 233
    and fig. 10.5b
    Athenian 259–63
    beauty as ugliness 279

Nikai 258, 261, 285
    comic 267–84
    described 257
    dramatic 263–7
    opposed to comedy 287
    Oresteia and 265–7
    siblings 257–58, 258–9, 264
    tragedy becomes 243
    on vases 260
    wings of 261
    See also Athena Nikê; victory
Nikêtêria 258–9
Nikias 260
Ninagawa, Y. 366–7
νοέω 19n.3
    See also ενοήσε
nomos / phusis 52
nouthesia 120
novel(s) 12
    discourse of 352
    'ideal' Greek 338
    vs. myth and tragedy 350, 352
    See also Longus; myth

Ober, J. 44 and n.22
Odyssey: in Euripides' work 125 and
    n.56
    See also Homer; Iliad; Index Locorum
Oedipus 2
    tragedy of family 132
    See also Sophocles
Oedipus vase 192
Old Comedy 241, 267–84
    See also Aristophanes; comedy; New
    Comedy
oligarchy 92–3
ὀλολυγή: in Eumenides 267n.36
Oltos (psykter painter) 152–3 and fig.
    6.1a-b, 155
Onchestos 90
    See also Boiotia
Orestes:
    described 171
    madness of 167–8, 169–70, 174
    See also Aeschylus; Euripides;
    Sophocles
Osborne, R. 259n.9, 301n.28
outside vs. inside: third option, 143, 144
    See also gender opposition

Ovid: *Metamorphoses* 368
  personifications in *Amores*, 249–51
  See also Index Locorum
Padel, R. 111n.18
Pagondas 66, 71, 86, 91n.54, 92, 93–4, 98
παιδαγωγός 190–1 and n.26; 197 and fig. 9.1, 202, 206–7, 209, 214, 217
paideia/pepaideumenos 4–5, 11, 235, 312–13
painting 151–62 *passim*
  inferior to verbal description 325
  superior to tragedy 329–32, 334
  verbal description 315, 325, 330–1
  parallels with tragedy 242, 328
  'translated' from tragedy 310, 311–28
  and viewer 331
  See also ecphrasis; tragedy; vases
pais amphithalês 83–4
Palatine Anthology 42–3
Pan 339
panêgyris 91
Pan Painter 161 and fig. 6.7
pantomime 253–4
  See also dance
paratragedy 119n.40, 121, 241, 273
  See also comedy; tragedy
parody:
  defined 119n.30, 121
  as parasite 121 and n.45
Parrhasius 45n.27
Partheneion 97
  fusion with epinician 85
  See also Index Locorum
'pathetic fallacy' 322
Pattoni, M. P. 343
Pausanias 49, 337
  on Daphnephoria 72, 74, 75, 76–7, 78, 85
  compared with Philostratus 336
peace: triumph of 279
  See also spondai
Pelopeia 180
Peloponnesian War 130
Pentheus 187, 313–14, 314–18, figs. 13.1, 13.2, and 13.3, 373
  H. Foley on 289n.4

performance:
  'buzz' about 36
  monuments of 35–6
  practicalities of today 357–78
  reperformance 240–1
  as 'temporary community' 360
  in Thasos 244
  of tragedy 354–7
  See also actor(s); audience; chorus; theatre; tragedy
Pericles 111nn. 20, 22
personification 235
  allegorical statues 244
  of comedy 223
  defined 222
  of elegy and tragedy 249–51
  of philosophy, 231
  of poetry 223
  of *thiasos* 249–50
  of tragedy 221–56
  in Plutarch 252–3
  and comedy with twin busts 55
  See also Kômôdia; Tragôidia
φαίνειν / δοκεῖν 169–70
Pherecrates: *Cheirôn* 223
Philostratus 11
  dualities in 32
  compared with Euripides 315–30
  Pausanias 336
  Pliny 336
  ecphrasis in 309–37
  Imagines 309–37
  parallel scenes in Homer and Aeschylus 329–33, 336
  'translation' in 310, 311
  use of pictures 335
  See also ecphrasis; painting
Phineus 172
Phobos 167, 168 and n.10, 174
  catharsis of 176
photography: ecphrasis as 333–4
  See also ecphrasis; painting
φρένες ('seat of feelings') 168
Phrygians: as Trojans 185 and n.15, fig. 8.4
Phrynichus 35n.1, 195
Phrixus 208, 209, 210
phthonos 85, 91, 92 and n.55, 96, 99, 100n.74

Pindar 9, 47, 61–2; fr. 94B, 84–101
and Herodotus, 92–3
Partheneion 2, 47, 85, 97
Pythian 9, 61
Theban poems 70–1
See also Index Locorum
pity:
Aristotle on 113
as solace in tragedy 110, 111 and
n.22, 113n.27
See also self-pity
Plataia, battle of 68, 69n.10
Plato 6, 11, 379
Phaedrus 242
Republic 231
See also Index Locorum
Plutarch:
on Athenian tragedy 252–3
on Athens and Thucydides 252
See also Index Locorum
Podlecki, A. 40
Poetry: personified 223
poetry:
into prose 310
lyric 339
See also individual poets; tragedy
Poinê 193
Polematas 82
polis:
comedy appropriates 268, 271, 281
vs. family 140
opposed to tribes 285
'political other' 111, 113, 125
political, the:
abandonment of 282, 283–4
vs. 'antipolitical' 107–8, 118
politics: and ritual 76–83
Polyneices 132, 139–40
Poseidon 22, 185, 258–9
on amphora, 290–2 and fig. 12.1, n.7
shrine at Onchestos 90, 91
See also gods
Prauscello, L. 83n.34
Priam:
and Achilles 28, 32
goes beyond epic 32
Proclus 66, 67n.6
on Daphnephoria 72–4, 79, 80
identity of 75–6n.28

prologist 247
See also actor(s)
Pronomos vase 4, 243
proxeniai 89–90
Pucci, P. 112n.26
pyrrhikê 59
Pythia, in *Eumenides*, 171–2
See also Apollo; Delphic Oracle

Reinhardt, K. 111
Reinhardt, M. 360, 368
Revermann, M. 284
reversal, tragic 35, 62, 103, 126, 134
See also tragedy
Reynolds, J.: *Sarah Siddons as the Tragic Muse* 255
rhêsis makra (great speech) 120
rhetoricians 7
ritual:
Dionysiac, revived 368
invented 369
Theban 72–84
and tragic chorus 100–101, 360
See also Daphnephoria; tragedy
Rönne-Linders, T. 293–4 and n.14

sacrifice 387
as celebratory 280
of ram on vase 208–10 and fig. 9.4
of Phrixus 210
prevented 209–10
of sheep 279 and n.75
of youth in tragedy 112–13, 140–2, 209–10
satyr drama 37, 222–3, 229–30, 231 and n.32, 235, 236–7, 248, 249, 354
separated from tetralogy, 237
satyr(s) 7, 227, 298–9 and n.21, 300, 304n.33
depicted on vases, 166 and figs. 12.4, 12.5, (Boston amphora) 180–3; 228–9, 229–30 and fig. 10.3, 232 and fig. 10.4, 233 and fig. 10.5b, 295 and n.14, fig. 12.3
Schachter, A. 66–7, 80–1
Schechner, R. 372–3
Schmidt, M. 201–2, 203
Schiller, F. von 360
Seaford, R. 132, 264–5 and n.30

Second Sophistic 5, 14, 312–13
seeing:
  carnage of battle 20–1
  delusion 328
  δρακεῖν 171
  gods 21
  meaning of 28
  metaphysics of 23–8
  retrospection 28–32
  stunned or wondrous 24
  See also sight
self-pity 112 and n.23
  See also pity
Selene 205
  Medea associated with 205 and n.10
Sellars, P. 367
Semnai Theai, see Eumenides
Seneca 5
Serban, A. 368–70
senses, in Philostratus 314n.14
  See also seeing; sight
Severyns, A. 80
Shakespeare, W.: *A Midsummer Night's Dream* 127 (epi.)
shields, relevant to imagery in *Seven against Thebes* 151–62
sight:
  during madness 238, 328
  making the 'unseeable' visible 165–6, 167, 169–72, 173–4, 176
  two kinds of 170
  vocabulary of 6–7
  See also seeing
Silk, M. S. 123n.51
similes, in *Iliad* 20–1, 28
  See also metaphor; personification
Simonides 40, 50n.36
Sirens 87, 88
Sitzenich, H., 255
'social poetics' 50
Solon 46, 48–9
Sommerstein, A. 277
sophiê 45, 53, 58, 59, 336
  sophiês horos 45, 59, 62
Sophocles 2
  Ajax 367
  Antigone 361–2
  on chorus 241
  Electra 367

Iambê 222–3
  intertextuality with Longus 342–3
  Oedipus at Colonus 217, 370–71
  Oedipus the King 6, 188, 360
  Women of Trachis 133–4
  See also Index Locorum; Oedipus
sophist: vs. poet 350
sophrosunê 348
space 49, 142, 173, 369, 378
  choral 35–62
  special effects on vases and 289–305
  walls as 147
  See also horos; *khoros*
sparagmos: ecphrasis from 313
Sparta 144–5
Sphinx 301n.26
spondai 119n.38, 126 and n.59
stasis 265, 269
  vs. war 264, 265
σταθμός 98
statue, of Tragôidia 243–4 and fig. 10.7
  See also art; *Index Locorum*; painting; vases
Stehle, E. 65n.3, 85n.39, 86n.41, 87, 98
Stein, P. 362
Stewart, A. 263n.25
Suda 50n.36, 97n.64, 166, 241
suicide 140–2, 143, 180
suspicion, Aeneas Tacticus on 146–7
symbolism:
  of Berlin Wall 128
  of clothing 175
  of hare 227–8
  of walls in Athens 130
  of wedding 98n.71, 99
  See also metaphor; personification; simile
symposium:
  imagery alternates with war motif 152–3
  vessels 152–63

Tadashi, S. 362 and n.13, 367
taenia: depicted on vase 208 and fig. 9.4, 210
θάμβος 27n.17
Taplin, O. 271n.51
Teichoskopiê 26

teichoskopiê 134–5, 139, 144
  See also Helen of Troy; Homer
Teiresias 140, 141
Telamon 343
Telson, Bob 370
terma: and *horos* 56–9
Thasos 243–4
θαῦμα 27, 28, 173
Theater Faction 359
theatre:
  'the metatheatrical' 268, 269, 271 and
    n.50, 374, 376–7
  vs. painting 334
  suggested by vase paintings 227
  and tragedy 228–9
  uniqueness of genre 6, 125
  See also audience; chorus;
    performance; tragedy
Thebes 8–9, 64, 99
  choral poetry of 63–101
  community building with
    Boiotia 71–84
  history of 68
  walls of in tragedy 131–47
  See also Boiotia; *koinon;* Oedipus
Themistocles 145
Theognis 41–2
  on wealth 53
Theocritus: in Longus 339, 350
  See also Index Locorum
Theodorides: Euripidean plays of
    241
Theodorus 240, 243, 244–7 and
    nn.76, 81, 252
  tomb of 244, 248
Thersites, on vase 193
thiasos 228, 232
  See also Dionysus; madness; maenad;
    tragedy
Thöne, C. 259 and n.10; 260 and nn.15,
    16, 263n.26
Thucydides 68, 69, 128, 339
  preoccupation with walls 144–6
  Plutarch on 252
  See also Index Locorum
Tragedy, Athenian 1–15
  adopted to gospel 370–1
  birth of 226, 374
  and civic ideology 106–8

compared with comedy 224, 237–8,
    239, 251, 265n.30
  conflict in both, 263–4
  defined 264
  within drama 8
  didacticism in 108–26
  elegy replaces 321
  encapsulated 330
  escape from Athens 238–43
  erôs in, vs. Longus's use of 338,
    339–49, 352
  excerpted highlights performed 240
  future of 248–56
  as generic entity 241
  and goats 351
  'happy endings' in 264–5 and n.30
  international 1–2, 238–42, 359–78
  vs. military (Athenian) 252–3
  on modern stage 5, 12, 353–78
  reception of 2–3, 11, 135, 322
  shifts epic perspective on *kleos* 28
  part of theatre 228–9
  and painting 151–62, 178–211
    passim, 209–37, 249 and n.84
  statue of 243–4
  from *thiasos* to *thasos* 243–8
  turns into art 252–3
  visualizing 13
    from outside 8–9, 221–4
  See also audience; chorus; comedy;
    individual characters; masks;
    tragedians; titles
tragôidein 351
Tragôidia 10, 224
  appearance today 255–6
  in Aristophanes, *Frogs* 223
  described 233 and fig. 10.6
  future of 248–56
  Hellenistic renditions of 249
  in Horace 249–51
  new mask of 243 and fig. 10.8
  no appearance in comedy 224
  in Plutarch 253
  range of personifications 256
  vase paintings of 225–38 and figs.
    10.1, 10.2, 10.3, 10.4, 10.5b
  See also Kômôidia; Kômos; masks;
    tragedy
tragôidia 351, 352

Tragôidos 243
Trendall, A. D. 177, 199n.3, 212
Tribes, in dithyramb competition 38
tripod:
  as *horos* 42, 43–5
  in Ismenion 77, 788100–101n.74
  as *martus* 45–46
  street of 284, 285
  'tripod verses' (dithyrambs) 38–42,
    58, 62
Troilus 158 and fig. 6.4
Trojans, called Phrygians 185
trophy 58
Troy: walls of, 131, 133–6
  See also Homer
trugôidia 119, 126
  See also comedy

Underworld Painter 190n.24
utopia 126

Valley, G. 346
vases:
  anonymous figures on 189–95
  artistic or literary? 178–9
  black-figure 166n.4, 228, 291 and
    figs.12.1, 12.2, 12.3, 12.4, 12.5,
    12.7, 304n.33
  Boston amphora 180–3 and figs. 8.1,
    8.2
  centaurs depicted on 155–62
  Erinyes depicted on 166 and n.4
  Hesione amphora 183–5 and figs.
    8.3, 8.4
  red-figure 177–96, figs. 10.1–10.6,
    260, 299n.21
  relevant to war imagery 151–64
  'theatrical' 177–8
  See also Index Locorum
Verfremdung 359
victory 10–11
  of Dicaeopolis (*Acharnians*) 271–7
  of peace 279
  in Peloponnesian war 268
  sought as personal name 260
  two levels of 270–1, 272
  visualized 257–9, 261–2
  See also Athena Nikê; Nikê
Vidal-Naquet, P. 152

Vision, *see* seeing; sight
Vita Aeschyli 165

Wachter, R.: on Corinthian cup 187n.18
Wagner, R. 5, 359–60
walls: symbolism of actual, 127–47
  See also Aeschylus: *Seven against
    Thebes*; Euripides: *Phoenician
    Women*
Wanamaker, Z. 353
war 88, 339
  and Athena Nikê 261
  imagery alternates with feasting 153
  imagery alternates with marriage 80–4
  Nikê engages in 262
  vs. *stasis* 264, 265
  on vases 152–62
  See also Aeschylus: *Seven against
    Thebes*
wealth 52, 53–4, 56, 57
wedding symbolism, *see hieros gamos;*
  marriage
wine 126 and n.61, 299n.21
  'story of' 299
  See also Dionysus; *spondai*
Witness, *see martus*
wom(a)(e)n:
  effect of debut of *Erinyes* on 165
  in Dionysiac scenes 228
  Theodorus performs as 246–7
  tragedy personified as 222
  See also gender opposition; *individual
    character names and titles*
Woodruff, R. 359

Xenophon *Cyropaidea,* 350. *See also
  Index Locorum*

Yeats, W. B., 360

Zeitlin, F. 35
  on *Choephoroi* 168n.12
  on mediation 137
  opus/accomplishments of, 12–16, 30
    and n.21, 63, 64, 131 and n.5, 136
    and n.12, 151, 152, 221, 222,
    224n.16, 264, 278, 309 and n.2,
    322n.29, 372
  'playing the other' 101, 231

quoted 288n.1
tribute to (Vernant) 373–9
tribute to (Vidal-Naquet) 380–9
Zeus 23 and n.13, 82, 124n.53
  Dios apatê 26–7 and n.16

and Hera 300n.24, 301 and nn. 26, 27
on vase 209 and fig. 9.4, 211, 304 and
  fig. 12.7
victory dance 258
See also gods

DATE DUE

MAY 1 4 2008	
JUN 1 0 2009	
JUN 1 0 2010	
STUDIES	
OCT 1 3 2021	

DEMCO, INC. 38-2971